History of the Great Reformation of the Sixteenth Century in Germany, Switzerland, Etc
by Jean Henri Merle D'aubigné

Address:
HardPress
8345 NW 66TH ST #2561
MIAMI FL 33166-2626
USA
Email: info@hardpress.net

HISTORY

OF THE

GREAT REFORMATION

OF THE

SIXTEENTH CENTURY

IN

GERMANY, SWITZERLAND, &c.

BY

J. H. MERLE D'AUBIGNÉ,

PRESIDENT OF THE THEOLOGICAL SCHOOL OF GENEVA, AND
MEMBER OF THE "SOCIETÉ EVANGELIQUE."

VOL. III.
EIGHTEENTH THOUSAND.

NEW YORK.
ROBERT CARTER, 58 CANAL STREET.
PITTSBURG—THOMAS CARTER.

1843.

7518.35.5

PREFACE.

AT a period when increased attention is everywhere drawn to those original documents which form the basis of Modern History, I gladly add my mite to the general stock.

In the former portion of this work, my attention was not confined to the historians of the time, but I judged it right to compare the testimony of the witnesses, letters, and earliest accounts; and had recourse to the authority of manuscripts, particularly one by Bullinger, which has since been printed.

But the necessity for recourse to unpublished documents became more urgent when I approached the Reformation in France. The printed materials for a history of the Reformed opinions in that country are few and scanty, owing to the state of continued trial in which the Reformed congregations have existed.

In the spring of 1838, I examined the various public libraries of Paris, and it will be seen that a manuscript preserved in the Royal Library, and never (as I believe,) before consulted, throws much light on the commencement of the Reformation.

In the autumn of 1839, I consulted the manuscripts in the library of the conclave of pastors of Neufchatel, a collection exceedingly rich in materials for the history of that age, since it includes the manuscripts of Farel's library. I am indebted to the kindness of the lord of the manor of Meuron, for the use of a manu-

script life of Farel, written by Choupard, in which
most of these documents are introduced.   These materials have enabled me to reconstruct an entire phase
of the Reformation in France.   In addition to the
above helps, and those supplied by the Library of Geneva, an appeal inserted by me in the columns of the
Archives du Christianisme, led to other communications
from private individuals, to whom I here return my
grateful acknowledgments,—and especially to M. La-
devese, pastor at Meaux.

It may be thought that I have treated at too much
detail the early progress of the Reformed opinions in
France: but those particulars are in truth very little
known.   The entire period occupying my Twelfth
Book has but four pages allotted to it by Beza; and
other historians have done little more than record the
political progress of the nation.

Many causes have combined to postpone the appearance of the present volume.   *Twice*—has heavy
affliction interrupted the labour of its composition, and
gathered my affections and my thoughts at the graves
of beloved children. The reflection that it was my duty
to glorify that adorable Master, who was dealing with
me by such moving appeals, and at the same time
ministering to me of His heavenly consolations, could
alone inspire me with the courage required for its
completion.

   Aux Eaux Vives
     pres Geneve

CONTENTS OF VOL. III

BOOK IX.—Page 9.

Aspect of the Church—Effects of Luther's Teaching—Wisdom of God Agitation of the People—Luther and Melancthon—Tidings of Luther's Safety—The Imperial Edict Powerless—The "Knight George"—A Safe Solitude—Luther's Sickness—Alarm of his Friends—The Confessional—Luther's Health—Feldkirchen's Marriage—Marriage of Priests—And of Friars—Monkery—Luther on Monastic Vows—Dedication to His Father—Sale of Indulgences Resumed—Luther's Letter to Spalatin—Luther to the Cardinal Elector—Effect of the Reformer's Letter—Albert to Luther—Joachim of Brandenburg—"The Last shall be First"—Luther's Fitness for the Work—Of Translating the Scriptures—Luther and Satan—Luther Quits the Wartburg—The Sorbonne—Luther's Visit to Wittemburg—Progress of the Reformation—The Monk Gabriel—Interference of the Elector—Frederic's Caution—Attack on Monkery—Thirteen Monks Quit the Convent—The Cordeliers Threatened—Decision of Monastic Vows—Carlstadt's Zeal—The Lord's Supper—Town Council of Wittemburg—Errors of Popery—Fanatics of Zwickau—The New Prophet Nicolas Hussman—Melancthon and Stubner—Melancthon's Perplexity—Carlstadt's Zeal—Contempt of Learning—Occupations of the Elector—Luther's Dejection—His Test of Inspiration—Edict of the Diet—Luther Leaves the Wartburg—Primitive Church—Two Swiss Students—A Strange Knight—Supper at the Inn—Luther on His Journey—Letter to the Elector—Reception at Wittemburg—Meditation—Luther Preaches—Faith and Love—God's Way—Luther on the Lord's Supper—Effect of Luther's Sermons—Luther's Moderation and Courage—Stubner and Cellarius—Order Restored—Scripture and Faith—The Visionary Pen—Publication of the New Testament—Effects of Luther's Translation—The "Loci Communes"—Original Sin—Free Will—Knowledge of Christ—Effect of Melancthon's Tract—Henry VIII—Catherine of Arragon—Bishop Fisher and Sir Thomas More—Cardinal Wolsey—Henry VIII. Writes against Luther—Royal Theology—The King's Vanity—Luther's Indignation—His Reply to Henry VIII—Literary Courtesy—More's Attack upon Luther—Henry's Attachment to More—Henry's Letter—Spread of the Reformation—The Augustine Monks—The Franciscans—The People and the Priests—The New Preachers—Power of the Scriptures—Religion and Literature—The Press—Spread of Luther's Writings—Luther at Zwickau—Duke Henry—Ibach at Rome Diffusion of the Light—University of Wittemburg—Principles of the Reformation—Transition State of the Church.

BOOK X.—Page 124.

Movement in Germany—War between Francis I. and Charles V—Inigo Lopez de Reculde—Siege of Pampeluna—Loyola's Armed Vigil—Enters a Dominican Convent—Mental Distress—"Strong Delusions"—"Belief of a Lie"—Amusement of the Pope—Death of

1*

Leo X—Character of Adrian VI—The Pope attempts a Reformation
—Opposition at Rome—Designs against Luther—Diet at Nuremburg
—Osiander at Nuremburg—The Pope's Candour—Resolution of the
Diet—Grievances—The Pope to the Elector—The Pope's Brief—The
Princes fear the Pope—" The Fiery Trial"—" The Failing Mines"—
The Augustine Convent—Mirisch and Probst—Persecution at Mil-
tenburg—The Inquisitors and the Confessors—The Fate of Lambert—
Luther's Sympathy—Hymn on the Martyrs—The Legate Campeggio
—Evasion of the Edict of Worms—Alarm of the Pope—The Dukes of
Bavaria—Conference at Ratisbon—Subtle Devices—Results of the
Ratisbon League—The Emperor's Edict—Martyrdom of Gaspard
Tauber—Cruelties in Wurtemburg—Persecution in Bavaria—Fa-
naticism in Holstein—The Prior and the Regent—Martyrdom of
Henry Zuphten—Luther and Carlstadt—Opinions on the Lord's
Supper—Carlstadt Leaves Wittemburg—Luther at Jena—Luther and
Carlstadt—Luther at Orlamund—Interview at Orlamund—On the
Worship of Images—Carlstadt Banished - Carlstadt Retires to Stras-
burg—Assembly at Spires—Abridgment of the Reformed Doctrine—
Albert of Brandenburg—The Word of God Not Bound—All Saints'
Church—Abolition of the Mass—Nature of Christianity—Letter to
Councillors—On the Use of Learning—Religion and the Arts—
Essence of Christianity—Music and Poetry—Abuses of Painting—
Insurrection of the Peasantry—The Reformation and Revolt—Fa-
naticism—" The Spirit"—Münzer Preaches Revolt—Liberty of Con-
science—Luther's View of the Revolt—Luther to the Peasantry—
Murder of Count Helfenstein—Warlike Exhortation—Gotz of Ber-
lichingen—" Radical Reform"—Defeat of the Rebels—Münzer at
Mulhausen—Anxieties at Wittemburg—The Landgrave Takes up
Arms—Defeat and Death of Münzer—Thirteenth Article—Luther
Calumniated—Rise of the New Church—The Revolt and the Refor-
mation—The Last Days of the Elector Frederic—The Elector and the
Reformer—Duke George's Confederacy—The Nuns of Nimptsch—
Catherine Bora—The Deserted Convent—Luther's Thoughts on
Matrimony—Luther's Marriage—Domestic Happiness—The Elector
John—The Landgrave Philip—Poliander's Hymn—New Ordination
—Diet at Augsburg—League of Torgau—The Evangelic Union—
* The Rulers Take Counsel Together"—The Emperor's Message—
The Reformation and the Papacy.

BOOK XI.—Page 235.

Spiritual Slavery—Christian Liberty—Effect of the Gospel on Zwingle
—Leo Judah at Zurich—The Challenge—Zwingle and Faber—
Zwingle Tempted by the Pope—" Zwingle's Passion"—Tract against
Images—Wooden Idols—The Unterwalders—Public Meeting—Hoff-
man's Defence of the Pope—The Mass—Schmidt of Kussnacht—
Results of the Conference—Oswald Myconius at Zurich—Thomas
Plater—The Swiss Aroused—Hottinger Arrested—His Martyrdom—
Persecution Invoked—Swiss and German Reformations—The Jewish
and Pagan Elements—Zwingle's and Luther's Tasks—The Council
and the People—Abduction of Œxlin—Riot and Conflagration—The
Wirths arrested—The Prisoners Surrendered—A Spectacle to the
World—" Cruel Mockings"—" Faithful unto Death"—Father and
Son on the Scaffold—Abolition of the Mass—The Lord's Supper—
Brotherly Love—Zwingle on Original Sin - Attack upon Zwingle—

The Gospel at Berne—Heim and Haller—Ordinance of the Government—St. Michael's Nunnery—The Convent of Königsfeld—Margaret Watteville's Letter—Liberation of the Nuns—Pretended Letter of Zwingle—Clara May and Nicolas Watteville—The Seat of Learning—Œcolampadius—Flight from the Convent—Œcolampadius at Basle—Jealousy of Erasmus—Hütten and Erasmus—Death of Hütten—Vacillation and Decision—Erasmus's Quatrain—Luther's Letter to Erasmus—Motives of Erasmus in Opposing the Reformation—Lamentations of Erasmus—Arguments for Free Will—Premature Exultation—A Test—God's Working—Jansenism—The Bible and Philosophy—The Three Days' Battle—Character of False Systems—Conrad Grebel — Extravagances — "The Little Jerusalem" — The Anabaptist Feast—Horrible Tragedy — Discussion on Baptism—Opinions not Punishable—Popish Immobility—Zwingle and Luther—Zwingle on the Lord's Supper—Consubstantiation—Luther's Great Principle—Carlstadt's Writings Prohibited—Zwingle's Commentary—The Suabian Syngramma—Need of Union in Adversity—Struggles of the Reformation—Tumult in the Toekenburg—Meeting at Hantz—Comander's Defence—Doctrine of the Sacrament—Proposed Public Discussion—Decision of the Diet—Zwingle in Danger—The Disputants at Baden—Contrast of the Parties—Eck and Œcolampadius—Zwingle's Share in the Contest—Murner of Lucerne—Haller and the Council of Berne—Reformation in St. Gall—Conrad Pellican—The Mountaineers—Alliance with Austria—Farel Appears.

BOOK XII.—Page 341.

THE FRENCH.—1500—1526.

The Reformation in France—Persecution of the Vaudois—Birthplace of Farel—La Saint Croix—The Priest's Wizard—Farel's Superstitious Faith—The Chevalier Bayard—Louis XII—The Two Valois—Lefevre—His Devotion—Farel's Reverence for the Pope—Farel and the Bible—Gleams of Light—Lefevre Turns to St. Paul—Lefevre on Works—University Amusements—Faith and Works—Paradoxical Truth—Farel and the Saints—Allman Refutes De Vio—Pierre Olivetan—Happy Change in Farel—Independence and Priority—Of the Reformation in France—Francis of Angoulême—Two Classes of Combatants—Margaret of Valois—Talents of the Queen of Navarre—The Bishop and the Bible—Francis Encourages Learning—Margaret Embraces the Gospel—Poetical Effusions—Of the Duchess of Alencon—Margaret's Danger—Violence of Beda—Louis Berquin—Opposition to the Gospel—The Concordat—The Concordat Resisted—Fanaticism and Timidity—The Three Maries—Beda and the University—The King and the Sorbonne—Briconnet in His Diocese—The Bishop and the Curates—Martial Mazurier—Margaret's Sorrows—Strength Under Trial—Death of Philibert of Nemours—Alone, Not Lonely—The Wandering Sheep—Briconnet's Hope and Prayer—Sufficiency of the Scriptures—Lefevre's French Bible—The People " Turned Aside"—Church of Landouzy—The Gospel and the French Court — Margaret's Lamentations — Briconnet Preaches Against the Monks—Two Despotisms—Briconnet Draws Back—Leclerc the Wool-Comber—Leclerc's Zeal and Sufferings—A Mother's Faith and Love—Secret Meetings for Worship—Berquin Imprisoned by the Parliament—Charges Against Berquin—Liberated

by the King—Pavanne's Recantation and Remorse—Zeal of Leclerc
and Chatelain—Peter Toussaint—Leclerc Breaks the Images—Up-
roar among the People—Martyrdom of Leclerc and Chatelain—The
Gospel Expelled from Gap—Anemond's Zeal—Farel Preaches to His
Countrymen—Pierre De Sebville—Anemond Visits Luther—Luther's
Letter to the Duke of Savoy—Farel's Arrival in Switzerland—Œco-
lampadius and Farel—Cowardice of Erasmus—French Frankness—
"Balaam"—Farel's Propositions—Faith and Scripture—The Refor-
mation Defended—Visits Strasburg—Ordination of Farel—Apostolical
Succession—Farel at Montbeliard—The Gospel at Lyons—Anthony
Papillon—Sebville Persecuted—Secret Meetings at Grenoble—Effects
of the Battle of Pavia—Trial and Arrest of Maigret—Evangelical
Association—Need of Unity—Christian Patriotism—Influence of
Tracts—The New Testament in French—Bible and Tract Societies
—Farel at Montbeliard—Oil and Wine—Toussaint's Trials—Farel
and Anemond—The Image of Saint Anthony—Death of Anemond—
Defeat and Captivity of Francis I—Consternation of the French—
Opposers of the Faith—The Queen-Mother and the Sorbonne—Cry
for "Heretical" Blood—Parliament Establishes the Inquisition—
Charges Against Briconnet—Cited Before the Inquisition—Dismay
of the Bishop—Refused a Trial by His Peers—Briconnet's Tempta-
tion and Fall—Retractation of Briconnet—Compared with Lefevre—
Beda Attacks Lefevre—Lefevre at Strasburg—Meets Farel—Berquin
Imprisoned—Erasmus Attacked by the Monks and the Sorbonne—
Appeals to the Parliament and the King—More Victims in Lorraine
—Bonaventure Rennel—Courage of Pastor Schuch—Martyrdom of
Schuch—Peter Caroli and Beda—The Martyrdom of James Pavanne
—The Hermit of Livry—Seized and Condemned—Resources of
Providence—John Calvin—The Family of Mommor—Calvin's Pa-
rentage—Calvin's Childhood—His Devotion to Study—Infant Eccle-
siastics—Calvin Proceeds to Paris—Reformation of Language—Pro-
testant France—System of Terror—The "Babylonish Captivity"—
Toussaint Goes to Paris—Toussaint in Prison—"Not accepting De-
liverance"—Spread of Persecution—Project of Margaret—For the
Deliverance of Francis—Margaret's Resolution—She Sails for Spain.

HISTORY OF THE REFORMATION.

BOOK IX.

It was now four years since the Church had heard again proclaimed a Truth which had formed part of her earliest teaching. The mighty word of a *Salvation by Grace*,—once 'fully preached' throughout Asia, Greece, and Italy by Paul and his companions, and discovered many ages after, in the pages of the Bible, by a monk of Wittemberg,—had resounded from the plains of Saxony, as far as Italy, France, and England; and the lofty mountains of Switzerland had echoed its inspiring accents. The springs of truth, liberty, and life were again opened: multitudes had drunk gladly of the waters; but those who had freely partaken of them had retained the same external appearance, and while all *within* was new, every thing *without* remained unchanged.

The constitution of the Church, its ritual, and its discipline had undergone no alteration. In Saxony—even at Wittemberg—and wherever the new opinions had spread, the papal ceremonies held on their accustomed course; the priest before the altar offering the host to God was believed to effect a mysterious transubstantiation; friars and nuns continued to present themselves at the convents to take upon them the monastic vows; pastors lived single; religious brotherhoods herded together; pilgrimages were undertaken; the faithful suspended their votive offerings on the pillars of the chapels; and all the accustomed ceremonies, down to the minutest observances, were celebrated as before. A voice had been heard in the world, but as yet it was not embodied forth in action.   The language of the priest accordingly presented the most striking contrast with his ministrations.   From his pulpit he might be heard to thunder against the mass as idolatrous, and then he might be seen to come down to the altar, and go scrupulously through the prescribed form of the service.   On every side, the recently recovered Gospel sounded in the midst of the ancient rites.   The officiating priest himself was unconscious of his inconsistency, and the populace, who listened with avidity to the bold discourses of the new preachers, continued devoutly observant of their long-established customs, as though they were never to abandon them.   All things continued unchanged at the domestic hearth, and in the social circle, as in the house of God.   A new faith was abroad, but new works were not yet seen. The vernal sun had risen, but winter still bound the earth; neither flower, nor leaf, nor any sign of vegetation was visible.   But this aspect of things was deceptive; a vigorous sap was secretly circulating beneath the surface, and was about to change the face of the world.

To this wisely-ordered progress, the Reformation may be indebted for its triumphs. Every revolution should be wrought out in men's minds before it takes the shape of action.   The contrast we have remarked did not at first fix Luther's attention.   He seemed to expect that while men received his writings with enthusiasm, they should continue devout observers of the corruptions those writings exposed.   One might be tempted to believe that he had planned his course beforehand, and was resolved to change the opinions of men before he ventured to remodel their forms of worship.   But this would be ascribing to Luther a wisdom, the honour of which is due to a higher Intelligence.   He was the appointed instrument for a purpose he had no power to conceive.   At a later period he could discern and comprehend these things, but he did not devise or arrange them. God led the way: the part assigned to Luther was to follow.

If Luther had begun by external reformation—if he had followed up his words by an attempt to abolish monastic vows, the mass, confession, the prescribed form of worship,—assuredly he would have encountered the most formidable resistance. Mankind need time to accommodate themselves to great changes. But Luther was not the imprudent and daring innovator that some historians[*] have depicted. The people, seeing no change in their daily devotions, followed undoubtingly their new leader—wondering at the assaults directed against a man who left unquestioned their mass, their beads, and their confessor; and disposed to ascribe such enmity to the petty jealousy of secret rivals, or to the hard injustice of powerful enemies. And yet the opinions that Luther put forth, fermented in the minds of men, moulded their thoughts, and so undermined the strong hold of prejudice that it, ere long, fell without being attacked. Such influence is, indeed, gradual. Opinions make their silent progress, like the waters which trickle behind our rocks, and loosen them from the mountains on which they rest: suddenly the hidden operation is revealed, and a single day suffices to lay bare the work of years, if not of centuries.

A new era had dawned upon the Reformation: already truth was recovered in its teaching; henceforward the teaching of the truth is to work truth in the Church and in society. The agitation was too great to allow of men's minds remaining at their then point of attainment; on the general faith in the dogmas so extensively undermined, customs had been established which now began to be disregarded, and were destined, with them, to pass away.

There was a courage and vitality in that age, which prevented its continuing silent in presence of proved error. The sacraments, public worship, the hierarchy, vows, constitutional forms, domestic and public life, all were on the eve of undergoing modification. The bark, slowly and laboriously con-

* Hume, &c.

tracted, was on the point of being lowered from the stocks, and launched on the open sea. It is for us to follow its progress through many shoals.

The captivity of Luther in the castle of Wartburg, separates these two periods. That Divine Providence which was about to give a mighty impulse to the Reformation, had prepared the means of its progress, by leading apart into profound seclusion, the man chosen to effect it. For a while, the work was as much lost sight of as the instrument of it: but the seed must be committed to the earth, if it is to bring forth fruit; and from this captivity, which might have seemed to close the Reformer's career, the Reformation was destined to go forth to new conquests, and spread rapidly through the world.

Until this period, the Reformation had indeed centered in the person of Luther. His appearance before the Diet of Worms was unquestionably the sublimest hour of his life. His character at that time seemed almost without a blemish; and this it is that has led some to the remark, that if God, who hid the Reformer for ten months within the walls of the Wartburg, had at that moment for ever removed him from the eyes of men, his end would have resembled an apotheosis. But God designs no apotheosis for His servants,—and Luther was preserved to the Church, that in him, and by his errors, the Church might learn that the faith of Christians should rest only on the word of God. He was hurried away and placed at a distance from the stage on which the great revolution of the sixteenth century was going on. The truth which he had for four years so energetically proclaimed, continued to produce its effect upon Christendom; and the work of which he had been the weak instrument, bore thenceforward the impress, not of man—but of God himself.

All Germany was moved by the news of Luther's captivity. Rumours, the most contradictory, were circulated in the provinces. Men's minds were more agitated by the absence of the Reformer, than they could possibly have been by his presence. On one side, it was affirmed that some of his friends, passing from the French territory, had carried him off, and lodged him in safety beyond the Rhine.* In another place, it was said that assassins had taken his life. Even in the smallest villages, inquiries were heard concerning Luther. Travellers were questioned, and groups of the curious assembled in the market-places. Sometimes a stranger, passing through, recounted how the Reformer had been carried off; depicting the brutal horsemen hastily tieing their prisoner's hands behind him, dragging him after them on foot, till his strength was spent, and deaf to his cries, though the blood forced its way from his fingers.† His body, said some, has been seen pierced through and through.‡ Such narratives drew forth exclamations of grief and horror. ‘Never more shall we behold him!’ said the gathered crowds; ‘never again shall we hear that bold man whose voice stirred the depths of our hearts!’ Luther's partisans, moved with indignation, swore to avenge his death. Women and children, men of peace, and aged people, foreboded new disturbances. The alarm of the Romish party was altogether unexampled. The priests and friars who had been at first unable to conceal their joy, believing their own triumph secured by the death of one man, and had carried themselves haughtily, would now willingly have hid themselves from the threatening anger of the populace.§ Those who had given free vent to their rage, so long as Luther was at large, now trembled with alarm, though Luther was in captivity.‖ Aleander, especially, was as if thunderstruck. “The only way of extricating ourselves,” wrote a Roman Catholic to the Archbishop of Mentz, “is to

---

* Hic . . . invalescit opinio, me esse ab amicis captum e Francia missis. (L. Epp. ii. 5.)

† Et iter festinantes cursu equites ipsum pedestrem raptim tractum sisse ut sanguis e digitis erumperet. (Cochlæus, p. 39.)

‡ Fuit qui testatus sit, visum à se Lutheri cadaver transfossum. . . . (Pallavicini Hist. Conc. Trid. i. p. 122.)

§ Molem vulgi imminentis ferre non possunt. (L. Epp. ii. p. 13.)

‖ Qui me libero insanierunt, nunc me captivo ita formidant ut incipiant mitigare. (Ibid.)

light our torches, and go searching through the earth for Luther, till we can restore him to the nation that *will* have him."*
It might have been thought that the pallid ghost of the Reformer, dragging his chain, was spreading terror around, and calling for vengeance. Luther's death, it was predicted, would occasion the effusion of torrents of human blood.†

Nowhere was there a stronger feeling displayed than in Worms itself. Bold remonstrances were heard both from nobles and people. Ulric Hütten and Hermann Busch filled the air with their plaintive lamentations and calls to war Loud accusations were brought against Charles V. and the Nuncios. The entire nation had espoused the cause of the monk whose energy of faith had made him its leader.

At Wittemberg, his colleagues and friends, and especially Melancthon, were at first lost in sadness. Luther had been the means of communicating to the young student the treasures of that divine knowledge which from that hour had taken possession of his whole soul. It was Luther who had given substance and life to that intellectual culture which Melancthon brought with him to Wittemberg. The depth of the Reformer's doctrine had impressed the young Grecian, and his bold advocacy of the claims of the unchanging Word against human traditions had called orth his enthusiasm. He had associated himself with him in his labours, and taking up the pen, with that finished style which he had imbibed in the study of ancient literature, he had made the authority of Fathers and of Councils to bend before the sovereignty of God's Word.

The prompt decision that Luther displayed in the trying occasions of life, Melancthon manifested in his pursuit of learning. Never were two men more strongly marked with diversity and agreement. "Scripture," said Melancthon, "satisfies the soul with holy and wondrous delight—it is a heavenly

---

* Nos vitam vix redempturos, nisi accensis candelis undique eum requiramus. (L. Epp. ii. p. 13.)

† Gerbelii Ep. in M. S. C. Heckelianis. Lindner, Leb. Luth. p. 244.

ambrosia!"* "The word of God," exclaimed Luther, "is a sword—an instrument of war and destruction,—it falls on the children of Ephraim like the lioness that darts from the forest." Thus one saw in Scripture chiefly its power to comfort;—and the other, a mighty energy opposed to the corruption of the world. But to both it was the sublimest of themes. In so far, there was a perfect agreement in their judgment. "Melancthon," observed Luther, "is a miracle in the estimation of all who know him. He is the most dreaded enemy of Satan and the schoolmen, for he knows all their 'foolishness, and he knows Christ as the rock. That young Grecian goes beyond me even in divine learning,—he will do you more good than many Luthers!" And he went on to say he was ready to give up an opinion if Philip disapproved it. Melancthon, on his part, full of admiration for Luther's knowledge of Scripture, ranked him far above the Fathers. He took pleasure in excusing the jesting which Luther was reproached for resorting to, and would, on such occasions, compare him to an earthen vase which holds a precious treasure in an unsightly vessel. "I would be careful how I blame him," said he.†

But behold the two friends so intimately united in affection, now parted one from the other. The two fellow-soldiers no longer march side by side to the rescue of the Church. Luther is absent,—and lost perhaps for ever! The consternation at Wittemberg was extreme:—as that of an army, gloomy and dejected, at sight of the bleeding corpse of the general who was leading it on to victory.

Suddenly news arrived of a more cheering character. "Our well-beloved father still lives,"‡ exclaimed Philip, exultingly, "take courage and stand firm." But ere long melancholy prognostications returned. Luther was indeed

---

* Mirabilis in iis voluptas, immo ambrosia quædam cœlestis. (Corp Ref. i. 128.)

† Spiritum Martiai nolim temere in hac causâ interpellare. (Ibid. p. 211.)

‡ Pater noster charissimus vivit. (Ibid. p. 389.)

living, but in close imprisonment. The edict of Worms, with
its menacing proscriptions,* was circulated by thousands
throughout the empire, and even in the Tyrolese mountains.†
Was not the Reformation on the very eve of destruction by
the iron hand impending over it? The gentle spirit of Melancthon recoiled with a thrill of horror.

But above the hand of man's power, a mightier hand was
making itself felt, and God was rendering powerless that
dreaded edict. The German princes, who had long sought
occasion to reduce the authority which Rome exercised in the
empire, took alarm at the alliance between the Emperor and
the Pope, lest it should work the ruin of their liberty.
Whilst, therefore, Charles, in journeying in the Low Countries, might see with a smile of irony the bonfires in which
flatterers and fanatics consumed the writings of Luther in the
public squares,—those writings were read in Germany with
continually increasing eagerness, and numerous pamphlets in
favour of the Reformation every day attacked the papal
authority.

The Nuncios could not control themselves when they found
that the edict, which it had cost them so much to obtain, produced so feeble an effect. "The ink of the signature," said
they, "has scarcely had time to dry, when, behold, on all
sides, the imperial decree is torn to pieces." The populace
were more and more won to the cause of the extraordinary
man who, without heeding the thunderbolts of Charles and
of the Pope, had made confession of his faith with the courage
of a martyr. It was said, "Has he not offered to retract if
refuted, and no one has had the hardihood to undertake to refute him. Does not that show that he has spoken the truth?"
Thus it was that the first emotions of fear were followed at
Wittemberg and throughout the empire by a movement of
enthusiasm. Even the archbishop of Mentz, beholding the
burst of national sympathy, durst not give permission to the

* Dicitur parari proscriptio horrenda. (Corp. Ref. i. p. 389.)
† Dicuntur signatæ chartæ proscriptionis bis mille missæ quoque ad
Insbruck. (Ibid.)

cordeliers to preach against the Reformer. The University, which might have been expected to yield to the storm, raised its head. The new doctrines had taken too deep root to suffer by Luther's absence, and the halls of the academies were crowded with auditors.*

Meanwhile, the Knight George, for this was the name of Luther, so long as he was in the Wartburg, was living solitary and unknown. "If you were to see me," wrote he to Melancthon, "truly you would take me for a knight; even you would scarcely know me again."† Luther, on his arrival, passed a short time in repose, enjoying a leisure which had not yet been allowed him. He was at large within the fortress; but he was not permitted to pass outside it.‡ All his wishes were complied with, and he had never been better treated.§ Many were the thoughts that occupied his mind, but none of them had power to disturb him. By turns he looked down upon the forests that surrounded him, and raised his eyes to heaven—"Strange captivity!" he exclaimed,— "a prisoner by consent, and yet against my will." ‖ "Pray for me," he wrote to Spalatin :—"I want nothing save your prayers : don't disturb me by what is said or thought of me in the world. At last I am quiet."¶ This letter, like many of that period is dated from the island of *Patmos.* Luther compared the Wartburg to the island celebrated as the scene of the banishment of St. John by the emperor Domitian.

* Scholastici quorum supra millia ibi tunc fuerunt. (Spalatini Annales, 1521, October.)

† Equitem videres ac ipse vix agnosceres. (L. Epp. ii. 11.)

‡ Nunc sum hic otiosus, sicut inter captivos liber. (Ibid. p. 3, 12 May.)

§ Quanquam et hilariter et libenter omnia mihi ministret. (Ibid. p. 13, 15 August.)

‖ Ego mirabilis captivus qui et volens et nolens hic sedeo. (L. Epp. ii. p. 4, 12 May.)

¶ Tu fac ut pro me ores: hac una re opus mihi est. Quicquid de me fit in publico, nihil moror ; ego in quiete tandem sedeo. (L. Epp. ii. p. 4, 10 June 1521.)

2*

After the stirring contests that had agitated his soul, the Reformer enjoyed repose in the heart of the gloomy forests of Thuringen. There he studied evangelic truth,—not for disputation, but as the means of regeneration and of life. The Reformation, in its beginning, was of necessity polemic;—other circumstances required new labours. After eradicating with the hoe the thorns and brambles, the time was arrived for peaceably sowing the word of God in men's hearts. If Luther had been all his life called to wage conflicts,—he would not have effected a lasting work in the Church. By his captivity he escaped a danger which might have ruined the cause of the Reformation,—that of always attacking and demolishing, without ever defending or building up.

This secluded retreat had one effect, perhaps still more beneficial. Lifted by his nation, like one raised upon a shield, he was but a hand's breadth from the abyss beyond, and the least degree of intoxication might have precipitated him headlong. Some of the foremost promoters of the Reformation in Germany, as well as in Switzerland, had made shipwreck on the shoals of spiritual pride and fanaticism. Luther was a man very subject to the weaknesses of our nature; and, as it was, he did not entirely escape these besetting dangers. Meanwhile, the hand of the Almighty, for a while, preserved him from them, by suddenly removing him from the intoxication of success, and plunging him in the depth of a retirement unknown to the world! There his soul gathered up itself to God,—there it was again tempered by adversity;—his sufferings, his humiliation, obliged him to walk, at least for a time, with the humble;—and the principles of the christian life thenceforward developed themselves in his soul with fresh energy and freedom.

Luther's tranquillity was not of long duration. Seated in solitude on the walls of the Wartburg, he passed whole days lost in meditation. At times, the Church rose before his vision, and spread out all her wretchedness;* at other times,

* Ego hic sedens tota die faciem Ecclesiæ ante me constituo. (L. Epp. ii. 1.)

lifting his eyes to heaven, he would say, "Canst Thou have made all men in vain?" Then letting go his confidence, he would add, dejectedly, "Alas! there is no one in this closing day of wrath to stand as a wall before the Lord, and save Israel!"

Then recurring to his own lot, he dreaded being charged with having deserted the field of battle;* the thought was insupportable. "Rather," exclaimed he, "would I be stretched on burning coals than stagnate here half dead."† Transported in thought to Worms—to Wittemberg—into the midst of his adversaries—he regretted that, yielding to his friends' entreaties, he had withdrawn himself from the world.‡ "Ah," said he, "nothing on earth do I more desire than to face my cruel enemies."§

Some gentler thoughts, however, brought a truce to such complainings. Luther's state of mind was not all tempest; his agitated spirit recovered at times a degree of calm and comfort. Next to the assurance of the Divine protection, one thing consoled him in his grief—it was the recollection of Melancthon. "If I perish," he wrote, "the Gospel will loose nothing‖—you will succeed me as Elisha succeeded Elijah, with a double portion of my spirit." But calling to mind the timidity of Melancthon, he ejaculated—"Minister of the Word! keep the walls and towers of Jerusalem till our enemies shall strike you down. We stand alone on the plain of battle; after me they will strike you down."¶

This thought of the final onset of Rome on the infant Church, threw him into renewed anxieties. The poor monk, —a prisoner and alone,—had many a struggle to pass through in his solitude; but suddenly he seemed to get a glimpse of

* Verebar ego ne aciem deserere viderer. (L. Epp. ii. 1.)
† Mallem inter carbones vivos ardere, quam solus semivivus, atque utinam non mortuus putere. (Ibid. 10.)
‡ Cervicem esse objectandam publico furori. (Ibid. 89.)
§ Nihil magis opto, quam furoribus adversariorum occurrere, objecto jugulo. (Ibid. 1.)
‖ Etiam si peream, nihil peribit Evangelia. (Ibid p. 30.)
¶ Nos soli adhuc stamus in acie: te quærent post me. (Ibid. p. 3.)

his deliverance. He thought he could foresee that the assaults of the papal power would rouse the nations of Germany; and that the soldiers of the Gospel, victorious over its enemies, and gathered under the walls of the Wartburg, would give liberty to its captive. "If the Pope," said he, "should stretch forth his hand against all who are on my side, there will be a violent commotion; the more he urges on our ruin, the sooner shall we see an end of him and his adherents! And as for me . . . . I shall be restored to your arms.* God is awakening many, and He it is who impels the nations. Only let our enemies take up our affair and try to stifle it in their arms,—and it will grow by their pressure, and come forth more formidable than ever!"

But sickness brought him down from these lofty heights to which his courage and faith would at times rise. He had already, when at Worms, suffered much; and his disorder had increased in solitude.† The food of the Wartburg was altogether unsuited to him; it was rather less ordinary in quality than that of his convent, and it was found needful to give him the poor diet to which he had been accustomed. He passed whole nights without sleep;—anxieties of mind were added to pain of body. No great work is accomplished without struggle and suffering. Luther, alone on his rock, endured in his vigorous frame a suffering that was needed, in order to the emancipation of mankind. "Sitting, at night, in my apartment," says he, "I uttered cries like a woman in travail."‡ Then, ceasing to complain, and touched with the thought that what he was undergoing was sent in mercy from God, he broke forth in accents of love: "Thanks to Thee, O Christ, that thou wilt not leave me without the precious relics of thy holy cross!"§ But soon, feeling indignation against him-

* Quo citus id tentaverit, hoc citius et ipse et sui peribunt, et ego revertar. (L. Epp. ii. p. 10.)

† Auctum est malum, quo Wormatiæ laborabam. (Ibid. p. 17.)

‡ Sedeo dolens, sicut puerpera, lacer et saucius et cruentus. (Ibid p. 50, 9 Sept.)

§ Gratias Christo, qui me sine reliquiis sanctæ Crucis non dereliquit. (Ibid.)

&en' wrought in his soul, he exclaimed, " Hardened fool that I am ; woe is me ! my prayers are few ; I wrestle but little with the Lord ; I bewail not the state of the Church of God ;* instead of being fervent in spirit, my passions take fire : I sink in sloth, in sleep, and indolence." Then, not knowing to what to ascribe his feelings, and accustomed to expect blessing through the affectionate remembrance of his friends, he exclaimed, in the bitterness of his soul, " O, my friends, do you then forget to pray for me ? that God can thus leave me to myself."

Those who were about him, as also his Wittemberg friends, and those at the Elector's court, were anxious and alarmed at his mental suffering. They trembled in the prospect of the life that had been snatched from the fires of the Pope, and the sword of Charles, so sadly sinking and expiring. The Wartburg then would be Luther's tomb ! " I fear," said Melancthon, " lest his grief for the condition of the Church should bring him down to the grave. He has lighted a candle in Israel ; if he dies, what hope is left us ? Would that by the sacrifice of my worthless life, I could retain in this world one who is surely its brightest ornament.† O, what a man !" he exclaimed, (as if already standing beside his grave,) "surely we never valued him as we ought."

What Luther termed the shameful indolence of his prison-life, was in reality, diligence beyond the strength of ordinary mortals. "Here am I," said he, on the 14th of May, "lapped in indolence and pleasures. [He doubtless refers to the quality of his food, which was at first less coarse than what he had been used to.] I am going through the Bible in Hebrew and Greek. I mean to write a discourse in German touching auricular confession ; also to continue the translation of the Psalms, and to compose a collection of sermons, as soon as I have received what I want from Wittemberg. My pen is never idle."‡ Even this was but a part of Luther's labours.

* Nihil gemens pro ecclesiâ Dei. (L. Epp. ii. p. 22, 13 July.)
† Utinam hac vili anima mea ipsius vitam emere queam. (Corp. Ref. 415, 6 July.) ‡ Sine intermissione scribo. (L. Epp. ii. 6 and 16.)

His enemies thought that, if not dead, at least he was effectually silenced; but their exultation was short, and, ere long, no doubt could exist that he still lived. A multitude of tracts, composed in the Wartburg, followed each other in rapid succession; and everywhere the well-known voice of the Reformer was enthusiastically responded to. Luther, at the same moment, put forth such writings as were adapted to build up the church, and controversial tracts which disturbed his opponents in their fancied security. For nearly a whole year, he, by turns, instructed, exhorted, rebuked, and thundered from his mountain height, and his astonished adversaries might well enquire whether indeed there was not something supernatural in so prodigious an activity—"He could not have allowed himself any rest,"* says Cochlæus. But the solution of the whole mystery was to be found in the rashness of the Romish party. They were in haste to profit by the decree of Worms, to put an end to the Reformation; and Luther, sentenced—placed under the ban of the empire,—and a prisoner in the Wartburg, stood up in the cause of sound doctrine, as if he were still at large and triumphant. It was especially at the tribunal of penance that the priests strove to rivet the fetters of their deluded parishioners;—hence it is the Confessional that Luther first assails. "They allege," says he, "that passage in St. James, 'confess your sins to one another;' a strange confessor this—his name is 'one another!' Whence it would follow that the confessors ought also to confess to their penitents; that every Christian should *in his turn* be pope, bishop, and priest, and that the pope himself should make confession before all."†

Scarcely had Luther finished this tract, when he commenced another. A divine of Louvain, named Latomos, already known by his opposition to Reuchlin and Erasmus, had impugned the Reformer's statements. Twelve days after, Luther's answer was ready, and it is one of his masterpieces. He first defends himself against the charge of want of mode

* Cum quiescere non posset. (Cochlæus, Acta Lutheri, p. 39.)
† Und der Papst müsse ihm beichten. (L. Opp. xvi. p. 701.)

ration. "The moderation of this age," says he, "consists in bending the knee before sacrilegious pontiffs and impious sophists, and saying, 'Gracious Lord, most worthy master.' Then, having so done, you may persecute who you will to the death; you may convulse the world,—all that shall not hinder your being a man of moderation! Away with such moderation, say I. Let me speak out, and delude no one. The shell may be rough, perhaps, but the nut is soft and tender."[*]

The health of Luther continued to decline; he began to think of leaving the Wartburg. But what to do; to appear in open day at the risk of his life? In the rear of the mountain on which the fortress was built, the country was intersected by numerous footpaths, bordered by tufts of wild strawberries. The massive gate of the castle was unclosed, and the prisoner ventured, not without fear, to gather some of the fruit.[†] Gradually, he became more venturesome, and, clothed in his knight's disguise, and attended by a rough-mannered but faithful guard from the castle, he extended his excursions in the neighbourhood. One day, stopping to rest at an inn, Luther laid aside his sword, which encumbered him, and took up some books that lay near. His natural disposition got the better of his prudence. His attendant took the alarm lest an action so unusual in a man of arms, should excite a suspicion that the doctor was not really a knight. Another time, the two companions descended the mountain, and entered the convent of Reichardsbrunn, in which, but a few months before, Luther had rested for a night, on his way to Worms.[‡] Suddenly, one of the lay-brothers uttered an exclamation of surprise—Luther had been recognised. His keeper, seeing how the matter stood, hurried him away, and it was not till they were galloping far from the cloisters, that the monk recovered from his astonishment.

* Cortex meus esse potest durior, sed nucleus meus mollis et dulcis est. (L. Opp. xvii. Lat. ii. p. 213.)

† Zu zeiten gehet er inn die Erdbeer am Schlossberg. (Mathesius, p. 33.)   ‡ See Vol. ii. p 214.

The life of the Doctor of Wittemberg, in his assumed character of knight, had, indeed, at times, a something about it truly theological. One day, the snares were made ready—the fortress gates thrown open—the sporting dogs let loose. Luther had expressed a wish to partake of the pleasures of the chase. The huntsmen were in high spirits; the dogs scoured the hills, driving the hares from the brushwood; but as the tumult swelled around him, the Knight George, motionless in the midst of it, felt his soul fill with solemn thoughts. Looking round him, his heart heaved with sorrow.* " Is it not," said he, "the very picture of the Devil, setting his dogs, the bishops, those messengers of antichrist, and sending them out to hunt down poor souls ?"† A young leveret had been snared: rejoicing to liberate it, Luther wrapped it in his mantle, and deposited it in the midst of a thicket; but scarcely had he left the spot, when the dogs scented it, and killed it. Drawn to the place by its cry, Luther uttered an exclamation of grief—" O, Pope! and thou, too, O Satan! it is thus that ye would compass the destruction of the souls that have been rescued from death !"‡

Whilst the Doctor of Wittemberg, dead to the world, was seeking to recruit his spirits by these occupations in the vicinity of the Wartburg, the great work was progressing, as if by its own power. The Reformation, in fact, was beginning to take effect. It was no longer limited to teaching; it now began to affect and mould the life.

Bernard Feldkirchen, the pastor of Kemberg, and the first, under Luther's direction, to expose the errors of Rome,∥ was also the first to throw off the yoke of her institutions:—he married!

* Theologisabar etiam ibi inter retia et canes . . . tantum misericordiæ et doloris miscuit mysterium. (L. Epp. ii. p. 43.)

† Quid enim ista imago, nisi Diabolum significat per insidias suas et impios magistros canes suos . . (Ibid.)

‡ Sic sævit Papa et Satan ut servatas etiam animas perdat. (L. Epp. ii. p. 44.)

∥ Vol. i. p. 189.

There is, in the German character, a strong love of family and domestic enjoyments:—hence, of all the injunctions of the Papal authority, none had had more lamentable results than the imposition of celibacy. Made obligatory on the heads of the clergy, this practice had prevented the fiefs of the church from passing into hereditary possessions. But extended by Gregory VII. to the inferior orders, its effects had been indeed deplorable. Many of the priests, in evading the obligation imposed upon them, by shameful disorders, had drawn down hatred and contempt on their profession; while those who had submitted to Hildebrand's law, were indignant that the Church, which lavished power, riches, and earthly possessions on its higher dignitaries, should impose on its humbler ministers, who were ever its most useful supporters, a denial so opposed to the Gospel.

"Neither the Pope, nor the Councils," said Feldkirchen, and another pastor, named Seidler, who followed his example, "can have a right to impose on the Church a command that endangers soul and body. The obligation to observe God's law compels us to throw aside traditions of men."[*] The reestablishment of marriage was, in the sixteenth century, an homage paid to the moral law. The ecclesiastical power, in alarm, instantly issued its mandates against the two priests. Seidler, who lived in the territory of Duke George, was given up to his superiors, and died in prison. But the Elector Frederic refused to surrender Feldkirchen to the Archbishop of Magdeburg. "His Highness," said Spalatin, "declines to act the part of a police-officer." Feldkirchen, therefore, continued to preside over his flock, though a *husband* and a *father !*

The first emotion of the Reformer, on receiving intelligence of these events, was one of joy. "I am all admiration," says he, "of the new bridegroom of Kemberg, who moves on fearlessly in the midst of all this hubbub." Luther was satisfied that priests *ought* to marry. But this question led

---

[*] Coegit me ergo ut humanas traditiones violarem, necessitas servandi juris divini. (Corp. Ref. I. p. 441.)

directly to another—the marriage of friars—and on this point Luther had to pass through one of those internal struggles, of which his life was full; for every reform was of necessity to be wrought out by a mental conflict. Melancthon and Carlstadt,—the one a layman, the other in priest's orders,—thought that the liberty of contracting the marriage bond ought to be as free to the friars as to the priests. Luther, himself a monk, did not at first agree with them in judgment. One day, when the commandant of the Wartburg had brought him some theses of Carlstadt, touching celibacy, "Good Heaven!" he exclaimed, "will our Wittemberg friends allow wives even to monks?" The thought overwhelmed him, and disturbed his spirit. For himself, he put far from him the liberty he claimed for others: "Ah," said he, indignantly, "at least they will not make *me* take a wife."* This expression is doubtless unknown to those who assert that Luther's object in the Reformation was that he might marry. Bent upon the truth, not from any desire of self-pleasing, but with upright intentions, he undertook the defence of that which appeared to him to be right, although it might be at variance with the general tendency of his doctrine. He worked his way through a mingled crowd of truths and errors, until the errors had altogether fallen, and truth alone remained standing in his mind.

There was indeed a broad distinction discernible between the two questions. The marriage of priests did not draw after it the downfall of the priesthood; on the contrary, it was of itself likely to win back popular respect to the secular clergy: but the marriage of friars involved the breaking up of the monastic institutions. The question then really was, whether it was right to disband the army that acknowledged themselves the soldiery of the Pope. "The priests," said Luther, writing to Melancthon, "are ordained by God, and therefore they are set above the commandments of men; but the friars have of their own accord chosen a life of celibacy,—

* At mihi non obtrudent uxorem. (L. Epp. ii. p. 40.)

they therefore are not at liberty to withdraw from the obligation they have laid themselves under."*

The Reformer was destined to advance a step further, and by a new struggle to carry also this post of the enemy. Already he had trampled under his feet many Romish corruptions; nay, even the authority of Rome herself. But monkery was still standing—monkery, which had in early times carried the spark of life to many a desert spot, and, passing through successive generations, now filled so many cloisters with sloth and luxury, seemed to find a voice and advocate in the castle of Thuringen, and to depend for life or death upon the agitated conscience of one man! Luther struggled for a while. at one moment on the point of rejecting it,—at another disposed to acknowledge it. At last, no longer able to support the contest, he threw himself in prayer at the feet of Christ, exclaiming, " Do thou teach us—do thou deliver us—establish us with thy free Spirit, in the liberty thou hast given us! for surely we are thy people!"†

And truly there was no long tarrying; a great change took place in the Reformer's thoughts, and again it was the great doctrine of *Justification by Faith* which gave victory.

This weapon, which had put down indulgences, baffled Romish intrigues, and humbled the Pope himself, dethroned monkery also from the place it held in the mind of Luther and of all Christendom. Luther was led to see that the monastic institutions were in flagrant opposition to the doctrines of Free Grace, and that the life led by the monks was entirely grounded on the assertion of human merit. Convinced from that instant, that the glory of Christ was at stake, his conscience incessantly repeated—'Monkery must yield.' So long as *Justification by Faith* is clearly held by the Church,

* Me enim vehementer movet, quod sacerdotum ordo, a Deo institutus, est liber, non autem monachorum qui sua sponte statum eligerunt. (L. Epp. ii. p. 34.)

† Dominus Jesus erudiat et liberet nos, per misericordiam suam, in libertatem nostram. (Melancthon on Celibacy, 6th Aug. 1521. ibid p. 40.)

not one of her members will become a monk.* This persuasion continued to gain strength in his mind, and as early
as the beginning of December, he addressed to the bishops
and deacons of the church of Wittemberg, the following
theses—-his declaration of war against monkery :—

" Whatsoever is not of *faith*, is sin.—Rom. xiv. 23.

" Whoever binds himself by a vow of celibacy, of chastity,
of service to God—without *faith*—vows, profanely and idola-
trously, a vow to the devil himself.

" To make such vows is worse than to be priests of Cybele,
or vestals of Pagan worship ; for the monks make their vows
in the thought that they shall be justified and saved by them ;
and that which should be ascribed to the alone mercy of God,
is thus ascribed to human deservings.   Such convents ought
to be razed to the foundation, as being abodes of the devil.
There is but one Order that is holy, and makes men holy,
and that is—Christianity or Faith.†

" To make the religious houses really useful, they should
be converted into schools, wherein children might be brought
up to manhood ; instead of which, they are establishments
where grown men are reduced to second childhood for the
rest of their lives."

We see that Luther at this period would have tolerated the
convents as houses of education ; but, ere long, his attack upon
them became more unsparing.

The immorality and shameful practices that disgraced the
cloisters, recurred forcibly to his thoughts.   " It is my great
aim," he wrote to Spalatin, on the 11th of November, " to
rescue the young from the hellish fires of celibacy ;"‡ and he
proceeded to compose a tract against monastic vows, which he
dedicated to his father.   " Do you desire," said he, in his
dedication to the old man at Mansfeld, " do you still feel a desire to extricate me from a monk's life ?   You have the right

* L. Opp. (W.) xxii. p. 1466.
† Es ist nicht mehr denn eine einige Geistlichkeit, die da heilig ist,
und heilig macht. . . . (L. Opp. xvii. p. 718.)
‡ Adolescentes liberare ex isto inferno coelibatus.   (Ibid. ii. 95.)

to do so, for you are still my father, and I am still your son.
But it is not needed: God has been beforehand with you, and
has Himself delivered me from it by his mighty arm. What
does it matter if I should lay aside the tonsure or the cowl?
Is it the cowl,—is it the tonsure that constitutes a monk?
'All things are yours,' said St. Paul, 'and you are Christ's.'
I belong not to the cowl, but the cowl to me ; I am a monk,
and yet no monk ; I am a new creature, not of the Pope, but
of Jesus Christ! Christ alone, and no mere go-between, is
my bishop, my abbot, my prior, my lord, my master,—and I
acknowledge no other! What matters it to me if the Pope
should sentence and put me to death ; he cannot summon me
from the grave, and take my life a second time. That great
day is nigh when the kingdom of abominations shall be overthrown. Would to God the Pope would do his worst, and
put us all to death ; our blood would cry to heaven against
him, and bring down swift destruction on him and his adherents."[*]

Luther himself was already transformed: he felt himself
no longer a friar. It was no outward circumstances, no human passions, no haste of the flesh that had brought about the
change. A struggle had been gone through : Luther had at
first sided with monkery, but truth had descended into the
arena, and monkery was overthrown. The triumphs of human passion are short-lived, but those of truth are decisive and
durable.

Whilst Luther was thus preparing the way for one of the
greatest changes which the Church was destined to pass
through, and the Reformation was beginning to manifest its
effects on the lives of Christians,—the partisans of Rome, with
that blind infatuation common to those who have long held
power, were pleasing themselves with the thought, that because Luther was in the Wartburg, the Reformation was for
ever at an end. They thought, therefore, quietly to resume

* Dass unser Blut möcht schreien, und dringen sein Gericht, dass
sein bald ein Ende würde. (L. Epp. ii. p. 105.)

2*

their former practices, which had been for an instant interrupted by the monk of Wittemberg. Albert, the Archbishop and Elector of Mentz, was one of those weak persons who, when things are nearly balanced, are found on the side of truth; but whenever their own interest is concerned, are quite willing to take up with error. His great aim was that his court should equal in splendour that of any of the German princes, that his equipages should be as rich, and his table as well served: the trade in indulgences was to him an admirable resource for the promotion of his favourite object. Accordingly, no sooner was the decree against Luther issued from the Imperial Chancellor's court, than Albert, who was then at Halle, attended by his courtiers, called together the vendors of indulgences, whose activity had been paralysed by the Reformer's preaching, and endeavoured to encourage them by such words as—" Do not fear, we have silenced him; go shear the flock in peace; the monk is in prison, under bolts and bars; and this time he will be clever indeed if he disturbs us at our work." The market was again opened, the wares spread out for sale, and again the churches of Halle resounded with the harangues of the mountebanks.

But Luther still lived; and his voice had power to pass beyond the walls and gratings behind which he was concealed. Nothing could have roused him to a higher pitch of indignation. " What!" thought he, " violent discussions have taken place, I have braved every danger, the truth has triumphed, and now they dare to trample it in the dust, as if it had been refuted. They shall again hear that voice which arrested their guilty traffic." " I will take no rest," wrote Luther to Spalatin, "till I have attacked the *idol* of Mentz, and its whoredoms at Halle."[*] He went instantly to work, caring little for the mystery in which some sought to envelope his seclusion in the Wartburg. He was like Elijah in the desert, forging new thunderbolts to hurl against the impious

---

[*] Non continebor quin idolum Moguntinum invadam, cum suo lupanari Hallensi. (L. Epp. ii. p. 59, 7th October.)

Ahab. On the 1st of November, he completed a tract "Against the new *Idol* of Halle."

The Archbishop had received information of Luther's intentions. Urged by his apprehensions, he, toward the middle of December, despatched two of his attendants, Capito and Auerbach, to Wittemberg, to ward off the blow. "It is indispensable," said they to Melancthon, who received them courteously, "it is quite indispensable that Luther should moderate his impetuosity." But Melancthon, though himself of gentler spirit, was not of the number of those who imagine wisdom to consist in perpetual concession, retracting, and silence. "God is making use of him," he replied, "and this age requires a bitter and pungent salt."[*] On this, Capito, addressing himself to Jonas, endeavoured, through him, to influence the Elector's councils.

The report of Luther's design had already spread thither, and produced great consternation. "What?" said the courtiers, "rekindle the flame that it cost so much trouble to subdue! The only safety for Luther is to withdraw into the shade; and see how he exalts himself against the greatest prince in the empire." "I will not suffer Luther to write against the Archbishop of Mentz, to the disturbance of the public tranquility,"[†] said the Elector.

When these words were reported to Luther, he was indignant. It is not enough, then, to confine his body, they would enchain his spirit, and the truth itself. Do they imagine he hides himself from fear? or that his retreat is a confession of defeat? On the contrary, he contends that it is a victory gained. Who then in Worms had dared to rise up against him, in opposition to the truth? Accordingly, when the captive of the Wartburg had finished reading Spalatin's letter apprizing him of the Elector's intention, he threw it aside, resolving to return no answer. But he could not contain his feelings; he again took it in hand. "And so, the Elector will not suffer, &c.!" wrote Luther in reply, "and I on my

[*] Huic seculo opus esse acerrimo sale. (Corp. Ref. i. 463.)
[†] Non passurum principem, scribi in Moguntinum. (L. Epr. ii. 94.)

part will not suffer that the Elector should *not* allow me to write.   Rather will I be the utter ruin of yourself, the Elector, and the whole world.*   If I have stood up against the Pope, who created your Cardinal, is it fitting that I should give way to his creature?   Truly, it is very fine to hear you say we ought not to disturb the public peace, while you permit the disturbance of the *Peace* that is from God.   It shall not be so, Spalatin!   O Prince it shall not stand!†   I send, with this, a tract I had written against the Cardinal, before I received your letter ;—please to hand it to Melancthon."

The reading of this manuscript alarmed Spalatin ;—he again urged on the Reformer the imprudence of a publication that would oblige the Imperial government to lay aside its affected ignorance of what had become of him, and to proceed to punish a prisoner who assailed the chief dignitary of the Church and Empire.   If Luther persisted, the general tranquility would be disturbed, and the cause of the Reformation endangered.   Luther, therefore, consented to delay the publication, and even gave Melancthon leave to strike out the more severe passages.‡   But growing indignant at his friend's timidity, he wrote to Spalatin,—" The Lord still lives—He reigns,—the Lord whom you counsellors of the court cannot trust, unless He so shapes his work, as that there be nothing left to trust Him in !"—and he forthwith resolved to write di rect to the Cardinal.

It is the Episcopal authority itself that Luther calls to the bar, of judgment in the person of the German primate.   His words are those of a bold man, burning with zeal in behalf of truth, and feeling that he speaks in the name of God himself.

" Your Electoral Highness," wrote he, from the depth of his retirement, " has seen fit again to set up at Halle the *idol* that engulphs the treasure and the souls of poor Christians. You think, perhaps, that I am disabled, and that the power of

* Potius te et principem ipsum perdam et omnem creaturam. (L. Epp. ii. p. 94.)

† Non sic, Spalatine, non sic, princeps.   (Ibid.)

‡ Ut acerbiora tradat (ib. p. 110.) doubtless *radat.*

he Emperor will easily silence the protest of a feeble monk.
. . . But know this,—I will fearlessly discharge the duty that
christian charity lays me under, dreading not the gates of hell !
—and much less, popes, bishops, or cardinals.

"Therefore, I humbly implore your Electoral Highness to
call to remembrance the origin of this business, and how from
one little spark came so fearful a conflagration.   Then also,
the world reposed in fancied security.   'That poor mendicant
friar,' thought they, 'who, unaided, would attack the Pope,
has undertaken a task above his strength.'   But God interposed his arm, and gave the Pope more disturbance and anxiety than he had known since first he sat in the temple of God,
and lorded it over God's church.   That same God still lives
—let none doubt it.*   He will know how to bring to nothing
the efforts of a Cardinal of Mentz, though he should be backed
by four emperors—for it is His pleasure to bring down the
lofty cedars, and humble the pride of the Pharaohs.

"For this cause I apprize your Highness that if the idol is not
removed, it will be ˙my duty, in obedience to God's teaching,
publicly to rebuke your Highness, as I have done the Pope
himself.   Let not your Highness neglect this notice.   I shall
wait fourteen days for an early and favourable answer.   Given
in my wilderness retreat, on Sunday after St. Catherine's day,
1521.   Your   Highness' devoted   and   humble, MARTIN
LUTHER."

This letter was forwarded to Wittemberg, and from thence
to Halle, where the Cardinal Elector was then resident; for
no one dared venture to intercept it, foreseeing the storm such
an act of audacity would have called forth.   But Melancthon
accompanied it by a letter to the prudent Capito, wherein he
laboured to give a favourable turn to so untoward a step.

It is not possible to describe the feelings of the young and
pusillanimous Archbishop on the receipt of the Reformer's
letter.   The forthcoming work against the *idol* of Halle was
like a sword suspended over his head.   And yet what must

* Derselbig Gott lebet noch, da zweifel nur niemand an . . . .
(L. Epp. ii. p. 113.)

have been, at the same time, the irritation produced by the insolence of the low-born and excommunicated monk, who dared address such language to a prince of the house of Brandenburg, and a primate of the German church. Capito besought the Archbishop to comply with Luther's advice. Fear, pride, and conscience, which he could not stifle, struggled long in Albert's soul. At length, dread of the threatened writing, joined, perhaps, to a feeling of remorse, prevailed. He stooped to humble himself, and put together such an answer as seemed likely to appease the man of the Wartburg, and scarcely had the fourteen days expired, when Luther received the following letter, more surprising even than his own terrifying epistle.

"My dear Doctor,—I have received and read your letter, and have taken it in good part, as being well intended : but I think the cause that has induced you to write to me in such a strain, has for a long time past had no existence. It is my desire, by God's help, to comport myself as a pious bishop, and a christian prince ; and I confess that for this, God's grace is necessary to me. I deny not that I am a sinful man, liable to sin, and apt to be led astray, and even sinning and going astray every day of my life. I know that, without God's grace, I am but worthless and loathsome mire, like others; if not worse. In replying to your letter, I would not omit to express the favour I bear you; for it is my most earnest desire, for Christ's sake, to show you all kindness and favour. I know how to receive the rebuke of a christian, and a brother. By my own hand. ALBERT."

Such was the strain in which the Elector Archbishop of Mentz and Magdeburg, commissioned to represent and maintain in Germany the constitution of the Church, wrote to the excommunicated prisoner of the Wartburg! In thus replying, did Albert obey the better dictates of his conscience, or was he swayed by his fears? On the former supposition, it is a noble letter; on the latter, it is contemptible. We would rather suppose it to have proceeded from a right motive. However that may be, it at least shows the vast superiority of the *servant of God* above the greatness of this world. Whilst Luther, solitary, a captive, and under sentence, derived from his faith an unconquerable courage, the Cardinal-archbishop, surrounded on all sides with the power and favour of the world, trembled in his chair. Again, and again, does this reflection present itself, and it affords the solution of the strange enigma offered by the history of the Reformation. The Christian is not called to calculate his resources, and count the means of success. His one concern is to know that his cause is the cause of God;—and that he himself has no aim but his Master's glory. Doubtless he has an enquiry to make, but it has reference only to his motives; the Christian looks in upon his heart,—not upon his arm: he regards right,—not strength. And that question once well settled,—his path is clear. It is for him to go boldly forward, though the world and all its armies should withstand his progress; in the firm persuasion that God himself will fight against the opposers.

Thus did the enemies of the Reformation pass at once from the harshest measures to pitiable weakness: they had done this at Worms, and these sudden changes are continually recurring in the conflict between truth and error. Every cause destined to succumb, carries with it an internal *malaise*, which occasions it to stagger and fluctuate between opposite extremes. Steadiness of purpose and energy could not sanctify a bad cause, but they might serve at least to gild its fall with what the world calls glory.

Joachim I., Elector of Brandenburg, Albert's brother, was an example of that decision of character so rare in our own times. Immoveable in his principles, decisive in action, knowing when needful how to resist the encroachments of the Pope, he opposed an iron hand to the progress of the Reformation. Long before this, when at Worms, he had urged that Luther should be refused a hearing, and brought to punishment, notwithstanding the safe-conduct with which he was furnished. Scarcely was the edict of Worms issued, when he directed that it should be rigorously enforced in his states. Luther could appreciate so decided a character, and,

drawing a distinction in favour of Joachim, when, speaking
of his other adversaries, remarked, "we may *still* pray for the
Elector of Brandenburg."* This disposition in the prince
seemed to communicate itself to his people. Berlin and
Brandenburg long continued closed to the reformed doctrines.
But that which is slowly received is firmly held; whilst
countries, which then hailed the Gospel with joy, as Belgium
and Westphalia, were ere long seen to abandon it; Brandenburg,—which was the latest of the German states to enter on
the way of faith,—was destined, at a later period, to stand
foremost in the cause of the Reformation.†

Luther was not without suspicion that the Cardinal's letter
was dictated by some insidious design suggested by Capito.
He returned no answer; he declared to the latter, that so long
as the Archbishop, unequal as he was to the care of a petty
parish, should hold to his pretensions as Cardinal, and his
episcopal state, instead of discharging the humble duty of a
minister of the Gospel, he could not be in the way of salvation.‡ Meanwhile, and at the very time that Luther contended against error, as if he were still in the thick of the conflict,
he was at work in his retirement as though regardless of all
that was happening outside its walls. The time had arrived
when the Reformation was to pass from the closet of divines,
into the private life of nations; and, nevertheless, the great
engine by which this advance was to be effected was not yet
brought forth. This mighty and wonder-working engine,
from whence a storm of missiles was to be discharged against
Rome, battering down its walls,—this engine, which was to
upheave the burthen, under which the Papacy then held down
the almost stifled Church, and to communicate to mankind an
impulse which, ages after, would still be felt, was ordained to
go forth from the old castle of the Wartburg, and enter, with

* Helwing, Gesch. der Brandeb. ii. p. 605.

† Hoc enim proprium est illorum hominum (ex March. Brandeburg)
ut quam semel in religione sententiam approbaverint, non facile deserant.
(Leutingeri Opp. i. 41.)

‡ Larvam cardinalatus et pompam episcopalem ablegare. (L. Epp.
ii. p. 132.)

the Reformer, on the world's stage on the same day that closed his captivity.

The further the Church was removed from the days in which Jesus, its true light, walked on this earth, the more did it need the candle of God's word to transmit to after times the unclouded knowledge of Jesus Christ. But that Divine Word was unknown to that age. Some fragments of translations from the Vulgate, made in 1477, 1490, and 1518, had been but coldly received, and were almost unintelligible, as well as, from their high price, beyond the reach of the common people. The giving the Scriptures to the Church in Germany in the vernacular tongue, had even been prohibited.* Added to which, the number of those who could read, became considerable, only when there existed in the German language a book of strong and general interest.

Luther was ordained to present his nation with the written word. That same God who had relegated St. John in Patmos, that he might there write what he had seen, had shut up Luther in the Wartburg, that he should there translate his Word. This great labour, which it would have been difficult for him to take in hand in the distracting occupations of Wittemberg, was to seat the new edifice on the solid rock, and, after the lapse of so many ages, recall Christians from scholastic subtleties to the pure and unadulterated fountains of redemption and salvation. The wants of the Church loudly called for this service, and Luther's deep experience had fitted him to render it. In truth, he had found in the faith, that rest for his own soul, which his fluctuating conscience and monkish prejudice had so long sought in merits and holiness of his own. The ordinary teaching of the Church, the theology of the schools knew nothing of the consolations which *faith* gives: but the Scriptures set them forth powerfully,— and it was in the Scriptures that he had discovered them. *Faith in God's word* had given him liberty! By faith he felt himself freed from the dogmatic authority of Church, hierarchy, tradition, the notions of the schools, the power of preju-

* Codex Diplom. Ecclesiæ Mogunt. iv. p. 460.

dice, and commandments of men! These manifold bonds which had for ages chained down and silenced all Christendom, were burst asunder, and he could raise his head freed from all authority save that of the Word. This independence of man,—this subjection to God, which he had learned in the Holy Scriptures,—he was anxious to communicate to the Church. But for this purpose it was needful that he should give to it God's own Revelations. There was a necessity that some strong hand should unclose the portals of that arsenal whence Luther had drawn his weapons, and that its recesses, which had for ages been unexplored, should be laid open to all christian people against the day of trial.

Luther had, before this time, translated some fragments of the Holy Scripture. The seven penitential psalms* had first occupied his pen. John the Baptist,—JESUS CHRIST,—and the Reformation—alike commenced by calling men to repentance. It is, indeed, the principle of every regeneration in human nature. These earlier essays had been eagerly bought up, and had awakened a general demand for more; and this desire on the part of the people was by Luther regarded as a call from God. He resolved to meet it. He was a captive enclosed within lofty walls; but what of that! he would devote his leisure to render the Word of God into the language of his nation. Soon shall we see that Word descending with him from the Wartburg—circulating among the families of Germany, and enriching them with spiritual treasure, that had hitherto been shut up within the hearts of a few pious persons. "Would that that book alone," he exclaimed, "were in all languages—before the eyes—in the ears —and in the hearts of all."† Admirable words, which a well-known society‡ engaged in translating the Bible into the vernacular dialect of every nation under heaven, has, after a lapse of three centuries, undertaken to realise. "Scripture,"

* Ps. 6, 32, 38, 51, 102, 130, 147.
† Et solus hic liber omnium linguâ, manû, oculis, auribus, cordibus, versaretur. (L. Epp. ii. p. 116.)
‡ The Bible Society.

says he again, "Scripture 'without comment is the sun whence all teachers receive their light.'"

Such are the true principles of Christianity and of the Reformation. Ado ting these memorable words, we are not to seek light from the Fathers, to interpret Scripture,—but to use Scripture to interpret the writings of the Fathers. The Reformers, as also the Apostles, hold forth the alone word of God as *light,* whilst they exalt the one offering of Christ as the only *righteousness.* To mingle commandments of men with this supreme authority of God, or any righteousness of man's own, with this perfect righteousness of Christ, is to corrupt the two great fundamental truths of the Gospel. Such were the two leading heresies of Rome: and the doctrines that certain teachers would introduce into the bosom of the Reformation, though not carried to such a length, have the same tendencies.

Luther, taking up the Greek originals of the inspired writers, entered on the difficult task of rendering them into his native tongue. Important moment in the history of the Reformation! thenceforth, it was no longer in the hands of the Reformer. The Bible was brought forward—and Luther held a secondary place. *God* showed himself; and man was seen as nothing. The Reformer placed the Boox in the hands of his contemporaries: thenceforward, each could hear God speaking to him,—and, as for himself, he mingled in the crowd, placing himself among those who came to draw from the common fountain of light and life.

In translating the Holy Scriptures, Luther had found that consolation and strength which met his need. Weak in body —solitary—depressed in spirit by the machinations of his enemies, and sometimes by the indiscretions of his friends—and sensible that his life was wasting in the gloom of the old castle, he had, at times, to pass through awful struggles. In those days, men were much disposed to carry into the visible world the conflicts that the soul sustains with its spiritual enemies. Luther's vivid imagination easily gave bodily shape to the emotions of his soul, and the superstitions of the middle ages

had still some hold upon his mind, so that it might be said of
him, as was said of Calvin, in reference to his judgment in
regard to heretics, that he had in him the remains of Popery.
To Luther, Satan was not simply an invisible, though really
existing, being; he thought that adversary of God was accustomed to appear in bodily form to man, as he had appeared to
Jesus Christ.   Although we may more than doubt the authenticity of the details given on such topics in his Table Talk
and elsewhere,* history must yet record this weakness in the
Reformer.   Never had these gloomy imaginations such
power over him as in his seclusion in the Wartburg.   At
Worms, when in the days of his strength, he had braved the
power of the devil,—but now, that strength was broken, and
his reputation tarnished.   He was thrown aside: Satan had
his turn—and in bitterness of soul, Luther imagined he saw
him rearing before him his gigantic form—lifting his finger
as if in threatening, grinning triumphantly, and grinding his
teeth in fearful rage.   One day in particular, as it is reported,
whilst Luther was engaged in translating the New Testament,
he thought he saw Satan, in detestation of his work, torment-
ing and vexing him, and moving round him like a lion ready
to spring upon his prey.   Luther, alarmed and aroused,
snatching up his inkstand, threw it at the head of his enemy.
The apparition vanished, and the ink-bottle was dashed to
pieces against the wall.†

His stay at the Wartburg began now to be insupportable to
him.   He was indignant at the timidity of his protectors.
Sometimes he remained all day lost in silent and deep meditation, and, awakening from it, he would utter the exclamation—
"Ah! would I were at Wittemberg!"   At length, he could
no longer restrain himself:—"Enough," thought he, "enough
of policy."   He must again see his friends—hear from their
lips how things were going on, and talk over all with them.

* M. Michelet, in his Memoirs of Luther, devotes no less than
thirty pages to the various accounts of this incident.

† The keeper of the Wartburg regularly points out to travellers the
mark made by Luther's inkstand.

True, he risked falling into the power of his enemies; but nothing could deter him. Toward the end of November, he secretly quitted the Wartburg, and set out for Wittemberg.[*]

A storm had just then burst forth against him. The Sorbonne had at length spoken out. This celebrated school of Paris—next in authority in the Church to the Pope himself— the ancient and venerable source whence theological teaching had gone forth, had just issued its verdict against the Reformation. The following were among the propositions it condemned :—Luther had said, "God ever pardons sin freely, and requires nothing from us in return, save that for the time to come we live according to righteousness." He had added— "The most mortal of all mortal sins is this: to wit, that a man should think that he is not guilty of damnable and mortal sin in the sight of God." He had also declared, that the practice of burning heretics was contrary to the will of the Holy Ghost. To these several propositions, as well as to many others which it quoted, the Faculty of Theology, in Paris, had replied by the word, "Heresy—let it be accursed."[†]

But there was a youth, a stripling of twenty-four years of age, of diffident and retiring manners, who ventured to take up the gauntlet that the first college in Europe had thrown down. It was no secret at Wittemberg, what was to be thought of those lofty censures;—it was known that Rome had allowed free course to the machinations of the Dominicans, and that the Sorbonne had been misled by the influence of two or three fanatical teachers who were designated in Paris by satirical nicknames.[‡] Accordingly, in his apology, Melancthon did not confine himself to defending Luther, but with the fearlessness which characterizes his writings, he car-

* Machete er sich heimlich aus seiner Patmo auf. (L. Opp. xviii. 238.)
† Determinatio theologorum Parisiensium super doctrina Lutherana. (Corp. Ref. i. p. 366 to 388.)
‡ Damnarunt triumviri Beda, Quercus, et Christophorus. Nomina sunt horum monstrorum etiam vulgo nunc nota Belua, Stercus, Christotomus. (Zwinglii Epp. i. p. 176.)

4*

ried the war into his adversaries' camp. "You say, 'he is a Manichean'—'he is a Montanist:' you call for fire and faggot to repress his madness. And who, I pray you, is Montanist? Luther, who would have men believe Scripture only? or yourselves, who would claim belief for the thoughts of men rather than for the word of God?"*

And truly the attaching more importance to man's teaching than to God's word was in substance the heresy of Montanus, as it is the real character of that of the Pope, and, indeed, of all who rank church authority or mystical impulses above the plain words of the Sacred Writings. Accordingly, the young master of arts, who had been heard to say—"I would rather die than relinquish the faith of the Gospel,"† did not stop there. He charged the doctors of the Sorbonne with having darkened the light of the Gospel,—put out the doctrine of Faith,—and substituted a vain philosophy in place of true Christianity.‡ The publication of this writing of Melancthon changed the position of the parties. He proved unanswerably that the heresy was in Paris and in Rome, and the Catholic truth at Wittemberg.

All this while, Luther, little regarding the censures of the Sorbonne, was journeying in his disguise as a knight toward the university city. Various rumours reached him in his journey, of a spirit of impatience and insubordination having manifested itself among certain of his adherents.§ He was deeply grieved at it.‖ At last he arrived at Wittemberg without having been recognized on the road thither, and stopped at the door of Amsdorff. Immediately his friends were secretly called together. Among the first was Melancthon, who

---

* Corp. Ref. i. p. 396.

† Scias me positurum animam citius quam fidem. (Corp. Ref. i. p. 396.)

‡ Evangelium obscuratum est . . . fides extincta . . . . Ex Christianismo, contra omnem sensum spiritus, facta est quædam philosophica vivendi ratio. (Ibid. p. 400.)

§ Per viam vexatus rumore vario de nostrorum quorumdam importunitate. (L. Epp. ii. p. 109,)

‖ Liess in der Stille seine Freunde fodern. (L. Opp. xviii. p. 238.)

had so often said, " I would rather die than be separated from him."* They met. What an interview! what joy! The captive of the Wartburg, surrounded by his friends, enjoyed the sweets of christian friendship. He learned the spread of the Reformation,—the hopes of his brethren,—and, delighted with what he saw and heard,† he kneeled down and prayed, gave thanks, and then, with brief delay, set forth, and returned to the Wartburg.

His joy was well founded. The work of the Reformation made, just then, a prodigious advance. Feldkirchen, ever in the van, had mounted the breach ; the whole body of those who held the new doctrines were in motion, and the energy which carried the Reformation from the range of teaching into the public worship, to private life, and the constitution of the Church, revealed itself by another explosion—more threatening to the papal power than that which had already happened.

Rome, having rid herself of the Reformer, thought she had extinguished the new heresy; but it was not long before a great change took place. Death removed the Pontiff who had put Luther under ban. Troubles broke out in Spain, and compelled Charles V. to recross the Pyrenees. War was declared between that prince and Francis the First; and (as if this were not enough to engross the Emperor's attention,) Solyman invaded Hungary. Charles, thus attacked on all sides, found himself compelled to leave unmolested the monk of Worms, and his religious novelties.

It was about this time, that the bark of the Reformed Faith, which, driven in every direction by the winds, had been well nigh swamped, righted itself, and rode above the waters.

It was in the convent of the Augustines, at Wittemberg, that the Reformation showed itself. We cannot wonder at this: the Reformer, it is true, was not within its walls, but no human power could expel from it the spirit that had animated him.

* Quo si mihi carendum est, mortem fortius tulero. (Corp. Ref. i. p. 453—455.)

† Omnia vehementer placent quæ video et audio. (L. Epp. ii. p. 109.)

Strange doctrines had for some time been occasionally heard in the church where Luther had so often preached. A zealous monk, who filled the office of college preacher, loudly urged on his hearers the necessity of a Reformation. As if Luther, whose name was on every one's lips, had reached too commanding an elevation and esteem, God seemed to be making choice of men, no way known for any strength of character or influence, to bring in the Reformation, for which the renowned doctor had opened a way. "Christ," said the preacher, "instituted the Sacrament of the Altar, in remembrance of his death, and not to make it an object of worship. To bow down to it is idolatry. The priest who communicates alone or in private, is guilty of a sin. No prior has the right to require a monk to say mass alone. Let one, two, or three officiate, and all the rest receive the Lord's Sacrament under both kinds."*

Such was the change called for by the monk Gabriel; and his bold words were heard with approbation by his brother monks, particularly those who came from the Low Countries.† As disciples of the Gospel, why should they not conform in everything to its directions? Had not Luther himself, in writing to Melancthon, in the month of August, remarked— "Henceforth, I will say no more private masses?"‡ Thus the friars, the very soldiers of the hierarchy, when made free by the Word of God, boldly took part against Rome.

In Wittemberg they encountered an unbending resistance from the Prior, and here they yielded,—at the same time protesting that to support the mass was to oppose the Gospel of God.

The Prior had carried the day. One man's authority had prevailed over all the rest. It might have been thought that this stir among the Augustines was but a capricious act of in-

* Einem 2 oder 3 befehlen Mess zu halten und die andern 12 von denen das Sacrament sub utraque specie mit empfahen. (Corp. Ref. i. p. 460.)

† Dermeiste Theil jener Parthei Niederlænder seyn. (Ibid. 475.)

‡ Sed et ego amplius non faciam missam privatim in æternum. (L. Epp. ii. p. 36.)

subordination, such as was often occurring in the convents; but in reality the Spirit of God itself was then moving christian hearts. A single voice proceeding from the seclusion of a monastery, found a thousand echoes; and that which men would have confined to the knowledge of the inhabitants of the convent, spread beyond its walls, and began to show itself in the heart of the city.

Rumours of the differences among the monks were soon circulated in the town: the burghers and students sided some with, and others against the mass. The Elector's court interposed. Frederic, in some surprise, despatched his Chancellor, Pontanus, to Wittemberg, with orders to reduce the monks to obedience, putting them, if necessary, upon bread and water;[*] and on the 12th October, a deputation of Professors, among whom was Melancthon, repairing to the convent, exhorted the monks to desist from all innovations,[†] or at least to wait the course of events. This did but rekindle their zeal; and all, with exception of their Prior, being of one mind in their faith, they appealed to Scripture, to the spiritual discernment of believers, and to the impartial judgment of divines,—and two days after, handed in a declaration in writing.

The Professors proceeded to examine the question more closely, and perceived that the monks had truth on their side. Having come to convince others, they were convinced themselves! What was to be done? Conscience pleaded—their perplexity was continually increasing; and at last, after long hesitation, they came to a courageous decision.

On the 20th of October, the University reported to the Elector, after setting forth the abuses of the mass: " Let your Electoral Highness," said they, " put an end to all corruptions; lest, in the day of judgment, Christ should apply to us the rebukes he once pronounced upon Capernaum."

Thus, it was no longer a handful of obscure monks who spoke,—it was the University, accredited by the most judi-

* Wollen die Mönche nicht Mess halten, sie werden's bald in der Küchen und Keller empfinden. (Corp. Ref. i. p. 461.)

† Mit dem Messhalten keine Neuerung machen. (Ibid.)

cious, as having, for years past, been the great school of national instruction: and thus, the very agency employed to
quell the spirit of the Reformation, was about to diffuse it far
and wide.

Melancthon, with that decision which he carried into learning, put forth fifty-five propositions calculated to enlighten the
minds of enquirers.

"Just," said he, "as gazing on a cross is no good work,
but the bare contemplation of a sign that reminds us of Christ's
death."

"Just as to behold the sun is not to do any good work, but
merely to look upon that which reminds us of Christ and his
Gospel."

"So, to partake of the Lord's Supper is not to do a good
work, but merely to make use of a sign which recalls to remembrance the grace bestowed upon us through Christ."

"But here is the difference; namely, that the symbols invented by men do *only* remind us of what they signify—
whilst the signs given by God, not merely recall the things
themselves, but assure our hearts in the will of God."

"As the sight of a cross does not justify, so the mass cannot justify."

"As the gazing on a cross is no sacrifice for our own or
others' sins, just so the mass is no sacrifice."

"There is but one sacrifice,—but one satisfaction,—Jesus
Christ. Beside him there is none other."

"Let such bishops as do not withstand the profanations of
the mass, be anathema."*

Thus spake the pious and gentle-spirited Philip.

The Elector was astounded. His intention had been to restore order among a few refractory friars, and lo! the entire
University, with Melancthon at their head, stand up to defend them. To wait the course of events, was ordinarily, in
his view, the most eligible course. He had no relish for ab-

---

* Signa ab hominibus reperta admonent tantum; signa a Deo tradita,
præterquam quod admonent, certificant etiam cor de voluntate Dei.
(Corp. Ref. i. p. 476.)

rupt changes, and it was his wish that all opinions should be left to work their own way. "Time alone," thought he, "throws light upon all things, and brings all to maturity." And yet the Reformation was advancing in spite of all his caution with rapid strides, and threatened to carry all before it. Frederic made indeed some efforts to arrest it. His authority,—the influence of his personal character,—and such arguments as appeared to him most conclusive, were all called into exercise: "Do not be hasty," said he, to the divines, "you are too few in number to effect such a change. If it is well founded in Scripture, others will be led to see it, and you will have the whole Church with you in putting an end to these corruptions. Speak of these things,—discuss and preach them as much as you will, but keep up the established services."

Such was the war waged relative to the mass. The monks had boldly mounted to the assault;—the divines, after a moment of indecision, had supported them. The prince and his counsellors alone defended the citadel. It has been said that the Reformation was brought about by the power and authority of the Elector; but so far from this being the case, we see the assailants drawing off their forces, in deference to the voice of the revered Frederic, and the mass, for a while, continuing to hold its place.

The heat of battle was already beginning to rage in another part of the field. The monk Gabriel did not relax in his fervid appeals from the pulpit of the Augustines. It was against the condition of monkery itself he now dealt his powerful strokes; and if the strength of Romish doctrines was principally in the mass, the monastic order formed the main support of her priestly hierarchy. Hence, these two posts were the first to be stormed. "No one," exclaimed Gabriel, according to the Prior's report, "not even a single inmate of a convent, keeps God's commandments."

"No one who wears a cowl can be saved.[*] Whoso enters a cloister, enters into the service of the Devil. Vows of chas-

---

[*] Kein Mönch werde in der Kappe selig. (Corp. Ref. i. p. 433.)

tity, poverty, and obedience to a superior, are contrary to the spirit of the Gospel."

These strange expressions were reported to the Prior, who took care not to be present in church to hear them.

"Gabriel," said his informants, "Gabriel insists that every possible means should be taken to clear out the cloisters; that when the friars are met in the street, they should be twitched by the cloak, and pointed out to ridicule; and that if that does not rout them from their convent, they should be expelled by main force. He cries, 'break open the monastaries, destroy them, raze them to their foundations, that no trace of them may remain, and that on the ground they cover, not one stone may be left of walls that have sheltered such sloth and superstition.' "*

The friars were astonished; their consciences whispered that the charge brought against them was but too true;—that the life of a monk was not agreeable to the will of God;—and that no man could have a claim to their implicit and unlimited obedience.

In one day, thirteen Augustine monks quitted the convent, and throwing aside the habit of their order, assumed the dress of the laity. Such of them as had the advantage of instruction continued their course of study, in the hope of being one day useful to the Church; and such as had profited little by study, sought a livelihood by working with their own hands, according to the precept of the Apostle, and after the example of the worthy burghers of Wittemberg.† One, who had some knowledge of carpentry, applied for the freedom of the city, resolving to marry and settle.

If Luther's entrance into the convent of the Augustines at Erfurth, had aid the seeds of the Reformation, the departure of the thirteen monks from the convent of the Augustines of Wittemberg was the signal of its taking possession of the

* Dass man nicht oben Stück von ernem Kloster da sey gestanden, merken möge. (Corp. Ref. i. p. 483.)

† "Etliche unter den Bürgern, etliche unter den Studenten," said the Prior, in his address to the Elector. (Ibid.)

nations of Christendom. For a period of thirty years, Erasmus had exposed the unprofitableness, fatuity, and vices of the friars; and all Europe had gone with him in his ridicule and contempt. Thirteen men of resolute character returned to their place in society;—and there, in service to their fellow men, sought to fulfil God's commandments. The marriage of Feldkirchen was one of humiliation to the hierarchy;—the emancipation of these thirteen Augustines followed close upon it, as a second. Monkery, which had established itself in the day when the Church entered on her long period of bondage and error, was doomed to fall whenever the time came which should restore liberty and truth.

This bold step occasioned a general ferment in Wittemberg. All marvelled at the men who thus came forward to share the labours of the common people, and welcomed them as brethren:—at the same time, cries were heard against those who obstinately clung to their indolent seclusion within the walls of their monastery. The monks, who adhered to the prior, trembled in their cells, and the prior himself, carried away by the general feeling, suspended the performance of private masses.

In a moment so critical, the least concession necessarily precipitated the course of events. The order issued by the Prior caused a strong sensation in the town and in the University, and produced an unforeseen explosion. Among the students and burghers of Wittemberg, were some of those turbulent spirits whom the least excitement inflames, and urges to criminal excesses. These men were indignant that the same masses, which were suspended by the devout Prior, should still be performed in the parish church; and on the 3d December, as mass was about to be chaunted, they suddenly made their way to the altar, bore off the books, and compelled the officiating priests to seek safety in flight. The Council and the University assembled to take severe measures against the authors of these disturbances. But the passions, once roused, are not easily calmed. The Cordeliers had taken no part in the Reformation that had begun to show itself among

the Augustines. Next day the students affixed to the gates of
their monastery a threatening placard. Soon after, forty of
their number forced their way into the chapel, and without
proceeding to violence, gave such free expression to their
ridicule, that the monks dared not proceed with the mass. In
the evening, notice came advising the friars to be on their
guard. "The students," it was said, "have planned to break
into the monastery." The monks in alarm, and seeing no
way of defence against these real or supposed attacks, sent in
haste to ask protection of the Council. Soldiers were placed
on guard, but the enemy did not make his appearance. The
University arrested the students who had taken part in these
disturbances. They were found to be from Erfürth, and
already noted for their insubordination.* The penalty annexed to their offence by the laws of the University was
imposed upon them.

Nevertheless, it was felt that a necessity had arisen for a
careful examination of the lawfulness of monastic vows. A
chapter, composed of the Augustine monks of Thuringen and
Misnia, assembled at Wittemberg in December following.
Luther's judgment was acquiesced in. They declared, on the
one hand, that monastic vows were not sinful, but, on the
other hand, that they were not obligatory. "In Christ," said
they, "there is neither layman nor monk,—each one is free
to leave the monastery or to abide in it. Let whoever leaves
it, beware how he abuses his liberty; let him who abides in
it, obey his superiors,—but with the obedience of love;" and
they proceeded to prohibit mendicity, and the saying masses
for money: they also determined that the more instructed
monks should devote themselves to teaching the word of God,
and that the rest should labour with their own hands for the
support of their brethren.†

Thus the question of Vows seemed to be settled, but that

* In summa es sollen die Aufruhr etliche Studenten von Erffurth
erwerckt haben. (Corp. Ref. i. p. 490.)

† Corp. Ref. i. p. 456.—The editors assign to this decree the date
of October, before the monks had forsaken their convent.

of the Mass was still undecided. The Elector continued to oppose the stream, and to defend an institution which he saw still standing in every nation where Christianity was professed. The moderation of this mild sovereign could not, however, for any length of time, hold in the public mind. Carlstadt, above all, took part in the general ferment. Zealous, upright, and fearless; prompt, like Luther, to sacrifice every thing for the truth; he had not the Reformer's wisdom and moderation: he was not free from vanity, and with a disposition that led him to go deeply into every question, he yet had but little power of judgment, and no great clearness of ideas. Luther had delivered him from the teaching of the schools, and had led him to study the Scriptures; but Carlstadt had not had patience to acquire a knowledge of the original languages, and had not, as his friend had done, acknowledged the sufficiency of God's word. Hence he was often taking up with singular interpretations. As long as Luther was at his side, the influence of the master restrained the disciple within due bounds; but Carlstadt was freed from this wholesome restraint. In the university,—in the chapel,—throughout Wittemberg,—the little tawny-complexioned Carlstadt, who had never excelled in eloquence, gave utterance to thoughts, at times, profound, but often enthusiastic and exaggerated. "What infatuated folly!" he exclaimed, "for men to think that the Reformation must be left to God's working. A new order of things is opening. The strength of man must be brought in, and woe to him who shall hold back instead of mounting the breach in the cause of the mighty God!"

The Archdeacon's speech communicated his own impatience to his auditory. "Whatever the Pope has set up is impious," exclaimed some men of sincere and upright minds, under the influence of his harangues. "Let us not make ourselves accomplices in these abominations by allowing them to exist. That which God's word condemns ought to be swept from the face of Christendom, without regarding the commandments of men. If the heads of the state and of the church will not do their duty, let us at least do ours. Let us leave thinking of negociation, conferences, theses, and discussions, and let us apply the true remedy to so many evils. We want a second Elijah to throw down the altars of Baal!"

The restoration of the Supper of the Lord in this moment of ferment and enthusiastic excitement, could not, doubtless, wear that character of solemnity and sacredness which was given to it by the Son of God in his institution of it 'the night that he was betrayed.' But if God was now using the weakness and passions of men, it was, not the less, His own hand which was engaged in re-establishing in the midst of His church the feast of His own love.

As early as the October previous, Carlstadt had privately celebrated the Lord's Supper, according to Christ's appointment, with twelve of his friends. On the Sunday before Christmas Day, he announced from the pulpit that, on New Year's Day, he would distribute the elements under the two kinds bread and wine, to all who should come to the altar; that he intended to omit all unnecessary ceremonies,* and should perform the service without cope or chasuble.

The Council, in perturbation, requested the counsellor Bergen to interfere, and prevent so disorderly a proceeding, whereupon Carlstadt resolved not to wait the time fixed. On Christmas Day, 1521, he preached, in the parochial church, on the duty of abandoning the mass, and receiving the sacrament under both kinds. The sermon being ended, he came down, took his place at the altar, and after pronouncing, in German, the words of institution, said solemnly, turning towards the people,—" If any one feels the burthen of his sins, and is hungering and thirsting for the grace of God, let him draw near, and receive the body and blood of the Lord."† Then, without elevating the host, he distributed to each one the bread and wine, saying, " This is the cup of my blood, the blood of the new and everlasting covenant."

---

* Und die anderen *Schirymstege* alle aussen lassen. (Corp. Ref. i. p. 512.)

† Wer mit Sünden beschwert und nach der Gnade Gottes hungrig und durstig. (Ibid. p. 540.)

Conflicting feelings reigned in the assembly. Some, in the sense that a further grace of God was given to the Church, drew near the altar in silent emotion. Others, attracted principally by the novelty of the occasion, approached in some confusion, and with a kind of impatience. Not more than five communicants had presented themselves in the confessional,—the rest took part only in the public confession of sins. Carlstadt gave to all the general absolution, laying upon them no other penance than this, " *Sin no more.*"—In conclusion, the communicants sang the *Agnus Dei.* *

Carlstadt met with no opposition : the changes we are narrating had already obtained general concurrence. The Archdeacon administered the Lord's Supper again on New Year's Day, and also on the Sunday following, and from that time the regular observance of it was kept up. Einsideln, one of the Elector's council, having rebuked Carlstadt for seeking his own exaltation, rather than the salvation of his hearers— " Noble Sir !" answered he, " I would meet death in any form, rather than desist from following the Scripture. The word has come to me so quick and powerful . . . . woe is me if I do not preach." † Soon after this, Carlstadt married.

In the month of January, the town-council of Wittemberg issued regulations for the celebration of the Supper according to the amended ritual. Steps were also taken to restore the influence of religion upon public morals ;—for it was the office of the Reformation to re-establish, simultaneously, faith, christian worship, and general morality. It was decreed that public beggars should be no longer tolerated, whether friars or others ; and that in each street, some man, well reported of for piety, should be commissioned to take care of the poor, and to summon before the University or the Council such as were guilty of disorders. ‡

* Wenn man communicirt hat, so singt man: *Agnus Dei* carmen. (Corp. Ref. i. p. 540.)

† Mir ist das Wort fast in grosser Geschwindigkeit eingefallen. (Ibid. p. 545.)

‡ Keinen offenbaren Sünder zu dulden . . . . (Ibid. p. 540.)

So fell that grand bulwark of Romish dominion,—the Mass. Thus it was that the Reformation passed beyond the sphere of teaching, into that of public worship. For three centuries, the mass and the doctrine of transubstantiation had been regularly established.* Throughout that long period, all things within the Church had a new tendency impressed upon them, and every thing conspired to favour the pride of man and the honour paid to the priest. The holy sacrament had been adored,—regular festivals had been instituted in honour of the most stupendous of miracles,—the worship of Mary had risen high in the scale of public estimation,—the priest, who in the consecration of the elements was supposed to receive mysterious power to change them into the very body of Christ, had been separated from the class of laity, and, to use the words of Thomas Aquinas, had become a 'mediator between God and man,'†—celibacy had been proclaimed as an inviolable law,—auricular confession was enforced upon the people, and the cup of blessing denied them,—for how, indeed, should common people be ranged on the same line with priests, honoured with the most solemn of all ministrations. The Mass cast reproach upon the Son of God; it was opposed to the perfect remission through his cross, and the spotless glory of his everlasting kingdom;—but, whilst it disparaged the glory of the Lord, it exalted the priest,—whom it invested with the inconceivable power of reproducing, in hand, and at will, the Sovereign Creator of all things!‡ Thenceforward the Church seemed to exist—not, to preach the Gospel, but only to reproduce Christ in the flesh! The Roman Pontiff, whose obedient vassals, at their pleasure, created the body of God himself,—took his seat as God, in the temple of God, and asserted his claim to a spiritual treasury, from whence to draw forth at will indulgences for the pardon of men's sins.

* By the Council of Lateran, in 1215.

† Sacerdos constituitur medius inter Deum et populum. (Th. Aquin. Summa iii. p. 22.)

‡ Perfectio hujus sacramenti non est in usu fidelium, sed in consecratione materiæ. (Th. Aquin. Summa, Quest. 80.)

Such were the gross errors which for a period of three centuries had established themselves in the Church in connection with the mass. The Reformation, by abolishing this thing of man's setting up, swept away all the abuses blended with it. The proceeding of the Archdeacon was therefore full of important results. The costly shows that amused the people, the worship of the Virgin, the pride of the clergy, and the papal authority, were all shaken. The glory was withdrawn from the priests, and returned to rest on JESUS,—and the Reformation advanced a step farther.

Nevertheless, prejudiced observers might have seen nothing in all that was going on, but what might be deemed the effect of passing enthusiasm. Facts were needed, that should give proof of the contrary, and demonstrate that there was a deep and broad distinction between a Reformation based on God's word and any mere fanatical excitement.

Whenever a great ferment is working in the Church, some impure elements are sure to mingle with the testimony given to truth; and some one or more pretended reforms arise out of man's imagination, and serve as evidences or countersigns of some *real* reformation in progress. Thus many false Messiahs in the first century of the Church, were an evidence that the true Messiah had already come. The Reformation of the sixteenth century could not run its course without presenting the like phenomenon, and it was first exhibited in the little village of Zwickau.

There were dwelling at Zwickau a few men, who, being deeply moved by the events passing around them, looked for special and direct revelations from the Deity, instead of desiring, in meekness and simplicity, the sanctification of their affections. These persons asserted that they were commissioned to complete that Reformation which in their view Luther had but feebly begun. "What is the use," asked they, "of such close application to the Bible? Nothing is heard of but the BIBLE. Can the Bible preach to us? Can it suffice for our instruction? If God had intended to instruct us by a book, would he not have given us a Bible direct from heaven?

It is only the Spirit that can enlighten! God himself speaks to us, and shows us what to do and say." Thus did these fanatics, playing into the hands of Rome, impugn the fundamental principle on which the whole Reformation is based; namely, the perfect sufficiency of the Word of God.

Nicolas Storch, a weaver, publicly declared that the angel Gabriel had appeared to him by night, and after revealing to him matters he was not allowed to divulge, had uttered the words—"Thou shalt sit on my throne!"[*] A senior student of Wittemberg, named Mark Stubner, joined Storch, and forthwith abandoned his studies,—for, according to his own statement, he had received immediately from God the ability to interpret holy Scripture. Mark Thomas, also a weaver, associated himself with them; and another of the initiated, by name Thomas Munzer, a man of fanatical turn of mind, gave to the new sect a regular organization. Resolving to act according to the example of Christ, Storch chose from among his followers twelve apostles and seventy disciples. All these loudly proclaimed, as we have lately heard it asserted by a sect of our own days, that Apostles and Prophets were at last restored to the Church.[†]

Ere long, the new prophets, in accordance with this plan of adhering to the example of those of holy writ, began to declare their mission—"Woe, woe!" they exclaimed, "a church under human governors, corrupted like the bishops, cannot be the church of Christ. The ungodly rulers of Christendom will soon be cast down. In five, six, or seven years, a time of universal desolation will come upon the earth. The Turk will get possession of Germany; the clergy, not even excepting those who have married, shall be slain. The ungodly sinners shall all be destroyed; and when the earth shall have been purified by blood, supreme power shall be given to Storch, to install the saints in the government of the

* Advolasse Gabrielem Angelum. (Camerarii Vita Melancthonis, p. 48.)
 † Breviter, de sese prædicant, viros esse propheticos et apostolicos. (Corp. Ref. i. p. 514.)

earth.* Then shall there be one Faith and one Baptism!
The day of the Lord draweth nigh, and the end of all things
is at hand. Woe! woe! woe!" Then publicly declaring
that infant baptism was of no avail, the new prophets called
upon all to draw near, and receive at their hands a true baptism, in token of their entrance into the new Church of
God.

Such preaching made a deep impression on the popular
mind. Not a few devout persons were startled by the thought
that prophets were again given to the Church, and those on
whom the love of the marvellous had most power, threw
themselves into the open arms of the eccentric preachers of
Zwickau.

But scarcely had this heresy, which had shown itself of
old in the days of Montanism, and again in the middle ages,
drawn together a handful of separatists, when it encountered
in the Reformation a strong opposing power. Nicolas Hauss-
man, to whom Luther gave that noble testimony—" *What we
teach, he acts,*"† was at this time the pastor of Zwickau.
This good man was not led away by the pretensions of the
false prophets. Supported by his two deacons, he successfully
resisted the innovations Storch and his followers were seeking
to introduce. The fanatics, repelled by the pastors of the
church, fell into another extravagance: they formed meetings,
in which doctrines subversive of order were publicly preached. The people caught the infection, and disturbances were
the consequence; a priest, bearing the sacrament, was pelted
with stones,‡ and the civil authority interfering, committed the
most violent of the party to prison.§ Indignant at this treatment, and intent upon justifying themselves and obtaining re-

---

* Ut rerum potiatur et instauret sacra et respublicas tradat sanctis
viris tenendas. (Camerar. Vit. Mel. p. 45.)

† Quod nos docemus, ille facit.

‡ Einen Priester der das Venerabile getragen mit Steinen geworfen.
(Seck. p. 482.)

§ Sunt et illic in vincula conjecti. (Mel. Corp. Ref. i. p. 513.)

dress, Storch, Mark Thomas, and Stubner, repaired to Wittemberg.*

They arrived on the 27th December, 1521. Storch, leading the way with the port and bearing of a Lanzknecht,† and Mark Thomas and Stubner following behind. The disorder that reigned in Wittemberg was favourable to their designs. The youth of the academies, and the class of citizens already roused and excited, were well prepared to give ear to the new teachers.

Making sure of co-operation, they waited upon the University Professors, to receive their sanction: "We," said they, "are sent by God to teach the people. The Lord has favoured us with special communications from Himself; we have the knowledge of things which are coming upon the earth.† In a word, we are Apostles and Prophets, and we appeal, for the truth of what we say, to Doctor Luther." The Professors were amazed.

"Who commissioned you to preach?" enquired Melancthon of Stubner, who had formerly studied under him, and whom he now received at his table.—"The Lord our God." —"Have you committed anything to writing?"—"The Lord our God has forbidden me to do so." Melancthon drew back, alarmed and astonished.

"There are indeed spirits of no ordinary kind in these men," said he; "but *what* spirits? . . . none but Luther can solve the doubt. On the one hand let us beware of quenching the Spirit of God, and on the other, of being seduced by the spirit of the devil."

Storch, who was of a restless disposition, soon left Wittemberg; Stubner remained behind. Actuated by an ardent desire to make proselytes, he went from house to house, conversing with one and another, and persuading many to

* Huc advolarunt tres viri, duo lanifices, literarum rudes, literatus tertius est. (Mel. Corp. Ref. i. p. 513.)

† Incedens more et habitu militum istorum quos *Lanzknecht* dicimus. (L. Epp. ii. p. 245.)

‡ Esse sibi cum Deo familiaria colloquia, videre futura . . . . , (Mel. Electori, 27th Dec. 1521. Corp. Ref. i. p. 514.)

acknowledge him as a prophet of God. He especially attached himself to Cellarius, a Suabian, a friend of Melancthon, and master of a school attended by a considerable number of young persons. Cellarius admitted, with blind confidence, the claims of the new Apostles.

Melancthon's perplexity and uneasiness continued to increase. It was not so much the visions of the prophets of Zwickau, as their doctrine concerning *Baptism*, that disturbed him. To him it seemed agreeable to reason,—and he thought it deserved to be examined into,—"for," observed he, "nothing should be lightly received or rejected."[*]

Such was the spirit of the Reformation. In this hesitation and struggle of Melancthon, we have an evidence of his uprightness, which does him more honour than a determined opposition could have done.

The Elector himself, whom Melancthon termed "the light of Israel,"[†] had his doubts. "Prophets and Apostles in the electorate of Saxony, as of old time in Jerusalem! It is a solemn question," said he, "and as a layman, I cannot decide it. But rather than fight against God, I would take to my staff, and descend from my throne!"

On reflection, he intimated by his counsellors, that Wittemberg had quite sufficient trouble in hand: that it was most likely the claims of the men of Zwickau were a temptation of the devil, and that the wisest course appeared to be to allow the whole matter to settle down,—that nevertheless whenever his Highness should clearly perceive what was God's will, he would not confer with flesh and blood, but was ready to endure every thing in the cause of truth.[‡]

Luther received in the Wartburg intelligence of the ferment at the court of Wittemberg. His informants apprized him of strange persons having made their appearance, and that, as to their message, it was not known from whence it came. The

[*] Censebat enim neque admittendum neque rejiciendum quicquam temeré. (Camer. Vit. Mel. p. 49.)

[†] Electori lucernæ Israel. (Ibid. p. 513.)

[‡] Daruber auch leiden was S. C. G. leiden sollt. (Ibid. p. 537.)

thought instantly occurred to him, that God had permitted
these deplorable events in order to humble his servants, and to
rouse them to seek higher degrees of sanctification. "Your
Highness," said he, in a letter to the Elector, "your Highness for many a year collected reliques far and wide; God
has heard your prayers, and sent you, at no cost or trouble of
your own, a *whole cross*, with nails, spears, and scourges.
God prosper the newly acquired relic! Only let your Highness spread out your arms, and endure the piercing of the
nails in your flesh. I always expected that Satan would send
us this plague."

Nevertheless, there was nothing, according to his judgment,
more urgent than to secure to others the liberty he claimed
for himself. He would have no divers weights or measures:
"Pray let them alone; don't imprison them," wrote he to
Spalatin; "let not our prince embrue his hands in the blood
of the prophets that have risen up."* Luther was far beyond
the age in which he lived, and even beyond many of the
Reformers in the matter of toleration.

Affairs were daily growing more serious in Wittemberg.†

Carlstadt did not receive many things taught by the new
teachers, and especially their anabaptist doctrine; but there is
something contagious in religious enthusiasm, which a head
like his could with difficulty withstand. From the time the
men of Zwickau arrived in Wittemberg, Carlstadt had accelerated his movements in the direction of violent changes: "It
is become necessary," cried he, "that we should exterminate
all the ungodly practices around us.‡ He brought forward
all the texts against image worship, and with increased vehemence declaimed against Romish idolatry—"People kneel,"
said he, "and crawl before those idols; burn tapers before
their shrines, and make offerings to them. Let us arise, and
drag the worshippers from their altars!"

Such appeals were not lost upon the populace. They broke

* Ne princeps manus cruentet in prophetis. (L. Epp. ii. p. 135.)
† Ubi fiebant omnia in dies difficiliora. (Camer: Vit. Mel. p. 49.)
‡ Irruendum et demoliendum statim. (Ibid.)

into churches, carried off the images, breaking them in pieces, and burning them.* Better would it have been to have awaited their abolition by authority; but the cautious advances of the leaders of the Reformation were thought to compromise its security.

It was not long before one who listened to these enthusiasts might have thought that there were no real Christians in all Wittemberg, save only those who refused to come to confession, persecuted the priests, and ate meat on fast days. The bare suspicion that he did not reject, one and all, the ceremonies of the Church as inventions of the devil, was enough to subject a man to the charge of being a worshipper of Baal. " We must form a church," they exclaimed, " that shall consist of the Saints alone!"

The burghers of Wittemberg presented to the Council certain regulations which it was compelled to sanction. Several of these regulations were conformable to christian morals The closing of places of amusement was particularly insisted upon.

But soon after this, Carlstadt went still greater lengths; he began to pour contempt upon human learning; and the students heard their aged tutor advising them, from his rostrum, to return to their homes, and resume the spade, or follow the plough, and cultivate the earth, because man was to eat bread in the sweat of his brow! George Mohr, master of the boys' school of Wittemberg, carried away by a similar madness, called from his window to the burghers outside to come and remove their children. Where indeed was the use of their pursuing their studies, since Storch and Stubner had never been at the University, and yet were prophets? A mechanic was just as well, nay perhaps better qualified than all the divines in the world, to preach the Gospel!

Thus it was that doctrines were put forth directly opposed to the Reformation. The revival of letters had opened a way for the reformed opinions. Furnished with theological learn-

* Die Bilder zu stürmen und aus den Kirchen zu werfen. (Math. p. 31.)

ing, Luther had joined issue with Rome;—and the Wittemberg enthusiasts, similar to those fanatical monks exposed by Erasmus and Reuchlin, pretended to trample under foot all human learning! Only let Vandalism once establish its sway, and the hopes of the world were gone; and another irruption of barbarians would quench the light which God had kindled among Christian people.

It was not long before the results of these strange lessons began to show themselves. Men's minds were diverted from the Gospel, or prejudiced against it: the school was almost broken up, the demoralised students burst the bands of discipline, and the states of Germany recalled such as belonged to their several jurisdictions.* Thus the men who aimed at reforming, and infusing new vigour into every thing, had brought all to the brink of ruin. "One more effort," thought the partisans of Rome, who, on all sides, were again lifting their heads, "and all will be ours!"†

The prompt repression of these fanatical excesses was the only means of saving the Reformation. But who should undertake the task? Melancthon? He was too young, too deficient in firmness, too much perplexed by this strange conjuncture of circumstances. The Elector? He was the most pacific man of his age. To build his castles of Altenburg, Weimar, Lochau, and Coburg, to adorn the churches with fine pictures by Lucas Cranach, to improve the chauntings in his chapels, to advance the prosperity of his university, and promote the happiness of his subjects; to stop in his walks and distribute little presents to playful children,—such were the tranquil occupations of his life; and now, in his declining years, to engage in conflict with fanatics, and oppose violence to violence,—how could the gracious and pious Frederic take such a step?

The evil, therefore, was gaining ground, and no one stept forward to arrest its progress. Luther was absent far from Wittemberg. Confusion and ruin impended over the city.

* Etliche Fürsten ihre Bewandten abgefordert. (Corp. Ref. i. p. 560.)
† Perdita et funditus diruta. (Cam. Vit. Mel. p. 52.)

The Reformation beheld, proceeding, as it were, from its own bosom, an enemy more to be dreaded than Popes and Emperors. It was as if on the brink of an abyss.

"Luther! Luther!" was the cry from one end of Wittemberg to the other. The burghers were clamorous for his re-appearance. Divines felt their need of the benefit of his judgment; even the prophets appealed to him. All united in entreating him to return.*

We may guess what was passing in the Reformer's mind. The harsh usage of Rome seemed nothing when compared with what now wrung his heart. It is from the very midst of the Reformation that its enemies have gone forth. It is preying upon its own vitals; and that teaching, which, by its power, had sufficed to restore peace to his troubled heart, he beholds perverted into an occasion of fatal dissensions in the Church.

"If I knew," said Luther, at an earlier period, "that my doctrine had injured one human being, however poor and unknown,—which it could not, for it is the very Gospel,—I would rather face death ten times over, than not retract it.† And lo! now, a whole city, and that city Wittemberg itself, is sinking fast into licentiousness." True, indeed, the doctrine he had taught had not been the cause of all this evil; but from every quarter of Germany voices were heard that accused him as the author of it. Some of the bitterest feelings he had ever known oppressed his spirit at this juncture, and his trial was of a different kind. Was this then, he asked himself, to be the issue of the great work of Reformation? Impossible! he utterly rejected the doubts that presented themselves. God has begun the work—God will fulfil it. "I prostrate myself in deep abasement before the Eternal," said he, "and I implore of Him that His name may rest upon this work, and

* Lutherum revocavimus ex heremo suo magnis de causis. (Corp. Ref. i. p. 566.)

† Möchte ich ehe zehn Tode leyden. (Wider Emser, L. Opp. xviii. p. 613.)

that if anything impure has mingled in the doing of it, He will remember that I am but a sinful man."[*]

The letters written to Luther, conveying reports of the inspiration of the pretended prophets and their exalted communion with the Lord, did not occasion him a moment's hesitation. He well knew the deep struggles and prostrations of the spiritual life; at Erfurth and at Wittemberg, he had had experience of the mighty power of God, which rendered him but little disposed to credit the statement that God had appeared visibly, and discoursed with his creature.

"Ask them," said he, in writing to Melancthon, "if they have known those spiritual heavings, those pangs of God's new creation, those deaths and hells, which accompany a real regeneration.[†] And if they speak only of soft and tranquil impressions, piety, and devotion, as they phrase it, don't believe them; not even though they should assert that they have been caught up into the third heaven! In order that Christ should enter into his glory, it behoved him to pass through the suffering of death : thus the believer must pass through the tribulation of his sin before he enters into his *Peace.* Would you learn when, where, and how, God speaks to men ? Listen to the word. ' *As a lion He has broken all my bones, —I am cast out from before His face, and my life is brought down to the gates of death.*' No, no, the Divine Majesty (as they term Him) does not speak face to face with man, for ' *no man,*' says He, ' *can see my face and live.*' "

But his firm conviction that the prophets were under a delusion did but aggravate Luther's grief. The solemn truth of Salvation by Grace seemed to have quickly lost its attraction, and men were turning aside after fables. He began to understand that the work was not so easy as he had once fondly thought. He stumbled at this first stone placed in his path by the fickleness of the human heart. Grief and anxiety weighed heavy on his spirit. He desired, though at the haz-

---

[*] Ich krieche zu seiner Gnaden.   (L. Opp. xviii. p. 615.)

[†] Quæras num experti sint spirituales illas angustias et nativitates divinas, mortes infernosque.   (L. Epp. ii. p. 215.)

and of his life, to remove the stumbling-block out of the way
of the people, and he resolved to return to Wittemberg.

It was a moment of considerable danger. The enemies of
the Reformation thought themselves on the very eve of destroying it. George of Saxony, who would neither connect
himself with Rome nor with Wittemberg, had written, as
early as the 15th October, 1521, to Duke John, the Elector's
brother, to induce him to side with those who opposed the
progress of the Reformation. " Some," wrote he, " deny the
immortality of the soul, others, and those friars too ! drag the
relics of St. Anthony through the streets, and throw them into
the gutters.* All this comes of Luther's teaching. Entreat
your brother either to make a public example of the impious
authors of these disorders, or, at least, publicly to declare his
opinion of them. Our grey hairs warn us that we are near
the end of our course, and that we ought speedily to put an
end to such evils."

After this, George took his departure to be present at the
sittings of the Imperial Government at Nuremberg. On arriving, he used every means to procure the adoption of severe
measures. The result was that, on the 21st of January, the
Diet published an edict, in which they complained bitterly
that the priests were accustomed to say mass without being
habited in priest's garments,—that they pronounced the words
of consecration in German,—administered it to such as had
not confessed themselves,—passed it into the hands of laymen,
without even troubling themselves to ascertain whether the
communicant came to it fasting.†

The Imperial Government directed the Bishops accordingly, to look after and punish severely the innovators within
their respective dioceses : and the Bishops were not slow in
following these directions.

; It was just at this moment that Luther decided to appear
again upon the stage. He clearly saw the critical position of

* Mit Schweinen und Schellen . . . . in Koth geworfen. (Weym.
Ajn Seck. p. 482.)

† In ihre laïsche Hände reiche. (L. Opp. xviii. p. 285.)

affairs, and foreboded wide-spreading calamity. "A time of trouble," said he, "is coming upon the empire which will sweep before it princes, magistrates, and bishops. People's eyes are opened; they cannot be driven by main force; Germany will be deluged with blood.[*] Let us take our stand as a wall of defence to our country in the day of God's anger."

So thought Luther: but he perceived a danger yet more imminent. At Wittemberg, the fire, instead of expiring, was burning every day more fiercely. From the summits of the Wartburg, Luther might discern in the horizon the lurid glare that gives notice of devastation flashing at intervals through the gloom. Who but himself can apply a remedy in the crisis? What should prevent his throwing himself into the heat of the conflagration, and exerting his influence to arrest its progress? He foresees his enemies preparing to strike him down, but his purpose is not shaken. Nor is he deterred by the Elector's entreaty that he would keep within the Wartburg, and there quietly prepare his justification at the approaching Diet. A more urgent necessity is pressing upon his soul; and it is to justify the Gospel itself. "The news from Wittemberg," wrote he, "is every day becoming more alarming. I am on the point of setting out. That state of things absolutely requires it."[†]

Accordingly, on the 3d of March, he finally decided on leaving the Wartburg. He bade farewell to its grey turrets and gloomy forests. He passed beyond those walls, within which the anathemas of Leo and the sword of Charles were alike powerless. He trod the path that wound to the foot of the mountain. The world which lay stretched before him, and on which he was once more about to appear, would soon perhaps ring with the clamours of those who sought his life. It matters not. On he goes rejoicing; for it is in the name of the Lord that he is bending his steps towards the haunts of men.[‡]

---

[*] Germaniam in sanguine natare. (L. Epp. ii. p. 157.)

[†] Ita enim res postulat ipsa. (Ibid. p. 135.)

[‡] So machte er sich mit unglaublicher Freudigkeit des Geistes, im Nahmen Gottes auf den Weg. (Seck. p. 458.)

Time had been busy. Luther was leaving the Wartburg for another cause and in a different character from that in which he had first entered it. He had arrived there as one who had attacked the received tradition, and its established teachers. He was quitting it for the *defence* of the doctrine of the Apostles against a new class of adversaries. He had entered the Wartburg as an innovator who had assailed the ancient hierarchy,—he was leaving it in the spirit of a conservator, that he might defend the faith of Christians. Until this period, Luther had seen in the success of his efforts but the triumph of the great truth of Justification by Faith; and, armed with this single weapon, he had beat down long standing superstitions. But if there had been a time for removing that which had encumbered the soil, a season must needs come for building up. Hidden under the ruins with which his assaults had strewed the plain, behind discredited letters of indulgence, broken tiaras and trampled cowls, beneath the many Romish errors and corruptions that his mind surveyed as the slain upon a battle-field, he discerned and brought forth to light the primitive Catholic Church, re-appearing still the same, and, as it were, emerging from a protracted struggle, with unchangeable doctrine and heavenly accents. He could appreciate the vast difference between Rome and that true Church which he hailed and embraced with joy. Luther wrought no new thing on the earth, as has been falsely charged upon him; he did not build for his own age an edifice that had no associations with the past; he discerned and let in the light upon those earlier foundations which were then overrun with thorns and brambles; while he persevered in reconstructing the temple, he did but build on the fundamental truths taught by the Apostles. Luther was aware that the ancient and primitive Apostolic Church must, on one hand, be restored and opposed to that papal power which had so long oppressed it,—and, on the other hand, be defended against enthusiasts and unbelievers, who affected to disown it, and were seeking to set up some new thing, regardless of all that God had done in past ages. Luther was, from that hour, no longer the representative of a single great truth—that of *Justification by Faith*, though, to the last, he gave to it the highest place; the whole theology of Christianity now occupied his thoughts:—and while he believed that, in its essence, the Church is the Congregation of Saints, he was careful not to despise the visible Church, and he therefore recognised those who were outwardly called, as constituting, in a certain sense, the kingdom of God. Accordingly, a great change took place in Luther, and, in his entrance into divine truth, and in that regenerative process which God was carrying on in the world. The hierarchy of Rome, acting upon him, might have goaded the Reformer to one extreme, had not the sects, which, at this time, lifted their heads so daringly, recalled him to just and moderate views. His residence in the Wartburg divides these two periods of the history of the Reformation.

Luther rode slowly on in the direction of Wittemberg. It was Shrove Tuesday, and the second day of his journey. Towards evening, a terrific storm came on, and the roads were flooded. Two young Swiss, who were travelling the same way, were hastening for shelter to the city of Jena. They had studied at Bale, and were attracted to Wittemberg by the renown of its university. Journeying on foot, tired, and wet through, John Kessler, of Saint Gall, and his comrade, quickened their steps. The town was in all the bustle and buffoonery of the carnival—dances, masquerades, and tumultuous feasting, engrossed the thoughts of the inhabitants, and the two travellers, on arriving, could find no room in any of the inns. After a while, they were directed to the Black Bear, outside the city gate. Harassed and depressed, they repaired thither. The landlord received them kindly.* Ashamed of their appearance, they sat down near the open door of the public room, unwilling to go further. Seated at

* See the narrative of Kessler, with its details, in the simple language of that age, in Bernet, Johann. Kessler, p. 27. Hahnhard Erzählungen, iii. p. 300, and Marheinecke Gesch. der Ref. ii. p. 331, 3d edit.

one of the tables, was a solitary man in the habit of a knight, his head covered with a red cap, and wearing small clothes, over which hung down the skirts of his doublet. His right hand rested on the pommel of his sword; his left grasped the hilt; a book lay open before him, and he seemed to be reading attentively.* At the noise made by their entrance, the stranger raised his head and saluted them courteously, inviting them to approach and take a seat with him at the table; then offering them a glass of beer, he said, alluding to their accent, "You are Swiss, I perceive; but from which of the Cantons?" —"From St. Gall."—"If you are going to Wittemberg, you will there meet one of your countrymen, Doctor Schurff." Encouraged by so much affability, they enquired—"Could you kindly inform us where Martin Luther now is?"—"I know for certain," answered the knight, "that Luther is not at Wittemberg, but probably he will be there shortly. Philip Melancthon is there. If you'll be advised by me, apply yourselves to the Greek and Hebrew, that you may understand the Holy Scriptures." "If our lives are spared," observed one of the Swiss, "we will not return without seeing and hearing Doctor Luther; it is for that purpose we have made the journey. We hear he wants to abolish the clergy and the mass, and as our parents always intended to bring us up to the church, we should like to know on what grounds he is acting." The knight was silent for a moment, and then enquired, "Where have you been studying hitherto?"—"At Bale."—"Is Erasmus still there? what is he doing?" They answered his questions; and a pause ensued. The two Swiss knew not what to make of their new acquaintance. "How strange," thought they, "that the conversation of a knight should be all about Schurff, Melancthon, and Erasmus, and the advantage of knowing Greek and Hebrew." "Tell me, my friends," said the stranger, suddenly breaking silence, "what is said of Luther in Switzerland?"—"Sir," replied Kessler, "opinions concerning him are greatly divided, as is the case every where. Some extol him, and others pronounce

* In einem rothen Schlöpli, in blossen Hosen und Wamms . (Ibid.)

him an abominable heretic."—" Aye, aye, the priests, no doubt,"
remarked the stranger.

The knight's cordiality had put the students completely at
their ease. Their curiosity was excited to know what book
he had been reading when they came in. The knight had
closed the volume. Kessler's comrade ventured to take it up:
what was his surprise at finding it to be the Hebrew Psalter.
Laying it down, he said, as if to divert attention from this
freedom, " Gladly would I give my little finger to understand
that language."—" You will surely have your wish," was the
stranger's reply, " if you will take the pains to acquire it."

A few minutes after, the landlord's voice was heard calling
Kessler. The poor Swiss began to fear something was
amiss; but the host whispered, " I hear you want to see
Luther; well, it is he who is seated beside you." Kessler's
first thought was that he was jesting. " You surely would
not deceive me," said he. " It is he, himself," replied the
landlord; "but don't let him see that you know him."
Kessler made no answer; but returned to the room, and
resumed his seat, eager to communicate the information to his
companion. To do this was not easy; at last he leaned forward, as if looking towards the door, and stooping close to
his friend's ear, whispered,—" The landlord says it is Luther
himself."—" Perhaps," returned his companion, " he said
Hutten ?"—" Probably so," said Kessler, " I may have
mistaken the one name for the other, for they resemble each
other in sound."

At that moment, the trampling of horses' feet was heard
outside: two travelling merchants, asking a night's lodging,
entered the room, laid aside their spurs, and threw off their
cloaks, and one of them deposited near him, on the table, an
unbound book, which attracted the knight's notice. " What
book may that be?" asked he. " It is a commentary on the
Gospels and Epistles, by Doctor Luther," was the traveller's
answer; " it has only just appeared."—" I shall get it shortly,"
remarked the knight.

Conversation was interrupted by the landlord's announcing

that supper was ready. The two students, not wishing to incur the expense of a meal in company with the knight Ulric Hutten, and two thriving merchants, took the landlord aside, and asked him to serve them with something apart. "Come along, my friends," said the innkeeper of the Black Bear, "sit ye down beside this gentleman; I will let you off easy."—"Come, come," said the knight, "I'll pay the score."

During supper, the mysterious stranger made many striking and instructive remarks. Both merchants and students listened in silence, more attentive to his words than to the dishes before them. In the course of conversation, one of the merchants exclaimed, "Luther must be either an angel from heaven, or a devil from hell!" and he followed up his exclamation by the remark,—"I would give ten florins for an opportunity of meeting him, and confessing to him."

Supper being over, the merchants rose from their seats; the two Swiss remained in company with the knight, who, taking up a large glass of beer, and raising it to his lips, said gravely, after the custom of the country,—"Swiss, one glass more, for thanks." And as Kessler was about to take the glass, the stranger, replacing it, handed him one filled with wine:—"You are not used to beer," said he.

This said, he rose from his seat, threw over his shoulders a military cloak, and extending his hand to the students, said, "When you reach Wittemberg, salute Doctor Jerome Schurff from me."—"With pleasure," replied they; "but whose name shall we give?"—"Do you tell him only, that he who is coming sends him greeting." With these words he departed leaving them delighted with his condescension and kindness.

Luther,—for he it was,—continued his journey. It will be remembered, that he had been placed under ban of the Empire: whoever met him might therefore seize his person. But in that critical moment, engaged as he was, in an enterprise replete with dangers, he was calm and serene, and conversed cheerfully with those whom he met with on his way.

It was not that he deceived himself as to immediate results,

He saw the horizon black with storms:—" Satan," said he, " is enraged; and all around me are plotting death and destruction.* But I go forward to throw myself in the way of the Emperor and the Pope, with no protector but God above. Go where I will, every man is at perfect liberty to put me to death wherever he may find me. Christ is Lord of all! if it be His will that my life should be taken, even so let it be."

That same day, being Ash Wednesday, Luther arrived at Borne, a small town in the neighbourhood of Leipsic. He felt that it became him to acquaint his prince with the bold step he was about to take, and accordingly wrote as follows, from the inn at which he had alighted:

" Grace and peace from God, our Father, and from our Lord Jesus Christ! Most Serene Elector, Gracious Prince,— the reproach brought upon the Gospel by the events that have taken place at Wittemberg, have so deeply grieved me, that I should have lost all hope, were I not assured that our cause is that of the truth.

" Your Highness knows full well,—or if not, be it known to you, I received the Gospel—not from man, but from heaven,—by our Lord Jesus Christ. It was not from any doubt as to the truth, that I formerly requested public discussions; I did so in humility, and in the hope to win over others. But since my humility is taken advantage of to the hindrance of the Gospel, my conscience urges me, at this time, to change my course of action. I have sufficiently shown my deference to your Highness, in withdrawing from the public gaze for a whole year. Satan knows that it was not from cowardice that I did so. I would have entered Worms, though there had been as many devils in the town, as there were tiles upon its roofs. Now Duke George, whom your Highness mentions as if to scare me, is much less to be dreaded than a single devil. If what is passing at Wittemberg were occurring at Leipsic, (the Duke's usual place of residence,) I would instantly mount my horse, and repair thither, even though—

* Furit Satanas; et fremunt vicini undique, nescio quot mortibus et infernis. (L. Epp. ii. p. 162.)

your Highness will, I trust, pardon the expression—it should rain Dukes George for nine days together, and every one should be nine times as fierce as he! What can he be thinking of in attacking me? Does he suppose that Christ, my Lord, is a man of straw?[*] May God avert from him the awful judgment that hangs over him.

"Be it known to your Highness, that I am repairing to Wittemberg, under a protection more powerful than that of an Elector. I have no thought of soliciting the aid of your Highness; and am so far from desiring _your_ protection, that it is rather my purpose to protect your Highness. If I knew that your Highness could or would take up my defence, I would not come to Wittemberg. No secular sword can advance this cause: God must do all, without the aid or co-operation of man. He who has most faith, is the most availing defence; but, as it seems to me, your Highness is as yet very weak in faith.

"But since your Highness desires to know what to do, I will humbly answer: Your Electoral Highness has already done _too much_, and should do nothing whatever; God neither wants nor will endure that you or I should take thought or part in the matter. Let your Highness follow this advice.

"In regard to myself, your Highness must remember your duty as Elector, and allow the instructions of his Imperial Majesty to be carried into effect in your towns and districts; offering no impediment to any who would seize or kill me;[†] for none may contend against the powers that be, save only He who has ordained them.

"Let your Highness accordingly leave the gates open, and respect safe-conducts, if my enemies in person, or by their envoys, should come to search for me in your Highness's states. Every thing may take its course, without trouble or prejudice to your Highness.

* Er hält meinen Herrn Christum für ein Mann aus Stroh geflochten. (L. Epp. ii. p. 139.)

† Und ja nicht wehren . . . so sie mich fahen oder tödten will. (L. Epp. p. 140.)

"I write this in haste, that you may not feel aggrieved by my coming. My business is with another kind of person from Duke George, one who knows me, and *whom I know well.*

"Written at Borne, at the inn of the *Guide,* on Ash Wednesday, 1522.

"Your Electoral Highness's
"Very humble servant,
"MARTIN LUTHER."

In this way, Luther made his approach to Wittemberg: he wrote to his prince, but not, as we have seen, to excuse the step he had taken. An unshaken confidence animated his heart. He saw God's hand engaged in the cause, and that sufficed him. The heroism of faith was perhaps never more fully acted out. In one of the editions of Luther's works, we read opposite this letter, the remark—"This is a wonderful writing of the third and latest Elias."[*]

It was on Friday, the 7th of March, that Luther re-entered Wittemberg, having been five days on his journey. Doctors, students, burghers, broke forth in rejoicings, for they had again among them the pilot who could best extricate the vessel from the reefs by which it was encompassed.

The Elector, who was then at Lochau, attended by his court, was much affected by the perusal of the Reformer's letter. In his desire to exculpate him before the Diet, he wrote to Schurff.—"Let Luther write to me, explaining his reasons for returning to Wittemberg, and introduce the statement that he came without my consent." Luther complied.

"Behold me ready to bear your Highness's disapprobation and the anger of the whole world. Are not the Wittembergers my own sheep? Has not God committed them to my care? and ought I not, if need be, to lay down my life for them? Besides, I dread lest we should see, throughout Germany, a revolt by which God shall punish our nation. Let your Highness be well assured, the decrees of heaven are not

[*] Der wahre, dritte und letzte Elias . . . (L. Opp. (L.) xviii. p. 271.)

like those of Nuremberg."* This letter was written on the same day that Luther reached Wittemberg.

The following day, being Easter Eve, Luther visited Jerome Schurff. He found Melancthon, Jonas, Amsdorff, Augustin Schurff, Jerome's brother, assembled. Luther put many questions to them, and while they recounted all that had taken place in his absence, two foreigners entered the room. The Swiss drew back timidly, on finding themselves in the midst of this company of learned Doctors; but they soon recovered their self-possession when they saw in the centre of the group, the knight whom they had met at the Black Bear. The latter advancing, accosted them as old friends, and said, smiling, as he pointed to one of the company,—" That is Philip Melancthon, whom I mentioned to you." The two Swiss spent that day in the society of the assembled friends, on the strength of the meeting at Jena.

One absorbing thought engrossed the Reformer's mind, and damped the pleasure he would otherwise have felt at finding himself once more surrounded by his friends. Doubtless, the stage on which he had chosen to appear was an obscure one. He was about to raise his voice in a petty town of Saxony; and yet his object was, in reality, so important, as to influence the destinies of the world, and be felt in its effects by many nations and people. The question to be decided was,—whether the teaching which he had derived from God's Word, and which was destined to produce so mighty an effect, would, in the trial, prove stronger than those disorganizing principles which threatened its extinction. It was now to be seen whether it was possible to reform without destroying,—to open a way to new developments without losing such as had already been evolved. To reduce to silence fanatics in the energy of the first bursts of enthusiasm,—to arrest the headlong course of a thoughtless multitude,—to calm their spirits, and restore order, peace, and reason,—to break the force of the torrent that beat against the as yet unsettled edifice of the Reformation,—such

* L. Epp. ii. p. 143. Luther altered this expression at the Elector's request.

was the object of Luther's return to Wittemberg.　　But would his influence accomplish all this ?　　Time must show.

The Reformer's heart thrilled at the thought of the struggle he was about to enter upon.　　He raised his head, as the lion shakes his brindled mane when roused to the fight.　　"The hour," said he, "is arrived, when we must trample under foot the power of Satan, and contend against the spirit of darkness. If our adversaries do not flee from us ;—Christ will know how to compel them.　　We who put our trust in the Lord of life and death, are lords both of life and of death !"*

But at the same time the impetuous Reformer, as if restrained by a higher power, refused to employ the anathemas and thunders of the Word, and set about his work in the spirit of an humble pastor—a tender shepherd of souls.　　"It is with *the Word* we must contend," observed he, "and by *the Word* we must refute and expel what has gained a footing by violence.　　I would not resort to force against such as are superstitious ;—nor even against unbelievers !　Whosoever believeth let him draw nigh, and whoso believeth not, stand afar off.　　Let there be no compulsion.　　Liberty is of the very essence of Faith."†

The next day was Sunday.　　That day the Doctor, whom the lofty walls of the Wartburg had for nearly a year hidden from the public eye, is to appear in the pulpit of the church of Wittemberg.　　"Luther is come back."　　"Luther is to preach to-day."　　The news, repeated from one to another, had of itself no slight effect in giving a turn to the thoughts by which the multitude were deluded.　　People hurried to and fro in all directions ; and on Sunday morning the church was filled to overflow with an attentive and impressed congregation.

Luther could comprehend the disposition of his hearers' minds.　　He ascended the pulpit.　　Behold him surrounded by the flock which had formerly followed him with one heart as

* Domini enim sumus vitæ et mortis.　(L. Epp. ii. p. 150.)

† Non enim ad fidem et ad ea quæ fidei sunt, ullus cogendus est. . . . (L. Epp. ii. p. 151.)

a docile sheep, but which has broken from him in the spirit of an untamed heifer. His address was simple and noble,—energetic and persuasive;—breathing the spirit of a tender father returning to his children, and enquiring into their conduct, while he communicates the reports that have reached him concerning them. He frankly commended their progress in the faith, and having thus prepared and gathered up their thoughts, he proceeded as follows :—

"But we need a something beyond Faith ; and that is Love. If a man who carries a sword is alone, it matters not whether he draw it or keep it sheathed ; but if he is in a crowd let him have a care lest he wound any of those about him.

"Observe a mother with her babe. She first gives it nothing but milk ; and then the most easily digestible food. What would be the consequence were she to begin by giving it meat or wine ?

"In like manner should we act toward our brother.—Have you been long at the breast ?—If so, well ;—only let your brother suck as long !

"Observe the Sun. He dispenses two gifts.—namely—*light* and *warmth.* The mightiest monarch cannot turn aside his rays ;—they come straight on, arriving upon this earth by a direct course. Meanwhile his warmth goes out and diffuses itself in every direction. So it is that Faith, like light, should ever be simple and unbending ;—whilst Love, like warmth, should beam forth on all sides, and bend to every necessity of our brethren."

Having thus engaged his hearers' attention, he proceeded to press them more closely :

"It is agreeable to Scripture, say you, to abolish the Mass. Be it so. But what order, what decency have you observed ? It became you to offer up earnest prayers to God; to apply to the authorities ; then, indeed, every one might have acknow-lodged that the thing was of the Lord."

Thus spake Luther. The fearless man who, at Worms, had stood forth against the princes of this world, made a deep impression on men's minds by these accents of wisdom and peace. Carlstadt and the prophets of Zwickau, from being extolled and all-powerful for a few weeks, and ruling to the disturbance of the public peace, had shrunk into insignificance beside the prisoner escaped from the Wartburg.

"The Mass," he continued, "is a bad thing. God is opposed to it. It ought to be abolished, and I would that every where the Supper of the Gospel were established in its stead. But let none be torn from it by force. We must leave results to God. It is not *we* that must work,—but HIS WORD. And why so? you will ask. Because the hearts of men are not in my hand as clay in the hand of the potter. We have a right to speak, but none whatever to compel. Let us preach;—the rest belongs to God. If I resort to force, what shall I gain? Grimace, fair appearances, apeings, cramped uniformity, and hypocrisy. But there will be no hearty sincerity,—no faith,—no love. Where these are wanting,—all is wanting; and I would not give a straw for such a victory!* Our first aim must be to win the heart; and to this end we must preach the Gospel. Then we shall find the Word impressing one to-day, another the next day; and the result will be, that each one will withdraw from the Mass, and cease to receive it. God does more by the simpler power of His word than you and I and the whole world could effect by all our efforts put together! God arrests the heart, and that once taken,—all is won!

"I say not this that you should restore the Mass. Since it is done away with, in God's name, let it not be revived. But was it right to go about it in such a manner? Paul, coming one day to the famous city of Athens, found there the altars of such as were no gods. He passed on from one to the other, observing them without touching one of them; but he made his way to the market-place, and testified to the people that all their gods were nought but images, graven by art and man's device. And that preached Word took possession of their hearts, and the idols fell, without his so much as touching them!

* Ich wollte nicht einen Birnstiel drauf geben. (L. Opp. (L.) xviii. p. 355.)

"I am ready to preach, argue, write,—but I will not constrain any one: for faith is a voluntary act. Call to mind what I have already done. I stood up against Pope, indulgences, and Papists; but without violence or tumult. I brought forward God's Word; I preached and wrote, and there I stopped. And whilst I laid me down and slept, or chatted with Amsdorff and Melancthon over our tankard of Wittemberg beer, the word I had preached brought down the power of the Pope to the ground, so that never prince or emperor had dealt it such a blow. For my part, I did next to nothing: the power of the Word did the whole business. Had I appealed to force, Germany might have been deluged with blood. But what would have been the consequence? Ruin and destruction of soul and body. Accordingly, I kept quiet, and let the Word run through the length and breadth of the land. Know you what the devil thinks when he sees men resort to violence to spread the Gospel through the world? Seated behind the fire of hell, and folding his arms, with malignant glance and horrid leer, Satan says, ' How good it is in yonder madmen to play into my hands.' But only let him see the Word of the Lord circulating, and working its way unaided on the field of the world, and at once he is disturbed at his work, his knees smite each other, he trembles, and is ready to die with fear."

On the Tuesday following, Luther again ascended the pulpit, and his powerful exhortation was once more heard, in the midst of an attentive audience. He preached again on Wednesday, Thursday, Friday, Saturday, and Sunday. He took a review of the destruction of images, the distinction of meats, the institution of the Supper, the restoration of the cup to the laity, and the abolition of the confessional. He showed that these points were of much less consequence than the Mass, and that the prime movers of the disorders of which Wittemberg had been the scene, had grossly abused their liberty. He passed by turns from accents of true Christian charity to bursts of holy indignation.

He especially declared himself against those who ventured

lightly to partake of the Supper of the Lord. "It is not the mere *pressing with the teeth*," said he, "it is the inward and spiritual partaking realized by faith which makes us Christians, and without which all outward acts are but show and grimace. But that faith consists in the firm belief that Jesus is the Son of God; that having himself borne our sins and our iniquities on the cross, he is, himself, the alone and all-sufficient expiation; that he now appears continually in the presence of God, reconciling us to the Father; and has given to us the sacrament of his body for the strengthening of our faith in this unspeakable mercy. Only let me believe this, and God is my defence; with Him for my buckler I defy sin, death, hell, and devils: they cannot harm me, nor even so much as ruffle a hair of my head! That spiritual bread is comfort to the afflicted, health to the sick, life to the dying, food to the hungry, and a treasury for the poor! The man who does not feel the burthen of his sins, ought, therefore, to abstain from approaching the altar. What can *he* have to do there? Ah! let conscience be heard; let our hearts be broken with the sense of our sins, and we shall not come to that holy sacrament in a spirit of presumption."

Crowds continually filled the church; many came even from the neighbouring towns and villages to hear this new Elijah. Among others Capito passed two days at Wittemberg, and heard the doctor preach twice. Never before had Luther and the cardinal's chaplain been so entirely agreed. Melancthon, magistrates, professors, and the whole population were overjoyed.* Schurff, delighted with such a termination of so unpromising a state of things, hastened to communicate the intelligence to the Elector. He wrote to him on Friday, the 15th of March, after hearing Luther's sixth discourse. "Oh, what joy has Doctor Martin's reappearance diffused among us! His words, through divine mercy, every day bring back into the way of truth our poor deluded people. It

* Grosse Freude und Frohlocken unter Gelahrten und Ungelahrten. (L. Opp. xviii. p. 266.)

is manifest that the Spirit of God is with him, and that his coming to Wittemberg is by His special providence."*

In truth these sermons are models of popular eloquence; but not such as, in the days of Demosthenes, or even in those of Savonarola, had led captive the hearts of the people. The task of the preacher of Wittemberg was one of greater difficulty. It is far easier to rouse the fury of a wild beast than to charm it down. What was needed to soothe a fanatic multitude, and to tame unruly passions; and in this Luther succeeded. In his first eight sermons, he allowed not a word to escape him against the originators of these disorders; no allusion likely to give pain,—not so much as a word by which their feelings could be wounded. But his moderation was his strength; and the more tenderly he dealt with the souls that had gone astray, the more perfectly did he vindicate that truth that was aggrieved. There was no withstanding the power of his eloquence. Men usually ascribe to timidity and cowardly compromise, exhortations that inculcate moderation. Here, how different was the case! In publicly standing forth before the inhabitants of Wittemberg, Luther braved the Pope's excommunication and the Emperor's proscription. He re-appeared, notwithstanding the Elector's prohibition, who had intimated that he could not protect him. Even at Worms his courage had not been so signally proved. He was exposing himself to the most imminent dangers; and hence his call was responded to. The man who braved the scaffold, might claim to be listened to when he inculcated submission. None better qualified to urge on his hearers the duty of obedience to God, than he who, in order that he might himself render such obedience, defied the most violent persecution of man. At Luther's appeal difficulties disappeared— tumult subsided—sedition was silenced, and the burghers of Wittemberg returned quietly to their dwellings.

Gabriel Didymus who, of all the Augustine monks, had manifested most enthusiasm, hung upon the Reformer's words. " Don't you think Luther a wonderful teacher?" inquired one

* Aus sonderlicher Schickung des Allmachtigen . . . (Ibid.)

of his hearers, who was himself deeply affected. "Ah!"
replied he, "I seem to be listening to the voice of an angel
rather than a man."[*]   Didymus, soon after this, publicly
confessed he had been deceived.   "He is quite a changed
man," said Luther.[†]

It was not so at first with Carlstadt.   Abandoning his
studies, and frequenting the workshops of artisans, that he might
there receive the true interpretation of the Scriptures, he was
mortified at beholding his party losing ground on the re-appearance of Luther.[‡]   In his view it was arresting the Reformation in the midst of its career.   Hence, his countenance
wore a constant air of dejection, sadness, and dissatisfaction.
Nevertheless, he sacrificed his self-love for the sake of peace,
restrained his desire to vindicate his doctrine, was reconciled,
at least in appearance, to his colleague, and soon after resumed
his studies in the university.[§]

The most noted of the prophets were not at Wittemberg
when Luther arrived there.   Nicolas Storch was on a progress through the country.   Mark Stubner had quitted the
hospitable roof of Melancthon.   Perhaps their spirit of pro-
phecy had left them without "voice or answer,"[||] from the
first tidings brought them that the new Elijah was turning his
steps toward their Mount Carmel.   Cellarius, the old schoolmaster, alone remained.   Meanwhile, Stubner, hearing that
his sheep were scattered, returned in haste to Wittemberg.
Those who had remained faithful to "the heavenly prophecy"
gathered round their master, repeated the substance of Luther's
sermons, and pressed him with anxious enquiries as to what
they ought to think and do.[¶]   Stubner exhorted them to stand
firm.   "Let him come forth," interposed Cellarius; "let him

* Imo, inquit, angeli, non hominis vocem mihi audisse videor.
(Camerarius, p. 12.)

† In alium virum mutatus est. (L. Epp. ii. p. 156.)

‡ Ego Carlstadium offendi, quod ordinationes suas cessavi. (L. Epp.
ii. p. 177.)

§ Philippi et Carlstadii lectiones, ut sunt optimæ . . (Ibid. p. 284.)

|| 1 Kings xviii.

¶ Rursum ad ipsum confugere . . . (Camerar. p. 52.)

give us the meeting; let him only afford us opportunity to declare our doctrine, and then we shall see . . . ."

Luther had but little wish to meet them. He knew them to be men of violent, hasty, and haughty temper, who would not endure even kind admonitions, but required that every one should, at the very first summons, submit to them as to a supreme authority.* Such are enthusiasts in every age. Nevertheless, as an interview was requested, Luther could not decline it. Besides, it might be doing service to the weak of the flock to unmask the imposture of the prophets. Accordingly the meeting took place. Stubner opened the conversation. He showed how he proposed to restore the Church and reform the world. Luther listened to him with great calmness.† "Of all you have been saying," replied he, at last, gravely, "there is nothing that I see to be based upon Scripture. It is a mere tissue of fiction." At these words Cellarius lost all self-possession. Raising his voice like one out of his mind, he trembled from head to foot, and striking the table with his fist, in a violent passion,‡ exclaimed against Luther's speech as an insult offered to a man of God. On this Luther remarked, "Paul declared that the signs of an apostle were wrought among the Corinthians, in signs and mighty deeds. Do you likewise prove your apostleship by miracles."—"We will do so," rejoined the prophets.§ "The God whom I serve," answered Luther, "will know how to bridle your gods." Stubner, who had hitherto preserved an imperturbable silence, now fixing his eyes on the Reformer, said, in a solemn tone, "Martin Luther, hear me while I declare what is passing at this moment in your soul. You are beginning to see that my doctrine is true." Luther was silent for a few moments, and then replied, "The Lord rebuke thee, Satan." Instantly the prophets lost all self-command. They shouted

* Vehementer superbus et impatiens . . . credi vult plena auctoritate, ad primam vocem . . . (L. Epp. ii. p. 179.)

† Audivit Lutherus placide . . . (Camer. p. 52.)

‡ Cum et solum pedibus et propositam mensulam manibus feriret. (Ibid.)

§ Quid pollicentes de mirabilibus affectionibus. (Ibid. p. 53.)

aloud, " The Spirit, the Spirit." The answer of Luther was
marked by the cool contempt and cutting homeliness of his
expressions: " I slap your spirit on the snout!"* said he.
Hereupon their outcries redoubled. Cellarius was more
violent than the rest. He stormed till he foamed at the
mouth,†——and their voices were inaudible from the tumult.
The result was that the pretended prophets abandoned the
field, and that very day they left Wittemberg.

Thus did Luther achieve the object for which he had left
his retirement. He had taken his stand against fanaticism,
and expelled from the bosom of the church the enthusiasm
and disorder which had invaded it. If the Reformation with
one hand dashed to the earth the dusty decretals of Rome,
with the other it put away from it the pretensions of the mystics, and established on the territory it had acquired the living
and sure Word of God. The character of the Reformation
was thus distinctly seen. Its mission was to keep constantly a
middle course between these extremes, remote alike from fanatical distortions and from the death-like slumber of the papal rule.

Here was an instance of a whole population passionately
excited, and misled to such a degree as to have cast off all
restraint, at once listening to reason, recovering calmness, and
returning to their accustomed submission, so that the most
perfect quiet again reigned in that very city which, but a few
days before, had been like the troubled ocean.

The most absolute liberty was forthwith established at Wittemberg. Luther continued to reside in the convent, and to
wear the monastic habit; but every one was free to lay it
aside. In coming to the Lord's Supper, persons might either
receive only the general absolution or they might apply for
a special one. It was recognised as a principle to reject nothing but what contradicted a clear and express declaration of
Scripture.‡ It was no indifference that dictated this course.

* Ihren Geist haue er über die Schnauze. (L. Opp. Altenburg.
Augs. iii. p. 137.)
† Spumabat et fremebat et furebat. (L. Epp. ii. p. 179.)
‡ Ganz klare und gründliche Schrift.

On the contrary, religion was recalled to its essential principle. Piety only withdrew from the accessary forms in which it had been well nigh lost, that it might rest on its true basis. Thus was the Reformation itself preserved, and the church's teaching progressively developed in love and truth.

No sooner was order re-established, when the Reformer turned to his beloved Melancthon, and requested his co-operation in the final revision of the translation of the New Testament, which he had brought with him from the Wartburg.* As early as the year 1519, Melancthon had laid down the grand principle that the Fathers must be explained conformably to the Scripture, and not Scripture according to the Fathers. Meditating daily on the books of the New Testament, he felt at once charmed by their simplicity, and solemnly impressed by the depth of their import. " In *them*, and them only," affirmed this adept in ancient philosophy, " do we find the true ' food of the soul.' " Gladly, therefore, did he comply with Luther's desire, and many were the hours the two friends, from that time, spent together, studying and translating the inspired Word. Often would they pause in their labours to give free expression to their wonder. " If Reason could speak," said Luther, " it would say, O, that I could once hear the voice of God! I should think it worth a journey to the very uttermost parts of the earth! Give ear, then, my fellow-man—God, the creator of heaven and earth, now speaks to thee !"

The printing of the New Testament was begun and carried on with an activity beyond all example.† One might have thought the very printers felt the importance of the work in hand. Three presses were constantly employed, and ten thousand sheets were struck off every day.*

At last, on the 21st Sept., appeared the complete edition of three thousand copies in two volumes, with the brief title,

* Verum omnia nunc elimare cœpimus Philippus et ego. (L. Epp. ii. p. 176.)

† Ingenti labore et studio. (L. Epp. p. 236.)

‡ Singulis diebus decies millia chartarum sub tribus prelis . . . (Ibid.)

" The New Testament in German ;—at Wittemberg." It bore no name of *man*. From that hour every German might obtain the Word of God at a small pecuniary cost.*

The new translation, written in the tone of the sacred books, in a language that was as yet in its virgin simplicity, and now first opening its full beauty, interested and delighted all classes, from the highest to the lowest. It was a national work—the people's book—nay, much more, it was the book of God. Even enemies could not withhold their commendation of this wonderful production, and there were some incautious partisans of the Reformation so carried away by the beauty of the new version, as to imagine they could recognize in it a second inspiration. It, indeed, served more than all Luther's own writings to diffuse a spirit of christian piety. The great work of the sixteenth century was now placed on a rock whence nothing could dislodge it. The Bible, restored to the people, recalled the mind of man, which had for ages wandered in the endless labyrinths of scholastic teaching, to the heavenly springs of salvation. Hence, the success that attended this step was prodigious. All the copies were quickly disposed of. In December following, a second edition appeared; and by the year 1533, no less than seventeen editions had issued from the presses of Wittemberg; thirteen from Augsburg; twelve from Bale; one from Erfurth; one from Grimma; one from Leipsic ; thirteen from Strasburg.†

Even while the first edition of the New Testament was passing through the press, Luther was already at work on a translation of the Old Testament. This labour, begun in 1522, was continued without intermission. He issued it in detached portions, as he finished them, in order to gratify the impatience of the public demand, and to make the purchase easy to the poor.

From Scripture and Faith, two streams issuing from one and the same spring, the life of the Gospel has flowed, and still diffuses itself through the world. They bore directly

---

* A florin and a half, about a half-crown.
† Gesch d. deutsch. Bibel Uebersetz.

against two established errors. Faith was met by the opposing Pelagian tendency of Catholicism. Scripture, in like manner, found arrayed against it the theory of tradition and the authority of Rome. Scripture led its reader to Faith, and Faith made him the disciple of the Word. "Man can do no meritorious work: the free grace of God, received through faith in Christ, alone saves him." Such was the doctrine proclaimed throughout Christendom. But this teaching must needs bring Christendom to the study of the Scripture. In truth, if faith in Christ is everything in Christianity, and if the observances and ordinances of the Church are nothing, it is not to the Church's teaching, but to Christ's word that we must adhere. The bond that unites to Christ will be everything to the believing soul. What signifies the outward link that connects him with a visible church, enslaved by the commandments of men? . . Thus, as the doctrine of the Bible had impelled Luther's contemporaries toward Jesus Christ, their love for Jesus Christ, in its turn, impelled them towards the Bible. It was not, as some in our days have supposed, from a philosophic necessity, or from doubt, or a spirit of inquiry that they reverted to Scripture, it was because they found *there* the words of *Him they loved.* "You have preached Christ," said they to the Reformer, "let us now hear him *himself.*" And they caught at the sheets given to the world, as a letter coming to them from heaven.

. . But if the Bible was thus joyfully welcomed by such as loved the Lord Jesus Christ, it was scornfully rejected by such as preferred the traditions and ordinances of men. This publication by Luther was the signal of violent persecution. Rome trembled at the report brought thither. The pen which transcribed the sacred oracles was in truth that visionary pen which Frederic had beheld in his dream, reaching to the seven hills, and discomposing the pope's tiara. The monk in his cell, the prince upon his throne, uttered a cry of anger. The ignorant priests were dismayed at the thought that burghers, and even rustics would now be able freely to discuss with them the precepts of the Lord. The king of England denounced the work to the Elector Frederic and to Duke George of Saxony.   But before this, and as early as the November previous, the Duke had commanded all his subjects to deliver up every copy of Luther's New Testament into the hands of the magistrate.   Bavaria, Brandenburg, Austria, and all the states in the interest of Rome passed similar decrees. In some parts, a sacrilegious bonfire, composed of the sacred books, was lighted in the public squares.*   Thus did Rome, in the sixteenth century, renew the efforts by which heathenism had attempted to uproot the religion of Jesus Christ, at the period when the reins were escaping from the hands of the Priests of Idol worship.   But what power can stay the triumphant progress of the Gospel?   " Even after I had prohibited the sale," wrote Duke George, " many thousand copies were sold and read in my states."

God even used, for the purpose of making known His word, the very hands that were essaying to destroy it.   The Romish divines, seeing they could not stop the circulation of the Reformer's work, themselves put forth a translation of the New Testament.   It was no other than Luther's, here and there altered by the new editors.   No hindrance was offered to the reading of it.   Rome had not yet experienced that wherever the Word of God took root, its own power began to totter.   Joachim of Brandenburg, gave license to his subjects to read any translation of the Bible, in Latin or in German, provided it were not from the presses of Wittemberg. The German nations, and more especially the people of Brandenburg, made, in this way, a decided advance in the knowledge of the truth.

The publication of the New Testament in the vernacular tongue, is among the memorable epochs of the Reformation. If the marriage of Feldkirchen had been the first step in the progress of its influence from the sphere of teaching to that of social life ;——if the abolition of monastic vows had been the second, and the establishment of the Supper of the Lord a third stage of this transition, the publication of the New Tes-

* Qui et alicubi in unum congesti rogum publice combusti sunt.

targent was, perhaps, even more important than all the rest
It wrought an entire change in the aspect of society—not
alone in the priest's presbytery—not merely in the monk's
cell and the noble's closet, but more than this, in the interior
of the dwellings of the nobles, citizens, and peasantry.   When
Christians began to read the Bible in their families, Christianity itself underwent a palpable change.   Thence ensued
changed habits,—improved morals,—other conversations,—in
short, a new life.   With the publication of the New Testament, it seemed as if the Reformation passed the threshold of
the college, and took its proper place at the hearths of the
people.

The effect that followed was incalculable.   The Christianity of the Primitive Church was, by the publication of the
Holy Scriptures, presented full before the eyes of the nation,
recovered from the oblivion in which for centuries it had lain
hid,—and the sight was, of itself, enough to justify the charges
that had been brought against Rome.   The least instructed,
provided they did but know how to read—women, artisans,
(we are quoting from one of that age who was bitterly opposed
to the Reformation,) studied the New Testament with eager
delight.*   They carried it about with them, learnt portions
by heart, and saw in its precious pages the proof of the perfect accordance of that Reformation which was Luther's aim,
with the revelation that God had given.

Meanwhile, it was in detached portions only that the teaching of the Bible and of the Reformation had till then been
set forth.   A certain truth had been declared in one tract—a
certain error exposed in another.   The field of the Church
presented the appearance of a plain, on which here and there
were seen, without order or arrangement, the ruins of the old,
and the materials of a new structure; but as yet the new
edifice was wanting.   True it is, that the publication of the
New Testament met this want.   The Reformation might say,
with that book in its hand—"Behold my system."   But as

*   .   .   . mulieres, et quilibet idiota '. . . avidissime legerent.
(Cochlæus, p. 50.)

8*

each individual may contend that his system is none other than that of the Bible, the Reformation seemed called to set forth in order what it found in Holy Scripture.   This was a work Melancthon now contributed in its name.

In the development of his theology, Melancthon's steps had been deliberate; but they were taken with firmness, and the result of his enquiries was courageously made known to all. As early as 1520, he had declared that some of the seven sacraments were, in his judgment, mere imitations of Jewish feasts; and that he considered the asserted infallibility of the Pope as a proud pretension, directly at variance with Scripture and sound judgment.   "We want more than a Hercules,"* remarked he, "to make a stand against such doctrines." Here we see that Melancthon had been led to the same conclusion as Luther by a more studious and calm process of conviction.   The time had now come that he in his turn should publicly confess his faith.

In 1521, during his friend's captivity in the Wartburg, his celebrated "*Loci Communes*" had presented to Christian Europe a body of doctrine, based on solid grounds, and admirably compacted.   The tracings of a simple and majestic outline appeared before the wondering minds of that generation.   As the translation of the New Testament had justified the Reformation to the people, so Melancthon's *Loci Communes* served to justify in it the judgment of the learned.

For fifteen centuries the Church had existed on the earth without having seen such a work.   Relinquishing the common argumentation of scholastic theology, the friend of Luther had at last given to Christendom a system of divinity, derived entirely from Scripture.   In it the reader was conscious of a breath of life, a quickness of understanding, a force of conviction, and a simplicity of statement, which strikingly contrasted with the subtle and pedantic method of the schools.   The coolest judgments, and the most exact divines, were alike impressed with admiration.

* Adversùs quas non uno nobis, ut ita dicam, Hercule opus est. (Corp. Ref. i. p. 137.)

Erasmus designated this work a wondrous army, ranged
in order of battle against the pharisaic tyranny of false teachers;* and while he confessed that on some points he did not
agree with the author, he nevertheless added, that having
always loved him, he had never loved him so much as after
reading this work. "So beautiful is the proof that it affords,"
said Calvin, when presenting it at a subsequent period to the
French people, "that the most perfect simplicity is the noblest
method of handling the Christian doctrine."†

But no one experienced a finer joy than Luther; to the
last this work was to him a theme of wonder. The occasional sounds his trembling hand had drawn, in the deep emotion
of his soul, from the chords of prophets and apostles, were
here blended together in entrancing harmony. Those solid
masses of truth which he had hewn from the quarry of Holy
Scripture, were here raised and compacted together in one
majestic edifice. He was never tired of commending the
work to the attention of the youths who came to study at
Wittemberg. "If you would wish to become divines," said
he, "read Melancthon."‡

In Melancthon's judgment, a deep sense of the wretched
state to which man is reduced by *sin*, is the foundation on
which we must build the teaching of Christian theology.
This universal evil is the primary fact, the leading truth
whence the science takes its departure; and it is *this* which
forms the peculiar distinction of theology from the sciences
which work their own advancement by the powers of reason.

The Christian divine, diving into the heart of man, revealed its laws and mysterious motions, as the philosopher in later
times has disclosed the laws and attractions of material bodies.
"Original sin," said he, "is an inclination born with us—an
impulse which is agreeable to us—a certain influence which

* Vide dogmatum aciem pulchre instructam adversus tyrannidem
pharisaïcam. (Er. Epp. p. 949.)

† La Somme de Theologie, par Philippe Melancthon. (Geneve,
1551. Jehan Calvin aux lecteurs.)

‡ "Librum invictum," said he another time, "non solum immor-
talitate sed et canone ecclesiastico dignum." (De servo arbitrio.)

leads us into the commission of sin, and which has passed from Adam upon all his posterity. Just as there is found in fire a native energy which mounts upward, just as in the loadstone we observe a natural power of attracting steel, just so do we find in man a primary impulse impelling him to that which is evil. I admit freely that in Socrates, Xenocrates, Zeno, were seen temperance and chastity; these exterior virtues were found in men whose hearts were unpurified, and they proceeded out of the love of self, hence we should regard them in reality, not as virtues, but vices."* Such language may sound harsh, but not so if we enter into Melancthon's real meaning. None more prompt than he to acknowledge virtues in the great men of antiquity, which entitled them to the esteem of men; but he laid down the solemn truth, that the highest law given by God to all his creatures is to *love Him above all things.* If then man is doing that which God commands, does it, not from love to God, but from love of self—can we think that God will accept him, thus daring to substitute *self* in place of His own infinite Majesty? And must it not be enough to vitiate any action, that it involves in it a direct rebellion against the sovereignty of God?

The Wittemberg divine proceeded to show how man is rescued from this wretched state: "The Apostle," said he, "invites thee to contemplate at the Father's right hand, the Son of God, our great Mediator, ever living to make intercession for us,† and he calls upon thee to believe assuredly that thy sins are pardoned, and thyself counted righteous and accepted by the Father, for the sake of that Son who died upon the cross."

A peculiar interest attaches to this first edition of the *Loci Communes,* from the manner in which the German divine speaks concerning Free Will. We find him recognising, even more clearly than had been done by Luther, (for he was more of a theologian,) that this doctrine could not be separated

* *Loci communes theologici.* Bale, 1521, p. 35,—a rare edition. See for the subsequent revisions, that of Erlangen, 1828, a reprint of that of Bale, 1561.

† Vult te intueri Filium Dei sedentem ad dextoram Patris, mediatorem interpellantem pro nobis. (Ibid.)

from that which constituted the very essence of the Reformation. Man's justification in the sight of God, is by FAITH
ALONE, was the first point. This faith wrought in man's
heart by the ALONE GRACE OF GOD, was the second. Melancthon saw clearly that to allow any ability in the natural
man *to believe*, would, in this second point, entirely set aside
that grand doctrine of Grace which is asserted in the first.
He was too discerning,—too deeply instructed in the Scriptures, to be misled on so important a question. But he went
too far: instead of confining himself to the religious bearing
of the question, he entered upon metaphysics. He laid down
a sort of fatalism, which might lead his readers to think of
God as the author of evil, and which consequently has no
foundation in Scripture:—" Since whatever happens," said he,
"happens by necessity, agreeably to the divine foreknowledge,
it is plain that our will hath no liberty whatever."[*]

But the principal object Melancthon had in view, was to
present theology as a system of devotion.—The schools had
so dried up the generally received creed, as to leave it destitute of life. The office of the Reformation was to reanimate
this lifeless creed. In succeeding editions, Melancthon felt the
necessity for great clearness in doctrinal statements.[†] In
1521, however, it was not so much the case. "The knowledge of Christ," said he, "is found in the knowledge of the
blessings derived through him. Paul, writing to the Romans,
and desiring to sum up the Christian doctrine, does not set
about treating philosophically of the Trinity, the Incarnation,
Creation, active or passive. What, then, are his themes?—the
Law, Sin, Grace. On our instruction in these, depends our
knowledge of Christ."[‡]

---

[*] Quandoquidem omnia quæ eveniunt, necessario eveniunt juxta
divinam prædestinationem, nulla est voluntatis nostræ libertas. Loci
comm. theol. Bale, 1521, p. 35.

[†] See the edition of 1561, reprinted in 1829, pages 14 to 44, the
several chapters,—De tribus personis;—De divinitate Filii;—De duabus
naturis in Christo;—Testimonia quod Filius sit persona; testimonia
refutantia Arianos; De discernendis proprietatibus humanæ et divinæ
naturæ Christi;—De Spiritu sancto, &c. &c.

[‡] Hoc est Christum cognoscere, beneficia ejus cognoscere, &c. (Ibid.)

The publication of this treatise was of singular service to the cause of truth. Calumnies stood refuted—prejudices were dissipated. Among the religious, the worldly, and the learned, the genius of Melancthon was admired, and his character esteemed and loved. Even such as had no personal knowledge of the author were conciliated to his creed by this work. The vigour and occasional violence of Luther's language had offended many; but in Melancthon, an elegance of composition, a discriminating judgment, and a remarkable clearness and arrangement were seen engaged in the exposition of those mighty truths that had aroused the slumbering world. The work was rapidly bought up, and read with avidity. His gentleness and modesty won all hearts, while his elevation of thought commanded their respect; and the higher classes, who had been hitherto undecided, were captivated by a wisdom which had at last found so noble an utterance.

On the other hand, such of the opposers of the truth as had not been humbled by the energy of Luther, were, for a while, silenced and disconcerted by the appearance of Melancthon's tract. They had found another man as worthy as Luther to be a mark for their hatred. "Alas!" they exclaimed, "alas, for Germany! to what new extremity shall we be brought by this last birth!"*

The *Loci Communes* passed through sixty-seven editions between 1521 and 1595, without including translations. Next to the Bible, this work may have mainly contributed to the establishment of the evangelical doctrine.

Whilst the "grammarian," Melancthon, was by this happy co-operation aiding the efforts of Luther, schemes of a violent character were again planning by his formidable enemies. At the news that he had effected his escape from the Wartburg, and appeared again on the world's stage, the rage of his former adversaries returned.

Luther had been rather more than three months at Wittemberg, when a rumour, repeated by common fame, brought him the intelligence that one of the greatest monarchs of

* Heu! infelicem hoc novo partû Germaniam! . . . (Cochl.)

Christendom had risen up against him. Henry VIII. head of the house of Tudor, a prince descended from the families of York and Lancaster, and in whom, after torrents of bloodshed, the red and white roses were at length united, the puissant king of England, who boldly advanced the obsolete authority of his crown over the continent, and more particularly over France—had put forth an answer to the poor monk of Wittemberg. "I hear much commendation of a little treatise by the king of England," wrote Luther to Lange, on the 26th of June 1522.*

Henry the Eighth was then in his thirty-first year,—"tall, strong-built, and proportioned, and had an air of authority and empire,"† and a countenance that expressed the vivacity of his mind. Vehement in temper, bearing down whatever stood in the way of his passions, and thirsting for distinctions, the defects of his character, were for a time, mistaken for the impetuosity of youth—and there was no lack of flatterers to confirm him in them. Often would he resort, accompanied by his favourite companions, to the house of his chaplain, Thomas Wolsey, the son of a butcher of Ipswich. This man, who was gifted with great abilities, of excessive ambition, and unbounded audacity, being patronised by the Bishop of Winchester, the king's chancellor, had rapidly risen in his master's favour. He would often allure the young prince to his residence by the attraction of riotous pleasures,‡ in which he would not have ventured to indulge within the walls of his own palace. This is recorded by Polydore Vergil, then subcollector of the pope's revenues in England. In these orgies, the chaplain outdid the licentiousness of the younger courtiers.

* Jactant libellum regis Angliæ; sed *leum* illum suspicor sub pelle *actum*—an allusion to Lee, Henry the Eighth's chaplain, punning on his name. (L. Epp. ii. p. 213.)

† He was tall, strong-built, and proportioned, and had an air of authority and empire. (Collier's Eccles. Hist. of Great Britain, fol. ii. 1.)

‡ Domi suæ voluptatum omnium sacrarium fecit, quo regem frequenter ducebat. (Polyd. Vergilius, Angl. Hist. Bale, 1570, fol. p. 633.)—Polydore Vergil seems to have been a sufferer by Wolsey's pride, and to have been, perhaps, inclined on that account, to exaggerate that minister's errors.

He sang, danced, laughed, played the buffoon, took part in indecent conversation, and fenced.* He soon attained the highest seat at the council board, and the whole kingly power passing into his hands, he was enabled to stipulate with foreign princes for a reward for his influence in affairs.

Henry passed whole days in balls, banqueting, and justing—thus squandering the treasure which the avarice of his father had accumulated. Splendid tournaments succeeded each other without intermission. On these occasions, the king, who was easily distinguished from the other combatants by his manly beauty, took the lead.† If the contest seemed for a moment doubtful, his expertness or strength, or else the skilful policy of his antagonist, decided the victory in his favour, and the arena resounded with shouts of applause. Such easy triumphs inflated the vanity of the young prince, and there was no pinnacle of earthly grandeur to which he would not have aspired. The Queen was often present on such occasions. Her grave deportment, melancholy look, and constrained and depressed manner, presented a marked contrast to the tumultuous glitter of such festivities. Henry VIII., soon after his accession, had, from political considerations, contracted marriage with Catherine of Arragon, five years older than himself, widow of his brother Arthur, and aunt to Charles V. While her husband followed his pleasures, the virtuous Catherine, whose piety was such as Spain has been noted for, was accustomed to leave her bed in the dead of the night to take a silent part in the prayers of the monks.‡ She

* Cum illis adolescentibus una psallebat, saltabat, sermones leporis plenos habebat, ridebat, jocabatur. (Polyd. Vergilius, Angl. Hist. Bale, 1570, fol. p. 633.)

† Eximia corporis forma præditus, in qua etiam regiæ majestatis angusta quædam species elucebat. (Sanderus de Schismate Anglicano, p. 4.)—The work of Sanders, the Pope's nuncio, must be read with much suspicion, for unfounded and calumnious statements are not wanting in it—as has been remarked by Cardinal Quirini and the Roman Catholic doctor Lingard.—(See the History of England, by this last, vol. vi. p. 173.)

‡ Surgebat media nocte ut nocturnis religiosorum precibus interesset. — (Sanders, p. 5.)

would kneel without cushion or carpet. At five, after taking a little rest, she would again rise, and assume the habit of St. Francis; for she had been admitted into the third order of that saint.* Then, hastily throwing over her the royal garments, she was in church at six, to join in the holy offices.

Two beings, living in such different atmospheres, could not long continue united.

Catherine, however, was not the only representative of Romish devotion at the court of Henry VIII. John Fisher, bishop of Rochester, then nearly seventy years of age, and distinguished alike for his learning and strict morals, was the object of universal veneration. He had been, for a long period, the oldest counsellor of Henry VII., and the Duchess of Richmond, grandmother to Henry VIII., had, on her death-bed, confided to him the youth and inexperience of her grandson. The king, in the midst of his excesses, long continued to revere the aged bishop as a father.

A much younger man than Fisher, a layman and civilian, had, at this time, attracted general attention by his genius and noble character. His name was Thomas More. He was the son of one of the judges of the Court of King's Bench. In poor circumstances, of temperate habits, and unwearied application, he, at the age of twenty, had sought to mortify the passions of youth by wearing a hair-shirt, and by self-inflicted scourgings. One day, when summoned to the presence of Henry VIII., at a moment when he was attending mass, he replied—"The king's service must give way to the service of God." Wolsey introduced him to Henry, who employed him in various embassies, and lavished on him much kindness. He would often send for him to converse with him on astronomy, and at other times concerning Wolsey, or on disputed points of theology.

The king was, to say the truth, not altogether unacquainted with the doctrines of Rome. It even appears, that, had prince Arthur lived to ascend the throne, Henry was destined to the archiepiscopal see of Canterbury. In his mind and life were

* Sub regio vestitû Divi Francisci habitu utebatur. (Sanders, p. 5.)

strangely blended Thomas Aquinas*—St. Bonaventura—tournaments—banquetings—Elizabeth Blount, and others of his
mistresses. Masses set to music by himself were chaunted in
his chapel.

From the time Henry VIII. first heard of Luther, his
indignation broke forth; and no sooner did the decree of the
Diet of Worms reach England than he gave orders that the
Pontiff's bull against the Reformer's writings should be carried into execution.† On the 12th of May, 1521, Thomas
Wolsey, who, together with the rank of Chancellor of England, held that of Cardinal and Roman Legate, repaired in
solemn procession to St. Paul's Church. Swollen by excess
of pride, he assumed to rival the pomp of royalty itself. He
was accustomed to seat himself in a gold chair, slept in a
golden bed, and dined on a table covered with cloth of gold.‡
On this occasion he displayed his utmost state. His household, to the number of 800 persons, comprising barons, knights,
sons of the first families, who had entered his service as a step
towards the service of the state, attended the haughty prelate.
His garments shone with gold and silk, (he was the first
ecclesiastic who had ventured to assume such sumptuous
apparel.)§ Even the horse-cloths and harness were of the
like costly materials. Before him walked a priest of lofty
stature, bearing a silver pillar, surmounted by a cross. Behind
him, another stately ecclesiastic, holding in his hand the
archiepiscopal crozier of York; a nobleman at his side,
carried his cardinal's hat.‖ Others of the nobility—the prelates—the ambassadors of the Pope and of the Emperor

* Legebat studiose libros divi Thomæ Aquinatis. (Polyd. Vergil,
p. 634.)

† Primum libros Lutheranos, quorum magnus jam numerus per
venerat in manus suorum Anglorum, comburendos curavit. (Ibid. p. 664.)

‡ Uti sella aurea, uti pulvino aureo, uti velo aureo ad mensam.
(Ibid. p. 664.)

§ Primus episcoporum et cardinalium, vestitum exteriorem sericum
sibi induit. (Polyd. Vergil, p. 633.)

‖ Galerum cardinalium, ordinis insignem, sublime a ministro præfe-
.... super altare collocabat .... (Ibid. p. 645.)

joined the cavalcade, and were followed by a long line of mules, bearing chests overhung with rich and brilliant stuffs; and in this pompous procession the several parties that composed it were carrying to the pile the writings of the poor monk of Wittemberg. On reaching the church, the proud priest deposited his cardinal's hat on the altar itself. The virtuous Bishop of Rochester took his place at the foot of the cross, and with accents of strong emotion, preached earnestly against heresy. After this, the attendants drew near bearing the writings of the heresiarch, and they were devoutly consumed in the presence of a vast concourse of spectators. Such was the first public announcement of the Reformation to the people of England.

Henry did not rest there. This prince, whose sword was ever uplifted against his adversaries, his wives, and his favourites, wrote to the Elector Palatine—" Surely, it is no other than the devil, who, by the agency of Luther, has kindled this wide-spreading conflagration. If Luther will not retract, let himself and his writings be committed to the flames."*

But this was not all. Convinced that the progress of heresy was mainly ascribable to the extreme ignorance of the German princes, Henry conceived that the moment was arrived for the exhibition of his own learning. The recollection of the triumphs of his battle-axe did not permit him to doubt of the victory he should gain by his pen. But another passion, vanity,—ever large in little minds,—spurred on the royal purpose. He was mortified by the circumstance, that he had no title to set against that of *Most Christian* and *Catholic*, borne by the kings of France and of Spain, and had for a long time solicited from the court of Rome a similar distinction. What course more likely to obtain it than an attack upon heresy! Henry, then, laid aside his royal dignity, and descended from his throne into the arena of theological dispute. He pressed into his service Thomas Aquinas, Peter Lombard, Alexander of Hale, and Bonaventura, and gave to the world

* Knapp's Nachlese, ii. p. 458.

his "*Defence of the Seven Sacraments, against Martin Luther, by the most Invincible King of England and of France, Lord of Ireland, Henry, the Eighth of that name.*"

"I will put myself in the forefront of the Church, to save her," said the king of England in this book;—"I will receive into my bosom the poisoned darts of her assailant;* what I hear constrains me to this. All the servants of Jesus Christ, whatever be their age, sex or rank, should rise up against the common enemy of Christendom."†

"Let us be doubly armed: with the heavenly armour to conquer with the arms of truth, him who fights with those of error; but also an earthly armour, so that, should he show himself obstinate in malice, the hand of the executioner may silence him; and thus, for once at least, he may be useful to the world, by the terrible example of his death."‡

Henry VIII. could not conceal the contempt which he entertained for his feeble adversary. "This man," says the royal theologian, "seems to be in pains of labour; he travails in birth; and lo! he brings forth but wind. Take away the audacious covering of proud words, with which he clothes his absurdities,—as an ape is clothed with purple,—and what remains?—a wretched and empty sophism."§

The king defends, successively, the mass, penance, confirmation, marriage, orders, and extreme unction. He is not sparing of hard epithets towards his adversary; styling him sometimes an infernal wolf, at others a venomous serpent, or a limb of the devil, and he even casts doubts on Luther's sincerity. In short, Henry VIII. crushes the mendicant monk with his royal anger, "and writes," says an historian, "as if were with his sceptre."‖

---

* Meque adversus venenata jacula hostis eam oppugnantis objicerem (*Assertio septem sacramentorum adv. M. Lutherum* in prologo.)

† Omnis Christi servus, omnis ætas, omnis sexus, omnis ordo consurgat. (Ibid.)

‡ Et qui nocuit verbo malitiæ, supplicii prosit exemplo. (Ibid.)

§ Mirum est quanto nixu parturiens, quam nihil peperit, nisi merus ventum. . . . (Ibid.)

‖ Collier. Eccl. Hist. Gr. Br. p. 17.

It must, however, be confessed, that the book was not ill written, considering the author and the age in which he wrote. The style is not altogether devoid of force. The public of the day set no bounds to its praises. The theological treatise of the powerful king of England, was received with a profusion of adulation. " The most learned work that ever the sun saw," is the expression of some.* " It can only be compared with the works of Saint Augustine," said others. " He is a Constantine, a Charlemagne,—nay more," echoed others, " he is a second Solomon."

These flattering reports soon reached the continent. Henry had desired his ambassador at Rome, John Clarke, dean of Windsor, to present his book to the Sovereign Pontiff. Leo X. received the ambassador in full consistory : Clarke presented the royal work to him with these words, " The king my master assures you, now that he has refuted the errors of Luther with the pen, he is ready to combat his adherents with the sword." Leo, touched with this promise, answered, that the king's book could not have been composed but by the aid of the Holy Spirit, and conferred upon Henry the title of " Defender of the Faith"—still borne by the Sovereigns of England !

The reception which the work met with at Rome, contributed not a little to attract the general attention. In a few months, many thousand copies, from different presses, got into circulation ;† so that, to use the words of Cochlæus, " the whole Christian world was filled with wonder and joy."‡

Such extravagant praises served to augment the already insufferable vanity of the head of the race of Tudor. He seemed himself to entertain no doubt, that he was inspired by the Holy Spirit.§ Henceforward he could not endure contradiction. Papal authority was in his view, no longer at Rome,

* Burnet, Hist of the Ref. of England, i. p. 30.
† Intra paucos menses, liber ejus a multis chalcographis in multa millia multiplicatus. (Cochlæus, p. 41.)
‡ Ut totum orbem christianum et gaudio et admiratione repleverit.
§ He was brought to fancy it was written with some degree of inspiration. (Burnet in præf.)

but at Greenwich,—and infallibility was vested in his own person.   This proud assumption served greatly to promote, at a later period, the Reformation in England.

Luther read Henry's book with a smile, mingled with disdain, impatience, and indignation.   The falsehoods and insults it contained, but above all the air of pity and contempt which the king affected, irritated the doctor of Wittemberg to the highest degree.   The thought that the Pope had publicly approved the book, and that on all sides the enemies of the Gospel, were triumphing over the Reformation and the Reformer, as already overthrown, increased his indignation:—and why indeed, thought he, should he temporise? Was he not contending in the cause of One greater than all the kings of this earth?   The gentleness that the Gospel inculcates seemed to him out of place.   An eye for an eye, a tooth for a tooth. And indeed he went beyond all bounds:—persecuted, railed at, hunted down, wounded,—the furious lion turned upon his pursuers, and set himself determinedly to crush his enemy. The Elector, Spalatin, Melancthon, Bugenhagen, essayed in vain to appease him.   They tried to dissuade him from replying; but nothing could stop him.   " I won't be gentle toward the king of England," said he: " I know it is useless to humble myself, to compromise, entreat and try peaceful methods.   I will show these wild beasts, who are every day running at me with their horns, how terrible I can be; I will turn upon my pursuers, I will provoke, and exasperate my adversary, until exhausting all his strength he falls and is for ever annihilated.* ' If this heretic does not retract,' says the new Thomas, Henry VIII., 'he must be burnt!' Such are the weapons which are now employed against me: the fury and the faggots of stupid asses and hogs of the Thomas Aquinas brood.† Well, then, be it so!   Let these swine come on, if

* (L. Epp. ii. p. 236.) Mea in ipsos exercebo cornua, irritaturus Satanam, donec effusis viribus et cornatibus corruat in se ipso.

† Ignis et furor insulsissimorum asinorum et Thomisticorum porcorum. (Contra Henricum Regem, Opp. Lat. ii. p. 331.) There is something in this way of speaking which recalls to our mind the language of the great agitator of Ireland, except that there is more force

they dare; aye, let them even burn me—here I am, awaiting them. My ashes, after death, though cast into a thousand seas, shall rise up in arms, and pursue, and swallow up their abominable troop. Living, I will be the enemy of the Papacy,—and burnt, I will be its ruin! Go then, swine of St. Thomas, do what you will. Ever will you find Luther, like a bear upon your road, and like a lion upon your path. He will fall upon you from all sides, and give you no rest until he shall have ground your iron brains, and pulverized your brazen foreheads!"

Luther begins by reproaching Henry VIII. with having supported his statements merely by decrees and doctrines of man. "As to me," says he, " I do not cease my cry of 'The Gospel! the Gospel!—Christ! Christ!'—and my enemies are as ready with their answer,—'Custom! custom!—Ordinances! ordinances!—Fathers! fathers!'—'*That your faith should not stand in the wisdom of men, but in the power of God*,' says St. Paul. And the Apostle, by this thunder-clap from heaven, at once overturns and disperses, as the wind scatters the dust, all the foolish thoughts of such a one as this Henry! Alarmed and confounded, the Aquinases, Papists, Henrys, fall prostrate before the power of those words."[*]

He proceeds to refute in detail the king's book, and exposes his arguments, one after the other, with remarkable clearness, energy, and knowledge of the Scriptures, and of Church history; but also with a boldness and contempt, and at times a violence, which need not surprise us.

Towards the end, Luther's indignation is again aroused, that his adversary should only have drawn his arguments from the Fathers; for on them was made to turn the whole controversy: "To all the decisions of Fathers, of men, of angels, of devils, I oppose," says he, "not the antiquity of custom, not the habits of the many, but the word of the Eternal God,— and nobility of thought in the orator of the sixteenth century, than in him of the nineteenth. (See *Revue Britannique*, Nov. 1835: 'The Reign of O'Connell'—"Soaped swine of civilised society," &c. p. 30.)

[*] Confusi et prostrati jacent a facie verborum istius tonitrui. (Contra Henricum regem. Opp. Lat. ii. p. 336.)

the Gospel,—which they themselves are obliged to admit. It is to this book that I keep,—upon it I rest,—in it I make my boast,—in it I triumph, and exult over Papists, Aquinases, Henrys, sophists, and all the swine of hell.* The King of Heaven is on my side,—therefore I fear nothing, though even a thousand Augustines, a thousand Cyprians, and a thousand such churches as that of which this Henry is Defender, should rise up against me. It is a small matter that I should despise and revile an earthly king, since he himself has not feared, by his writings, to blaspheme the King of Heaven, and profane his Holy name by the most daring lies."†

"Papists!" he exclaims in conclusion, "will you never have done with your vain attempts? Do, then, what ye list. Notwithstanding, it must still come to pass, that popes, bishops, priests, monks, princes, devils, death, sin,—and all that is not Jesus Christ, or in Jesus Christ,—must fall and perish before the power of this Gospel, which I, Martin Luther, have preached."‡

Thus spake an unfriended monk. His violence certainly cannot be excused, if we judge of it according to the rule to which he himself was ever appealing, namely, God's Word. It cannot even be justified, by pleading in extenuation, the grossness of the age,—(for Melancthon knew how to observe courtesy of language in his writings,)—nor can we plead the energy of his character. If something is allowed for this, more must be ascribed to the violence of his passions. It is better, then, that we should give our judgment against it. Nevertheless, justice requires the remark, that in the sixteenth century this extravagant language was not so strange as it would be at this time. The learned were, like the nobles, a kind of estate. Henry, in attacking Luther, had put himself in the rank of a man of letters. Luther replied to him

* Hic sto, hic sedeo, hic maneo, hic glorior, hic triumpho, hic insulto papistis . . . . (Contra Henricum regem. Opp. Lat. ii. p. 342.)

† Nec magnum si ego regem terræ contemno. (Cont. Hen. reg. p. 344. verso.)

‡ 3 L. Opp. Leipz. xviii. p. 209.

according to the law which obtained in the republic of letters viz. that the truth of what is stated is to be considered, and not the condition in life of him who states it.   Let it be added, also, that when this same king turned against the Pope, the insults heaped upon him by the Romish writers, and by the Pope himself, far exceeded all that Luther had ever fulminated against him.

Besides,—if Luther did call Doctor Eck an ass, and Henry VIII. a hog, he indignantly rejected the intervention of the secular arm; at the time that the former was writing a dissertation to show that heretics ought to be burned, and the latter was erecting scaffolds that he might follow out the precepts of the chancellor of Ingolstadt.

Great was the emotion at the king's court, when Luther's reply arrived.   Surrey, Wolsey, and the rest of the courtiers put a stop to the fetes and pageantry at Greenwich, to vent their indignation in sarcasms and abuse.   The aged Bishop of Rochester, who had looked on with delight at the young prince, formerly confided to his care, breaking a lance in defence of the Church, was stung to the quick by the monk's attack.   He replied to it at the moment.   His words gave a good idea of the age, and of the Church:—"Take us the little foxes that spoil the vines, says Christ in Solomon's Song; from this we learn," said Fisher, "that we ought to lay hands upon heretics, *before they grow big.*   Luther is become a large fox, so old, so cunning, so mischievous, that it is very difficult to catch him.   What do I say, a fox?   He is a mad dog, a ravening wolf, a cruel she-bear; or rather, all these put together, for the monster includes many beasts within him."*

Thomas More also descended into the arena to engage with the monk of Wittemberg.   Although a laic, his zeal against the Reformation amounted to fanaticism, if it would not have led him even to the shedding of blood.   When young men of family take up the cause of the Papacy, they often, in their

* Canem dixissem rabidum, imo lupum rapacissimum, aut sævissimam quamdam ursam. (Cochlæus, p. 60.)

violence, outdo the clergy themselves. "Reverend brother father tippler, Luther, apostate of the order of St. Augustine, (misshapen bacchanalian) of either faculty, unlearned doctor of sacred theology."[*] Thus it is the Reformer is addressed by one of the most illustrious men of the age. Then he goes on to say, in explanation of the way in which Luther had composed his book against Henry VIII. :—" He assembled his companions, and bid them go each his own way to pick up scurrilities and insults. One frequented the public carriages and barges; another the baths and gambling houses; this one, the barber's shops and low taverns; that one, the manufactory and the house of ill fame. They took down in their pocket-books all that they heard of insolence, of filthiness, of infamy, and bringing back all these insults and impurities, they filled with them that dirty sink which is called "*Luther's wit.*" Then he continues: " If he retracts these lies and calumnies, if he puts away these fooleries and this rage, if he swallows down his excrements again,[†] .... he will find one who will soberly discuss with him. But if he continues as he has begun, joking, taunting, fooling, calumniating, vomiting out sinks and sewers .... [‡] let others do what they choose; for ourselves we prefer leaving the little man to his own anger and dirtiness."[§] Thomas More would have done better to restrain his own coarseness; Luther never descended to such a style, neither did he return it any answer. This work increased Henry's attachment to More. He even used to go and visit him at his humble residence at Chelsea. After dinner,—his arm leaning on the shoulder of

---

[*] Reverendus frater, pater, potator, Lutherus. (Cochlæus, p. 61.)

[†] Si .. suas resorbeat et sua relingat stercora. (Ibid. p. 62.)

[‡] Sentinas, cloacas, latrinas ... stercora. (Ibid. p. 63.)

[§] Cum suis ..... et stercoribus ... relinquere. (Ibid.) Cochlæus indeed glories in the citation of these passages, choosing what, according to his taste, he thinks the finest parts of the work of Thomas More. M. Nisard, on the contrary, confesses in his book on More, whose defence he undertakes with so much warmth and learning, that, in this writing, the expressions dictated by the anger of the Catholic are such, that the translation of them is impossible.

his favourite, the king would walk round the garden with him,
whilst the astonished wife of his flattered host, concealed
behind a lattice, with her children, could not but keep her
eyes fixed on them. After one of these walks, More, who
well knew the man he had to deal with, said to his wife, "If
my head could gain for him a single castle in France, he
would not hesitate a moment to take it off."

The king, thus defended by the Bishop of Rochester, and
by his future chancellor, needed not any more to resume his
pen. Confounded at the thought of being treated, in the face
of Europe, as any common writer, Henry VIII. abandoned
the dangerous position he had taken, and laying aside the pen
of the theologian, had recourse to the more effectual measures
of diplomacy.

An ambassador was despatched from his court at Greenwich, with a letter to the Elector, and to the Dukes of Saxony.
"The true serpent cast down from heaven, even Luther,"
says Henry, "casts out a flood of poison upon the earth. He
excites revolt in the Church of Jesus Christ, he abolishes its
laws, insults the authorities, inflames the laity against the
priesthood, both of these against the Pope, the people against
kings, and asks nothing better than to see Christians fighting
against, and destroying one another, and the enemies of our
faith enjoying, with a savage grin, the scene of carnage.*

"What is this doctrine, which he calls evangelical, other
than the doctrine of Wicklif? Now, most honoured uncles,
I know how your ancestors have laboured to destroy it; they
pursued it, as a wild beast, in Bohemia, and driving it, till it
fell into a pit, they shut it in there, and barricaded it. You
will not, I am sure, let it escape through your negligence,
lest, making its way into Saxony, it should become master of
the whole of Germany, and, with smoking nostrils, vomiting
forth the fire of hell, spread that conflagration far and wide,

* So ergiest er, gleichwie eine Schlang vom Himmel geworfen. (L.
Opp. xviii. p. 212.) The original is in Latin—Velut a cœlo dejectus
serpens, virus effundit in terras.

which your nation has so often wished to extinguish in its blood.*

"Therefore it is, most worthy lords, I feel obliged to exhort you, and even to beseech you, by all that is most sacred, promptly to extinguish the cursed sect of Luther. Shed no blood, if it can be avoided; but if this heretical doctrine lasts, shed it without hesitation, in order that this abominable sect may disappear from under the heaven."†

The Elector and his brother referred the king to the approaching council. Henry VIII. was thus as far as ever from his object. "So renowned a name mixed up in the dispute," says Paolo Sarpi, "served to give it a greater zest, and to conciliate general favour towards Luther, as is usually the case in combats and tournaments, where the spectators have always a leaning to the weakest, and delight to exaggerate the merit of his actions."‡

In fact, an immense movement was in progress. The Reformation, which, after the Diet of Worms, had been thought to be confined, together with its great teacher, in the turret-chamber of a strong castle, was breaking forth on all sides in the empire, and even throughout Christendom. The two parties, until now, mixed up together, were beginning to separate, and the partisans of a monk, who had nothing on his side but the power of his words, were fearlessly taking their stand in the face of the followers of Charles V. and Leo X. Luther had only just left the Wartburg,—the Pope had excommunicated all his adherents,—the Imperial Diet had just condemned his doctrine,—the princes were active in putting it down throughout the greatest part of the German states,— the Romish priests were setting the public against it by their violent invective,—foreign nations were requiring that Germany should sacrifice a man whose attacks were formidable even at a distance,—and yet, this new sect, few in number, and

* Und durch sein schädlich Anblasen das höllische Feuer ausspracke.
(L. Opp. xviii. p. 213.)
† Oder aber auch mit Blut vergiessen. (Ibid.)
‡ Hist. of the Council of Trent, p. 15, 16.

among whose numbers there was no organization, no acting in concert, nothing, in short, of concentrated power, was already, by the energy of the faith engaged in it, and the rapidity of its conquests of the minds of men, beginning to cause alarm to the vast, ancient, and powerful sovereignty of Rome. Everywhere was to be seen, as in the first appearance of spring-time, the seed bursting forth from the earth, spontaneously and without effort. Every day some progress might be remarked. Individuals, village populations, country towns, nay, large cities, joined in this new confession of the name of Jesus Christ. It was met by strong opposition and fierce persecution, but the mysterious power which animated these people was irresistible; and, though persecuted, they still went forward, facing the terrors of exile, imprisonment, or the stake, and were every where more than conquerors over their persecutors.

The monastic orders, which Rome had planted over the whole of Christendom, like nets for catching souls and retaining them in their meshes, were among the first to burst their fetters, and to propagate the new doctrine in every part of the Western Church. The Augustines of Saxony had gone along with Luther, and, like him, formed that intimate acquaintance with the Word of Truth, which, making God their portion, disabused their minds from the delusions of Rome and its lofty pretensions. But in other convents of this order, the light of the Gospel had also shone forth: sometimes, among the aged, who, like Staupitz, had preserved, in the midst of a leavened Christianity, the sound doctrines of truth, and were now asking of God that they might depart in peace, since their eyes had seen his salvation; sometimes, among the young, among those who had imbibed Luther's instructions with the characteristic eagerness of their years. At Nuremberg, Osnabruck, Dillingen, Ratisbon, in Hesse, in Wirtemburg, at Strasburgh, at Antwerp, the convents of the Augustines were returning to the faith of Christ, and by their courageous confession exciting the indignation of Rome.

But the movement was not confined to the Augustines.

Men of decided character among the other orders followed
their example; and, notwithstanding the clamours of their
fellow-monks, who were unwilling to abandon their carnal
observances, and undeterred by their anger and contempt, or
by censure, discipline, and claustral imprisonment, they fearlessly lifted up their voices in favour of that holy and precious
truth, which, after so many toilsome researches, so many distressing doubts, and inward conflicts, they had at last found.
In the majority of the cloisters, the most spiritual, devout, and
instructed monks declared themselves in favour of the Reformation. Eberlin and Kettenbach attacked, from the convents
of the Franciscans at Ulm, the *service of bondage* of monkery,
and the superstitious practices of the Church, with an eloquence that might have drawn a whole nation after it. They
introduced in their petition, in the same sentence, a request for
the abolition of the houses of the monks, and of those of pros-
titution. Another Franciscan, Stephen Kempe, preached the
Gospel at Hamburg, and, though alone, set his face like a
flint against the hatred, envy, threats, cunning, and violence
of the priests,—enraged to see the congregations forsake their
altars, and flock with enthusiasm to his preachings.*

Sometimes it was the superiors themselves who were first
won over to the Reformation. The Priors at Halberstadt, at
Neuenwerk, at Halle, at Sagan, set the example, in this respect, to those under their authority; at least, they declared
that if a monk felt his conscience burdened by his monastic
vows, so far from insisting on his remaining in the convent,
they would themselves carry him out on their shoulders.†

In fact, in all parts of Germany might be seen monks leaving, at the gates of their monastery, their frock and cowl. Of
these, some had been expelled by the violence of their fellows,
or of their superiors; others, of a gentle and peaceable spirit,
could no longer endure the continually recurring disputes, insults, recriminations, and animosities, which pursued them from

* Der übrigen Prediger Feindschafft, Neid, Nachstellungen, Pra-
ticken und Schrecken. (Seckendorf, p. 559.)
† Seckendorf, p. 811. Stentzel. Script. Rer Silen, I. p. 45.

morning till night.   Of all these, the greater number were convinced that the monastic vows were inconsistent with the will of God and the Christian life.   Some had gradually been led to this conviction; others had reached it at once by considering a single text.   The indolent, heavy ignorance which generally marked the mendicant orders communicated a feeling of disgust to men of more intelligent minds, who could no longer endure the society of such associates.   A Franciscan, begging his way, one day presented himself, box in hand, at a blacksmith's shop, in Nuremberg.   "Why don't you get your bread by working with your own hands?" inquired the blacksmith.   Thus invited, the sturdy monk, tossing from him his habit, lifted the hammer, and brought it down again with force upon the anvil.   Behold the useless mendicant transformed into the industrious workman!   The box and monk's gown were sent back to the monastery.*

It was not, however, the monks only, who ranged themselves under the standard of evangelical truth: a far greater number of priests proclaimed the new doctrine.   But it needed not to be promulgated by human organs; it often acted upon men's minds and aroused them from their deep slumber, without the instrumentality of a preacher.

Luther's writings were read in the boroughs, cities, and hamlets; even the village schoolmaster had his fire-side audience.   Some persons in each locality, impressed with what they had heard, consulted the Bible to relieve their uncertainty, and were struck with the marked contrast between the Christianity of Scripture and that which they had imbibed.   Fluctuating for a while between Romanism and Holy Writ, they ere long took refuge in that living Word which had beamed into their minds with such new and cheering lustre.   While these changes were passing in their minds, an evangelical preacher—he might be a priest, or, perhaps, a monk—would appear.   He speaks with eloquence and authority,† proclaiming that Christ has fully atoned for the sins of his people, and

* Ranke, Deutsche Geschichte, ii. p. 70.
† Eaque omnia prompte, alacriter, eloquenter.   (Cochlæus, p. 52.)

proves from the sacred Word the vanity of human works and
penance. Such preaching excited terrible opposition; the
clergy, in numerous instances, aided by the magistrates, used
every effort to bring back those whose souls were escaping
from bondage. But there was in the new preaching an accordance with Scripture, and a secret, but irresistible energy,
which won the heart and subdued the most rebellious. Risk
ing the loss of property, and, if needful, the loss of life itself,
men deserted the barren fanatical preachers of the Papacy,
and enrolled themselves under the Gospel banner.* Sometimes the people, irritated at the thought how long they had
been duped, drove away the priests; but more frequently these
latter, forsaken by their flocks, without tithes or offerings,
went off, with desponding hearts, to earn a livelihood in distant places.† Whilst the defenders of the ancient hierarchy
withdrew in sullen dejection, pronouncing maledictions as they
took leave of their former flocks,—the people, whom truth
and liberty filled with transports of joy, surrounded the new
preachers with acclamations, and in their eagerness to hear
the Word, bore them, as in triumph, into the churches and
pulpits.‡

A word of Power from God himself, was remoulding so
ciety. In many instances, the people, or the principal citi
zens, wrote to a man whose faith they knew, urging him to
come and instruct them; and he, for the love of the truth,
would, at their call, at once leave his worldly interests, his family, friends, and country.§ Persecution often compelled the
favourers of the Reformation to abandon their dwellings;
—they arrive in a place where the new doctrines have never
yet been heard of; they find there some hospitable roof, offering shelter to houseless travellers; there they speak of the

* Populo odibiles catholici concionatores. (Cochlæus, p. 52.)
† Ad extremam redacti inopiam, aliunde sibi victum quærere coge-
rentur. (Ibid. p. 53.)
‡ Triumphantibus novis prædicatoribus qui sequacem populum verbo
novi Evangelii sui ducebant. (Ibid.)
§ Multi, omissa re domestica, in speciem veri Evangelii, parentes et
amicos relinquebant. (Ibid.)

Gospel, and read a few pages to the listening townsmen, and perhaps, by the intercession of their new acquaintances, obtain leave to preach a sermon in the church. Immediately, the Word spreads like fire through the town, and no efforts can stay its progress.* If not permitted to preach in the church, the preaching took place elsewhere, and every place became a temple. At Husum in Holstein, Herman Tast, then on his way from Wittembeŕg, and to whom the parochial clergy denied the use of the church, preached to an immense multitude, under the shade of two large trees adjoining the churchyard, not far from the spot where, seven centuries before, Anschar had first proclaimed the Gospel to a Heathen auditory. At Armstadt, Gaspard Gittel, an Augustine friar, preached in the market-place. At Dantzic, the Gospel was proclaimed from an eminence outside the city. At Gosslar, a student of Wittemberg opened the new doctrines, in a plain planted with lime-trees, from which circumstance the evangelical Christians there obtained the appellation of *The Lime-tree Brethren.*

Whilst the Priests were exposing, before the eyes of the people, their sordid avidity, the new preachers, in addressing them, said : " Freely we have received—freely do we give."† The observation often dropt by the new preachers in the pulpit, that Rome had of old given to the nations a corrupted Gospel, so that Germany now first heard the Word of Christ in its divine and primitive beauty, made a deep impression upon all ;‡ and the grand thought of the equality of all men in the universal brotherhood of Jesus Christ, elevated the souls which had so long borne the yoke of the feudality and papacy of the middle ages.§

Simple Christians were often seen with the New Testament in hand, offering to justify the doctrine of the Reformation.

* Ubi vero aliquos nacti fuissent amicos in ea civitate . . . . (Cochlæus, p. 54.)

† Mira eis erat liberalitas. (Ibid.)

‡ Eam usque diem nunquam germane prædicatam. (Cochlæus, p. 53.)

§ Omnes æquales et fratres in Christo. (Ibid.)

The Catholics, who adhered to Rome, drew back in dismay; for the study of Holy Scripture was reserved to the priests and monks alone. The latter being thus compelled to come forward, discussion ensued; but the priests and monks were soon overwhelmed with the Scriptures quoted by the laity, and at a loss how to meet them.* "Unhappily," says Cochlæus, "Luther had persuaded his followers that their faith ought only to be given to the oracles of Holy Writ." Often clamours were heard in the crowd, denouncing the shameful ignorance of the old theologians, who had till then been regarded by their own party as among the most eminently learned.†

Men of the humblest capacity, and even the weaker sex, by the help of the knowledge of the Word, persuaded, and prevailed with many. Extraordinary times produced extraordinary actions. At Ingolstadt a young weaver read the works of Luther to a crowded congregation, in the very place where Doctor Eck was residing. The university council of the same town, having resolved to oblige a disciple of Melancthon to retract,—a woman, named Argula de Staufen, volunteered to defend him, and challenged the doctors to a public disputation. Women, children, artizans, and soldiers, had acquired a greater knowledge of the Bible than learned doctors or surpliced priests.

Christianity was presented in two-fold array, and under aspects strikingly contrasted. Opposed to the old defenders of the hierarchy, who had neglected the acquirement of the languages and the cultivation of literature, (we have it on the authority of one of themselves) was a generous-minded youth, most of them devoted to study and the investigation of the Scriptures, and acquainted with the literary treasures of antiquity.‡ Gifted with quickness of apprehension, elevation of soul, and intrepidity of heart these youths soon attained such

---

* A laicis lutheranis, plures scripturæ locos, quam a monachis et presbyteris. (Ibid. p. 54.)

† Reputabantur catholici ab illis ignari Scripturarum. (Ibid.)

‡ Totam vero juventutem, eloquentiæ litteris, linguarumque studio deditam ... in partem suam traxit. (Cochlæus. p. 54.)

proficiency that none could compete with them. It was not only the vigour of their faith which raised them above their contemporaries, but an elegance of style, a perfume of antiquity, a sound philosophy, and a knowledge of the world, of which the theologians, *veteris farinæ* (as Cochlæus himself terms them) were altogether destitute. So that on public occasions, on which these youthful defenders of the Reformation encountered the Romish doctors, their assault was carried on with an ease and confidence that embarrassed the dulness of their adversaries, and exposed them before all to deserved contempt.

The ancient structure of the Church was thus tottering under the weight of superstition and ignorance, while the new edifice was rising from its foundations of faith and learning. The elements of a new life were diffused among the general body of the people. Listless dulness was everywhere succeeded by an inquiring disposition and a thirst for information. An active enlightened and living faith, took the place of superstitious piety, and ascetic meditations. Works of true devotedness, superseded mere outward observance and penances. The pulpit prevailed over the mummeries of the altar, and the ancient and supreme authority of God's word, was at length, re-established in the Church.

The art of printing, that mighty engine, the discovery of which marks the fifteenth century, came to the assistance of the efforts we are now recording ; and its weighty missiles were continually discharged against the enemy's walls.

The impulse which the Reformation gave to popular literature, in Germany, was prodigious. Whilst the year 1513 saw only thirty-five publications, and 1517 but thirty-seven, the number of books increased with astonishing rapidity after the appearance of Luther's theses. We find, in 1518, seventy-one various publications recorded ; in 1519, one hundred and eleven ; in 1520, two hundred and eight ; in 1521, two hundred and eleven ; in 1522, three hundred and forty-seven ; and in 1523, four hundred and ninety-eight. And where were all these books published ? Almost invariably at Wittemberg. And who was the author of them ? For the most part, Luther. The year 1522, saw one hundred and thirty publications from the pen of the Reformer alone ; and the following year, one hundred and eighty-three ; whilst in this latter year, the total number of Roman Catholic publications amounted to but twenty.* Thus, the literature of Germany was formed *in the din of controversy,* as its religion arose in the midst of conflicts. Already it gave evidence of that learned, profound, bold, and stirring spirit that latter times have seen in it. The genius of the nation now, for the first time, displayed itself without mixture, and in the very hour of its birth it received a baptism of fire from christian enthusiasm.

Whatever Luther and his friends composed, others disseminated far and wide. Monks, who had been led to see the unlawfulness of the monastic obligations, and desirous of exchanging a life of indolence for one of activity, but too ignorant to be able themselves to proclaim the Word of God, traversed the provinces, and, visiting the hamlets and cottages, sold the writings of Luther and his friends. Germany was, ere long, overrun with these enterprising colporteurs.† Printers and booksellers eagerly received whatever writings were directed to the defence of the Reformation, but would not look at those of the opposite party, as savouring generally of ignorance and barbarism.‡ If any of these men, however, ventured to sell a book in favour of Papacy, or to offer it for sale at Frankfort or elsewhere, he drew upon himself a torrent of ridicule and sarcasm from dealers, publishers, and scholars.§ Vainly had the Emperor and the reigning princes fulminated severe edicts against the writings of the Reformers. As soon as an inquisitorial visit was determined on, the dealers, (who secretly obtained information of it) would conceal the books which it

* Panzer's Annalen der Deutsch Litt.—Ranke's Deutsch Gesch. ii. p. 79.

† Apostatarum, monasteriis relictis, infinitus jam erat numerus, in speciem bibliopolarum. (Cochlæus, p. 54.)

‡ Catholicorum, velut indocta et veteris barbarici trivialia scripta, contemnebant. (Cochlæus, p. 54.)

§ In publicis mercatibus Francofordiæ et alibi, vexabantur ac ridebuntur. (Ibid.)

was intended to proscribe; and the people, ever eager to possess that of which authority would deprive them, would afterwards buy them up, and read them with redoubled ardour. It was not alone Germany that was the theatre of such incidents, the writings of Luther were translated into French, Spanish, English, and Italian, and were circulated among those nations.

If instruments so despised could yet inflict such disaster on the power of Rome, what was it when the monk of Wittemberg was heard to raise his voice? Shortly after the discomfiture of the strange prophets, Luther traversed the territory of Duke George, in a waggon, attired in plain clothes. His gown was carefully concealed, and the Reformer wore the disguise of a countryman. Had he been recognised, and so fallen into the hands of the exasperated Duke, it had, perhaps, been all over with him. He was on his way to preach at Zwickau, the birth-place of the pretended prophets. Scarcely was it known at Schneeberg, Annaberg, and the neighbouring towns, when numbers flocked to hear him. Fourteen thousand persons arrived in the town, and as there was no edifice which could contain so great a multitude, Luther preached from the balcony of the Town-hall to twenty-five thousand auditors, who thronged the market-place,—and of whom several had climbed to the top of some stones that lay heaped together near the hall.* The servant of Jesus Christ was expatiating with fervour on the election of grace, when suddenly a shriek proceeded from the midst of the rivetted auditory. An old woman of haggard mien, who had stationed herself on a large block of stones, was seen motioning with her lank arms as though she would controul the multitude just about to fall prostrate at the feet of Jesus. Her wild yells interrupted the preacher. "It was the devil," says Seckendorf, "who took the form of an old woman, in order to excite a tumult."† But vain was the effort; the Reformer's word put the evil

* Von dem Rathhaus unter einem Zulauf von 25,000 Menschen (Secb. p. 539.)

† Der Teufel indem er sich in Gestalt eines alten Weibes . . . (Ibid.)

spirit to silence;—an enthusiasm communicated itself from one to another, looks and warm greetings were exchanged; the people pressed each other by the hand, and the friars, not knowing what to make of what they saw, and unable to charm down the tempest, soon found it necessary to take their departure from Zwickau.

In the Castle of Freyberg resided Duke Henry, brother of Duke George. His wife, the Princess of Mecklenburg, had, the preceding year, presented him with a son, who was christened Maurice. Duke Henry united the bluntness and coarse manners of the soldier to a passion for the pleasures of the table, and the pursuits of dissipation. He was, withal, pious after the manner of the age in which he lived; he had visited the Holy Land, and had also gone on pilgrimage to the shrine of St. James at Compostella. He would often say, " When I was at Compostella, I deposited a hundred golden florins on the altar of the Saint, and I said to him,—'O! St. James, it is to gain your favour I have made this journey. I make you a present of this money; but if those knaves (the priests) steal it from you, I can't help it; so take you care of it.' "*

Two friars, (a Franciscan and a Dominican) disciples of Luther, had been for some time preaching the Gospel at Freyberg. The Duchess, whose piety had inspired her with a horror of heresy, attended their sermons, and was all astonishment at discovering that what she had been taught so much to dread, was the gracious word of a *Saviour.* Gradually, her eyes were opened; and she found peace in Jesus Christ. The moment Duke George learned that the Gospel was preached at Freyberg, he begged his brother to resist the introduction of such novelties. The Chancellor Stehelin and the canons seconded these representations with their fanatical zeal. A violent explosion took place at the court of Freyberg. Duke Henry sternly reprimanded and reproached his wife, and more than once the pious Duchess was known to shed tears over the cradle of her babe. By slow degrees, however, her gentle entreaties melted the heart of her husband. This man, so

* Lasst du dir's die Buben nehmen .... (Ibid. p. 490)

stern by nature, softened down. A sweet harmony was established between them: at length, they were enabled to join in prayer beside their infant son. Great and untold destinies hovered above that son; and from that cradle, where the christian mother had so often poured out her sorrows, was to come forth one whom God in his own time would use as a defender of the Reformation.

The intrepidity of Luther had made a deep impression on the inhabitants of Worms. The Imperial Decree overawed the magistrates; the churches were all closed; but a preacher, taking his stand on a rudely-constructed pulpit, in a square thronged with an immense multitude, proclaimed the glad tidings with persuasive earnestness. If the authorities showed a disposition to interfere, the people dispersed in an instant, hastily carrying off their pulpit; but no sooner had the officers of authority passed by, than they again erected their pulpit in some more retired spot, to which the multitude would again flock together, to hear more of the Word of Jesus Christ. This temporary pulpit was every day set up in one spot or another, and served as a rallying point for the people who were still under the influence of the emotions awakened by the drama lately enacted in Worms.*

At Frankfort on the Maine, one of the most considerable free cities of the empire, all was commotion. A courageous evangelist, Ibach, preached salvation by Jesus Christ. The clergy, among whom was Cochlæus, known by his writings and his opposition to the Reformation, irritated by the daring intrusion of such a colleague, denounced him to the Archbishop of Mentz. The Council, though with some timidity, nevertheless supported him; but without avail. The clergy expelled the evangelical minister, and obliged him to quit Frankfort. Rome appeared triumphant; all seemed lost; and private Christians began to fear that they were for ever deprived of the preaching of the Word: but at the very moment when the citizens seemed disposed to submit to the ty-

* So liessen sie eine Canzel machen, die man von einem Ort zum andern . . . (Seck. p. 436.)

ranny of their priests, certain nobles suddenly declared themselves for the Gospel.   Max of Molnheim, Harmut of Cronberg, George of Stockheim, and Emeric of Reiffenstein,
whose estates lay near Frankfort, wrote to the Council:—
" We are constrained to make a stand against those spiritual
wolves."   And, in addressing the clergy, they said:—" Either
embrace evangelical doctrines and recall Ibach, or we will
pay no more tithes."

The common people, who listened gladly to the reformed
opinions, emboldened by this language of the nobles, showed
symptoms of agitation; and one day when Peter Mayer, the
persecutor of Ibach, and who of all the priests was the most
hostile to the new opinions, was on the point of preaching
against heretics, a violent tumult broke forth, and Mayer in
alarm retreated from the pulpit.   This popular movement
decided the determination of the Council.   An ordinance was
published, enjoining all ministers to preach the pure Word of
God, or to quit the town.

The light which shone forth from Wittemberg, as from the
heart of the nation, was thus diffusing itself throughout the
empire.   In the west,—Berg, Cleves, Lippstadt, Munster,
Wesel, Miltenberg, Mentz, Deux Ponts, and Strasburg, heard
the 'joyful sound.'   In the south,—Hof, Schlesstadt, Bamberg, Esslingen, Hall (in Suabia), Heilbrunn, Augsburg, Ulm,
and many other places, welcomed it with joy.   In the east,—
the Duchy of Liegnitz, Prussia and Pomerania, received it
with open arms.   In the north,—Brunswick, Halberstadt,
Gosslar, Zell, Friesland, Bremen, Hamburg, Holstein, and
even Denmark, and other adjacent countries, moved at the
sounds of the new teaching.

The Elector had declared that he would give full liberty to
the bishops to preach in his dominions; but that he would not
deliver any one into their hands.   Accordingly, the evangelical preachers, persecuted in other countries, were soon
driven to take refuge in Saxony.   Among these were—
Ibach, from Frankfort, Eberlin, from Ulm, Kanadorff, from

Magdeburg, Valentine Musteus.* whom the canons of Halberstadt had horribly mutilated, and other faithful ministers, from all parts of Germany, flocked to Wittemberg, as to the only asylum of which they felt secure. Here they could hold converse with the leading Reformers, thereby strengthening themselves in the faith, and at the same time communicating the experience each one had gained, together with the information he had acquired. It is thus that the waters of our rivers return, borne in the clouds from the vast expanse of ocean, to feed the glaciers whence they first descended, to flow through the plain.

The work which was at this time developing itself at Wittemberg, composed, as has been seen, of various elements, became from day to day increasingly the work of that nation, of Europe, and of Christendom. The school which Frederic had founded, and into which Luther had introduced the Word of Life, was the centre of that wide-spreading revolution which regenerated the Church; and from it the Reformation derived a true and a living unity, far above the semblance of unity that might be seen in Rome. The Bible was the supreme authority at Wittemberg, and there its doctrines were heard on all sides. This academy, though the most recent of all in its origin, had acquired a rank and influence throughout Christendom which hitherto had exclusively appertained to the ancient University of Paris. The crowds of students which resorted to Wittemberg, from all parts of Europe, brought thither the report of the wants of the Church and of the people, and in quitting those walls, become sacred in their esteem, they bore with them, to the Church and people, that Word of Grace, which is for the healing and salvation of the nations.

In contemplating these happy results, Luther felt his confidence increased. He had seen a feeble effort, begun

* Aliquot ministri canonicorum capiunt D. Valentinum Mustæum et vinctum manibus pedibusque, injecto in ejus os freno, deferunt per trabes in inferiores cœnobii partes, ibique in cella cerevisiaria eum castrant. (Hamelmann, Hist. renati Evangelii, p. 880.)

amidst so many fears and struggles, change the face of the christian world; and he himself was astonished at a result which he never anticipated when he first entered the lists against Tetzel.   Prostrate before the God whom he adored, he confessed that the work was His; and he rejoiced in the assurance of victory which no power could prevent.   "Our enemies threaten us with death," said he, to the Chevalier Harmut of Cronberg—"if their wisdom were equal to their folly, it is with life they would threaten us.   What an absurdity and insult it is to affect to denounce death against Christ and Christians, who are themselves the conquerors of death!* It is as if I would seek to affright a rider by saddling his courser, and helping him to mount.   Do they not know that Christ is raised from the dead? So far as they see, He is yet lying in the grave, nay—even in hell.   But we know that He lives."   He was grieved whenever he thought that and one should look upon him as the author of a work, of which the most minute details disclosed to him the finger of God.   "Some there are," said he, "who believe because *I* believe.   But *they* only truly believe, who would continue faithful even though they should hear (which may God forbid!) that I had denied Christ.   True disciples believe—not in Luther—but in Jesus Christ.   Even I myself care little for Luther.†   Let him be counted a saint or a cheat, what care I? It is not him that I preach; it is Christ. If the devil can seize Luther, let him do so! But let Christ abide with us, and we shall abide also."

Surely it is idle to explain such a principle as here speaks out, by the mere circumstances of human affairs.   Men of letters might sharpen their wits, and shoot their poisoned arrows against pope and friars—the gathering cry for freedom, which Germany had so often sent forth against Italian tyranny, might again echo in the castles and provinces;—the people might again delight in the familiar voice of the Wittemberg nightingale‡ heralding the spring that was everywhere burst

* Herren und Siegmänner des Todes.   (L. Epp. ii. p. 164.)
† Ich kenne auch selbst nicht den Luther.   (Ibid.)
‡ Wittemberger Nachtigall, poem of Hans Sachs, 1523.

ing forth ;—but it was no change in mere outward circumstances, like such as is the effect of a craving for earthly liberty, that was then accomplishing. Those who assert that the Reformation was brought about by bribing the reigning princes with the prospect of convent treasure,—the clergy, with the licence of marriage,—or the people with the boon of freedom, are strangely mistaken in its nature. Doubtless, a profitable use of resources which hitherto had maintained the monks in idleness,—doubtless, marriage and liberty, God's gifts, might conduce to the progress of the Reformation,—but the moving power was not in these things. An interior revolution was going on in the deep privacy of men's hearts : Christians were again learning to love and to forgive, to pray, to suffer affliction, and, if need be, to die for the sake of that Truth which yet held out no prospect of rest on this side heaven ! The Church was in a state of transition. Christianity was bursting the shroud in which it had so long been veiled, and resuming its place in a world which had well nigh forgotten its former power. He who made the earth, now 'turned his hand,' and the Gospel,—emerging from eclipse,— went forward, notwithstanding the repeated efforts of priests and of kings,—like the Ocean, which, when the hand of God presses on its bosom, rises in majestic calmness along its shores, so that no power of man is able to resist its movement.

BOOK X

THE Reformation, which had taken its rise in a few pious hearts, had worked its way into the public worship and the private life of the Church ; it was to be expected that it would, as it advanced, penetrate into civil relationships. Its progress was constantly, from within,—*outward*. We are about to contemplate this great change taking possession of the political life of nations.

For a period of nearly eight centuries, Europe had formed one vast sacerdotal state. Its emperors and kings had been under the patronage of its popes. If France and Germany had afforded examples of energetic resistance to audacious pretensions, still, Rome, in the result, had prevailed, and the world had seen temporal princes, consenting to act as executioners of her terrible sentences, contend in defence of her power against private Christians living under their rule, and shed, in her cause, the blood of the children of their people.

No infringement of this vast ecclesiastical polity but must affect, in a greater or less degree, established political relations.

Two leading desires then agitated the minds of the Germans. On one hand, the people aspired after a revival of the faith ; on the other, they demanded a national government wherein the German states might be represented, and which should serve as a counterpoise to the Imperial power.[*]

[*] Pfeffel Droit publ. de l'Allemagne, 590.—Robertson, Charles V. vol. iii. p. 114.—Ranke, Deutsche Gesch.

The Elector Frederic had urged this demand at the time of the election of Maximilian's successor, and the youthful Charles had consented. A national government had, in consequence, been chosen, consisting of the Imperial chief and representatives of the various electors and circles.

Thus while Luther was reforming the Church, Frederic was engaged in reforming the State.

But when, simultaneously with a change in religion, important modifications of political relationships were introduced by the authorities, it was to be apprehended that the commonalty would exhibit a disposition to revolt,—thereby bringing into jeopardy the Reformation both of Church and of State.

This violent and fanatical irruption of the people, under certain chosen leaders, unavoidable where society is in a state of crisis,—did not fail to happen in the times we are recording.

Other circumstances there were which tended to these disorders.

The Emperor and the Pope had combined against the Reformation, and it might appear to be doomed to fall beneath the strokes of such powerful enemies. Policy—interest—ambition obliged Charles V. and Leo X. to extirpate it. But such motives are feeble defences against the power of Truth. A devoted assertion of a cause deemed sacred can be conquered only by a like devotedness opposed to it. But the Romans, quick to catch Leo's enthusiasm for a sonnet or a musical composition, had no pulse to beat response to the religion of Jesus Christ: or, if at times some graver thoughts would intervene, instead of their being such as might purify their hearts, and imbue them with the Christianity of the apostles, they turned upon alliances, or conquests, or treaties that added new provinces to the Papal states; and Rome, with cold disdain, left to the Reformation to awaken on all sides a religious enthusiasm, and to go forward in triumphant progress to new victories. The foe that she had sworn to crush, in the church of Worms, was before her in the confidence of courage and strength. The contest must be sharp: blood must flow.

11*

Nevertheless some of the dangers that threatened the Reformation seemed, just then, to be less pressing.   The youthful Charles, standing one day, a little before the publication of the edict of Worms, in a window of his palace in conversation with his confessor, had, it is true, said with emphasis, laying his hand upon his heart, " I swear that I will hang up before this window the first man who, after the publication of my edict, shall declare himself a Lutheran."*   But it was not long before his zeal cooled.   His plan for restoring the ancient glory of the empire, or, in other words, enlarging his own dominions, was coldly received ;† and taking umbrage with his German subjects, he passed the Rhine, and retired to the Low Countries, availing himself of his sojourn there, to afford the friars some gratifications that he found himself unable to give them in the empire.   At Ghent, Luther's writings were burned by the public executioner with the utmost solemnity.   More than fifty thousand spectators attended this auto-da-fe, and the presence of the Emperor himself, marked his approval of the proceedings.‡

Just at this time, Francis the First, who eagerly sought a pretext for attacking his rival, had thrown down the gauntlet. Under pretence of re-establishing in their patrimony the children of John of Albret, king of Navarre, he had commenced a bloody contest, destined to last all his life :—sending an army to invade that kingdom, under command of Lesparra, who rapidly pushed his victorious advance to the gates of Pampeluna.

On the walls of this fortress was to be enkindled an enthusiasm which, in after years, should withstand the aggressive enthusiasm of the Reformer, and breathe through the Papal

* Sancte juro. . . . . eum ex hac fenestrâ meo jussu suspensum iri. (Pallavicini, i. p. 130.)

† Essendo tornato dalla Dieta che sua Maestà haveva fatta in Wormatia, escluso d'ogni conclusione buona d'ajuti e di favori che si fussi proposto d'ottenere in essa.   (Instruttione al card. Farnese. Manuscript of the Bibl. Corsini, published by Ranke.)

‡ Ipso Cæsare, ore subridenti, spectaculo plausit.   (Pallavicini, i. p. 130.)

system a new energy of devotedness and control. Pampeluna was to be the cradle of a rival to the Wittemberg monk.

The spirit of chivalry, which had so long reigned in the Christian world, still survived in Spain. The wars with the Moors, recently terminated in that Peninsula, but continually recurring in Africa—and distant and adventurous expeditions beyond sea, kept alive in the Castilian youth the enthusiastic and simple valour of which Amadis had been the ideal exhibition.

Among the garrison of Pampeluna was a young man named Don Inigo Lopez de Recalde, the youngest of a family of thirteen. Recalde had been brought up at the court of Ferdinand the Catholic. Remarkable for a fine person,* and expert in the use of sword and lance, he was ardently ambitious of chivalrous renown. Clothed in dazzling armour, and mounted on a prancing steed, he took delight in exposing himself to the glittering dangers of the tournament,† engaging in hazardous enterprizes, taking part in the impassioned struggles of opposing factions,‡ and manifesting as much devotion to St. Peter as to his lady-love. Such was the life led by the young knight.

The governor of Navarre, having gone into Spain to obtain succours, had left to Inigo and a few nobles the charge of defending Pampeluna. These latter, learning the superior numbers of the French troops, decided on retiring. Inigo entreated them to stand firm and resist Lesparra; but, not being able to prevail on them, he indignantly reproached them with their cowardice and perfidy, and then threw himself into the citadel, resolved to defend it at the sacrifice of his life.§

When the French, who had been received with enthusiasm in Pampeluna, proposed to the commandant of the fortress to

---

* Cum esset in corporis ornatû elegantissimus. (Maffei, Vita Loyolæ, 1586, p. 3.)

† Equorumque et armorum usû præcelleret. (Ibid.)

‡ Partim in factionum rixarumque periculis, partim in amatoria vesania . . . tempus consumeret. (Maffei, Vita Loyolæ, 1586, p. 3.)

§ Ardentibus oculis, detestatus ignaviam perfidiamque spectantibus omnibus, in arcem solus introit. (Ibid. p. 6.)

capitulate, " Let us endure everything,"* boldly exclaimed
Inigo, "rather than surrender!" On this the French began
to batter the walls with their formidable artillery, and in a
short time they attempted to storm it. The bravery and exhortations of Inigo gave fresh courage to the Spaniards ; they
drove back the assailants by their arrows, swords, or halberds.
Inigo led them on. Taking his stand on the ramparts, with
eyes flaming with rage, the young knight brandished his
sword, and felled the assailants to the earth. Suddenly a ball
struck the wall, just where he stood ; a stone shivered from
the ramparts, wounded the knight severely in the right leg,
at the same moment as the ball, rebounding from the violence
of the shock, broke his left. Inigo fell senseless.† The garrison immediately surrendered ; and the French, admiring
the courage of their youthful adversary, bore him in a litter
to his relatives in the castle of Loyola. In this lordly mansion, from which his name was afterwards derived, Inigo had
been born of one of the most illustrious families of that country,
eight years after the birth of Luther.

A painful operation became necessary. In the most acute
suffering, Inigo firmly clenched his hands but uttered no complaint.‡

Constrained to a repose which he could ill endure, he found
it needful to employ, in some way, his ardent imagination.
In the absence of the romances which he had been accustomed
to devour, they gave him the Life of Christ, and the Flores
Sanctorum. The reading of these works, in his state of
solitude and sickness, produced an extraordinary effect upon
his mind. The stirring life of tournaments and battles, which
had occupied his youth, to the exclusion of every thing beside,
seemed as if receding and fading from view, while a career
of brighter glory appeared to open before him. The humble
labours of the saints, and their heroic patience were, all of a

* Tam acri ac vehementi oratione commilitonibus dissuasit. (Maf.
Vita Loyolæ, 1586, p. 6.)

† Ut e vestigio semianimis alienata mente corruerit. (Ibid. p. 7.)

‡ Nullum aliud indicium dedit doloris, nisi ut coactus in pugnam
digitos valde constringeret. (Ibid. p. 8.)

sudden, seen to be far more worthy of praise than all the high deeds of chivalry. Stretched upon his couch, and still under the effects of fever, he indulged in the most conflicting thoughts. The world he was planning to renounce, and that life of holy mortification which he contemplated, both appeared before him—the one soliciting by its pleasures, the other by its severities;—and fearful was the struggle in his conscience between these two opposing worlds. "What," thought he, "if I were to act like St. Francis or St. Dominic?"[*] But the recollection of the lady to whom he had pledged his love recurred to his mind. "She is neither countess nor duchess," said he to himself, with a kind of simple vanity, "she is *much more* than either."[†] But thoughts like these were sure to fill him with distress and impatience, while the idea of imitating the example of the saints caused his heart to overflow with peace and joy.

From this period his resolution was taken. Scarcely had he risen from his sick-bed, when he decided to retire from the world. As Luther had done, he once more invited to a repast his companions in arms; and then, without divulging his design, set out, unattended,[‡] for the lonely cells excavated by the Benedictine monks, in the rocks of the mountains of Montserrat. Impelled, not by the sense of his sin, or of his need of the grace of God, but by the wish to become "knight of the Virgin Mary," and to be renowned for mortifications and works, after the example of the army of saints,—he confessed for three successive days, gave away his costly attire to a mendicant,[§] clothed himself in sackcloth, and girled himself with a rope. Then, calling to mind the armed vigil of Amadis of Gaul, he suspended his sword at the shrine of Mary, passed the night in watching, in his new and strange

[*] Quid si ego hoc agerem quod fecit b. Franciscus, quid si hoc quod b. Dominicus? (Acta Sanctorum, vii. p. 634.)

[†] Non era condessa, ni duquessa, mas era su estado mas alto . . (Ib.)

[‡] Ibi duce amicisque ita salutatis, ut arcana consiliorum suorum quam accuratissime tegeret. (Maf. p. 16.)

[§] Pretiosa vestimenta quibus erat ornatus, pannoso cuidam largitus sacco seso alacer induit ac fune præcinxit. (Ibid. p. 20.)

costume; and sometimes on his knees, and then standing, but ever absorbed in prayer, and with his pilgrim's staff in hand, went through all the devout practices of which the illustrious Amadis had set the example. "Thus," remarks the Jesuit, Maffei, one of the biographers of the saint, "while Satan was stirring up Martin Luther to rebellion against all laws, divine and human, and whilst that heretic stood up at Worms, declaring impious war against the Apostolic See, Christ, by his heavenly providence, called forth this new champion, and binding him by after vows to obedience to the Roman Pontiff, opposed him to the licentiousness and fury of heretical perversity."[*]

Loyola, who was still lame in one of his legs, journeyed slowly by circuitous and secluded paths till he arrived at Manresa. There he entered a convent of Dominicans, resolving in this retired spot to give himself up to the most rigid penances. Like Luther, he daily went from door to door begging his bread.[†] Seven hours he was on his knees, and thrice every day did he flagellate himself. Again at midnight he was accustomed to rise and pray. He allowed his hair and nails to grow; and it would have been hard, indeed, to recognise in the pale and lank visage of the monk of Manresa, the young and brilliant knight of Pampeluna.

Yet the moment had arrived when the ideas of religion, which hitherto had been to Inigo little more than a form of chivalric devotion, were to reveal themselves to him as having an importance, and exercising a power of which, till then, he had been entirely unconscious. Suddenly, without any thing that might give intimation of an approaching change of feeling, the joy he had experienced left him.[‡] In vain did he have recourse to prayer and chaunting psalms; he could not rest.[§] His imagination ceased to present nothing but pleasing

---

[*] Furori ac libidini hæreticæ pravitatis opponeret. (Maf. p. 21.)

[†] Victum osteatim precibus, infimis emendicare quotidie. (Ib. p. 23.)

[‡] Tunc subito nulla præcedente significatione prorsus exui nudarique se omni gaudio sentiret. (Ibid. p. 27.)

[§] Nec jam in precibus, neque in psalmis . . . . . ullam inveniret delectationem aut requiem. (Ibid.)

illusions,—he was *alone with his conscience.* He did not know what to make of a state of feeling so new to him; and he shuddered as he asked whether God could still be against him, after all the sacrifices he had made. Day and night, gloomy terrors disturbed him,—bitter were the tears he shed, and urgent was his cry for that peace which he had lost—but all in vain.* He again ran over the long confession he had made at Montserrat. "Possibly," thought he, "I may have forgotten something." But that confession did but aggravate his distress of heart, for it revived the thought of former transgressions. He wandered about, melancholy and dejected, his conscience accusing him of having, all his life, done nought but heap sin upon sin, and the wretched man—a prey to overwhelming terrors—filled the cloisters with the sound of his sighs.

Strange thoughts, at this crisis, found access to his heart. Obtaining no relief in the confessional, and the various ordinances of the Church,† he began, as Luther had done, to doubt their efficacy. But, instead of turning from man's works, and seeking to the finished work of Christ,—he considered whether he should not once more plunge into the vanities of the age. His soul panted eagerly for that world that he had solemnly renounced;‡ but instantly he recoiled, awestruck.

And was there, at this moment, any difference between the monk of Manresa and the monk of Erfurth? Doubtless, in secondary points; but their condition of soul was alike. Both were deeply sensible of their sins; both sought peace with God, and desired to have the assurance of it in their hearts. If another Staupitz, with the Bible in his hand, had presented himself at the convent of Manresa, perhaps Inigo might have been known to us as the Luther of the Peninsula. These two remarkable men of the sixteenth century, the founders of two

---

* Vanis agitari terroribus, dies noctesque fletibus jungere. (Maf. p. 28.)

† Ut nulla jam res mitigare dolorem posse videretur. (Ibid. p. 29.)

‡ Et sæculi commodis repetendis magno quodam impetu cogitaverit. (Ibid. p. 30.)

opposing spiritual empires, which, for three centuries, have
warred one against the other, were, at this period, *brothers;*
and, perhaps, if they had been thrown together, Luther and
Loyola would have rushed into each other's embrace, and
mingled their tears and their prayers.

But, from this moment, the two monks were to take opposite courses.

Inigo, instead of regarding his remorse as sent to urge him
to the foot of the cross, deluded himself with the belief that
his inward compunctions were not from God, but the mere
suggestions of the devil; and he resolved not to think any
longer of his sins, but to obliterate them for ever from his memory!*   Luther looked to Christ—Loyola did but turn inward on himself.

It was not long before visionary attestations came in confirmation of Inigo's self-imposed convictions.   His own resolutions had been to him in place of the Lord's grace, and he had
suffered the imaginations of his own heart to take the place
of God's word.   He had counted the voice of God, speaking
to him in his conscience, as the voice of the devil; and hence,
we see him, in the remainder of his history, the dupe of delusions of the power of darkness.

One day, Loyola chanced to meet an old woman; as Luther, when his soul was under trial and exercise, had received
a visit from an old man.   But the Spanish crone, instead of
testifying of Remission of Sins to the penitent of Manresa,
predicted certain appearances of Jesus.   This was the sort of
Christianity to which Loyola, like the prophets of Zwickau,
had recourse.   Inigo did not seek truth from the Holy Scriptures, but invented in their place certain direct communications
from the world of spirits.   He soon passed his whole time
absorbed in extacy and abstraction.

Once, when on his way to the church of St. Paul, outside
the city, he followed, lost in thought, the course of the Llobre-
gat, and stopped, for a moment, to seat himself on its bank.

* Sine ulla dubitatione constituit præteritæ vitæ labes perpetua
oblivione conterere. (Maf. p. 31.)

He fixed his eyes on the river which rolled its deep waters in silence before him. He soon lost all consciousness of surrounding objects. Of a sudden, he fell into an extacy. Things were revealed to his sight, such as ordinary men comprehend only after much reading and long watching, and study [*] He rose from his seat. As he stood by the bank of the river, he seemed to himself a new man. He proceeded to throw himself on his knees before a crucifix erected near the spot, decided to devote his life in service to that cause, the mysteries of which had just been revealed to his soul.

From this time, his visions were more frequent. Sitting one day on the steps of St. Dominic, at Manresa, singing hymns to the Virgin, his thoughts were all of a sudden arrested, and, wrapt in extacy of motionless abstraction, while the mystery of the Holy Trinity[†] was revealed before his vision, under symbols of glory and magnificence. His tears flowed—his bosom heaved with sobs of emotion, and all that day he never ceased speaking of that ineffable vision.

Such repeated apparitions had overcome and dissipated all his doubts. He believed, not as Luther, because the things of Faith were written in the Word of God,—but because of the visions he himself had had. " Even though no Bible had existed,"[‡] say his apologists, "even though those mysteries should never have been revealed in Scripture, he would have believed them, for God had disclosed Himself to him."[§] Luther, become a doctor of divinity, had pledged his oath to the sacred Scriptures—and the alone infallible rule of God's word was become the fundamental principle of the Reformation. Loyola, at the time we are recording, bound himself to dreams, and apparitions;—and visionary delusions became the moving principles of his life, and the grounds of his confidence.

Luther's sojourn in the convent of Erfurth, and that of Loyola at Manresa explain to us the principle of the Refor

[*] Quæ vix demum solent homines intelligentia comprehendere. (Maf. p. 32.)
[†] En figuras de tres teclas.
[‡] Quod etsi nulla scriptura, mysteria illa fidei doceret. (Acta Sanct.)
[§] Quæ Deo sibi aperiente cognoverat. (Maf. p. 34.)

mation, and the character of modern Popery. We will not follow,—in his journey to Jerusalem, whither he repaired on leaving the convent,—the monk who was to be a means of re-animating the expiring power of Rome. We shall meet with him again in the further progress of this history.

Whilst these things were passing in Spain, Rome herself appeared to wear a graver aspect. The great patron of music, hunting, and feasting was removed from the throne of the Pontiff, and succeeded by a pious and grave monk.

Leo X. had been greatly pleased by the intelligence of the edict of Worms, and of Luther's captivity; and in sign of his triumph had caused the Reformer to be publicly burnt in effigy, together with his writings.* It was the second or third time that the Papacy had indulged itself in this harmless satisfaction. At the same time, Leo, to show his gratitude to the Emperor, united his army with the Imperial forces. The French were compelled to evacuate Parma, Placentia, and Milan; and Cardinal Giulio de Medici, cousin to the Pope, made a public entry into the latter city. The Pope appeared on the point of attaining the summit of human greatness.

The winter of the year 1521 was just commencing. It was customary with Leo X. to spend the autumn in the country. At that season, he would leave Rome without surplice, and also, what, remarks his master of the ceremonies, was a yet greater impropriety, wearing boots! At Viterbo, he would amuse himself with hawking; at Corneto, he hunted; the lake of Bolsena afforded him the pleasures of fishing. Leaving these, he would pass some time at his favourite residence, Malliana, in a round of festivities. Musicians, improvisatori, and other Roman artists, whose talents might add to the charms of this delightful villa, there gathered round the Sovereign Pontiff. He was residing there, when news was brought him of the taking of Milan. A tumult of joy ensued in the town. The courtiers and officers could not contain their exultation;

---

* Comburi jussit alteram vultus in ejus statua, alteram animi ejus in libris. (Pallavicini, i. p. 128.)

the Swiss discharged their carbines, and Leo incautiously
passed the night in walking backward and forward in his
chamber, and looking out of the window at the rejoicings of
the people. He returned to Rome, exhausted in body, and
in the intoxication of success. Scarcely had he re-entered the
Vatican, when he was suddenly taken ill. "Pray for me,"
said he to his attendants. He had not even time to receive the
last sacraments, and died, in the prime of life, at the age of
forty-seven—in a moment of victory, and amid the sounds of
public joy.

The crowd that followed the hearse of the Sovereign Pontiff gave utterance to curses. They could not pardon his
having died without the sacraments,—leaving behind him the
debts incurred by his vast expenditure. "Thou didst win the
pontificate like a fox—heldst it like a lion—and hast left it
like a dog," said the Romans.

Such was the mourning with which Rome honoured the
Pope who excommunicated the Reformation ; and one whose
name yet serves to designate a remarkable period in history.

Meanwhile a feeble reaction against the temper of Leo and
of Rome was already beginning in Rome itself. A few men
of piety had opened a place of prayer in order to mutual edification,—not far from the spot in which tradition reports the
first Christians of Rome to have held their meetings.* Con-
tarini, who had been present on Luther's appearance at
Worms, took the lead in these little meetings. Thus, almost
at the same time as at Wittemberg, a kind of movement toward a reformation manifested itself at Rome. Truly has it
been remarked, that wherever there are the seeds of 'love to
God,' there are also the germs of reformation. But these
well-meant efforts were soon to come to nothing.

In other times, the choice of a successor to Leo X. would
surely have fallen upon a Gregory VII. or an Innocent III.,
if men like them had been to be found ; but now the Imperial

* Si unirono in un oratorio, chiamato del divino amore, circa sessanta
di loro. (Caracciolo Vita da Paolo IV. MSC. Ranke.)

interest was stronger than that of the Church, and Charles V. required a Pope who should be devoted to his interests.

The Cardinal de Medici, afterwards Clement VII., seeing that he had no chance of obtaining the tiara, exclaimed aloud —" Choose the Cardinal Tortosa, an old man whom every one regards as a saint." The result was, that this prelate, who was a native of Utrecht, and of humble birth, was actually chosen, and reigned under the name of Adrian VI. He had been professor at Louvain, and afterwards tutor to Charles. In 1517, through the Emperor's influence, he had been invested with the Roman purple. Cardinal de Vio supported his nomination. " Adrian," said he, " was very useful in persuading the doctors of Louvain to put forth their condemnation of Luther."* The conclave, tired out and taken by surprise, nominated the ultramontane Cardinal. " But soon coming to their senses," observes an old chronicler, " they were ready to die with fear of the consequences." The thought that the native of the Netherlands might not accept of the tiara, brought them temporary relief; but it was soon dissipated. Pasquin represented the elect Pontiff under the character of a schoolmaster, and the Cardinals as boys under the discipline of the rod. The irritation of the populace was such that the members of the conclave thought themselves fortunate to escape being thrown into the river.† In Holland, it was a subject of general rejoicing that they had given a head to the Church. Inscribed on banners, suspended from the houses, were the words, " Utrecht planted—Louvain watered—the Emperor gave the increase." One added underneath, the words,—" and God had nothing to do with it !"

Notwithstanding the dissatisfaction which was at first manifested by the inhabitants of Rome, Adrian VI. repaired thither in August, 1522, and was well received. It was whispered from one to another that he had five thousand benefices in his gift, and each reckoned on some advantage to himself. For

---

* Doctores Lovanienses accepisse consilium a tam conspicuo alumno. (Pallavicini, p. 136.)

† Sleidan. Hist. de la Ref. i. p. 124.

a long time, the Papal chair had not been filled by such a man. He was upright, industrious, learned, pious, sincere, irreproachable in morals, and neither misled by favouritism, nor blinded by passion. He brought with him to the Vatican, his old house-keeper, whom he charged to continue to provide frugally for his daily wants in that palace which Leo had filled with luxury and dissipation. He was a stranger to the tastes of his predecessor. When they showed him the noble group of Laocoon, discovered only a few years before, and purchased by Julius II. at an enormous cost—he turned away, coolly observing, " They are the idols of the heathen :" and in one of his letters, he wrote, " I would far rather serve God in my priory at Louvain, than be pope at Rome."

Adrian, alarmed by the danger to which the religion, which had come down to them through the middle ages, was exposed from the spread of the Reformation ; and not, like the Italians, fearing the discredit into which Rome and her hierarchy were brought by it,—earnestly desired to oppose and arrest its progress ; and he judged that the best means to that end was to be found in a reformation of the Church by herself. " The Church," said he, " stands in need of a reformation ; but we must take one step at a time." " The Pope," said Luther, "advises that a few centuries should be permitted to intervene between the first and the second step." In truth, the Church had for ages tended toward a reformation. It was now no time for temporising. It was necessary to act !

Adhering to his plan, Adrian set about banishing from the city the profane, the perjurers, and the usurers. It was no easy task, for they composed a considerable proportion of the population.

At first the Romans derided him, but ere long they hated him. Priestly rule and the vast gains it brought, the power, and influence of Rome, its games and its festivals, the luxury that everywhere reigned in it, all would be irretrievably lost, if there were a return to apostolic simplicity.

The restoration of discipline everywhere encountered strong opposition. " To produce the desired effect," said the chief

Cardinal Penitentiaria, " it would-be necessary to begin by
reviving the ' first love' of Christians : the remedy is more
than the patient can bear; it will be death to him.   Take
care, lest in your desire to preserve Germany you should
lose Italy."*   And, indeed, it was not long before Adrian had
even more to fear from Romanism than Lutheranism itself.

Those about him attempted to lead him back to the path he
had abandoned.   The old and practised Cardinal Soderinus
of Volterra, the intimate friend of Alexander VI., of Julius II.,
and of Leo X.,† would often drop expressions well suited to
prepare him for that part, to him so strange, which he was
reserved to act.   " Heretics," observed he, " have, in all ages,
declaimed against the morals of the Roman Court; and yet
the Popes have never changed them.   It has never been by
reforms that heresies have been extinguished, but by crusades."
" Oh, how wretched is the position of the Popes," replied the
Pontiff, sighing deeply, " since they have not even liberty to
do right."‡

On the 23d March, 1522, and before Adrian's entry into
Rome, the Diet assembled at Nuremberg.   Already the
bishops of Mersburg and Misnia had petitioned the Elector
of Saxony to allow a visitation of the convents and churches
in his states.   Frederic, thinking that truth had nothing to
fear, had consented, and the visitation took place.   The bishops and doctors preached vehemently against the new opinions, exhorting, alarming, and entreating, but their arguments
seemed to have no effect; and when looking about them for
more effectual methods, they requested the secular authorities
to carry their directions into execution, the Elector's council
returned for answer, that the question was one that required
to be examined by the Word of God, and that the Elector, at
his advanced age, could not engage in theological investigation.   These expedients of the bishops did not reclaim a

* Sarpi Histoire du Concile de Trente, p. 20.
† Per longa esperienza delle cose del mundo, molto prudente e
accorto.   (Nardi. Hist. Fior., lib. 7.)
‡ Sarpi Hist. du Conc. de Tr., p. 21.

single soul to the fold of Rome; and Luther, who passed over the same ground, shortly afterwards, preaching from place to place, dispelled, by his powerful exhortation, the slight impression that had here and there been produced.

It was to be feared that the Archduke Ferdinand, brother to the Emperor, would do what Frederic had declined doing. That young prince, who presided at several sittings of the Diet, gradually acquiring decision of purpose, might, in his zeal, boldly unsheathe the sword that his more prudent and politic brother wisely left in the scabbard. In fact, Ferdinand, in his hereditary states of Austria, had already commenced a cruel persecution against those who were favourable to the Reformation. But God, on various occasions, made instrumental, in the deliverance of reviving Christianity, the very same agency that had been employed for the destruction of corrupt Christianity. The Crescent suddenly appeared in the panic-struck provinces of Hungary. On the 9th of August, after a siege of six weeks, Belgrade, the advanced post of that kingdom, and of the empire, was taken by assault by Soliman. The followers of Mahomet, after retiring from Spain, seemed intent on re-entering Europe from the East. The Diet of Nuremberg turned its attention from the Monk of Worms to the Sultan of Constantinople. But Charles V. kept both antagonists in view. In writing to the Pope from Valladolid on the 31st October, he said, " We must arrest the progress of the Turks,—and punish by the sword, all who favour the pestilent doctrines of Luther."*

It was not long before the thunder clouds which had seemed to pass by and roll eastward, again gathered over the Reformer. His re-appearance and activity at Wittemberg had revived the by-gone hatred. "Now that we know where to lay hands on him," said Duke George, "why not carry into effect the sentence of Worms?" It was confidently affirmed in Germany, that Charles V. and Adrian had in a meeting at

* Das man die Nachfolger derselben vergiften Lehre, mit dem Schwert strafen mag. (L. Opp. xvii. p. 321.)

Nuremberg concerted the measures to be adopted.* "Satan feels the wound that has been inflicted on him," said Luther, " and thence his rage. But Christ has already put forth his power, and will ere long trample him under foot, in spite of the gates of hell."†

In the month of December, 1522, the Diet again assembled at Nuremberg. Everything announced that, as Soliman had been the great enemy that had fixed attention in the spring session, Luther would be its principal object during the winter sittings. Adrian VI., by birth a German, hoped to find that favour from his own nation which a Pope of Italian origin could not expect.‡ He, in consequence, commissioned Chieregati, whom he had known in Spain, to repair to Nuremberg. At the opening of the Diet, several of the princes spoke strongly against Luther. The Cardinal Archbishop of Salzburg, who was high in the confidence of the Emperor, urged the adoption of prompt and vigorous measures, before the arrival of the Elector of Saxony. The Elector Joachim of Brandenburg, inflexible in his purpose, and the Chancellor of Treves, jointly insisted that the edict of Worms should be carried into effect. The rest of the princes were in great part undecided, and divided in opinion. The dilemma in which the church was placed, filled its faithful adherents with anguish. " I would give one of my fingers," exclaimed the Bishop of Strasburg, in open assembly of the Diet, "I would give one of my fingers to be no priest."§

Chieregati, supported by the Cardinal of Salzburg, insisted that Luther should be put to death. " It is necessary," said he, speaking in the Pope's name, and holding the Pope's brief in his hand, " It is indispensable that we should sever from the body that gangrened member.‖ Your forefathers

* Cumfama sit fortis et Cæsarem et Papam Nurnbergam conventuros. (L. Epp. ii. p. 214.)

† Sed Christus qui cœpit conteret eum. (L. Epp. ii. p. 215.)

‡ Quod ex ea regione venirent, unde nobis secundum carnem origo est. (See the Pope's brief L. Opp. lat. ii. p. 352.)

§ Er wollte einen Finger drum geben. (Seck. p. 568.)

‖ Resecandos uti membra jam putrida a sano corpore. (Pall. i. 158.

punished with death John Huss and Jerome of Prague, at Constance, but both these are now risen up in Luther. Follow the glorious example of your ancestors, and by the help of God, and of St. Peter, gain a signal victory over this serpent of hell."

On hearing the brief of the pious and mild Adrian read in the assembly, the majority of the princes were not a little alarmed.* Many began to see more in Luther's arguments; and they had hoped better things from the Pope. Thus then Rome, though under the presidency of an Adrian, cannot be brought to acknowledge her delinquency, but still hurls her thunderbolts, and the fields of Germany are again about to be deluged with blood. Whilst the princes maintained a gloomy silence, the prelates, and such members of the Diet as were in the interest of Rome, tumultuously urged the adoption of a decision. " Let him be put to death,"† cried they,—as we learn from the Saxon envoy who was present at this sitting.

Very different were the sounds heard in the churches of Nuremberg. The chapel of the hospital, and the churches of the Augustines, St. Sebald and St. Lorenzo, were crowded with multitudes flocking to hear the preaching of the Gospel. Andrew Osiander preached powerfully at St. Lorenzo's. Many princes attended, especially Albert, Margrave of Brandenburg, who, in his quality of Grand Master of the Teutonic order, took rank immediately next to the archbishops. Monks, abandoning the religious houses in the city, applied themselves to learn various trades, in order to gain their livelihood by their labour.

Chieregati could not endure such daring disobedience. He insisted that the priests and refractory monks should be imprisoned. The Diet, notwithstanding the remonstrances of the ambassadors of the Elector of Saxony and the Margrave Casimir, decided to seize the persons of the monks, but consented to communicate previously to Osiander and his col-

* Einen grossen Schrecken eingejagt. (Seck. p. 552.)
† Nicht anders geschrien denn: *Crucifige! Crucifige!* (L. Opp. xviii. p. 367.)

leagues the Nuncio's complaint. A committee, under the direction of the fanatical Cardinal of Salzburg, was charged with the matter. The danger was imminent—the conflict was on the point of commencing, and it was the great Council of the nation that provoked it.

Yet the people interposed. Whilst the Diet was engaged in deliberating what should be done with these ministers, the town council was considering what steps should be taken in regard to the decision of the Diet. The council came to a resolution which did not overstep the limits assigned to it by the laws,—that if force were employed to deprive them of their preachers, recourse should be had to force to set them at liberty. Such a resolution was full of significance. The astonished Diet returned an answer to the Nuncio that it was not lawful to arrest the preachers of the free city of Nuremberg without previously convicting them of heresy.

Chieregati was strangely disconcerted by this fresh insult to the supreme authority of the Papacy.—"Very well," said he, haughtily, addressing himself to Ferdinand, "do you then do nothing,—leave me to act,—I will seize the preachers in the Pope's name."[*] When the Cardinal-Archbishop Albert of Mentz, and the Margrave Casimir were apprized of this startling determination, they came in haste to the Legate, imploring him to abandon his intention. The latter was, at first, inflexible, affirming that, in the bosom of Christendom, obedience to the Pope could not be dispensed with. The two Princes retired:—"If you persist in your intention," said they, "we require you to send us notice, for we will quit the city before you venture to lay hands on the preachers."[†] The Legate abandoned his project.

Despairing of success by authoritative measures, he now decided to have recourse to expedients of another kind, and, with this purpose, communicated to the Diet the Pontiff's intentions and orders, which he had hitherto kept private.

* Sese auctoritate pontifica curaturum ut isti caperentur. (Corp. Ref. L. p. 606.)

† Priusquam illi caperentur, se urbe cessurosesse. (Ibid.)

But the well-intentioned Adrian, little used to the ways of the world, did injury even by his candour to the cause he had at heart. "We are well aware," said he, in the 'resolutions' forwarded to his Legate, "that for many years past, the holy city has been a scene of many corruptions and abominations.* The infection has spread from the head through the members, and has descended from the Popes to the rest of the clergy. It is our desire to reform that court of Rome, whence so many evils are seen to flow,—the whole world desires it, and it is in order that we may do this, that we consented to ascend the throne of the pontiffs."

The supporters of Rome blushed to hear these unlooked-for words. "They thought," as Pallavicini says, "that such admissions were too sincere."† The friends of the Reformation, on the contrary, rejoiced to hear Rome herself proclaiming her corruption. Who could doubt that Luther had truth on his side, now that the Pope declared it!

The answer of the Diet shewed how greatly the authority of the chief Pontiff had lost ground in the Empire. Luther's spirit seemed to have taken possession of the hearts of the nation's representatives. The moment was auspicious.— Adrian's ear seemed open,—the Emperor was at a distance ;— the Diet resolved to enumerate in one document the various wrongs that Germany had for centuries endured from Rome, and to address their memorial to the Pope.

The Legate was alarmed at this determination. He used threats and entreaties, but both were unavailing. The secular states adhered to their purpose, and the ecclesiastical did not venture to offer opposition. Eighty grievances were therefore set forth. The corruption and arts of the Popes and of the court of Rome, in order to squeeze revenue from Germany,—the scandals and profanations of the clerical orders,—

---

* In eam sedem aliquot jam annos quædam vitia irrepsisse, abusus in rebus sacris, in legibus violationes, in cunctis denique perversionem. (Pallav. i. p. 160. See also Sarpi, p. 25. L. Opp. xviii. p. 329, &c.)

† Liberioris tamen quam par erat, sinceritatis fuisse visum est, ea conventui patefacere. (Ibid. p. 162.)

the disorders and simony of the ecclesiastical courts,—the encroachments on the civil power to the restriction of liberty of conscience, were detailed with equal freedom and force. The States distinctly intimated that traditions of men were the source of all this abuse, and they ended by saying,—"If these grievances are not redressed within a limited time, we will consult together, and seek some other means of deliverance from our sufferings and our wrongs."* Chieregati, having a presentiment that the report the Diet would prepare would be couched in strong language, hastily took his departure from Nuremberg, thus avoiding being himself the bearer of so disappointing and insolent a communication.

After all, was it not still to be feared that the Diet would endeavour to make some amends for this bold measure, by the sacrifice of Luther himself? At first, there were some apprehensions of such a policy,—but a spirit of justice and sincerity had been breathed on the assembly. Following the example of Luther, it demanded the convocation of a free Council in the Empire, and decreed that until such Council should assemble, nothing should be preached but the simple Gospel, and nothing put forth in print, without the sanction of a certain number of men of character and learning.† These resolutions afford us some means of estimating the vast advance the Reformation had made since the Diet of Worms,—and yet the Saxon envoy, the knight Frelitsch, recorded a formal protest against the censorship prescribed by the Diet, moderate as that censorship might seem. The decree of the Diet was a first victory gained by the Reformation, which was the presage of future triumphs. Even the Swiss, in the depths of their mountains, shared in the general exultation. "The Roman Pontiff has been defeated in Germany!" said Zwingle; "All that remains to be done is to deprive him of his armour. It is for this that we must now fight, and the battle will be

* Wie sie solcher Beschwerung und Drangsal entladen werden. (L. Opp. xviii. p. 354.)
† Ut pie placideque purum Evangelium prædicaretur. (Pal. i. p. 166. Sleiden, i. p. 135.)

fiercer than before. But we have Christ present with us in the conflict."* Luther loudly affirmed that the edict the Princes had put forth was by inspiration of God himself.†

Great was the indignation at the Vatican among the Pope's council. "What! it is not enough to have to bear with a Pope who disappoints the expectation of the Romans, in whose palace no sound of song or amusement is ever heard, but, in addition to this, secular princes are to be suffered to hold a language that Rome abhors, and refuse to deliver up the monk of Wittemberg to the executioner!"

Adrian himself was indignant at the events in Germany, and it was on the head of the Elector of Saxony that he now poured out his anger. Never had the Roman Pontiffs uttered a cry of alarm more energetic, more sincere, or more affecting.

"We have waited long—perhaps too long," said the pious Adrian, in his brief addressed to the Elector: "It was our desire to see whether God would visit thy soul, so that thou mightest at the last be delivered from the snares of the devil. But where we had hoped to gather grapes there have we found nothing but wild grapes. The Spirit's promptings have been despised; thy wickedness has not been subdued. Open then thine eyes to behold the greatness of thy fall!

"If the unity of the Church is gone—if the simple have been turned out of the way of that faith which they had sucked from their mothers' breasts—if the churches are deserted—if the people are without priests, and the priests have not the honour due to them,—if christians are without Christ, to whom is it owing but to thee?‡ .... If christian peace has forsaken the earth—if, on every side, discord, rebellion, pillage, violence, and midnight conflagrations prevail—if the

* Victus est ac ferme profligatus e Germania romanus pontifex. (Zw. Epp. 313. 11th Oct. 1523.)

† Gott habe solches E. G. eingeben. (L. Opp. xviii. 476.)

‡ Dass die Kirchen ohne Volk sind, dass die Völker ohne Priester sind, dass die Priester ohne Ehre sind, und dass die Christen ohne Christo sind. (L. Opp. xviii. p. 371.)

ary of war is heard from east to west,—if universal conflict is at hand,—it is thou thyself who art the author of all these.

"Seest thou not that sacrilegious man (Luther,) how he rends with wicked hands, and profanely tramples under foot, the pictures of the saints, and even the holy cross of Jesus? . . . . Seest thou not how, in his infamous rage, he incites the laity to shed the blood of the priests, and overturn the temples of the Lord.

"And what, if the priests he assails are disorderly in conduct? Has not the Lord said, ' *Whatsoever they bid you, that observe and do, but do not after their works*'—thus instructing us in the honour that belongs to them, even though their lives should be disorderly.*

"Rebellious apostate! he does not blush to defile vessels dedicated to God; he forces from the sanctuaries virgins consecrated to Christ, delivering them over to the devil; he getteth into his power the priests of the Lord, and gives them to abandoned women. Awful profanation! which even the heathen would have reprobated in the priests of their idol worship.

"What punishment, what infliction, dost thou think we judge thee to deserve? Have pity on thyself,—have pity on thy poor Saxons; for surely, if thou dost not turn from the evil of thy way, God will bring down His vengeance upon thee.

"In the name of the Almighty God and our Saviour Jesus Christ, of whom I am vicegerent on earth, I warn thee that thou wilt be judged in this world, and be cast into the lake of everlasting fire in that which is to come. Repent and be converted. Both swords are impending over thy head,—the sword of the Empire, and that of the Papal authority."

The pious Frederic shuddered as he read this menacing brief. A little before he had written to the Emperor to say that his age and bodily indisposition incapacitated him for attending to such matters; and the answer returned was one of

* Wenn sie gleich eines verdammten Lebens sind. (L. Opp. xviii. p. 379.)

the most insolent letters a reigning prince had ever received. Infirm and aged as he was, his eyes rested upon the sword he had received at the holy sepulchre in the days of youthful vigour. A thought crossed his mind that it might be necessary to unsheathe it in defence of the conscience of his subjects, and that, near as his life was to its close, he should not descend to the grave in peace. He forthwith wrote to Wittemberg to have the judgment of the fathers of the Reformation as to what should be done.

There, also, forebodings of commotion and persecution were rife. " What can I say," exclaimed the mild Melancthon, " whither can I turn?[*] Hatred presses us to the earth—the world is up in arms against us." Luther, Link, Melancthon, Bugenhagen and Amsdorff, held a consultation on the answer to be returned to the Elector. They drew up a reply, each in terms nearly identical, and the advice they gave is not a little remarkable.

" No prince," said they, " can undertake a war without the consent of the people from whose hands he has received his authority.[†] But the people have no heart to fight for the Gospel, for they do not believe. Therefore, let not princes take up arms; they are rulers of the *nations*, that is to say, of *unbelievers.*" Here we find the impetuous Luther soliciting the discreet Frederic to restore his sword to its scabbard. No better answer could be given to the Pope's charge that he stirred up the laity to embrue their hands in the blood of the priests. Few characters have been more misunderstood than his. This advice was dated the 8th February, 1523. Frederic submitted in silence.

It was not long before the effects of the Pope's anger began to be seen. The princes who had recapitulated their grievances, now dreading the consequences, sought to make amends by compliances. Some, there were, who reflected that victory would probably declare for the Pontiff, seeing that he, to all

* Quid dicam ? quo me vertam ? (Corp. Ref. i. p. 627.)
† Principi nullum licet suscipere bellum, nisi consentiente populo, a quo accepit imperium. (Ibid. p. 601.)

appearance, was the stronger of the two. " In our days," observed Luther, " princes are content to say three times three make nine, or twice seven make fourteen,—right, the counsel shall stand. Then the Lord our God arises and speaks: ' What then do you allow for My power ?' . . . . It may be *naught* . . . . And immediately He confuses the figures, and their calculations are proved false."*

The stream of fire poured forth by the humble and gentle Adrian kindled a conflagration, and the rising flame spread far and wide in Christendom a deep agitation. Persecution, which had slackened for a while, was now renewed. Luther trembled for Germany, and sought to allay the tempest. " If the princes make war against the truth," said he, " there will be such confusion as will be the ruin of princes, magistrates, clergy, and people. I tremble at the thought that all Germany may, in a little while, be deluged with blood.† Let us stand as a rampart for our country against the wrath of our God. Nations are not now as formerly.‡ The sword of civil war is impending over kings :—they are bent on destroying Luther—but Luther is bent on saving them ; Christ lives and reigns, and *I shall reign with him*."§

These words were spoken to the winds. Rome was pressing forward to scaffolds and the shedding of blood. The Reformation in this resembled Jesus Christ,—that it came not to send peace on the earth, but a sword. Persecution was necessary in the counsels of God. As certain substances are hardened in the fire that they may be less liable to be affected by atmospheric changes, so the fiery trial was designed to arm and defend the truth of the Gospel from the influence of the world. But that fiery trial did yet more ;—it served,

* So kehrt er ihnen auch die Rechnung gar um. (L. Opp. xxii. 1831.)

† Ut videar mihi videre Germaniam in sanguine natare. (L. Epp. ii. p. 156.)

‡ Cogitent populos non esse tales modo, quales hactenus fuerunt. (Ibid. p. 157.)

§ Christus meus vivit et regnat, et ego vivam et regnabo. (Ibid. p 158.)

as in the early days of Christianity, to kindle in men's hearts
an universal enthusiasm for a cause against which such rage
was let loose.   There is in man, when first introduced to the
knowledge of the truth, a holy indignation against violence
and injustice.   An instinct received from God impels him to
range himself on the side of the oppressed ; and, at the same
time, the faith of the martyrs exalts, controls, and leads him to
that saving truth which gifts its followers with so much courage and tranquillity.

Duke George openly took the lead in the persecution.   But
he was not content to carry it on among his own subjects ; he
desired, above all, to see it extend itself to electoral Saxony,
the focus of heresy, and he laboured hard to move the Elector
Frederic and Duke John.   In writing to them from Nuremberg, he observed, " Certain merchants, recently from Saxony,
bring reports from thence of strange things, and such as are most
opposed to the honour of God, and the saints.   It seems, they
take the holy sacrament in their hands—consecrate the bread
and wine in the common speech of the people—pour the blood
of Christ into a common cup.   It is said that at Eulenberg, a
man, who sought occasion to insult the officiating priest, rode
into the church mounted on an ass.   And what do we hear to be
the consequence ?   The mines, with which God had enriched
Saxony, are become less productive ever since this preaching
of Luther's innovations.   Would to God that those who boast
that they have restored the Gospel in the electorate had employed themselves in carrying the testimony of it to Constantinople.   Luther's speech is gentle and specious, but it draws
after it a sting which is sharper than a scorpion's.   Let us
make ready our hands to fight.   Let us cast these apostate
monks and ungodly priests into prison ; let us do so at once ;
for the hairs of our heads are turning as grey as our beards,
and admonish us that we have not long to live."*

So wrote Duke George to the Elector.   The latter answered
decidedly, yet mildly, that whoever should commit any crime

* Wie ihre Bärt und Haare ausweisen.   (Seckend. p. 482.)
13*

within his state should not go unpunished; but that, as to matters of conscience, they must be left to the judgment of God.*

Failing in his endeavour to persuade Frederic, George pressed his severities against such as lay within his reach. He imprisoned the monks and priests who were known to adhere to Luther's doctrines,—recalled to their families the students who had gone from his states to pursue their studies in the universities to which the Reformation had extended, and required his subjects to deliver up to the magistrates all copies of the New Testament in the vernacular tongue. Similar measures were put in force in Austria, Wurtemberg, and the Duchy of Brunswick.

But it was in the Low Countries, under the immediate rule of Charles V., that the persecution broke out with most violence. The convent of the Augustines, at Antwerp, contained within it many monks who had hailed with joy the truths of the Gospel. Several of the brothers had passed some time at Wittemberg, and ever since 1519, Salvation, by Grace had been preached in their church with unusual power. Toward the close of the year 1521, James Probst, the prior, a man of ardent temperament, and Melchior Mirisch, who was remarkable for the opposite qualities of experience and prudence, were arrested and carried to Brussels. They were there brought before Aleander, Glapio, and several other prelates. Taken unawares, disconcerted, and dreading consequences, Probst recanted. Melchior Mirisch found means to appease his judges; and, while he avoided a recantation, escaped condemnation.

These proceedings no way overawed the monks who remained in the convent of Antwerp. They continued to preach the Gospel with earnestness. The people crowded to hear, and the church of the Augustines at Antwerp was unable to contain the hearers, as had been the case at Wittemberg. In October, 1522, the storm which had been gathering

* Müsse man solche Dinge Gott überlassen. (Seckend. p. 485.)

over their heads suddenly burst forth. The convent was closed, and the monks imprisoned and sentenced to die.[*] A few effected their escape. Some women, roused into forgetfulness of the natural timidity of their sex, rescued one of them, by name Henry Zuphten, from the hands of the executioners.[†] Three of the younger monks, Henry Voe, John Eesch, and Lambert Thorn, evaded for a time the search of the inquisitors. The sacred vessels of the convent were publicly sold, the entrance to the church barricaded, the holy sacrament was carried forth as if from a place of pollution, and Margaret, who then governed the Low Countries, solemnly received it into the church of the Holy Virgin.[‡] An order was given that not one stone should be left upon another of that heretical monastery; and several private citizens and women who had joyfully received the Gospel were thrown into prison.[§]

Luther was deeply grieved on receiving intelligence of these events. " The cause we have in hand," said he, " is no longer a mere trial of strength ; it demands the sacrifice of our lives, and must be cemented by our blood."[||]

Mirisch and Probst were reserved for a very different fate. The politic Mirisch soon became the docile slave of Rome, and was employed in carrying into execution the Imperial orders against the favourers of the Reformation.[¶] Probst, on the contrary, escaping out of the hands of the inquisitors, wept bitterly over his failure, retraced his recantation, and boldly preached, at Bruges in Flanders, the doctrine he had abjured. Being again arrested and cast into prison at Brussels, death seemed inevitable.[**] A Franciscan took pity upon him, assisted him in his flight, and Probst, "saved by a miracle

---

[*] Zum Tode verurtheilet. (Seck. p. 548.)
[†] Quomodo mulieres vi Henricum liberarint. (L. Epp. ii. p. 265.)
[‡] Susceptum honorifice a domina Margareta. (Ibid.)
[§] Cives aliquos, et mulieres vexatæ et punitæ. (Ibid.)
[||] Et vitam exiget et sanguinem. (Ibid. 181.)
[¶] Est executor Cæsaris contra nostros. (Ibid. p. 207.)
[**] Domo captum, exustum credimus. (Ibid. p. 214.)

of God," says Luther, reached Wittemberg, where all hearts were filled with joy at his second deliverance.[*]

On every side the priests of Rome were under arms. The town of Miltenberg on the Maine, in the jurisdiction of the Elector Archbishop of Mentz, had, of all the towns of Germany, received the Word of God with most joy. The inhabitants were much attached to their pastor, John Draco, one of the most enlightened men of his time. He was compelled to leave the city; but the Roman clergy withdrew at the same time, dreading the vengeance of the people. An evangelical deacon remained behind, and comforted their hearts. At the same time the soldiery of Mentz were introduced and dispersed through the city, vomiting blasphemies, brandishing their swords, and giving themselves up to debauchery.[†]

Some of the evangelical Christians fell victims to their violence,[‡] others were seized and thrown into dungeons, the rites of Romish worship was restored, the reading of the Scriptures prohibited, and the inhabitants forbidden to speak of the Gospel, even in their family meetings. The deacon had taken refuge with a poor widow, on the entrance of the troops. Information was given to the commanding officer, and a soldier despatched to take him. The humble deacon, hearing the steps of the soldier who sought his life, advancing quietly waited for him, and just as the door of the chamber

---

[*] Jacobus, Dei miraculo liberatus qui nunc agit nobiscum. (L. Epp. ii. p. 182.) This letter, which is found in M. De Wette's collection, under the date of April 14, must be subsequent to the month of June,— since, on the 26th of June, we find Luther saying that Probst has been again taken, and was expected to be burnt. The supposition that would solve the difficulty, by supposing Probst to have been at Wittemberg between these two captures, is not admissible, for Luther would not have said of a Christian who had been saved from death by his recantation, that he had been delivered by a miracle of God. Perhaps we should read the date, &c. of this letter, instead of ' *in die S. Tiburtii*,'—' *in die Turiaji*.'—which would place it in July 13—the probable date, in my opinion.

[†] So sie doch schändlicher leben denn Huren und Buben. (L. Epp. ii. p. 482.)

[‡] Schlug etliche todt. (Seck. p. 604.)

was abruptly pushed open, he came forward, and, embracing him, said, " I bid you welcome, brother. Here I am : plunge your sword in my bosom."* The stern soldier, in astonishment, dropt his weapon, and contrived to save the pious evangelist from further molestation.

Meanwhile, the inquisitors of the Low Countries, thirsting for blood, scoured the neighbouring country, searching everywhere for the young Augustines who had escaped from the Antwerp persecution. Esch, Voes, and Lambert, were at last discovered, put in chains, and conducted to Brussels. Egmondanus, Hochstraten, and several other inquisitors, summoned them to their presence. " Do you retract your opinion," inquired Hochstraten, "that the priest has no power to forgive sins, but that that power belongs to God alone ?"—and then he went on to enumerate the other Gospel truths which he required them to abjure. " No : we will retract nothing," exclaimed Esch and Voes, firmly ; " we will not disown God's Word ; we will rather die for the faith!"

THE INQUISITOR.—" Confess that you have been deceived by Luther."

THE YOUNG AUGUSTINES.—" As the apostles were deceived by Jesus Christ."

THE INQUISITORS.—" We declare you to be heretics, worthy of being burnt alive ; and we deliver you over to the secular arm."

Lambert was silent. The prospect of death terrified him : distress and uncertainty agitated his heart. " I request four days' respite," said he, in stifled emotion. He was taken back to prison. As soon as this respite was expired, Esch and Voes were degraded from their priestly office, and handed over to the council of the reigning governess of the Low Countries. The council delivered them, bound, to the executioner. Hochstraten and three other inquisitors accompanied them to the place of execution.†

Arriving at the scaffold, the young martyrs contemplated it

* Sey gegrüsst, mein Bruder. (Scultet. ann. i. p. 173.)
† Facta est hæc res Bruxellæ in publico foro. (L. Epp. ii. p. 361.)

with calmness. Their constancy, their piety, and their youth, drew tears from the inquisitors themselves. When they were bound to the stake,* the confessors drew near, "Once more we ask you if you will receive the Christian faith ?"

THE MARTYRS.—"We believe in the Christian Church, but not in your Church."

Half-an-hour elapsed. It was a pause of hesitation. A hope had been cherished that the near prospect of such a death would intimidate these youths. But, alone tranquil of all the crowd that thronged the square, they began to sing psalms,—stopping from time to time to declare that they were resolved to die for the name of Jesus Christ.

"Be converted—be converted," cried the inquisitors, "or you will die in the name of the devil." "No," answered the martyrs; "we will die like Christians, and for the truth of the Gospel."

The pile was then lighted. Whilst the flame slowly ascended, a heavenly peace dilated their hearts; and one of them could even say, "I seem to be on a bed of roses."† The solemn hour was come—death was at hand. The two martyrs cried with a loud voice, "O Lord Jesus, Son of David, have mercy upon us !" and then they began to recite their creed.‡ At last the flames reached them; but the fire consumed the cords which fastened them to the stake before their breath was gone. One of them, feeling his liberty, dropped upon his knees in the midst of the flames, and then, in worship to his Lord, exclaimed, clasping his hands, "Lord Jesus, Son of David, have mercy on us !"§

Their bodies were quickly wrapped in flame; they shouted " *Te Deum laudamus.*" Soon their voices were stifled,—and their ashes alone remained.

* Nondum triginta annorum. (L. Epp. ii. p. 361.)

† Dit schijnen mij als roosen te zijn. (Brandt Hist. der Reformatie, i. p. 79.)

‡ Admoto igni, canere cœperunt symbolum fidei, says Erasmus. (Epp. i. p. 1278.)

§ Da ist der eine im Feuer auf die Knie gefallen. (L. Opp. xviii. p. 481.)

This execution had lasted four hours. It was on the 1st of July, 1523, that the first martyrs of the Reformation laid down their lives for the Gospel.

All good men shuddered when they heard of these events. The future was big with fearful anticipations. " The executions have begun,"* said Erasmus. " At length," exclaimed Luther, " Christ is gathering some fruits of our preaching, and preparing new martyrs."

But the joy of Luther in the constancy of these young Christians was disturbed by the thoughts of Lambert. Of the three, Lambert possessed most learning ; he had been chosen to fill the place of Probst, as preacher at Antwerp. Finding no peace in his dungeon, he was terrified at the prospect of death ; but still more by conscience, which reproached him with his cowardice, and urged him to confess the Gospel. Delivered, ere long, from his fears, he boldly proclaimed the truth, and died like his brethren.†

A noble harvest sprung up from the blood of these martyrs. Brussels manifested a willingness to receive the Gospel.‡ "Wherever Aleander lights a pile," remarked Erasmus, " there it seems as if he had sowed heretics."§

" I am bound with you in your bonds," exclaimed Luther : " Your dungeons, and your burnings my soul takes part in.‖ All of us are with you in spirit; and the Lord is above it all !"

He proceeded to compose a hymn commemorative of the death of the young monks ; and soon, in every direction, throughout Germany and the Low Countries, in towns and in

* Cœpta est carnificina. (Epp. i. p. 129.)

† Quarta post exustus est tertius frater Lambertus. (L. Epp. ii. p. 361.)

‡ Ea mors multos fecit lutheranos. (Er. Epp. p. 952.) Tum demum cœpit civitas favere Luthero. (Ibid. p. 1676. Erasmus to Duke George.) Ea civitas antea purissima. (Ibid. p. 1430.)

§ Ubicumque fumos excitavit nuntius, ibi diceres fuisse factam hæreseon sementem. (Ibid.)

‖ Vestra vincula mea sunt, vestri carceres et ignes mei sunt. (L. Epp. ii. p. 464.)

villages, were heard accents of song which communicated an enthusiasm for the faith of the martyrs.*

> Flung to the heedless winds,
> Or on the waters cast,
> Their ashes shall be watched,
> And gathered at the last.
> And from that scattered dust,
> Around us and abroad,
> Shall spring a plenteous seed
> Of witnesses for God.
>
> Jesus hath now received
> Their latest living breath,—
> Yet vain is Satan's boast
> Of victory in their death.
> Still—still—though dead, they speak,
> And trumpet-tongued proclaim
> To many a wakening land,
> The one availing Name.

Doubtless Adrian would have persisted in these violent measures;—the failure of his efforts to arrest the progress of the Reformation—his own orthodoxy—his zeal—his inflexibility—even his conscientiousness would have made him an unrelenting persecutor. Providence ordained otherwise. He expired on the 14th of September, 1523; and the Romans, overjoyed at being rid of the stern foreigner, suspended a crown of flowers at the door of his physician, with an inscription—"*to the saviour of his country.*"

Julio de Medicis, cousin to Leo X., succeeded Adrian under the name of Clement VII. From the day of his election, all ideas of religious reformation were at an end. The new Pope, like many of his predecessors, thought only of

---

* Die Asche will nicht lassen ab,
 Sie stäubt in allen Landen,
 Hie hilft kein Bach, Loch, noch Grab . . . . (L. Opp. xviii. p. 464.)
 Obligingly rendered by John Alex. Messenger; to whose friendly pen the publisher is indebted for the touching hymns of Zwingle (see Vol. ii. p. 329—332): as well as for the translation of a considerable portion of the Second Volume, besides other assistance and many valuable suggestions.

maintaining the privileges of the Papacy, and employing its resources for his own aggrandisement.

Anxious to repair the indiscretions of Adrian, Clement despatched a legate of a character resembling his own, Cardinal Campeggio, the ablest prelate of his court, and a man of large experience, well acquainted with most of the German Princes. After a pompous reception in his passage through the Italian cities, the Legate soon noticed the change that had taken place in the Empire. On entering Augsburg, he proposed, according to custom, to give his benediction to the people; but those to whom he spoke met the proposal by a smile. The hint was enough; and he entered Nuremberg incognito, without repairing to St. Sebalde's church, where the clergy were waiting for him. No priests in sacerdotal vestments were seen advancing to greet him;—no cross was borne in solemn state before him; but one might have thought a private individual was taking his journey through the city.[*] Every thing indicated that the reign of the Papacy was drawing to its close.

The Diet had met again in session, at Nuremberg, in January, 1525. A storm was impending over the government of the nation, owing to the firmness of Frederic. The Suabian league, comprising the richest cities of the empire, and, above all, Charles the Fifth, had combined for his destruction. He was charged with favouring the newly-broached heresy. Accordingly, it was decided that the executive powers should be so entirely changed as not to retain one of the old members. Frederic, overwhelmed with grief, instantly took his departure from Nuremberg.

Easter drew nigh. Osiander and the gospel preachers redoubled their activity. The former preached publicly to the effect, that *Antichrist* entered Rome the very day that Constantine had quitted it to fix his residence at Constantinople. The ceremony of Palm Sunday and others were omitted: four thousand persons partook of the supper under both kinds;

---

[*] Communi habitu quod per sylvas et campos ierat, per mediam urbem . . . sine clero, sine prævia cruce. (Cochl. p. 82.)

and the Queen of Denmark, sister to the Emperor, publicly received it in like manner at the Castle. "Oh!" exclaimed the Archduke Ferdinand, losing all self-command, "would that you were not my sister."—"The same mother bore us," replied the Queen; "and I would give up every thing but God's truth to serve you."[*]

Campeggio trembled at witnessing such audacity; nevertheless, affecting to despise the jeers of the people, and the harangues of the preachers,—and relying on the authority of the Emperor and of the Pope, he referred the Diet to the edict of Worms, and demanded that the Reformation should be put down by force. On hearing this, some of the princes and deputies gave vent to their indignation. "And pray," asked they, addressing Campeggio, "what has become of the memorial of grievances presented to the Pope by the people of Germany?" The Legate, acting upon his instructions, assumed an air of bland surprise: "Three versions of that memorial have been received in Rome," said he; "but it has never been officially communicated; and I could never believe that so unseemly a paper could have emanated from your Highnesses."

The Diet was stung by this reply. If this be the spirit in which the Pope receives their representations, they also know what reception to give to such as he should address to them. Several deputies remarked that such was the eagerness of the people for the Word of God, that the attempt to deprive them of it would occasion torrents of bloodshed.

The Diet straightway set about preparing an answer to the Pope. As it was not possible to get rid of the edict of Worms, a clause was added to it, which had the effect of rendering it null. "We require," said they, "that all should conform to it—*so far as is possible.*"[†] But several of the states had declared that it was *impossible* to enforce it. At the same time calling to mind the unwelcome remembrance of the Councils

* Wolle sich des Wortes Gottes halten. (Seckend. p. 613.)
† Quantum eis possibile sit . . . (Cochl. p. 84.)

of Constance and of Bale, the Diet demanded the convocation in Germany of a General Council of Christendom.

The friends of the Reformation did not stop there. What could they look for from a Council which might perhaps never be called together, and which, in any case, would be sure to be composed of bishops of all nations? Will Germany humble her anti-Roman inclinations in deference to prelates assembled from Spain, France, England, and Italy? The government of the nation has been already set aside. It is necessary that in its place should be a 'national assembly' charged with the defence of the popular interest.

Vainly did Hannart, the Spanish envoy of Charles, supported by the adherents of Rome and of the Emperor, oppose the suggestion; the majority of the Diet were unshaken. It was arranged that a diet or secular assembly should meet in November at Spires, to regulate all questions of religion, and that the States should invite their divines to prepare a list of controverted points to be laid before that august assembly.

No time was lost. Each province prepared its memorial, and never had Rome reason to apprehend so great an explosion. Franconia, Brandenburg, Henneberg, Windsheim, Wertheim, Nuremberg, declared for the truth of the Gospel as opposed to the seven sacraments, the corruptions of the mass, the worship of the saints, and the Pope's supremacy. " There is coin for you of the genuine stamp," said Luther. Not one of the questions which engaged the popular mind seemed likely to be passed over in silence, in that council of the nation. The majority would make a stand for general measures. The unity of Germany, its independence, and its reformation, would yet be safe!

When news of what was passing reached the Pope, he could not restrain his anger. What! do any presume to set up a secular tribunal to decide questions of religion in contempt of his authority?* If this unprecedented step be taken, doubtless Germany will be saved,—but Rome is ruined! A consistory

* Pontifex ægerrime tulit. . . . intelligens novum de religione tribunal eo pacto excitari citra ipsius auctoritatem. (Pallav. i. p. 182.)

was hastily called together, and one who watched the dismay of the senators might have thought the Germans were in full march upon the Capitol. " As to the Elector Frederic," exclaimed Aleander, " we must take off his head ;" and another Cardinal gave counsel that the kings of England and of Spain should overawe the free cities by threatening to break off all commercial intercourse with them. In conclusion, the consistory came to the decision that the only way of safety lay in moving heaven and earth to prevent the proposed assembly at Spires.

The Pope wrote directly to the Emperor :—" If I am called to be foremost in making head against the storm, it is not because I am the only one threatened by the tempest, but because I am at the helm. The imperial authority is yet more invaded than even the dignity of the court of Rome."

Whilst the Pope was sending this letter to Castile, he was seeking to strengthen himself by alliances in Germany. It was not long before he gained over one of the most powerful reigning families of the Empire, the Dukes of Bavaria. The edict of Worms had been as much a dead letter there as elsewhere ; and the doctrine of the Gospel had made its way extensively. But subsequent to the close of 1521, the princes of the country, urged on by Doctor Eck, who was chancellor in their university of Ingolstadt, had again made advances towards Rome, and passed a law enjoining their subjects to adhere faithful to the religion of their forefathers.*

The Bavarian bishops showed some signs of alarm at this intervention of the secular authority. Eck set out immediately for Rome to solicit from the Pope an extension of the authority lodged in the princes. The Pope granted all their desires, and even went so far as to make over to them a fifth of the revenues of the church in their country.

Here we see Roman Catholicism, at a time when the Reformation had no regular settlement, resorting to established institutions for support, and Catholic princes, aided by the

* Erstes baierisches Religions Mandat. (Winter, Gesch. der Evang. Lehre in Baiern, i p. 310.)

Pope, seizing the revenues of the Church long before the Reformation had ventured to touch them. What then must be thought of the oft-repeated charges of Catholics on this head!

Clement VII. was secure of the assistance of Bavaria in quelling the dreaded assembly of Spires. It was not long before the Archduke Ferdinand, the Archbishop of Salzburg, and others of the princes were likewise gained over.

But Campeggio was bent on something more. His aim was to divide Germany into two hostile camps;—Germans were to be opposed to Germans.

During a previous residence at Stutgard, the Legate had concerted with Ferdinand the project of a league against the Reformation. "There is no telling what may be the result of an assembly in which the voice of the people will be heard," observed he: "The Diet of Spires may be the ruin of Rome and the salvation of Wittemberg. Let us close our ranks and be prepared for the onset."* It was settled that Ratisbon should be the point of rendezvous.

Prevailing over the jealousies that estranged the reigning houses of Bavaria and Austria, Campeggio contrived to assemble in that city, toward the end of 1524, the Duke of Bavaria and the Archduke Ferdinand. The Archbishop of Salzburg and the Bishops of Trent and of Ratisbon, joined them. The Bishops of Spires, Bamberg, Augsburg, Strasburg, Bale, Constance, Freesingen, Passau, and Brixen, sent deputies to the assembly.

The Legate opened the subject of the meeting, depicting in moving language the dangers resulting from the Reformation both to princes and the clergy, and concluded by calling upon them to extirpate heresy and rescue the Church.

For fifteen days the conferences were continued in the townhall of Ratisbon. At the expiration of that time, a ball, which continued till daybreak, served as a relaxation to the first Catholic assembly convened by the Papacy to resist the infant

* Winter, Gesch. der Evang. Lehre in Baiern, i. p. 156.

Reformation,[*]—and, after this, measures were agreed upon for the destruction of the heretics.

The Princes and Bishops bound themselves to enforce the edicts of Worms and Nuremberg—to allow of no innovations in public worship—to tolerate no married priest—to recall the students of their states who might be resident in Wittemberg, and to employ all the means in their power for the extirpation of heresy. They enjoined the preachers to take for their guides, in interpreting difficult scriptures, the Latin Fathers, Ambrose, Jerome, Augustine, and Gregory. Not daring, in the face of the Reformation, to invoke again the authority of the Schools, they contented themselves with laying the foundations of *Roman* orthodoxy.

But, not able to close their eyes against the scandals and profligate morals of the clergy,[†] they agreed on a programme of reform in which they studiously selected such grievances of the Germans as least involved or affected the court of Rome. They prohibited priests from dealings in the way of barter, from frequenting taverns, being present " at dances," and disputing over their bottle about points of faith !

This was the issue of the confederation of Ratisbon.[‡] In the very act of taking up arms against the Reformation, Rome yet conceded a something ;—and we discern in these regulations the earliest influence of the Reformation, in inducing an interior renovation in Catholicism itself. Wherever the Gospel develops its resources, its enemies are sure to have their counterfeits at hand. Emser had produced a translation of the Bible to counteract that by Luther. Eck, in like manner, put forth his *Loci Communes* in opposition to Melancthon's,[§] —and then it was that Rome began to oppose to the Reformation those partial changes which have given to Roman Catholicism its present aspect. But, in truth, these expedients were

---

* Ranke, Deutsche Gesch. ii. p. 159.

† Improbis clericorum abusibus et perditis moribus. (Cochl. p. 91.)

‡ Ut Lutheranæ factioni efficacius resistere possint, ultronea confoederatione sese constrixerunt. (Ibid.)

§ Enchiridion, seu loci communes contra hæreticos.

but subtle devices to escape impending dangers. Branches, plucked indeed from the tree of the Reformation, but set in a soil which doomed them to decay : the principle of *life* was wanting, and thus it will ever be with all similar attempts.

Another fact is here presented to us. The Romanist party, by the league which they formed at Ratisbon, were the first to violate the unity of Germany. It was in the Pope's camp that the signal of battle was given. Ratisbon was the birthplace of that schism and political rending of their country which so many of the Germans to this hour deplore. The national assembly of Spires was called to ensure the unity of the Empire by sanctioning and extending the Reformation of the Church. The conventicle of separatists that met at Ratisbon for ever divided the nation in two parties.* Yet the schemes of Campeggio were not at first attended with the results anticipated. But few of the chiefs responded to the call. The most decided opponents of Luther, Duke George of Saxony, the elector Joachim of Brandenburg, the ecclesiastical Electors, and the imperial cities, declined taking any part. An opinion prevailed that the Pope's legate was forming a Romanist faction opposed to the national mind. The popular sympathies counterbalanced the antipathies of religion ; and it was not long before the *Ratisbon Reformation* was an object of public ridicule. But a first step had been taken,—an example had been set. It was expected that, with a little pains, it would be easy eventually to confirm and enlarge this Roman league. Those who then hesitated would be decided by the course of events. To the legate, Campeggio, is ascribed the glory of having laid the train which was to bring little less than destruction upon the liberties of Germany, and the safety of the Empire, and the Reformation. From that hour the cause of Luther was no longer of a nature purely religious ; and the contest with the Wittemberg monk ranked among the political events of Europe. Luther in this new sphere, would pass under eclipse, and Charles V., the Pope, and the reigning Princes, would be the chief actors on the stage where

* Ranke Deutsche Gesch. ii. p. 163.

the grand drama of the sixteenth century was to be performed.

But the prospect of the assembly at Spires was continually present to the minds of the people. Its measures might remedy the mischiefs that Campeggio had occasioned at Ratisbon. Accordingly, Rome strained every nerve to prevent its assembling. "What!" exclaimed the Pope's deputies to Charles V., as also to his ally Henry VIII., and other princes, "will these presumptuous Germans pretend to decide points of faith in a national assembly! They seem to expect that kings, the imperial authority, all Christendom, and the whole world, are to bend to their decisions."

The moment was not ill chosen for influencing the Emperor. The war between that prince and Francis the First was at its height. Pescara and the Constable of Bourbon had left Italy, and entering France in the month of May, laid siege to Marseilles. The Pope, who looked with an evil eye on this attack, might effect a powerful diversion in the rear of the Imperial forces. Charles, who, under these circumstances, must have feared to give umbrage to his Holiness, did not hesitate to sacrifice the independence of the Empire, that he might purchase the favour of Rome, and humble his rival the king of France.

On the 15th July, Charles issued an edict, dated at Burgos in Castile, "in which he haughtily and angrily declared that to the Pope alone belonged the right to convoke a Council, and to the Emperor that of demanding one : that the meeting appointed to be held at Spires neither ought to be, nor could be allowed : that it was strange that the German people should undertake to do that, which all the nations of the earth, with the Pope at their head, could not lawfully do : and that it was necessary, without delay, to carry into effect the decree of Worms against the modern Mahomet."

Thus it was from Spain and Italy the blow was struck which arrested the development of the Gospel among the people of Germany. Charles was not satisfied with this. In 1519 he had offered to duke John, the Elector's brother, to give his sister, the Archduchess Catharine, in marriage to his son, John Frederic, heir to the electorate.   But was not that reigning house of Saxony the grand support of those principles of religious and political independence which Charles detested ? He decided to break off all intercourse with the troublesome and guilty champion of Gospel principles and the nation's wishes,—and accordingly gave his sister in marriage to John III. king of Portugal.   Frederic, who in 1519 had manifested some indifference to the overtures of the king of Spain, was enabled in 1524, to suppress his indignation at this conduct of the Emperor.   But Duke John haughtily intimated his feeling of the affront put upon him.

Thus, an observer might have distinguished, as they fell slowly into the line, the rival hosts by whose struggle for mastery the Empire was to be so long convulsed.

The Romanists went a step further.   The compact of Ratisbon was to be no empty form ; it was necessary that it should be sealed with blood.   Ferdinand and Campeggio descended the Danube from Ratisbon to Vienna, and, during their journey, mutually pledged themselves to cruel measures.   Instantly a persecution was set on foot in the Austrian provinces.

A citizen of Vienna, by name Gaspard Tauber, had circulated Luther's writings, and had himself written against the invocation of saints, purgatory, and transubstantiation.* Being thrown into prison, he was required by his judges, both divines and jurisconsults, to retract his errors.   It was believed that he had given way, and every preparation was made in Vienna to gratify the populace with the solemn spectacle of his recantation.   On St. Mary's day, two pulpits were erected over the cemetery of St. Stephen's, the one for the leader of the choir, whose office was to chaunt the heretic's repentance, the other for Tauber himself.   The formula of his recantation was put into his hands.†   The people, the choristers, and the priests were in silent expectation.   Whether it was that

---

* Atque etiam proprios ipse tractatus perscripserim. (Cochlæus, p. 92, verso.)

† See Cochl., Ib. Cum igitur ego Casparus Tauber, etc.

Tauber had given no promise to recant, or whether, in the appointed moment of abjuration, he suddenly received fresh energy of faith,—he exclaimed aloud, "*I am not convinced*, and I appeal to the holy Roman Empire." Ecclesiastics, choristers, and by-standers, were struck with astonishment and dismay. But Tauber continued calling for death rather than that he should deny the Gospel. He was beheaded,—his body burned :*—and his firmness left an indelible impression on the memory of the citizens of Vienna.

At Buda, in Hungary, a bookseller, named John, who had received the truth in the love of it, had distributed copies of the New Testament, and also some of Luther's writings. The persecutors bound him to a stake, and then forming a pile of his books, so as to enclose him within them, set fire to the whole. The poor man manifested an unshaken courage, rejoicing, amidst the flames, that he was counted worthy to suffer for his Lord's name. "Blood follows blood," cried Luther, when he heard of this martyrdom,† "but that innocent blood that Rome delights to shed, will one day choke the Pope, with his kings and their kingdoms.‡"

The zeal of the fanatics burnt every day more fiercely. Gospel preachers were expelled, magistrates banished, and sometimes the most horrible torments were inflicted. In Wurtemberg an inquisitor, named Reichler, caused the Lutherans, especially their preachers, to be hanged upon the trees. Monsters were found, who deliberately nailed by their tongues to the stake the ministers of God's word,—so that the sufferers, tearing themselves in their agony from the wood to which they were fastened, endured a frightful mutilation in their efforts to liberate themselves,—and were thus deprived of that

---

* Credo te vidisse Casparis Tauber historiam martyris novi Viennæ, quem cæsum capite scribunt et igne exustum pro verbo Dei. (Luther to Hausmann, 12 Nov. 1524, ii. p. 563.)

† Idem accidit Budæ in Ungaria bibliopolæ cuidam Johanni, simul cum libris circa eum positis exusto, fortissimeque passo pro Domino. (Ibid.)

‡ Sanguis sanguinem tangit, qui suffocabit papam cum regibus et regnis suis. (Ibid.)

gift of speech which they had long used in the preaching of the Gospel.*

The same persecutions were set on foot in the other states of the Catholic League. In the neighbourhood of Salzburg, a minister of the Gospel, who had been sentenced to imprisonment for life, was on his way to the prison; whilst the constables who had charge of him were stopping to drink at a house by the wayside, two country youths, moved with compassion, contrived, by eluding their vigilance, to favour the escape of the pastor. The rage of the Archbishop broke forth against these poor people, and without so much as any form of trial, he commanded that they should be beheaded. They were secretly taken outside the town, at an early hour. Coming to the plain where they were to die, the executioner's heart failed him:—" For," said he, " they have not been condemned." " Do your duty," said the Archbishop's emissary, sternly, " and leave to the Prince to answer for it:"—and the heads of the youths were immediately struck off.†

The persecution raged with most violence in the states of the Duke of Bavaria. Priests were degraded; nobles expelled from their castles; spies traversed the country; and suspicion and terror filled the hearts of all. Bernard Fichtel, a magistrate, was on his way to Nuremberg, called thither by the Duke's affairs; on the road, he was joined by Francis Bourkard, a professor, from Ingolstadt, and a friend of Eck. Bourkard accosted him, and they travelled in company. After supping together, the professor began to speak on matters of religion. Fichtel having some knowledge of his company, reminded him that the recent edict prohibited such topics of conversation. "Between us," answered Bourkard, "there is nothing to fear." On this Fichtel remarked, " I don't think the edict can be enforced;" and he went on to express himself in a tone of doubt respecting purgatory, observing, " that it was a dreadful thing to visit religious differences with death." At hearing this, Bourkard could not control him-

* Ranke, Deutsche Gesch. ii. p. 174.
† Zauner, Salzburger Chronik IV. p. 381.

self. " What more just," exclaimed he, " than to strike off
the heads of all those scoundrel Lutherans ?" He soon took a
kind leave of Fichtel ;—but hastened to lodge information
against him. Fichtel was thrown into prison, and the unhappy man, who had no desire of the martyr's crown—his
religious convictions not being at all deep—escaped death
only by a shameful recantation. Confidence was at an end;
and no one was safe.

But that death which Fichtel avoided, others met. It was
in vain that the Gospel was now only privately preached.[*]
The Duke urged on its pursuers; following it even in the
darkness, in secret places, in private dwellings, and mountain
recesses.

" The cross and persecution are in full career in Bavaria,"
said Luther: " those wild beasts are carrying all before
them."[†]

Even the north of Germany was not exempted from these
atrocities. Bogislas, Duke of Pomerania, dying, his son, who
had been brought up in the court of Duke George, set on
foot a persecution of the Gospel. Suaven and Knipstrow
were compelled to seek refuge in flight.

But it was in Holstein, that one of the most memorable instances of fanaticism occurred.

Henry Zuphten, who, as has been seen, had escaped from
the convent at Antwerp, was engaged in preaching the Gospel at Bremen. Nicholas Boye, pastor at Mehldorf, in the
country of the Dittmarches, and several devout persons of the
neighbouring districts, having invited him to come over and
declare Jesus Christ; he complied. Immediately, the prior
of the Dominicans and the vicar of the official of Hamburg
concerted measures. " If he is allowed to preach, and the
people give ear," said they, "we are undone." The prior
passed a disturbed night; and, rising early in the morning,
repaired to the wild and barren heath on which the forty-eight
regents of the country are accustomed to hold their meetings,

---

* Verbi non palam seminati. (L. Epp. ii. p. 559.)

† In Bavaria multum regnat crux et persecutio . . . . (Ibid.)

" The monk from Bremen is come amongst us," said he, addressing them, "and will bring ruin on the Dittmarches."
Those forty-eight simple-minded and unlearned men, deceived
into the belief that they would earn imperishable renown by
delivering the world from the heretical monk, decided on
putting him to death without so much as giving him a hearing.

It was Saturday—and the prior was bent on preventing
Henry's preaching on the following Sunday. In the middle
of the night he knocked at the door of the pastor Boye, armed
with the mandate of the forty-eight regents. " If it be the
will of God that I should die among the Dittmarches," said
Henry Zuphten ; " Heaven is as easily reached from thence
as from anywhere else.*   I will preach."

He ascended the pulpit, and spoke with earnestness. His
hearers, moved and roused by his christian eloquence, had
scarcely quitted the church, when the prior delivered to them
the mandate of the forty-eight regents forbidding the monk to
preach.   They immediately sent a deputation to the heath, and
the Dittmarches, after long discussion, agreed that, considering
their total ignorance, further measures should be deferred till
Easter.   But the prior, irritated at this, approached certain of
the regents, and stirred up their zeal afresh.   " We will write
to him," said they.   " Have nothing to do with him," replied
the prior ; " if he begins to speak, we shall not be able to
withstand him.   We must seize him during the night, and
burn him without giving him time to open his lips."

Every thing was arranged accordingly.   The day after
Conception day, at nightfall, *Ave Maria* was rung.   At the
signal, all the peasants of the adjacent villages assembled, to
the number of five hundred, and their leaders having broach-
ed three butts of Hamburg beer, by this means stimulated their
resolution.   The hour of midnight struck as the party entered
Mehldorf ; the peasants were under arms ; the monks carried
torches ; all went forward in disorder, exchanging shouts of
fury.   Arrived at the village, there was a deep silence lest

* Der Himmel wäre da so nahe als anderswo.   (L. Opp. xix. 330.)

Henry, receiving intimation of danger, should effect his escape.

Of a sudden, the gates of the parsonage were burst open—the drunken peasantry rushed within, striking everything in their way—tossing pell-mell, dishes, kettles, cups, and articles of apparel. They seized any money that they could find, and then rushing on the poor pastor, they struck him down, shouting " Kill him! kill him !" and then threw him into the mud. But Henry was their chief object in the attack. They pulled him out of bed, tied his hands behind him, and dragged him after them, naked as he was, in the piercing cold. " What are you come here for ?" cried they ; and as Henry answered meekly, they exclaimed, " Down with him! down with him! if we listen to him we shall become heretics like himself." They had dragged him naked over ice and snow, his feet were bleeding profusely, and he begged to be set on horseback. " A fine thing truly," said they, "for us to furnish horses for heretics! On, on"—and they continued dragging him behind them till they arrived at the heath. A woman, who stood at the door of the house just as the servant of God was passing, burst into tears. " My good woman," said Henry, " weep not for me." The bailiff pronounced his sentence. Then one of his ferocious escort, with a sword, smote the preacher of Jesus Christ on the head. Another struck him with a club. A monk was ordered to approach, and receive his confession. " My brother," said Henry, " have I done *you* any wrong ?" " None," replied the monk. " Then," returned Henry, " I have nothing to confess to you, and you have nothing to forgive." The monk retired in confusion. Many attempts were made to set fire to the pile; but the wood would not catch. For two hours the martyr stood thus in presence of the infuriated peasantry—calm, and lifting his eyes to heaven. While they were binding him, that they might cast him into the flame, he began to confess his faith. " First burn," said a countryman, dealing him a blow with his fist on the mouth; " burn ; and after that, speak." They threw him on the pile, but he rolled down on one side. John Holme, seizing a club, struck

him upon the breast, and laid him dead upon the burning
coals. "Such is the true story of the sufferings of that holy
martyr, Henry Zuphten."*

Whilst the Romanists were, on all sides, unsheathing the
sword against the Reformation, the work itself was passing
through new stages of development. Not to Zurich—nor
Geneva, but to Wittemberg, the focus of Luther's revival, must
we go to find the beginnings of that Reformed Church, of
which Calvin ranks as the most distinguished doctor. There
was a time when these two great families of believers slept in
the same cradle. Concord ought to have crowned their ma-
tured age; but when once the question of the Supper was
raised, Luther threw away the proper element of the Reformation, and took his stand for himself and his church in an
exclusive Lutheranism. The mortification he experienced
from this rival teaching was shown in his loss of much of that
kindness of manner which was so natural to him, and communicated in its stead a mistrust, an habitual dissatisfaction, and
an irritability which he had never before manifested.

It was between the two early friends—the two champions
who, at Leipsic, had fought side by side against Rome,—between Carlstadt and Luther that the controversy broke forth.
Their attachment to contrary views was the result, with each
of them, of a turn of mind that has its value. Indeed, there
are two extremes in religious views; the one tends to materialize all things; the other, to spiritualize every thing. The
former characterized Rome; the latter is seen in the Mystics.
Religion resembles man himself in this—namely, that it consists of a body and a soul; pure idealists, equally with mate-
rialists in questions of religion, as of philosophy—both err.

This was the great question which lay hid in the dispute
concerning the Supper. Whilst a superficial observer sees in
it nothing but a paltry strife about words, a deeper observation discerns in it one of the most important controversies that
can engage the mind of man.

* Das ist die wahre Historie, etc. (L. Opp. (L.) xix. p. 333.)

Here the Reformers diverge, and form two camps; but each camp carries away a portion of the truth. Luther, with his adherents, think they are resisting an exaggerated spiritualism. Carlstadt, and those of the reformed opinion, believe they are opposing a detestable materialism. Each turns against the error which, to his mind, seems most noxious, and in assailing it, goes—it may be—beyond the truth. But this being admitted, it is still true that both are right in the prevailing turn of their thoughts, and though ranking in different hosts, the two great teachers are nevertheless found under the same standard—that of Jesus Christ, who alone is TRUTH in the full import of that word.

Carlstadt was of opinion that nothing could be more prejudicial to genuine piety than to lean upon outward observances, and a sort of mysterious efficacy in the sacraments. "The outward participation in the Supper brings Salvation," had been the language of Rome; and that doctrine had sufficed to materialize religion. Carlstadt saw no better course for again exalting its spiritual character than to deny all presence of Christ's body; and he taught that the Supper was simply a pledge to believers of their redemption.

As to Luther, he now took an exactly opposite direction. He had at first contended for the sense we have endeavoured to open. In his tract on the Mass, published in 1520, he thus expressed himself:—"I can every day enjoy the advantages of the Sacraments, if I do but call to mind the word and promise of Christ, and with them feed and strengthen my faith." Neither Carlstadt, nor Zwingle, nor Calvin have said any thing more strong than this. It appears, indeed, that at that period the thought would often occur to him, that a symbolical explanation of the Supper would be the mightiest engine to overturn the Papal system; for, in 1525, we find him saying, that five years before, he had gone through much trial of mind on account of this doctrine;* and that any one who could then have proved to him that there is only the bread

---

* Ich habe wohl so harte Anfechtungen da erlitten. (L. Epp. ii. p. 577.)

and wine in the Supper would have done him the greatest
service.

But new circumstances arose, and threw him into a position in which he was led to oppose, and sometimes with much
heat, opinions to which he had made so near an approach.
The fanaticism of the Anabaptists may account for the turn
which Luther then took. These enthusiasts were not content
with disparaging what they termed the outward Word—that
is, the Bible, and setting up a claim to special communications of the Holy Spirit, they went so far as to despise the
Sacrament of the Supper as an external act, and to speak of
the inward as the only true communion. From that time, in
every attempt to exhibit the symbolical import of the Supper,
Luther saw only the danger of weakening the authority of
the Scriptures, and of admitting, instead of their true meaning, mere arbitrary allegories spiritualizing all religion, and
making it consist, not in the gifts of God, but in man's impressions; and, by this means, substituting, in place of genuine
Christianity, a mystic doctrine, or theosophy, or fanaticism
which would be sure to be its grave. It must be confessed,
that, but for the energetic resistance of Luther, this tendency to
mysticism (enthusiastic and subjective in its character,) might
have rapidly extended itself, and turned back the tide of blessings which the Reformation was to pour upon the world.

Carlstadt, impatient at finding himself hindered from opening his views without reserve in Wittemberg; and having no
rest in his spirit, from his desire to combat a system which, in
his view, "lowered the value of Christ's death, and set aside
his righteousness," resolved "to give a public testimony for
the advantage of poor deluded Christians." He left Wittemberg, in the beginning of the year 1524, without previous intimation of his intention to the university or the chapter, and
repaired to the small town of Orlamund, the church of which
was placed under his superintendence. Dismissing the vicar,
he procured himself to be appointed its pastor, and in opposition to the wishes of the chapter, of the university, and of the
Elector, established himself in his new office.

He soon began to disseminate his doctrines : " It is not possible," said he, " to name any advantage derived from the *real presence*, which does not already flow from faith—it is, therefore, useless." To explain Christ's words in the institution of the Supper, he resorted to an interpretation which is not received in the Reformed churches. Luther, during the discussion at Leipsic, had explained the words—" *Thou art Peter, and on this rock I will build my church*"—separating the two propositions, and applying the latter to the person of the Saviour. " Just so," said Carlstadt, " ' *take eat*' was spoken in reference to the bread ; but ' *this is my body*' is to be understood of Jesus Christ, who then pointed to himself,—and intimated by the symbol of the broken bread, that that body was about to be broken."

Carlstadt did not stop there. Scarce had he emancipated himself from Luther's oversight, when he felt his zeal revive against the use of images. His bold addresses and enthusiastic appeals were but too likely to madden the minds of men in these agitated times. The people, thinking they heard a second Elijah, proceeded to throw down the idols of Baal. The excitement soon spread to the neighbouring villages. The Elector interfered ; but the peasants answered that it was right to obey God rather than men. On this, the Prince decided to despatch Luther to Orlamund, to restore tranquillity. Luther looked upon Carlstadt as a man urged on by a love of notoriety ;* a fanatic who would even go the length of raising war against Christ himself. Perhaps Frederic might have made a wiser choice. Luther, however, set forth ; and Carlstadt saw his troublesome rival once more appear in order to baffle his projects of reform and arrest his impetuosity.

Jena lay in the road to Orlamund. Arriving in that town on the 23rd August, Luther ascended the pulpit on the 24th, at seven in the morning. He preached an hour and a half to a numerous auditory against fanatics, rebels, the breakers of images, and the despisers of the real presence, protesting with

* Huc perpulit eum insana gloriæ et laudis libido. (L. Epp. ii. p. 551.)

ehemence against the innovations at Orlamund. He did not refer to Carlstadt by name, but every one understood whom he had in his eye.

Either by accident or design, Carlstadt was then at Jena, and among the crowd of Luther's hearers. He lost no time in calling the preacher to account. Luther was at dinner with the prior of Wittemberg, the burgomaster, the secretary, the pastor of Jena, and several officers in the service of the Emperor and of the Margrave, when a letter was handed to him from Carlstadt, requesting an interview. He passed it to those near him, and returned a message by the bearer : " If Doctor Carlstadt wishes to see me, let him come in ;—if not, I have no wish to see him." Carlstadt entered. His appearance produced a lively sensation in the whole assembly. The majority, eager to see the two lions encounter one another, suspended their repast, and were all eyes, while the more timid turned pale with apprehension.

Carlstadt, at Luther's invitation, took a seat opposite to him, and then said, " Doctor, you have in your sermon of this day classed me with those who inculcate revolt and assassination. I declare that such a charge is false."

LUTHER.—" I did not name you ; but since the cap fits, you may wear it."

A momentary pause ensued.—Carlstadt resumed : " I am prepared to show that in the doctrine of the sacrament you have contradicted yourself, and that from the days of the apostles, no one has preached that doctrine so purely as I have done."

LUTHER.—" Write then—establish your point."

CARLSTADT.—" I offer you a public discussion at Wittemberg or at Erfurth, if you promise me a safe-conduct."

LUTHER.—" Never fear, Doctor !"

CARLSTADT.—" You bind me hand and foot, and when you have deprived me of the power to defend myself, you strike."*

Silence ensued.—Luther resumed :—

* Ihr bandet mir Hände et Füsse, darnach schlugt Ihr mich. (L. Opp. xix. p. 150.

" Write against me—but openly—and not in secret."

CARLSTADT.—" If I were but assured you were in earnest in what you say, I would do so."

LUTHER.—" Set about it ;—here—take this florin."

CARLSTADT.—" Where is it ?   I accept the challenge."

At these words, Luther thrust his hand in his pocket, and producing a gold florin, said, as he gave it to Carlstadt, " Take it, and attack me like a man."

Carlstadt, holding the gold florin in his hand, and turning to the assembly, said, " Dear brethren, this is to me *arabo*, a pledge that I have authority to write against Luther ; I call you all to witness this."

Then bending the florin, that he might know it again, he put it into his purse, and held out his hand to Luther.   The latter pledged him.   Carlstadt returned his civility.   " The more vigorous your attacks, the better I shall like them," resumed Luther.

" If I fail," answered Carlstadt, " the fault will be mine."

They once more shook each other by the hand, and Carlstadt returned to his lodging.

Thus, says an historian, as from a single spark a fire often originates which consumes in its progress the vast forest, so, from this small beginning, a great division in the Church took its rise.*

Luther set forward for Orlamund, and arrived there but in differently prepared by the scene at Jena.   He assembled the council and the church, and said, " Neither the Elector nor the University will acknowledge Carlstadt as your pastor."— " If Carlstadt is not our pastor," replied the treasurer of the town-council, " why then, St. Paul is a false teacher, and your writings are mere falsehood,—for *we* have chosen him."†

---

* Sicut una scintilla sæpe totam sylvam comburit. (M. Adam, Vit. Carlst. p. 83.)   Our account is chiefly derived from the *Acts of Rein-hard*, pastor of Jena, an eye-witness,—but a friend of Carlstadt,—and taxed with inaccuracy by Luther.

† How remarkable is this incident !   On this passage the translator had made a note which he will here insert for the confirmation of those who, though only ' two or three' in any one place, are acting in con-

As he said this, Carlstadt entered the room. Some of those who happened to be next to Luther, made signs to him to be seated, but Carlstadt, going straight up to Luther, said, " Dear Doctor, if you will allow me, I will give you induction."

LUTHER.—" You are my antagonist. I have fixed you by the pledge of a florin."

CARLSTADT.—" I will be your antagonist so long as you are opposed to God and his truth."

LUTHER.—" Leave the room; I cannot allow of your being present."

CARLSTADT.—" This is an open meeting,—if your cause is good, why fear me ?"

LUTHER, to his attendant :—" Go,—put the horses to : I

fidence in the sufficiency of 'God and the word of His grace' to 'build them up.'

If the conference had been really carried on in the reverential sense of the presence of the Spirit, (Acts i. 24, Eph. ii. 22.) it might have been asked, and so have come down to us, on what passage in St. Paul these persons grounded their choosing of their pastor.

But would not the recognition of His *presence* have led to the acknowledgment of His 'dividing' gifts to the mutually dependant members, (1 Cor. xii. 25. xiv. 31.) 'according to His own will'? (1 Cor. xii. 11.) and so have prevented the assertion of a right on their part to elect,—much less to elect to *exclusive* pastorship ?

Luther was a brother, and one not meanly gifted for service to the body ;—might it not have been expected that Carlstadt, calling to mind Romans xii. and 1 Cor. xiv. 3, 31, would have welcomed the word of Luther in the little church of Orlamünd,—and that that word would have been just the very corrective, or rather *complement*, needed by the peculiarity of Carlstadt's teaching,—for as M. D'Aubigné has observed, the turn of mind of *each* had its value.

Instead of this, we find the Great Reformer saying, " The Elector and the University will not acknowledge Carlstadt as your pastor;" and the church of Orlamünd replying. " *We* have chosen him ;"— the two forms of disobedient *limiting* of the teaching of the Spirit, with which Christians have become so familiar,—and which, in their want of faith, almost all are helping to perpetuate.

See the reflections at the opening of the XIth Book of this history. The heart that is exercised by these things should consider John xiv. 16, 26 ; xvi. 7 ; xvii. 21 ; Acts v. 3 ; Rom. viii. 9 ; 1 Cor. xi. 2 ; xiv. 37 ; Eph. iv. 16 ; 1 Th. iv. 18 ; v. 11 ; Heb. iii. 13.

have nothing to say here to Carlstadt; and since he will not leave, I shall go."*   Luther rose from his seat, upon which Carlstadt withdrew.

After a moment's silence, Luther resumed :—" Only prove from the Scripture that it is our duty to destroy images."

ONE OF THE TOWN COUNCIL.—" Doctor, you will allow, I suppose, that Moses was acquainted with God's commandments."   This said, he opened his Bible.   " Well, here are his words,—' *Thou shalt not make to thyself any graven image, nor any likeness,*' " &c.

LUTHER.—" The passage refers only to images for idolatrous worship.   If I hang up, in my chamber, a crucifix, and do not worship it; what harm can it do me ?"

A SHOEMAKER.—" I have often touched my hat before an image which was in my room, or on my mantlepiece.   It is an act of idolatry which robs God of the glory due to Him alone."

LUTHER.—" Would you think it necessary, then, because they are abused, to put your women to death, and pour your wine into the gutter."†

ANOTHER MEMBER OF THE CHURCH.—" No: they are God's creatures, which we are not commanded to destroy."

The conference had lasted some time.   Luther and his attendant returned to their carriage, astonished at the scene they had witnessed, and having failed to convince the inhabitants, who claimed for themselves the right of interpreting and freely expounding the Scripture.   Agitation reigned in Orlamund. The people insulted Luther ; and some even called after him, —" Begone ! in the name of all the devils ; and may you break your neck before you are out of our town."‡   Never had the Reformer had to undergo such contemptuous treatment.

* Spann an, spann an.   (L. Opp. xix. p. 154.)
† So muss du des Missbrauchs halber auch.   (Ibid. p. 155.)
‡ Two of the most distinguished living historians of Germany add, that Luther was pelted by the inhabitants; but Luther tells us the contrary :—" Dass ich nit mit Steinen und Dreck ausgeworffen ward." (L. Epp. ii. p. 579.)

He repaired thence to Kale, the pastor of which place had also embraced the views of Carlstadt. He resolved to preach a sermon there; but on entering the pulpit, he found the broken fragments of a crucifix. At first his emotion overcame him; but recovering himself, he gathered up the pieces into one corner of the pulpit, and delivered a discourse in which he made no allusion to the circumstance. "I determined," said he, speaking of it in after life, "to revenge myself on the devil by this *contempt for him.*"

The nearer the Elector's life drew to a close, the more did he appear to dread lest men should go too far in the work of Reformation. He issued orders to deprive Carlstadt of his appointments, and banished him, not only from Orlamund, but from the states of the Electorate. It was in vain that the Church of Orlamund interceded in his behalf,—in vain did they petition that he might be permitted to reside among them as a private citizen, with leave occasionally to preach,—in vain did they represent that the word of God was dearer to them than the whole world, or even a thousand worlds.* Frederic was deaf to their entreaties, and he even went the length of refusing the unhappy Carlstadt the funds necessarily required for his journey. Luther had nothing to do with this sternness on the part of the Prince: it was foreign to his disposition,—and this he afterwards proved. But Carlstadt looked at him as the author of his disgrace, and filled Germany with his complaints and lamentations. He wrote a farewell letter to his friends at Orlamund. The bells were tolled, and the letter read in presence of the sorrowing Church.† It was signed—"Andrew Bodenstein, expelled by Luther, unconvicted, and without even a hearing."

It is impossible not to feel a pain at contemplating these two men, once friends, and both worthy of our esteem, thus angrily opposed. Sadness took possession of the souls of the disciples of the Reformation. What would be the end of it,

---

* Hoher als tausend Welten. (Seck. p. 628.)

† Quæ publice vocatis per campanas lectæ sunt omnibus simul flentibus. (L. Epp. ii. 558.)

when thus its bravest defenders turned one against another? Luther could discern these fears, and endeavoured to allay them. "Let us contend," said he, "as those who fight for another. It is God's cause :* the *care* of it belongs to God,—the work, the victory, and the glory, all are His. He will fight for it, and prevail, though we should stand still. Whatever He decrees should fall, let it fall,—whatever He wills should stand, let that stand. It is no cause of our own that is at stake; and we seek not our own glory."

Carlstadt sought refuge at Strasburg, where he published several writings. "He was well acquainted," says Doctor Scheur, "with Latin, Greek, and Hebrew;" and Luther acknowledged him to be his superior in learning. Endowed with great powers of mind, he sacrificed to his convictions fame, station, country, and even his bread. At a later period of his life he visited Switzerland. There, it might seem, he ought to have commenced his teaching. The independence of his spirit needed the free air breathed by the Œcolampadiuses and Zwingles. His instructions soon attracted an attention nearly equal to that which had been excited by the earliest theses put forth by Luther. Switzerland seemed almost gained over to his doctrine. Bucer and Capito also appeared to adopt his views.

Then it was that Luther's indignation rose to its height; and he put forth one of the most powerful but also most outrageous of his controversial writings,—his book "*Against the Celestial Prophets.*"

Thus the Reformation, hunted down by the Pope, the Emperor, and the Princes, began to tear its own vitals. It seemed to be sinking under accumulated evils; and surely it would have been lost if it had been a work of man. soon from the very brink of ruin it rose again in renewed energy.

The Catholic League of Ratisbon, and the persecutions that followed close upon it, created a powerful popular re-action. The Germans were not disposed to surrender that word of

* Causa Dei est, cura Dei est, opus Dei est, victoria Dei est, gloria Dei est, (L. Epp. ii. p. 556.)

God of which they had recovered possession; and when orders to that effect came to them from Charles V., though backed by papal bulls and the faggots of Ferdinand, and other Catholic Princes, they returned for an answer,—" We will not give it up."

No sooner had the members of the League taken their departure from Ratisbon, when the deputies of the towns whose bishops had taken part in that alliance, surprised and indignant, assembled at Spires, and passed a law, that, notwithstanding the episcopal prohibitions, their preachers should confine themselves to the proclamation of the Gospel, and the Gospel only, according to the doctrine of the apostles and prophets. They proceeded to prepare a report, couched in firm and consistent terms, to be presented to the assembly of their nation.

The Emperor's letter, dated from Burgos, came unseasonably to disturb their plans. Nevertheless, toward the close of that year, the deputies of the towns and many nobles assembling at Ulm, bound themselves by solemn oath to assist one another, in case of an attack.

Thus the free cities opposed to the camp that had been formed by Austria, Bavaria, and the bishops, another, in which the standard of the Gospel and of the national liberties was unfurled.

Whilst the cities were placing themselves in the van of the Reformation, several princes were, about the same time, gained over to its ranks. In the beginning of June, 1524, Melancthon was returning, on horseback, from a visit to his mother, in company with Camerarius and some other friends, when, approaching Frankfort, he met a brilliant retinue ;—it was Philip, Landgrave of Hesse, who, three years previously, had visited Luther at Worms, and who now on his way to the games of Heidelberg, where most of the princes of Germany were expected to be present.

Thus did Providence bring Philip successively in contact with the two leading Reformers. It was known that the celebrated Doctor was gone on a journey to his birth-place. One of the horsemen who accompanied the Landgrave remarked,

——"It is Melancthon, I think." Immediately the young Prince put spurs to his horse, and coming up with the Doctor, enquired,—"Is your name Philip?" "It is," replied he, drawing back timidly, and preparing respectfully to alight.[*] "Keep your saddle," said the Prince, "turn your horse's head, and come stay one night with me; there are some things I want to speak with you about. Fear nothing." "What can I fear from a prince like yourself!" rejoined the Doctor. "Ah, ah!" said the Landgrave, laughing, "if I were only to carry you off, and hand you over to Campeggio, he would not be a little pleased, I suspect." The two Philips rode onward, side by side,—the Prince asking questions and the Doctor answering; and the Landgrave delighted with the clear and impressive views that were opened before him. At length, Melancthon entreating him to permit him to continue his journey, Philip reluctantly parted with him. "On one condition," said he, "and that is, that, on your return home, you should treat fully the questions we have discussed,[†] and send me your thoughts in writing." Melancthon promised. "Go, then," said Philip, "and pass freely through my states."

Melancthon, with his accustomed talent, prepared an *Abridgment of the Reformed Doctrine of Christianity*;[‡] and this tract, remarkable for its conciseness and force of argument, made a decided impression upon the mind of the Landgrave. Shortly after his return from the Heidelberg games, this Prince issued an edict, in which, without connecting himself with the free towns, he opposed the League of Ratisbon, and directed that the Gospel should be preached in all its purity. He embraced it himself, with the energy that marked his character. "Rather," exclaimed he, "would I sacrifice my body, my life, my estates, and my subjects, than the word of God!" A Franciscan friar, named Ferber, perceiving this inclination of the Prince in favour of the Refor-

---

* Honoris causa de equo descensurus. (Camerarius, p. 94.)

† Ut de quæstionibus quas audiisset moveri, aliquid diligenter conscriptum curaret. (Ibid.)

‡ Epitome renovatæ ecclesiasticæ doctrinæ.

mation, wrote him a letter filled with reproaches and entreaties to continue faithful to Rome. "I am resolved," answered Philip, "to be faithful to the ancient doctrine,—but as I find it set forth in the Scriptures:" and he proceeded to prove, with much clearness of statement, that man is justified by faith alone. The monk, confounded, made no reply.* The Landgrave was commonly spoken of as "the disciple of Melancthon."†

Other Princes followed the same course. The Elector Palatine refused to countenance the slightest persecution; the Duke of Luneburg, nephew of the Elector of Saxony, began the Reformation in his dominions; and the King of Denmark gave orders that, throughout Sleswick and Holstein, every one should be at liberty to worship God according as his conscience dictated.

The Reformation gained a victory yet more important. A Prince, whose conversion to Gospel truth involved consequences most momentous to our own times, now evinced a disposition to withdraw from Rome. One day, towards the end of June, shortly after the return of Melancthon to Wittemberg, Albert, Margrave of Brandenburg, and Grand Master of the Teutonic Order, entered Luther's apartment. This chief of the monastic knights of Germany, who then governed Prussia, had repaired to the Diet of Nuremberg, to invoke the aid of the Empire against Poland. He returned broken in spirit. On one hand, Osiander's preaching, and the reading of the New Testament, had convinced him that his monk's vow was contrary to the word of God; on the other, the suppression of the national government in Germany had deprived him of all hope of obtaining the assistance which he had come to solicit. What was to be done . . . . ? The Saxon councillor, De Planitz, in whose company he had left Nuremberg, proposed to him to seek an interview with the Reformer. "What think you," said the anxious and agitated Prince to Luther, "of the rule of our order?" Luther did not hesitate; he saw

* Seckendorf, p. 738.
† Princeps ille discipulus Philippi fuit a quibusdam appellatus. (Camer. p. 95.)

that a course of conduct in conformity with the Gospel was, also, the only means of saving Prussia. "Look to God for assistance," said he, to the Grand Master, "and reject the senseless and inconsistent rule of your order; put an end to your detestable hermaphrodite principality, neither religious nor secular;* away with mere pretended chastity, and seek that which is the true. Take a wife—and become the founder of a legitimate empire, in the place of that anomalous monster."† These words set clearly before the mind of the Grand Master a state of things which he had as yet seen but indistinctly. A smile lighted up his countenance; but he was too prudent to give utterance to his thoughts.‡ Melancthon, who was present, spoke to the same effect as Luther, and the Prince set out to return to his dominions, leaving the Reformers in the confident hope that the seed which they had sown would sink down into his heart, and one day bring forth fruit.

Thus, as we have seen, Charles the Fifth and the Pope had opposed the national assembly at Spires, fearing lest the Word of God should win over all present; but the Word of God was not bound. It was denied a hearing in a hall of a town of the Lower Palatinate. But what then?—it burst forth and spread throughout the provinces, stirring the hearts of the people, enlightening the Princes and developing that Divine power of which neither Bulls nor Ordinances can ever divest it.

Whilst nations and their rulers were thus coming to the light, the Reformers were endeavouring to remould every thing by the infusion of the true principles of Christianity Public worship first engaged their attention. The moment, anticipated by the Reformer, when returning from the Wartburg, had arrived: "Now," said he, "that hearts have been fortified by Divine Grace, we must put away those things which defile the Lord's kingdom, and attempt to do something in the Name of Jesus." He required that the communion should be

* Ut loco illius abominabilis principatus, qui hermaphrodita quidam. (L. Epp. ii. p. 527.)
† Ut contempta ista stulta confusaque regula, uxorem duceret. (Ibid.)
‡ Ille tum arrisit, sed nihil respondit. (Ibid.)

taken under both kinds ; that the Supper should be cleared of every thing which gave to it the character of a sacrifice ;[*] that Christians should never assemble themselves together without having the word of God preached to them ;[†] that the flock, or at least the priests and students, should meet every morning at four or five o'clock, to read the Old Testament, and every evening at five or six o'clock, to read the New Testament ; that on Sundays the whole church should meet together, morning and afternoon, and that the great object of the services should be to sound abroad the Word of God.[‡]

The church of All Saints, at Wittemberg, especially called forth his indignation. In it, (to quote the words of Seckendorf,) 9,901 masses were annually celebrated, and 35,570 lbs. of wax annually consumed. Luther called it " the sacrilege of Tophet." " There are," said he, "only three or four lazy monks who still worship this shameful Mammon ; and if I had not restrained the people, this abode of all Saints, or rather of all Devils, would have been brought down with a crash such as the world has never yet heard."

It was in connection with this church that the conflict began. It resembled those ancient sanctuaries of heathen worship in Egypt, Gaul, and Germany, which were ordained to fall, that Christianity might be established in their place.

Luther, earnestly desiring that the mass should be abolished in this cathedral, addressed to the chapter on the 1st March, 1523, a requisition to that effect, following it up by a second letter dated the 11th July.[§] The canons having pleaded the Elector's orders,—" What, in this case, have we to do with the prince's orders?" remarked Luther : " he is but a secular prince ; his business is to bear the sword, and not to interfere in the ministry of the Gospel."[‖] Luther here clearly marks

* Weise christliche Messe zu halten. (L. Opp. (L.) xxii. p. 232.)

† Die christliche Gemeine nimmer soll zusammen kommen, es werde lenn daselbst Gottes Wort geprediget. (L. Opp. xxii. 226.)

‡ Dass das Wort im Schwange gehe. (Ibid.)

§ L. Epp. ii. p. 303, and 854.

‖ Welchem gebührt das Schwerd, nicht das Predigtamt zu versorgen. (L. Opp. xviii. p. 497.)

16*

the distinction between the State and the Church. "There is," said he again, "but one sacrifice to put away sins,—Christ, who has offered himself *once for all;* and we are partakers thereof, not by any works or sacrifices of ours,—but solely through belief of the word of God."

The Elector, feeling his end approaching, was averse from further change.

But entreaties from other quarters came in aid of those of Luther. "It is high time to act," wrote the cathedral provost, Jonas, to the Elector: "such a shining forth of Gospel truth, as that which we have at this hour, does not ordinarily last longer than a sunbeam. Let us then lose no time."*

This letter of Jonas, not having changed the Elector's views, Luther became impatient; he judged that the time had come to strike the final blow, and he addressed a letter of menace to the chapter. "I beg of you, as a friend;—I desire and seriously urge it upon you to put an end to this sectarian worship. If you refuse to do so, you shall, God helping, receive the punishment which you will have deserved. I say this for your guidance, and I request an immediate reply—yes, or no—before Sunday next, in order that I may consider what I have to do. God give you grace to follow His light.†

MARTIN LUTHER.

"Thursday, Dec 8th, 1524."   "Preacher at Wittemberg."

At this juncture the rector, two burgomasters, and ten councillors, waited upon the Dean, and begged him, in the name of the university, of the council, and of the commune of Wittemberg, "to abolish the great and horrible impiety committed against the majesty of God, in the celebration of mass."

The chapter found it necessary to give way, and declared that, enlightened by the word of God,‡ they acknowledged the abuses which had been denounced, and published a new

---

* Corp. Ref. i. p. 636.
† L. Epp. ii. p. 565.
‡ Durch das Licht des heiligen göttlichen Wortes. . . . . (L. Opp. xviii. p. 502.)

order of service, which began to be observed on Christmas Day, 1524.

Thus fell the Mass, in this renowned sanctuary, where it had so long held out against the reiterated attacks of the Reformers. The Elector Frederic, suffering from gout, and drawing near his end, could not, by any efforts of his, retard this great triumph of the Reformation. He saw in it the will of God, and submitted to it. The cessation of Romish observances, in the church of All Saints, hastened their abolition in many of the churches of Christendom. In all quarters there was similar resistance, but also the like victory. Vainly did priests, and even princes in many places, try to interpose obstacles; they could effect nothing.

It was not alone in public worship that the Reformation was ordained to work a change. Education was very early associated with the Reformed Church, and these two institutions, in their power to regenerate mankind, were alike invigorated by its influence. It was in intimate alliance with letters that the Reformation had made its appearance in the world; and, in the hour of its triumph, it did not forget its ally.

Christianity is not a mere expansion of Judaism; its great end is not again to envelop man, as the Papacy seeks to do, in the swaddling bands of outward ordinances and man's teaching. Christianity is a new creation; it takes possession of the inward man, and transforms him in the innermost principles of his nature; so that he needeth not human teaching, but, by God's help, is able, of himself, and by himself, to discern that which is true, and to do that which is right."*

To bring man to that maturity which Christ has purchased for him, and to emancipate him from the tutelage in which Rome had so long held him bound, the Reformation must needs develop the whole man; and, while by the Word of God it regenerated his heart and will, it enlightened his understanding by the study of sacred and profane literature.

Luther understood this; he felt that to consolidate the Reformation, he must work on the minds of the rising genera-

* Heb. chap. viii. 11.

tion, remodel the schools, and propagate throughout Christendom the knowledge necessary for a deep study of the Holy Scriptures. This, therefore, was one of the objects of his life. He was especially impressed with this conviction, at this period of his history, and, accordingly, he addressed a letter to the councillors of all the towns in Germany, urging them to found Christian schools. " Dear sirs," said he, " so much money is annually expended in arquebuses, making roads, and constructing dykes,—how is it that a little is not expended in paying one or two schoolmasters to instruct our poor children? God stands at the door, and knocks; blessed are we if we open to Him! Now-a-days, there is no famine of God's word. My dear countrymen, buy, buy, whilst the market is opened before your dwellings. The Word of God and His grace resembles a shower which falls and passes on. It fell among the Jews; but it passed away, and now they have it no longer. Paul bore it with him to Greece; but there also it is passed, and Mahometanism prevails in its place. It came to Rome and the Latin territories; but from thence it likewise departed, and now Rome has the Pope.* O! Germans, think not that you will never have that Word taken away from you. The little value you put upon it will cause it to be withdrawn. Therefore, he who would have it, must lay hold upon and keep it.

"Let our youth be the objects of your care," he continued, addressing the magistrates, "for many parents are like the ostrich, their hearts are hardened against their young, and, satisfied with having laid the egg, they give themselves no further trouble about it. The prosperity of a town does not consist in amassing wealth, erecting walls, building mansions, and the possession of arms. If attacked by a party of madmen, its ruin and devastation would only be the more terrible. The true well-being of a town, its security, its strength, is to number within it many learned, serious, kind, and well-educated citizens. And who is to blame that there are found, in our days, so few of this stamp, but you, magistrates, who have suffered our youth to grow up like the neglected growth of the forest?"

* Aber hin ist hin; sie haben nun den Papst. (L. Opp. W. x. 535.)

Luther especially insisted on the necessity for the study of literature and languages : " We are asked," says he, " what is the use of learning Latin, Greek, and Hebrew, when we can read the Bible in German ?   But, for the languages," he replied, " we should never have received the Gospel . . Languages are the scabbard in which the sword of the Spirit* is found ; they are the casket which holds the jewels ; they are the vessels which contain the new wine ; they are the baskets in which are kept the loaves and fishes which are to feed the multitude.   If we cease to study languages, we shall not only lose the Gospel, but, eventually, we shall be unable either to speak or write in Latin or in German.   From the hour we throw them aside, Christianity may date its decline, even to falling again under the dominion of the Pope.   But now that languages are once more held in estimation, they diffuse such light that all mankind are astonished—and that every one may see that the Gospel we preach is almost as pure as that of the Apostles themselves.   The holy Fathers of other days, made many mistakes by reason of their ignorance of languages ; in our time, some, like the Vaudois of Piedmont, do not attach value to the study of them ; but though their doctrine may be sound, they often fail of the real meaning of the Sacred Text ; they are without a safeguard against error, and I much fear that their faith will not continue pure.†   If a knowledge of languages had not given me the certainty of the true sense of the Word, I might have been a pious monk, quietly preaching the Truth in the obscurity of the cloister; but I should have left Pope, sophists, and their anti-christian power in the ascendant."‡

But Luther's attention was not limited to the education of ecclesiastics ;—he was desirous that learning should no longer be confined to the Church alone ; and proposed to extend it to

* Die Sprachen sind die Scheide, darinnen dies Messer des Geistes stecket. (L. Opp. W. x. p. 535.)

† Es sey oder werde nicht lauter bleiben. (L. Opp. W. x. p. 535.)

‡ Ich hätte wohl auch können fromm seyn und in der Stille rechte predigen. (Ibid)

the laity, who had hitherto been debarred from it.   He sug
gested the establishment of libraries, not limited merely to
works and commentaries of scholastic divines and Fathers of
the Church, but furnished with the productions of orators and
poets, even though heathens, as also with books of literature,
law, medicine, and history.   "Such writings," said he, "are
of use to make known the wonderful works of God."

This effort of Luther is one of the most important the Reformation produced.   It wrested learning from the hands of
the priests, who had monopolised it, like those of Egypt in ancient times,—and rendered it accessible to all.   From this impulse, derived from the Reformation, some of the greatest developments of later ages have proceeded.   Literary men, and
scholars of the laity, who now-a-days decry the Reformation,
forget that they are themselves its offspring ; and that, but for
its influence, they would at this hour be like half-educated children, subject to the tyrannical authority of the clergy.   The
Reformation recognised the intimate connection of all branches
of learning, receiving all to learn, and opening all the avenues
to learning.   "They who despise general literature," said
Melancthon, "make no more account of sacred theology.
Their affected contempt is but a pretext to conceal their indo
lence."*

The Reformation not only communicated a mighty impulse
to literature, but served to elevate the Arts, although Protestantism has often been reproached as their enemy.   Many
Protestants have willingly taken up and borne this reproach.
We will not examine whether or not the Reformation ought
to glory in it; but will merely remark, that impartial history
does not confirm the premises on which the clergy rests.   Let
Roman Catholicism pride itself in being more favourable than
Protestantism to the arts.   Be it so : Paganism was even more
so; while Protestantism hath somewhat else to glory in.
There are some religions in which the disposition in man to a
taste for the fine arts has a place assigned it above that given
to his moral nature.   Christianity is distinguished from these

    * Hunc titulum ignaviæ suæ prætextunt.   (Corp. Ref. i. p. 613.)

by the fact that the moral element is its essence. Christian principle manifests itself, not in productions of the fine arts, but in the fruits of a Christian life. Every sect that forgets this bearing of Christianity upon morals, forfeits its claim to the name of Christian. Rome has not entirely renounced this essential characteristic, but Protestantism cherishes it in far greater purity. It takes pleasure in deep acquaintance with morals, discriminating religious actions not by their outward appearance and effect upon the imagination, but according to their inherent worth, and their bearing upon the conscience; so that, if the Papacy is strongly marked as an esthetic system, as has been proved by an able writer,* Protestantism is equally characterised as a moral sytem.

Nevertheless, the Reformation, while primarily appealing to the moral sense, addressed the whole man. We have seen how it spoke to his understanding, and what it did for literature: it spoke also to his *sensibility* and *imagination*, and thereby contributed to the development of the Arts. The Church was no longer composed exclusively of priests and friars; it was the assembly of the faithful; all were to take part in the worship; and congregational singing was to take the place of the priests' chaunting. Luther, in translating the Psalms, had in view their adaptation to be sung in the churches. Thus a taste for Music was disseminated throughout the nation.

" Next to theology," said Luther, " it is to *Music* that I give the highest place and the greatest honour.† A schoolmaster," he added, " ought to know how to sing; without this qualification I would have nothing to do with him."

One day, when some fine music was performing, ne exclaimed in transport, " If our Lord God has shed forth such wondrous gifts on this earth, which is no better than a dark nook, what may we not expect in that eternal life in which we shall be perfected." From the days of Luther, the con-

* Chateaubriand, Genie du Christianisme.
† Ich gebe nach der Theologie, der Musica den nähesten Locum und höchste Ehre. (L. Opp. W. xxii. p. 2253.)

gregated worshippers have taken part in the singing; the
Bible has been the great theme of their songs, and the impulse
communicated at that period of the Reformation, has more recently produced those noble Oratorios, which have carried the
art to its highest point of attainment.

Poetry participated in the movement. In singing the praises
of God, Christians were not willing to restrict themselves to
simple renderings of ancient hymns. The souls of Luther
and his contemporaries, elevated by faith to the most sublime
contemplations, roused to enthusiasm by the dangers and
struggles which incessantly threatened the infant Church, inspired by the poetry of the Old, and the hope of the New
Testament, soon began to pour out their feelings in religious
songs, in which poetry and music joined, and blended their
most heavenly accents ; and thus were heard reviving, in the
sixteenth century, the hymns which, in the first century
soothed the sufferings of the martyrs. In 1523, Luther, as
we have already said, consecrated it to commemorate the martyrs of Brussels; others of the children of the Reformation
followed his example. Many were the hymns composed, and
rapidly circulated among the people, and greatly did they
contribute to arouse their slumbering minds. It was in this
same year Hans Sach composed the " *Nightingale of Wittemberg.*" It represented the teaching that had been current
in the Church for four centuries as a moonlight time of wandering in the deserts. But the nightingale proclaimed the
dawn, and soaring above the morning mist, sang the praise
of day.

Whilst lyric poesy was thus deriving from the Reformation its loftiest inspiration, satirical verses and dramas, from
the pen of Hütten, Murner, and Manuel were attacking the
most flagrant corruptions.

It is to the Reformation that the great poets of England,
Germany, and perhaps of France, are indebted for the highest
flights of their muse.

Painting was, of all the arts, the least affected by the Reformation. This, nevertheless, was renovated, and, as it were,

hallowed by that universal movement which was then com-municated to all the powers of man. The great master of that age, Lucas Cranach, settled at Wittemberg, and became the painter of the Reformation. We have seen how he repre-sented the points of contrast between Christ and Antichrist (the Pope,) and was thus among the most influential instru-ments in that change by which the nation was transformed. As soon as he had received new convictions, he devoted his chastened pencil solely to paintings in harmony with the thoughts of a Christian, and gave to groups of children, repre-sented as blessed by the Saviour, that peculiar grace with which he had previously invested legendary saints.

Albert Durer was one of those who were attracted by the Word of Truth, and from that time, a new impulse was given to his genius. His master-pieces were produced subsequently to conversion. It might have been discerned, from the style in which he thenceforward depicted the Evangelists and Apostles, that the Bible had been restored to the people, and that the painter derived thence a depth, power, life, and dignity, which he never would have found within himself.[*]

It must, however, be admitted, that, of all the arts, Paint-ing is that one whose influence upon religion is most open to well founded and strong objection. We see it con-tinually connected with grievous immorality or pernicious error ; and those who have studied history, or visited Italy, will look for nothing in this art of benefit to human-kind. Our general remark holds good however, notwithstanding this exception.

Thus every thing progressed, arts, literature, purity of worship—and the minds of prince and people. But this glo-rious harmony, which the Gospel, in its revival, every where produced, was on the eve of being disturbed. The melody of the Wittemberg Nightingale was to be broken in upon by the howling of the tempest, and the roaring of lions. In a mo-ment a cloud overspread Germany, and a brilliant day was succeeded by a night of profound darkness.

* Ranke, Deutsche Geschichte, ii. p. 85.

A political ferment, very different from that which the Gospel brings with it, had long been secretly working in the Empire. Sinking under secular and ecclesiastical oppression, and, in some of the states, forming part of the seigneurial property and liable to sale with it, the people began to threaten to rise in insurrection, and burst their fetters. This spirit of resistance had shown itself long before the Reformation, by various symptoms; and even at that time a feeling of religion had mingled with the political elements of resistance. It was impossible, in the sixteenth century, to keep asunder two principles so intimately associated with the existence of nations. In Holland, at the close of the preceding century, the peasantry had made an insurrection, representing on their banners a loaf of bread and a cheese, the two staple articles of their poor country. The " *alliance of the shoes,*" showed itself first in the neighbourhood of Spires, in 1503; and in 1513, being encouraged by the priests, it was re-acted at Brisgau. In 1514, Wurtemburg was the scene of " the league of poor Conrad," which had for its object to sustain, by the revolt, " the right of God." In 1515, Carinthia and Hungary had been the theatre of terrible commotions. These seditious movements had been arrested by torrents of blood; but no relief had been afforded to the people. A political reform was, therefore, not less evidently needed than religious reform. In this the people were right; but it must be admitted, that they were not ripe for its enjoyment.

Since the commencement of the Reformation these popular ferments had not been repeated; men's minds were absorbed with other thoughts. Luther, whose penetrating eye had discerned the condition of people's minds, had, from his tower in the Wartburg, addressed to them some serious exhortations, of a nature to pacify their agitated feelings :—

" Rebellion," he observed, " never obtains for us the benefit we seek, and God condemns it. What is rebellion? is it not to revenge oneself? The devil tries hard to stir up to rebellion such as embrace the Gospel, that it may be covered with reproach; but they who have rightly received the truths I have preached, will not be found in rebellion."*

The aspect of things gave cause to fear that the popular ferment could not be much longer restrained. The government which Frederic of Saxony had taken pains to form, and which possessed the nation's confidence, was broken up. The Emperor, whose energy would perhaps have supplied the place of the influence of the national administration, was absent; the princes, whose union had always constituted the strength of Germany, were at variance; and the new manifestoes of Charles the Fifth against Luther, by excluding all hope of a future reconciliation, deprived the Reformer of much of the moral influence, by which, in 1522, he had succeeded in calming the tempest. The barrier, which had hitherto withstood the torrent, being swept away, its fury could no longer be restrained.

The religious movement did not give birth to the political agitation; but in some quarters it was drawn into, and went along with its swelling tide. We might perhaps, go farther, and acknowledge that the movement which the Reformation communicated to the popular mind, added strength to the discontent which was everywhere fermenting. The vehemence of Luther's writings, his bold words and actions, and the stern truth he spake, not only to the Pope and the prelates, but even to the nobles, must needs have contributed to inflame minds that were already in a state of considerable excitement. Thus Erasmus failed not to remind him,—"We are now gathering the fruits of your teaching."† Moreover the animating truths of the Gospel, now fully brought to light, stirred all bosoms, and filled them with hopeful anticipations. But there were many unrenewed hearts which were not prepared by a change of thought for the faith and liberty of a Christian. They were quite willing to cast off the yoke of Rome, but they had no desire to take upon them the yoke of Christ. Thus, when the Princes who espoused the cause of Rome endeavoured, in

---

* Luther's treue Ermahnung an alle Christen sich vor Aufruhr und Empörung zu hüten. (Opp. xviii. p. 288.)

† Habemus fructum tui spiritus. (Erasm. Hyperasp. B. 4.)

their anger, to crush the Reformation, those who were really Christians were enabled patiently to endure those cruel persecutions,—while the majority were roused to resistance, and broke forth in tumults ; and, finding their desires opposed in one direction, they sought vent for them in another. "Why is it," said they, "when the Church invites all men to a glorious liberty, that servitude is perpetuated in the state? When the Gospel inculcates nothing but gentleness, why should Governments rule only by force?" Unhappily, at the very period when a reformation of religion was hailed with joy, alike by nobles and people, a political reformation, on the contrary, encountered the opposition of the most powerful of the nation. And whilst the former had the Gospel for its rule and basis, the latter had ere long no principles or motives but violence and insubjection. Hence,—while the one was kept within the bounds of truth, the other rapidly overpassed all bounds.—like an impetuous torrent bursting its banks. But to deny that the Reformation exerted an indirect influence on the commotions which then disturbed the Empire, would subject the historian to the charge of partiality. A fire had been lighted up in Germany by religious discussions, from which it was scarcely possible but that some sparks should escape which were likely to inflame the popular minds.

The pretensions of a handful of fanatics to Divine inspiration added to the danger. Whilst the Reformation constantly appealed from the authority claimed by the Church to the real authority of the Sacred Word, those enthusiasts rejected, not only the authority of the Church, but that of Scripture also; they began to speak only of an inward Word—an internal revelation from God ; and, unmindful of the natural corruption of their hearts, they abandoned themselves to the intoxication of spiritual pride, and imagined themselves to be saints.

"The Sacred Writings," said Luther, "were treated by them as a dead letter, and their cry was, 'the Spirit! the Spirit!' But assuredly, I, for one, will not follow whither their spirit is leading them! May God, in His mercy, pre serve me from a Church in which there are only such saints.[*] I wish to be in fellowship with the humble, the weak, the sick, who know and feel their sin, and sigh and cry continually to God from the bottom of their hearts to obtain comfort and deliverance." These words of Luther have a depth of meaning, and indicate the change which his views were undergoing as to the nature of the Church. They, at the same time, show how opposed the religious principles of the rebels were to the religious principles of the Reformation.

The most noted of these enthusiasts was Thomas Münzer ; he was not without talent; had read his Bible, was of a zealous temperament, and might have done good, if he had been able to gather up his agitated thoughts, and attain to settled peace of conscience. But with little knowledge of his own heart, and wanting in true humility, he was taken up with the desire of reforming the world, and, like the generality of enthusiasts, forgot that it was with himself, he should begin. Certain mystical writings, which he had read in his youth, had given a false direction to his thoughts. He made his first appearance in public at Zwickau ;—quitted Wittemberg on Luther's return thither,—not satisfied to hold a secondary place in the general esteem, and became pastor of the small town of Alstadt, in Thuringia. Here he could not long remain quiet, but publicly charged the Reformers with establishing by their adherence to the written Word, a species of Popery, and with forming churches which were not pure and holy.

"Luther," said he, "has liberated men's consciences from the Papal yoke ; but he has left them in a carnal liberty, and has not led them forward in spirit towards God."[†]

He considered himself as called of God to remedy this great evil. The revelations of the *Spirit*, according to him, were the means by which the Reformation he was charged with should be effected. "He who hath the Spirit," said he, "hath true faith, although he should never once in all his life see the

* Der barmherzige Gott behüte mich ja für der christlichen Kirche, daren eitel heilige sind. (Upon John i. 2. L. Opp. (W.) vii. p. 1469.)

† Führete sie nicht weiter in Geist und zu Gott. (L. Opp. xix. 294.)

Holy Scriptures. The heathen and the Turks are better prepared to receive the Spirit than many of those Christians who call us enthusiasts." This remark was directed against Luther. " In order to receive the Spirit," continued he, " we must mortify the flesh—wear sackcloth—neglect the body—be of a sad countenance—keep silence*—forsake the haunts of men—and implore God to vouchsafe to us an assurance of His favour. Then it is that God will come unto us, and talk with us, as he did of old with Abraham, Isaac, and Jacob. If He were not to do so, he would not deserve our regard.† I have received from God the commission to gather together His elect in a holy and eternal union."

The agitation and ferment which were working in men's minds were not a little favourable to the spread of these enthusiastic ideas. Men love the marvellous and whatever flatters their pride. Münzer having inoculated with his own views, a portion of his flock, abolished the practice of chaunting, and all the other ceremonies annexed to public worship. He maintained that to obey princes " devoid of understanding," was to serve, at one and the same time, God and Belial; and then setting off at the head of his parishioners to a chapel in the neighbourhood of Alstadt, to which pilgrims were accustomed to resort from all quarters, he totally demolished it. After this exploit, being obliged to leave the country, he wandered from place to place in Germany, and came as far as Switzerland, everywhere carrying with him, and communicating to all who gave ear to him, the project of a general revolution. Wherever he went he found men's minds prepared. His words were like gunpowder cast upon burning coals, and a violent explosion quickly ensued.

Luther, who had rejected the warlike enterprises of Sickingen,‡ could not be led away by the tumultuous movements of

---

* Saur sehen, den Bart nicht abschneiden. (L. Opp. xix. p. 294.)
† The expression used by Münzer is low and irreverent: Er wollt in Gott scheissen wenn er nicht mit ihm redet, wie mit Abraham. (Hist. of Münzer, by Melancthon.—Ibid. p. 295.)
‡ Vol. I. book i. p. 113.

the peasantry. Happily for social order, the *Gospel* kept him from falling into this error; for what would have been the consequences, had he cast his extensive influence into the scale ? . . . He resolutely maintained the distinction between spiritual and secular matters; constantly affirming, that it was to immortal souls that Christ gave liberty by His word; and while on the one hand he impugned the authority of the Church, he on the other, with equal courage, stood up for the power of rulers. "A Christian," said he, "ought to suffer a hundred deaths, rather than be mixed up in the least degree with the revolted peasantry." He wrote to the Elector—"It gives me indescribable satisfaction that these enthusiasts themselves boast, to all who will give ear to them, that they do not belong to us. ' It is,' say they, 'the Spirit which impels us;' to which I reply, ' that it must be an evil spirit, that bears no other fruits than the pillage of convents and churches;' the greatest robbers on this earth might easily do as much as that."

At the same time, Luther, who desired for others the liberty that he claimed for himself, was dissuading the Prince from resorting to severe measures. "Let them preach what they will, and against whom they please," said he, "for it is the Word of God alone which must go forth and give them battle. If the spirit *in them* be the true Spirit, any severities of ours will be unavailing; but if our Spirit be the true, He will not fear their violence! Let us leave the Spirits to struggle and contend.* A few, perhaps, may be seduced. In every battle there are some wounded; but he who is faithful in the fight shall receive the crown. Nevertheless, if they have recourse to the sword, let your Highness prohibit it, and command them to quit your dominions."

The insurrection commenced in the districts of the Black Forest, near the sources of the Danube, a country that had been often the theatre of popular commotions. On the 19th July, 1524, the Thurgovian peasantry rose against the Abbot

* Man lasse die Geister auf einander platzen und treffen. (L. Epp. ii. p. 547.)

of Reichenau, who had refused to appoint over them an evangelical preacher. Shortly after this, several thousands of them collected round the small town of Tenger,—their object being to liberate an ecclesiastic who was there imprisoned. The insurrection spread, with inconceivable rapidity, from Suabia as far as the Rhenish provinces, Franconia, Thuringia, and Saxony. In January, 1525, all these countries were in a state of open insurrection.

Towards the close of that month, the peasantry put forth a declaration in twelve articles, wherein they claimed the liberty of choosing their own pastors, the abolition of small tithes, servitude, and the taxes on inheritance; the right to hunt, fish, cut wood, &c. Each demand was backed by a passage from the Bible: and they concluded with the words,—" If we are wrong, let Luther set us right by the Scriptures."

They requested to have the opinion of the divines of Wittemberg. Melancthon and Luther each gave his judgment separately; and the decision of each reminds us of the difference that marked their characters. Melancthon, who regarded any disturbance as a serious crime, overstepped the limits of his habitual mildness, and seemed to labour to express the strength of his indignation. According to him, the peasantry were public criminals, on whom he invoked all laws,—divine and human. If amicable communications should fail of effect, he would have the magistrates to pursue them, as they would robbers and assassins. " Nevertheless," adds he, —(and some one feature, at least, we need to find, that shall remind us of Melancthon,)—" think of the *orphans* before you have recourse to capital punishment!"

Luther took the same view of the revolt as Melancthon; but he had a heart which deeply felt for the miseries of the people. He manifested, on this occasion, a noble impartiality and frankly spoke truth to both parties. He first addressed the princes,—and more particularly the bishops :—

" It is you," said he, " who have caused the revolt; it is your declamations against the Gospel, it is your guilty oppression of the poor of the flock,—which have driven the people to despair. My dear Lords, it is not the peasants who have risen against you,—it is God Himself who is opposing your madness.* The peasants are but instruments He is employing to humble you. Think not you can escape the punishment reserved for you. Even though you should succeed in exterminating all the peasantry, God could from these stones raise up others to chastise your pride. If I were bent on avenging my own wrongs, I might laugh in my sleeve,—and quietly look on, while the peasantry were acting,—or even inflame their rage,—but the Lord keep me from it! My dear Lords, for the love of God! calm your irritation;—grant reasonable conditions to these poor people, as phrenzied and misled persons;—appease these commotions by gentle methods, lest they give birth to a conflagration which shall set all Germany in a flame. Some of their twelve articles contain just and reasonable demands."

Such an exordium was calculated to gain for Luther the confidence of the peasantry, and to induce them to listen to the truths which he was about to press upon them. After admitting that some of their demands were founded in justice, he declared that rebellion was the act of heathens: that Christians were called to suffer, not to fight: that if they persisted in their revolt in the name of the Gospel, but contrary to the very precepts of the Gospel, he should consider them as worse enemies than the Pope. "The Pope and the Emperor," continued he, "combined against me; but the more the Emperor and the Pope stormed, the more did the Gospel make its way. Why was this? Because I neither took up the sword, nor called for vengeance, nor had recourse to tumult or revolt; I committed all to God,—and waited for Him to interpose by His mighty power. The Christian conflict is not to be carried on by sword or arquebuss, but by endurance and the cross. Christ, their Captain, would not have his servants smite with the sword,—he was hanged upon a tree."

But in vain did Luther inculcate these Christian precepts. The people, under the influence of the inflammatory haran-

* Gott ist's selber der setzt sich wider euch. (L. Opp. xix. p. 254.)

gues of the leaders of the revolt, were deaf to the words of the Reformer. "He is playing the hypocrite," said they, "and flatters the nobles:—he has himself made war against the Pope, and yet expects that we should submit to our oppressors."

Instead of subsiding, the insurrection grew more formidable. At Weinsberg, Count Louis of Helfenstein, and the seventy men under his command, were doomed to death. A body of peasantry drew up in close ranks, with advanced pikes, whilst others drove the Count and his retainers against the points of this forest of weapons.* The wife of the ill-fated Helfenstein, a natural daughter of the Emperor Maximilian, holding her infant in her arms, implored them, on bended knees, to spare the life of her husband, and vainly endeavoured to avert this barbarous murder. A lad who had served under the Count, and had afterwards joined the rebels, gamboled in mockery before him, and played the dead march upon his fife, as if he had been leading his victims in a dance. All perished; the infant was wounded in its mother's arms, and she herself thrown upon a dung-cart, and thus conveyed to Heilbronn.

At the news of these atrocities, a cry of horror was uttered by the friends of the Reformation, and Luther's feeling heart was violently agitated. On one hand, the peasantry, ridiculing his counsel, asserted that they had a revelation from Heaven,—impiously perverted the threatenings contained in the Old Testament,—proclaimed an equality of conditions, and a community of goods,—defended their cause with fire and sword, and rioted in barbarous executions. On the other hand, the enemies of the Reformation, with malicious sneer, enquired if the Reformer did not know that it was easier to kindle a fire than to extinguish it. Indignant at these excesses, and alarmed at the thought that they might check the progress of the Gospel, Luther no longer hesitated; he laid aside his former forbearance, and denounced the rebels with all the energy of his character, overpassing, perhaps, the just bounds within which he should have contained himself.

* Und fechten ein Grassen durch die Spiesse. (Mathesius, p. 46.)

"The peasantry," said he, "are guilty of three horrible crimes against God and men; and thus deserve both the death of the body and that of the soul. In the first place, they rebel against their rulers, to whom they have sworn allegiance; next, they rob and plunder convents and castles; and, to crown all, they cloak their crimes under the profession of the Gospel! If you neglect to shoot a mad dog, yourself and all your neighbours will perish. He who dies in the cause of the magistrates will be a true martyr, provided he fight with a good conscience."

Luther then proceeds to comment severely upon the guilty violence of the peasantry, in compelling simple and peaceable men to join their ranks, and thus bringing them into the same condemnation. He then proceeds: "On this account, my dear Lords, I conjure you to interpose for the deliverance of these poor people. I say to him who can bear arms, strike, and kill. If thou shouldst fall, thou canst not have a more blessed end; for thou meetest death in the service of God, and to save thy neighbour from hell."*

Neither gentle nor violent measures could arrest the popular torrent. The church bells were rung no longer for divine worship. Whenever their deep and prolonged sounds were heard in country places, it was known as the tocsin, and all flew to arms.

The people of the Black Forest had enrolled themselves under John Muller of Bulgenbach. With an imposing aspect, wrapped in a red cloak, and wearing a red cap, this chief daringly proceeded from village to village, followed by his peasantry. Behind him, on a waggon, decorated with boughs and ribands, was exhibited a tri-coloured flag, black, red, and white,—the standard of revolt. A herald, similarly decorated, read aloud the twelve articles, and invited the people to join in the insurrection. Whoever refused to do so, was banished from the community.

Their progress, which at first was pacific, became more and more alarming. "We must," they exclaimed, "compel the

* Deinen Nehesten zu retten aus der Hölle. (L. Opp. xix. p. 266.)

lords of the soil to submit to our conditions"—and by way of bringing them to compliance they proceeded to break open the granaries, empty the cellars, draw the fish-ponds, demolish the castles of the nobles, and set fire to the convents. Opposition had inflamed to frenzy these misguided men: Equality could no longer satisfy them;—they thirsted for blood; and swore to make every man who wore a spur bite the dust.

At the approach of the peasantry, those towns which were incapable of withstanding a siege opened their gates, and made common cause with them. In every place they entered, the images of the saints were defaced—the crucifixes broken to pieces,—while women, armed with weapons, passed through the streets threatening the lives of the monks. Beaten and repulsed in one place, they re-assembled in another, and braved the most formidable regular troops.

A committee chosen by the peasants stationed themselves at Heilbrun. The Counts of Lowenstein were captured, stript, and clothed in common blouse, a white staff was placed in their hands, and they were compelled to swear adhesion to the twelve articles. "*Brother* George, and you, brother Albert," said a brazier to the Counts of Hohenlohe, who visited their camp, "swear to us to act the part of brothers—for yourselves are now peasants and no longer lords." Equality of ranks, that dream of democrats, was established in aristocratic Germany.

Many persons of the upper classes, some from fear, and some from motives of ambition, joined the insurrection. The celebrated Gotz of Berlichingen finding himself unable to maintain his authority over his vassals, prepared to seek a refuge in the states of the Elector of Saxony, but his wife, who was then in child-bed, wishing to keep him at home, concealed from him the Elector's letter. Gotz, hemmed in on all sides, was compelled to put himself at the head of the rebel forces. On the 7th of May, the peasants entered Wurtzburg, where they were received with acclamations. The troops of the princes and of the knights of Suabia and Franconia, who were stationed in that city, evacuated it, and withdrew in confusion within the citadel,—the last refuge of the nobility,

But already had the commotion spread to other parts of Germany. Spires, the Palatinate, Alsace, Hesse, had adopted the twelve articles, and the peasants threatened Bavaria, Westphalia, the Tyrol, Saxony, and Lorraine. The Margrave of Baden, having scornfully rejected the articles, was compelled to seek refuge in flight. The Coadjutor of Fulda acceded to them with a laugh. The smaller towns submitted, alleging that they had no spears to resist the insurgents. Mentz, Treves, Frankfort, obtained the immunities on which they had insisted.

Throughout the Empire, a wide-spreading revolution was in full career. The ecclesiastical and secular privileges, which bore so heavily on the peasantry, were to be suppressed; church property was to be diverted to secular uses, to indemnify the chiefs, and meet the exigencies of the state; taxes were to be abolished, with exception of a tribute payable every ten years; the power of the Emperor, as recognised by the New Testament, was to be maintained supreme; all other reigning princes were to come down to the level of citizens; sixty-four free courts were to be instituted, and men of all ranks to be eligible as judges; all conditions were to return to their primitive positions; the clergy were to be restricted to the pastorship of their several churches; princes and knights were to be defenders of the weak; uniform weights and measures were to be introduced; and one coin to be struck, and be the only currency of the whole Empire.

Meanwhile, the nobles were recovering from their first stupor, and George Truchsess, commander-in-chief of the Imperial forces, advanced in the direction of the lake of Constance. On the 7th of May, he drove back the peasants at Beblingen, and directed his march upon the town of Weinsberg, where the unfortunate Count of Helfenstein had lost his life. He set fire to it, and burned it to the ground, giving orders that its ruins should be left as a lasting memorial of the treason of its inhabitants. At Furfeld, he effected a junction with the Elector Palatine and the Elector of Treves, and the combined army advanced upon Franconia.

The Frauenberg, the citadel of Wurtzburg, had held out for the cause of the nobles, and the main army of the peasants still lay before its walls. On receiving intelligence of the approach of Truchsess, they resolved on an assault, and on the 15th of May, at nine in the evening, the trumpets sounded, the tri-colour flag was unfurled, and the peasants rushed to the assault with frightful shouts. Sebastian Rotenhan, one of the staunchest partisans of the Reformation, was commandant in the castle. He had organized the means of defence on an efficient footing, and when he harangued the soldiers and exhorted them to repel the attack, they had all sworn to do so, raising their three fingers towards heaven. A fierce struggle ensued. The reckless and despairing efforts of the peasants were answered from the walls of the fortress by petards and showers of sulphur and boiling pitch, and discharges of cannon. The peasants, thus struck by their unseen enemy from behind the ramparts, for an instant faltered, but their fury rose above it all. Night closed in, and the contest still raged. The fortress, lighted up by a thousand battle-fires, seemed, in the darkness of the night, to resemble a towering giant pouring forth flames, and contending in the midst of bursts of thunder for the salvation of the Empire from the savage bravery of infuriated hordes. At two in the morning, the peasants, failing in all their efforts, at last retreated.

They tried to open negociations with the garrison, on the one side, and with Truchsess, who was approaching at the head of his army, on the other. But negociation was not their forte. Violence and conquest offered their only chance of safety. After some hesitation, they decided to advance against the Imperial forces; but the cannon and charges of the Imperial cavalry made fearful havoc in their ranks. On reaching Konigshofen, they were completely routed. Then it was that the princes, nobles, and bishops, cruelly abusing their victory, gave loose to unheard-of cruelties. Those who were taken prisoners, were hanged at the road-side. The bishop of Wurtzburg, who had taken flight, returning to his diocese, passed over it, attended by executioners, who shed, without distinction, the blood of rebels, and of such as were living quietly in subjection to God's word. Gotz de Berlichingen was sentenced to imprisonment for life. The Margrave Casimir of Anspach, deprived of their sight no less than eighty peasants, who, in the rebellion, had declared, with an oath, that their eyes should never look upon that prince,—casting the victims of his cruelty on the wide world, blind, and holding each other by the hand, to grope their way, and beg their bread. The unfortunate youth who had played, on his fife, the death-march of Helfenstein, was chained to a stake, and a fire lighted round him,—the knights being present, and laughing at his horrid contortions.

Everywhere public worship was restored, under its ancient forms. In the most flourishing and populous districts of the Empire, the traveller was horror-struck with the sight of heaps of dead bodies and smoking ruins. Fifty thousand had perished; and almost everywhere the people lost what little liberty they had previously possessed. Such, in Southern Germany, was the dreadful result of the Revolt.

But the evil was not confined to the south and west of Germany. Münzer, after traversing part of Switzerland, Alsace, and Suabia, had again turned his steps toward Saxony. Some townsmen of Mulhausen, in Thuringia, invited him to their town, and elected him as their pastor. The Town-council having offered resistance, Münzer degraded it,—appointing another in its stead, composed of his own friends, and presided over by himself. Contemning the Christ full of grace, whom Luther preached, and resolved on recourse to violent means, his cry was,—" We must exterminate with the sword, like Joshua, the Canaanitish nations." He set on foot a commu-nity of goods,* and pillaged the convents. " Münzer," wrote Luther to Amsdorff, on the 11th of April, 1525, " Münzer is king, and emperor of Mulhausen, and no longer its pastor." The lowest classes ceased to work. If any one wanted a piece of cloth, or a supply of corn, he asked his richer neigh

* Omnia simul communia. (L. Opp. xix. p. 292.)

hour : if the latter refused, the penalty was hanging. Mulhausen being a free town, Münzer exercised his power, unmolested for nearly a year. The revolt of Southern Germany led him to imagine that the time was come to extend his new kingdom. He cast some large guns in the convent of the Franciscans, and exerted himself to raise the peasantry and miners of Mansfeld. " When will you shake off your slumbers," said he, in a fanatical address: " Arise, and fight the battle of the Lord !——The time is come.——France, Germany, and Italy, are up and doing. Forward, Forward, Forward !——*Dran, Dran, Dran!* Heed not the cries of the ungodly. They will weep like children,—but be you pitiless.——*Dran, Dran, Dran !*——Fire burns ;—let your swords be ever tinged with blood !*——*Dran, Dran, Dran !*——Work while it is day." The letter was signed " Münzer, God's servant against the ungodly."

The country people, eager for plunder, flocked in crowds to his standard. Throughout the districts of Mansfeld, Stolberg, Schwarzburg, Hesse, and Brunswick, the peasantry rose *en masse*. The convents of Michelstein, Ilsenburg, Walkenried, Rossleben, and many others in the neighbourhood of the Hartz mountains, or in the plains of Thuringia were plundered. At Reinhardsbrunn, the place which Luther had once visited, the tombs of the ancient landgraves were violated, and the library destroyed.

Terror spread far and wide. Even at Wittemberg, some anxiety began to be felt. The Doctors who had not feared Emperors nor Pope felt themselves tremble in presence of a madman. Curiosity was all alive to the accounts of what was going on, and watched every step in the progress of the insurrection. Melancthon wrote—" We are here in imminent danger. If Münzer be successful, it is all over with us ; unless Christ should appear for our deliverance. Münzer's progress is marked by more than Scythian cruelty.† His threats are more dreadful than I can tell you."

---

* Lasset euer Schwerdt nicht kalt werden von Blut. (L. Opp. xix. 289)

† Moncerus plus quam Scythicam crudelitatem prœ se fert. (Corp. Ref. i. p. 741.)

The pious Elector had hesitated long what steps he should take. Münzer had exhorted him, as well as the other reigning princes, to be converted : " For," said he, "their time is come :" and he had signed his letters—" Munzer, armed with the sword of Gideon." It was Frederic's earnest desire to try gentle methods for reclaiming these deluded men. Dangerously ill, he had written on the 14th of April, to his brother John—" Possibly, more than one cause for insurrection has been given to these wretched people. Oh, in many ways are the poor oppressed by their temporal, as well as by their spiritual rulers !" And when his councillors adverted to the humiliation, confusions, and dangers to which he would expose himself by neglecting to stifle the rebellion in its infancy, he made answer—" In my time, I have been a potent Elector, with horses and chariots in great abundance,—if, at this time, God will take them away, I will go on foot."*

Phillip, the young Landgrave of Hesse, was the first of the reigning princes who took up arms. His knights and retainers swore to live or die with him. Having put the affairs of his states in order, he moved towards Saxony. On their side, Duke John, the Elector's brother, Duke George of Saxony, and Duke Henry of Brunswick, advancing, effected a junction with the Hessian troops. As the combined force came into sight, the peasants, in alarm, took their station on a hill, and, without observing any discipline, set about constructing a sort of rampart, composed of their waggons. Münzer had not even provided powder for his immense guns. No help appeared—the troops hemmed them in, and a panic spread through the rebel host. The princes from motives of humanity, proposed to them to capitulate—and they showed signs of willingness to do so. Then it was, that Münzer had recourse to the most powerful lever of enthusiasm : " This day," said he, " this day we shall behold the mighty arm of God, and destruction shall fall upon our enemies !" Just at that moment, a rainbow was seen in the clouds—and the fanatic multitude, whose standard bore the representation of a rainbow, beheld in

* So wolle er hinkünftig zu fuss gehen. (Seck. p. 685.)

18*

it a sure omen of the Divine protection. Münzer took advantage of it : "Never fear," said he, to the burghers and peasantry ; " I will receive all their balls in my sleeve :"* and at the same moment, he gave direction that a young gentleman, Maternus Geholfen, an envoy from the princes, should be cruelly put to death, in order that the rebels might thus know themselves beyond the hope of pardon.

The Landgrave harangued his soldiers—"I well know," said he, "that we princes are often to blame—for we are but men ; but it is God's will that the powers that be should be respected. Let us save our wives and children from the fury of these murderers. The Lord will give us the victory, for. hath He not said, 'He that resisteth the power, resisteth the ordinance of God.' " Philip then gave the signal for the attack. It was the 15th of May, 1525. The army put itself in motion—but the crowd of peasants standing still, struck up the hymn, " Come, Holy Spirit,"—expecting Heaven to interpose in their behalf. But the artillery soon opened a breach in their rude fortification, and scattered confusion and death in their midst. On this, their fanaticism and resolution at once forsook them ; a panic spread throughout their host, and breaking from their ranks they fled in the utmost disorder. Five thousand were slain in the pursuit. After the battle the princes and their victorious troops entered Frankenhausen. A soldier, who had mounted to the loft of the house in which he was quartered, perceived a man crouching in concealment.† "Who are you?" demanded he ; "are you one of the rebels ?"—then catching sight of a writing-case, he opened it, and found therein letters addressed to Thomas Münzer—"Is that your name?" inquired the trooper.—"No," answered the sick man. But the soldier, uttering dreadful threats, Münzer —for he it was—confessed he was the man. "You are my prisoner," rejoined the other. Being taken before Duke George and the Landgrave, Münzer persisted in maintaining

* Ihr sollt sehen dass ich alle Büchsensteine in Ermel fassen will. (L. Opp. xix. p. 297.)

† So findet er einen am Bett.

that he was justified in chastising the nobles, since they were opposers of the Gospel. "Wretch!" said they, "think of those whose death thou hast occasioned." But he made answer, smiling in the midst of his anguish, "They would have it so." He took the sacrament under one kind, and was beheaded on the same day as his lieutenant Pfeiffer. Mulhausen was taken, and the peasants loaded with chains.

One of the nobles, who had remarked in the crowd of prisoners a peasant whose appearance interested him, drew near, and said,—"Well, my boy, what government is most to your mind,—the peasants or the princes?" The poor youth, sighing deeply, replied,—"Ah, my dear lord, no edge of sword inflicts such suffering as the rule of a peasant over his fellow."*

What remained of the rebellion was quenched in blood: Duke George was particularly inflexible. In the states of the Elector, there were neither executions nor punishments;† God's word, preached in its purity, had been proved sufficient to control the tumultuous passions of the people.

In truth, Luther had, from its very beginning, withstood the rebellion; which to him appeared the forerunner of final judgments. He had spared neither advice, entreaties, nor irony. To the twelve articles which the rebels had drawn up at Erfurth, he had subjoined as a thirteenth: "*Item*, the following article omitted above. From this day forth the honourable Council shall be powerless,—its functions shall be to do nothing,—it shall sit as an idol or as a log,—the commune shall chew its meat for it, and it shall govern bound hand and foot. From this day, the waggon shall guide the horses, the horses shall hold the reins, and all shall go on prosperously, in conformity with the glorious system set forth in the foregoing articles."

Luther was not satisfied with using his pen. Just when the confusion was at its height, he left Wittemberg, and trav-

* Kein Messer scherpfer schirrt denn wenn ein Baur des andern Herr wird. (Mathesius, p. 48.)

† Hic nulla carnificina, nullum supplicium. (Corp. Ref. i. p. 752.)

ersed some of the districts where the agitation was greatest. He preached, he laboured to soften the hearts of his hearers, and being strengthened from above in his work, he guided, quieted, and brought back into their accustomed channels, the impetuous and overflowing torrents.

The reformed teachers everywhere exerted a similar influence. At Halle, Brentz, by the power of the divine promises, revived the drooping spirits of its inhabitants, and four thousand of the peasants fled before six hundred of its citizens.* At Ichterhausen, where a body of peasants had met, intending to demolish certain castles, and put their owners to death, Frederic Myconius ventured alone among them, and such was the power of his eloquence, that they at once abandoned their purpose.†

Such was the part taken by the Reformers and the Reformation during the continuance of the revolt. They contended, as far as they were enabled, by the sword of the Word, and boldly asserted the principles which alone have power at all times to preserve order and subjection among nations. Hence we find Luther asserting that if the wholesome influence of sound doctrine had not withstood the madness of the people, the revolt would have extended its ravages far more widely, and would everywhere have overturned both Church and State. Every thing inclines us to believe that this melancholy anticipation would have been realised.

If, as we have seen, the Reformers stood up against sedition they nevertheless did not escape without being wounded. That moral agony which Luther had first undergone in his cell at Erfurth, was perhaps at its height after the revolt of the peasants. On the side of the princes it was repeated, and in many quarters believed, that Luther's teaching had been the cause of the rebellion; and groundless as was the charge, the Reformer could not but feel deeply affected by the credit

---

* Eorum animos fractos et perturbatos verbo Dei erexit. (M. Adam. Vit. Brentii, p. 441.)

† Agmen rusticorum qui convenerant ad demoliendas arces, unica oratione sic compescuit. (M. Adam. Vit. Fred. Myconii, p. 178.)

attached to it. On the side of the people, Münzer and all the leaders of the sedition represented him as a vile hypocrite and flatterer of the great,[*] and their calumnies easily obtained belief. The strength with which Luther had declared against the rebels, had given offence even to men of moderate opinions. The partisans of Rome exulted;[†] all seemed against him, and he bore the indignation of that generation : but what most grieved him was that the work of heaven should be thus degraded by being classed with the dreams of fanatics. He contemplated the bitter cup presented to him, and foreseeing that ere long he would be forsaken by all, he exclaimed, "Soon shall I also have to say, 'All ye shall be offended because of me in that night !' "

Yet, in the midst of this bitter experience, his faith was unshaken. "He," said he, "who has enabled me to tread the enemy under foot when he came against me as a roaring lion, will not suffer that enemy to crush me, now that he approaches with the treacherous leer of the basilisk.[‡] I mourn over the late calamities. Again and again have I asked myself whether it might not have been better to have allowed the Papacy to pursue its course unmolested, rather than be a witness to the breaking out of such commotions. But no ;—it is better to have extricated a few from the jaws of the devil, than that all should be left under his murderous fangs."

At this period we must note the completion of that change in Luther's views which had commenced at the time of his return from the Wartburg. A principle of internal life no longer satisfied him ; the Church and her institutions assumed a high importance in his estimate. The fearlessness with which he had thrown down all that stood in the way of his reforms, drew back in the prospect of a work of destruction,

* Quod adulator principum vocer. (L. Epp. ii. p. 671.)

† Gaudent papistæ de nostro dissidio. (Ibid. p. 612.)

‡ Qui cum toties hactenus sub pedibus meis calcavit et contrivit leonem et draconem, non sinet etiam basiliscum super me calcare. (Ibid. p. 671.)

§ Es ist besser einige aus dem Rachen des Teufels herausreissen. (L. Opp. ii. Ed. ix. p. 961.)

far more radical and sweeping: he felt the necessity for preserving, ruling, building up,—and it was in the centre of the blood-watered ruins with which the war of the peasants had covered Germany, that the structure of the new Church rose slowly from its foundations.

The troubles we have been narrating left a deep and enduring impression on the minds of that age. Nations were struck with consternation. The masses who had sought in the Reformation nothing but political freedom, withdrew from it of their own accord, when they saw that spiritual liberty was the only liberty it offered. Luther's opposition to the peasants involved the renunciation of the inconstant favour of the people. It was not long before a seeming tranquillity was restored, and the silence of terror* succeeded to the outbreaks of enthusiasm and sedition.

Thus the popular passions, the cause of revolution, and radical equality, were quelled and passed away; but the Reformation did not pass away. The two movements, by many confounded with each other, were exhibited in the distinctness of their character by the diversity of their results. The revolt was a thing of earthly origin, the Reformation was from above—some cannon and soldiers sufficed to put down the former, but the latter never ceased to grow and strengthen, in spite of the reiterated assaults of the imperial or ecclesiastical powers.

And yet the cause of the Reformation itself seemed likely to perish in the gulph in which the liberties of the people were lost. A melancholy event appeared likely to hasten its ruin. At the time the princes were in full march against Münzer, and ten days before the final defeat of the peasants, the aged Elector of Saxony, the man whom God had raised up to defend the Reformation against external dangers, descended to the tomb.

His strength had been daily declining; and his feeling

* Ea res incussit .... vulgo terrorem, ut nihil usquam moveatur. (Corp. Ref. i. p. 752.)

heart was wrung by the atrocities which stained the progress of the war of the peasants. "Oh!" cried he, with a deep sigh, "if it were the will of God, I would gladly be released from this life. I see nothing left, neither love, truth, or faith, or any thing good upon this earth."[*]

Turning from the thought of the confusions that prevailed throughout Germany, the pious prince quietly prepared himself to depart. He had taken up his abode in his castle of Lochau. On the 4th of May, he asked for his chaplain, the faithful Spalatin : "You do well to visit me," said he to him as he entered the room, "for it is well to visit the sick." Then directing that his couch should be moved toward the table where Spalatin was seated, he desired his attendants to leave the room, and affectionately taking his friend's hand, spoke to him familiarly of Luther, of the peasants, and of his approaching end. At eight that same evening Spalatin returned; the aged prince opened his mind to him, and confessed his sins, in the presence of God. The next morning, the 5th, he received the communion under both kinds. No member of his family was present : his brother and his nephew had both left with the army ; but, according to the ancient custom of those times, his domestics stood round the bed gazing in tears[†] upon the venerable prince whom it had been their sweet privilege to serve : "My little children," said he, tenderly, "if I have offended any one of you forgive me for the love of God ; for we princes often offend against such little ones, and it ought not so to be." In this way did Frederic conform himself to the apostle's direction that the rich humble himself when he is brought low, "because as the flower of the grass he shall pass away."[‡]

Spalatin never left him. He set before him with glowing earnestness the glorious promises of the Gospel ; and the pious Elector drank in its strong consolations with unspeakable peace. That evangelic doctrine was then to his soul no longer

* Noch etwas gutes mehr in der Welt. (Seckend. p. 702.)
† Dass alle Umstehende zum weinen bewegt. (Ibid.)
‡ St. James, 1 ch. 10th ver.

a sword, turned against false teaching, searching it in all its refuges of lies, and triumphing over it at every turn : it was a shower—a gentle dew, distilling on his heart, and causing it to overflow with hope and joy. God and eternity were alone present to his thought.

Feeling his death rapidly drawing nigh, he destroyed a will he had made some years before, in which he had commended his soul to "the Mother of God," and dictated another in which he cast himself on the spotless and availing merit of Jesus Christ "for the forgiveness of his sins," and expressed his firm assurance that "he was redeemed by the precious blood of his beloved Saviour."[*] This done, he added,—"My strength fails me, I can say no more;" and at five the same evening he "fell asleep." "He was a son of Peace," remarked his physician, "and in peace he is departed."—"Oh! said Luther, "how bitter *to his survivors* was that death."[†]

It is remarkable that Luther, who just at that time was on a mission of peace, trying to allay the excitement left, by recent events, on the minds of the people of Thuringia, had never seen the Elector, but at a distance,—as at Worms, when the latter was seated beside Charles the Fifth. But from the moment the Reformation appeared, these two remarkable men had been together in spirit. Frederic in quest of the national interest and independence,—Luther in quest of truth and reformation. It cannot be doubted that the Reformation was, *in principle*, a work of the Spirit; but, in order to its gaining footing on the earth, it was, perhaps, necessary that it should be linked with a something connected with the interests of the nation. Hence,—no sooner had Luther stood up against indulgences, than the alliance between the Monk and the Prince was tacitly concluded,—an alliance in its nature simply moral, without form of contract, without writing, without even verbal communication,—an alliance in which the stronger lent no aid to the weaker party, but that which consisted in leaving him

* Durch das theure Blut meines allerliebsten Heylandes erlöset. (Seck. p. 703.)

† O mors amara! (L. Epp. ii. p. 659.)

unmolested to his work. But now that the mighty oak, under the shelter of which the Reformation had grown up, was felled to the dust,—now that the opposers of the Gospel gave more free expression to their hatred, and its supporters were obliged to retire or to be silent, it seemed as if nothing was left to defend it against the sword of those who were pursuing it.

The confederates of Ratisbon, after the complete defeat of the peasants of the southern and western provinces, proceeded to vent their revenge on the Reformation, as well as on those who had taken part in the revolt. At Wurtzburg, at Bamberg, inoffensive citizens were put to death,—including some who had even opposed themselves to the peasants. "It matters not," it was openly said, "they were of the Gospellers," —and they were beheaded.*

Duke George sought opportunity to infuse into the minds of the Landgrave and Duke John his own prejudices and antipathies. "See," said he, after the rout of the peasants, pointing to the field of carnage, "see what miseries Luther has occasioned." John and Philip showed signs of acquiescence. "Duke George," remarked the Reformer, "flatters himself he shall succeed, now that Frederic is dead; but Christ still reigns in the midst of his enemies. Gnash their teeth as they will, the desire of them shall perish."†

George lost no time in forming, in northern Germany, a confederacy similar to that of Ratisbon. The Electors of Mentz and Brandenburg,—Dukes Henry, Eric, and George, assembled at Dessau, and there concluded a treaty of alliance in the interest of Rome.‡ In the month of July, George urged the new Elector and his son-in-law, the Landgrave, to accede to it. Then, as if to give intimation of the objects of the confederation, he beheaded two citizens of Leipsic, who had been proved to have in their possession the Reformer's writings.

* Ranke, Deutsche Gesch. ii. p. 226.
† Dux Gorgius, mortuo Frederico, putat se omnia posse. (L. Epp. iii. p. 22.)
‡ Habito conciliabulo conjuraverunt restituros esse esse omnia . . . (Ibid.)

Just at this time letters from Charles the Fifth, dated from Toledo, reached Germany, by which another Diet was convoked at Augsburg. Charles wished to give the Empire such a constitution as would allow him to dispose, at will, of the military force of Germany. The divisions in religion favoured his design. He had but to let loose the Catholics against the Gospellers; and when both should have exhausted their strength, he might gain an easy victory over both. " Away with the Lutherans,"* was therefore the cry of the Emperor.

Thus, all conspired against the Reformation. Never could Luther's spirit have been bowed down by such manifold apprehensions. The surviving sectaries of Münzer had vowed to take his life. His sole protector was no more. " Duke George," wrote some, " intended to arrest him in Wittemberg itself."† The Princes who could have defended him, one after another bowed before the storm, and seemed to be abandoning the cause of the Gospel. The University, already lowered in credit by the recent confusions, was, according to rumour, on the point of being suppressed by the new Elector. Charles, after his victory at Pavia, had just convoked another Diet, that a finishing blow might be dealt against the Reformation. What dangers, then, must he not have foreseen? The anxious mental struggles that had so often drawn sobs from his bosom again wrung his heart. How should he bear up against such multiplied enemies? In the very crisis of this agitation, with all these accumulated dangers staring him in the face,—the corpse of Frederic scarcely cold, and the plains of Germany still strewed with the unburied bodies of the peasants—Luther,—none surely could have imagined such a thing,—Luther married!

In the monastery of Nimptsch, near Grimma, in Saxony, resided, in the year 1523, nine nuns, who had devoted themselves to the reading of God's word, and had discerned the contrast that existed between the christian life and the daily

* Sleidan. Hist. de la Ref. i. p. 214.
† Keil. Luther's Leben, p. 160.

routine of their cloister. The names of these nuns were Magdalene Staupitz, Elisa Canitz, Ave Grossen, Ave and Margaret Schonfeld, Laneta Golis, Margaret and Catherine Zeschau, and Catherine Bora. The first step taken by these young women, after their minds were delivered from the superstitions of their monastery, was to write to their relations—"Our continuance in a cloister," said they, "is incompatible with the salvation of our souls."* Their parents, dreading the trouble such a resolution was likely to occasion to themselves, repelled with harshness the entreaties of their children. The poor nuns were overwhelmed with distress. How to leave their nunnery! their timidity took alarm at so desperate a decision. At last, their horror of the Papal services prevailed, and they mutually promised not to part company, but together to find their way to some respectable quarter with decency and order.† Two respected and pious citizens of Torgau, Leonard Koppe and Wolff Tomitzch, tendered their assistance‡—they welcomed it as of God's sending, and quitted the convent of Nimptsch without any hindrance being interposed, as if the hand of the Lord had set open its gates.§ Koppe and Tomitzch were in waiting to receive them in their waggon—and on the 7th of April, the nine nuns, amazed at their own boldness, drew up in deep emotion at the gate of the old convent of the Augustines where Luther resided.

"This is not my doing," said Luther, as he received them, "but would to God I could, in this way, give liberty to enslaved consciences, and empty the cloisters of their tenants. A breach is made, however."‖ Several persons proposed to the doctor to receive the nuns into their houses, and Catherine Bora found a welcome in the family of the burgomaster of Wittemberg.

If Luther had then before him the prospect of any solemn

* Der Seelen Seligkeit halber. (L. Epp. ii. p. 323.)
† Mit aller Zucht und Ehre an redliche Stätte und Orte kommen. (Ibid. p. 322.)
‡ Per honestos cives Torgavienses adductæ. (Ibid. p. 319.)
§ Mirabiliter evaserunt. (Ibid.)
‖ Und alle Klöster ledig machen. (Ibid. p. 322.)

erent, it was that he should be called to ascend the scaffold, not the steps of the altar. Many months after this, he answered those who spoke of marriage—"God may change my purpose, if such be His pleasure; but at present I have no thought of taking a wife; not that I am insensible to the charms of a married life; I am neither wood nor stone; but I every day expect death and the punishment of a heretic."*

And yet all was moving onward in the church. The habits of monastic life, invented by man, were on all sides giving place to the habits of domestic life, instituted by God. On Sunday, the 9th of October, Luther, on rising, laid aside his monk's gown, assumed the garb of a secular priest, and then made his appearance in the church, where this transformation caused a lively satisfaction. Christianity, in its renewed youth, hailed with transport everything that announced that the old things were passed away.

It was not long before the last monk quitted the convent. Luther remained behind; his footsteps alone re-echoed in its long corridors—he sat silent and alone in the refectory, so lately vocal with the babble of the monks. A speaking silence! attesting the triumph of the Word of God. The convent had, indeed, ceased to have any existence. Luther, toward the end of December, 1524, transmitted to the Elector the keys of the monastery, together with a message, that himself would see where it might be God's will to feed him.† The Elector made over the convent to the university, and desired Luther to continue to reside in it. The abode of the monks was, ere long, to become the home of a Christian family.

Luther, who had a heart happily constituted for relishing the sweetness of domestic life, honoured and loved the marriage state. It is even likely that he had some preference for Catherine Bora. For a long while, his scruples and the thought of the calumnies which such a step would occasion,

* Cum expectam quotidie mortem et meritum hæretici supplicium (L. Epp. ii. p. 570, 30th Nov. 1524.)

† Muss und will Ich gehen wo mich Gott ernähret. —(Ibid. p. 589.)

had hindered his thinking of her; and he had offered the hand of poor Catherine first to Baumgartner of Nuremberg,[*] and afterwards to Doctor Glatz, of Orlamund.   But when Baumgartner declined, and Catherine herself refused Glatz, he began more seriously to consider whether he himself ought not to think of making her his wife.

His aged father, who had been so much grieved when he first took upon him the profession of an ecclesiastic, urged him to marry.[†]   But one thought above all was present in much power to the conscience of Luther.   Marriage is God's appointment—celibacy is man's.   He abhorred whatever bore the stamp of Rome.   " I desire," said he, to his friends, " to have nothing left of my papistic life."[‡]   Night and day he besought the Lord to put an end to his uncertainty.   At last a thought came to break the last ties which held him back.   To all the considerations of consistency and personal obedience which taught him to apply to himself that word of God—*It is not good that man should be alone*[§]—was added a higher and more powerful motive.   He recognized that if as a man he was called to the marriage state, he was also called to it as a Reformer.   This thought decided him.

" If that monk marries," said his friend Schurff the juris-consult, " he will cause men and devils to shout with laughter,[‖] and bring ruin upon all that he has hitherto effected."   This remark had upon Luther an effect the very reverse of what might have been expected.   To brave the world, the devil, and his enemies, and, by an act in man's judgment the most likely to ruin the Reformation, make it evident that its triumph was not to be ascribed to him, was the very thing he most of all desired.   Accordingly, lifting up his head, he boldly replied,—" I'll do it!   I will play this trick to the world and the devil!—I'll content my father and marry Catherine!"

* Si vis Ketam tuam a Bora tenere.   (L. Epp. ii. p. 553.)
† Aus Begehren meines lieben Vaters.   (Ibid. iii. p. 2.)
‡ Ibid. p. 1.   § Genesis ii. 18.
‖ Risuros mundum universum et diabolum ipsum.   (M. Ad. Vit. Luth. p. 130.)

Luther, by his marriage, broke even more irrevocably with the institutions of the Papacy. He sealed his doctrine by his own example,—and emboldened the timid to an entire renunciation of their delusions.* Rome had seemed to be here and there recovering the ground she had lost, and might have been indulging in dreams of victory;—but here was a loud explosion that carried wonder and terror into her ranks, and discovered, more clearly than ever, the courage of the enemy she had pictured to herself defeated and depressed. "I am determined," said Luther, "to bear witness to the Gospel, not by my words alone, but by my actions. I am determined, in the face of my enemies, who already are triumphing and exulting over me, to marry a nun,—that they may know that they have not conquered me.† I do not take a wife that I may live long with her; but, seeing people and princes letting loose their fury against me,—in the prospect of death, and of their again trampling my doctrine under foot, I am resolved to edify the weak, by leaving on record a striking confirmation of the truth of what I have taught."‡

On the 11th of June, Luther repaired to the house of his friend and colleague Amsdorff. He requested Pomeranus, whom he dignified with the special character of *the* Pastor, to give them the nuptial benediction. Lucas Cranach and Doctor John Apelles witnessed their marriage. Melancthon was not present.

No sooner had Luther's marriage taken place than all Christendom was roused by the report of it. On all sides accusations and calumnies were heaped upon him. "It is incest," exclaimed Henry the Eighth. "A monk has married a vestal!"§ said some. "Antichrist must be the fruit of such a union," said others; "for it has been predicted that he will

* Ut confirmem facto quæ docui, tam multos invenio pusillanimes in tanta luce Evangelii. (L. Epp. iii. p. 13.)

† Nonna ducta uxore in despectum triumphantium et clamantium Jo! Jo! hostium. (Ibid. p. 21.)

‡ Non duxi uxorem ut diu viverem, sed quod nunc propiorem finem meum suspicarer. (Ibid. p. 32.)

§ Monachus cum vestali copularetur. (M. Ad. Vit. Luth. p. 131.)

be the offspring of a monk and a nun." To which Erasmus made answer, with malicious sneer. " If that prophecy be true, what thousands of Antichrists the world has before now seen."[*] But while these attacks were directed against Luther, some prudent and moderate men, in the communion of the Church of Rome, undertook his defence. " Luther," said Erasmus, " has taken to wife a female of the noble house of Bora,—but she brought him no dowry."[†] One whose testimony carries still more weight, bore witness in his favour. Philip Melancthon, the honoured teacher of Germany, who had at first been alarmed by so bold a step, now remarked with that grave conscientiousness which commanded respect even from his enemies : " If it is asserted that there has been anything unbecoming in the affair of Luther's marriage, it is a false slander.[‡] It is my opinion, that, in marrying, he must have done violence to his inclination. The marriage state, I allow, is one of humility,—but it is also one of sanctity—if there be any sanctity in this world ; and the Scriptures everywhere speak of it as honourable in God's sight."

At first Luther was disturbed by the reproaches and indignities showered upon him. Melancthon showed more than his usual kindness and affection towards him ;[§] and it was not long before the Reformer was enabled to discern, in men's opposition, one mark of God's approval. " If the *world* were not scandalized by what I have done," said he, " I should have reason to fear that it was not according to God's mind."[¶]

Eight years had elapsed between the period when Luther first preached against indulgences, and the time of his union with Catherine Bora. It would be difficult to attribute, as is sometimes done, his zeal against the corruptions of the Church

* Quot Antichristorum millia jam olim habet mundus. (Er. Epp. p. 789.)

† Erasmus adds :—Partu maturo sponsæ vanus erat rumor. (Er. Epp. p. 780, 789.)

‡ Ὅτι ψεῦδος τοῦτο καὶ διαβολή ἐστι. (Corp. Ref. i. p. 753 ad Cam.)

§ Πᾶσα σπουδῇ καὶ εὐνοία. (Ibid.)

¶ Offenditur etiam in carne ipsius divinitatis et creatoris, he adds. (L. Epp. iii. p. 32.)

to an eager desire to enter into the marriage state.   He was
already turned forty-two ; and Catherine had passed two years
at Wittemberg since leaving the convent.

Luther's marriage was a happy one : " The greatest of
earthly blessings," said he, " is a pious and amiable wife,—
who fears God and loves her family, one with whom a man
may live in peace and in whom he may repose perfect confidence."

Some time after, in writing to one of his friends, he intimated that his Catherine might soon present him with a child ;*
and, in fact, just one year after their marriage, Catherine was
delivered of a boy.†   The charms of domestic life soon dispelled the dark clouds raised around him by the wrath of his
adversaries.   His Ketha, as he called her, manifested towards
him the tenderest affection, comforting him, when cast down,
by reciting passages of the Bible, relieving him from the cares
of the household, sitting by him in his intervals of leisure,
while she worked his portrait in embroidery, or reminded him
of the friends he had neglected to write to, and amused him by
the simplicity of her questions.   A sort of dignity seems to
have marked her deportment, for Luther occasionally spoke
of her as " *My Lord Catherine.*"   One one occasion he said,
jesting, that if ever he had to marry again, he would chisel an
obedient wife in stone, for, added he, " there is no possi-
bility of finding a real one."   His letters were full of tenderness for Catherine, whom he styled, " *his dear and gracious
wife*,"—" *his dear and amiable Ketha.*"   Luther's manner
acquired more playfulness from the society of his Catherine ;
and that happy flow of spirits continued from that time, and
was never lost even in the most trying circumstances.

Such was the almost universal corruption of the clergy, that
the priestly office had fallen into almost general disrepute : the
isolated virtue of a few faithful servants of God had not sufficed

* 21st Oct. 1525.   Catena mea simulat vel vere implet illud Genes 3.
Tu dolore gravida eris.   (L. Epp. iii. p. 35.)
† Mir meine liebe Kethe einen Hansen Luther bracht hat, gestern
um zwei. (8th June, 1526. Ibid. p. 119.)

to redeem it from contempt. Family peace and conjugal fidelity were continually being disturbed, both in towns and rural districts, by the gross passions of priests and monks;—none were safe from their seductions. The free access allowed them to families, and sometimes even the confidence of the confessional, was basely perverted into an opportunity of instilling deadly poison, that they might gratify their guilty desires. The Reformation, by abolishing the celibacy of the ecclesiastics, restored the sanctity of wedlock. The marriage of the clergy put an end to an untold amount of secret profligacy. The Reformers became examples to their flocks in the most endearing and important of all human relationships,—and it was not long before the people rejoiced to see the ministers of religion in the character of husbands and fathers.

On a hasty view, Luther's marriage had indeed seemed to multiply the difficulties in the way of the Reformation. It was still suffering from the effects of the revolt of the peasants; the sword of the Emperor and of the princes was unsheathed against it; and its friends, the Landgrave Philip, and the new Elector John, appeared discouraged and silenced.

Nevertheless, this state of things was of no long duration. The young Landgrave ere long, boldly raised his head. Ardent and fearless as Luther, the manly spirit of the Reformer had won his emulation. He threw himself with youthful daring into the ranks of the Reformation, while he at the same time studied its character with the grave intelligence of a thoughtful mind.

In Saxony, the loss of Frederic's prudence and influence was but ill supplied by his successor ; but the Elector's brother, Duke John, instead of confining himself to the office of a protector, intervened directly and courageously in matters affecting religion : " I desire," said he, in a speech communicated to the assembled clergy, on the 16th August, 1525, as he was on the point of quitting Weimar, "that you will in future preach the pure word of God, apart from those things which man has added." Some of the older clergy, not knowing how to set about obeying his directions, answered with simplicity,

—"But we are not forbidden to say mass for the dead, or to bless the water and salt?"—"Every thing,—no matter what," —replied the Elector, "must be conformed to God's word."

Soon after, the young Landgrave conceived the romantic hope of converting Duke George, his father-in-law. Sometimes he would demonstrate the sufficiency of the Scriptures— another time he would expose the Mass, the Papacy, and compulsory vows. His letters followed quick upon each other, and the various testimony of God's word was all brought to bear upon the old Duke's faith.*

These efforts were not without results. Duke George's son was won to the new opinions. But Philip failed with the father.—"A hundred years hence," said the latter, "and you will see who is right."—"Awful speech!" observed the Elector of Saxony: "What can be the worth, I pray you, of a faith that needs so much previous reflection?†—Poor Duke! he will hold back long—I fear God has hardened his heart, as Pharaoh's, in old time."

In Philip, the friends of the Gospel possessed a leader, at once bold, intelligent, and capable of making head against the formidable assaults its enemies were planning. But is it not sad to think, that from this moment the leader of the Reformation should be a soldier, and not simply a disciple of God's word? Man's part in the work was seen in due expansion, and its spiritual element was proportionably contracted. The work itself suffered in consequence, for every work should be permitted to develop itself, according to the laws of its own nature,—and the Reformation was of a nature essentially spiritual.

God was multiplying external supports. Already a powerful state on the German frontier—Prussia—unfurled with joy the standard of the Gospel. The chivalrous and religious spirit that had founded the Teutonic order, had gradually become extinct with the memory of the ages in which it arose.

* Rommels Urkundenbuch. I. p. 2.
† Was das für ein Glaube sey, der eine solche Erfahrung erfordert. (Seckend. p. 739.)

The knights, intent only upon their private interests, had given dissatisfaction to the people over whom they presided. Poland had seized the opportunity to impose her suzerainty on the order. People, knights, grand master, Polish influence, were so many different interests continually conflicting, and rendering the prosperity of the country impossible.

In this state of things, the Reformation found them, and all men saw in it the only way of deliverance for that unfortunate people. Brisman, Speratus, Poliander, (who had been secretary to Eck, at the time of the Leipsic discussion,) and others besides, preached the Gospel in Prussia.

One day a beggar, coming from the lands under the rule of the Teutonic knights, arrived in Wittemberg; and, stopping before the residence of Luther, sang slowly that noble hymn of Poliander's,

"At length redemption's come."*

The Reformer, who had never heard this Christian hymn, listened, rapt in astonishment. The foreign accent of the singer heightened his joy. "Again, again," cried he, when the beggar had ended. Afterwards he enquired where he had learned that hymn, and tears filled his eyes, when he heard from the poor man that it was from the shores of the Baltic that this shout of deliverance was sounding as far as Wittemberg:—then, clasping his hands, he gave thanks to God.†

In truth Redemption *was* come even thither !

"Take compassion on our weakness," said the people of Prussia to the Grand Master, "and send us preachers who may proclaim the pure Gospel of Jesus Christ." Albert at first gave no answer, but he entered into parley with Sigismund king of Poland, his uncle and suzerain lord.

The latter acknowledged him as hereditary Duke of Prussia,‡ and the new prince made his entry into his capital of Konigsberg, amidst the ringing of bells, and acclamations

* Es ist das Heyl uns kommen her.
† Dankte Gott mit Freuden. (Seck. p. 668.)
‡ Sleidan, Hist. de la Ref. p. 290.

of the inhabitants, who had decorated their houses, and strewed
their streets with flowers.   "There is but One religious order,"
said Albert, "and it is as comprehensive as Christianity itself!"
The monastic orders vanished, and that divinely appointed
order was restored.

The bishops surrendered their secular rights to the new
Duke; the convents were converted into hospitals; and the
Gospel carried into the poorest villages; and in the year fol-
lowing, Albert married Dorothy, daughter of the king of
Denmark, whose faith in the one Saviour was unshaken.

The Pope called upon the Emperor to take measures
against the "apostate" monk;—and Charles placed Albert
under interdict.

Another prince of the house of Brandenburg, the Cardinal-
Archbishop of Mentz, was just then on the point of following
his relation's example.   The revolt of the peasants was especially menacing in its aspect toward the ecclesiastical principalities; the Elector, Luther, and all Germany thought a
great revolution was at hand.   The Archbishop seeing no
better way to preserve his principality than to render it secular, privately requested Luther to sound the minds of the people
preparatory to so decided a step,*—which Luther accordingly
did, in a letter written with a view to its being made public,
wherein he said that the hand of God was heavy on the clergy,
and that nothing could save them.†   However the War of the
peasants having been brought to an earlier termination than
had been looked for: the Cardinal retained possession of his
temporalities—his uneasiness subsided, and all thoughts of se-
cularizing his position were dismissed !

Whilst John of Saxony, Philip of Hesse, and Albert of
Prussia, were openly taking part with the Reformation, and
thus, in place of the cautious Frederic, three princes of bold
and decided character were standing forward in its support,
the blessed Word was working its way in the Church, and
among the nations.   Luther besought the Elector to establish

* Seckend. p. 712.
† Er muss herunter.   (L. Epp. ii. p. 674.)

generally the preaching of the Gospel in place of the ministrations of Romish priests, and to direct a general visitation of
the churches.* About the same time at Wittemberg they
began to exercise the episcopal function, and ordain ministers;
" Let not the Pope, the bishops, or the monks, exclaim against
us," said Melancthon, " *we* are the Church ;—he who separates from us separates himself from the Church. There is
no other Church—save the assembly of those who have the
word of God, and who are purified by it."†

All this could not be said and done without occasioning a
strong reaction. Rome had thought the Reformation extinguished in the blood of the rebel peasants—but in all quarters
its flame was rising more bright and powerful than ever. She
decided on making one more effort. The Pope and the Emperor wrote menacing letters, the former from Rome, the latter from Spain. The Imperial government took measures
for restoring the ancient order of things, and preparations
were made for finally crushing the Reformation at the approaching Diet.

The electoral Prince of Saxony, and the Landgrave, in
some alarm, met on the 7th of November in the castle of
Friedewalt, and came to an agreement that their deputies at
the Diet should act in concert. Thus in the forest of Sullin-
gen arose the earliest elements of an evangelical association
in opposition to the leagues of Ratisbon and Dessau.

The Diet opened on the 11th of December, at Augsburg.
The princes favourable to the Gospel were not present, but
the deputies from Saxony and Hesse spoke out fearlessly :
" The rising of the peasants," said they, " was the effect of
impolitic and harsh usage. God's truth is not to be torn from
the heart by fire and sword : if you are bent on resorting to
violence against the reformed opinions, you will bring down
upon us calamities more terrible than those from which we
have but just escaped."

* L. Epp. iii. p. 28, 38, 51, &c.
† Dass Kirche sey allein diejenige, so Gottes Wort haben und damit
gereiniget werden. (Corp. Ref. i. p. 766.)

It was felt that the resolution of the Diet must be most important in its results. Every one desired, by postponing the decisive moment, to gain time to strengthen his own position. It was accordingly resolved, that the Diet should re-assemble at Spires in the month of May following; and in the meanwhile the rescript of Nuremberg was to continue in force. " When the Diet meet again," said they, " we will go fully into the questions of ' the holy faith,—public rights,—and the general peace.' "

The Landgrave pursued his plan. Toward the end of February, 1526, he had a conference with the Elector at Gotha. The two princes came to an understanding, that if attacked on account of the word of God, they would unite their forces to resist their adversaries. This alliance was formally ratified at Torgau, and was destined to be fruitful in important consequences.

However, the alliance he had concluded was of itself not enough to satisfy the Landgrave. Convinced that Charles was at work to compact a league " against Christ and his holy word," he addressed letter after letter to the Elector, urging upon him the necessity of uniting with other states: " For myself," said he, " rather would I die than deny the word of God, and allow myself to be driven from my throne."*

At the Elector's court much uncertainty prevailed. In fact, a serious difficulty stood in the way of union between the princes favourable to the Gospel; and this difficulty originated with Luther and Melancthon. Luther insisted that the doctrine of the Gospel should be defended by *God* alone. He thought that the less man meddled in the work, the more striking would be God's intervention in its behalf. All the politic precautions suggested, were in his view attributable to unworthy fear and sinful mistrust. Melancthon dreaded lest an alliance between the evangelical princes should hasten that very struggle which it was their object to avert.

The Landgrave was not to be deterred by such considerations, and laboured to gain over the neighbouring states to the

* Seckendorf, p. 768.

alliance, but he failed in his endeavours. The Elector of
Treves abandoned the ranks of the opposition, and accepted a
pension from the Emperor. Even the Elector Palatine,
whose disposition was known to be favourable to the Gospel,
declined Philip's advances.

Thus, in the direction of the Rhine, the Landgrave had
completely failed; but the Elector, in opposition to the advice
of the reformed divines, opened negociations with the princes
who had in all times gathered round the standard of the powerful chief of Saxony. On the 12th day of June, the Elector
and his son, the Dukes Philip, Ernest, Otho and Francis of
Brunswick and Lunenburg, Duke Henry of Mecklenburg,
Prince Wolf of Anhalt, Counts Albert and Gebhard of Mansfeld, assembled at Magdeburg, and there, under the presidence
of the Elector, they contracted an alliance similar to that of
Torgau.

"Almighty God," said the princes, "having in his unspeakable mercy again brought forward among men his holy
and eternal word, the food of our souls, and our richest treasure
on this earth,—and great efforts being made by the clergy
and their adherents to suppress and extirpate it,—we,—being
well assured that He who has sent it forth to glorify his name
upon earth, will know how to maintain it, mutually engage
to preserve that blessed word to our people, and to employ for
this end our goods, and our lives, the resources of our states,
and the arms of our subjects, and all that we have, putting our
trust not in our armies, but solely in the almighty power of
the Lord, of whom we desire to be but the instruments."* So
spoke the princes.

Two days after, the city of Magdeburg was received into
the alliance, and Albert of Brandenburg, the new Duke of
Prussia, acceded to it by a separate convention.

The Evangelic Union was formed; but the dangers it was
destined to ward off seemed every day to become more threatening. The priests, and such of the princes as adhered to the

* Allein auf Gott den Allmächtigen, als dessen Werkzeuge sie
handeln. (Hortleber, Ursache des deutschen Krieges, i. p. 1490.)

Romish party, had seen the Reformation, which they had thought stifled, suddenly growing up before them to a formidable height. Already the partisans of the Reformation were nearly as numerous as those of the Pope. If they should form a majority in the Diet, the consequences to the ecclesiastical states might be imagined. Now or never! It was no longer a heresy to be refuted, but a powerful party to be withstood. Victories of a different kind from those of Eck were needed on this occasion.

Vigorous measures had been already taken. The metropolitan chapter of the church of Mentz had convoked an assembly of its suffragans, and adopted the resolution to send a deputation to the Emperor and the Pope, entreating them to interpose for the deliverance of the Church.

At the same time, Duke George of Saxony, Duke Henry of Brunswick, and the Cardinal-Elector Albert, had met at Halle, and addressed a memorial to Charles. "The detestable doctrine of Luther," said they, " is making extensive progress ; every day attempts are made to seduce ourselves, and, failing to persuade us, they seek to compel us by exciting our subjects to revolt. We implore the Emperor's intervention."* On the breaking up of this conference, Brunswick himself set out for Spain to induce Charles to take the decisive step.

He could not have arrived at a more favourable juncture : the Emperor had just concluded with France the famous peace of Madrid. He seemed to have nothing left to apprehend from that quarter, and his undivided attention was now directed to the affairs of Germany. Francis the First had offered to defray half the expences of a war either against the heretics or against the Turks !

The Emperor was at Seville ;——he was on the eve of marriage with a princess of Portugal, and the banks of the Guadalquiver resounded with joyous festivity. A dazzling train of nobles, and vast crowds of people thronged the ancient capital of the Moors. The pomp and ceremonies of the Church were displayed under the roofs of its noble cathedral. A Le-

* Schmidt, Deutsche Gesch. viii. p. 202.

gate from the Pope officiated; and never before, even under Arabian rule, had Andalusia witnessed a spectacle of more magnificence and solemnity.

Just at that time, Henry of Brunswick arrived from Germany, and solicited Charles to save the Church and the Empire from the attacks of the monk of Wittemberg. His request was immediately taken into consideration, and the Emperor resolved on vigorous measures.

On the 23d of March, 1526, he addressed letters to several of the princes and free cities that still adhered to Rome. He also specially commissioned the Duke of Brunswick to communicate to them that he had learned with grief that the continued progress of Luther's heresy threatened to fill Germany with sacrilege, havoc, and bloodshed; and at the same time, to express the great pleasure he felt in the fidelity of the majority of the States, and to acquaint them that, laying aside all other business, he was about to leave Spain and repair to Rome, to concert measures with the Pope, and from thence to pass into Germany, and there oppose that abominable Wittemberg pest; adding, that it behoved them to continue steadfast in their faith, and in the event of the Lutherans seeking to seduce or oblige them to a renunciation of it, to repel their attempts by a united and courageous resistance: that he himself would shortly be among them and support them with all his power.[*]

When Brunswick returned into Germany, the Catholic party joyfully lifted up their heads. The Dukes of Brunswick, Pomerania, Albert of Mecklenburg, John of Juliers, George of Saxony, the Dukes of Bavaria, and all the dignitaries of the Church, on reading the menacing letters of the conqueror of Francis the First, thought their triumph secure. It was decided they should attend the approaching Diet, and humble the heretical princes; and in the event of the latter resisting, quell them with the sword. " I may be Elector of Saxony *any day I please*,"[†] was an expression ascribed by

* Archives of Weimar. (Seckend. p. 768.)
† Ranke, Deutsch Gesch. ii. p. 349. Rommel Urkunden, p. 22.

report to Duke George—words to which he afterwards endeavoured to attach another meaning. "The Lutheran party cannot long hold together," said his Chancellor to the Duke, in a tone of exultation; "let them mind what they are about:" —and truly Luther was on his guard, though not in the sense their words conveyed. He attentively observed the designs of the opposers of God's word: he, like Melancthon, expected that thousands of swords would ere long be unsheathed against the Gospel. But he sought a strength far above the strength of men. Writing to Frederic Myconius, he observed, "Satan is raging : ungodly priests take counsel together, and we are threatened with war. Exhort the people to contend earnestly before the throne of the Lord, by faith and prayer, that our adversaries, being overcome by the Spirit of God, may be constrained to peace. The most urgent of our wants—the very first thing we have to do, is to *pray :* let the people know that they are at this hour exposed to the edge of the sword, and the rage of the devil : let them *pray.*"*

Thus every thing indicated a decisive conflict. The Reformation had on its side the prayers of Christians, the sympathy of the people, and an ascendant in men's minds that no power could stay. The Papacy had with it the established order, the force of early habit, the zeal and hatred of powerful princes, and the authority of an Emperor whose dominion extended over both hemispheres, and who had just before deeply humbled the pride of Francis the First.

Such was the condition of affairs when the Diet of Spires was opened. Let us now turn our attention to Switzerland.

* Ut in mediis gladiis et furoribus Satanæ posito et periclitanti. (L. Epp. iii. p. 100.)

BOOK XI.

WE are about to contemplate the diversities, or, as they have been since called, *variations* of the Reformation. These diversities are among its most essential characters.

Unity in diversity, and diversity in unity—is a law of Nature, and also of the Church.

Truth may be compared to the light of the Sun. The light comes from heaven colourless, and ever the same; and yet it takes different hues on earth, varying according to the objects on which it falls. Thus different formularies may sometimes express the same christian Truth, viewed under different aspects.

How dull would be this visible creation, if all its boundless variety of shape and colour were to give place to an unbroken uniformity! And may we not add how melancholy would be its aspect, if all created beings did but compose a solitary and vast *Unity!*

The unity which comes from Heaven doubtless has its place,—but the diversity of *human nature* has its proper place also. In religion we must neither leave out God nor man. Without unity your religion cannot be *of God,*—without diversity, it cannot be the religion *of man.* And it ought to be of both. Would you banish from creation a law that its Divine Author has imposed upon it, namely,—that of boundless diversity? "Things without life giving sound," said Paul, "whether pipe or harp, except they give a *distinction* in the sounds, how shall it be known what is piped or harped?"* But, if in religion there is a diversity, the result of distinction of individuality, and which, by consequence, must subsist even in heaven,—there is a diversity which is the fruit of man's rebellion,—and this last is indeed a serious evil.

There are two opposite tendencies which may equally mislead us. The one consists in the exaggeration of *diversity*,—the other, in extending the *unity*. The great doctrines of man's salvation are as a line of demarcation between these two errors. To require more than the reception of those doctrines, is to disallow the diversity:—to require any thing less, is to infringe the unity.

This latter departure is that of rash and unruly minds looking beyond, or out of Jesus Christ, in the desire to set up systems and doctrines of men.

The former appears in various exclusive sects and is more especially seen in that of Rome.

It is the duty of the Church to reject Error from her bosom. If this be neglected, Christianity can not be upheld; but, pushed to an extreme, it would follow that the Church should take proceedings against the smallest deviations, and intervene in mere disputes about words; faith would be silenced, and christian feeling reduced to slavery. Not such was the condition of the Church in those times of real Catholicity,—the first ages. It cast out the sects which impugned the fundamental truths of the Gospel, but where these were received, it left full liberty to faith. Rome soon departed from these wise precedents, and, in proportion as an authoritative teaching of man established itself within the Church, there appeared a Unity of man's imposing.

A system of human appointment being once devised, rigour went on increasing from age to age. Christian liberty, respected by the catholicity of the earliest ages, was first limited, then chained, and finally stifled. Conviction, which, by the laws of our nature, as well as of God's word, should be freely formed in the heart and understanding, was imposed by exter-

* 1 Cor. xiv. 7.

mal authority, ready framed and squared by the masters of mankind. Thought, will, and feeling, all those faculties of our nature, which, once subjected to the Word and Spirit of God, should be left free in their working, were hindered of their proper liberty, and compelled to find vent in forms that had been previously settled. The mind of man became a sort of mirror wherein impressions to which it was a stranger were reproduced, but which, of itself, presented nothing! Doubtless there were those who were taught of God,—but the great majority of Christians received the convictions of other men; —a personal faith was a thing of rare occurrence: the Reformation it was that restored this treasure to the Church.

And yet there was, for a while, a space within which the human mind was permitted to move at large,—certain opinions, at least, which Christians were at liberty to receive or reject at will. But, as a besieging army, day by day, contracts its lines, compelling the garrison to confine their movements within the narrow enclosure of the fortress, and, at last, obliging it to surrender at discretion, just so, the hierarchy, from age to age, and almost from year to year, has gone on restricting the liberty allowed for a time to the human mind, until, at last, by successive encroachments, there remained no liberty at all. That which was to be believed,—loved,—or done,— was regulated and decreed in the courts of the Roman chancery. The faithful were relieved from the trouble of examining, reflecting, and combating; all they had to do was to repeat the formularies that had been taught them!

From that period, whenever, in the bosom of Roman Catholicism, a man has appeared inheriting the Catholicity of apostolic times, such a one, feeling his inability to act out the life imparted to him, in the bonds in which he is held, has been led to burst those bonds, and give to the astonished world another example of a Christian walking at liberty in the acknowledgment of no law but the law of God.

The Reformation, in restoring liberty to the Church, must therefore restore to it its original diversity, and people it with families united by the great features of resemblance derived from their common head, but varying in secondary features, and reminding us of the varieties inherent in human nature. Perhaps it might have been desirable that this diversity should have been allowed to subsist in the Universal Church without leading to sectarian divisions, and yet we must remember that *Sects* are only the expression of this diversity.

Switzerland, and Germany, which had till now developed themselves independently, came in contact with each other in the years we are about to retrace, and they afforded an example of that diversity of which we have spoken, and which was to be one of the characteristics of Protestantism. We shall have occasion to behold men perfectly agreeing in the great doctrines of the Faith yet differing on certain secondary questions. True it is that human passion found an entrance into these discussions, but while deploring such minglings of evil, Protestantism, far from seeking to disguise the diversity, publishes and proclaims it. Its path to unity is indeed long and difficult, but the unity it proposes is *real*.

Zwingle was advancing in the christian life. Whilst the Gospel had to Luther brought deliverance from the deep melancholy in which he had been plunged when in the convent of Erfurth, and developed in him a cheerfulness which often amounted to gaiety, and of which, from that time, the Reformer gave such repeated evidence, even when exposed to the greatest dangers,—Christianity had had quite a contrary effect on the joyous child of the mountains of the Tockenburg. Reclaiming Zwingle from his thoughtless and worldly career, it had stamped upon his character a seriousness which was not natural to him. This seriousness was indeed most needed. We have seen how, toward the close of 1522, numerous enemies appeared to rise against the Reformation.[*] From all sides reproaches were heaped upon Zwingle, and contentions would at times take place even in the churches.

Leo Juda, who, to adopt the words of an historian, was a man of small stature,[†] with a heart full of love for the poor,

[*] Vol. II. Book 8, to the end,

[†] Er war ein kurzer Mann. (Füsslin Beyträge, iv. p. 44.)

and zeal against false teachers, had arrived in Zurich about the end of 1522, to take the duty of pastor of St. Peter's church. He had been replaced at Einsidlen by Oswald Myconius.* His coming was a valuable acquisition to Zwingle and the Reformation.

One day, soon after his arrival, being at church, he heard an Augustine monk preaching with great earnestness that man was competent by his own strength to satisfy the righteousness of God. "Reverend father Prior," exclaimed Leo, "listen to me for an instant; and you, my dear fellow-citizens, keep your seats,—I will speak as becomes a Christian:" and he proceeded to show the unscriptural character of the teaching he had just been listening to.† A great disturbance ensued in the church.—Instantly several persons angrily attacked the "little priest" from Einsidlen. Zwingle, repairing to the Council, presented himself before them, and requested permission to give an account of his doctrine, in presence of the bishop's deputies;—and the Council, desiring to terminate the dissensions, convoked a conference for the 29th of January. The news spread rapidly throughout Switzerland. "A vagabond diet," observed his mortified adversaries, "is to be held at Zurich. All the vagrants from the high-road will be there."

Wishing to prepare for the struggle, Zwingle put forth sixty-seven theses. In them the mountaineer of the Tockenburg boldly assailed the Pope, in the face of all Switzerland. "They," said he, "who assert that the Gospel is nothing until confirmed to us by the Church, blaspheme God."

"Jesus Christ is the only way of salvation for all who have been, are, or shall be."

"Christians are all the brethren of Christ, and of one another; and they have no 'fathers,' upon earth;—away, therefore, with religious orders, sects, and parties."

"No compulsion should be employed in the case of such as do not acknowledge their error,—unless by their seditious conduct they disturb the peace of others."

* Ut post abitum Leonis, monachis aliquid legam. (Zw. Epp. p. 253.)
† J. J. Hottinger, Helw. Kirch. Gesch. iii. p. 105.

Such were some of the propositions put forth by Zwingle.

On the morning of Thursday, the 29th January, more than six hundred persons were collected in the hall of the Great Council, at Zurich. Many from the neighbouring cantons, as well as Zurichers, the learned, the higher classes, and the clergy, had responded to the call of the Council. "What will be the end of all this?"* was the question asked. None ventured to answer; but the breathless attention, deep feeling, and agitation, which reigned in the meeting, sufficiently showed that important results were looked for.

The burgomaster Roust, who had fought in the battle of Marignan, presided at the conference. The knight James Anwyl, grand master of the bishop's court at Constance, Faber the vicar-general, and several doctors of divinity, attended on the part of the bishop. Schaffhausen had deputed Doctor Sebastian Hofmeister; he was the only deputy from the cantons,—so weak, as yet, was the Reformation in Switzerland. On a table in the centre of the hall was deposited a Bible, and seated before it was Zwingle. "I am driven and beset on all sides," he had said, "yet I stand firm,† leaning on no strength of my own, but on Christ, the rock, by whose help I can do all things."

Zwingle stood up. "I have proclaimed," said he, "that salvation is to be found in Christ alone; and it is for this that, throughout Switzerland, I am charged with being a heretic, a seducer, and rebellious man. Here, then, I stand in God's name!"‡

On this, all eyes were turned to Faber, who, rising from his seat, thus replied:—"I am not sent to dispute,—but to report." The assembly in surprise, began to smile. "The Diet of Nuremberg," continued Faber, "has promised a Council within one year: we must wait for its assembling."

* Ein grosses Verwunderen, was doch nss der Sach werden wollte. (Bullinger, Chron. i. p. 97.)

† Immotus tamen maneo, non meis nervis nixus, sed petra Christo, in quo omnia possum. (Zw. Epp. p. 261.)

‡ Nun wohlan in dem Namen Gottes, hie bin ich. (Bullinger. Chron. p. 98.)

"What!" said Zwingle, "is not this large and intelligent meeting as competent as a Council?" then turning to those who presided, he added,—"Gracious Lords; defend the word of God."

A solemn silence ensued on this appeal. At last it was interrupted by the burgomaster. "If any one present has anything to say," said he, "let him say on." Still all were silent. "I implore all those who have accused me,—and I know that some are here present," said Zwingle, "to come forward and rebuke me for the truth's sake." Not a word! Again and again Zwingle repeated his request, but to no purpose. Faber, thus brought to close quarters, lost sight, for an instant, of the reserve he had imposed on himself, and stated that he had convicted of his error the pastor of Filispach, who was at that time in durance; but, having said this, he again relapsed into silence. It was all in vain that he was urged to bring forward the arguments by which he had convinced that pastor; he would give no answer. This silence on the part of the Romish doctors mortified the impatience of the assembly. A voice from the further end of the hall was heard exclaiming, —"Where have they got to—those braggarts, whose voices are so loud in our streets.* Come forward: there's the man you want." On this the burgomaster observed, smiling, "It seems that the sharp-edged sword that succeeded against the pastor of Filispach is fast fixed in its scabbard:"—and he proceeded to break up the meeting.

In the afternoon, the parties being again assembled, the Council resolved that master Ulric Zwingle, not being reproved by any one, was at liberty to continue to preach the Gospel; and that the rest of the clergy of the canton should be enjoined to advance nothing but what they could establish by the Scriptures.

"Thanks be to God, who will cause his word to prevail in heaven and in earth!" exclaimed Zwingle. On this Faber could not suppress his indignation. "The theses of master

* *i.e.*—the monks. Wo sind nun die grossen Hansen . . . . (Zw. Opp. i. p. 124.)

Ulric," said he, " are incompatible with the honour due to the
Church, and opposed to the doctrine of Christ,—and I can
prove it." " Do so," retorted Zwingle. But Faber declined,
except it should be in Paris, Cologne, or Friburg. " I acknowledge no authority but that of the Gospel," said Zwingle :
" Before you can shake one word of that, the earth itself will
open before you."* " That's always the cry," remarked Faber; " the Gospel,—nothing but the Gospel! Men might
lead holy lives in peace and charity if there were no Gospel!"† At these words the auditors indignantly rose from
their seats, and the meeting finally broke up.

The Reformation was gaining ground. It was at this period called to new conquests. After the skirmish at Zurich,
in which the ablest champions of the Papacy had kept silence,
who would be so bold as to oppose the new doctrines? But
methods of another kind were tried. The firmness of Zwingle,
and the republican freedom of his bearing, overawed his enemies. Accordingly, recourse was had to suitable methods for
subduing him. Whilst Rome was pursuing Luther with
anathemas, she laboured to win the Reformer of Zurich by
persuasions. Scarcely was the conference closed over when
Zwingle was surprised by a visit from the captain of the
Pope's guards—the son of the burgomaster Roust, accompanied by Einsius the legate, who was the bearer of a brief
from the Pontiff,—in which Adrian addressed Zwingle as his
" well-beloved son," and assured him of his special favour.
At the same time the Pope set others upon urging Zink to influence Zwingle.‡ " And what," enquired Oswald Myconias,
"does the Pope authorise you to offer him ?" " Everything
short of the Pontiff's chair,"§ answered Zink, earnestly."

* Es müss das Erdrych brechen. (Zw. Opp. i. p. 148.)
† Man möcht denocht früntlich, fridlich und tugendlich läben,
wenn glich kein Evangelium were. (Bull. Chron. p. 107. Zw. Opp.
i. p. 152.)
‡ Cum de tua egregia virtute specialiter nobis sit cognitum. (Zw.
Epp. p. 266.)
§ Serio respondit : Omnia certe præter eadem papalem. (Vit. Zwingli
per Osw. Myc.)

There was nothing, whether mitre, crozier, or cardinal's hat, which the Pope would not have given to buy over the Reformer of Zurich. But Rome altogether mistook her man —and vain were all her advances. In Zwingle, the Church of Rome had a foe even more determined than Luther. He had less regard for the long established notions and the ceremonies of former ages—it was enough to draw down his hostility that a custom, innocent in itself had been connected with some existing abuses. In his judgment the word of God alone was to be exalted.

But if Rome had so little understanding of the events then in progress in Christendom she wanted not for counsellors to give her the needful information.

Faber, irritated at the Pope's thus humbling himself before his adversary—lost no time in advising him. A courtier, dressed in smiles, with honied words upon his tongue, those who listened to him might have thought him friendly toward all, and even to those whom he charged with heresy,—but his hatred was mortal. Luther, playing on his name (Faber,) was accustomed to say—"The vicar of Constance is a blacksmith . . . . of lies. Let him take up arms like a man, and see how Christ defends us."[*]

These words were no uncalled-for bravado—for all the while that the Pope in his communications with Zwingle was complimenting him on his distinguished virtues, and the special confidence he reposed in him, the Reformer's enemies were multiplying throughout Switzerland. The veteran soldiers, the higher families, and the herdsmen of the mountains, were combined in aversion to a doctrine which ran counter to all their inclinations. At Lucerne, public notice was given of the performance of *Zwingle's passion;* and the people dragged about an effigy of the Reformer, shouting that they were going to put the heretic to death; and laying violent hands on some Zurichers who were then at Lucerne, compelled them to be spectators of this mock execution. "They shall not disturb my peace," observed Zwingle; "Christ will

[*] Prodeant volo, palamque arma capiant . . . . (Zw. Epp. p. 292.)

never fail those who are his." Even in the Diet threats against him were heard.[*] "Beloved Confederates," said the Councillor of Mullinen, addressing the cantons, "make a stand against Lutheranism while there is yet time. At Zurich no man is master in his own house."

This agitation in the enemies' ranks proclaimed, more loudly than any thing else could have done, what was passing in Zurich. In truth victory was already bearing fruits, the victorious party were gradually taking possession of the country; and every day the Gospel made some new progress. Twenty four canons, and a considerable number of the chaplains came of their own accord to petition the Council for a reform of their statutes. It was decided to replace those sluggish priests by men of learning and piety, whose duty it should be to instruct the youth of Zurich, and to establish, instead of their vespers and Latin masses, a daily exposition of a chapter in the Bible, from the Hebrew, and Greek texts, first for the learned, and then for the people.

Unhappily there are found in every army ungovernable spirits, who leave their ranks, and make onset too early, on points which it would be better for a while to leave unattacked. Louis Ketzer, a young priest, having put forth a tract in German, entitled the *Judgment of God against Images*, a great sensation was produced, and a portion of the people could think of nothing else. It is ever to the injury of essentials that the mind of man is pre-occupied with secondary matters. Outside one of the city gates, at a place called Stadelhofen, was stationed a crucifix elaborately carved, and richly ornamented. The more ardent of the Reformed, provoked at the superstitious veneration still paid this image, could not suppress their indignation whenever they had occasion to pass that way. A citizen, by name Claudius Hottinger, "a man of family," says Bullinger, "and well acquainted with the Scriptures," meeting the miller of Stadelhofen, to whom the crucifix belonged, enquired when he meant to take away his idol. "No one requires you to worship them," was the miller's

* Christum suis nunquam defecturum. (Zw. Epp. p. 273.)

reply. "But do you not know," retorted Hottinger, "that God's word forbids us to have graven images?" "Very well," replied the miller, "If you are empowered to remove them, I leave you to do so." Hottinger thought himself authorized to act, and he was soon after seen to leave the city, accompanied by a number of the citizens. On arriving at the crucifix, they deliberately dug round the image until, yielding to their efforts, it came down with a loud crash to the earth.

This daring action spread alarm far and wide. One might have thought religion itself had been overturned with the crucifix of Stadelhofen. "They are sacrilegious disturbers, —they are worthy of death," exclaimed the partisans of Rome. The Council caused the iconoclasts to be arrested.

"No," exclaimed Zwingle, speaking from his pulpit, "Hottinger and his friends have not sinned against God, nor are they deserving of death*——but they may be justly punished for having resorted to violence without the sanction of the magistrates."†

Meanwhile acts of a similar kind were continually recurring. A vicar of St. Peter's one day observing before the porch of that church a number of poor persons ill clad and famished, remarked to one of his colleagues, as he glanced at the images of the saints decked in costly attire——"I should like to strip those wooden idols and clothe those poor members of Jesus Christ." A few days after, at three o'clock in the morning, the saints and their fine trappings were missing. The Council sent the vicar to prison, although he protested that he had no hand in removing them. "Is it these blocks of wood," exclaimed the people, "that Jesus enjoined us to clothe? Is it of such images as these that he will say to the righteous—"*I was naked, and ye clothed Me?*" . . . Thus the Reformation, when resisted, rose to a greater height; and

. * The same principles are seen in the speeches of M. M. de Broglie and Royer-Collard, on occasion of the celebrated debates on the law of Sacrilege.

† Dorum habend ir unser Herren kein racht zuinen, sv zu töden. (Bull. Chr. p. 127.)

the more it was compressed, with the more force did it break forth and threaten to carry all before it.

These excesses conduced to some beneficial results. Another struggle was needed to issue in further progress—for in spiritual things as in the affairs of earthly kingdoms, there can be no conquest without a struggle—and since the adherents of Rome were inert, events were so ordered that the conflict was begun by the irregular soldiery of the Reformation. In fact, the magistrates were perplexed and undecided: they felt the need of more light in the matter; and for this end they resolved on appointing a second public meeting, to discuss in German, and on grounds of Scripture, the question as to images.

The bishops of Coira, Constance, and Bale, the university of the latter city, and the twelve cantons, were accordingly requested to send deputies to Zurich. But the bishops declined compliance, recollecting the little credit their deputies had brought them on occasion of the first meeting, and having no wish for a repetition of so humiliating a scene. Let the Gospel party discuss if they will—but let it be among themselves. On the former occasion, silence had been their policy—on this they will not even add importance to the meeting by their presence. Rome thought perhaps that the combat would pass over for want of combatants. The bishops were not alone in refusing to attend. The men of Unterwald returned for answer that they had no philosophers among them—but kind and pious priests alone—who would persevere in explaining the Gospel as their fathers had done; that they accordingly must decline sending a deputy to Zwingle and the like of him; but that only let him fall into their hands, and they would handle him after a fashion to cure him of his inclination for such irregularities. The only cantons that sent representatives were Schaffhausen* and Saint Gall.

On Monday, the 26th of October, more than nine hundred persons—among whom were the members of the Grand

---

* So wollten wir Ihm den Lohn geben, dass er's nimmer mehr thäte. (Simmler Samml. M.S.C. ix.)

Council—and no less than three hundred and fifty priests, were assembled after sermon in the large room of the Town Hall. Zwingle and Leo Juda were seated at a table on which lay the Old and New Testaments in the originals. Zwingle spoke first, and soon disposing of the authority of the hierarchy and its councils, he laid down the rights of every Christian church, and claimed the liberty of the first ages, when the Church had as yet no council either œcumenical or provincial. "The Universal Church," said he, "is diffused throughout the world, wherever faith in Jesus Christ has spread: in India as well as in Zurich . . . And as to particular churches, we have them at Berne, at Schaffhausen, and even here. But the Popes, with their cardinals and councils, are neither the Universal Church nor a particular Church.* This assembly which hears me," exclaimed he, with energy, "is the church of Zurich—it desires to hear the word of God, and can rightfully decree whatever it shall see to be conformable to the Scriptures."

Here we see Zwingle relying on the Church—but on the true Church,—not on the clergy, but on the assembly of believers. He applied to particular churches all those passages of Scripture that speak of the Church Catholic. He could not allow that a church that listened with docility to God's word could fall into error. The Church was, in his judgment, represented both politically and ecclesiastically by the Great Council.† He began by explaining each subject from the pulpit; and when the minds of his hearers were convinced, he proposed the different questions to the Council, who, in conformity with the ministers of the Church, recorded such decisions as they called for.‡

* Der Päbste, Cardinäle und Bischöffe Concilia sind nicht die christliche Kirche. (Füssl Beytr. III. p. 20.)

† Diacosion Senatus summa est potestas Ecclesiæ vice. (Zw. Opp. III. p. 339.)

‡ Ante omnia multitudinem de quæstione probe docere ita factum est, ut quidquid diacosii (the grand council,) cum verbi ministris ordinarent, jamdudum in animis fidelium ordinatum esset. (Zw. Opp. III. p. 339.)

In the absence of the bishops' deputies, Conrad Hoffman, an aged canon, undertook to defend the Pope. He maintained that the Church, the flock, the "third estate," was not author ized to discuss such matters. "I resided," said he, "for no less than twelve years at Heidelberg in the house of a man of extensive learning, named Doctor Joss—a kind and pious man—with whom I boarded and lived quietly for a long time, but then he always said that it was not proper to make such matters a subject of discussion; you see, therefore!" . On this every one began to laugh. "Thus," continued Hoff man, "let us wait for a Council—at present I shall decline taking part in any discussion whatever, but shall act accord· ing to the bishop's orders, even though he himself were a knave!"

"Wait for a Council!" interrupted Zwingle, "and who, think you, will attend a Council?—the Pope and some sleepy and ill-taught bishops, who will do nothing but what pleases them. No, that is not the Church: Hong and Küssnacht (two villages in the neighbourhood of Zurich,) are more of a Church than all the bishops and popes put together."

Thus did Zwingle assert the rights of Christians in general, whom Rome had stript of their inheritance. The assembly he addressed was in his view not so much the church of Zurich as its earliest representative. Here we see the beginnings of the Presbyterian system. Zwingle was engaged in delivering Zurich from the jurisdiction of the bishops of Constance—he was likewise detaching it from the hierarchy of Rome; and on this thought of *the flock* and the *assembly of believers*, he was laying the foundations of a new church order, to which other countries would afterwards adhere. ·

The discussion was continued. Several priests having defended the use of images, without deriving their arguments from Scripture, Zwingle, and the rest of the Reformers, refuted them by passages from the Bible. "If," said one of the presidents, "no one defends the images by the Scriptures, we shall call upon some of their advocates by name." No one coming forward, the curate of Wadischwyl was called. "He

is asleep," exclaimed one of the crowd. The curate of Hor-
gen was next called. "He has sent me in his stead," said his
vicar, "but I cannot answer for him." It was plain that the
power of the word of God was felt in the assembly. The
partisans of the Reformation were buoyant with liberty and
joy; their adversaries, on the contrary, were silent, uneasy,
and depressed. The curates of Laufen, Glattfelden, and Wet-
zikon, the rector and curate of Pfaffikon, the dean of Elgg,
the curate of Baretschwyl, the Dominicans and Cordeliers,
known for their preaching in defence of image worship and
the saints, were one after another invited to stand forward.
They all made answer that they had nothing to say in their
defence, and that, in future, they would apply themselves to
the study of the truth. "Until to-day," said one, "I have put
my faith in the ancient doctors, but now I will transfer my
faith to the new."—"It is not *us*," interrupted Zwingle, "that
you should believe. It is *God's word*. It is only the Scriptures of God that never can mislead us." The sitting had
been protracted,—night was closing in. The president, Hofmeister of Schaffhausen, rose and said: Blessed be God the
Almighty and Eternal, who, in all things, giveth us the victory,"—and he ended by exhorting the Town-Council of Zurich to abolish the worship of images.

On Tuesday, the assembly again met, Vadian being president, to discuss the doctrine of the Mass. "My brethren in
Christ," said Zwingle, "far from us be the thought that there
is any thing unreal in the body and blood of Christ.* Our
only aim is to prove that the Mass is not a sacrifice that can
be offered to God by one man for his fellow, unless indeed any
will be bold enough to say that a man can eat and drink for
his friend."

Vadian having twice inquired if any of those present had
any thing to say in defence of the doctrine impugned, and no
one coming forward, the canons of Zurich, the chaplains, and
several ecclesiastics declared themselves of Zwingle's opinion.

* Dass einigerly Betrug oder Falsch syg in dem reinen Blut und
Fleisch Christi. (Zw. Opp. i. p. 498.)

But scarcely had the Reformers overcome the partisans of the ancient doctrines, when they were called to contend against the impatient spirits of men clamorously demanding abrupt and violent changes, instead of prudent and gradual reformation. The unfortunate Conrad Grebel rose, and said: "It is not sufficient that we should talk about the Mass; it is our duty to do away with the abuses of it."—"The Council," answered Zwingle, "will put forth an edict on the subject." On this, Simon Stumpf exclaimed, "The Spirit of God has already decided,—why then refer the matter to the Council's decision?"*

The commandant Schmidt, of Kussnacht, rose gravely, and, in a speech marked by much wisdom, said,—"Let us teach Christians to receive Christ into their hearts.† Until this hour you have all been led away after idols. The dwellers in the plain have made pilgrimages to the hills,—those of the hill country have gone on pilgrimage to the plain; the French have made journeys into Germany, and the Germans into France. You now know whither you ought to go. God has lodged all things in Christ. Worthy Zurichers, go to the true source, and let Jesus Christ re-enter your territory, and resume his ancient authority."

This speech made a deep impression, and no one standing up to oppose it, Zwingle rose with emotion, and spoke as follows:—"My gracious lords, God is with us,—He will defend His own cause. Now then, in the name of our God, let us go forward." Here Zwingle's feelings overcame him;—he wept, and many of those near him also shed tears.

Thus ended the conference. The president rose;—the burgomaster thanked them, and the veteran, turning to the Council, said in a grave tone, with that voice that had been so often heard in the field of battle,—"Now then, let us take in hand the sword of the Word . . . . and may God prosper his own work!"

* Der Geist Gottes urtheilet. (Zw. Opp. i. p. 529.)
† Wie sy Christum in iren Herzen sollind bilden und machen. (Ibid. p. 534.)

This dispute, which took place in the month of October. 1523, was decisive in its consequences. The greater number of the priests, who were present at it, returned full of zeal to their stations in different parts of the canton ; and the effect of those memorable days was felt in every corner of Switzerland. The church of Zurich, which, in its connexion with the see of Constance, had always maintained a certain measure of independence was now completely emancipated. Instead of resting, through the bishop, on the Pope, it rested henceforth, through the people, on the Word of God. Zurich had recovered the rights of which Rome had deprived her. The city and its rural territory vied with each other in zeal for the work of the Reformation, and the Great Council merely obeyed the impulse of the people at large. On every important occasion, the city and the villages signified the result of their separate deliberations. Luther had restored the Bible to the Christian community,—Zwingle went further—he restored their rights. This is a characteristic feature of the Reformation in Switzerland. The maintenance of sound doctrine was entrusted, under God, to the people ; and recent events have shown that the people can discharge that trust better than priests or pontiffs.

Zwingle did not allow himself to be elated by victory ; on the contrary, the Reformation, under his guidance, was carried on with much moderation. " God knows my heart," said he, when the Council demanded his opinion, " He knows that I am inclined to build up, and not to cast down. There are timid spirits whom it is needful to treat tenderly ; let the mass, therefore, for some time longer, be read on Sundays in the churches, and let those who celebrate it be carefully protected from insult."*

The Council issued a decree to this effect. Hottinger and Hochrutiner, one of his friends, were banished from the canton for two years, and forbidden to return without an express permission.

* Ohne dass jemand sich unterstehe die Messpriester zu beschimpfen. (Wirtz H. K. G. v. p. 208.)

The Reformation at Zurich proceeded thus in a steady and Christian course. Raising the city day by day to a higher pitch of moral elevation, it cast a glory round her in the eyes of all who loved the word of God. Throughout Switzerland, therefore, those who welcomed the day-spring which had visited the Church, felt themselves powerfully attracted to Zurich. Oswald Myconius, after his expulsion from Lucerne, had spent six months in the valley of Einsidlen, when, returning one day, wearied and overpowered by the heat of the weather, from a journey to Glaris, he was met on the road by his young son, Felix,* who had run out to bring him tidings of his having been invited to Zurich, to take charge of one of the schools there. Oswald could hardly credit the happy intelligence, and hesitated for a while between hope and fear.† "I am thine," was the reply which, at length, he addressed to Zwingle. Geroldsek dismissed him with regret, for gloomy thoughts had taken possession of his mind. "Ah!" said he, "all who confess Christ are flocking to Zurich : I fear that one day we shall all perish there together."‡ A melancholy foreboding, which was but too fully realized when Geroldsek, and so many other friends of the Gospel lost their lives on the plain of Cappel.

At Zurich, Myconius had at last found a secure retreat. His predecessor, nicknamed at Paris, on account of his stature, "the tall devil," had neglected his duty. Oswald devoted his whole heart and his whole strength to the fulfilment of his. He explained the Greek and Latin classics; he taught rhetoric and logic; and the youth of the city listened to him with delight.§ Myconius was to become, to the rising generation, all that Zwingle was already to those of maturer years.

At first Myconius felt some alarm at the number of full-grown scholars committed to his care; but by degrees he

---

* Inesperato nuntio excepit me filius redeuntem ex Glareana. (Zw. Epp. p. 322.)

† Inter spem ac metum. (Ibid.)

‡ Ac deinde omnes simul pereamus. (Ibid. p. 323.)

§ Fuventus illum lubens audit. (Ibid. p. 361.)

gathered courage, and it was not long before he distinguished among his pupils a young man of four-and-twenty, whose intelligent looks gave sufficient indication of his love of study. This young man, whose name was Thomas Plater, was a native of the Valais. In that beautiful valley, through which the torrent of the Viege rolls its tumultuous waters, after escaping from the sea of glaciers and snow that encircles Mount Rosa,—seated between St. Nicholas and Standen, upon the hill that rises on the right of the river, is still to be seen the village of Grächen. This was Plater's birth-place. From under the shadow of those colossal Alps emerged one of the most remarkable of all the characters that figured in the great drama of the sixteenth century. At the age of nine he had been consigned to the care of a curate, a kinsman of his own, —by whom the little rustic was often so severely beaten, that his cries, he tells us himself, were like those of a kid under the hands of the butcher. One of his cousins took him along with him to visit the schools of Germany. But removing in this way from school to school, when he had reached the age of twenty, he scarcely knew how to read!* On his arrival at Zurich, he made it his fixed determination that he would be ignorant no longer, took his post at a desk in one corner of the school over which Myconius presided, and said to himself, "Here thou shalt learn, or here thou shalt die." The light of the Gospel quickly found its way to his heart. One morning, when it was very cold, and fuel was wanting to heat the school-room stove, which it was his office to tend, he said to himself, "Why need I be at a loss for wood, when there are so many idols in the church?" The church was then empty, though Zwingle was expected to preach, and the bells were already ringing to summon the congregation. Plater entered with a noiseless step, grappled an image of Saint John, which stood over one of the altars, carried it off, and thrust it into the stove, saying, as he did so, "Down with thee,—for in thou must go." Certainly neither Myconius nor Zwingle would have applauded such an act.

* See his Autobiography.

It was by other and better means that unbelief and superstition were to be driven from the field.   Zwingle and his
colleagues had stretched out the hand of fellowship to Myconius; and the latter now expounded the New Testament in
the Church of the Virgin, to a numerous and eager auditory.[*]
Another public disputation, held on the 13th and 14th January, 1524, terminated in renewed discomfiture to the cause of
Rome; and the appeal of the canon Koch, who exclaimed,
" Popes, cardinals, bishops, councils,—these are the church
for me!" awakened no sympathetic response.

Everything was moving forward at Zurich; men's minds
were becoming more enlightened,—their hearts more stedfast.
The Reformation was gaining strength.   Zurich was a fortress in which the new doctrine had entrenched itself, and
from within whose enclosure it was ready to pour itself
abroad over the whole confederation.

The enemies were aware of this.   They felt that they must
no longer delay to strike a vigorous blow.   They had remained quiet long enough.   The strong men of Switzerland,
her iron-sheathed warriors,—were up at last, and stirring;
and who could doubt, when they were once aroused, that the
struggle must end in blood ?

The Diet was assembled at Lucerne.   The priests made a
strenuous effort to engage that great council of the nation in
their favour.   Friburg and the Forest Cantons proved themselves their docile instruments.   Berne, Basle, Soleure, Glaris,
and Appenzel, hung doubtfully in the balance.   Schaffhausen
was almost decided for the Gospel ; but Zurich alone assumed
a determined attitude as its defender.   The partisans of Rome
urged the assembly to yield to their pretensions and adopt their
prejudices.   " Let an edict be issued," said they, " enjoining all
persons to refrain from inculcating or repeating any new or Lutheran doctrine, either secretly or in public; and from talking
or disputing on such matters in taverns, or over their wine."[†]

* Weise Füsslin Beyter. iv. p. 66.
† Es soll uieman in den Wirtzhůseren oder sunst hinter dem Wyn
von Lutherischen oder newen Sachen uzid reden.   (Bull. Chr. p. 144.)

Such was the new ecclesiastical law which it was attempted to establish throughout the confederation.

Nineteen articles to this effect were drawn up in due form,—ratified, on the 26th January, 1523, by all the states—Zurich excepted, and transmitted to all the bailiffs, with injunctions that they should be strictly enforced,—"which caused," says Bullinger, "great joy among the priests, and great grief among the faithful." A persecution, regularly organized by the supreme authority of the confederation, was thus set on foot.

One of the first who received the mandate of the Diet was Henry Flackenstein of Lucerne, the bailiff of Baden. It was to his district that Hottinger had retired when banished from Zurich, after having overthrown the crucifix at Stadelhofen; and he had here given free utterance to his sentiments. One day, when he was dining at the Angel Tavern, at Zurzach, he had said that the priests expounded Holy Scriptures amiss, and that trust ought to be reposed in none but God alone.* - The host, who was frequently coming into the room to bring bread or wine, lent an attentive ear to what seemed to him very strange discourse. On another occasion, when Hottinger was paying a visit to one of his friends—John Schutz of Schneyssingen,—" Tell me," said Schutz, after they had finished their repast, " what is this new religion that the priests of Zurich are preaching?"—" They preach," replied Hottinger, "that Christ has offered himself up *once only* for all believers, and by that one sacrifice has purified them and redeemed them from all iniquity; and they prove by Holy Scripture that the Mass is a mere delusion."

Hottinger had afterwards (in February, 1523,) quitted Switzerland, and repaired on some occasion of business, to Waldshut, on the other side of the Rhine. In the meanwhile, measures had been taken to secure his person; and when the poor Zuricher, suspecting no danger, recrossed the Rhine about the end of February, he had no sooner reached Co-

* Wie wir unser pitt Hoffnung und Trost allein uf Gott. (Bull. Chr. p. 146.)

klentz, a village on the left bank of the river, than he was arrested. He was conveyed to Klingenau, and as he there fearlessly confessed his belief, Flackenstein said, in an angry tone, " I will take you to a place where you shall meet with those who will give you a fitting answer." Accordingly the bailiff dragged his prisoner first before the magistrates of Klingenau, next before the superior tribunal of Baden, and ultimately, since he could not elsewhere obtain a sentence of condemnation against him, before the Diet asssembled at Lucerne. He was resolved that in one quarter or another he would find judges to pronounce him guilty.

The Diet was prompt in its proceedings, and condemned Hottinger to lose his head. When this sentence was communicated to him, he gave glory to Jesus Christ. "Enough, enough," cried Jacob Troger, one of the judges, " we do not sit here to listen to sermons—thou shalt babble some other time."—" He must have his head taken off for this once," said the bailiff Am-Ort, with a laugh, " but if he should recover it again, we will all embrace his creed."—" May God forgive those who have condemned me !" exclaimed the prisoner ; and when a monk presented a crucifix to his lips, " It is the heart," said he, pushing it away, " that must receive Jesus Christ."

When he was led forth to death, there were many among the spectators who could not restrain their tears. He turned towards them, and said, " I am going to everlasting happiness." On reaching the place of execution, he lifted up his eyes to heaven, saying, " Oh, my Redeemer, into thy hands I commend my spirit !"—and a moment after, his head rolled upon the scaffold.

No sooner had the blood of Hottinger been shed than the enemies of the Reformation seized the opportunity of inflaming the anger of the confederates to a higher pitch. It was in Zurich that the root of the mischief must be crushed. So terrible an example as that which had now been set, could not fail to intimidate Zwingle and his followers. One vigorous effort more,—and the Reformation itself would share the fate of Hottinger.   The Diet immediately resolved that a deputation should be sent to Zurich, to call on the councils and the citizens to renounce their new faith.

The deputies were admitted to an audience on the 21st of March. "The ancient unity of the Christian Church is broken," said they; "the evil is gaining ground; the clergy of the four Forest Cantons have already intimated to the magistrates that aid must be afforded them, or their functions must cease.   Confederates of Zurich! join your efforts to ours; root out this new religion;* dismiss Zwingle and his disciples; and then let us all unite to remedy the abuses which have arisen from the encroachments of popes and their courtiers."

Such was the language of the adversary.   How would the men of Zurich now demean themselves?   Would their hearts fail them?   Had their courage ebbed away with the blood of their fellow-citizens?

The men of Zurich left neither friends nor enemies long in suspense.   The reply of the Council was calm and dignified. They could make no concessions in what concerned the word of God.   And their very next act was a reply more emphatic still.

It had been the custom ever since the year 1351, that, on Whit Monday, a numerous company of pilgrims, each bearing a cross, should go in procession to Einsidlen, to worship the Virgin.   This festival,† instituted in commemoration of the battle of Tatwyll, was commonly attended with great disorders.   It would fall, this year, on the 7th May.   At the instance of the three pastors, it was now abolished, and all the other customary processions were successively brought under due regulation.

Nor did the Council stop here.   The relics, which had given

* Zurich selbigen ausreuten und untertrucken helfe.   (Holt Helv. K. G. iii. p. 170.)

† Uff einen creitzgang sieben unehelicher kinden überkommen wurdend.   (Bullinger Chr. p. 160.)

22*

occasion to so many superstitions, were honourably interred.[*] And then, on the further requisition of the three pastors, an edict was issued, decreeing that, inasmuch as God alone ought to be honoured, the images should be removed from all the churches of the canton, and their ornaments applied to the relief of the poor. Accordingly, twelve councillors,—one for each tribe, the three pastors, and the city architect,—with some smiths, carpenters, and masons, visited the several churches; and having first closed the doors, took down the crosses, obliterated the paintings, whitewashed the walls, and carried away the images, to the great joy of the faithful, who regarded this proceeding, Bullinger tells us, as a glorious act of homage to the true God. In some of the country parishes the ornaments of the churches were committed to the flames, "to the honour and glory of God." Soon after this, the organs were suppressed, on account of their connection with many superstitious observances; and a new form of baptism was established, from which everything unscriptural was carefully excluded.[†]

The triumph of the Reformation threw a joyful radiance over the last hours of the burgomaster Roust and his colleague. They had lived long enough; and they both died within a few days after the restoration of a purer mode of worship.

The Swiss Reformation here presents itself to us under an aspect rather different from that assumed by the Reformation in Germany. Luther had severely rebuked the excesses of those who broke down the images in the churches of Wittemberg;—and here we behold Zwingle, presiding in person over the removal of images from the temples of Zurich. This difference is explained by the different light in which the two Reformers viewed the same object. Luther was desirous of retaining in the Church all that was not expressly contradicted by Scripture,—while Zwingle was intent on abolishing all that could not be proved by Scripture. The German Reformer wished to remain united to the Church of

* Und es eerlich bestattet hat. (Bull. Chr. p. 161.)
† Habend die nach inen zu beschlossen.

all preceding ages, and sought only to purify it from everything that was repugnant to the word of God.   The Reformer of Zurich passed back over every intervening age till he
reached the times of the apostles ; and, subjecting the Church
to an entire transformation, laboured to restore it to its primitive condition.

Zwingle's Reformation, therefore, was the more complete.
The work which Divine Providence had entrusted to Luther,
—the re-establishment of the doctrine of Justification by Faith,
was undoubtedly the great work of the Reformation ; but
when this was accomplished, other ends, of real, if not of primary importance, remained to be achieved ; and to these, the
efforts of Zwingle were more especially devoted.

Two mighty tasks, in fact, had been assigned to the Reformers.   Christian Catholicism taking its rise amidst Jewish
Pharisaism, on the one hand, and the Paganism of Greece, on
the other, had, by degrees, contracted something of the spirit
of each of those systems, and had thus been transformed into
Roman Catholicism.   The Reformation, therefore, whose
mission it was to purify the church, had to clear it alike from
the Jewish and the Pagan element.

The Jewish element had incorporated itself chiefly with that
portion of Christian doctrine which relates to man.   Catholicism had borrowed from Judaism the pharisaic notions of inherent righteousness, and salvation obtainable by human
strength or works.

The Pagan element had allied itself principally with that
other portion of Christian doctrine which relates to God.   Paganism had corrupted the catholic notion of an infinite Deity,
whose power, being absolutely all-sufficient, acts everywhere
and at every moment.   It had set up in the church the dominion of symbols, images, and ceremonies ; and the saints
had become the demi-gods of Popery.

The Reformation, in the hands of Luther, was directed essentially against the Jewish element.   With this he had been
compelled to struggle at the outset, when an audacious monk,

on behalf of the Pope, was bartering the salvation of souls for paltry coin.

The Reformation, as conducted by Zwingle, was directed mainly against the Pagan element. It was this that he had first encountered, in the chapel of the Virgin at Einsidlen, when crowds of worshippers, benighted as those of old who thronged the temple of Ephesian Diana, were gathered from every side to cast themselves down before a gilded idol.

The Reformer of Germany proclaimed the great doctrine of justification by faith,—and, in so doing, inflicted a death blow on the pharisaic righteousness of Rome. The Swiss Reformer, undoubtedly, did the same. The inability of man to save himself is the fundamental truth on which all reformers have taken their stand. But Zwingle did something more. He brought forward, as practical principles, the existence of God, and His sovereign, universal, and exclusive agency ; and by the working out of these principles, Rome was utterly bereft of all the props that had supported her paganized worship.

Roman Catholicism had exalted man and degraded God. Luther reduced man to his proper level of abasement ; and Zwingle restored God, (if we may so speak,) to his unlimited and undivided supremacy.

Of these two distinct tasks, which were specially, though not exclusively, allotted to the two Reformers, each was necessary to the completion of the other. It was Luther's part to lay the foundation of the edifice—Zwingle's to rear the superstructure.

To an intellect gifted with a still more capacious grasp, was the office reserved of developing on the shores of the Leman, the peculiar characters of the Swiss and the German Reformation,—blending them together and imprinting them thus combined, on the Reformation as a whole.*

But while Zwingle was thus carrying on the great work, the disposition of the cantons was daily becoming more hostile. The government of Zurich felt how necessary it was to assure itself of the support of the people. The people, more-

* Litterarischer Anzeiger, 1840, No. 27.

over,—that is to say, "the assembly of believers," was, according to Zwingle's principles, the highest earthly authority to which an appeal could be made. The Council resolved, therefore, to test the state of public opinion, and instructed the bailiffs to demand of all the townships, whether they were ready to endure everything for the sake of our Lord Jesus Christ, "who shed his precious blood," said the Council, "for us poor sinners."[*] The whole canton followed close upon the city in the career of Reformation,—and, in many places, the houses of the peasants had become schools of Christian instruction, in which the Holy Scriptures were constantly read.

The proclamation of the Council was received by all the townships with enthusiasm: "Only let our magistrates hold fast and fearlessly to the word of God," answered they, "we will help them to maintain it;[†] and, if any should seek to molest them, we will come like brave and loyal citizens to their aid." The peasantry of Zurich showed, on that occasion, as they have recently shown again, that the strength of the Church is in the Christian people.

But the people were not alone. The man whom God had placed at their head, answered worthily to their call. Zwingle seemed to multiply himself for the service of God. Whosoever, in any of the cantons of Switzerland, suffered persecution for the Gospel's sake, addressed himself to him [‡] The weight of business, the care of the churches,[§] the solicitude inspired by that glorious struggle which was now beginning to be waged in every valley of his native land—all pressed heavily on the Evangelist of Zurich. At Wittemberg, the tidings of his courageous deportment were received with joy. Luther

* Der sin rosenfarw blüt alein für uns arme sunder vergossen hat. (Bull. Chr. p. 180.)

† Meine Herrn sollten auch nur dapfer bey dem Gottsworte verbleiben. (Füssl. Beytr. iv. p. 107. where the answer given by each township is recorded.)

‡ Scribunt e Helvetiis ferme omnes qui propter Christum premuntur. (Zw. Epp. p. 348.)

§ Negotiorum strepitus et ecclesiarum curæ ita me undique quatiunt. (Ibid.)

and Zwingle were the two great luminaries of Upper and
Lower Germany; and the doctrine of salvation, which they
proclaimed so powerfully, was fast diffusing itself over all
those vast tracts of country that stretch from the summit
of the Alps to the shores of the Baltic and the German
Ocean.

While the word of God was pursuing its victorious course
over these spacious regions, we cannot wonder that the Pope
in his palace, the inferior clergy in their presbyteries, the magistrates of Switzerland in their councils, should have viewed
its triumphs with alarm and indignation.   Their consternation
increased every day.   The people had been consulted;—the
Christian people had again become something in the Christian
Church ; their sympathies and their faith were now appealed
to, instead of the decrees of the Roman chancery.   An attack
so formidable as this must be met by a resistance more formidable still.   On the 18th April, the Pope addressed a brief to
the Confederates ; and, in the month of July, the Diet assembled at Zug, yielding to the urgent exhortations of the Pontiff,
sent a deputation to Zurich, Schaffhausen, and Appenzel, to
notify to those states their fixed determination that the new
doctrine should be entirely suppressed, and its adherents subjected to the forfeiture of property, honours, and even life itself.   Such an announcement could not fail to excite a strong
sensation at Zurich ; but a resolute answer was returned from
that canton,—that in matters of faith, the word of God alone
must be obeyed.   When this reply was communicated to the
assembly, the liveliest resentment was manifested on the part
of Lucerne, Schwitz, Uri, Unterwalden, Friburg, and Zug,
and, forgetting the reputation and the strength which the accession of Zurich had formerly, imparted to the infant Confederation, forgetting the precedence which had been assigned to
her, the simple and solemn oaths of fidelity by which they
were bound to her,—the many victories and reverses they had
shared with her,—these states declared that they would no
longer sit with Zurich in the Diet.   In Switzerland, therefore, as well as in Germany, the partisans of Rome were the

first to rend asunder the federal union. But threats and breaches of alliance were not enough. The fanaticism of the cantons was clamorous for blood; and it soon appeared what were the weapons which Popery intended to wield against the word of God.

The excellent Œxlin,[*] a friend of Zwingle, was the pastor of Burg, a village in the vicinity of Stein, upon the Rhine. The bailiff Am-Berg, who had previously appeared to favour the cause of the Gospel,[†] being anxious to obtain that bailiwick, had pledged himself to the leading men of the canton of Schwitz, that he would put down the new religion. Œxlin, though not resident within his jurisdiction, was the first object of his persecution.

On the night of the 7th July, 1524, near midnight, a loud knocking was heard at the pastor's door; it was opened;— they were the soldiers of the bailiff. They seized him and dragged him away prisoner, in spite of his cries. Œxlin, believing that they meant to put him to death, shrieked out 'Murder!'' The inhabitants rose from their beds in affright, and the whole village immediately became a scene of tumult, the noise of which was heard as far as Stein. The sentinel posted at the castle of Hohenklingen fired the alarm gun, the tocsin was sounded, and the inhabitants of Stein, Stammheim, and the adjacent places, were shortly all a-foot and clustering together in the dark, to ask each other what was the matter.

Stammheim was the residence of the deputy-bailiff Wirth, whose two eldest sons, Adrian and John, young priests full of piety and courage, were zealously engaged in preaching the Gospel. John especially was gifted with a fervent faith, and stood prepared to offer up his life in the cause of his Saviour. It was a household of the patriarchal cast. Anna, the mother, who had brought the bailiff a numerous family, and reared them up in the fear of God, was revered for her virtues through the whole country round. At the sound of the tu-

* See Vol. ii. p. 296.
† Der war anfangs dem Evangelio günstig. (Bull. Chr. p. 180.)

mult in Burg, the father and his two sons came abroad like their neighbours. The father was incensed when he found that the bailiff of Frauenfeld had exercised his authority in a manner repugnant to the laws of his country. The sons were grieved by the tidings that their friend and brother, whose good example they delighted to follow, had been carried off like a criminal. Each of the three seized a halberd, and regardless of the fears of a tender wife and mother, father and sons joined the troop of townspeople who had sallied out from Stein with the resolute purpose of setting their pastor at liberty. Unfortunately, a band of those ill-disposed persons who never fail to make their appearance in a moment of disorder, had mingled with the burghers in their march. The bailiff's serjeants were hotly followed; but warned by the tocsin and the shouts of alarm which echoed on every side, they redoubled their speed, dragging their prisoner along with them, and in a little time the Thur was interposed between them and their pursuers.

When the people of Stein and Stammheim reached the bank of the river and found no means of crossing it, they halted on the spot, and resolved to send a deputation to Frauenfeld. "Oh!" said the bailiff Wirth, "the pastor of Stein is so dear to us that I would willingly sacrifice all I possess,— my liberty,—my very heart's blood—for his sake."[*] The rabble, meanwhile, finding themselves in the neighbourhood of the convent of Ittingen, occupied by a community of Carthusians, who were generally believed to have encouraged the bailiff Am-Berg in his tyranny, entered the building and took possession of the refectory. They immediately gave themselves up to excess, and a scene of riot ensued. In vain did Wirth entreat them to quit the place;[†] he was in danger of personal ill treatment among them. His son Adrian had remained outside of the monastery; John entered it, but shocked by what he beheld within, came out again imme-

---

[*] Sunder die kuttlen in Buch fur In wagen. (Bull. Chr. p. 193.)

[†] Und badt sy um Gottes willen uss dem Kloster zu gand. (Ibid. p. 193.)

diately.[*] The inebriated peasants proceeded to pillage the cellars and granaries, to break the furniture to pieces, and to burn the books.

As soon as the news of these disorders reached Zurich, the deputies of the Council were summoned in haste, and orders issued for all persons belonging to the canton who had left their homes to return to them immediately. These orders were obeyed. But a crowd of Thurgovians, drawn together by the tumult, now established themselves in the convent for the sake of the good cheer which they found there. A fire suddenly broke out, no one could tell how,—and the edifice was reduced to ashes.

Five days after, the deputies of the cantons were convened at Zug. Nothing was heard in this assembly but threats of vengeance and death. "Let us march," said they, "with our banners spread, against Stein and Stammheim, and put the inhabitants to the sword." The deputy-bailiff and his two sons had long been objects of especial dislike on account of their faith. "If any one is guilty," said the deputy from Zurich, "he must be punished; but let it be by the rules of justice, not by violence." Vadian, the deputy from St. Gall, spoke to the same effect. Hereupon the avoyer John Hug of Lucerne, unable any longer to contain himself, broke out into frightful imprecations.[†] "The heretic Zwingle is the father of all these rebellions; and you, Doctor of St. Gall, you favour his hateful cause, and labour for its advancement. You shall sit here with us no longer!" The deputy for Zug endeavoured to restore order, but in vain. Vadian retired; and knowing that his life was in danger from some of the lower order of the people, secretly left the town, and, by a circuitous road, reached the convent of Cappel in safety.

The magistrates of Zurich, intent upon repressing all commotion, resolved upon a provisional arrest of the individuals against whom the anger of the confederates had been more particularly manifested. Wirth and his sons were living

* Dan es im leid was. (Bull. Chr. p. 195.)
† Mit fluchen und witen. (Ibid. p. 194.)

quietly at Stammheim. "Never," said Adrian Wirth from
the pulpit, "can the friends of God have any thing to fear
from His enemies." The father was warned of the fate that
awaited him, and advised to make his escape along with his
sons. "No," he replied, "I put my trust in God, and will
wait for the serjeants here." When at length a party of
soldiers presented themselves at his door—"Their worships
of Zurich," said he, "might have spared themselves this
trouble;—had they only sent a child to fetch me, I would have
obeyed their bidding."* The three Wirths were carried to
Zurich and lodged in the prison. Rutiman, the bailiff of
Nussbaum, shared their confinement. They underwent a
rigid examination; but the conduct they were proved to have
held furnished no ground of complaint against them.

As soon as the deputies of the cantons were apprized of the
imprisonment of these four citizens, they demanded that they
should be sent to Baden, and decreed that, in case of a refusal,
an armed power should march upon Zurich, and carry them
off by force. "It belongs of right to Zurich," replied the
deputies of that canton, "to determine whether these men are
guilty or not, and we find no fault in them." Hereupon, the
deputies of the cantons cried out, "Will you surrender them
to us, or not?—answer yes or no—in a single word." Two
of the deputies of Zurich mounted their horses at once, and
repaired with all speed to their constituents.

Their arrival threw the whole town into the utmost agitation. If the authorities of Zurich should refuse to give up the
prisoners, the confederates would soon appear in arms at their
gates, and, on the other hand, to give them up, was, in effect,
to consent to their death. Opinions were divided. Zwingle
insisted on a refusal. "Zurich," said he, "must remain
faithful to its ancient laws." At last a kind of compromise
was suggested. "We will deliver up the prisoners," said
they to the Diet, "but on this condition, that you shall examine them regarding the affair of Ittingen only, and not with
reference to their faith." The Diet agreed to this proposition;

* Dann hättind sy mir ein kind geschikt. (Bull. Chr. p. 186.)

and on the Friday before St. Bartholomew's day, (August, 1524,) the three Wirths and their friend took their departure from Zurich under the escort of four Councillors of State and a few soldiers.

The deepest concern was manifested on this occasion by the whole body of the people. The fate which awaited the two old men and the two brothers was distinctly foreseen. Nothing but sobs was heard as they passed along. "Alas!" exclaims a contemporary writer, "what a woeful journey was that!"[*] The churches were all thronged. "God will punish us," cried Zwingle,—"He will surely punish us. Let us at least beseech Him to visit those poor prisoners with comfort, and strengthen them in the true faith."[†]

On the Friday evening, the prisoners arrived at Baden, where an immense crowd was awaiting to receive them. They were taken first to an inn, and afterwards to the jail. The people pressed so closely round to see them that they could scarcely move. The father, who walked first, turned round towards his sons, and meekly said,—"See, my dear children, we are like those of whom the Apostle speaks,—men appointed to death, a spectacle to the world, to angels and to men."—(1 Cor. iv. 9.) Just then he chanced to observe, among the crowd, the bailiff Am-Berg, his mortal enemy, and the prime author of all his misfortunes. He went up to him, held out his hand, and, grasping Am-Berg's,—though the bailiff would have turned away,—said, with much composure, "There is a God above us, and He knows all things."

The examination began the next morning. Wirth, the father, was the first who was brought before the tribunal. Without the least consideration for his character or for his age, he was put to the torture; but he persisted in declaring that he was innocent both of the pillage and the burning of Ittingen. A charge was then brought against him of having destroyed an image representing St. Anne. As to the other

* O weh! was elender Fahrt war das! (Bern. Weyss. Füssl. Beyt. iv. p. 56.)
† Sy troste und in warem glouben starckte. (Bull. Chr. p. 188.)

prisoners,—nothing could be substantiated against them, except that Adrian Wirth was married, and that he was accustomed to preach after the manner of Zwingle and Luther; and that John Wirth had given the holy sacrament to a sick man without candle or bell![*]

But the more conclusively their innocence was established, the more furious became the excitement of their adversaries. From morning till noon of that day, the old man was made to endure all the severity of torture. His tears were of no avail to soften the hearts of his judges. John Wirth was still more cruelly tormented. "Tell us," said they, in the midst of his agonies, "from whom didst thou learn thy heretical creed? Was it Zwingle, or who else, that taught it thee?" And when he was heard to exclaim, "O merciful and everlasting God! grant me help and comfort!" "Aha!" said one of the deputies, "where is your *Christ* now?" When Adrian was brought forward, Sebastian von Stein, a deputy of Berne, addressing him thus :—"Young man, tell us the truth, for if you refuse to do so, I swear by my knighthood,—the knighthood I received on the very spot where God suffered martyrdom,—we will open all the veins in your body, one by one." The young man was then hoisted up by a cord, and while he was swinging in the air, "Young master," said Stein, with a fiendish smile,[†] "this is our wedding gift;" alluding to the marriage which the youthful ecclesiastic had recently contracted.

The examination being now concluded, the deputies returned to their several cantons to make their report, and did not assemble again until four weeks had expired. The bailiff's wife,—the mother of the two young priests,—repaired to Baden, carrying a child in her arms, to appeal to the compassion of the judges. John Escher, of Zurich, accompanied her as her advocate. The latter recognised among the judges Jerome

[*] On Kertzen, schellen und andern so bissher güüpt ist. (Bull. Chr. p. 196.)

[†] Alls man inn am folter seyl uffzog, sagt der zum Stein: Herrli, das ist die gaab diewir üch zu üwer Hussfrowen schänckend. (Ibid. p. 190.)

Stocker, the landamman of Zug, who had twice been bailiff of Frauenfeld. "Landamman," said he, accosting him, "you remember the bailiff Wirth; you know that he has always been an honest man." "It is most true, my good friend Escher," replied Stocker; "he never did any one an injury: countrymen and strangers alike were sure to find a hearty welcome at his table; his house was a convent,—inn,—hospital, all in one.* And knowing this, as I do, had he committed a robbery or a murder, I would have spared no effort to obtain his pardon; but since he has burned St. Anne, the grandmother of Christ, it is but right that he should die!"— "Then God take pity on us!" ejaculated Escher.

The gates were now shut, (this was on the 28th of September,) and the deputies of Berne, Lucerne, Uri, Schwitz, Underwald, Zug, Glaris, Friburg, and Soleure, having proceeded agreeably to usage, to deliberate on their judgment with closed doors, sentence of death was passed upon the bailiff Wirth, his son John, who, of all the accused, was the firmest in his faith, and who appeared to have gained over the others, and the bailiff Rutiman. They spared the life of Adrian, the younger of Wirth's sons, as a boon to his weeping mother.

The prisoners were now brought forth from the tower in which they had been confined. "My son," said the father to Adrian, "we die an undeserved death, but never do thou think of avenging it." Adrian wept bitterly. "My brother," said John, "where Christ's word comes his *cross* must follow."†

After the sentence had been read to them, the three christian sufferers were led back to prison; John Wirth walking first, the two bailiffs next, and a vicar behind them. As they crossed the castle bridge, on which there was a chapel dedicated to St. Joseph, the vicar called out to the two old men—"Fall on your knees and invoke the saints." At these words, John Wirth, turning round, said, "Father, be firm! You know there is but one Mediator between God and man—Christ

* Sin huus ist allwey gsin wie ein Kloster, wirtshuus und Spitall. (Bull. Chr. p. 198.)

† Doch allwäg das crütz darbey. (Ibid.)

Jesus."—"Assuredly, my son," replied the old man, "and by the help of His grace, I will continue faithful to Him, even to the end." On this, they all three began to repeat the Lord's Prayer, "Our Father who art in heaven" . . . And so they crossed the bridge.

They were next conducted to the scaffold. John Wirth, whose heart was filled with the tenderest solicitude for his father, bade him a solemn farewell. "My beloved father," said he, "henceforth thou art my father no longer, and I am no longer thy son;—but we are brothers still in Christ our Lord, for whose name's sake we are doomed to suffer death.* So now, if such be God's will, my beloved brother, let us depart to be with Him who is the father of us all. Fear nothing!"—"Amen!" answered the old man, "and may God Almighty bless thee, my beloved son, and brother in Christ."

Thus, on the threshold of eternity did father and son take their leave of each other, with joyful anticipations of that unseen state in which they should be united anew by imperishable ties. There were but few among the multitude around whose tears did not flow profusely. The bailiff Rutiman prayed in silence.† All three then knelt down "in Christ's name,"—and their heads were severed from their bodies.

The crowd, observing the marks of torture on their persons, uttered loud expressions of grief. The two bailiffs left behind them twenty-two children, and forty-five grand-children. Anna was obliged to pay twelve golden crowns to the executioner by whom her husband and son had been deprived of life.

Now at length blood had been spilt—innocent blood. Switzerland and the Reformation were baptized with the blood of the martyrs. The great enemy of the Gospel had effected his purpose; but in effecting it he had struck a mortal blow against his own power. The death of the Wirths was an appointed means of hastening the triumph of the Reformation.

---

* Furohin bist du nitt me min Vatter und ich din sun, sondern wir sind brüdern in Christo. (Bull. Chr. p. 204.)

† Des gnadens weyneten vil Lüthen herzlich. (Ibid.)

The Reformers of Zurich had abstained from abolishing the mass when they suppressed the use of images; but the moment for doing so seemed now to have arrived.

Not only had the light of the Gospel been diffused among the people—but the violence of the enemy called upon the friends of God's word to reply by some striking demonstration of their unshaken constancy. As often as Rome shall erect a scaffold, and heads shall drop upon it, so often shall the Reformation exalt the Lord's holy Word, and crush some hitherto untouched corruption. When Hottinger was executed, Zurich put down the worship of images, and now that the Wirths have been sacrificed, Zurich shall reply by the abolition of the *Mass.* While Rome fills up the measure of her severities, the Reformation shall be conscious of a perpetual accession of strength.

On the 11th of August, 1525, the three pastors of Zurich, accompanied by Megander, and Oswald and Myconius, presented themselves before the Great Council, and demanded the re-establishment of the Lord's Supper. Their discourse was a weighty one,* and was listened to with the deepest attention; —every one felt how important was the decision which the Council was called upon to pronounce. The mass—that mysterious rite which for three successive centuries had constituted the animating principle in the worship of the Latin Church— was now to be abrogated,—the corporeal presence of Christ was to be declared an illusion, and of that illusion, the minds of the people were to be dispossessed; some courage was needed for such a resolution as this, and there were individuals in the Council who shuddered at the contemplation of so audacious a design. Joachim Am-Grüt, the under-secretary of state, was alarmed by the demand of the pastors, and opposed it with all his might. "The words, *This is my body,*" said he, "prove beyond all dispute that the bread is the very body of Christ himself." Zwingle argued that there is no other word in the Greek language than *εστι* (is) to express *signifies,* and he quoted several instances of the employment of that

* Und vermandend die ernstlich. (Bull. Chr. p. 363.)

word in a figurative sense. The Great Council was convinced by his reasoning, and hesitated no longer. The evangelical doctrine had sunk deep into every heart, and moreover, since a separation from the Church of Rome had taken place, there was a kind of satisfaction felt in making that separation as complete as possible, and digging a gulf as it were between the Reformation and her. The Council decreed therefore that the *mass* should be abolished, and it was determined that on the following day, which was Maundy Thursday, the Lord's Supper should be celebrated in conformity to the apostolic model.

Zwingle's mind had been deeply engaged in these proceedings; and at night, when he closed his eyes, he was still searching for arguments with which to confront his adversaries. The subject that had occupied him during the day, presented itself to him again in a dream. He thought that he was disputing with Am-Grüt, and could not find an answer to his principal objection. Suddenly some one stood before him in his dream and said, " Why dost not thou quote the 11th verse of the 12th chapter of Exodus : *Ye shall eat the Lamb in haste ; it is the Lord's Passover ?*" Zwingle awoke, rose from his bed, took up the Septuagint translation, and turning to the verse found the same word εστι (is) whose import in that passage, by universal admission, can be no other than *signifies.*

Here then, in the very constitution of the paschal feast under the old covenant, was the phrase employed in that identical sense which Zwingle assigned to it—who could resist the conclusion that the two passages are parallel ?

On the following day, Zwingle took the verse just mentioned as the text of his discourse, and reasoned so forcibly from it that the doubts of his hearers were dispelled.

The incident which has now been related, and which is so naturally explained—and the particular expression* used by Zwingle to intimate that he had no recollection of the aspect of the person whom he saw in his dream, have given rise to

* Ater fugrit ap albus nihil meamini, somnium enim matra.

the assertion that the doctrine promulgated by the Reformer was delivered to him by the devil!

The altars disappeared; some plain tables, covered with the sacramental bread and wine, occupied their places, and a crowd of eager communicants was gathered round them. There was something exceedingly solemn in that assemblage. Our Lord's death was commemorated on three different days, by different portions of the community:—on Maunday Thursday, by the young people; on Good Friday, the day of his passion, by those who had reached the middle stage of life; on Easter Sunday, by the aged.*

After the deacons had read aloud such passages of Scripture as relate to this sacrament, the pastors addressed their flock in the language of pressing admonition,—charging all those whose wilful indulgence in sin would bring dishonour on the body of Christ to withdraw from that holy feast. The people then fell on their knees; the bread was carried round on large wooden dishes or platters, and every one broke off a morsel for himself; the wine was distributed in wooden drinking cups; the resemblance to the primitive Supper was thought to be the closer. The hearts of those who celebrated this ordinance were affected with alternate emotions of wonder and joy.†

Such was the progress of the Reformation at Zurich. The simple commemoration of our Lord's death caused a fresh overflow in the Church, of love to God, and love to the brethren. The words of Jesus Christ were once more proved to be 'spirit and life.' Whereas the different orders and sections of the Church of Rome had kept up incessant disputes among themselves, the first effect of the Gospel, on its reappearance in the Church, was the revival of brotherly charity. The *Love* which had glowed so brightly in the first ages of Christianity, was now kindled anew. Men, who had before been at variance, were found renouncing their long-

---

* Fusslin Beytr. iv. p. 64.

† Mit grossem verwundern viler Lüthen und noch mit vil grössem fröuden der glöubigen. (Bull. Chr. p. 264.)

cherished enmity, and cordially embracing each other, after having broken bread together at the table of the Lord. Zwingle rejoiced at these affecting manifestations of grace, and returned thanks to God that the Lord's Supper was again working those miracles of charity, which had long since ceased to be displayed in connection with the sacrifice of the mass.*

"Our city," said he, "continues at peace. There is no fraud, no dissension, no envy, no wrangling among us. Where shall we discover the cause of this agreement except in the Lord's good pleasure, and the harmlessness and meekness of the doctrine we profess?"†

Charity and unity were there—but not uniformity. Zwingle, in his " Commentary on true and false religion,"‡ which he dedicated to Francis the First, in March, 1525, the year of the battle of Pavia, had stated some truths in a manner that seemed adapted to recommend them to human reason, following in that respect the example of several of the most distinguished among the scholastic theologians. In this way he had attached to original corruption the appellation of a disease, reserving the name of sin for the actual violation of law.§ But these statements, though they gave rise to some objections, yet occasioned no breach of brotherly charity; for Zwingle, while he persisted in calling original sin a disease, added, by that disease, all men were ruined, and that the sole remedy was in Jesus Christ.‖ Here then was no taint of Pelagian error.

But whilst in Zurich the celebration of the sacrament was followed by the re-establishment of Christian brotherhood,

---

* Expositio fidei. (Zw. Opp. ii. p. 241.)

† Ut tranquillitatis et innocentiæ studiosos reddat. (Zw. Epp. p. 390.)

‡ De verâ et falsâ religione commentarius. (Zw. Opp. iii. p. 145, 325.)

§ Peccatum ergo morbus est cognatus nobis, quo fugimus aspera et gravia, sectamur jucunda et voluptuosa: secundo loco accipitur peccatum pro eo quod contra legem fit. (Ibid. p. 204.)

‖ Originali morbo perdimur omnes; remedio verò quod contra ipsum invenit Deus, incolumitati restituimur. (De peccato originali declaratio ad Urbanum Rhegium. (Ibid. p. 632.)

Zwingle and his friends had to sustain a harder struggle than ever against their adversaries without. Zwingle was not only a Christian teacher, he was a true patriot also; and we know how zealously he always opposed the capitulations, and foreign pensions, and alliances. He was persuaded that this extraneous influence was destructive to piety, contributed to the maintenance of error, and was a fruitful source of civil discord. But his courageous protests on this head were destined to impede the progress of the Reformation. In almost every canton, the leading men, who received the foreign pensions, and the officers under whose command the youth of Switzerland were led out to battle, were knit together in powerful factions and oligarchies, which attacked the Reformation, not so much in the spirit of religious animosity, as in the belief that its success would be detrimental to their own pecuniary and political interests. They had already gained a triumph in Schwitz, and that canton, in which Zwingle, Leo Juda, and Oswald Myconius had preached the truth, and which seemed disposed to follow the example of Zurich, had, on a sudden, renewed the mercenary capitulations, and closed the door against the Gospel.

In Zurich itself, a few worthless persons, instigated to mischief by foreign agency, made an attack upon Zwingle, in the middle of the night, throwing stones at his house, breaking the windows, and calling aloud for "red haired Uli, the vulture of Glaris,"—so that Zwingle started from his sleep, and caught up his sword.* The action is characteristic of the man.

But these desultory assaults could not counteract the impulse by which Zurich was carried onward, and which was beginning to vibrate throughout the whole of Switzerland. They were like pebbles thrown to check the course of a torrent. The waters of the torrent meanwhile were swelling, and the mightiest of its obstacles were likely soon to be swept away.

The people of Berne having intimated to the citizens of Zurich, that several of the cantons had refused to sit with them any longer in the Diet :—" Well," replied the men of

* Interea surgere Zuinglius ad ensem suum. (Zw. Opp. iii. p. 411.)

Zurich, with calm dignity, raising (as in times past the men of Rutli had done) their hands towards heaven, " we are persuaded that God the Father, Son, and Holy Ghost, in whose name the Confederation has been formed, will not forsake us, and will, at last, in his mercy, make us to sit at the right hand of His majesty."*

With such a faithful spirit, there was nothing to fear for the Reformation. But would it make similar progress in the other states of the Confederation? Might not Zurich be single on the side of the word of God? Berne, Basle, and other cantons, would they remain in their subjection to Rome? It is this we are now to see. Let us then turn towards Berne, and contemplate the march of the Reformation in the most influential of the confederated states.

No where was the contest likely to be so sharp as at Berne, for the Gospel had there both powerful friends and determined opponents. At the head of the reforming party was the banneret John Weingarten. Bartholomew May, member of the lesser Council, his sons, Wolfgang and Claudius, his grandsons, James and Benedict, and, above all, the family of the Wattevilles. James Watteville, the magistrate, who, since 1512, had presided over the republic, had read the writings of Luther and Zwingle, at the time of their publication, and had often conversed concerning the Gospel with John Haller, pastor at Anseltingen, whom he had protected from his persecutors.

His son, Nicholas, then thirty-one years of age, had, for two years, filled the office of provost in the church of Berne; and, as such, by virtue of papal ordinances, enjoyed distinguished privileges; so that, Berthold Haller, in speaking of him, would call him "our Bishop."†

The prelates and the Pope used every effort to bind him to the interests of Rome,‡ and the circumstances in which he was

* Bey ihm zuletzt sitzen. (Kirchhofer. Ref. v. Bern. p. 55.)

† Episcopus noster *Vadivillius.* (Zw. Epp. p. 285.)

‡ Tantum favoris et amicitiæ quæ tibi cum tanto summorum pontificum et potentissimorum episcoporum cœtu hactenus intercessit. (Zw. Opp. i. ed. lat. p. 305.)

placed, seemed likely to keep him from the knowledge of the Gospel; but the workings of God's Spirit were more powerful than the flatteries of man. " Watteville," says Zwingle,[*] " was turned from darkness to the sweet light of the Gospel." As the friend of Berthold Haller, he was accustomed to read the letters which he received from Zwingle, for whom he expressed the highest admiration.[†]

It was natural to suppose that the influence of the two Wattevilles, the one being at the head of the state, and the other of the church, would draw after it the republic over which they presided. But the opposite party was scarcely less powerful.

Among its chiefs were the schultheiss of Erlach, the banneret Willading, and many persons of high family, whose interests were identified with those of the convents placed under their administration. Backing these influential leaders was an ignorant and corrupted clergy, who went the length of calling Gospel truth, "an invention of hell." "Beloved colleagues," said the counsellor of Mullinen, at a full conference, held in the month of July, "be on your guard, lest this Reformation should creep in upon us. There is no safety at Zurich in one's own house: people are obliged to have soldiers to guard them." In consequence, they invited to Berne the lecturer of the Dominicans at Mentz, John Heim, who, taking his stand in the pulpit, poured forth all the eloquence of St. Thomas Aquinas against the Reformation.[‡]

Thus, then, the two parties were in presence of each other; a struggle seemed inevitable, but already there were indications with whom the victory would remain. In fact, a common faith united a part of the people to those distinguished families who espoused the Reformation. Berthold Haller exclaimed, full of confidence in the future, " Unless, indeed,

---

 * Ex obscuris ignorantiæ tenebris in amœnam Evangelii lucem productum. (Zw. Opp. i. ed. lat. p. 305.)

 † Epistolas tuæ et eruditionis et humanitatis testes locupletissimas. (Zw. Epp. p. 287.)

 ‡ Suo Thomistico Marte omnia invertere. (Ibid.)

the wrath of God should show itself against us, it is not possible that the word of the Lord should be banished from the
city, for the Bernese are hungering after it."*

Two acts of the government soon appeared to incline the
balance in favour of the new opinions.   The Bishop of Lausanne had given notice of an episcopal visitation; the Council
sent a message to him by the provost, Watteville, desiring
him to abstain from it.†   And, in the mean time, the government put forth an ordinance, which, whilst in appearance it
left the enemies of the truth in possession of some of their
advantages, at the same time sanctioned the principles on
which the Reformation was founded.   They directed that the
ministers should preach, clear of all additions,—freely and
openly,—the Gospel and the doctrine of God, as it is found in
the books of the Old and New Testaments; and that they
should not allude to any doctrine, disputation, or writing
coming from Luther or other teachers.‡

Great was the surprise of the enemies of the truth, when
they saw the ministers of the Gospel appealing with confidence to this decree.   This ordinance, which was to furnish
the ground for all those that succeeded, was, legally speaking,
the commencement of the Reformation at Berne.   From that
time, there was more decision in the progress of this canton;
and Zwingle, who attentively observed all that was passing in
Switzerland, was able to write to the provost de Watteville,
"Christians are all exulting on account of the faith which the
pious city of Berne has just received."§   "The cause is that
of Christ," exclaimed the friends of the Gospel, and they
exerted themselves to advance it with increased confidence.‖
The enemies of the Reformation, alarmed at these first advan-

* Famem verbi Bernates habent.   (Zw. Epp. p. 295.)
† Ut nec oppidum, nec pagos Bernatum visitare pretendat omnino.
(Ibid,)
‡ Alsim das heilig Evangelium und die leer Gottes frey, offentlich
und unverborgen.   (Bull. Chr. p. 111.)
§ Alle Christen sich allenthalben fröuwend des Glaubens. . . . .
(Zw. Opp. i. p. 426.)
‖ Christi negotium agitur.   (Zw. Epp. 9th May, 1523)

teges, closed their ranks, and resolved on striking a blow which should ensure victory on their side. They conceived the project of getting rid of those ministers whose bold preaching was turning all the ancient customs upside down; and a favourable occasion was not long wanting. There was, at Berne, in the place where now stands the hospital de l'Ile, a convent of nuns of the Dominican order, consecrated to St. Michael St. Michael's day, (29th of September,) was always a solemn festival to the inmates of the nunnery. On this anniversary, many of the clergy were present, and, among others, Wittembach de Bienne, Sebastian Meyer, and Berthold Haller. This latter, having entered into conversation with the nuns, among whom was Clara, the daughter of Claudius May, (one of those who maintained the new doctrines,) he remarked to her, in the presence of her grandmother, "the merits of the monastic state are but imaginary, whilst marriage is honourable, and instituted by God himself." Some nuns, to whom Clara related this conversation of Berthold, received it with outcries. It was soon rumoured in the city that Haller had asserted that "the nuns were all children of the devil." The opportunity that the enemies of the Reformation had waited for, was now arrived; and they presented themselves before the lesser Council. Referring to an ancient law, which enacted that whosoever should carry off a nun from her convent should lose his head, they proposed that the "sentence should be mitigated" so far, as that, without hearing the three accused ministers in their defence, they should be banished for life! The lesser Council granted the petition, and the matter was immediately carried to the grand Council.

Thus, then, Berne was threatened with the loss of her Reformers. The intrigues of the Popish party seemed successful. But Rome, triumphant when she played her game with the higher orders, was beaten when she had to do with the people or their representatives. Hardly were the names of Haller, of Meyer, of Wittembach—those names held in veneration by all the Swiss,—pronounced in the grand Council, before an energetic opposition was manifested against the lesser Council

and the clergy. "We cannot," said Tillman, "condemn the
accused unheard! ... Surely their own testimony may be received against that of a few women." The ministers were
called up. There seemed no way of settling matters. "Let
us admit the statements of both parties," said John Weingart-
en. They did so, and discharged the accused ministers,—at
the same time desiring them to confine themselves to the duties
of their pulpits, and not to trouble themselves concerning the
cloisters. But the pulpit was all they wanted: their accusers
had taken nothing by their motion. It was counted a great
victory gained by the Reforming party, insomuch that one of
the leading men exclaimed, "It is all over now—Luther's
work must go forward."*

And go forward it did,—and that in places where it could least
have been expected. At Königsfeld upon the river Aar, near
the castle of Hapsburg, stood a monastery adorned with all
the magnificence of the middle ages, and in which reposed the
ashes of many of that illustrious house which had so often
given an Emperor to Germany. To this place the noble families of Switzerland and of Suabia used to send their daughters
to take the veil. It was in the neighbourhood of this convent
that the Emperor Albert had fallen by the hand of his nephew,
John of Suabia, on the 1st of May, 1308; and the beautiful
stained windows of the church at Königsfeld represented the
horrible tortures which had been inflicted upon the relations
and dependants of the prepetrators of the murder. Catherine of
Waldburg-Truchsess, abbess of the convent at the period of
the Reformation, numbered among her nuns Beatrice Landen-
berg, sister of the Bishop of Constance, Agnes Mullinen,
Catherine Bonnstetten, and Margaret Watteville, sister of the
provost. The liberty enjoyed in this convent, a liberty which
in earlier times had given occasion to scandalous disorders,
had favoured the introduction not only of the Bible, but of the
writings of Luther and Zwingle; and soon a new spring of

* Es ist nun gethan. Der Lutherische Handel muss vorgehen.
(Anshelm. Wirtz. K. G. V. p. 290.)

life and joy changed the aspect of its interior. Nigh to that cell to which Queen Agnes, daughter of Albert, had retired, after bathing in torrents of blood "as in Maydews;" and where, dividing her time between spinning wool and embroidering tapestry for the church, she had mingled thoughts of vengeance with devotional exercises,—Margaret Watteville had only thoughts of peace,—read the Scriptures,—and found time, in her spare moments, to compound, of certain salutary ingredients, an excellent electuary. Retiring to her cell, the youthful nun took courage to write to the Reformer of Switzerland. Her letter discovers to us, better than any reflections could do, the Christian spirit which existed among those pious women, —still, even in our days, so much calumniated.

"Grace and peace, in the Lord Jesus Christ, be given and multiplied towards you always, by God our heavenly Father," was the language of the nun of Königsfeld to Zwingle: "Very learned, reverend, and most dear Sir, I pray you to take in good part this letter which I now address to you. The love of Christ constrains me ;—especially since I have learned that the doctrines of grace are spreading from day to day through your preaching of the word of God. For this cause I give thanks to the Eternal God, for that he has enlightened us anew, and has sent us, by His Holy Spirit, so many heralds of His blessed word; and at the same time I present before him my earnest prayers, that He will be pleased to clothe with His strength, both you and all those who publish His glad tidings,—and that arming you against all enemies of the truth, He will cause His Divine Word to grow in all men. Most learned Sir, I take the liberty of sending to your reverence this little mark of my affection ; I pray you do not despise it, for it is an offering of Christian love. If this electuary should be useful to you, and you should wish to have more, pray let me know, for it would be a joy to my heart to do anything that would be agreeable to you. I am writing not my own feelings only, but those of all in our convent of Königsfeld who love the Gospel. They salute you in Jesus Christ, and we together cease not to commend you to His Almighty protection.*

"Saturday before *Lætare*, 1528."

Such was the pious letter which the nun of Königsfeld wrote to the Reformer of Switzerland.

A convent into which the light of the Gospel had penetrated in such power, could not long continue to adhere to monastic observances. Margaret Watteville and her sisters, persuaded that they should better serve God in their families than in a cloister, solicited permission to leave it. The Council of Berne, in some alarm, took measures to bring the nuns to reason, and the provincial and abbess alternately tried promises and threats, but the sisters, Margaret, Agnes, and Catherine, and their friends, could not be dissuaded. On this, the discipline of the convent was relaxed,—the nuns being exempted from fasting and matins, and their allowance increased. "We desire," said they, in reply to the Council, "not 'the *liberty of the flesh*,' but that of *the spirit*. We, *your* poor, unoffending prisoners, beseech you to take compassion on us."—"*Our* prisoners ! *our* prisoners," exclaimed the banneret, Krauchthaler; "*I* have no wish to detain them prisoners!" This speech, coming from a firm defender of the convents, decided the Council. The gates were opened ; and a short time afterwards Catherine Bonnstetten married William von Diesbach.

Nevertheless, Berne, instead of openly taking part with the Reformation, did but hold a middle course, and pursue a system of vacillation. An incident soon occurred which made this apparent. Sebastian Meyer, lecturer of the Franciscans, put forth a recantation of Romish errors, which produced an immense sensation ; and, in which, depicting the condition of the inmates of convents, he said, "The living in them is more impure, the falls more frequent, the recoveries more tardy, the habitual walk more unsteady, the moral slumber in them more dangerous, the grace toward offenders more rare, and

* Cujus præsidio auxilioque præsentissimo, nos vestram dignitatem assidue commendamus. (Zw. Epp. p. 280.)

the cleansing from sin more slow, the death more despairing, and the condemnation more severe."[*]   At the very time when Meyer was thus declaring himself against the cloisters, John Heim, lecturer of the Dominicans, exclaimed from the pulpit, "*No!* Christ has not, as the Evangelicals tell us, made satisfaction *once for all*, to his Father.   God must still further every day be reconciled to men by good works and the sacrifice of the mass."   Two burghers, who happened to be in the church, interrupted him with the words, "That's not true." The interruption caused a great disturbance in the church; and Heim remained silent.   Some pressed him to go on; but he left the pulpit without finishing his sermon.   The next day the Grand Council struck a blow at once against Rome and the Reformation!   They banished from the city the two leading controversialists, Meyer and Heim.   It was remarked of the Bernese, "They are neither clear nor muddy,"[†]—taking in a double sense the name of Luther, which in old German signified *clear*.[‡]

[*] Langsamer gereiniget, verzweifelter stirbt, härter verdammet. (Kirchhofer Reform. v. Bern. p. 48.)

[†] Dass sie weder luther noch trüb seyen.   (Ibid. p. 50.)

[‡] Romish writers, and particularly M. de Haller, have mentioned, following Salat and Tschudi, enemies of the Reformation, a pretended letter of Zwingle, addressed, at this juncture, to Kolb at Berne.   It is as follows:—"Health and blessing from God our Saviour.   Dear Francis, move gently in the matter.   At first only throw one sour pear to the bear, amongst a great many sweet ones; afterwards two, then three; and as soon as he begins to eat them, throw more and more,—sweet and bitter all together.   Empty the sack entirely.   Soft, hard, sweet, bitter, he will eat them all, and will no longer allow either that they be taken, or be driven away.—Zurich, Monday before St. George, 1525.

"Your servant in Christ, ULRICH ZWINGLE."

We can oppose convincing arguments against the authenticity of this letter.   First,—In 1525, Kolb was pastor at Wertheimer.   He did not come to Berne until 1527.—(See Zw. Epp. 526.)   M. de Haller substitutes, indeed, but quite arbitrarily, 1527 for 1525.   This correction, doubtless, *had its object;* but, unfortunately, in making it, M. de Haller puts himself in direct contradiction of Salat and Tschudi, who, though they do not agree as to the day on which this letter was mentioned in the diet, agree as to the year, which, with both, is clearly 1525.   Sec-

But it was in vain to attempt to smother the Reformation at Berne. It made progress on all sides. The nuns of the convent de l'Ile had not forgotten Haller's visit. Clara May and many of her friends, pressed in their consciences to know what to do, wrote to the learned Henry Bullinger. In answer, he said, "Saint Paul enjoins young women not to take upon them vows, but to marry, instead of living in idleness, under a false show of piety. (1 Tim. v. 13, 14.) Follow Jesus in humility, charity, patience, purity, and kindness."* Clara, looking to heaven for guidance, resolved to act on the advice, and renounce a manner of life at variance with the word of God,—of man's invention,—and beset with snares. Her grandfather Bartholomew, who had served for fifty years in the field and the council-hall, heard with joy of the resolution she had formed. Clara quitted the convent.

The provost, Nicholas Watteville, connected by strong ties of interest to the Roman hierarchy, and who was to have been nominated to the first vacant bishopric in Switzerland, also gave up his titles, revenues, and expectations, that he might keep a clear conscience; and, breaking through all the en

ondly,—There is no agreement as to the way in which the letter itself got abroad. According to one account, it was intercepted; another version tells us that Kolb's parishioners communicated it to an inhabitant of the small cantons, who happened to be at Berne. Thirdly,—The original is in German. Now Zwingle wrote always in Latin to his friends who could understand that language: moreover, he used to salute them as *brother*, and not as *servant*. Fourthly,—In reading Zwingle's correspondence it is impossible not to perceive that his style is quite different from that of the pretended letter. Zwingle never would have written a letter to say so little. His letters in general are long and full of news. To call the little jeu d'esprit picked up by Salat *a letter*, is but trifling. Fifthly, —Salat deserves but little confidence as an historian; and Tschudi appears to have copied him, with a few variations. Possibly a man of the small cantons may have had communication, from some inhabitant of Berne, of the latter from Zwingle to Haller, which we have before mentioned, (see vol. ii.,) wherein Zwingle employs, with a good deal of dignity, the comparison of the bears,—which is found in all authors of that age. This may have given the idea to some wit to invent this letter which has been supposed to have passed from Zwingle to Kolb.

* Euerem Herrn Jesu nachfolget in Demuth. (Kirchh. Ref. v. B. 60.]

tanglements in which the popes had sought to bind him, he too entered into that state, which had been, from the beginning, instituted by God. Nicholas Watteville took to wife Clara May; and his sister Margaret, the nun of Königsfeld, was, about the same time, united to Lucius Tscharner of Coira.*

Everything gave intimation of the victory which the Reformation would soon obtain at Berne. A city not less important, and which then ranked as the Athens of Switzerland —Basle, was also beginning to take part in the memorable struggle of the sixteenth century.

Each of the cities of the Confederation had its own peculiar character. Berne was distinguished as the place of residence of the chief families; and the question was one that seemed likely to be decided by the part taken by certain of the leading nobles. At Zurich, the ministers of the Word, such men as Zwingle, Leo Juda, Myconius, and Schmidt, exercised a commanding influence over a powerful middle class of society. Lucerne was the city of arms,—a centre of military organization. Basle was the seat of learning, and its accompaniment, —printing-presses. Erasmus, the acknowledged head of the republic of letters in the sixteenth century, had there fixed his residence, and, preferring the liberty it afforded him to the flattering invitations of popes and kings, he had become a centre of attraction to a concourse of men of learning.

However, a man inferior to Erasmus in natural genius, but humble, gentle, and pious, was, ere long, to exercise, in that very city, an influence more powerful than that possessed by this prince of scholars. Christopher von Utenheim, bishop of Basle, who agreed in judgment with Erasmus, sought to surround himself with men disposed to co-operate in a sort of half-way Reformation. With this view he had called to his aid Capito and Œcolampadius. The latter had a something savouring of monkery in his habit of mind, and this often clashed with the views of the philosopher. Œcolampadius,

* Zw. Epp. annotatio, p. 451. It is from this union that the Tscharners of Berne derive their descent.

however, on his part, soon became enthusiastically attached to Erasmus; and it is probable he would have lost all independence of mind in this intimacy, if Providence had not separated him from his idol. He returned, in 1517, to his native city, Weinsberg. Here he was disgusted with the disorders and the profanity which prevailed among the priests; and he has left a noble record of the serious spirit which from that time actuated him, in his work entitled "The Humours of Easter," which appears to have been written about this period.[*]

Called to Augsburg, towards the end of 1518, to fill the post of preacher in its cathedral, he found that city still under the effects of the memorable discussion which had been held there, in the previous May, between Luther and the Pope's legate. It was necessary that he should choose his side, and Œcolampadius did not hesitate to declare himself on the side of the Reformer. Such candour on his part soon drew down upon him much opposition, and being convinced that his natural timidity, and the feebleness of his voice, rendered it impossible for him to succeed in public, he looked around him for a place of retreat, and his thoughts rested on a convent of monks of Saint Bridget, near Augsburg, renowned for the piety, as well as for the profound and liberal studies of its monks. Feeling the need of repose, of leisure, and, at the same time, of quiet occupation and prayer, he addressed himself to this community, and inquired, "Can I live in your convent according to the word of God?" The answer being in the affirmative, Œcolampadius entered its gates on the 23d April, 1520, having expressly stipulated that he should be free, if ever the ministry of the word of God should require his service elsewhere.

It was well that the Reformer of Basle should, like Luther, become acquainted with that monastic life, which presented the fullest exhibition of the working of Roman Catholicism. But *rest* was what he could not find there; his friends blamed the step; and he himself declared frankly that Luther was nearer to the truth than his adversaries. No wonder, there-

[*] Herzog. Studien und Kritiken, 1840. p. 334.

fore, that Eck and other Romish doctors pursued him with menaces even in this his quiet retreat.

At the time we are recording, Œcolampadius was neither one of the Reformed, nor yet a blind follower of Rome; what he most desired was a sort of purified Catholicism, which is no where to be found in history,—but the idea of which has, to many, served as a bridge of passage to better things. He set himself to correct, by reference to the word of God, the statutes of his order. " I conjure you," said he, to the confraternity, " not to think more highly of your statutes, than of the ordinances and commandments of the Lord." " We have no wish," replied his brethren, " for other rules than those of the Saviour. Take our books, and mark, as in the presence of Christ himself, whatever you find therein contrary to his word." Œcolampadius began the task imposed ; but he was almost wearied by it. " O Almighty God !" he exclaimed, " what abominations has not Rome sanctioned in these statutes."

Hardly had he pointed out some of them, when the anger of the fraternity was aroused. " Thou heretic—thou apostate," was their cry, " thou deservest to be thrown into a lonesome dungeon for the rest of thy days." They would not allow him to come to prayers. Meanwhile, outside the walls, still greater danger awaited him. Eck, and his party, had not relinquished their schemes. " In three days," it was told him, " they will be here to arrest you." " Do you intend," asked he, " to deliver me up to assassins ?" The monks were silent and irresolute . . . ; neither willing to save him, nor yet to give him up. At this juncture, some friends of Œcolampadius approached the convent, bringing with them horses to conduct him to a place of safety. At the news, the monks decided to allow the departure of one who had brought the seeds of trouble into their convent. " *Farewell*," said he. Behold him at liberty !

He had remained nearly two years in the convent of Saint Bridget.

Œcolampadius was saved—he began to breathe. " I have sacrificed the monk," said he, writing to a friend, " and have regained the Christian." But his flight from the convent, and his heretical writings were everywhere proclaimed. People on all sides drew back at his approach. He knew not which way to turn, when Sickingen offered him an asylum. This was in the spring of the year 1522. He accepted it.

His mind, oppressed during his confinement within the monastery, recovered its elasticity amongst the noble warriors of Ebernburg. " Christ is our liberty !" burst from his lips, " and that which men consider as their greatest misfortune,— death itself,—is for us a real gain." He directly commenced reading to the people the Gospels and Epistles in German. " No sooner will these trumpets sound abroad," said he, " than the walls of Jericho will crumble to the ground."

Thus the most humble man of his time was preparing, in a fortress on the banks of the Rhine, in the midst of unpolished warriors, for that change of worship which Christianity was shortly to undergo. Nevertheless, Ebernburg was not a field large enough for his plans; besides, he felt the need of other society than such as he was in the midst of. Cratander, the bookseller, invited him to take up his abode at Basle; Sickingen offered no impediment; and Œcolampadius, glad at the thought of seeing his old friends, arrived there on the 16th November, 1522. After having lived there some time, simply as a man of learning, without any public vocation, he was nominated vicar of the church of St. Martin, and his acceptance of this humble engagement* perhaps decided the Reformation at Basle. Whenever Œcolampadius was to preach a great crowd filled the church.† At the same time, the public lectures given by him, and by Pellican, were crowned with so much success, that Erasmus himself felt constrained to exclaim, " Œcolampadius triumphs !"‡

" In fact, this gentle, and firm man, says Zwingle, " diffused,

---

* Meis sumtibus non sine contemptu et invidia. (Œcol. ad Pirckh. de Eucharistia.)

† Dass er kein Predigt thate, er hatte ein mächtig Volk darinn, says Peter Ryf, his contemporary. (Wirtz. v. 350.)

‡ Œcolampadius apud nos triumphat. (Eras. ad Zwing. Zw. Epp. p. 312.)

all around him, the sweet savour of Christ; and all who assembled about him grew in the truth."* Often a report prevailed that he was on the point of being obliged to quit Basle, and begin again his hazardous flights. On these occasions his friends,—and above all Zwingle,—would be in consternation; but then came tidings of fresh advantages gained by Œcolampadius, dissipating their fears, and raising their hopes. The renown of his labours spread even to Wittemberg, and rejoiced Luther, who would often talk with Melancthon concerning him. But the Saxon Reformer was not without anxiety on his account. Erasmus was at Basle,—and Erasmus was the friend of Œcolampadius . . . Luther thought it his duty to put one whom he loved on his guard. "I fear much," wrote he, "that, like Moses, Erasmus will die in the country of Moab, and never lead us into the land of promise."†

Erasmus had retired to Basle, as to a quiet city, situated in the centre of the intellectual activity of the age,—from whence, by means of the printing-press of Frobenius, he could act upon France, Germany, Switzerland, Italy, and England. But he liked not to be interfered with; and if the neighbourhood of Œcolampadius was not entirely agreeable to him, another man there was whose presence inspired him with still more apprehension. Ulric Hutten had followed Œcolampadius to Basle. For some time he had been attacking the Pope, as one knight tilts with another. "The axe," said he, "is already laid at the root of the tree. Faint not, my countrymen, in the heat of the battle: the lot is cast; the charge is begun . . . Hurrah for liberty!" He laid aside the Latin, and now wrote only in German; for his object was to get at the hearts of the people.

His views were grand and generous. According to his plan, there was to be a yearly meeting of bishops, to regulate the interests of the church. Christian institutions, and above

* Illi magis ac magis in omni bono augescunt. (Eras. ad Zwing. Zw. Epp. p. 312.)

† Et in terram promissionis ducere non potest. (L. Epp. ii. p. 358.)

all, a Christian spirit, was to go forth from Germany, as
formerly from Judea, and spread through the whole world.
Charles V. was the young hero destined to realise this golden
age; but Hutten's hopes having been blasted in that quarter,
he turned towards Sickingen, and sought from knighthood that
which the Imperial authority refused him.

Sickingen, as a leading chieftain, had acted a distinguished
part in Germany; but soon after the nobles had besieged him
in the castle of Landstein, and the ancient walls of that fortress had yielded to the strange power of cannon and musket-
ry,—then only recently invented. The taking of Landstein
had been the final defeat of the power of the knights,—the
triumph of the art of modern warfare over that of the middle
ages. Thus, the last exploits of the knights had been on the
side of the Reformation, while the earliest use of the newly-
invented engines was against it. The steel-clad warriors,
whose bodies fell beneath the unlooked-for storm of balls,
made way for other soldiery. Other conflicts were opening.
A spiritual knighthood was taking the place of the Du
Guesclins and Bayards; and those battered ramparts, broken
walls, and expiring warriors, told, more plainly than Luther
had been able to do, that it was not by such allies or such
weapons that the Gospel of the Prince of Peace was destined
to prevail.

The hopes of Hutten had died with the fall of Landstein,
and the ruin of the power of the knights. As he stood by
the corpse of his friend Sickingen, he bade adieu to his dream
of brighter days to come, and losing all confidence in men, he
sought only for retirement and repose. In quest of these, he
visited Erasmus in Switzerland. An early friendship had
subsisted between them; but the rough and overbearing knight
regardless of the opinions of others, quick to grasp the sword
and dealing his blows on all sides, wherever he came, could
scarcely be expected to ' walk together' with the fastidious and
timid Erasmus, with all his refinement, politeness, love of
praise, his readiness to sacrifice all for the sake of it, and his
fear, above all, of controversy.

On his arrival at Basle, Hutten, poor, suffering in bodily health, and a fugitive, immediately sought out his old friend. But Erasmus shrunk from the thought of receiving at his table a man who was placed under ban by the Pope and the Emperor,—a man who,[*] in his conversation, would spare no one, and, besides borrowing money of him, would no doubt be followed by others of the "Gospel party," whom Erasmus dreaded more and more. He declined to see him,—and the magistrates of Basle desired Hutten to leave the city. Wounded to the quick, and irritated by the timid prudence of his friend, Hutten repaired to Mulhausen, and there circulated a violent diatribe against Erasmus,—to which the latter put forth a reply replete with talent. The knight had, as it were, with both hands, seized his sword, and felled his adversary to the earth; the philosopher, recovering his feet, had replied to the strokes of his adversary by peckings with his beak.[†]

Hutten was again compelled to flight. He reached Zurich, and there found a kind reception at the hospitable hearth of Zwingle. Intrigues again obliged him to quit that city; and after passing some time at the baths of Pfeffers, he repaired, provided with a letter from the Swiss Reformer, to the pastor, John Schnapp, who resided in the little island of Uffnan, on the lake of Zurich. That humble minister of God's word received the sick and homeless knight with the tenderest charity. And in that tranquil and unknown seclusion, Ulric Hutten, one of the most remarkable men of his age, expired about the end of August, after an agitated life, in the course of which he had been expelled by one party, persecuted by another, and deserted by nearly all;—having all his life contended against superstition, without, as it would seem, ever arriving at the knowledge of the truth. The poor minister who had gained some experience in the healing art, had be-

---

* Ille egens et omnibus rebus destitutus quærebat nidum aliquem ubi moveretur. Erat mihi gloriosus ille miles cum sua scabie in ædes recipiendus, simulque recipiendus ille chorus titulo *Evangelicorum*, writes Erasmus to Melancthon in a letter in which he seeks to excuse himself. (Er. Epp. p. 949.

† Expostulatio Hutteni.—Erasmi spongia.

stowed upon him the utmost attention. He left behind him
neither money nor furniture, nor books,—nothing, save his
pen.* So broken was that steel-clad arm that he had dared
to put forward to support the ark of God.

But there was one man in Germany more formidable in
the eyes of Erasmus than the ill-fated knight,—and that man
was Luther. The time had come when the two great combatants of the age were to measure their strength in the lists.
They were the leaders of two very different reformations.
Whilst Luther was bent on a complete reformation, Erasmus
as the advocate of a middle course, was seeking certain concessions from the hierarchy, that might have the effect of con-
ciliating the opposing parties. Luther was disgusted with the
vacillation and inconsistency of Erasmus. " You are trying
to walk on eggs without breaking them," said he.†

At the same time, he met these vacillations of Erasmus
with the most entire and unfaltering decision. " We Christians," said he, " ought to be well persuaded of what we teach,
and to be able to say *yes* and *no*. To object to our affirming
with full conviction what we believe, is to strip us of our faith
itself. The Holy Spirit is no spirit of doubt.‡ And he has
written in our hearts a firm and peaceful assurance, which
makes us as sure of the object of faith as we are of our existence."

These words suffice to show on which side strength was to
be found. To effect a change in religion, there is need of
firm and living faith. A salutary revolution in the Church
is never to be derived from philosophic views and thoughts of
man. To restore fertility to the earth after a long drought,
the lightning must strike the cloud, and the windows of
heaven must be opened. Critical acuteness, philosophy, and
even history, may prepare the ground for a true faith, but
never can they fill its place. Vainly would you cleanse the

* Libros nullos habuit, supellectilem nullam, præter calamum. (Zw
Epp. p. 313.)
† Auf Eyern gehen und keines zutreten. (L. Opp. xix. p. 11.)
‡ Der heilige Geist ist kein Scepticus. (Ibid. p. 8.)

aqueduct or build up your embankments, so long as the rain cometh not down from heaven. The learning of man without faith is but as the dry channel.

Much and essentially as Luther and Erasmus differed one from the other, a hope was long cherished by Luther's friends, and even by himself, that both would one day be united in resistance of Rome. Expressions, dropt in his caustic humour, were commonly reported, which showed the philosopher dissenting, in his opinion, from the most devoted adherents of Catholicism. For instance, it is related, that, when in England, he was one day in earnest conversation with Thomas More on the subject of transubstantiation. "Only believe," said More, "that you receive the body of Christ, and you really have it." Erasmus was silent. Shortly after this, when Erasmus was leaving England, More lent him a horse to convey him to the port where he was to embark; but Erasmus took it abroad with him. When More heard of it, he reproached him with much warmth; but the only answer Erasmus gave him was in the following quatrain:—*

"Only believe thou sharest Christ's feast, say you,
And never doubt the fact is therefore true:
So write I of thy horse;—if thou art able
But to believe it, he is in thy stable."†

Erasmus's sentiments having got wind, not only in Germany and England, but in other countries, it was said at Paris that "Luther wanted to force open the door, of which Erasmus had already picked the lock."‡

* There is surely profanity as well as levity in this. May the reader be preserved from any sympathy with such a way of dealing with a belief which, right or wrong, is reverential.—TR.

† "Quod mihi dixisti nuper de corpore Christi:
    Crede quod habes et habes;
  Hoc tibi rescribo tantum de tuo caballo:
    Crede quod habes et habes."
                  (Paravicini, Singularia, p. 71.)

‡ Histoire Cathol. denotre temps, par S. Fontaine de l'ordre de St. Francois, Paris, 1562.

The position taken by Erasmus was a difficult one. "I will not be unfaithful to the cause of Christ," wrote he to Zwingle, "at least *so far* as the times will allow."[*] Just in proportion as he saw Rome rising up against the favourers of the Reformation, he prudently drew back from them. All parties looked to him. Pope, emperor, kings, nobles, men of learning, and even his most intimate friends, entreated him to take up his pen against the Reformer.[†] "You cannot possibly undertake a work more acceptable to God and more worthy of your genius," wrote the Pope.[‡]

Erasmus for a long time held out against these solicitations. He could not conceal from himself that the cause of the Reformation was that of Religion as well as of Learning. Moreover, Luther was an adversary he dreaded to find himself opposed to. "It is an easy thing for you to say, Write against Luther," said he to a Romish divine, "but the matter is full of hazard."[§] He knew not which way to move.

This hesitation on the part of Erasmus drew upon him the most violent of both parties. Luther himself scarcely knew how to make his respect for Erasmus's learning consist with the indignation his timid policy awakened in him. He resolved to break through the painful restraint he had hitherto imposed on himself, and wrote to him, in April, 1524, a letter which he commissioned Camerarius to deliver to him.

"*You* have not yet received from the Lord the courage requisite for marching side by side with us against the Papists. We bear with your weakness. If learning prospers, and if, by its means, the treasury of Scripture is unlocked to all comers, it is a gift which God has given us by you—a noble gift, for which our praise ascends to heaven. But do not desert the post assigned you, to take up your quarters in our camp. No doubt your eloquence and genius might be useful

* Quantum hoc seculum patitur. (Zw. Epp. p. 221.)
† A Pontifice, a Cæsare, a regibus et principus, a doctissimis etiam et carissimis amicis huc provocor. (Erasm. Zw. Epp. p. 308.)
‡ Nulla te et ingenio, eruditione, eloquentiaque tua dignior esse potest. (Adrianus Papa, Epp. Er. p. 1202.)
§ Res est periculi plena. (Er. Epp. p. 758.)

to us; but, since your courage fails you, remain where you are. If I could have my will, those who are acting with me should leave your old age in peace, to fall asleep in the Lord. The greatness of our cause has long ago surpassed your strength. But then, dear Erasmus, cease, I pray you, to scatter, with open hands, the biting satire you are so skilled to clothe in flowery rhetoric, for the slightest stroke of your pen inflicts more pain than the being ground to powder by all the Papists put together. Be satisfied to be a spectator of our tragedy:* only abstain from writing against me, and I will not attack you."

Here we see Luther, whose spirit breathed the breath of conflict, asking for peace and amity! Erasmus, the man of peace, broke it.

This communication of the Reformer was received by Erasmus as the keenest of insults, and if he had not previously resolved on publishing against Luther, it is probable that resolution was then taken. "Perhaps," was his reply, "perhaps Erasmus will better serve the Gospel by writing against you, than certain senseless writers on your† own side, whose doctrines do not allow me to be any longer a mere spectator of the tragedy."

But other motives were not wanting. Henry VIII. and the leading nobility of England, pressed him to declare himself openly against the Reformation, and Erasmus, in a moment of more than usual boldness, gave a promise to that effect. His questionable position had, besides, become a source of continual trouble to him; he loved ease, and the necessity he was continually brought under of vindicating his conduct was a constant disturbance. He loved the praise of men, and he heard himself charged with fearing Luther, and being unable to answer him—he clung to the uppermost seat,—and the plain monk of Wittemberg had dethroned the powerful Erasmus from his pre-eminence. It was his aim, by a bold step, to regain the place he had lost. The established Christianity

---

* Spectator tantum sis tragœdiæ nostræ. (L. Epp. ii. p. 501.)

† Quidam stolidi scribentes pro te. (Unschuldige Nachricht, p. 545.)

of his age, with one voice, invited him to the attempt. A man of large capacity, and of the highest reputation in that age, was wanted to oppose to the Reformation. Erasmus gave himself to the work.

But with what weapons will he arm for the encounter? Will he call forth the former thunders of the Vatican? Will he undertake the vindication of the corruptions which are the disgrace of the Papacy? Erasmus could not act such a part. The grand movement which then swelled all hearts, after the death-like stupor of so many centuries, filled him with joy, and he would have shrunk from shackling its progress. Unable to be the champion of Roman Catholicism in that which it has *added* to Christianity, he undertook the defence of it in the particulars wherein it has *taken away* from it. Erasmus chose for the ground of his attack upon Luther, that point wherein Catholicism makes common cause with Rationalism, the doctrine of Free Will, or the power of man by nature. Accordingly, although undertaking thus to defend the Church, Erasmus was also gratifying the men of this world; and, although fighting the battle on behalf of the Pope, he was also contending on the side of the philosophic party. It has been said that he acted injudiciously in thus restricting himself to an intricate and unprofitable question.* Luther,—the Reformers generally,—and, indeed, that age were of a different opinion; and we agree with them. "I must acknowledge," said Luther, "that, in this great controversy, you alone have taken the bull by the horns. I thank you with all my heart, for I prefer to be occupied with that theme rather than such secondary questions as Pope, purgatory, and indulgences, with which the enemies of the Gospel have hitherto dogged my steps."†

His own experience, and the attentive study of the Holy Scriptures, and of St. Augustine, had convinced Luther that

---

* "It is humbling to mankind," says M. Nisard—see Revue des deux mondes, iii. p. 411,—" to contemplate men capable of grasping eternal truths, fencing and debating in such trivialities, like gladiators fighting with flies."   † L. Opp. xix. p. 146.

the powers of man's nature are so strongly inclined to evil, that, in his own strength, he can attain no more than an outward decency, of no value or sufficiency in the sight of God. He had, at the same time, recognised that it was God, who, by his Holy Spirit, bestowing freely on man the gift of 'faith' communicated to him a real righteousness. This doctrine had become the vital principle of his religion, the predominant tenet of his theology, and the pivot on which the entire Reformation turned.

Whilst Luther maintained that every thing good in man came down from God, Erasmus sided with those who thought that this good came out from man himself. God or man— good or evil—these are no unimportant themes; and if there is '*triviality*,' it is assuredly not in such solemn questions.

It was in the autumn of 1524, that Erasmus published his famous tract, entitled " Diatribe on the Freedom of the Will," and as soon as it saw the light, the philosopher could hardly credit his own boldness. With his eyes rivetted on the arena, he watched, with trembling, the gauntlet he had flung to his adversary. " The die is cast," he wrote to Henry VIII., with emotion ; " the book on *free will* is published. I have done a bold thing, believe me. I expect nothing less than to be stoned for it. But I take comfort from your majesty's example, whom the rage of these people has not spared."[*]

His alarm soon increased to such a degree, that he bitterly lamented the step he had taken " Why," he ejaculated, " why was I not permitted to grow old in the mount of the Muses ! Here am I, at sixty years of age, forcibly thrust forward into the arena, and I am throwing the cestus and the net, instead of handling the lyre! I am aware," said he to the Bishop of Rochester, " that in writing upon free will, I was going out of my sphere ; you congratulate me on my triumphs. Ah ! I do not know over whom. The faction (the Reformation) gathers strength daily.[†] Was it then my fate, at my time of

---

[*] Jacta est alea . . . audax, mihi crede, facinus . . . expecto lapidationem. (Er. Epp. p. 811.)

[†] Quomodo triumphans nescio . . . Factio crescit in dies latius. (Ibid. p. 809.)

life, to pass from my place as a friend of the Muses, to that of a miserable gladiator!"

Doubtless it was no small matter for the timid Erasmus to have stood forth against Luther; nevertheless, he had not spoken out with any extraordinary boldness. He seems, in his book, to ascribe but little to man's will, and to leave to Grace the greater part of the work; but then he chooses his arguments so as to make it seem as if man did every thing, and God nothing. Not daring openly to express his opinions, he seems to affirm one thing, and to prove another; so that one may be allowed to suppose that he believed what he proved, not what he asserted.

He distinguishes three several sentiments opposed to different degrees of Pelagianism: "Some think," said he, "that man can neither will, nor begin, still less perform any thing good, without the special and constant aid of Divine grace; and this opinion seems probable enough. Others teach that the will of man has no power but for evil, and that it is grace alone that works any good in us; and, lastly, there are some who assert that there never has been any free will, either in angels, or in Adam, or in us, whether before or after grace received; but that God works in man whether it be good or evil, and that every thing that happens, happens from an absolute necessity."*

Erasmus, whilst seeming to admit the first of these opinions, uses arguments that are opposed to it, and which might be employed by the most determined Pelagian. It is thus that, quoting the passages of Scripture, in which God offers to man the choice between good and evil, he adds: "Man then must needs have a power to will and to choose; for it would be folly to say to any one, Choose! were it not in his power to do so?"

Luther feared nothing from Erasmus: "Truth," said he, "is more powerful than words. The victory will remain with him who with stammering lips shall teach the truth, and

* De libero arbitrio Διατριβή. (Erasmi. Opp. ix. p. 1215, sq.)

not to him who eloquently puts forward a lie."* But when he received Erasmus' book in the month of October, 1524, he considered it to be so feebly argued, that he hesitated whether to answer it. "What!" he exclaimed, "all this eloquence in so bad a cause! It is as if a man should serve up mud on gold and silver dishes.† One cannot get any hold upon you. You are like an eel that slips through one's fingers; or, like the fabled Proteus, who changes his form when in the very arms of him who would strangle him."

Luther making no reply, the monks and theologians of the schools broke forth in exultation: "Well, where is your Luther now? Where is the great Maccabeus? Let him enter the lists! let him come forward! Ah! ah! he has at last found his match! He has had a lesson to keep in the back ground! he has learnt to be silent."‡

Luther saw that he must answer Erasmus; but it was not till the end of the year 1525 that he prepared to do so; and Melancthon having told Erasmus that Luther would write with moderation, the philosopher was greatly alarmed. "If I write with moderation," said he, "it is my natural character; but there is in Luther's character the indignation of the son of Peleus. And how can it be otherwise? The vessel that braves such a storm as that which rages round Luther, needs anchor, ballast, and rudder to keep it from bearing down out of its course—If therefore he should answer more temperately than suits his character—the sycophants will exclaim that we understand one another."—We shall see that Erasmus was soon relieved from this last fear.

The doctrine of God's election as the sole cause of man's salvation, had long been dear to the Reformer:—but hitherto he had only considered its practical influence. In his answer

* Victoria est penes balbutientem veritatem, non apud mendacem eloquentiam. (L. Epp. ii. p. 200.)

† Als wenn einer in silbern oder guldern Schüsseln wolte mist und Unflath Auftragen. (L. Opp. xix. p. 4.)

‡ Sehet, sehet nun da zu! wo ist nun Luther. (Ibid. p. 3.)

to Erasmus he investigated it especially in a speculative point of view, and laboured to establish, by such arguments as seemed to him most conclusive, that God works every thing in man's conversion, and that our heart is so alienated from the love of God, that it can only have a sincere desire after righteousness by the regenerating action of the Holy Spirit.

"To call our will a Free will," said he, "is to imitate those princes who accumulate long titles, styling themselves sovereigns of this or that kingdom, principality, and distant island, (of Rhodes, Cyprus, and Jerusalem,) over which they do not exercise the least authority." Nevertheless, Luther here makes an important distinction which shews that he by no means participated in the third opinion which Erasmus had raised to notoriety by attributing it to him. "Man's will," said he, "may indeed be said to be free, not indeed in relation to what is above him,—that is, to God,—but in relation to what is beneath him,—that is, to the things of this world. In any matter affecting my property, my lands, my house, or my farm, I find myself able to act, do, and manage freely; but in every thing that has reference to his salvation, man is a captive; he is subject to the will of God,—or rather to that of the devil.* Show me," cries he, "only one among all those who teach the doctrine of free will, who has been able *in himself* to find strength to endure a slight insult, a passionate assault, nay, even the hostile look of his enemy, and that joyfully,— and without so much as asking whether he is willing to give up his body, his life, his goods, his honour, and all that he has,—I will acknowledge that you have gained your cause."†

Luther had too much penetration not to discern the contradictions into which his adversary had fallen. He, therefore, in his answer, laboured to enclose the philosopher in the net in which he had entangled himself. "If the passages you quote," said he, "establish the principle that it is easy for us to do good, wherefore is it that we are disputing? And what need can we have of *Christ*, or the *Holy Spirit?* Christ would then have shed his blood without necessity to obtain

* L. Opp. xix. p. 33.   † Ibid. p. 32.

for us a power which we already had in our own nature."
In truth the passages quoted by Erasmus are to be understood
in quite a different sense. This much debated question is
more simple than it at first sight appears. When the Bible
says to man, 'Choose,' it is because it assumes the assistance
of God's grace, by which alone he can obey the command.
God, in giving the commandment gives also the strength to
fulfil it. If Christ said to Lazarus, 'Come forth,' it was not
that Lazarus could restore himself to life, but that Christ, in
commanding him to come forth, gave him the ability to do so,
and accompanied his word with his creative power. He
speaks, and it is done. Moreover it is quite true that the man
to whom God speaks, must will to do; it is he himself, and
not another, that must will;—he can receive this will from
none but God; but surely in him it must be; and the very
command which God brings to him, and which, according to
Erasmus, proves the power to be in man, is so perfectly
reconcilable with God's working, that it is, in fact, the very
means by which that work of God is wrought out. It is
by saying to the man " Be converted," that God converts him.

But the idea which Luther especially kept in view in his
answer is, that the passages quoted by Erasmus are designed
not to make known to men this pretended power which is
attributed to them, but to show them their duty, and their total
inability to fulfil it. " How often does it happen," says
Luther, "that a father calls to him his feeble child, saying,
'Will you come, my son? come then,'—in order that the
child may learn to call for his assistance and allow himself to
be carried."*

After having combated Erasmus's arguments in favour of
free will, Luther defends his own against the attacks of his
opponent. " Dear Diatribe," says he, ironically, "mighty
heroine, you who pride yourself on having explained away
those words of our Lord in St. John's Gospel, ' *Without me
ye can do* NOTHING,' although you acknowledge their force
and call them Luther's Achilles, listen to me—Unless you

* L. Opp. xix. p. 55.

prove that this word *nothing* not only may, but must signify a
little, all your sounding words, all your famous examples,
have no more effect than if a man were to attempt to oppose a
mighty conflagration with a handful of straw.   What matter
to us such assertions as, *This may mean, this may be thus
understood*, whilst you ought to prove to us that it *must* be
so understood.   Unless you do this we take the declaration in
its *literal* meaning, and laugh at all your examples, your fine
exordiums, and self-complacent boastings."[*]

Subsequently, Luther shows, still from the Scriptures, that
the grace of God does all in Conversion.   He concludes thus:
" In short, since the Scripture every where contrasts Christ
with that which has not the spirit of Christ; since it declares
that every thing which is not Christ, and in Christ, is under
the power of delusion, darkness, the devil, death, sin, and the
wrath of God; *it follows that every passage in the Bible
which speaks of Christ is against your doctrine of free will.*
Now such passages are innumerable, the Holy Scriptures are
full of them."[†]

We perceive that the discussion which arose between Luther and Erasmus, is the same as that which occurred a century
later between the Jansenists and Jesuits,—between Pascal and
Molina.[‡]   Wherefore, then, while the Reformation has had
such immense results, did Jansenism, though adorned by the
finest geniuses, go out in weakness?   It is because Jansenism
went back to St. Augustine, and rested for support on the Fathers; whilst the Reformation went back to THE BIBLE, and was
based on the word of God;—because Jansenism made a compromise with Rome, and would have pursued a middle course
between truth and error; whereas, the Reformation, relying
on God alone, cleared the soil, swept away the incrustations
of past ages, and laid bare the primitive rock.   To stop half
way in any work is useless; in every undertaking we must

* L. Opp. xix. p. 116.   † Ibid. p. 143.
  ‡ It is scarcely necessary to say that I do not speak of personal
discussions between these two men, of whom, the one died in 1600, and
the other was not born till 1623.

go through. Hence, while Jansenism has passed away, Evangelical Christianity presides over the destinies of the world.

After having energetically refuted the errors of Erasmus, Luther, renders a high sounding, but perhaps somewhat malicious, homage to his genius. "I confess," says he, "that you are a great man: in whom have we ever beheld more learning, intelligence, or readiness, both in speaking and writing? As to me, I possess none of these qualities; in one thing only can I glory—I am a Christian. May God raise you infinitely above me in the knowledge of His Gospel, so that you may surpass me in that respect as much as you already do in every other."[*]

Erasmus was incensed beyond measure by the perusal of Luther's answer, and looked upon his encomiums as the honey of a poisoned cup, or the embrace of a serpent at the moment he fixes his deadly fang. He immediately wrote to the Elector of Saxony, demanding justice; and, when Luther wished to appease him, he lost his usual temper, and, in the words of one of his most zealous apologists, began "to pour forth invectives in a feeble voice and with hoary hairs."[†]

Erasmus was conquered. Moderation had, till this occasion, been his strength; and now this left him. Anger was the only weapon he could oppose to Luther's energy. The wisdom of the philosopher, on this occasion, failed him. He replied, publicly, in his *Hyperapistes*, in which he accuses the Reformer of barbarism, falsehood, and blasphemy. The philosopher even ventured on prophecy: "I predict," said he, "that no name under heaven will hereafter be more execrated than Luther's." The jubilee of 1817 has replied to this prophecy, after a lapse of three centuries, by the enthusiasm and acclamations of the entire Protestant world.

Thus, while Luther, with the Bible in his hand, was placing himself in the van of his age, Erasmus, in opposition to him, sought that station for himself and philosophy. Of these two

* L. Opp. xix. p. 146, 147.
† M. Nisard. Erasme, p. 419.

chiefs, which has been followed? Both, undoubtedly. Nevertheless, Luther's influence on the nations of Christendom has been infinitely greater than that of Erasmus. Even those who did not well comprehend the matter in dispute, seeing the full conviction of one antagonist, and the doubts of the other, could not refrain from believing that the former had truth on his side, and that the latter was in the wrong. It has been said that the three last centuries, the 16th, 17th and 18th, may be considered as a protracted battle of three days' duration.* We willingly adopt the comparison, but not the part that is allotted to each of these days. The same struggle, it is said, marked the sixteenth and the eighteenth centuries. On the first day, as on the last, we are told that it was philosophy that broke the ranks. The sixteenth century philosophical! Strange mistake! No, each of those days had its marked and peculiar characteristic. On the first, the Word of God, the Gospel of Christ triumphed, and Rome was defeated; and Philosophy, in the person of Erasmus, and her other champions, shared in the defeat. On the second, we admit that Rome, her authority, her discipline, and her doctrine, are again seen on the point of obtaining the victory, through the intrigues of a far-famed society, and the power of the scaffold, aided by certain leaders of eminent character, and others of lofty genius. The third day, human Philosophy arises in all its pride, and finding the battle field occupied, not by the Gospel, but by Rome, it quickly storms every entrenchment, and gains an easy conquest. The first day's battle was for God, the second for the Priest, the third for Reason—what shall the fourth be? . . . . The confused struggle, the hard fought conflict, as we believe, of all these powers together, which will end in the triumph of Him to whom triumph belongs.

But the battle which the Reformation fought in the great day of the sixteenth century was not one and single,—but manifold. The Reformation had to combat at once several enemies; and after having protested against the decretals and

* Port Royal, par Sainte Beuve, vol. i. p. 20.

the sovereignty of the Popes,—then against the cold apophthegms of rationalists, philosophers, and school-men,—it took the field against the reveries of enthusiasm and the hallucinations of mysticism; opposing alike to these three powers the sword and the buckler of God's Holy Revelation.

We cannot but discern a great resemblance,—a striking unity,—between these three powerful adversaries. The false systems which, in every age, have been the most adverse to evangelical Christianity, have ever been distinguished by their making religious knowledge to emanate from man himself. Rationalism makes it proceed from reason; Mysticism from a certain internal illumination; Roman Catholicism from an illumination derived from the Pope. These three errors look for truth in man; Evangelical Christianity looks for it in God alone: and while Rationalism, Mysticism, and Roman Catholicism acknowledge a permanent inspiration in men like ourselves, and thus make room for every species of extravagance and schism,—Evangelical Christianity recognises this inspiration only in the writings of the Apostles and Prophets, and alone presents that great, noble, and living unity which continues to exist unchanged throughout all ages.

The office of the Reformation has been to re-establish the rights of the word of God, in opposition, not only to Roman Catholicism, but also to Rationalism and Mysticism.

The fanaticism of the Anabaptists, which had been extinguished in Germany, by Luther's return to Wittemberg, reappeared in vigour in Switzerland, where it threatened the edifice which Zwingle, Haller, and Œcolampadius had erected on the foundation of the word of God. Thomas Münzer, obliged to quit Saxony in 1521, had reached the frontiers of Switzerland. Conrad Grebel, whose ardent and restless disposition we have already remarked, had joined him, as had also Felix Mantz, a canon's son, and several other natives of Zurich. Grebel endeavoured to gain over Zwingle. It was in vain that the latter had gone further than Luther; he saw a party spring up which desired to proceed to yet greater lengths. "Let us," said Grebel, "form a community of true believers; for it is to

26*

them alone that the promise belongs; and let us establish a church, which shall be without sin."* "It is not possible," replied Zwingle, "to make a heaven upon earth; and Christ has taught us to let the tares grow among the wheat."†

Grebel, unsuccessful with the Reformer, wished to appeal from him to the people. "The whole community of Zurich," said he, "is entitled to decide finally in all matters of faith." But Zwingle dreaded the influence which violent enthusiasts might exercise in a popular assembly. He believed that, except on some extraordinary occasions, where the people might be called on to give their support, it was more desirable to confide the interests of religion to a college, which might be considered the chosen representatives of the church. Consequently, the Council of Two Hundred, which then exercised the supreme political authority in Zurich, was also entrusted with the ecclesiastical power, on the express condition that it should conform, in all things, to the rule of the Holy Scriptures. Undoubtedly it would have been preferable to have organised the church complete, and called on it to name representatives, to whom no interests save the religious interests of the people should be confided; for he who is qualified for affairs of state, may be very unskilful in administering those of the church,—just as the reverse of this is also true. Nevertheless, the inconvenience was not then so serious as it would be in our days, for the members of the Grand Council had heartily embarked in the religious movement. However this may be, Zwingle, in his appeal to the church, would not bring it too prominently forward; and preferred a system of representation to the active sovereignty of the general body. It is the same policy which, after three centuries, the states of Europe have adopted, in reference to earthly politics.

Meeting with a repulse from Zwingle, Grebel turned in another direction. Roubli, an aged minister of Basle, Brödtlein, minister at Zollikon, and Lewis Herzer, welcomed his advances. They resolved on forming an independent body in

---

* Vermeintend ein Kirchen zu versammlen die one Sünd wär. (Zw. Opp. ii. p. 231.) † Zw. Opp. iii. p. 362.

the centre of the general community,—a church within the church. A new baptism was to be their instrument for gathering their congregation, which was to consist exclusively of true believers. "The baptism of infants," said they, "is a horrible abomination,—a flagrant impiety, invented by the evil spirit and by Pope Nicholas II."[*]

The Council of Zurich, in some alarm, directed that a public discussion should be held; and as the Anabaptists still refused to relinquish their errors, some of them, who were natives of Zurich, were imprisoned, and others, who were foreigners, were banished. But persecution only inflamed their zeal. "It is not by words alone," cried they, "but by our blood, that we are ready to bear testimony to the truth of our cause." Some of them, girding themselves with ropes or rods of osier, ran through the streets, crying, "Yet a few days and Zurich will be destroyed! Woe to thee, Zurich! woe! woe!" Several there were who uttered blasphemies: "Baptism," said they, "is but the washing of a dog. To baptize a child is of no more use than baptizing a cat."[†] Fourteen men, including Felix Mantz, and seven women, were arrested, and, in spite of Zwingle's entreaties, imprisoned, on an allowance of bread and water, in the heretics' tower. After a fortnight's confinement they managed, by removing some planks in the floor, to effect their escape during the night. "An angel," they said, "had opened their prison doors, and set them free."[‡]

They were joined by George Jacob of Coira, a monk, who had absconded from his convent, and who was surnamed Blaurock, as it would seem from his constantly wearing a blue dress. His eloquence had obtained for him the appellation of a *second Paul.* This intrepid monk travelled from place to place, constraining many, by the fervour of his ap-

---

† Impietatem manifestissimam, a caco dæmone, a Nicolao II. esse. (Hottinger, iii. p. 219.)

† Nutzete eben so viel als wenn man eine Katze taufet. (Füssl. Beytr. i. p. 243.)

‡ Wie die Apostel von dem Engel Gottes gelediget. (Bull. Chr. p. 261.)

peals, to receive his baptism. One Sunday, at Zollikon, whilst the deacon was preaching, the impetuous Anabaptist, suddenly interrupting him, exclaimed in a voice of thunder, " It is written. *My house is a house of prayer, but ye have made it a den of thieves.*" Then, raising the staff he carried in his hand, he struck it four times violently on the ground.

" I am a door," exclaimed he; " by me if any man enter in he shall find pasture. I am a good shepherd. My body I give to the prison; my life to the sword, the axe, and the wheel. I am the beginning of the baptism and of the bread of the Lord."*

While Zwingle was attempting to stem the torrent of Anabaptism at Zurich, it quickly inundated St. Gall. Grebel arrived there, and was received by the brethren with acclamations; and on Palm Sunday he proceeded to the banks of the Sitter, attended by a great number of his adherents, whom he there baptized.

The news soon spread through the neighbouring cantons, and a great multitude from Zurich, Appenzell, and various other places, flocked to "the little Jerusalem."

Zwingle was deeply afflicted by this agitation. He saw a storm descending on the land where the seeds of the Gospel had as yet scarcely begun to take root.† Resolving to oppose these disorders, he composed a tract " on Baptism,"‡ which the Council of St. Gall, to whom he dedicated it, caused to be read in the church in the hearing of the people.

" Dear brethren in the Lord," said Zwingle, "the waters of the torrents which rush from our rocks hurry with them every thing within their reach. At first, small stones only are put in motion, but these are driven violently against larger ones, until the torrent acquires such strength that it carries

* Ich bin ein Anfanger der Taufe und des Herrn Brodes. (Fussl. Beytr. i. p. 264.)

† Mich beduret seer das ungewitter. (Zw. to the Council of St. Gall, ii. p. 230.)

‡ Vom Touf, vom Widertouf, und vom Kindertouf. (Zw. Opp. ii. p. 230.)

away every thing it encounters in its course, leaving behind lamentations, vain regrets, and fertile meadows changed into a wilderness. The spirit of disputation and self-righteousness acts in a similar manner, it occasions disturbances, banishes charity, and where it found fair and prosperous churches, leaves behind it nothing but mourning and desolate flocks."

Thus wrote Zwingle—the child of the mountains of the Tockenburg. " Give us the word of God," exclaimed an Anabaptist who was present in church, " and not the word of Zwingle." Immediately confused voices arose : " Away with the book ! away with the book !" cried the Anabaptists. Then rising, they quitted the church, exclaiming, " Do you keep the doctrine of Zwingle ; as for us, we will keep the word of God."*

Then it was that this fanaticism broke forth in lamentable disorders. Alleging, in excuse, that the Saviour had exhorted us to become as little children, these poor creatures began to go dancing through the streets, clapping their hands, footing it in a circle, seating themselves on the ground together, and tumbling each other in the sand. Some there were who threw the New Testament into the fire, exclaiming, " The letter killeth, the spirit giveth life ;" and several, falling into convulsions, pretended to have revelations from the Holy Spirit.

In a solitary house situated on the Müllegg, near St. Gall, lived an aged farmer, John Schucker, with his five sons. The whole family, including the servants, had received the new baptism ; and two of the sons, Thomas and Leonard, were distinguished for their fanaticism. On the 7th of February, 1526, being Shrove Tuesday, they invited a large party of Anabaptists to their house, and the father had a calf killed for the feast. The good cheer, the wine, and their numbers altogether, heated their imaginations ; and they spent the whole night in fanatical excitement, convulsions, visions, and revelations.†

* So wollen wir Gottes Wort haben. (Zw. Opp. ii. p. 237.)
† Mit wunderbaren geperden und gesprächen, verzucken, gesichten, und offenbarungen. (Bulling. Chr. i. p. 324.)

In the morning, Thomas, still agitated by that night of disorder, and having even,—as it would seem,—lost his senses, took the calf's bladder, and placing part of the gall in it, in imitation of the symbolical language of the prophets, approached his brother Leonard, and said to him gloomily, "Thus bitter is the death thou art to suffer!" Then he added, "Brother Leonard, fall on thy knees;" Leonard knelt down;—presently, "Brother Leonard, arise!" Leonard arose. Their father, brothers, and the other Anabaptists, looked on with astonishment, asking themselves what God would do. Soon Thomas resumed: "Leonard, kneel down again!" Leonard obeyed. The spectators, terrified at the gloomy countenance of the wretched Thomas, said to him, "Reflect on what thou art about to do; take care that no mischief happens."—"Fear not," answered Thomas, "nothing will happen without the will of the Father." At the same moment he hastily snatched a sword, and bringing it down with all his force on the neck of his brother, who was kneeling before him, like a criminal before the executioner, he severed his head from his body, crying out, "Now is the will of the Father accomplished!" The bystanders recoiled in horror; the farm resounded with shrieks and lamentations. Thomas, who had nothing on him but his shirt and drawers, rushed out of the house bare-footed, and with his head uncovered, and running towards St. Gall with frenzied gestures, entered the house of the burgomaster, Joachim Vadian, with haggard looks, shouting, "I proclaim to thee the *day of the Lord*." The dreadful tidings spread throughout St. Gall—"He has killed his brother as Cain killed Abel," said the crowd.* The criminal was seized.—"True," he repeated continually, "I did it, but it was God who did it by my hand." On the 16th of February, the unhappy wretch was beheaded by the executioner. Fanaticism had run its course to the utmost. Men's eyes were opened, and, to adopt the words of an early historian, "the same blow took off the head of Thomas Schucker, and of Anabaptism in St. Gall."

* Glych wie Kain den Abel sinen bruder ermort hat! (Bull. Chr. i. 394.)

At Zurich, however, it still prevailed. On the 6th of No
vember, in the preceding year, a public discussion had taken
place, in order to content the Anabaptists, who were constantly
complaining that the innocent were condemned unheard. The
three following theses were put forth by Zwingle and his
friends, as subjects of the conference, and triumphantly maintained by them in the Council hall.

" The children of believing parents are children of God,
even as those who were born under the Old Testament; and
consequently they may receive Baptism."

" Baptism is, under the New Testament, what Circumcision
was under the Old. Consequently, Baptism is now to be administered to children, as Circumcision was formerly."

" The custom of repeating Baptism cannot be justified either
by examples, precepts, or arguments drawn from Scripture;
and those who are re-baptized, crucify Jesus Christ afresh."

But the Anabaptists did not confine themselves to questions
purely religious; they demanded the abolition of tithes,
" since," said they, "they are not of divine appointment."
Zwingle replied that the tithes were necessary for the maintenance of the churches and schools. He desired a complete
religious reformation, but he was resolved not to allow the
least invasion of public order or political institutions. This
was the limit at which he discerned, written by the hand of
God, that word from heaven, " Thus far shalt thou go, and no
farther."* Somewhere, it was necessary to make a stand;
and it was at this point that Zwingle and the Reformers took
their stand, in spite of the efforts made by rash and impetuous
men to hurry them beyond it.

But when the Reformers themselves stopped, they could not
stop the enthusiasts, who seem as if brought into contact with
them in order to set off by contrast their wisdom and sober-
mindedness. It was not enough for the Anabaptists to have
formed their church;—in their eyes that church was itself
the State. Did any one summon them before the tribunals,—
they refused to recognise the civil authority, maintaining that

* Job xxxviii. 11.

it was a remnant of Paganism, and that they would obey no power but that of God!   They taught that it was unlawful for Christians to fill public offices or bear the sword,—and, resembling in another respect certain irreligious enthusiasts of our own days, they esteemed a 'community of goods' as the perfection of humanity.[*]

Thus the evil was increasing; Civil Society was endangered.   It arose to cast out from its bosom those elements that threatened it with destruction.   The Government, in its alarm, suffered itself to be hurried into strange measures.   Resolved on making an example, they condemned Mantz to be drowned. On the 5th January, 1527, he was put into a boat; his mother, (the aged concubine of his father, the canon,) together with his brother, mingled in the crowd which accompanied him to the water's edge.   "Be faithful unto death," was their exhortation.   At the moment when the executioner prepared to throw Mantz into the lake, his brother burst into tears; but his mother, calm and undaunted, witnessed, with eyes dry and flashing fire, the martyrdom of her son.[†]

The same day, Blaurock was scourged with rods.   As he was led outside the city, he shook his blue dress, and the dust from off his feet, against it.[‡]   This unhappy man was, it would appear, burnt alive two years after this by the Roman Catholics of the Tyrol.

Undoubtedly, a spirit of rebellion existed among the Anabaptists; undoubtedly, the ancient ecclesiastical law, which condemned heretics to capital punishments, was still in force, and the Reformation could not, in the space of one or two years, reform every thing; nor can we doubt that the Catholic states would have accused their Protestant neighbours of encouraging insubjection, if the latter had not resorted to severe measures against these enthusiasts; but though such conside-

* Füssl. Beytr. i. p. 229—258; ii. p. 263.
† Ohne das er oder die Mutter, sondern nur der Bruder geweinet. (Hott. Helv. K. Gesch. iii. p. 385.)
‡ Und schüttlet sinen blauen rock und sine schüh über die Statt Zurich. (Bull. Chr. i. p. 382.)

rations serve to account for the rigour of the magistrate, they
never can justify it. Measures might be taken against an infringement of the civil constitution, but religious errors, being
combated by the teachers of religion, should be altogether
exempt from the jurisdiction of civil tribunals. Such opinions
are not to be expelled by whippings, nor are they drowned
in the waters into which those who profess them may be cast:
they again come forth from the depth of the abyss; and the
fire but serves to kindle in those who adhere to them a fiercer
enthusiasm, and thirst for martyrdom. Zwingle, whose sentiments on this subject we have already seen, took no part in
these severities.*

But it was not only on the subject of baptism that dissensions were to arise; yet more serious differences appeared,
touching the doctrine of the Lord's Supper.

The human mind, freed from the yoke which had so long
weighed it down, made use of its liberty; and, if Romanism
is hemmed in by the shoals of despotic authority, Protestantism
has to steer clear of those of anarchy. One characteristic distinction of Protestantism is progress, while that of Romanism
is immobility.

Roman Catholicism, possessing in the papal authority a
means of, at any time, establishing new doctrines, appears, at
first view, to have in it a principle eminently favourable to
change. It has, indeed, largely availed itself of this power,
and, century after century, we see Rome bringing forward, or
confirming new dogmas. But its system once completed, Roman Catholicism has declared itself the champion of immobility. Therein lies its safety: it resembles a shaky building,
from which nothing can be taken without bringing the whole
down to the ground. Permit the priests to marry, or strike a
blow against the doctrine of transubstantiation, and the whole
system totters—the entire edifice falls to pieces.

It is not thus with Evangelical Christianity. Its principle

* Quod homines seditiosi, rei-publicæ turbatores, magistratuum hostes,
justâ Senatus sententiâ, damnati sunt, num id Zwinglio fraudi esse
poterit? (Rod. Gualtheri Epist. ad lectorem, Opp. 1544. ii.)

is much less favourable to *change*, much more so to *progress* and *life*. On the one hand, it recognises no other fountain of truth than Scripture, one and immutably the same, from the very beginning of the Church to the end of time; how, then, should it vary, as Popery has varied? But, on the other hand, every individual Christian is to draw for himself from this fountain; and hence spring progress and liberty. Accordingly, Evangelical Christianity, although in the nineteenth century the same that it was in the sixteenth, and in the first, is,—at all times,—full of spontaneity and action; and is, at this moment, filling the wide world with its researches and its labours, its Bibles and its missionaries, with light, salvation, and life!

It is a gross error which would class together, and almost confound, rationalism and mysticism with Christianity, and, in so doing, charge upon it the extravagances of both. Progress belongs to the nature of Christian Protestantism: it has nothing in common with immobility and a state of deadness; but its movement is that of healthful vitality, and not the aberration of madmen, or the restlessness of disease. We shall see this character manifesting itself in relation to the doctrine of the Lord's Supper.

What ensued might have been expected. This doctrine had been understood in very various ways in the early ages of the Church: and the difference of opinion continued up to the time when the doctrine of transubstantiation and the scholastic theology began, at about the same period, their reign over the mind of the middle ages. But that dominion was now shaken to its base, and the former differences were again to appear.

Zwingle and Luther, who had at first gone forward, each in his separate course,—the one in Switzerland, the other in Saxony,—were one day to find themselves brought, as it were, face to face. The same mind, and, in many respects, the same character, might be discerned in them. Both were full of love for truth and hatred of injustice; both were naturally violent; and in both that violence was tempered by sincere piety. But there was one feature in the character of Zwingle which tended to carry him beyond Luther. He loved liberty, not only as a man, but as a republican, and the fellow-countryman of Tell. Accustomed to the decision of a free state, he was not stopped by considerations before which Luther drew back. He had, moreover, given less time to the study of the theology of the schools, and found himself, in consequence. less shackled in his modes of thinking. Both ardently attached to their own convictions,—both resolute in defending them,—and little accustomed to bend to the convictions of others, they were now to come in contact, like two proud chargers rushing from opposite ranks and encountering on the field of battle.

A practical tendency predominated in the character of Zwingle and of the Reformation which he had begun, and this tendency was directed to two great ends—simplicity in worship and sanctification in life. To adapt the form of worship to the wants of the soul, seeking not outward ceremonies, but things invisible, was Zwingle's first object. The idea of Christ's real presence in the Eucharist, which had given rise to so many ceremonies and superstitions in the Church, must, therefore, be abolished. But the other great desire of the Swiss Reformer led him directly to the same result. He judged that the Romish doctrine respecting the Supper, and even that held by Luther, implied a belief of a certain mystical influence, which belief, he thought, stood in the way of sanctification ;—he feared lest the Christian, thinking that he received Christ in the consecrated bread, should no longer earnestly seek to be united to him by faith in the heart. "Faith," said he, "is not knowledge, opinion, imagination ;— it is a reality.* It involves in it a real participation in divine things." Thus, whatever the adversaries of Zwingle may have asserted, it was no leaning towards rationalism, but a deep religious view of the subject which conducted him to the doctrines he maintained.

The result of Zwingle's studies were in accordance with hese tendencies. In studying the Scriptures, not only in

* Fidem rem esse, non scientiam, opinionem vel imaginationem. Comment de verâ relig. Zw. Opp. iii. p. 230.)

detached passages, but as a whole, and having recourse to classical antiquity to solve the difficulties of language, he arrived at the conviction, that the word "is" in the words of institution of this sacrament, should be taken in the sense of "*signifies;*" and, as early as the year 1523, he wrote to a friend, that the bread and wine in the Lord's Supper are exactly what the water is in baptism.* "In vain," added he, "would you plunge a thousand times under the water a man who does not believe. *Faith* is the one thing needful."

Luther, at first, set out from principles nearly similar to those of the Reformer of Zurich. "It is not the sacrament which sanctifies," said he, "it is *faith* in the sacrament." But the extravagances of the Anabaptists, whose mysticism spiritualized every thing, produced a great change in his views. When he saw enthusiasts, who pretended to inspiration, destroying images, rejecting baptism, and denying the presence of Christ in the Eucharist, he was affrighted; he had a kind of prophetic presentiment of the dangers which would threaten the Church if this tendency to over-spiritualize, should gain the ascendant; hence he took a totally different course, like the boatman, who, to restore the balance of his foundering skiff, throws all his weight on the side opposed to the storm.

Thenceforward, Luther assigned to the sacraments a higher importance. He maintained they were not only signs by which Christians were outwardly distinguished, but evidences of the Divine will, adapted to strengthen our faith. He went farther: Christ, according to him, desired to give to believers a full assurance of salvation, and, in order to seal this promise to them with most effect, had added thereto his real body in the bread and wine. "Just," continued he, "as iron and fire, though two different substances, meet and are blended in a red hot bar, so that in every part of it there is at once iron and fire; so, *à fortiori*, the glorified body of Christ exists in every part of the bread."

Thus, at this period of his career, Luther made, perhaps, a

* Haud aliter hic panem et vinum esse puto quam aqua est in baptismo. (Ad Wittenbachium Epp. 15th June, 1523.)

partial return to the scholastic theology. He had openly divorced himself from it on the doctrine of *justification by faith;* but on the doctrine of this Sacrament, he gave up but one point, viz. *transubstantiation,* and retained the other, the *real presence.* He even went so far as to say that he would rather receive the mere *blood* with the Pope than the mere *wine* with Zwingle.

Luther's great principle was never to depart from the doctrines or customs of the Church, unless the words of Scripture absolutely required him to do so. "Where has Christ commanded us to elevate the host, and exhibit it to the people?" had been Carlstadt's question. "Where has he forbidden it?" was Luther's reply. Herein lies the difference of the two Reformations we are considering. The traditions of the Church were dear to the Saxon Reformer. If he separated from them on many points, it was not till after much conflict of mind, and because, above all, he saw the necessity of obeying the word of God. But wherever the letter of God's word appeared to him in accordance with the tradition and practice of the Church, he adhered to it with unalterable resolution. Now this was the case in the question concerning the Lord's Supper. He did not deny that the word "*is*" might be taken in the sense ascribed to it by Zwingle. He admitted, for example, that it must be so understood in the passage, "*That rock was Christ;*"* but what he did deny was that the word should be taken in this sense in the institution of the Lord's Supper.

In one of the later schoolmen, Occam, whom he preferred to all others,† he found an opinion which he embraced. With Occam, he gave up the continually repeated miracle, in virtue whereof, according to the Romish Church, the body and blood take the place of the bread and wine after every act of consecration by the priest,—and with Occam, substituted for it a universal miracle, wrought once for all,—that is, the ubi-

---

* 1 Cor. x. 4.

† Diu multumque legit scripta Occam cujus acumen anteferebat Thomæ et Scoto. (Melancth. Vita Luth.)

quity or omnipresence of Christ's body. "Christ," said he, " is present in the bread and wine, because he is present every where,—and in an especial manner where he wills to be."[*]

The inclination of Zwingle was the reverse of Luther's He attached less importance to the preserving a union, in a certain sense, with the universal church, and thus maintaining our hold upon the tradition of past ages. As a theologian, he looked to Scripture alone; and thence only would he freely, and without any intermediary channel, derive his faith; not stopping to trouble himself with what others had in former times believed. As a republican, he looked to the commune of Zurich. His mind was occupied with the idea of the church of his own time, not with that of other days. He re‐ lied especially on the words of St. Paul,—"*Because there is but one bread, we being many are One body;*[†] and he saw in the supper the sign of a spiritual communion between Christ and all Christians. "Whoever," said he, "acts unworthily, is guilty of sin against the body of Christ, of which he is a mem‐ ber." Such a thought had a great practical power over the minds of communicants; and the effects it wrought in the lives of many, was to Zwingle the confirmation of it.

Thus Luther and Zwingle had insensibly separated from one another. Nevertheless peace, perhaps, might have con‐ tinued between them, if the turbulent Carlstadt, who spent some time in passing to and fro between Germany and Switz‐ erland, had not inflamed their conflicting opinions.

A step, taken with a view to preserve peace, led to the ex‐ plosion. The Council of Zurich, wishing to put a stop to controversy, prohibited the sale of Carlstadt's writings. Zwingle, though he disapproved the violence of Carlstadt, and blamed his mystic and obscure expressions,[‡] upon this thought it right to defend his doctrine, both from the pulpit and before

---

[*] Occam und Luther. *Studien und Kritiken.* 1839, p. 69.

[†] The passage referred to is 1 Cor. x. 17, and the original stands thus:—Ὅτι εἷς ἄρτος, ἓν σῶμα οἱ πολλοί ἐσμεν. (Tr.)

[‡] Quod morosior est (Carlstadius) in cæremoniis non ferendis, non admodum probo. (Zw. Epp. p. 369.)

the Council; and soon afterwards he wrote a letter to the minister, Albert of Reutlingen, in which he said: "Whether or
not Christ is speaking of the sacrament in the sixth chapter
of St. John's gospel, it is, at least, evident, that he therein
teaches a mode of eating his flesh and drinking his blood, in
which there is nothing corporeal."* He then endeavoured to
prove that the Supper of the Lord, by reminding the faithful,
according to Christ's design, of his body which 'was broken'
for them, is the procuring cause of that spiritual-manducation,
which is alone truly beneficial to them.

Nevertheless, Zwingle still shrunk from a rupture with
Luther. He trembled at the thought that distressing discussions would rend asunder the little company of believers
forming in the midst of effete Christendom. Not so with
Luther. He did not hesitate to include Zwingle in the ranks
of those enthusiasts with whom he had already broken so
many lances. He did not reflect that if images had been removed from the churches of Zurich, it had been done legally,
and by public authority. Accustomed to the forms of the
German principalities, he knew but little of the manner of proceeding in the Swiss republics; and he declared against the
grave Swiss divines, just as he had done against the Müntzers
and the Carlstadts.

Luther having put forth his discourse "*against celestial
prophets,*" Zwingle's resolution was taken; and he published
almost immediately after, his *Letter to Albert,* and his *Commentary on true and false Religion,* dedicated to Francis I.
In it he said, "Since Christ, in the sixth of John, attributes to
faith the power of communicating eternal life, and uniting the
believer to him in the most intimate of all unions, what more
can we need? Why should we think that he would afterwards attribute that efficacy to His flesh, when He himself
declares that the flesh profiteth nothing? So far as the suffering death for us, the flesh of Christ is of unspeakable benefit

* A manducatione cibi, qui ventrem implet, transiit ad verbi man-
ducationem, quam cibum vocat cœlestem, qui mundum vivificet. (Zw.
Opp. iii. p. 573.)

to us,—for it saves us from perdition ;—but as being eaten by us, it is altogether useless."

The contest began. Pomeranus, Luther's friend, took the field, and attacked the Evangelist of Zurich somewhat too contemptuously. Then it was that Œcolampadius began to blush that he had so long struggled with his doubts, and preached doctrines which were already giving way in his own mind. Taking courage, he wrote from Basle to Zwingle. " The dogma of the ' real presence' is the fortress and strong hold of their impiety ; so long as they cleave to this *idol*, none can overcome them." After this, he, too, entered the lists, by publishing a tract on the import of the Lord's words, " *This is my body*." *

The bare fact that Œcolampadius had joined the Reformer of Zurich, excited an immense sensation, not only at Basle, but throughout all Germany. Luther was deeply affected by it. Brentz, Schnepff, and twelve other ministers in Suabia, to whom Œcolampadius had dedicated his tract, and who had almost all been disciples under him, testified the most lively sorrow. In taking up the pen to answer him, Brentz said, " Even at this moment, when I am separating from him for just reasons, I honour and admire him as much as it is possible to do. The tie of love is not severed because we differ in judgment." And he proceeded, in concert with his friends, to publish the celebrated *Suabian Syngramma*, in which he replied to the arguments of Œcolampadius with boldness, but with respect and affection. " If an emperor," say the authors of the Syngramma, " were to give a baton or a wand to a judge, saying, ' Take—this is the power of judging :'—the wand, no doubt, is a mere sign ; but, the words being added thereto, the judge has not merely the sign of the power, he has the *power* itself."

The true children of the Reformation might admit this illustration. The *Syngramma* was received with acclamations, and its authors were looked upon as the defenders of the truth.

* He retained the usual signification of the word *is*, but he understood, by *body*, a sign of the body.

Several divines, and even some laymen, in their desire to share in their glory, undertook the defence of the doctrine that was assailed, and wrote against Œcolampadius.

Then it was Strasburg interposed, and sought to mediate between Switzerland and Germany. Capito and Bucer were disposed for peace; and, in their view, the question under discussion was of secondary importance. Accordingly stepping between the two parties, they sent George Cassel, one of their colleagues, to Luther, to conjure him not to snap the link of brotherhood which united him with the Swiss divines.

No where does Luther's character display itself more strikingly than in this controversy on the Lord's Supper. Never did it more clearly appear with what firmness he maintained the convictions he believed to be those of a Christian,—with what faithfulness he established them on the authority of Scripture alone,—his sagacity in defending them, and his animated, eloquent, and often overpowering argumentation. But, on the other hand, never was there a more abundant exhibition of the obstinacy with which he brought up every argument for his own opinion, the little attention he gave to his opponents' reasoning, and the uncharitable haste with which he attributed their errors to the wickedness of their hearts, and the machinations of the devil. To the mediator of Strasburg he said,—"Either the one party or the other,—either the Swiss or we,—must be ministers of Satan."

Such were what Capito termed "the furies of the Saxon Orestes;" and these furies were succeeded by exhaustion. Luther's health suffered. One day he fainted in the arms of his wife and friends; and, for a whole week, he was as if "in death and hell."* He had lost Jesus Christ, he said, and was driven hither and thither by tempests of despair. The world was about to pass away, and prodigies announced that the last day was at hand.

But these divisions among the friends of the Reformation were to have after consequences yet more to be deplored. The Romish divines in Switzerland especially boasted of being

* In morte et in inferno jactatus. (L. Epp. iii. p. 132.)

able to oppose Luther to Zwingle. And yet, if,—now that three centuries have passed away,—the recollection of these divisions should teach Evangelical Christians the precious lesson of Unity in diversity, and Love in liberty, they will not have happened in vain. Even at the time,—the Reformers, by thus opposing one another, proved that they were not governed by blind hatred of Rome, but that Truth was the great object of their hearts. It must be admitted that there is something generous in such conduct; and its disinterestedness did not fail to produce some fruit, and extort from enemies themselves a tribute of interest and esteem.

But we may go further, and here again we discern the Sovereign hand which governs all events, and allows nothing to happen but what makes part of its own wise plan. Notwithstanding his opposition to the Papacy, Luther had a strong conservative instinct. Zwingle, on the contrary, was predisposed to radical reforms. Both these divergent tendencies were needed. If Luther and his followers had been alone in the work, it would have stopped short in its progress; and the principle of Reformation would not have wrought its destined effect. If, on the other hand, Zwingle had been alone, —the thread would have been snapped too abruptly, and the Reformation would have found itself isolated from the ages which had gone before.

These two tendencies, which, on a superficial view, might seem present only to conflict together, were, on the contrary, ordained to be the complement of each other,—and now that three centuries have passed away, we can say that they have fulfilled their mission.

Thus, on all sides, the Reformation had to encounter resistance; and, after combating the rationalist philosophy of Erasmus, and the fanatical enthusiasm of the Anabaptists, it had, in addition, to settle matters at home. But its great and lasting struggle was against the Papacy;—and the assault, commenced in the cities of the plain, was now carried to the most distant mountains.

The summit of Tockenburg had heard the sound of the

Gospel), and three ecclesiastics were prosecuted by order of
the bishop, as tainted with heresy. "Only convince us by the
word of God," said Militus, Doring, and Farer, "and we
will humble ourselves, not only before the chapter, but before
the very least of the brethren of Jesus Christ. Otherwise,
we will obey no one; not even the greatest among men."*

The genuine spirit of Zwingle and of the Reformation
speaks out in these words. It was not long before a new incident occurred to inflame the minds of the mountaineers. A
meeting of the people took place on St. Catherine's day; the
townsmen gathered in groups, and two men of Schwitz, whose
business had called them to the Tockenburg, were seated together at one of the tables. They entered into conversation:
—"Ulric Zwingle," exclaimed one of them, "is a heretic and
a robber." The Secretary Steiger defended the Reformation.
Their loud voices attracted the attention of the meeting.
George Bruggman, uncle to Zwingle, who was seated at an
adjoining table, angrily left his seat, exclaiming, "Surely
they are speaking of Master Ulric;" on which the guests all
rose up and followed, apprehending a disturbance.† The
tumult increased; the bailiff hastily collected the Town-
council in the open street, and Bruggman was requested, for
the sake of peace, to content himself with saying, "If you do
not retract your words, it is yourselves who are liars and
thieves." "Recollect what you have just said," answered the
men of Schwitz, "we will not forget it." This said, they
mounted their horses, and set forward at full speed for
Schwitz.‡

The government of Schwitz addressed to the inhabitants
of the Tockenburg, a letter, which spread terror wherever it
came. "Stand firm and fear nothing,"§ wrote Zwingle to

* Ne potentissimo quidem, sed soli Deo ejusque verbo. (Zw. Epp.
p. 370.)

† Totumque convivium sequi, grandem conflictum timentes. (Ibid.
p. 371.)

‡ Auf solches, ritten sie wieder heim. (Ibid. p. 374.)

§ Macti animo este et interriti. (Zw. Epp. p. 351.)

the Council of his native place: "Let not the lies they circulate concerning me disturb you. There is no brawler but has the power to call me heretic; but do you avoid all insulting language, tumults, excesses, and mercenary war. Relieve the poor; espouse the cause of the oppressed; and whatever insults may be heaped upon you, hold fast your confidence in Almighty God."[*]

Zwingle's exhortations had the desired effect. The Council were still hesitating; but the people gathering together in their several parishes, unanimously resolved that the Mass should be abolished and the word of God adhered to.[†]

The progress of the work was not less marked in Rhetia, from whence Salandronius had been compelled to take his departure, but where Comander was preaching with much boldness. It is true that the Anabaptists, by their fanatical preachings in the country of the Grisons, had at first been a great hindrance to the progress of the Reformation. The people had split into three parties. Some had embraced the doctrines of those pretended prophets: others in silent astonishment meditated with anxiety on the schism that had declared itself. And, lastly, the partisans of Rome were loud in their exultations.[‡]

A meeting was held at Ilantz, in the Grison league, for the purpose of a discussion. The supporters of the Papacy, on one hand, the favourers of the Reformation on the other, collected their forces. The bishop's vicar at first laboured to avoid the dispute. "Such disputations are attended with considerable expenses," said he; "I am ready to put down ten thousand florins, in order to defray them, but I expect the op-

---

* Verbis diris abstinete .... opem ferte egenis .... spem certissimam in Deo reponatis omnipotente. (Ibid.) Either the date of one of the letters, 14th and 23d of 1524, must be a mistake, or one letter from Zwingle to his fellow-countrymen of the Tockenburg must be lost.

† Parochiæ uno consensu statuerunt in verbo Dei manere. (Zw. Epp. p. 423.)

‡ Pars tertia papistarum est in immensum gloriantium de schismate inter nos facto. (Ibid. p. 400.)

posite party to do as much." "If the bishop has ten thousand florins at his disposal," exclaimed the rough voice of a countryman in the crowd, "it is from us he has extorted them; to give such poor priests as much more would be a little too bad." "We are a poor set of people," said Comander, the pastor of Coira, "we can scarcely pay for our soup, where then can we raise ten thousand florins."* Every one laughed at this stratagem, and the business proceeded.

Among those present were Sebastian Hofmeister and James Amman of Zurich. They held in their hands the Holy Scriptures, in Hebrew and Greek. The bishop's vicar moved that strangers be desired to withdraw. Hofmeister understood this to be directed against him. "We have come provided," said he, "with a Hebrew and Greek Bible, in order that none may in any way do violence to the Scripture. However, sooner than stand in the way of the conference we are willing to retire." "Ah!" cried the curate of Diatzen, as he glanced at the books the two Zurichers held in their hands, "if the Hebrew and Greek languages had never obtained entrance into our country, there would be fewer heresies among us."† "St. Jerome," observed another, "has translated the Bible for us, and we don't want the Jewish books." "If the Zurichers are excluded," said the banneret of Ilantz, the commune will move in the affair." "Well," replied the others, "let them listen, but let them be silent." The Zurichers were accordingly allowed to remain, and their Bible with them.

Comander, rising in his place, read from the first of his published theses—"The Christian Church is born of the word of God. Its duty is to hold fast that Word, and not to give ear to any other voice." He proceeded to establish what he advanced by numerous passages from the Scriptures. "He went boldly forward," says an eye-witness, "planting

* Sie wären gute arme Gesellen mit lehren Secklen. (Füssl. Beytr i. p. 358.)

† Wäre die Griechische und Hebraische Sprache nicht in das Land gekommen. (Ibid. p. 360.)

his foot, at every step, with the firmness of an ox's tread."* " This will last all day," said the vicar.——" When he is at table with his friends, listening to those who play the flute, he does not grudge the time,"† remarked Hofmeister.

Just then one of the spectators left his seat, and elbowing his passage through the crowd, forced his way up to Comander, waving his arms, scowling on the Reformer, and knitting his brows. He seemed like one beside himself; and as he bustled up to Comander, many thought he was going to strike him.‡ He was a schoolmaster of Coira. " I have written down various questions for you to answer," said he to Comander: " answer them directly." " I stand here," said the Reformer of the Grisons, " to defend my teaching. Do you attack it, and I will answer you; or, if not, go back to your place. I will reply to you when I have done." The schoolmaster deliberated for an instant. " Well," said he, at last,——and returned to his seat.

It was proposed to proceed to consider the doctrine of the Sacrament. The abbot of St. Luke's declared that it was not without awe that he approached such a subject; and the vicar devoutly crossed himself in fear.

The schoolmaster of Coira, who had before showed his readiness to attack Comander, with much volubility began to argue for the received doctrine of the Sacrament, grounding what he said on the words,——" This is my body." " My dear Berre," said Comander to him, " how do you understand these words,——John is Elias?" " I understand," replied Berre, who saw Comander's object in the question, " I understand that he was truly and essentially Elias." " And why then," continued Comander, " did John the Baptist himself say to the Pharisees that he was not Elias?" The schoolmaster was silent; and at last ejaculated,——" It is true." All laughed,——even the friends who had urged him to speak.

* Satzte den Fuss wie ein müder Ochs. (Füssl. Beytr. i. p. 362.)
† Den Pfeiffern zuzuhören, die . . . . wie den Fürsten hofierten. (Ibid.)
‡ Blintzete mit den Augen, rumpfete die Stirne. (Füssl. Beytr. i. p. 368.)

The abbot of Saint Luke's spoke at much length on the Supper; and the conference was finally closed. Seven priests embraced the Gospel. The most perfect religious liberty was proclaimed; and in several of the churches the Romish worship was abolished. "Christ," to use the words of Salandronius, "grew up every where in the mountains, like the tender grass of the spring, and his ministers were like living fountains, watering those Alpine pastures."[*]

The Reformation was advancing, with yet more rapid strides, in Zurich. Dominicans, Augustines, Capucins, so long opposed to each other, were reduced to the necessity of living together;—an anticipated *purgatory* for these poor monks. In place of those degenerated institutions were founded schools, an hospital, a theological seminary. Learning and charity everywhere took the place of sloth and selfishness.

These triumphs of the Reformation could not escape notice. The monks, the priests, and their prelates, not knowing how to move, everywhere felt that the ground was passing from under their feet; and that the Church was on the point of sinking under its unprecedented dangers. The oligarchs of the cantons,—the hired supporters of foreign capitulations, perceived there was no time to be lost, if they wished to preserve their own privileges; and at the moment when the Church, in her terror, was sinking into the earth, they again tendered her the support of their arms bristling with steel. A John Faber was reinforced by a Stein or John Hug of Lucerne, and the civil authority came forward to assist that power of the hierarchy which opens his mouth to blaspheme and makes war against the saints.[†]

Public opinion had for a long while demanded a conference. No other way appeared of quelling the people.[‡] "Only convince us from the Scriptures," said the Council of Zurich to the Diet, "and we will fall in with your desires." "The

---

[*] Vita, moribus et doctrina herbescenti Christo apud Rhœtos fons irrigans. (Zw. Epp. p. 485.) [†] Rev. xiii.

[‡] Das der gmein man, one eine offne disputation, nitt zü stillen. was. (Bulling. Chr. i. p. 331.)

Zurichers," said the people, "have given you their promise; if you are able to refute them from the Scriptures, why not do it? And if not able, why not yourselves conform to the Bible?"

The conferences at Zurich had had a mighty influence; it seemed politic to oppose to them a conference held in a city in the interest of Rome; taking at the same time all necessary precautions to secure the victory to the Pope's party.

It is true that the same party had declared such discussions unlawful,—but a door of evasion was found to escape that difficulty; for, said they, all that it is proposed to do is to declare and condemn the pestilent doctrine of Zwingle.* This difficulty obviated, they looked about them for a sturdy disputant and Doctor Eck offered himself. He had no fear of the issue. "Zwingle, no doubt, has more knowledge of cows than of books,"† observed he, as Hofmeister reports.

The Grand Council of Zurich despatched a safe-conduct for Eck to repair direct to Zurich; but Eck answered that he would await the answer of the Confederation. Zwingle, on this, proposed to dispute at St. Gall, or at Schaffhausen, but the Council, grounding its decision on an article in the federal compact, which provided that any person accused of misdemeanor should be tried in the place of his abode, enjoined Zwingle to retract his offer.

The Diet at length came to the decision that a conference should take place at Baden, and appointed the 16th of May 1526. This meeting promised important consequences; for it was the result and the seal of that alliance that had just been concluded between the power of the Church and the aristocrats of the Confederation. "See," said Zwingle to Vadian, "what these oligarchs and Faber‡ are daring enough to attempt."

Accordingly, the decision to be expected from the Diet was a question of deep interest in Switzerland. None could doubt

---

* Diet of Lucerne, 13th of March, 1526.

† Er habe wohl mehr Kühe gemolken als Bücher gelesen. (Zw. Opp. ii. p. 405.)

‡ Vide nunc quid audeant oligarchi atque Faber. (Zw. Epp. p. 484.)

that a conference held under such auspices would be any thing but auspicious to the Reformation. Were not the five cantons most devoted to the Pope's views paramount in influence in Baden? Had they not already condemned Zwingle's doctrine, and pursued it with fire and sword? At Lucerne had he not been burnt in effigy with every expression of contempt? At Friburg had not his writings been consigned to the flames? Throughout the five cantons was not his death demanded by popular clamour? The cantons that exercised a sort of suzerainty in Baden, had they not declared that Zwingle should be seized if he set foot on any part of their territory?* Had not Uberlinger, one of their chiefs, declared that he only wished he had him in his power that he might hang him, though he should be called an executioner as long as he lived?† And Doctor Eck himself, had he not for years past called for fire and sword as the only methods to be resorted to against heretics?——What then must be the end of this conference, and what result can it have but the death of the Reformer?

Such were the fears that agitated the commission appointed at Zurich, to examine into the matter. Zwingle, beholding their agitation rose and said, "You know what happened at Baden to the valiant men of Stammheim, and how the blood of the Wirths stained the scaffold—and yet we are summoned to the very place of their execution! Let Zurich, Berne, Saint Gall, or, if they will, Basle, Constance, or Schaffhausen be chosen for the conference; let it be agreed that none but essential points shall be discussed, that the word of God shall be the only standard of authority which nothing shall be allowed to supersede, and then I am ready to come forward."‡

Meanwhile, fanaticism was already aroused and was striking down her victims. On the 10th of May, 1526, that is, about a week before the discussion at Baden, a consistory, headed by

* Zwingli in ihrem Gebiet, wo er betreten werde, gefangen zu nehmen. (Zw. Opp. ii. p. 422.)

† Da wollte er gern all sein Lebtag ein Henker genannt werden. (Ibid. p. 454.)

‡ Wellend wir ganz geneigt syn ze erschynen. (Zw. Opp. ii. 423.)

28*

the same Faber who challenged Zwingle, condemned to the flames, as a heretic, an evangelical minister named John Hügle, pastor of Lindau,* who sang the *Te Deum* while walking to the place of execution. At the same time, another minister, named Peter Spengler was drowned at Friburg, by order of the bishop of Constance.

Gloomy tidings reached Zwingle from all sides. His brother-in-law, Leonard Tremp, wrote to him from Berne: "I conjure you as you value your life, not to repair to Baden. I know that they will not respect your safe-conduct."†

It was confidently asserted that a project had been formed to seize, gag, and throw him into a boat which should carry him off to some secret place.‡ Taking into consideration these threats of danger and death, the Council of Zurich resolved that Zwingle should not go to Baden.§

The day for the discussion being fixed for the 19th of May, the disputants and representatives of the cantons and bishops slowly collected. First, on the side of the Roman Catholics, appeared the pompous and boastful Eck; on the Protestant side, the modest and gentle Œcolampadius. The latter was fully sensible of the perils attending this discussion:—"Long had he hesitated," says an ancient historian, "like a timid stag, worried by furious dogs;" at length he decided on proceeding to Baden; first making this solemn protestation—"I recognise no other rule of judgment than the word of God." He had, at first, much wished that Zwingle should share his perils;∥ but he soon saw reason to believe that if the intrepid doctor had shown himself in that fanatical city, the anger of the Roman Catholics, kindling at the sight of him, would have involved them both in destruction.

The first step was to determine the laws which should re-

* Hunc hominem hæreticum damnamus, projicimus et conculcamus (Hotting. Helv. K. Gesch. iii. p. 300.)

† Caveatis per caput vestrum. (Zw. Epp. p. 483.)

‡ Navigio captum, ore mox obturato, clam fuisse deportandum. (Osw. Myc. Vit. Zw.)

§ Zwinglium Senatus Tigurinus Badenam dimittere recusavit. (Ibid.)

∥ Si periclitaberis, periclitabimur omnes tecum. (Zw. Epp. p. 312.)

gulate the controversy. Eck proposed that the deputies of the Forest Cantons should be authorized to pronounce the final judgment,—a proposal which, if it had been adopted, would have decided beforehand the condemnation of the reformed doctrines. Thomas Plater, who had come from Zurich to attend the conference, was despatched by Œcolampadius to ask Zwingle's advice. Arriving at night, he was with difficulty admitted into the Reformer's house. Zwingle, waking up and rubbing his eyes, exclaimed, " You are an unseasonable visitant,—what news do you bring ? For these six weeks past, I have had no rest ; thanks to this dispute."* Plater stated what Eck required. " And how," replied Zwingle, " can those peasants be made to understand such matters ? they would be much more at home in milking their cows."†

On the 21st of May the conference began. Eck and Faber, accompanied by prelates, magistrates, and doctors, robed in damask and silk, and bedizened with rings, chains, and crosses,‡ repaired to the church. Eck haughtily ascended a pulpit superbly decorated, whilst the humble Œcolampadius, meanly clad, sat facing his adversary upon a rudely constructed platform. " During the whole time the conference lasted," says the chronicler Bullinger, " Eck and his party were lodged in the parsonage house of Baden, faring sumptuously, living gaily and disorderly, drinking freely the wine with which they were supplied by the abbot of Wettingen.§ Eck, it was said, takes the baths at Baden, but it is *in wine* that he bathes. The Reformers, on the contrary, made but a sorry appearance, and were scoffed at as a troop of mendicants. Their manner of life afforded a striking contrast to that of the Pope's champions. The landlord of the *Pike*, the inn at which Œcolampadius lodged, curious to see how the latter spent his time in his room, reported that whenever he looked in on him,

* Ich bin in 6 Wochen nie in das Beth Kommen. (Plater's Leben. p. 263.)
† Sie verstunden sich bas auf Kuh mälken. (Ibid.)
‡ Mit Syden, Damast und Sammet bekleydet. (Bull. Chr. i. p. 351.)
§ Verbruchten vil wyn. (Ibid.)

he found him either reading or praying. It must be confessed, said he, that he is a very pious heretic."

The discussion lasted eighteen days; and every morning
the clergy of Baden went in solemn procession, chaunting
litanies, in order to ensure victory. Eck was the only one
who spoke in defence of the Romish doctrines. He was at
Baden exactly what he was at Leipsic, with the same German twang, the same broad shoulders and sonorous voice, reminding one of a town-crier, and in appearance more like a
butcher than a divine. He was vehement in disputing, according to his usual custom; trying to wound his opponents
by insulting language, and even now and then breaking out
in an oath.* The president never called him to order—

> Eck stamps his feet. and claps his hands,
> He raves, he swears, he scolds;
> "I do," cries he, "what Rome commands,
> And teach what'er she holds."†

Œcolampadius, on the contrary, with his serene countenance, his noble and patriarchal air, spoke with so much mildness, but at the same time with so much ability and courage,
that even his antagonists, affected and impressed, whispered to
one another, "Oh that the tall sallow man were on our side."‡
Sometimes, indeed, he was moved at beholding the hatred and
violence of his auditors: "Oh," said he, "with what impatience do they listen to me; but God will not forego His
glory, and it is that only that we seek."§

Œcolampadius having combated Eck's first thesis, which
turned on the real presence, Haller, who had reached Baden
after the commencement of the discussion, entered the lists
against the second. Little used to such discussions, constitutionally timid, fettered by the instructions of his government,

* So entwuscht imm ettwan ein Schür.   (Bull. Chr. i. p. 381.)
    † Egg zablet mit fussen und henden
        Fing an schelken und schenden, etc.
    (Contemporaneous Poems of Nicholas Manuel of Berne.)
    ‡ O were der lange gäl man uff unser syten.   (Bull. Chr. i. p. 353.)
    § Domino suam gloriam, quam salvam cupimus ne utiquam deserimus.
(Zw. Epp. p. 511.)

and embarrassed by the presence of its chief magistrate, Gaspard Mullinen, a bitter enemy of the Reformation, Haller had none of the confident bearing of his antagonist ; but he had more real strength.   When Haller had concluded, Œcolampadius again entered the lists, and pressed Eck so closely, that the latter was compelled to fall back upon the custom of the church.   "In our Switzerland," answered Œcolampadius, "custom is of no force unless it be according to the constitution ; now, in all matters of faith, the *Bible* is our constitution."

The third thesis, regarding invocation of saints ; the fourth, in images; the fifth, on purgatory, were successively discussed.   No one came forward to dispute the two last theses, which bore reference to original sin and baptism.

Zwingle took an important part in the whole of the discussion.   The Catholic party had appointed four secretaries, and prohibited all other persons from taking notes on pain of death.*   Nevertheless, a student from the Valais, named Jerome Wälsch, gifted with a retentive memory, carefully impressed upon his mind all that he heard, and upon leaving the assembly privately committed his recollections to writing. Thomas Plater, and Zimmermann of Winterthur, carried these notes to Zwingle every day, as also letters from Œcolampadius, and brought back the Reformer's answers.   The gates of Baden were guarded by halberdiers, and it was only by inventing different excuses that the two messengers could evade the questions of the soldiers, who were at a loss to comprehend why these youths so frequently entered and quitted the city.†   Thus Zwingle, though absent from Baden in bodily presence, was with them in spirit.

He advised and strengthened his friends, and refuted his adversaries.   "Zwingle," says Oswald Myconius, "has la-

* Man sollte einem ohne aller weiter Urtheilen, den Kopf abhauen. (Thom. Plateri. Lebens Beschreib. p. 262.)

† When I was asked, "What are you going to do ?" I replied, "I am carrying chickens to sell to the gentlemen who are come to the baths :" - the chickens were given me at Zurich, and the guards could not understand how it was that I always got them so fresh, and in so short a time. (Plater's Autobiography.)

boured more in meditating upon and watching the contest, and transmitting his advice to Baden, than he could have done by disputing in person in the midst of his enemies."[*]

During the whole time of the conference the Roman Catholics were in a ferment, publishing abroad the report of advantages gained by them. " Œcolampadius," cried they, " vanquished by Eck, lies prostrate on the field, and sues for quarter ;[†] the Pope's authority will be every where restored."[‡] These statements were industriously circulated throughout the cantons, and the many, prompt to believe every rumour, gave credit to these vauntings of the partisans of Rome.

The discussion being concluded, the monk Murner of Lucerne, nicknamed the " tom-cat," came forward and read forty articles of accusation against Zwingle. " I thought," said he, " that the dastard would appear and answer for himself, but he has not done so: I am therefore justified by every law, both human and divine, in declaring forty times over, that the tyrant of Zurich and all his partisans are rebels, liars, perjured persons, adulterers, infidels, thieves, robbers of temples, fit only for the gallows; and that any honest man must disgrace himself if he hold any intercourse with them, of what kind soever." Such was the opprobrious language which, at that time, was honoured with the name of " Christian controversy," by divines whom the Church of Rome herself might well blush to acknowledge.

Great agitation prevailed at Baden; the general feeling was that the Reformers were overcome not by force of arguments, but by power of lungs.[§] Only Œcolampadius and ten of his friends signed a protest against the theses of Eck,

[*] Quam laborasset disputando vel inter medios hostes. (Osw. Myc. Vit. Zw.) See the various writings composed by Zwingle relative to the Baden conference. (Opp. ii. p. 398, 520.

[†] Œcolampadius victus jacet in arena prostratus ab Eccio, herbam porrexit. (Zw. Epp. p. 514.)

[‡] Spem concipiunt lætam fore ut regnum ipsorum restituatur. (Ibid. p. 513.)

[§] Die Evangelische weren wol uberschryen, nicht aber uberwunden worden. (Hotting. Helv. K. Gesch. iii. p. 320.)

whilst they were adopted by no less than eighty persons, including those who had presided at the discussion, and all the monks of Wittengen.   Haller had left Baden before the termination of the conference.

The majority of the Diet then decreed, that as Zwingle, the leader in these pernicious doctrines, refused to appear, and as the ministers who had come to Baden hardened themselves against conviction, both the one and the others were in consequence cast out from the bosom of the church.*

But this celebrated contest, which had originated in the zeal of the oligarchs and the clergy, was yet in its effects to be fatal to both.   Those who had contended for the Gospel, returning to their homes, infused into their fellow-citizens an enthusiasm for the cause they had defended; and Berne and Basle, two of the most influential cantons of the Helvetic confederation, began thenceforth to fall away from the ranks of the Papacy.

It was to be expected that Œcolampadius would be the first to suffer, the rather as he was not a native of Switzerland; and it was not without some fear that he returned to Basle. But his alarm was quickly dissipated.   His gentle words had sunk deeply into those unprejudiced minds which had been closed against the vociferations of Eck; and he was received with acclamations by all men of piety.   His adversaries, it is true, used all their efforts to exclude him from the pulpit, but in vain: he taught and preached with greater energy than before, and never had the people manifested a more ardent thirst for the word of the Lord.†

The course of events at Berne was of a similar character. The conference at Baden, which it had been hoped would stifle the Reformation, gave to it a new impulse in this the most powerful of the Swiss cantons.   No sooner had Haller arrived in the capital, than the inferior Council summoned him before them, and commanded him to celebrate mass.   Haller asked leave to answer before the Grand Council; and the people came together, thinking it behoved them to defend their

* Von gemeiner Kylchen ussgestossen.   (Bull. Chr. p. 355.)
† Plebe Verbi Domini admodum sitiente.   (Zw. Epp. p. 518.)

pastor. Haller, in alarm, declared that he would rather quit the city than be the innocent occasion of disorders. Upon this, tranquillity being restored, "If," said the Reformer, "I am required to perform mass I must resign my office: the honour of God and the truth of His holy Word lie nearer to my heart than any care what 'I shall eat, or wherewithal I shall be clothed.'" Haller uttered these words with much emotion; the members of the Council were affected; even some of his opponents were moved to tears.* Once more was moderation found to be strength. To meet in some measure the requirements of Rome, Haller was removed from his office of canon, but appointed preacher. His most violent enemies, Lewis and Anthony von Diesbach and Anthony von Erlach, indignant at this decision, immediately withdrew from the Council and the city, and threw up their rank as citizens. "Berne stumbled," said Haller, "but she has risen up in greater strength than ever." This firmness of the Bernese made a powerful impression in Switzerland.†

But the effects of the conference of Baden were not confined to Berne and Basle. While these events were occurring in those powerful cities, a movement more or less of the same character was in progress in several other states of the Confederation. The preachers of St. Gall, on their return from Baden, proclaimed the Gospel.‡ At the conclusion of a public meeting, the images were removed from the parish church of St. Lawrence, and the inhabitants parted with their costly dresses, jewels, rings, and gold chains, that they might employ the money in works of charity. The Reformation did, it is true, strip men of their possessions, but it was in order that the poor might be clothed; and the only worldly goods it claimed the surrender of were those of the Reformed themselves.§

* Tillier, Gesch. v. Bern., iii. p. 242.
† Profuit hic nobis Bernates tam dextre in servando Berchtoldo suo egisse. (Eccl. ad. Zw. Epp. p. 518.)
‡ San Gallenses officiis suis restitutos. (Zw. Epp. p. 518.)
§ Kostbare Kleider, Kleinodien, Ring, Ketten, etc. freywillig verkauft. (Hott. iii, p. 338.)

At Mulhausen the preaching was continued with unwearied boldness. Thurgovia and the Rhenish provinces daily drew nearer to the doctrine held in Zurich. Immediately after the conference, Zurzach abolished the use of images in its churches, and almost the whole district of Baden received the Gospel.

Nothing can show more clearly than such facts as these which party had really triumphed. Hence we find Zwingle, contemplating what was passing around him, giving thanks to God :—" Manifold are their attacks," said he, " but the Lord is above all their threatenings and all their violence ;—a wonderful unanimity in behalf of the Gospel prevails in the city and canton of Zurich—we shall overcome all things by the prayer of faith."* Shortly afterwards, writing to Haller, he expressed himself thus: " Every thing here below follows its appointed course :—after the rude northern blast comes the gentle breeze. The scorching heat of summer is succeeded by the treasures of autumn. And now after stern contests, the Creator of all things, whom we serve, has opened for us a passage into the enemy's camp. We are at last permitted to receive among us the Christian doctrine, that dove so long denied entrance, but which has never ceased to watch for the hour when she might return. Be thou the Noah to receive and shelter her."

This same year Zurich made an important acquisition. Conrad Pellican, superior of the Franciscan convent at Basle, professor of theology when only twenty-four years of age, had, through the interest of Zwingle, been chosen to fill the office of Hebrew professor at Zurich. On his arrival he said, " I have long since renounced the Pope, and desired to live to Christ."† Pellican's critical talents rendered him one of the most useful labourers in the great work of the Reformation.

Early in 1527, Zurich, still excluded from the Diet by the Romish cantons, and wishing to take advantage of the more favourable disposition manifested by some of the confederates,

* Fideli enim oratione omnia superabimus. (Zw. Epp. p. 519.)

† Jamdudum papæ renuntiavi et Christo vivere concupivi. (Ibid. p. 455.)

convened an assembly within her own walls. It was attended
by deputies from Berne, Basle, Schaffhausen, Appenzell
and Saint Gall. "We require," said the deputies of Zurich,
"that God's word, which alone leads us to Christ crucified, be
the one thing preached, taught, and exalted. We renounce
all doctrines of men, whatever may have been the custom of
our forefathers; being well assured that if they had been
visited by this divine light of the Word, which we enjoy, they
would have embraced it with more reverence than we, their
unworthy descendants."* The deputies present promised to
take into consideration the representations made by their
brethren of Zurich.

Thus the breach in the walls of Rome was every day
widened. The Baden conference it was hoped would have
repaired it; but, on the contrary, from that time forward the
cantons that had hitherto been only doubtful appeared willing
to make common cause with Zurich. The Reformation was
already spreading among the inhabitants of the plain, and beginning to ascend the sides of the mountains;—and the more
ancient cantons, which had been as the cradle and are still the
citadel of Switzerland—seemed in their alpine inclosures alone
to adhere faithfully to the religion of their fathers. These
mountaineers, constantly exposed to violent storms, avalanches,
and overflowing torrents, are all their lives obliged to struggle
against these formidable enemies, and to sacrifice every thing
for the preservation of the pastures where their flocks graze,
and the roofs which shelter them from the tempest, and which
at any moment may be swept away by an inundation. Hence
a conservative principle is strikingly developed among them,
and has been transmitted from generation to generation. With
these children of the mountains, wisdom consists in preserving
what they have inherited from their fathers.

At the period we are recording these rude Helvetians struggled against the Reformation that came to change their faith
and worship, as at this very hour they contend against the

* Mit höherem Werth und mehr Dankbarkeit denn wir angenommen.
(Zurich Archiv. Absch. Sonntag nach Lichtmesse.)   (___)

roaring waters which tumble from their snow-clad hills, or against those modern notions and politics which have established themselves in the adjoining cantons. They will probably be the very last to lay down their arms before that twofold power which has already planted its standard on the adjacent hills, and is steadily gaining ground upon these conservative communities.

Accordingly, these cantons, yet more irritated against Berne than against Zurich, and trembling lest that powerful state should desert their interests, assembled their deputies in Berne itself, eight days after the conference at Zurich. They called on the Council to deprive the innovating teachers of their office, to proscribe their doctrines, and to maintain the ancient and true Christian faith, as confirmed by past ages and sealed by the blood of martyrs. " Convene all the bailiwicks of the canton," added they, " if you refuse to do this, we will take it upon ourselves." The Bernese were irritated, and replied, " We require no assistance in the directing of those who hold authority under us."

This answer only inflamed the anger of the Forest Cantons; and those very cantons, which had been the cradle of the *political* liberty of Switzerland, affrighted at the progress of *religious* liberty, began to seek even foreign alliances in order to destroy it. In opposing the enemies of the capitulations it seemed to them reasonable to seek the aid of capitulations; and if the oligarchs of Switzerland were not sufficiently powerful, it was natural to have recourse to the princes their allies. Austria, who had found it impossible to maintain her own authority in the Confederation, was ready to interfere to strengthen the power of Rome. Berne learnt with terror that Ferdinand, brother of Charles V., was preparing to march against Zurich, and all those who took part with the Reformation.*

Circumstances were becoming more trying. A succession of events, more or less adverse, such as the excesses of the Ana-

* Berne à Zurich, le lundi apres *Misericorde* (Kirchoff. B. Haller. p. 85.)

baptists, the disputes with Luther concerning the Lord's Supper, and other causes, seemed to have compromised the prospects of the Reformation in Switzerland. The conference at Baden had disappointed the hopes of the Papists, and the sword which they had brandished against their opponents had been shivered in their hands; but their animosity and rage did but increase, and they began to prepare for a fresh effort. The Imperial power was in motion; and the Austrian bands, which had been compelled to shameful flight from the defiles of Morgarten and the heights of Sempach, stood ready to enter Switzerland with flying banners, to confirm the tottering authority of Rome. The moment was critical: it was no longer possible to halt between two opinions;—to be " neither clear nor muddy." Berne and other cantons which had so long hesitated were reduced to the necessity of decision, either to return without loss of time to the Papal ranks, or to take their stand with boldness on the side of Christ.

Just then William Farel, a Frenchman from the mountains of Dauphiny, communicated a powerful impulse to Switzerland,—decided the reformation of the western cantons, hitherto sunk in a profound slumber, and so caused the balance to incline in favour of the new doctrines throughout the Confederation. Farel's coming resembled the arrival of those fresh troops, who, just when the battle hangs doubtfully, appear upon the field, throw themselves into the thick of the fight and decide the victory. He led the way in Switzerland for another Frenchman, whose austere faith and commanding genius were ordained to terminate the Reformation, and render the work complete. In the persons of these distinguished men France took her part in that vast commotion which agitated Christendom. It is therefore time that we should turn our attention to France.

BOOK XII.

ONE essential character of Christianity, is its Universality. Very different in this respect are the religions of particular countries that men have invented. Adapting themselves to this or that nation, and the point of progress which it has reached, they hold it fixed and motionless at that point—or if from any extraordinary cause the people are carried forward, their religion is left behind, and so becomes useless to them.

There has been a religion of Egypt—of Greece—of Rome, and even of Judea. Christianity is the only religion of *Mankind*.

It has for its origin in man—Sin; and this is a character that appertains not merely to one race, but which is the inheritance of all mankind. Hence, as meeting the highest necessities of our common nature, the Gospel is received as from God, at once by the most barbarous nations, and the most civilized communities. Without deifying national peculiarities, like the religions of antiquity, it nevertheless does not destroy them, as modern cosmopolism aims to do. It does better, for it sanctifies, ennobles, and raises them to a holy oneness, by the new and living principle it communicates to them.

The introduction of the Christian religion into the world has produced an incalculable change in history. There had previously been only a history of nations,—there is now a history of mankind; and the idea of an education of human nature as a whole,—an education, the work of Jesus Christ

29*

himself,—is become like a compass for the historian, the key of history, and the hope of nations.

But the effects of the Christian religion are seen not merely among all nations, but in all the successive periods of their progress.

When it first appeared, the world resembled a torch about to expire in darkness, and Christianity called forth anew a heavenly flame.

In a later age, the barbarian nations had rushed upon the Roman territories, carrying havoc and confusion wherever they came; and Christianity, holding up the cross against the desolating torrent, had subdued, by its influence, the half-savage children of the north, and moulded society anew.

Yet an element of corruption lay hidden in the religion carried by devoted missionaries among these rude populations. Their faith had come to them almost as much from Rome as from the Bible.   Ere long that element expanded; man every where usurped the place of God,—the distinguishing character of the church of Rome; and a revival of religion became necessary.   This Christianity gave to man in the age of which we are treating.

The progress of the Reformation in the countries we have hitherto surveyed has shown us the new teaching rejecting the excesses of the Anabaptists, and the newly arisen prophets: but it is the shallows of Incredulity which it especially encountered in the country to which we are now to turn our attention.   Nowhere had bolder protests been heard against the superstitions and abuses of the Church.   Nowhere had there been a more striking exhibition of that love of learning, apart from, or independent of, Christianity, which often leads to irreligion.   France bore within it at once two reformations, —the one of man, the other of God.   " Two nations were in her womb, and two manner of people were to be separated from her bowels."*

In France not only had the Reformation to combat incredulity as well as superstition, it found a third antagonist which

* Gen. xxv. 23.

it had not encountered, at least in so much strength, among the Germanic population, and this was immorality. Profligacy in the church was great. Debauchery sat upon the throne of Francis the First and Catherine de Medicis; and the rigid virtues of the Reformers provoked the anger of the Sardanapaluses.* Wherever it came, doubtless,—but especially in France—the Reformation was necessarily not only dogmatic and ecclesiastical, but, moreover, moral.

These violent opposing influences, which the Reformation encountered at one and the same moment among the French people, gave to it a character altogether peculiar. Nowhere did it so often have its dwelling in dungeons, or bear so marked a resemblance to the Christianity of the first ages in faith and love, and in the number of its martyrs. If in those countries of which we have heretofore spoken the Reformation was more illustrated by its triumphs, in those we are about to speak of it was more glorious in its reverses! If elsewhere it might point to more thrones and council chambers, here it could appeal to more scaffolds and hill-side meetings. Whoever knows in what consists the real glory of Christianity upon earth, and the features that assimilate it to its Author, will study with a deep feeling of veneration and affection the history, often marked with blood, which we are now to recount.

Of those who have afterwards shone on the stage of life, the greater number have been born and have grown up in the provinces. Paris is like a tree which spreads out to view its flowers and its fruit, but of which the roots draw from a distance and from hidden depths of the soil the nutritive juices which they transform. The Reformation followed this law.

The Alps, which had witnessed the rise of fearless Christian men in every canton, and almost in every valley of Switzerland, were destined in France also to shelter, with their lengthened shadows, the infancy of some of the earliest Reformers. For ages they had preserved their treasure more or less pure in their lofty valleys, among the inhabitants of the

* Sardanapalus (Henry II.) inter scorta. (Calvini Epp. M.S.)

Piedmontese districts of Luzerne, Angrogne, and Peyrouse. The truth, which Rome had not been able to wrest from them, had spread from the heights to the hollows and base of the mountains in Provence and in Dauphiny.

The year after the accession of Charles VIII., the son of Louis XI. and a youth of feeble health and timid character —Innocent VIII. had been invested with the Pontiff's tiara. (1484.)   He had seven or eight sons by different women :— hence, according to an epigram of that age, the Romans unani mously gave him the name of *Father.**

There was, at this time, on the southern declivities of the Alps of Dauphiny and along the banks of the Durance, an after-growth of the ancient Vaudois opinions. " The roots," says an old chronicler, "were continually putting forth fresh shoots in all directions."†   Bold men were heard to desig- nate the Church of Rome the ' church of evil spirits,' and to maintain that it was quite as profitable to pray in a stable as in a church.

The clergy, the bishops, and the Roman legates were loud in their outcries, and on the 5th of May, 1487, Innocent VIII. the 'Father' of the Romans, issued a bull against these hum- ble Christians.   " To arms," said the Pontiff, " to arms ! and trample those heretics under your feet as you would crush the venomous serpent."‡

At the approach of the Legate, at the head of an army of eighteen thousand men, and a host of voluntaries, drawn to- gether by the hope of sharing in the plunder of the Vaudois, the latter abandoned their dwellings and retired to the moun- tains, caverns, and clefts of the rocks, as the birds flee for shelter when a storm is rising.   Not a valley, a thicket, or

---

* Octo nocens pueros genuit totidemque puellas.
    Hunc merito poterit dicere Roma Patrem.
 -† In Ebredunensi archiepiscopatu veteres Waldensium hæreticorum fibra repullularunt. (Raynald.   Annales Ecclesiast. ad. ann. 1487.)
   ‡ Armis insurgant, eosque veluti aspides venenosos . . . conculcent. (Bull of Innocent VIII. preserved at Cambridge.   Leger Histoire des Eglises Vaudoises, ii. p. 8.)

a rock escaped their persecutors' search. Throughout the adjacent Alps, and especially on the side of Italy, these defenceless disciples of Christ were tracked like hunted deer. At last the Pope's satellites were worn out with the pursuit; their strength was exhausted, their feet could no longer scale the inaccessible retreats of the "heretics," and their arms refused their office.

In these Alpine solitudes, then disturbed by Roman fanaticism, three leagues from the ancient town of Gap,* in the direction of Grenoble, not far from the flowery turf that clothes the table land of Bayard's mountain, at the foot of the Mont de l'Aiguille, and near to the Col de Glaize, toward the source of the Buzon, stood, and still stands, a group of houses, half hidden by surrounding trees, and known by the name of Farel, or, in patois, *Fareau*.† On an extended plain above the neighbouring cottages, stood a house of the class to which, in France, the appellation of "*gentilhommiere*" is attached,— a country gentleman's habitation.‡ It was surrounded by an orchard, which formed an avenue to the village. Here, in those troublous times, lived a family bearing the name of Farel, of long-established reputation for piety, and, as it would seem, of noble descent.§ In the year 1489, at a time when Dauphiny was groaning under a weight of papal oppression, exceeding what it had ever before endured, a son was born in this modest mansion, who received the name of William. Three brothers, Daniel, Walter, and Claude, and a sister,

* Principal town of the High Alps.

† Revue du Dauphiné, July 1837, p. 35.

‡ Grenoble to Gap, distant a quarter of an hour's journey from the last posthouse, and a stone's throw to the right from the high road is the village of the Farels. The site of the house which belonged to the father of the Farel is still pointed out. Though it is now occupied by a cottage only, its dimensions are sufficient to prove that the original structure must have been a dwelling of a superior order. The present inhabitant of the cottage bears the name of Farel. For these particulars I am indebted to M. Blanc, the pastor of Mens.

§ Gulielmum Farellum Delphinatem, nobili familia ortum. (Beza Icones.) Calvin, writing to Cardinal Sadolet, dwells upon the disinterestedness of Farel,—*a man of such noble birth.* (Opuscula, p. 148.)

grew up with William, and shared his sports on the banks of the Buzon, and at the foot of Mount Bayard.

His infancy and boyhood were passed on the same spot. His parents were among the most submissive thralls of Popery. "My father and mother believed every thing,"* he tells us himself; and accordingly they brought up their children in the strictest observances of Romish devotion.

God had endowed William Farel with many exalted qualities, fitted to give him an ascendancy over his fellow-men. Gifted at once with a penetrating judgment, and a lively imagination, sincere and upright in his deportment, characterised by a loftiness of soul which never, under any temptation, allowed him to dissemble the convictions of his heart;—he was still more remarkable for the earnestness, the ardour, the unflinching courage which bore him up and carried him forward in spite of every hindrance. But, at the same time, he had the faults allied to these noble qualities, and his parents found frequent occasion to repress the violence of his disposition.

William threw himself with his whole soul into the same superstitious course which his credulous family had followed before him. "I am horror struck," said he, at a later period, ' when I think on the *hours*, the prayers, the divine honours, which I have offered myself, and caused others to offer, to the cross, and such like vanities."†

Four leagues distant from Gap, to the south, near Tallard, on a hill which overlooks the impetuous waters of the Durance, was a place in high repute at that time, called La Sainte Croix. William was but seven or eight years old when his parents thought fit to take him thither on a pilgrimage.‡ "The cross you will see there," said they, "is made of the wood of the very cross on which Jesus Christ was crucified."

The family set forth on their journey, and, on reaching the

* Du vray usage de la croix, par Guillaume Farel, p. 237.
† Du vray usage de la croix, par Guillaume Farel, p. 232.
‡ J'estoye fort petit et à peine je savoye lire. (Ibid. p. 237.) Le premier pelerinage auquel j'ai este a esté à la saincte croix. (Ibid. p. 233.)

object of their veneration, cast themselves prostrate before it. After they had gazed awhile on the holy wood of the cross, and the copper appertaining to it,—the latter, as the priest told them, "made of the basin in which our Saviour washed the feet of his disciples,"—the pilgrims cast their eyes on a little crucifix which was attached to the cross. "When the devils send us hail and thunder," resumed the priest, "this crucifix moves so violently, that one would think it wanted to get loose from the cross to put the devils to flight, and all the while it keeps throwing out sparks of fire against the storm; were it not for this, the whole country would be swept bare."*

These pious pilgrims were greatly affected at the recital of such prodigies. "Nobody," continued the priest, "sees or knows any thing of these things, except myself and this man here . . . ." The pilgrims turned their heads, and saw a strange looking man standing beside them. "It would have frightened you to look at him," says Farel: "the pupils of both his eyes seemed to be covered with white specks; whether they were so in reality, or that Satan gave them that appearance."† This uncouth looking man, whom the unbelieving called the "priest's wizard," on being appealed to by the latter, bore testimony at once to the truth of the miracle.‡

A new episode was now accidentally introduced to complete the picture, and mingle suggestions of guilty excess with the dreams of superstition. "Up comes a young woman on some errand very different from devotion to the cross, carrying a little child wrapped in a cloak. And, behold, the priest, goes to meet her, and takes hold of her and the child, and carries them straight into the chapel : never, believe me, did couple in a dance amble off more lovingly than did these two. But so blinded were we that we took no heed of their gestures or their glances, and even had their behaviour been still more unseemly, we should have deemed it altogether right and reverent:—of a truth, both the damsel and the priest

* Du vray usage de la croix, par Guillaume Farel, p. 235—239.
† Ibid. p. 237.   ‡ Ibid. p. 238.

understood the miracle thoroughly, and how to turn a pilgrim's visit to fair account."[*]

Here we are presented with a faithful picture of the religion and manners of France at the commencement of the Reformation. Morals and belief had alike been vitiated, and each stood in need of a thorough renovation. In proportion as a higher value was attached to outward rites, the sanctification of the heart had become less and less an object of concern;—dead ordinances had every where usurped the place of a christian life; and, by a revolting yet natural alliance, the most scandalous debauchery had been combined with the most superstitious devotion. Instances are on record of theft committed at the altar,—seduction practised in the confessional, —poison mingled with the eucharist,—adultery perpetrated at the foot of a cross! Superstition, while ruining Christian doctrine, had ruined morality also.

There were, however, numerous exceptions to this pitiable state of things in the Christianity of the middle ages. Even a superstitious faith may be a sincere one. William Farel is an example of this. The same zeal which afterwards urged him to travel incessantly from place to place, that he might spread the knowledge of Jesus Christ, then incited him to visit every spot where the church exhibited a miracle, or exacted a tribute of adoration. Dauphiny could boast of her seven wonders, which had long been sanctified in the imagination of the people.[†] But the beauties of nature, by which he was surrounded, had also their influence in raising his thoughts to the Creator.

The magnificent chain of the Alps,—the pinnacles covered with eternal snow,—the enormous rocks, sometimes rearing their pointed summits to the sky,—sometimes stretching their naked ridges on-and-on above the level clouds, and presenting the appearance of an island suspended in the air,—all these

[*] Du vray usage de la croix, par Guillaume Farel, p. 235. Some phrases of this narrative have been a little softened.

[†] The boiling spring, the cisterns of Sassenage, the manner of Briancon, &c.

wonders of creation, which, even then, were dilating the soul of Ulric Zwingle, in the Tockenburg, spoke with equal force to the heart of William Farel, among the mountains of Dauphiny. He thirsted for life,—for knowledge—for light; he aspired to be something great: he asked permission to study.

It was an unwelcome surprise to his father, who thought that a young noble should know nothing beyond his rosary and his sword. The universal theme of conversation at that time was the prowess of a young countryman of William's, a native of Dauphiny, like himself, named Du Terrail, but better known by the name of Bayard, who had recently performed astonishing feats of valour in the battle of Tar, on the other side of the Alps. "Such sons as he," it was currently remarked, "are like arrows in the hand of a mighty man. Blessed is the man who has his quiver full of them!" Accordingly, Farel's father resisted his wish to become a scholar. But the youth's resolution was not to be shaken. God designed him for nobler conquests than any that are to be achieved by such as Bayard. He urged his request with repeated importunity, and the old gentleman at length gave way.*

Farel immediately applied himself to study with surprising ardour. The masters whom he found in Dauphiny were of little service to him; and he had to contend with all the disadvantages of imperfect methods of tuition and incapable teachers.† But difficulties stimulated instead of discouraging him; and he soon surmounted these impediments. His brothers followed his example. Daniel subsequently entered on the career of politics, and was employed on some important negociations concerning religion.‡ Walter was admitted into the confidence of the Count of Furstemberg.

Farel, ever eager in the pursuit of knowledge, having learned all that was to be learned in his native province,

---

* Cum a parentibus vix impetrassem ad litteras concessum. (Farel Natali Galeoto, 1527. MS. Letters of the conclave of Neuchâtel.)

† A præceptoribus præcipue in Latina lingua ineptissimis institutus. (Farelli Epist.)

‡ Life of Farel, MS. at Geneva.

turned his eyes elsewhere. The fame of the university of Paris had long resounded through the Christiain world. He was anxious to see "this mother of all the sciences, this true luminary of the Church, which never knew eclipses,—this pure and polished mirror of the faith, dimmed by no cloud, sullied by no foul touch.* He obtained permission from his parents, and set out for the capital of France.

In the course of the year 1510, or shortly after the close of that year, the young Dauphinese arrived in Paris. His native province had sent him forth a devoted adherent of the Papacy, —the capital was to convert him into something far different. In France the Reformation was not destined, as in Germany, to take its rise in a petty city. By whatever movement the population of the former country may at any time be agitated; the impulse is always to be traced to the metropolis. A concurrence of providential circumstances had made Paris, at the commencement of the sixteenth century, the focus from which a spark of vivifying fire might easily be emitted. The stranger from the neighbourhood of Gap, who had just found his way to the great city, an obscure and ill-instructed youth, was to receive that spark into his bosom, and to share it with many around him.

Lous XII., the father of his people, had just convened an assembly of the representatives of the French clergy at Tours. This prince seems to have anticipated the times of the Reformation, so that if that great revolution had taken place during his reign, all France, probably, would have become Protestant. The assembly at Tours had declared that the King had a right to make war against the Pope, and to carry into effect the decrees of the Council of Basle. These decisions were the subject of general conversation in the colleges, as well as in the city, and at the court, and they could not fail to make a deep impression on the mind of young Farel.

Two children of royal blood were then growing up in the

* Universitatem Parisiensem matrem omnium scientiarum . . . . speculum fidei tersum et politum . . . (Prima Apellat Universit. an. 1396, Bulœus, iv. p. 806.)

court of Louis. The one was a young prince of tall stature,
and a striking cast of features, who evinced little moderation
of character, and yielded himself unreflectingly to the mastery
of his passions, so that the king was often heard to say, "That
great boy will spoil all."* This was Francis of Angoulême,
Duke of Valois, the king's cousin. Boisy, his governor, had
taught him, however, to show great respect to letters.

The companion of Francis was his sister Margaret, who
was two years older than himself. "A princess," says Brantôme, "of vigorous understanding, and great talents, both
natural and acquired."† Accordingly, Louis had spared no
pains in her education, and the most learned men in the kingdom,
were prepared to acknowledge Margaret as their patroness.

Already, indeed, a group of illustrious men was collected
round the two Valois. William Budé, who, in his youth, had
given himself up to self-indulgence of every kind, and especially to the enjoyment of the chase,—living among his
hawks, and horses, and hounds; and who, at the age of
twenty-three, had suddenly altered his course of life, sold off
his equipage, and applied himself to study with all the eagerness he had formerly displayed when cheering on his pack to
follow the scent through field and forest.‡—Cop, the physician,
—Francis Vatable, whose proficiency in Hebrew learning
was admired by the Jewish doctors themselves,—James
Tusan, the celebrated Hellenist;—these and other men of
letters besides,—encouraged by Stephen Poncher, the bishop
of Paris, Louis Ruzé, the "Lieutenant-Civil," and Francis de
Luynes, and already protected by the two young Valois,—
maintained their ground against the violent attacks of the
Sorbonne, who regarded the study of Greek and Hebrew as
the most fearful heresy. At Paris, as in Germany and
Switzerland, the restoration of religious truth was preceded by
the revival of letters. But in France the hands that prepared
the materials were not appointed to construct the edifice.

* Mezeray, vol. iv. p. 127.
† Brant. Dames Illustres, p. 331.
‡ His wife and sons came to Geneva in 1510, after his death.

Among all the doctors who then adorned the French metropolis, one of the most remarkable was a man of diminutive
stature, of mean appearance, and humble birth;* whose wit,
erudition, and eloquence had an indescribable charm for all
who approached him. The name of this doctor was Lefevre;
he was born in 1455 at Etables, a little town in Picardy. He
had received only an indifferent education,—a barbarous one,
Theodore Beza calls it; but his genius had supplied the want
of masters; and his piety, his learning, and the nobility of his
soul shone with a lustre so much the brighter.   He had been
a great traveller,—it would even appear that his desire to
acquire knowledge had led him into Asia and Africa.† So
early as the year 1493, Lefevre, being then a doctor of theology, occupied the station of a professor in the University of
Paris. He immediately assumed a distinguished place among
his colleagues, and in the estimation of Erasmus ranked above
them all.‡

Lefevre soon discovered that he had a peculiar task to
fulfil. Though attached to the practices of the Romish
church, he conceived a desire to reform the barbarous system
which then prevailed in the University;§ he accordingly
began to teach the various branches of philosophy with a
precision hitherto unknown. He laboured to revive the study
of languages and classical antiquities. He went further than
this; he perceived that when a mental regeneration is aimed
at, philosophy and literature are insufficient instruments.
Abandoning, therefore, the scholastic theology, which for so
many ages had held an undisputed sway in the seats of learning, he applied himself to the Bible, and again introduced the
study of the Holy Scriptures and evangelical science.   They

* Homunculi unius neque genere insignis. (Bezæ Icones.)

† In the 2nd chapter of his Commentary on the Second Epistle to the
Thessalonians is a curious story regarding Mecca and the temple there,
which he relates in the style of a traveller.

‡ Fabro, viro quo vix in multis millibus reperias vel integriorem vel
humaniorem, says Erasmus. (Er. Epp. p. 174.)

§ Barbariem nobilissimæ academiæ . . . . . incumbentem detrudi.
(Bezæ Icones.)

were no barren researches to which he addicted himself; he went straight to the heart of the Bible. His eloquence, his candour, his affability, captivated every heart. Earnest and fervent in the pulpit,—in his private intercourse with his pupils he condescended to the most engaging familiarity. " He loves me exceedingly," was the language of Glareanus, one of the number, when writing to his friend Zwingle; " he is all frankness and kindness,—he sings, he plays, he disputes, and then laughs with me."* Accordingly, a great number of disciples from every country were gathered around his chair.

This man, learned as he was, submitted himself all the while, with childlike simplicity, to the ordinances of the church. He passed as much time in the churches as in his closet,—so that a sympathetic union seemed established beforehand between the old doctor of Picardy and the young student of Dauphiny. When two natures, so congenial as these, are brought within the same sphere, though it be the wide and agitated circle of a capital city, their reciprocal attraction must at last place them in contact with each other. In his pious pilgrimages, young Farel soon observed an old man, by whose devotion he was greatly interested. He remarked how he fell on his knees before the images, how long he remained in that posture, how fervently he seemed to pray, and how devoutly he repeated his *hours*. " Never," says Farel, " had I heard a chanter chant the mass more reverently."† This was Lefevre. Farel immediately felt a strong desire to become acquainted with him ;—and great, indeed, was his joy when the venerable man met his approaches with kindness. He had now found what he had come to the capital to seek. Henceforth his chief delight was to converse with the doctor of Etaples, to listen to his instructions, to practise his admirable precepts, and to kneel with him in pious adoration at the same shrine. Often were the aged Lefevre

* Supra modum me amat totus integer et candidus, mecum cantillat ludit, disputat, ridet mecum. (Zw. Epp. p. 26.)

† Ep. de Farel à tous seigneurs, peuples et pasteurs.

and his youthful disciple seen assisting each other to adorn the image of the Virgin with flowers,—while far removed from Paris, far removed from the throng of the collegiate hall, they murmured in concert their earnest prayers to the blessed Mary.*

The attachment of Farel to Lefevre was generally noticed, and the respect inspired by the old doctor was reflected on his pupil. This illustrious connection was the means of with-drawing the young Dauphinese from his obscurity. He soon acquired a reputation for his zeal; and many pious persons of the wealthier order entrusted him with sums of money, to be applied to the support of poor students.†

Some time elapsed before Lefevre and his disciple attained to a clear perception of the truth. It was neither the hope of a rich benefice, nor any propensity to an irregular life, that bound Farel so firmly to the cause of Popery: a spirit like his was not to be influenced by motives so sordid. The Pope, in his eyes, was the visible chief of the church,—a sort of divinity, at whose bidding, souls were rescued from perdition. If any one, in his hearing, presumed to say a word against the venerated Pontiff, he gnashed his teeth like a raging wolf, and, if he could, would have called down thunder from heaven to overwhelm the guilty wretch in ruin and confusion. "I believe," he said, "in the cross, in pilgrimages, in images, in vows, in relics. What the priest holds in his hands, shuts up in the box, eats himself, and gives to be eaten by others,— *that* is my only true God,—and to me there is no God beside, in heaven or on earth?"‡ "Satan," he says afterwards, "had lodged the Pope, and Popery, and all that is of himself, so deeply in my heart, that, even in the Pope's own heart, they could have sunk no deeper."

And thus it was, that while Farel seemed to be seeking God, his piety decayed, and superstition gathered strength in his soul. He has himself, in forcible language, described his

---

* Floribus jubebat Marianum idolum, dumuna soli murmuraretur preces Marianas ad idolum, ornari. (Farellus Pellicano, an 1556.)

† Manuscript at Geneva.

‡ Ep. de Farel,—à tous seigneurs, peuples et pasteurs.

condition at that time.* "Oh!" says he, "how I shudder at myself and my sins, when I think on it all; and how great and wonderful a work of God it is, that man should ever be delivered from such an abyss!"

The deliverance in his own case was wrought by little and little. In the course of his reading, his attention had at first been engaged by profane authors; but, finding no food for his piety in these, he had set himself to study the lives of the saints: infatuation had led him to these legends, and he quitted them more miserably infatuated still.† He then addressed himself to several of the celebrated doctors of the age; but these, instead of imparting tranquillity to his mind, only aggravated his wretchedness. He next resolved to study the ancient philosophers, and attempted to learn Christianity from Aristotle; but again his hopes were frustrated. Books, images, relics, Aristotle, the Virgin, and the saints,—all were unavailing. His eager spirit wandered from one broken cistern of human wisdom to another, and turned away from each in succession, unrelieved of the thirst that consumed it.

At last, remembering that the Pope allowed the writings of the Old and New Testament to be called the "*Holy Bible*," Farel betook himself to the perusal of these, as Luther, in the cloister of Erfurth had done before him; and then, to his dismay,‡ he found that the existing state of things was such as could in no way be reconciled with the rule of Scripture. He was now, we might think, on the very point of coming at the truth, when, all at once, the darkness rolled back upon him with redoubled weight, and the depths closed over him again. "Satan," says he, "started up in haste, that he might not lose his possession, and wrought in me as he was wont."§ A terrible struggle between the word of God and the word of the Church now ensued in his heart. If he fell in with any pas-

* Quo plus pergere et promovere adnitebar, eo amplius retrocedebam. (Far. Galeoto, MS. Letters at Neuchâtel.)

† Quæ de sanctis conscripta offendebam, verum ex stulto insanum faciebant. (Ibid.)

‡ Farel à tous seigneurs.   § Ibid.

sage of Scripture opposed to the practice of the Romish Church, he cast down his eyes in perplexity, not daring to credit what he read.* "Ah!" he would say, shrinking away from the Bible, "I do not well understand these things;—I must put a different construction on these passages from that which they seem to me to bear. I must hold to the interpretation of the Church,—or rather, of the Pope!"

One day, when he was reading the Bible, a doctor, who chanced to come in, rebuked him sharply. "No one," said he, "ought to read the Holy Scriptures until he has studied philosophy, and taken his degree in *arts*." This was a preparation the Apostles had never required;—but Farel believed him. "I was the most unhappy of men," he tells us, "for I turned away my eyes from the light."†

The young Dauphinese was now visited with a fresh paroxysm of Romish fervor. His imagination was inflamed by the legends of the saints. The severities of monastic discipline were to him a powerful attraction. There was a cluster of gloomy cells in a wood not far distant from Paris, occupied by an establishment of Carthusians: hither he often repaired as an humble visitor, and took part in the austerities of the monks. "I was busied day and night," he says, "in serving the devil after the fashion of the Pope,—that man of sin. I had my Pantheon in my heart, and so many intercessors, so many saviours, so many gods, that I might well have passed for a Popish register."

The darkness could never grow thicker,—but now the morning star was to arise; and the voice of Lefevre was to give the signal of its appearance. The Doctor of Etaples had already caught some gleams of light: an inward conviction assured him that the Church could not remain in the state in which she then was;—and often on his way homeward, after chanting the mass, or paying adoration to an image, the old man would turn to his youthful disciple, and say in a solemn tone, as he grasped him by the hand:—"My dear William

* Oculos demittens, visis non credebam. (Farel Natali Galeoto.)
† Oculos a luce avertebam.

God will change the face of the world,—and you will see it !"*
Farel did not properly conceive his meaning. But Lefevre
did not stop at these mysterious words ; and the great change
which was wrought in his mind about this time was appointed
to produce a similar change in the mind of his pupil.

The old Doctor had undertaken a task of immense labour ;
he was carefully collecting the legends of the saints and martyrs, and arranging them in the order in which their names
are inserted in the calendar.   Two months had already been
printed, when one of those rays of light that come from on high
flashed on a sudden into his soul.   He could no longer overcome the disgust which superstitions so puerile must ever excite in a christian heart.   The grandeur of the word of God
made him perceive the wretched folly of such fables.   They
now appeared to him but as " brimstone, fit only to kindle the
fire of idolatry."†   He abandoned his work, and, casting aside
all these legends, turned affectionately to the Holy Scriptures.
At that moment, when Lefevre, forsaking the marvellous his-
tories of the saints, laid his hand on the word of God, a new
era opened in France,—and the Reformation commenced its
course.

Weaned, as we have seen, from the fictions of the Breviary,
Lefevre began to study the Epistles of St. Paul : the light
grew rapidly in his heart, and he soon communicated to his
disciples that knowledge of the truth, which we find in his
Commentaries.‡   Those were strange doctrines for the schools
and for the world around him, which were then first heard
in Paris, and disseminated by printing presses through all

* A tous seigneurs.—See also his letter to Pellican. Ante annos plus
minus quadraginta, me manu apprehensum ita alloquebatur :—" Guil-
lelme, oportet orbem immutari et tu videbis !"

† A tous seigneurs, peuples et pasteurs.

‡ The first edition of his Commentary on the Epistles of St. Paul bears
the date, if I mistake not, of 1512.   There is a copy of it in the Royal
Library at Paris.   The second edition is that to which my citations refer.   The learned Simon, in his observations on the New Testament,
says, " James Lefevre must be ranked among the most able commenta-
tors of his age."

Christendom. We may imagine that the young students who listened were aroused, impressed, and changed; and that in this way the aurora of a brighter day had dawned upon France prior to the year 1512.

The great truth of Justification by Faith, which at once overturns the subtilties of the schools and the Popish doctrine of the efficacy of works, was boldly proclaimed in the very bosom of Sorbonne itself. " It is God alone," said the teacher, (and it might have seemed as if the very roofs of the university would cry out against such new sounds,) " It is God alone, who by His grace justifies unto *eternal life.*[*] There is a righteousness of our own works, and a righteousness which is of grace,—the one a thing of man's invention, the other coming from God,—the one earthly and passing away, the other divine and everlasting,—the one the shadow and semblance, the other the light and the truth,—the one discovering sin and bringing the fear of death—the other revealing grace for the attainment of life !"[†]

" What will you then say ?" enquired the hearers, to whom such sounds appeared to contradict the teaching of four centuries, " will you say that any one man was ever justified without works ?"—" *One*, do you ask ?" returned Lefevre, " why they are innumerable. How many shameful sinners have eagerly asked to be baptized, having nothing but faith in Christ alone, and who, if they died the moment after, entered into the life of the blessed without works."—" If, then, we are not justified by works, it is in vain that we should do them," replied some. To this the Doctor made answer,—and possibly the other Reformers might not have altogether gone with him in his reply:—" Quite the contrary,—it is not in vain. If I hold up a mirror to the Sun, it receives in it his image : the more I polish and clean the mirror, the brighter does the reflection of the sun shine in it; but if I suffer it to tarnish and

---

[*] Solus enim Deus est qui hanc justitiam per fidem tradit, qui sola gratia ad vitam justificat æternam. (Fabri Comm. in Epp. Pauli, p. 70.)

[†] Illa umbratile vestigium atque signum, hæc lux et veritas est. (Fabri Comm. in Epp. Pauli, p. 70.)

dull, the solar brilliancy is lost. So it is with Justification in those who lead an unholy life." In this passage, Lefevre, like St. Augustin, in several parts of his writings, does not perhaps sufficiently mark the distinction between justification and sanctification. The Doctor of Etaples often reminds us of him of Hippone. Those who lead an unholy life have never received justification,—hence such cannot lose it. But Lefevre perhaps intended to say that the Christian, when he falls into any sin, loses the assurance of his salvation, and not his salvation itself.* To this way of stating it there would be nothing to object.

Thus a new life and a new character of teaching had penetrated within the University of Paris. The doctrine of Faith, which in the first ages had been preached in Gaul by Potinus and Irenæus, was again heard. Thenceforward there were two different parties and two different peoples in that celebrated school. The instructions given by Lefevre,—the zeal of his disciples, formed a striking contrast to the dry teaching of the majority of its doctors, and the frivolous conversation of the generality of the students. In the colleges, more time was lost in committing to memory different parts in comedies, masquerading, and mountebank farces, than was given to the study of God's word. In such farces it not unfrequently happened that the respect due to the higher classes, the nobility, and even royalty itself, was forgotten. At the very time we are writing of, the Parliament intervened, and summoning before them the principals of several of the colleges, prohibited those indulgent tutors from suffering such comedies to be acted in their houses.†

But a mightier intervention than the mandates of Parliament came to the correction of these disorders in the Univer-

* The believer may well bless God for this truth, namely, that he may lose the ('*sentiment*') assurance of his salvation without his salvation being endangered. The cloud may, and it is believed often has, involved the vessel during the greater part of her course, which is not the less advancing unto the haven where she would be. Is Christ in the vessel?—is that which concerns us.—TR.

† Crevier Hist. de l'Université, V. p. 95.

sity: CHRIST was preached among its inmates. Great was
the commotion on its benches; and the minds of the students
were almost as generally occupied with discussions of the doctrines of the Gospel, as in scholastic subtilties or theatrical ex-
hibitions. Some of those whose lives were least able to bear
the light, were yet heard taking the part of works, and feeling
instinctively that the doctrine of Faith condemned the licentiousness of their lives,—they maintained that St. James, in his
epistle, was at variance with the writings of St. Paul. Lefevre, resolving to stand by and protect the treasure he had
found, showed how the two Apostles agreed : " Does not St.
James say," asked he "that every good and perfect gift cometh
down *from above*,—and who will contest that justification is
the perfect gift, the excellent grace ? . . . If we see a man
moving, the breathing we see in him is *to us* the sign of life.
Thus works are necessary, but only as signs of that living
faith which is accompanied by justification.* Is it the eye-
salve or lotion which gives light to the eye ? No ; it is the light
of the sun. Just so our works are but as eye-salves and lo-
tions; the beam that the sun sends forth from above is justification itself."†

Farel hung upon these sounds with intense interest. Instantly this word of a Salvation by Grace had upon his soul
an unspeakable power of attraction. Every objection fell,—
every difficulty vanished. Scarcely had Lefevre brought forward this doctrine, when Farel embraced it with all his heart
and mind. He had known enough of labour and conflict to
be convinced that he had no power to save himself; therefore,
when he saw in God's word that God saves FREELY, he believed God. " Lefevre," exclaimed he, " extricated me from
the delusive thought of human deservings, and taught me how
that all is of *Grace*,—which I believed as soon as it was
spoken."‡ Thus was gained to the faith by a conversion as

* Opera signa vivæ fidei, quam justificatio sequitur. (Fabri Comm.
in Epp. Pauli, p. 73.)
† Sed radius desuper a sole vibratus, justificatio est. (Ibid. p. 73.)
‡ Farel A tous seigneurs.

prompt and decisive as that of St. Paul himself, that Farel who, to use the words of Theodore Beza, undismayed by threatening, despising the shame and enduring his cross, won for Christ,—Montbelliard, Neufchatel, Lausanne, Aigle, and at last Geneva itself.*

Meanwhile Lefevre, following up his teaching, and taking delight in employing contrasts and paradoxes, embodying weighty truths, extolled the sublime mysteries of redemption. "Oh!" he exclaimed, "the unspeakable greatness of that exchange,—the sinless One is condemned, and he who is guilty goes free,—the Blessing bears the curse, and the cursed is brought into blessing,—the Life dies, and the dead live,—the Glory is whelmed in darkness, and he who knew nothing but confusion of face is clothed with glory."† The pious teacher, going yet deeper into his theme, recognised that all salvation emanates from the sovereignty of God's love: "They who are saved," said he, "are saved by the electing grace and will of God, not by their own will. *Our* election, *our* will, *our* working is all in vain; the alone election of God is all powerful! When we are converted, it is not our conversion which makes us the elect of God, but it is the grace, will, and election of God which work our conversion."‡

But Lefevre did not stop short in doctrines; if he gave to God the glory,—he turned to man for "the obedience," and urged the obligations flowing from the exceeding privileges of the Christian. "If thou art a member of Christ's church," said he, "thou art a member of his body; if thou art of his body, then thou art full of the Divine nature, for the 'fulness of the Godhead dwelleth in him bodily.' Oh! if men could but enter into the understanding of this privilege, how purely, chastely, and holily would they live, and how contemptible, when compared with the glory within them,—that glory

---

* Nullis difficultatibus fractus, nullis minis, conviciis, verberibus denique inflictis territus. (Bezæ Icones.)

† O ineffabile commercium! . . . (Fabri Comm. 145 verso.)

‡ Inefficax est ad hoc ipsum nostra voluntas, nostra electio; Dei autem electio efficacissima et potentissima, &c. (Ibid. p. 89. verso.)

which the eye of flesh cannot see,—would they deem all the glory of this world."*

Lefevre felt that the office of a teacher in heavenly things was a high distinction : he discharged that office with unvarying fidelity.   The dissolute morals of the age, and more especially of the clergy, roused his indignation, and was the theme of many a stern rebuke : "What a reproach," said he, "to hear a bishop asking persons to drink with him, gambling, shaking the dice, and spending his whole time in hawking, sporting, hunting, hallooing in the chase of wild beasts, and sometimes with his feet in houses of ill-fame.† . . . O men worthy of a more signal retribution than Sardanapalus himself!"

Such was the preaching of Lefevre.   Farel listened, trembling with emotion,—received all into his soul, and went forward in that new path now suddenly made plain before him. Nevertheless there was one article of his former creed which he could not as yet entirely relinquish ; it was the invocation of the saints.   The noblest minds have often these lingering remains of darkness after the light has broken in upon them. Farel heard with astonishment the teacher declare that Christ alone should be invoked : "Our religion," said Lefevre, "has only one foundation, one object, one head, Jesus Christ, blessed for ever ! he hath trodden the winepress alone.   Let us not then take the name of Paul, of Apollos, or of Peter.   The cross of Christ alone opens heaven, and shuts the gate of hell." These words wakened a struggle in the soul of Farel.   On the one hand he beheld the whole army of saints with the Church,—on the other, Jesus Christ and His preacher.   One moment he inclined to the one side, the next to the other.   It was the last hold of ancient error, and his final struggle.   He hesitated ; still clinging to those venerated names before which Rome bends adoringly.   At last the decisive blow was struck from above ; the scales fell from his eyes ; Jesus was seen by

* Si de corpore Christi, divinitate repletus es.   (Fabri Comm. p. 176. verso.)

† Et virgunculas gremio tenentem, cum suaviis sermones miscentem. (Ibid. p. 209.)

him as the only object of adoration. "From that moment," said he, "the Papacy was dethroned from my mind. I began to abhor it as devilish, and the holy word of God held the supreme place in my heart."[*]

Events in the great world accelerated the advance of Farel and his friends. Thomas De Vio, who was subsequently opposed at Augsburg against Luther, having contended in a printed work that the Pope was absolute monarch of the Church, Louis XII. called the attention of the University of Paris to the work in February, 1512. James Allman, one of the youngest of its doctors, a man of rare genius and unwearied application, read at one of the meetings of the faculty of theology a refutation of the Cardinal's arguments, which drew forth the plaudits of the assembly.[†]

What must have been the effect of such discussions on the young disciples of Lefevre? Could they hesitate when the university itself manifested an impatience of the Papal yoke? If the main body were in motion should not they be skirmishing at the advanced posts? "It was necessary," said Farel, "that the Papal authority should be very gradually expelled from my mind, for the first shock did not bring it down."[‡] He contemplated the abyss of superstitions in which he had been plunged; standing on its brink, he again surveyed its gloomy depths, and drew back with a feeling of terror:— Oh!" ejaculated he, "what horror do I feel for myself and my sins when I think of the past.[§] Lord," he continued, "would that my soul served Thee with living faith after the example of thy faithful servants! Would that I had sought after and honoured Thee as I have yielded my heart to the mass, and served that magic wafer,—giving all honour to that!" Grieving over his past life, he with tears repeated those words of St. Augustine, "I have come too late to the knowledge of Thee! too late have I begun to love Thee!"

Farel had found Christ; and safe in harbour he reposed in

----

[*] Farel. A tous seigneurs.
[†] Crevier Hist. de l'Universite de Paris, v. p. 81.
[‡] Farel. A tous seigneurs.   [§] Ibid.

peace after the storm.* "Now," said he, "every thing appears to me to wear a different aspect.† Scripture is elucidated, prophecy is opened, and the epistles carry wonderful light into my soul.‡ A voice before unknown—the voice of Christ, my shepherd and my teacher, speaks to me with power."§ So great was the change in him that "instead of the murderous heart of a ravening wolf," he came back, as he himself tells us, "like a gentle and harmless lamb, with his heart entirely withdrawn from the Pope and given to Jesus Christ."‖

Escaped from so great an evil, he turned toward the Bible,¶ and applied himself zealously to the acquirement of Greek and Hebrew.** He was unremitting in his study of the Holy Scriptures, esteeming them more and more, and daily receiving more light. He continued to resort to the churches of the established worship—but what did he there hear?—Responses and chauntings innumerable, words spoken without understanding.†† Often, when standing among the throng that gathered round an image or an altar, he would exclaim,— "Thou alone art God! Thou alone art wise! Thou alone art good!‡‡ Nothing should be taken away—nothing added to thy holy law—for Thou only art the Lord, and it is Thou alone who claimest and hast a right to our obedience."

Thus all human teachers were brought down from the height to which his imagination had raised them, and he recognized no authority but God and his word. The doctors of Paris, by their persecution of Lefevre, had long since lost

---

* Animus per varia jactatus, verum nactus portum, soli hæsit. (Fare Galeoto.)

† Jam rerum nova facies. (Ibid.)

‡ Notior scriptura, apertiores prophetæ, lucidiores apostoli. (Ibid.)

§ Agnita pastoris, magistri et præceptoris Christi vox. (Ibid.)

‖ Farel. A tous seigneurs.

¶ Lego sacra ut causam inveniam. (Farel Galeoto.)

** Life of Farel. MSS. of Geneva and of Choupard.

†† Clamores multi, cantiones innumeræ. (Farel Galeoto, MSS. of Neufchâtel.)

‡‡ Vere tu solus Deus! (Ibid.)

all place in his esteem ; but ere long Lefevre himself, his well-beloved guide and counsellor, was no more to him than his fellow-man : he loved and venerated him as long as he lived—but God alone was become his teacher.

Of all the Reformers, Farel and Luther are the two best known to us in their early spiritual history, and most memorable for the struggles they had to pass through. Earnest and energetic, men of conflict and strife, they bore the brunt of many an onset before they were permitted to be at peace. Farel is the pioneer of the Reformation in Switzerland and in France. He threw himself into the wood, and with his axe cleared a passage through a forest of abuses. Calvin followed, as Luther was followed by Melancthon, resembling him in his office of theologian and " master-builder." These two men,—who bear some resemblance to the legislators of antiquity, the one in its graceful, the other in its severer style,— settle, establish, and give laws to the territory won by the two former. And yet if Farel reminds us of Luther, we must allow that it is only in one aspect of the latter that we are reminded of him. Luther, besides his superior genius, had, in a'l that concerned the Church, a moderation and prudence, an acquaintance with past experience, a comprehensive judgment, and even a power of order, which was not found in an equal degree in the Reformer of Dauphiny.

Farel was not the only young Frenchman into whose soul a new light was, at this time, introduced. The doctrines which flowed from the lips of the far-famed doctor of Etaples fermented among the crowd of his hearers; and in his school were formed and trained the bold men who were ordained to struggle, even to the very foot of the scaffold. They listened, compared, discussed, and argued with characteristic vivacity. It is a probable conjecture, that we may number among the handful of scholars who then espoused the Truth, young Pierre Olivetan, born at Noyon, at the end of the fifteenth century, who afterwards revised Lefevre's translation of the Bible into French, and seems to have been the first who so presented the doctrine of the Gospel as to draw the attention

31*

of a youth of his family, also a native of Noyon, who became the most distinguished of all the leaders of the Reformation.*

Thus, before 1512, at a time when Luther had made no impression on the world, but was taking a journey to Rome on some business touching the interests of some monks, and when Zwingle had not even begun to apply himself in earnest to Biblical studies, but was traversing the Alps, in company with the confederated forces, to fight under the Pope's banner, —Paris and France heard the sound of those life-giving truths, whence the Reformation was destined to come forth—and there were found souls prepared to propagate those sounds, who received them with holy affection. Accordingly, Theodore Beza, in speaking of Lefevre of Etaples, observes that " it was he who boldly began the revival of the holy religion of Jesus Christ :"† and he remarks that, " as in ancient times, the school of Isocrates had the reputation of furnishing the best orators, so, from the lecture-rooms of the doctor of Etaples, went forth many of the best men of the age, and of the Church."‡

The Reformation was not, therefore, in France, an importation from strangers ; it took its birth on the French territory. Its seed germinated in Paris—its earliest shoots were struck in the University itself, that ranked second in power in Romanized Christendom. God deposited the first principles of the work in the kindly hearts of some inhabitants of Picardy and Dauphiny, before it had begun in any other country of the globe. The Swiss Reformation was, as we have seen,‡ independent of that of Germany ; the French Reformation was, in like manner, independent of that of Switzerland, and that of Germany. The work sprung up in these different countries at one and the same time, without communication between them, as in a field of battle, the various divisions that compose

* Biographie Universelle, Article *Olivetan*. Histoire du Calvinisme, par Maimbourg, 53.

† Et purioris religionis instaurationem fortiter agressus. (Beza Icones.)

‡ Sic ex Stap ulensis auditorio praestantissimi viri plurimi prodierint, (Ibid.)

§ Vol. ii. p. 367.

the army are seen in motion at the same instant, although the order to advance has not passed from one to the other, but all have heard the word of command proceeding from a higher authority. The time had come—the nations were ripe, and God was everywhere beginning the revival of His Church.

If we regard dates, we must then confess that neither to Switzerland nor to Germany belongs the honour of having been first in the work, although, hitherto, only those countries have contended for it. That honour belongs to France. This is a fact that we are the more careful to establish, because it has possibly, until now, been overlooked. Without dwelling upon the influence exercised by Lefevre, directly or indirectly, on many persons, and especially on Calvin,—let us consider that which he had on one of his disciples, Farel himself,— and the energy of action which that servant of God from that hour manifested. Can we, after that, withhold our conviction that even though Zwingle and Luther should never have been born, there would still have been a movement of Reformation in France? It is, of course, impossible to estimate how far it might have extended: we must even acknowledge that the report of what was passing on the other side of the Rhine and the Jura, afterwards accelerated and animated the progress of the Reformers of France. But it was they who were first awakened by the voice of that trumpet which sounded from heaven in the sixteenth century, and who were earliest in the field, on foot, and under arms.

Nevertheless, Luther is the great workman of the sixteenth century, and, in the fullest import of the term, the *first* Reformer. Lefevre is not as complete as Calvin, Farel, or Luther. There is about him that which reminds us of Wittemberg—of Geneva—but a something besides, that tells of the Sorbonne; he is the foremost Catholic in the Reformation movement, and the latest of the Reformers in the Catholic movement. To the last, he continues a go between,—a mediator,—not well understood; reminding us that there is some connection between the old things and the new, which might seem for ever separated as by a great gulf. Repulsed and persecuted by Rome, he yet holds to Rome, by a slender thread which he is unwilling to sever. Lefevre of Etaples has a place to himself in the theology of the sixteenth century: he is the connecting link between ancient and modern times, and the man in whom the theology of the middle ages passed into the theology of the Reformation.

Thus, in the University, the truth was already working. But the Reformation was not to be an affair of college life. It was to establish its power among the great ones of the earth, and to have some witnesses even at the King's court.

The young Francis of Angoulême, cousin-german and son-in-law to Louis XII., succeeded him on the throne. His manly beauty and address, his courage, and his love of pleasure, rendered him the most accomplished knight of his time. His ambition, however, rose higher; it was his aim to be a great and even a gracious prince; provided only that all should bend before his sovereign authority. Valour, taste for literature, and gallantry, are three words that well express the genius of Francis, and of the age in which he figured. At a somewhat later period, the like features appear in Henry IV. and Louis XIV. These princes wanted that which the Gospel communicates; and, although there has been no time when the nation did not contain in it the elements of sanctity and of Christian elevation, it may be said that these great monarchs of modern France have, in a measure, stamped upon that people the impress of their own characters, if it be not more correct to say that they themselves were the faithful expression of the character of the nation over which they presided. If the evangelic doctrine had entered France under the auspices of the most famed of the Valois princes, it might have brought with it to the nation that which France has not,—a spiritual turn of mind, a christian purity, and an intelligence in heavenly things, which would have been the completion of the national character in what most contributes to the strength and greatness of a people.

It was under the rule of Francis I. that Europe, as well as France, passed from the middle ages to the range of modern history. It was then that that new world which was bursting forth on all sides when that prince ascended the throne, grew and entered upon possession. Two different classes of men exercised an influence in moulding the new order of society. On the one hand were the men of faith, who were also men of wisdom and moral purity, and close to them, the writers of the court,—the friends of this world and its profligacy,—who by their licentious principles, contributed to the depravation of morals as much as the former served to reform them.

If, in the days of Francis the First, Europe had not witnessed the rise of the Reformers, but had been given up by God's righteous judgment to the uncontrolled influence of unbelieving innovators, her fate and that of Christianity had been decided. The danger seemed great. For a considerable time, the two classes of combatants, the opposers of the Pope, and those who opposed the Gospel, were mixed up together; and as both claimed *liberty*, they seemed to resort to the same arms against the same enemies. In the cloud of dust raised on the field, an unpractised eye could not distinguish between them. If the former had allowed themselves to be led away by the latter all would have been lost. Those who assailed the hierarchy passed quickly into extremes of impiety, urging on the people to a frightful catastrophe. The Papacy itself contributed to bring about that catastrophe, accelerating by its ambition and disorders the extinction of any truth and life still left in the Church.

But God called forth the Reformation,—and Christianity was preserved. The Reformers who had shouted for liberty, were, ere long, heard calling to *obedience*. The very men who had cast down that throne whence the Roman Pontiff issued his oracles, prostrated themselves before the ' word of the Lord.' Then was seen a clear and definite separation, and war was declared between the two divisions of the assailants. The one party had desired liberty only that themselves might be free,—the others had claimed it for the word of God. The Reformation became the most formidable antagonist of that incredulity to which Rome can show leniency.

Having restored liberty to the Church, the Reformers restored religion to society; and this last was, of the two, the
gift most needed.

The votaries of incredulity, for a while, hoped to reckon
among their number Margaret of Valois, Duchess of Alençon, whom Francis loved with especial tenderness, and, as
Brantôme informs us, used to call his "darling."* The same
tastes and general information distinguished both brother and
sister. Of fine person like Francis, Margaret united to those
eminent qualities, which in their combination constitutes remarkable characters, these gentler virtues which win the
affection. In the gay world, the festive entertainment, the royal
the imperial court, she shone in queenly splendour, charming
and captivating all hearts. Passionately fond of literature
and gifted with no ordinary genius, it was her delight to shut
herself in her apartment, and there indulge in the pleasures
of reflection, study, and meditation. But her ruling desire
was to do good and prevent evil. When ambassadors from
foreign countries had presented themselves before the king,
they were accustomed afterwards to pay their respects to Margaret, and "they were greatly pleased with her," observes
Brantôme, "and returning to their homes, noised abroad the
fame of her: and he adds that "the king would often hand
over to her matters of importance, leaving them for her to
decide."†

This celebrated princess was through life distinguished by
her strict morals; but whilst many who carry austerity on
their lips, indulge laxity in conduct, the very reverse of this
was seen in Margaret. Blameless in conduct, she was not
altogether irreproachable in the use of her pen. Far from
wondering at this, we might rather wonder that a woman
dissolute as was Louisa of Savoy, should have a daughter so
pure as Margaret. Attending the court, in its progress through
the provinces, she employed herself in describing the manners of the time, and especially those of the priests and monks.

* Vie des Dames Illustres, p. 333, Haye 1740.
† Ibid. p. 337.

" On these occasions," says Brantôme, " I often used to hear her recount stories to my grandmother, who constantly accompanied her in her litter, as *dame d'honneur*, and had charge of her writing desk."[*]   According to some, we have here the origin of the Heptameron; but more recent and esteemed critics have satisfied themselves that Margaret had no hand in forming that collection, in some parts chargeable with worse than levity, but that it was the work of Desperiers, her gentleman of the chamber.[†]

This Margaret, so charming, so full of wit, and living in so polluted an atmosphere, was to be one of the first won over by the religious impulse just then communicated to France. But how, in the centre of so profane a court, and amid the sounds of its licentious gossip was the Duchess of Alençon to be reached by the Reformation? Her soul, led to look to heaven, was conscious of wants that the Gospel alone could meet. Grace can act in every place, and Christianity,—which even before an apostle had appeared in Rome, had some followers among the household of Narcissus, and in the palace of Nero,[‡]—in the day of its revival rapidly made its way to the court of Francis the First. There were ladies and lords who spoke to that princess concerning the things of faith, and the sun which was then rising on France, sent forth one of its

[*] Vie des Dames Illustres, p. 346.

[†] This is proved by one of the most distinguished critics of the age, M. Ch. Nodier, in the *Revue des Deux Mondes*, t. xx. wherein he observes, p. 350—" Desperiers is in reality and almost exclusively author of the Heptameron. I scruple not to say I have no doubt of this, and entirely coincide in the opinion of Bouistuan, who, solely on this account, omitted and withheld the name of the Queen of Navarre." If, as I think, Margaret did compose some tales, doubtless the most harmless of those in the Heptameron, it must have been in her youth—just after her marriage with the Duke of Alençon (1509). The circumstances mentioned by Brantome, p. 316, that the king's mother and Madame de Savoy " being young," wished to " imitate" Margaret, is a proof of this. To this may be added the evidence of De Thou, who says, " Si tempora et juvenilem ætatem in qua scriptum est respicias, non prorsus damnandum, certe gravitate tantæ heroinæ et extrema vita minus dignum." (Thuanus, t. vi. p. 117.) Brantome and De Thou are two unobjectionable witnesses.

[‡] Romans xvi. 11.   Phil. iv. 22.

earliest beams on a man of eminent station by whom its light
was immediately reflected on the Duchess of Alençon.

Among the most distinguished lords of the court was Count
William of Montbrun, a son of Cardinal Briçonnet of St.
Malo, who had entered the church on his being left a widower.
Count William, devoted to studious pursuits, himself also took
orders, and was bishop, first of Lodeva, and afterwards of
Meaux. Although twice sent on an embassy to Rome, he
returned to Paris unseduced by the attractions and splendours
of Leo X.

At the period of his return to France, a ferment was beginning to manifest itself. Farel, as Master of Arts, was lecturing
in the college of Cardinal Lemoine, one of the four leading
establishments of the faculty of theology of Paris, ranking
equal with the Sorbonne. Two countrymen of Lefevre, Arnaud and Gerard Roussel, and some others, enlarged this little
circle of free and noble spirits. Briçonnet, who had so recently quitted the festivals of Rome, was all amazement at
what had been doing in Paris during his absence. Thirsting after the truth, he renewed his former intercourse with
Lefevre, and soon passed precious hours in company with the
Doctor of the Sorbonne, Farel, the two Roussels, and their
friends.* Full of humility, the illustrious prelate sought instruction from the very humblest, but, above all, he sought it
of the Lord himself. "*I* am all dark," said he, " waiting for
the grace of the divine favour, from which my sins have banished me." His mind was as if dazzled by the glory of the
Gospel. His eye-lids sunk under its unheard-of brightness.
"The eyes of all mankind," exclaimed he, " cannot take in
the whole light of that sun !"†

Lefevre had commended the Bishop to the Bible,—he had

* Histoire de la Révocat. de l'edit de Nantes, vol. i. p. 7. Maimbourg. Hist. du Calv. p. 12.

† These expressions of Briçonnet are from a manuscript in the Royal
Library at Paris—entitled Letters of Margaret Queen of Navarre, and
which is marked S. F. 337. I shall more than once have occasion to
quote this manuscript, which I found not easy to decipher. I quote the
language of the time.

pointed to it as that guiding clue which ever brings us back to the original truth of Christianity, such as it existed before all schools, sects, ordinances, and traditions, and as that mighty agent by means of which the religion of Jesus Christ is renewed in power. Briçonnet read the Scriptures. " Such is the sweetness of that heavenly manna," said he, " that it never cloys; the more we taste of it, the more we long for it."* The simple and prevailing truth of SALVATION filled him with joy;—he had found Christ, he had found God Himself. " What vessel," he exclaimed, " is capable of receiving into it such vast and inexhaustible grace. But the mansion expands with our desire to lodge the good guest. FAITH is the quartermaster who alone can find room for him, or rather who alone can enable us to dwell *in him*." But, at the same time, the excellent bishop grieved to see that living word which the Reformation gave to the world so slighted at court, in the city, and among the people; and he exclaimed, "Singular innovation, so worthy of acceptation, and yet so ill received!"

Thus did evangelic truth open itself a way into the midst of the frivolous, dissolute, and literary court of Francis I. Several of those who composed it and enjoyed the unlimited confidence of that prince,—as John du Bellay, du Budé, Cop, the court physician, and even Petit, the king's confessor, seemed favourable to the views of Briçonnet and Lefevre. Francis, who loved learning, and invited to his court scholars "suspected" of Lutheranism, " in the thought," observes Erasmus, "that he should, in that way, adorn and illustrate his reign better than he could do by trophies, pyramids, or buildings,"—was himself persuaded by his sister, by Briçonnet, and the learned of his court and colleges. He was present at the discussions of the learned,—enjoyed listening to their discourse at table,—and would call them " his children." He assisted to prepare the way for the word of God, by founding professorships of Hebrew and Greek,—accordingly, Theodore Beza thus speaks, when placing his portrait at the head of the Re-

* Ibid.

formers,—"Pious Reader! do not shudder at the sight of this adversary. Ought not he to have his part in this honour who banished barbarism from society, and with firm hand established in its place the cultivation of three languages and profitable studies that should serve as the portals of that new structure that was shortly to arise."*

But there was at the court of Francis I. one soul which seemed prepared for the reception of the evangelic doctrines of the teachers of Etaples and of Meaux. Margaret, hesitating and not knowing on what to lean in the midst of the profligate society that surrounded her, sought somewhat on which her soul might rest,—and found it in the Gospel. She turned toward that fresh breath of life which was then reviving the world, and inhaled it with delight as coming from heaven. She gathered from some of the ladies of her court the teaching of the new preachers. Some there were who lent her their writings, and certain little books, called, in the language of the time, "*tracts ;*"—they spoke of "the primitive church, of the pure word of God, of a worship ' in spirit and truth,' of a Christian liberty that rejected the yoke of human traditions and superstitions, that it might adhere singly to God."† It was not long before this princess sought interviews with Lefevre, Farel, and Roussel. Their zeal, piety, and walk, and all she saw of them, impressed her,—but it was her old friend the bishop of Meaux, who was her guide in the path of faith.

Thus, at the glittering court of Francis I.—and in the dissolute house of Louisa of Savoy, was wrought one of those conversions of the heart which in every age are the work of the word of God. Margaret subsequently recorded in her poetical effusions the various emotions of her soul at this important period of her life, and we may there trace the course by which she was led. We see that the sense of sin had taken strong hold

* Neque rex potentissime pudeat . . . quasi atrienses hujus ædis futuras. (Bezæ Icones.)—Disputationibus eorum ipse interfuit. (Flos Ramundi, Hist. de ortu hæresum. vii. p. 2.)

† Maimbourg. Hist. du Calvinisme, p. 16.

apon her, and that she bewailed the levity with which she had once viewed the scandals of the court.

> Is there in the abyss's lowest depth
> A punishment that equals e'en the tenth
> Of all my sin.

The corruption which she had so long overlooked, now that her eyes were opened, was seen in every thing about her—

> Surely in *me* there dwells that evil root
> That putteth forth *in others* branch and fruit.*

But amid all the horror she felt at her own state of heart, she yet acknowledged that a God of Peace had manifested himself to her soul—

> Thou, O my God, hast in thy *Grace* come down
> To me, a worm of earth, who strength had none.†

And soon a sense of the love of God in Christ was shed abroad in her heart :—

> My Father, then,—but what a Father thou,
> Unseen,—that changest not,—endless of days,
>   Who graciously forgivest all my sins.
> Dear Lord Emanuel, behold me fall
> Low at thy sacred feet, a criminal !
>   Pity me, Father,—perfect in Thy love !
> Thou art the sacrifice, and mercy-seat,
> And Thou hast made for us an offering meet,
>   Well pleasing unto Thee, oh God above.‡

Margaret had found the faith, and her soul in its joy gave free expression to holy delight,—

> Oh Saviour Jesus—oh most holy Word
> Only begotten of thy Father God
> The First—the Last—for whom all things were made—
> Bishop and King, set over all as Head,

* Marguerites de la Marguerite des princesses (Lyon 1547). tome 1er, Miroir de l'âme pecheresse, p. 15. The copy I have used seems to have belonged to the Queen of Navarre herself, and some notes appearing in it are, it is said, in her handwriting. It is now in the possession of a friend.

† Ibid. p. 18, 19.   ‡ Ibid. Oraison à J. C., p. 143.

> Through death, from fear of death thou sett'st us free!
> Making us children by our Faith in Thee,
> Righteous and pure and good by faith to be.
> Faith plants our souls in innocence again,
> Faith makes us kings with Christ as kings to reign,
> Faith gives us all things in our Head to gain.[*]

From that time a great change was seen in the Duchess of Alençon—

> Though poor, untaught, and weak I be,
> Yet feel I rich, wise, strong in Thee.[†]

However, the power of sin was not yet subdued—Her soul was still conscious of a want of blessed harmony, and of a degree of inward struggle that perplexed her—

> By spirit noble, yet by nature serf,
> Of heavenly seed,—begotten here on earth;
> God's temple,—wherein things unclean find room;
> Immortal,—and yet hastening to the tomb;
> Though fed by God,—in earthly pastures roving;
> Shrinking from ill,—yet sinful pleasures loving;
>   Cherishing truth—yet not to truth conformed;
> Long as my days on earth prolonged are,
> Life can have nought for me but constant war.[‡]

Margaret, seeking in nature symbols that might express the felt want and desire of her soul, chose for her emblem, says Brantôme, the *marigold*, " which in its flower and leaf has most resemblance to the sun, and, turning, follows it in its course."[§] She added this device, *Non inferiora secutus*—I seek not things below—" signifying," continues the annalist of the court, " that her actions, thoughts, purposes, and desires were directed to that exalted Sun, namely God,—whereupon it was suspected that she had imbibed the religion of Luther."[‖]

In fact, the princess shortly after experienced the truth of that word, " *All that will live godly in Jesus Christ shall suffer persecution.*" The new opinions of Margaret were the sub-

* Marguerites de la Marguerite des princesses (Lyon 1547), tome 1er, Miroir de l'âme pecheresse, p. 15.   Discord de l'Esprit et de la chair, p. 73.
† Ibid.   Miroir de l'âme, p. 22.
‡ Ibid.   Discord de l'Esprit et de la chair, p. 71.
§ Vies des Femmes Illustres. p. 33.
‖ Ibid. p. 33.

ject of conversation at court, and great was the sensation ;—
What! could the king's sister be one of those people?—For a
moment it might have been feared that Margaret's disgrace
was certain. But the king who loved his sister, affected to
disregard the rumour of the court. The conduct of Margaret
gradually dissipated the opposition ;—" Every one loved her,
for," says Brantöme, " she was very kind, gentle, condescend-
ing, and charitable, very easy of access, giving away much in
alms, overlooking no one, but winning all hearts by her gracious deportment."*

In the midst of the corruption and frivolity of that age, the
mind may joyfully contemplate this elect soul, which the grace
of God gathered from beneath all its pomps and vanities. But
her feminine character held her back. If Francis the First
had had the convictions of his sister, we can hardly doubt he
would have followed them out. The fearful heart of the princess trembled at the thought of facing the anger of her king.
She continued to fluctuate between her brother and her Saviour, unwilling to give up either one or the other. We do
not recognise in her the Christian who has attained to the perfect liberty of God's children, but the exact type of those souls
—at all times so numerous, and especially among her sex,—
who, drawn powerfully to look to heaven, have not strength
sufficient to disengage themselves entirely from the bondage
of earth.

Nevertheless, such as she is here seen, her appearance is a
touching vision on the stage of history. Neither Germany
nor England presents such a picture as Margaret of Valois.
She is a star, slightly clouded, doubtless, but shedding a peculiarly soft light. And at the period we are contemplating,
her light even shines forth with much radiance. Not till
afterwards, when the angry glance of Francis the First de-
nounces a mortal hatred of the Gospel, will his sister spread a
veil over her holy faith. But at this period she is seen erec-
in the midst of a degraded court, and moving in it as the bride
of Jesus Christ. The respect paid to her, the high opinion

* Vies des Femmes Illustres, p. 341.

32*

entertained of her understanding and character, pleads more persuasively than any preacher, the cause of the Gospel at the court of France, and the power of this gentle female influence gains admission for the new doctrines. Perhaps it is to this period we may trace the disposition of the noblesse to embrace Protestantism. If Francis had followed in the steps of his sister, if the entire nation had opened its arms to Christianity, the conversion of Margaret might have been the channel of salvation to France. But whilst the nobles welcomed the Gospel, the throne and the people adhered faithful to Rome,—and a day came when it was a source of heavy misfortune to the Reformation to have numbered in its ranks the names of Navarre and Condé.

Thus already had the Gospel made converts in France. Lefevre, Briçonnet, Farel, Margaret, in Paris, joyfully followed in the direction of the movement. It seemed as if Francis himself were more attracted by the light of learning than repelled by the purity of the Gospel. The friends of God's word encouraged the most hopeful anticipations, and were pleasing themselves with the thought that the heavenly doctrine would spread, unresisted, through their country, when suddenly a powerful opposition was concocted in the Sorbonne, and at the court. France, which was to signalize herself among Roman Catholic states by three centuries of persecution of the Reformed opinions, arose against the Reformation with pitiless sternness. If the seventeenth century was, in France, an age of bloody persecution, the sixteenth was that of cruel struggle. In no country, perhaps, have those who professed the reformed faith met with more merciless opposers on the very spots where they brought the Gospel. In Germany the anger of the enemy came upon them from other states, where the storm had been gathering. In Switzerland, it fell upon them from the neighbouring cantons; but in France it everywhere met them face to face. A dissolute woman and a rapacious minister then took the lead in the long line of enemies of the Reformation.

Louisa of Savoy, mother of the king and of Margaret, notorious for her gallantries, of overbearing temper, and surrounded by ladies of honour, whose licentiousness was the beginning of a long train of immorality and infamy at the court of France, naturally ranged herself on the side of the opposers of God's word. What rendered her more formidable was the almost unbounded influence she possessed over her son. But the Gospel encountered a still more formidable enemy in Anthony Duprat, Louisa's favourite, and, by her influence, elevated to the rank of chancellor of the kingdom. This man, whom a contemporary historian has designated as the most vicious of bipeds,* was yet more noted for avarice than Louisa for her dissolute life. Having begun with enriching himself by perverting justice, he sought to add to his wealth at the cost of religion ; and took orders with a view to get possession of the richest benefices.

Luxury and avarice thus characterized these two persons, who, being both devoted to the Pope, sought to cover the infamy of their lives by the shedding the blood of heretics.†

One of their first steps was to hand over the kingdom to the ecclesiastical supremacy of the Pope. The king, after the battle of Marignan, had a meeting with Leo X. at Bologna, and in that place was concluded the memorable Concordat, in virtue of which those two princes divided between them the spoils of the Church. They annulled the supremacy of Councils to ascribe supremacy to the *Pope*, and took from the respective churches the power of nominating to bishoprics, to give that power to the *king*. After this, Francis the First, supporting the Pontiff's train, repaired publicly to the cathedral church of Bologna to ratify the treaty. Sensible of the iniquity of the Concordat, he turned to Duprat, and whispered in his ear,—" There is enough in this to damn us both."‡ But what signified to him salvation,—money and the Pope's alliance was what he sought.

The Parliament met the Concordat with a vigorous resist-

* Bipedum omnium nequissimus. (Belcarius, xv. p. 435.)
† Sismondi. Hist. des Francais, xvi. p. 387.
‡ Mathieu, i. p. 16.

ance. The king, after keeping its deputies waiting for some weeks at Amboise, sent for them one day into his presence, upon rising from table, and said: " There is a king in France, and I don't at all understand that any men should form a senate after the manner of Venice." He then ordered them to depart before sunset. From such a prince, Gospel liberty had nothing to hope. Three days afterwards, the Grand Chamberlain la Tremouille appeared in Parliament, and directed that the Concordat should be enregistered.

On this, the University was in motion. On the 18th of March, 1518, a solemn procession, at which were present the whole body of students and bachelors in their corps, repaired to the church of St. Catherine of Scholars, to implore God to preserve the liberties of the Church and kingdom.* " The halls of the different colleges were closed; strong bodies of students went armed through the streets, threatening and in some instances maltreating consequential persons, engaged pursuant to the king's directions, in making known the Concordat, and carrying it into effect."† However, in the result, the University allowed the compact to be fulfilled, but without rescinding the resolutions in which their opposition to it was declared; and "from that time," says the Venetian ambassador Correro, "the king began to give away bishoprics at the solicitation of the ladies of the court, and to bestow abbey lands on his soldiers, so that at the French court bishoprics and abbeys were counted merchandise, just as among the Venetians they trade in pepper and cinnamon."‡

Whilst Louisa and Duprat were taking their measures to root up the Gospel by the destruction of the Gallican Church, a powerful party of fanatics were gathering together against the Bible. The truth of the Gospel has ever had two great adversaries,—the profligacy of the world, and the fanaticism of the priests. The scholastic Sorbonne and a shameless court, were now about to go forward hand in hand against the confessors of Jesus Christ. The unbelieving Sadducees, and

* Crevier, v. p. 110.
† Fontaine, Hist. Cathol. Paris, 1562, p. 16.
‡ Raumer, Gesch. Europ. i. p. 270.

the hypocritical Pharisees, in the early days of the Gospel were the fiercest enemies of Christianity, and they are alike in every age.   At their head stood Noël Bedier, commonly called Beda, a native of Picardy, syndic of the Sorbonne, who had the reputation of the first blusterer and most factious disturber of his time.   Educated in the dry maxims of scholastic morality, he had grown up in the constant hearing of the *theses* and *antitheses* of his college, and had more veneration for the hair-breadth distinctions of the school, than for God's word, so that his anger was readily excited whenever any one ventured to give utterance to other thoughts.   Of a restless disposition, that required continually to be engaged in pursuit of new objects, he was a torment to all about him ; his very element was trouble ; he seemed born for contention ; and when adversaries were not at hand, he would fall upon his friends.   Boastful and impetuous, he filled the city and the university with the noise of his disputation,—with his invectives against learning and the innovations of that age,—as also against those, who, in his opinion, did not sufficiently oppose them.   Some laughed, others gave ear to the fierce talker, and in the Sorbonne his violence gave him the mastery.   He seemed to be ever seeking some opponent, or some victim to drag to the scaffold—hence, before the "heretics" began to show themselves, his imagination had created them, and he had required that the vicar-general of Paris, Merlin, should be brought to the stake, on the charge of having defended Origen.   But when he caught sight of the new teachers, he bounded like a wild beast that suddenly comes within view of its unsuspecting prey.   "There are three thousand monks in one Beda," remarked the wary Erasmus.*

Yet his violence injured the cause he laboured to advance. "What! can the Romish Church rest for her support on such an Atlas as that?†   Whence all this commotion but from the insane violence of Beda?" was the reflection of the wisest.

In truth the invectives that terrified the weak, revolted

* In uno Beda sunt tria millia monachorum.   (Erasmi Epp. p. 373.)
† Talibus Atlantibus nititur Ecclesia romana.   (Ibid. p. 113.

nobler minds. At the court of Francis the First, was a gentleman of Artois, by name Louis Berquin, about thirty years of age, who was never married. The purity of his life,[*] his accurate knowledge, which had won him the appellation of "most learned among the noble,"[†] his ingenuousness, compassion for the poor, and unbounded attachment to his friends distinguished him above his equals.[‡] The rites of the Church its fasts, festivals, and masses, had not a more devout observer,[§] and he held in especial horror everything heretical. His devotion was indeed the wonder of the whole court.

It seemed as if nothing could have given this man a turn in favour of the Reformation; nevertheless, some points of his character disposed him toward the Gospel. He had a horror of all dissimulation, and having himself no ill-will to any, he could not endure injustice in others. The overbearing violence of Beda and other fanatics, their shuffling and persecutions disgusted his generous heart, and, as he was accustomed in every thing to go heartily to work, he, ere long, wherever he came, in the city and at court, even in the first circles,[‖] was heard vehemently protesting against the tyranny of those doctors, and pursuing into their very holes the pestilent hornets who then kept the world in fear.[¶]

But this was not all: for his opposition to injustice led Berquin to enquire after the truth. He resolved on knowing more of that Holy Scripture so dear to the men against whom Beda and his party were conspiring;—and scarcely had he begun to study it, than his heart was won by it. Berquin immediately sought the intimacy of Margaret, Briçonnet, Lefevre, and those who loved the truth; and in their society

---

* Ut ne rumusculus quidem impudicitiæ sit unquam in illum exortus. (Erasmi Epp. p. 1278.)

† Gaillard Hist. de Francois 1er.

‡ Mirere benignus in egenos et amicos. (Er. Epp. p. 1238.)

§ Constitutionum ac rituum ecclesiasticorum observantissimus . . . . (Ibid.)

‖ Actes des Martyrs de Crespin, p. 103.

¶ Ut maxime omnium tunc metuendos crabones in ipsis eorum cavis . . . (Bezæ Icones.)

tasted of the purest delight. He became sensible that he had something else to do than to stand up against the Sorbonne, and gladly would he have communicated to all France the new convictions of his soul. With this view he sat down to compose and translate into French certain christian writings. To him it seemed as if every one must confess and embrace the truth as promptly as he himself had done. The impatient zeal that Beda brought to the service of traditions of men, Berquin employed in the cause of God's truth. Somewhat younger than the syndic of the Sorbonne, less wary, less acute, he had in his favour the noble incentive of a love of truth. Berquin had a higher object than victory over his antagonist when he stood up against Beda. It was his aim to let loose the flood of truth among his countrymen. On this account, Theodore Beza observes, " that if Francis the First had been another Elector, Berquin might have come down to us as another Luther."*

Many were the obstacles in his way. Fanaticism finds disciples everywhere,—it is a contagious infection. The monks and ignorant priests sided with the syndic of the Sorbonne. An esprit de corps pervaded their whole company, governed by a few intriguing and fanatical leaders, who knew how to work upon the credulity and vanity of their colleagues, and by that means communicate to them their own animosities. At all their meetings these persons took the lead, lording it over others, and reducing to silence the timid and moderate of their body. Hardly could they propose any thing, when this party exclaimed, in an overbearing tone, " Now we shall see who are of Luther's faction."† If the latter offered any reasonable suggestion, instantly a shudder passed from Beda to Lecouturier, Duchesne, and the rest, and all exclaimed, " Why they are worse than Luther." The manœuvre answered their purpose, and the timid, who prefer quiet to disputation, and are willing to give up their own opinion for their own ease,—

* Gallia fortassis alterum esset Lutherum nacta. (Bezæ Icones.)
† Hic inquiunt, apparebit qui sint Lutheranæ factionis. (Er. Epp. p. 889.)

those who do not understand the very simplest questions,—
and, lastly, such as are easily turned round by mere clamour,
were led away by Beda and his followers. Some silently, and
some assenting aloud, submitted to the influence exercised over
ordinary spirits by one proud and tyrannical mind. Such was
the state of this association, regarded as venerable, and which,
at this time, was found among the most determined opposers
of the Christianity of the Gospel. Often would one glance
within the interior of such bodies suffice to enable us to estimate at its true value the war they wage against truth.

Thus the University which, under Louis XII., had applauded
the first inklings of independence in Allman, abruptly plunged
once more, under the guidance of Duprat and Louisa of
Savoy, into fanaticism and servility. If we except the Jansenists, and a few others, no where in the Gallican clergy do
we find a noble and genuine independence. It has done no
more than vibrate between servility to the court, and servility
to the Pope. If, under Louis XII. or Louis XIV., we notice some faint semblance of liberty, it is because its master in
Paris was at strife with its master in Rome. Herein we have
the solution of the change we have noticed. The University
and the Bishops forgot their rights and obligations, the moment the King ceased to enjoin the assertion of them!

Beda had long cherished ill-will against Lefevre. The renown of the doctor of Picardy irritated and ruffled the pride
of his countryman, who would gladly have silenced him.
Once before, Beda had attacked the doctor of Etaples, and,
having as yet but little discernment of the true point of the
evangelic doctrines, he had assailed his colleague on a point
which, strange as it must to us appear, was very near sending
Lefevre to the scaffold.* The doctor had asserted that Mary
the sister of Lazarus, Mary Magdalen, and the woman who
was a sinner, (mentioned by Luke in his seventh chapter,)
were three distinct persons. The Greek fathers had considered them as distinct, but the fathers of the *Latin* Church had
spoken of them as one and the same. This shocking heresy,

* Gaillard Hist. de Francois Ier iv. p. 228.

In relation to the three Maries, set Beda and all his clique in motion. Christendom itself was roused. Fisher, bishop of Rochester, and one of the most eminent prelates of the age, wrote against Lefevre, and the whole Church declared against a judgment that is now universally received among Roman Catholics themselves. Already, Lefevre, condemned by the Sorbonne, was prosecuted by the Parliament on the charge of heresy, when Francis I., not sorry to have an opportunity of striking a blow at the Sorbonne, and humbling the monks, interfered, and rescued him from the hands of his persecutors.

Beda, enraged at seeing his victim thus snatched from his grasp, resolved on taking his next measures more cunningly. The name of Luther was beginning to be noised in France. The Reformer, after disputing against Eck at Leipsic, had agreed to acknowledge the universities of Erfurth and of Paris as his judges. The zeal displayed by the University against the Concordat doubtless led him to expect an impartial verdict. But a change had taken place, and the more decided their opposition to the encroachments of Rome, the more did the members of the University seem to have it at heart to make proof of their orthodoxy. Beda, accordingly, found them quite disposed to enter into all his views.

On the 20th of January, 1520, the questor of France purchased twenty copies of Luther's conference with Eck, to distribute them among the members of the commission charged to make its report on the matter. More than a year was taken up in the investigation. The German Reformation was beginning to produce a strong sensation in France. The several universities, then truly Catholic institutions, resorted to from all parts of Christendom, maintained a more direct and intimate intercourse, on topics of theology and philosophy, between Germany, France, and England, than exists in our own day. The report, brought to Paris, of Luther's labours and success, strengthened the hands of such men as Lefevre, Briçonnet, and Farel. Some of the divines of the Sorbonne were struck by the truths they saw in the writings of the Wittemberg monk. Now and then a bold confession was heard;

but there was also fierce opposers. "Europe," says Crevier, a was all expectation of the decision of the University of Paris." The issue seemed doubtful,—but Beda finally triumphed. In April, 1521, the University decreed that the writings of Luther should be publicly committed to the flames, and that the author should be compelled to retract.

Further measures were resolved on. Luther's disciples had crossed the Rhine, even before his writings. Maimbourg tells us that the University was quickly filled with foreigners, who, having obtained a reputation on the strength of some know ledge of Hebrew, and more of Greek, crept into the houses of persons of distinction, and took upon them the liberty of explaining the Scriptures.* The faculty, therefore, sent a deputation to the king to call attention to these disorders.

Francis the First, caring little for theological dissensions, was then pursuing the career of his pleasures. Passing from one chateau to another, in company with his gentlemen and the ladies of his mother's and his sister's court, he indulged in every species of dissolute excess, out of the range of the troublesome observation of his capital. In this way he passed through Brittany, Anjou, Guienne, Angoumois, Poitou, requiring, in villages and forests, the same attention and luxury as if he had been in the Chateau des Tournelles at Paris. Nothing was heard of but tournaments, single combats, masquerades, shows, and feastings, "such," says Brantôme, "that Lucullus himself never saw the like."*

Suspending for a moment the course of his pleasures, he gave audience to the grave deputies of the Sorbonne; but he saw only men of learning in those whom the faculty designated as heretics; and should a prince, who boasts of having eclipsed and put *hors de page* the kings of France, stoop to humour a clique of fanatical doctors. "I command you," was his answer, "not to molest those people. To persecute those who teach us would prevent able scholars from settling in our country."‡

* Histoire du Calvinisme, p. 10.
·† Vie des Hommes Illustres, i. p. 326.   ‡ Maimbourg, p. 11.

The deputation quitted the royal presence in a rage. What then is to be the consequence ? The danger is every day greater, already the heretical sentiments are counted as those of the best informed classes,—the devouring flame is circulating between the rafters,—the conflagration will presently burst forth, and the structure of the established faith will fall, with sudden crash, to the earth.

Beda and his party, failing to obtain the king's permission to resort to scaffolds, had recourse to more quiet persecution. There was no kind of annoyance to which the evangelic teachers were not subjected. Every day brought with it new rumours and new charges. The aged Lefevre, wearied out by these ignorant zealots, panted for quiet. The pious Briçonnet, who was unremitting in his attentions to the Doctor of Etaples,* offered him an asylum. Lefevre, therefore, took leave of Paris, and repaired to Meaux. It was a first advantage gained by the enemies of the Gospel, and thenceforth it was seen that if the party cannot enlist the civil power on its side, it has ever a secret and fanatical police, which it knows how to use, so as to ensure the attainment of its ends.

Thus Paris was beginning to rise against the Reformation, and to trace, as it were, the first lines of that enclosure which, for three centuries, was to bar the entrance of the Reformation. God had appointed that in Paris itself its first glimmering should appear ; but men arose who hastily extinguished it ;—the spirit of the sixteen chiefs was already working, and other cities in the kingdom were about to receive that light which the capital itself rejected.

Briçonnet, on returning to his diocese, there manifested the zeal of a Christian and of a bishop. He visited all the parishes, and having called together the deans, curates, vicars, church-wardens, and principal parishioners, he made enquiries respecting the teaching and manner of life of the preachers. " At the time of the gathering," they replied, " the Franciscans of Meaux sally forth ; a single preacher goes over

* Pro innumeris beneficiis, pro tantis ad studia commodis. (Epist. dedicatoria Epp. Pauli.)

four or five parishes in one day; repeating as many times the same sermon, not to feed the souls of his hearers, but to fill his belly, and enrich his convent.* The scrip once replenished, the object is answered; the preaching is at an end, and the monks are not seen again in the churches until begging time comes round again. The only thing these shepherds attend to is the shearing of their flocks."†

The majority of the curates lived upon their incomes at Paris. "Oh!" exclaimed the pious bishop, on finding the presbytery he had come to visit deserted, "must we not regard those who thus forsake the service of Christ,‡ traitors to him?" Briçonnet resolved to apply a remedy to these evils, and convoked a synod of all his clergy for the 13th of October, 1519. But these worldly priests, who gave but little heed to the remonstrances of their bishop, and for whom Paris possessed so many attractions, took advantage of a custom, by virtue of which they were allowed to substitute one or more vicars to look after their flocks in their absence. Out of a hundred and twenty-seven vicars, Briçonnet upon examination, found only fourteen whom he could approve.

Earthly-minded curates, imbecile vicars, monks whose God was their belly, such, then, was the state of the church. Briçonnet forbade the pulpit to the Franciscans,§ and, being persuaded that the only method of supplying able ministers in his diocese, was himself to train them, he determined to found a school of theology at Meaux, under the superintendence of pious and learned doctors. It became necessary to look around for such persons. Beda, however, supplied him with them.

This fanatic and his troop continued their efforts, and complaining bitterly against the government for tolerating the new

* Eo solum doceri quæ ad cœnobium illorum ac ventrem explendum pertinerent. (Acta Mart p. 334.)

† MS. de Meaux. I am indebted to M. Ladeveze, pastor of Meaux, for the communication of a copy of this MS. preserved in that city.

‡ MS. de Meaux.

§ Eis in universa diocesi sua prædicationem interdixit. (Act Mart. p. 334.)

teachers, declared they would wage war against their doctrines without, and even against its orders. Lefevre had indeed quitted the capital, but were not Farel and his friends still there. Farel, it is true, did not preach, for he was not in priest's orders; but in the university, in the city, with professors, priests, students, and citizens, he boldly maintained the cause of the Reformation. Others, emboldened by his example, circulated more freely the word of God. Martial Mazurier, president of St. Michael's college, and distinguished as a preacher, unsparingly depicted the disorders of the time, in the darkest and yet the truest colours, and it seemed scarce possible to withstand the force of his eloquence.* The rage of Beda, and those divines who acted with him, was at its height. " If we suffer these innovators," said Beda, " they will spread through our whole company, and there will be an end of our teaching and tradition, as well as of our places, and the respect France and all Christendom have hitherto paid us."

The doctors of the Sorbonne were the stronger party. Farel, Mazurier, Gerard Roussel, and his brother Arnaud, soon found their active service every where counteracted. The Bishop of Meaux pressed his friends to rejoin Lefevre,— and these worthy men, persecuted and hunted by the Sorbonne, and hoping to form with Briçonnet a sacred phalanx for the triumph of truth, accepted the bishop's invitation, and repaired to Meaux.† Thus, the light of the Gospel was gradually withdrawn from the capital where Providence had kindled its first sparks. " *This is the condemnation that light is come into the world, and men love darkness rather than light, because their deeds are evil.*"‡ It is impossible not to discern that Paris then drew down upon it that judgment of God which is here conveyed in the words of Jesus Christ.

* Frequentissimas de reformandis hominum moribus conciones habuit. (Lannoi, Navarræ gymnasii Hist. p. 261.)
† It was the persecution which arose against them in Paris, in 1521, which compelled them to leave that city. (Vie de Farel, par Chaupard.)
‡ St. John iii. 19.

Margaret of Valois, successively deprived of Briçonnet,
Lefevre, and their friends, found herself alone in the centre of
Paris, and of the dissolute court of Francis I.   A young princess, sister to her mother, Philibert of Savoy, lived on intimacy with her.   Philibert, whom the king of France had
given in marriage to Julian the Magnificent, brother of Leo X.,
in confirmation of the Concordat, had, after her nuptials, repaired to Rome, where the Pope, delighted with so illustrious
an alliance, had expended no less than 150,000 ducats in festive entertainments on the occasion.*   In 1516, Julian, who
then commanded the Papal forces, died, leaving his widow
only eighteen.   She attached herself to Margaret, being attracted by the influence which the character and virtues of
that princess gave her over all about her.   The grief of Philibert unclosed her heart to the voice of religion.   Margaret
imparted to her the fruit of her reading, and the widow of the
lieutenant-general of the Church began to taste the sweetness
of the saving truth.   But Philibert had as yet too little experience to be a support to her friend, and often did Margaret
tremble at the thought of her own extreme weakness.   If the
love she bore her king, and her fear of offending him, led her
to any action contrary to her conscience, instantly her soul
was troubled, and, turning in sorrow to the Lord, she found
in him a master and brother more gracious and sweet to her
heart than Francis himself.   It was in such a season she
breathed forth those feelings :—

> Sweet Brother, who, in place of chastenings meet,
> Lead'st gently home thy wandering sister's feet,
> Giving thy Grace and Love in recompense
> Of murmurings, presumption, and offence.
> Too much, my Brother,—too much hast thou done :
> The blessing is too vast for such an one.†

When she saw all her friends retiring to Meaux, Margaret
turned after them a look of sorrow from the midst of the fes-

* Guichemon. Hist. gén. de Savoie, ii. p. 180.
† Miroir de l'âme pécheresse.   Marguerites de la Marguerite, &c. i.
p. 36.

tivities of the court. She seemed deserted of all,—her husband the Duke of Alençon was setting out for the army,—her young aunt Philibert was returning to Savoy. The Duchess wrote to Briçonnet, as follows :—

"Monsieur de Meaux,—Knowing that God is all-sufficient, I apply to you to ask your prayers that He will conduct in safety, according to His holy will, M. d'Alençon, who is about to take his departure, by order of the king, as lieutenant-general of his army, which I apprehend will not break up without a war ; and, thinking that, besides the public good of the kingdom, you have an interest in all that concerns his and my salvation, I request your spiritual aid. To-morrow, my aunt leaves Nemours for Savoy. I must be mixed up with many things which I dread. Therefore, if you should know that master Michael could make a journey hither, it would be a comfort to me, which I desire only for the honour of God."[*]

Michaël Arand, whose counsel Margaret desired, was one of the members of the evangelic assembly at Meaux, who, at a later period, exposed himself to many dangers in preaching the Gospel.

The pious princess trembled to see an opposition gathering strength against the truth. Duprat and the retainers of the government, Beda and those who adhered to the University, inspired her with terror. Briçonnet wrote cheeringly—"It is the war which the gentle Jesus said he was come to send upon earth,—the fire, the fierce fire which transforms earthliness into that which is heavenly. With all my heart do I desire to help you, Madam ; but do not expect from my weakness any more than the will to serve you. Whoever has faith, hope, love, has all that is necessary, and needeth not any other help or protection. God will be all,—and out of Him we can hope for nothing. Take with you into the conflict that mighty giant, unconquerable Love. The war is led on by Love. Jesus requires to have our hearts in his presence: woe befals

* Lettres de Marguerite, reine de Navarre. (Bibl. Royale Manuscript, S.F. 337. 1521.)

the Christian who parts company from Him.   He who is
present in person in the battle is sure of victory; but if the
battle is fought out of His own presence, he will often lose
ground."*

The Bishop of Meaux was then beginning to experience
what it is to contend for the word of God.   The theologians
and monks, irritated by the shelter he had afforded to the
friends of the Reformation, vehemently accused him, so that
his brother, the Bishop of St. Malo, came to Paris to enquire
into the charges brought against him.†   Hence Margaret
was the more touched by the comfortings which Briçonnet
addressed to her; and she answered by offering him her assistance.

"If in any thing," wrote she, "you think that I can be of
service to you or your's, be assured that I shall find comfort
in doing all I can.   Everlasting Peace be given to you after
the long struggles you have waged for the faith—in the which
cause *pray* that you may live and die.

"Your devoted daughter, MARGARET."‡

Happy would it have been if Briçonnet had died while contending for the truth.   Yet was he still full of zeal.   Philibert
of Nemours, universally respected for her piety, charity, and
blameless life, read with increasing interest the evangelical
writings sent her from time to time by the Bishop of Meaux.
"I have received all the tracts you forwarded, wrote Margaret
to Briçonnet, "of which my aunt of Nemours has taken some,
and I mean to send her the last, for she is now in Savoy,
called thither by her brother's marriage.   Her absence is no
small loss to me;—think of my loneliness in your prayers."
Unhappily, Philibert did not live to declare herself openly in
favour of the Reformation.   She died, in 1524, at the castle
of Virieu le Grand in Bugey, at the age of twenty-six.§   Mar-

* Lettres de Marguerite, reine de Navarre.   (Bibl. Royale Manuscript, S.F. 337.   12th June, 1521.)

† MS. de Meaux.

‡ MS. S.F. 227, de la Bibl. royale.

§ Guichemon. Hist. de la maison de Savoie, ii. p. 181.

garet was deeply sensible of the loss of one who was to her a friend—a sister; one who could, indeed, enter into her thoughts. Perhaps no loss by death was the occasion of more sorrow to her, if we except that of her brother.

Alas! nor earth nor heaven above appears
To my sad eyes, so ceaseless are the tears
That from them flow.*

Margaret, feeling her own weakness to bear up under her grief, and against the seductions of the court, applied to Briçonnet to exhort her to the love of God:—" The gentle and gracious Jesus, who wills, and who alone is able to work that which he wills, in his infinite mercy, visit your heart, and lead it to love him with an undivided love. None but He, Madam, hath power to do this, and we must not seek light from darkness, nor warmth from cold. When he draws, he kindles, and by the warmth draws us after him, enlarging our hearts. You write to me to pity you because you are alone; I do not understand that word. The heart that is in the world, and resting in it, is indeed lonely,—for many and evil are they who compass it about. But she whose heart is closed against the world and awake to the gentle and gracious Jesus, her true and faithful spouse, is *really* alone, living on supplies from One who is all to her,—and yet not alone, because never left by Him who replenishes and preserves all. I cannot and ought not to pity such solitude as this, which is more to be prized than the whole world around us, from which I am confident that God hath in his love delivered you, so that you are no longer its child. Continue, Madam, —alone,—abiding in Him who is your all, and who humbled himself to a painful and ignominious death.

" In commending myself to your favour, I humbly entreat you not to use the words of your last letters. You are the daughter and the spouse of God only. No other father hath any claim upon you. I exhort and admonish you to be to Him such and so good daughter as He is to you a Father;

* Chanson spirituelle après la mort du Roi. (Marguerites, i. p. 473.)

and since you cannot attain to this, by reason that finite cannot compare with infinite, I pray Him to strengthen you, that you may love and serve Him with all your heart."*

Notwithstanding these counsels, Margaret was not yet comforted. She grieved over the loss of those spiritual guides who had been removed from her. The new pastors set over her to reclaim her, did not possess her confidence; and notwithstanding what the bishop had said, she felt alone amidst the court, and all around her seemed like a desolate wilderness. She wrote to Briçonnet as follows:—"As a sheep wandering in a strange land, and turning from her pasture in distrust of her new shepherds, naturally lifts her head to catch the breeze from that quarter of the field where the chief shepherd once led her to the tender grass, just so am I constrained to implore your love. Come down from your mountain, and look in pity on the blindest of all your fold, astray among a people living in darkness.

(Signed) 'MARGUERITE."†

The Bishop of Meaux, in his reply, taking up the comparison of a wandering sheep, under which Margaret had pictured herself, uses it to depict the mysteries of Salvation under the figure of a wood. "The sheep," says he, "on entering this wood under the guidance of the Holy Spirit, is at once charmed by the goodness, beauty, height, length, breadth, depth, and refreshing odours of the forest, and looking round about, sees only Him in all, and all in Him; and hastening onward through its green alleys, finds it so sweet, that the way becomes life, joy, and consolation."‡ The bishop then describes the sheep trying in vain to penetrate to the bounds of the forest (as a soul would fathom the deep things of God,) meeting with mountains which it in vain endeavours to ascend, being stopped on all sides by "inaccessible heights." He then shows the way by which the soul, inquiring after God, surmounts the difficulties, and how the sheep among all

* MSC., S.F. 337, de la Bibl. royale, 10th July.
† Ibid.   ‡ Ibid.

the hirelings, finds out "the Chief Shepherd's nook," and "enters on the wing of meditation by faith;" then all is made plain and easy, and she begins to sing, "I have found him whom my soul loveth."

Thus wrote the Bishop of Meaux. In the fervour of his zeal he would at this time have rejoiced to see France regenerated by the Gospel.* Often would he dwell especially on those three individuals who seemed called to preside over the destinies of his country; namely, the king, his mother, and his sister. He thought that if the royal family were but enlightened, the whole nation would be so; and that the clergy, aroused to emulation, would awake from their death-like stupor. "Madam," wrote he to Margaret, "I humbly pray God that He will please, in His goodness, to kindle a fire in the hearts of the king, his mother, and yourself, so that from you three a flame may go forth through the nation, and reanimate especially that class, which, by its coldness, chills all the others."

Margaret did not share in these hopes. She says nothing of her mother, nor yet of her brother. These were themes she did not dare to touch; but in her answer to the bishop, in January, 1522, oppressed at heart by the indifference and worldliness all around her, she said,—" The times are so cold, the heart so frozen up;" and she signed herself—" Your cold-hearted, hungering and thirsting daughter, "MARGARET."

This letter did not discourage Briçonnet, but it put him upon reflection; and feeling how much he who sought to reanimate others required to be reanimated himself, he asked the prayers of Margaret and of Madame de Nemours. "Madam, said he, with perfect simplicity, "I pray you to re-awaken by your prayers the poor drowsy one."†

And such, in 1521, were the expressions interchanged at the court of France. Strange words, doubtless; and which now, after a lapse of above three centuries, a manuscript in the

* Studio veritatis aliis declarandæ inflammatus. (Act. Martyrum, p. 334.)
† MSC. de la Bibl. royale.

Royal Library reveals to us.   Was this influence in high
places favourable to the Reformation, or adverse to it ?   The
spur of truth was felt indeed at the court, but perhaps did but
arouse the slumbering beast,—exciting him to rage,—and
causing him to dart more furiously on the weak ones of the flock.

In truth the time was drawing nigh when the storm was to
burst upon the Reformation; but first it was destined to scatter
some seeds and gather in some sheaves.   This city of Meaux
which a century and a half later was to be honoured by the
residence of the noble defender of the Gallican church against
the claims of Rome, was called to be the first town in France
wherein regenerated Christianity should establish its hold.   It
was at this time the field on which the labourers profusely
scattered their seed, and into which they had already put the
sickle.   Briçonnet, less given to slumber than he had said,
cheered, watched, and directed every thing.   His fortune was
equal to his zeal.   Never did any one make a more noble use
of his means—and never did so noble a devotion promise at
first to yield such abundant fruit.   Assembled at Meaux, the
pious teachers took their measures thenceforward with more
liberty.   The word of God was not bound; and the Reformation made a great advance in France.   Lefevre, with unwonted
energy, proclaimed that Gospel with which he would gladly
have filled the world—" Kings, princes, nobles, the people,
and all nations," he exclaimed, "ought to think and aspire
only after Jesus Christ.*   Every priest should resemble that
angel seen by John in the Apocalypse, flying through the
air, having in his hand the everlasting Gospel, to preach to
every nation, and kindred, and tongue, and people.   Draw
near, ye pontiffs, kings, and generous hearts.   Awake, ye
nations, to the light of the Gospel, and receive the breath of
eternal life.†   Sufficient is the word of God!"‡

* Reges, principes, magnates omnes et subinde omnium nationum
populi, ut nihil aliud cogitent . . . ac Christum . . . (Fabri Comment.
in Evang. præfat.)

† Ubivis gentium expergiscimini ad Evangelii lucem . . . (Ibid.)

‡ Verbum Dei sufficit.   (Ibid.)

Such, in truth, was the motto of the new school: *sufficient is the word of God.* The whole Reformation is embodied in that truth. "To know Christ and his word," said Lefevre, Roussel, Farel, "is the only true, living, and universal Theology. He who knows that, knows everything."[*]

The truth produced a deep impression at Meaux. At first private meetings took place, then conferences, and lastly the Gospel was proclaimed in the churches. But a yet more formidable blow was struck against the authority of Rome.

Lefevre resolved to put it in the power of the Christians of France to read the Scriptures. On the 30th of October he published the French translation of the four Gospels; on the 6th of November the remaining books of the New Testament; and on the 12th of November, 1524, the whole of these collected in one volume at Meaux; and in 1525 a French version of the Psalms.[†] Thus in France, and almost at the same time as in Germany, we have the commencement of that publication of the Scriptures, in the vernacular tongue, which, after a lapse of three centuries, was to receive such wonderful development. In France, as in the countries, beyond the Rhine, the Bible produced a decided effect. Many there were who had learned by experience that when they sought the knowledge of divine things, darkness and doubt encompassed them on all sides. How many were the passing moments,— perhaps even years,—in which they had been tempted to regard the most certain truths as mere illusions. We want a ray from heaven to enlighten our darkness. Such was the longing desire of many souls at the period of the Reformation. With feelings of this sort many received the Scriptures from the hands of Lefevre. They read them in their families and in private. The Bible became increasingly the subject of conversation. Christ appeared to these souls, so long misled, as the sun and centre of all discovery. No longer did they want

---

[*] Hæc est universa et sola vivifica Theologia . . . Christum et verbum ejus esse omnia. (Ibid. in Ev. Johan. p. 271.)

[†] Le Long. Biblioth. sacrée, 2 edit. p. 42.

evidence that Scripture was of the Lord : they knew it, for it had delivered them from darkness into light.

Such was the course by which some remarkable persons in France were at this time brought to know God. But there were yet humbler and more ordinary steps by which many of the poorer sort arrived at the knowledge of the truth. The city of Meaux was almost entirely peopled with artizans and dealers in woollen cloth. "Many," says a chronicler of the sixteenth century, "were taken with so ardent a desire to know the way of salvation, that artisans, carders, fullers, and combers, while at work with their hands, had their thoughts engaged in conversation on the word of God, and getting comfort from thence. On Sunday and on festivals, especially, they employed themselves in reading the Scriptures and in quiring into the good pleasure of the Lord."*

Briçonnet rejoiced to see true piety take the place of superstition in his diocese. "Lefevre, availing himself of his great reputation for learning," observes a contemporary historian,† "managed so to cajole and impose upon Messire Guillaume Briçonnet by his specious words, that he turned him aside into gross error, so that it has been found impossible to cleanse the town and diocese of Meaux from that wicked doctrine from that time to this, when it has marvellously spread abroad. The subverting of that good bishop was a sad event, for he had, before that, been very devout in his service to God and the Virgin Mary." However, not all had been so grossly 'turned aside,' to adopt the expression of the Franciscan. The townspeople were divided in two parties. On one side, were the Franciscan monks, and the partisans of Romanism : on the other, Briçonnet, Lefevre, Farel, and those who loved the new preaching. A man of low station, named Leclerc was one of the most servile adherents of the monks ; but his wife and his two sons, Peter and John, had joyfully received the Gospel ; and John, who was by trade a wool-carder, soon at-

* Act des Mart. p. 182.
† Hist. Cathol. de notre temps, par Fontaine, de l'ordre de Saint Francois.   Paris, 1562.

tracted notice among the infant congregations. James Pavanne, a native of Picardy, a young man of open and upright character evinced an ardent zeal for the Reformed opinions. Meaux was become a focus of light. Persons called thither by business, and who there heard the Gospel, returning, bore it with them to their respective homes. It was not merely in the city that the Scripture was the subject of inquiry ; "many of the adjacent villages were awakened," says a chronicler, "so that in that diocese seemed to shine forth a sort of image of the regenerated church."

The environs of Meaux were, in autumn, clothed with rich harvests, and a crowd of labouring people resorted thither from the surrounding countries. Resting themselves, in the heat of the day, they would talk with the people of those parts of a seed-time and harvest of another kind. Certain peasantry, who had come from Thierachia, and more particularly from Landouzy, after their return home continued in the doctrine they had heard, and, ere long, an evangelic church was formed in this latter place,*—a church which is among the most ancient in the kingdom. "The report of this unspeakable blessing spread through France, says the chronicler.† Briçonnet himself preached the Gospel from the pulpit, and laboured to diffuse, far and wide, that "free, gracious, true, and clear light, which dazzles and illuminates every creature capable of receiving it; and, while it enlightens him, raises him by adoption to the dignity of a child of God."‡ He besought his hearers not to listen to those who would turn them aside from the Word. "Though an angel from heaven," exclaimed he, "should preach any other Gospel, do not give ear to him." At times melancholy thoughts presented themselves to his mind. He did not feel confident in his own stedfastness, and he recoiled from the thought of the fatal consequences that

* These facts are derived from old and much damaged papers discovered in the church of Laudouzy-la-Ville (Aisne), by M. Colany, during the time he filled the office of pastor in that town.

† Actes des Mart. p. 182.

‡ MS. in the Royal Library, S.F. No. 337.

might result from any failure of faith on his part. Forewarning his hearers, he would say, "Though I, your bishop, should change my voice and doctrine, take heed that you change not with me."* At that moment nothing foreboded such a calamity. "Not only," says the chronicler, "the word of God was preached, but it was practised: all kinds of works of charity and love were visible; the morals of the city were reformed, and its superstitions disappeared."†

Still indulging in the thought of gaining over the king and his mother, the bishop sent to Margaret a translation of St. Paul's Epistles, richly illuminated, humbly soliciting her to present it to the king, "which, coming through your hands," added he, cannot fail to be acceptable. They make a truly royal dish," continued the worthy bishop, "of a fatness that never corrupts, and having a power to restore from all manner of sickness. The more we taste them the more we hunger after them, with desires that are ever fed and never cloyed."‡

What dearer commission could Margaret receive . . . . ? The moment seemed auspicious. Michel d'Arande was at Paris, detained there by command of the king's mother, for whom he was translating portions of the Scriptures.§ But Margaret would have preferred that Briçonnet should himself present St. Paul to her brother : "You would do well to come," wrote she, "for you know the confidence the king and his mother have in you."‖

Thus at this time (in 1522 and 1523) was God's word placed before the eyes of Francis the First and Louisa of Savoy. They were thus brought in contact with that Gospel of which they were afterwards to be the persecutors. We see nothing to indicate that that Word made on them any saving impression; curiosity led them to unclose that Bible which was

* Hist. Cathol. de Fontaine.
† Actes des Mart. p. 182.
‡ MS. in the Royal Library, S.F. No. 337.
§ Par le commandement de Madame a quy il a lyvré quelque chose de la saincte Escripture qu'elle desire parfaire.   (Ibid.)
‖ Ibid.

the subject of so much discussion; but they soon closed it again as they had opened it.

Margaret herself with difficulty struggled against the worldliness which surrounded her. Her tender regard for her brother, respect for her mother, the flattery of the court, all conspired against the love she had vowed to Jesus Christ. Many indeed were her temptations. At times, the soul of Margaret, assailed by so many enemies, and dizzy with the tumult of life, turned aside from her Lord. Then becoming conscious of her sin, the princess shut herself in her apartments, and gave vent to her grief in sounds very different from those with which Francis and the young lords who were the companions of his pleasures, filled the royal palaces in their carousings :—

> I have forsaken thee, for pleasure erring;
> In place of thee, my evil choice preferring;
> And from thee wandering, whither am I come?
> Among the cursed,—to the place of doom.
> I have forsaken thee, oh Friend sincere;
> And from thy love, the better to get free,
> Have clung to things most contrary to thee.*

After this, Margaret, turning in the direction of Meaux, wrote, in her distress,—"I again turn toward you, Mons. 'Fabry,' and your companions, desiring you in your prayers to entreat of the unspeakable mercy an alarum that shall rouse the unwatchful weak one from her heavy and deathlike slumbers."†

The friends of the Reformation were beginning to indulge in cheering anticipations. Who would be able to resist the Gospel if the authority of Francis the First should open the way for it. The corrupting influence of the court would be succeeded by a sanctifying example, and France would acquire a moral power which would constitute her the benefactress of nations.

But the Romish party on their side had caught the alarm.

* Les Marguerites, i. p. 40.
† MS. in the Royal Library, S. F. No. 337.

One of their party at Meaux, was a Jacobin monk, of the name of Roma. One day, when Lefevre, Farel, and their friends were in conversation with him, and certain other partisans of the Papacy, Lefevre incautiously gave utterance to his hopes: "Already," said he, "the Gospel is winning the hearts of the nobles and the common people, and ere long we shall see it spreading throughout France, and casting down the inventions that men have set up." The aged doctor was warmed by his theme, his eyes sparkled, and his feeble voice seemed to put forth new power, resembling the aged Simeon giving thanks to the Lord because his eyes had seen His salvation. Lefevre's friends partook of his emotion; the opposers were amazed and silent .... Suddenly Roma rose from his seat, exclaiming, "Then I and all the monks will preach a crusade—we will raise the people, and if the king suffers the preaching of your Gospel, we will expel him from his kingdom by his own subjects."* Thus did a monk venture to stand up against the knightly monarch. The Franciscans applauded his boldness. It was necessary to prevent the fulfilment of the aged doctor's predictions. Already the mendicant friars found their daily gatherings fall off. The Franciscans in alarm distributed themselves in private families. "Those new teachers are heretics," said they, "they call in question the holiest practices, and deny the most sacred mysteries." Then, growing bolder, the more violent of the party, sallying forth from their cloister, presented themselves at the bishop's residence, and being admitted,—"Make haste," said they, "to crush this heresy, or the pestilence which now afflicts Meaux will extend its ravages through the kingdom."

Briçonnet was roused, and for a moment disturbed by this invasion of his privacy; but he did not give way. Despising the interested clamour of a set of ignorant monks, he ascended the pulpit and preached in vindication of Lefevre, designating the monks as pharisees and hypocrites. Still this opposition from without had already awakened anxiety and conflict in his soul. He tried to quiet his fears by persuading himself that it was necessary to pass through such spiritual

* Farel. Epitre au Duc de Lorraine. Gen. 1634.

struggles. "By such conflict," said he, in expressions that sound mystical to our ears, "we are brought to a death that ushers into life, and, while ever mortifying life,—living we die, and dying, live."* The way had been more sure, if, turning to the Saviour, as the apostles, when "driven by the winds and tossed," he had cried out,—"Lord! save us, or we perish."

The monks of Meaux, enraged at this repulse, resolved to carry their complaint before a higher tribunal. An appeal lay open to them; and if the bishop should be contumacious, he may be reduced to compliance. Their leaders set forth for Paris, and concerted measures with Beda and Duchesne. They presented themselves before the Parliament, and lodged information against the bishop and the heretical teachers. "The town," said they, "and all the neighbouring country, is infected with heresy, and the muddy waters go forth from the bishop's palace."

Thus France began to hear the cry of persecution raised against the Gospel. The priestly and the civil power,—the Sorbonne and the Parliament laid their hands upon the sword, and that sword was destined to be stained with blood. Christianity had taught men that there are duties anterior to all civil relationships; it had emancipated the religious mind, laid the foundations of liberty of conscience, and wrought an important change in society;—for Antiquity, everywhere recognizing the *citizen* and nowhere the *man*, had made of religion a matter of mere state regulation. But scarcely had these ideas of liberty been given to the world when the Papacy corrupted them. In place of the despotism of the prince, it substituted that of the priest. Often, indeed, had both prince and priest been by it stirred up against the Christian people. A new emancipation was needed: the sixteenth century produced it. Wherever the Reformation established itself, the yoke of Rome was thrown off, and liberty of conscience restored. Yet is there such a proneness in man to exalt him-

---

* MS. in the Royal Library S.F. No. 337.

self above the truth, that even among many Protestant nations
of our own time, the Church, freed from the arbitrary power
of the priest, is near falling again into subserviency to the
civil authority ; thus, like its divine Founder, bandied from
one despotism to another ; still passing from Caiaphas to Pilate, and from Pilate to Caiaphas !

Briçonnet, who enjoyed a high reputation at Paris, easily
cleared himself. But in vain did he seek to defend his friends ;
the monks were resolved not to return to Meaux empty
handed. If the bishop would escape, he must sacrifice his
brethren. Of a character naturally timid, and but little prepared for ' Christ's sake' to give up his possessions and standing,—alarmed, agitated, and desponding, he was still further
misled by treacherous advisers : " If the evangelical divines
should leave Meaux," said some, " they will carry the Reformation elsewhere." His heart was torn by a painful struggle.
At length the wisdom of this world prevailed : on the 12th
of April, 1523, he published an *ordonnance* by which he deprived those pious teachers of their licence to preach. This
was the first step in Briçonnet's downward career.

Lefevre was the chief object of enmity. His commentary
on the four Gospels, and especially the epistle " to Christian
readers," which he had prefixed to it, inflamed the wrath of
Beda and his fellows. They denounced the work to the
faculty—" Has he not ventured," said the fiery syndic, " to
recommend to all the faithful the reading of the Holy Scriptures ? Does he not affirm that whosoever loves not the word
of Christ is no Christian ;* and again, that the word of God
is sufficient of itself to lead us to eternal life ?"

But Francis I. saw nothing more in this accusation than a
theological squabble. He appointed a commission, before
which Lefevre successfully defended himself, and was honourably acquitted.

Farel, who had fewer protectors at court, found himself
obliged to quit Meaux. It appears that he at first repaired to

* **Qui verbum ejus hoc modo non diligunt, quo pacto hi Christiani
essent.** (Præf. Comm. in Evang.)

Paris,* and that having there unsparingly assailed the errors of Rome, he again found himself obliged to remove, and left that city, retiring to Dauphiny, whither he was desirous of carrying the Gospel.

To have intimidated Lefevre, and caused Briçonnet to draw back, and Farel to seek refuge in flight, was a victory gained, so that the Sorbonne already believed they had mastered the movement. Monks and doctors exchanged congratulations; but enough was not done in their opinion,—blood had not flowed. They went, therefore, again to their work, and blood, since they were bent on shedding it, was now to slake the thirst of Roman fanaticism.

The evangelical Christians of Meaux, seeing their pastors dispersed, sought to edify one another. A wool-carder, John Leclerc, who had imbibed the true christian doctrine from the instructions of the divines, the reading of the Bible, and some tracts,† distinguished himself by his zeal and his expounding of the Scripture. He was one of those men whom the Spirit of God inspires with courage,‡ and places in the foremost rank of a religious movement. The Church of Meaux soon came to regard him as its minister.

The idea of one universal priesthood, known in such living power to the first Christians had been revived by Luther§ in the sixteenth century. But this idea seems then to have dwelt only in theory in the Lutheran Church, and was really acted out only among the congregations of the Reformed Churches. The Lutheran congregations (agreeing in this point with the Anglican Church) took, it seems, a middle course between the Romish and the Reformed Churches. Among the Lutherans, everything proceeded from the pastor or priest; and nothing was counted valid in the Church but what was regularly conveyed through its rulers. But the Reformed Churches,

* "Farel, après avoir subsisté tant qu'il put à Paris." (Bezæ Hist. Eccles. i. 6.)
† Aliis pauculis libellis diligenter lectis. (Bezæ Icones.)
‡ Animosæ fidei plenus. (Ibid.)
  Vide vol. ii. pp. 87, 88.

while they maintained the divine appointment of the ministry —by some sects denied,—approached nearer to the primitive condition of the apostolical communities. From this time forward, they recognized and proclaimed that the flock are not to rest satisfied with receiving what the priest gives out; that, since the Bible is in the hands of every one, the members of the Church, as well as those who take the lead, possess the key of that treasury whence the latter derive their instructions; that the gifts of God, the spirit of faith, of wisdom, of consolation, and of knowledge are not imparted to the minister alone; but that each is called upon to employ for the good of all whatever gift he has received: and that it may often happen that some gift needful for the edification of the Church may be denied to the pastor, and granted to some member of his flock. Thus the mere passive state of the Churches was changed into one of general activity; and it was in France especially that this transformation took place. In other countries, the Reformers are found almost exclusively among the ministers and doctors; but in France, the men who had read or studied had for fellow-labourers men of the lowest class. Among God's chosen servants in that country we have a doctor of the Sorbonne and a wool-comber.

Leclerc began to visit from house to house, strengthening and confirming the disciples in their faith. But not resting satisfied with these ordinary labours, he longed to see the papal edifice overthrown, and France coming forward to embrace the Gospel. His ungovernable zeal was such as to remind an observer of Hottinger at Zurich, and Carlstadt at Wittemberg. He wrote a proclamation against the Antichrist of Rome, in which he announced that the Lord was about to consume that wicked one with the spirit of his mouth, and proceeded boldly to post his placard at the very door of the cathedral.* Soon all was confusion in the neighbourhood of the ancient edifice. The faithful were amazed, the priests

---

* Cet hérétique écrivit des pancartes qu'il attacha aux portes de la grande église de Meaux (MS de Meaux.) See also Bèze Icones, Crespin, Actes des Martyrs, &c.

enraged. What! shall a base wool-comber be allowed to
assail the Pope? The Franciscans were furious. They
insisted that at least on this occasion a terrible example should
be made,—Leclerc was thrown into prison.*

His trial took place in the presence of Briçonnet himself,
who was now to witness and endure all that was done. The
wool-comber was condemned to be publicly whipped through
the city, three successive days, and on the third day to be
branded on the forehead. The mournful spectacle began.
Leclerc was led through the streets, his hands bound, his back
bare, and receiving from the executioners the blows he had
drawn upon himself by his opposition to the bishop of Rome.
A great crowd followed the martyr's progress, which was
marked by his blood: some pursued the heretic with yells:
others, by their silence, gave no doubtful signs of sympathy
with him; and one woman encouraged the martyr by her
looks and words—she was his mother.

At length, on the third day, when the bloody procession
was over, Leclerc was made to stop at the usual place of execution. The executioner prepared to fire, heated the iron
which was to sear the flesh of the minister of the Gospel, and
approaching him branded him as a heretic on his forehead.
Just then a shriek was uttered—but it came not from the
martyr. His mother, a witness of the dreadful sight, wrung
with anguish, endured a violent struggle between the enthusiasm of faith and maternal feelings; but her faith overcame,
and she exclaimed in a voice that made the adversaries tremble, "Glory be to Jesus Christ and his witnesses."* Thus
did this Frenchwoman of the 16th century have respect to
that word of the Son of God,—"Whosoever loveth his son
more than me is not worthy of me." So daring a courage at
such a moment might have seemed to demand instant punishment; but that Christian mother had struck powerless the
hearts of priests and soldiers. Their fury was restrained by
a mightier arm than theirs. The crowd falling back and

* Hist. Ecclés. de Th. de Bezæ, p. 4. Hist. des Martyrs de Crespin,
p. 93.

making way for her, allowed the mother to regain, with faltering step, her humble dwelling. Monks, and even the town-serjeants themselves, gazed on her without moving; "not one of her enemies," says Theodore Beza, "dared put forth his hand against her." After this punishment, Leclerc, being set at liberty, withdrew, first to Rosay en Bric, a town six leagues from Meaux, and subsequently to Metz, where we shall again meet with him.

The enemy was triumphant. "The Cordeliers having regained possession of the pulpit, propagated their accustomed falsehoods and absurdities."[*] But the poor working-people of Meaux, no longer permitted to hear the word of God in regular assemblies, began to hold their meetings in private, "imitating," says the chronicler, "the sons of the prophets in the days of Ahab, and the Christians of the early church; assembling, as opportunity offered, at one time in a house, at another in a cavern, and at times in a vineyard or a wood. On such occasions, he among them who was most conversant with the Holy Scriptures, exhorted the rest; and this being done, they all prayed together with much fervency, cheered by the hope that the Gospel would be received in France, and the tyranny of Antichrist be at an end."[†] Where is the power can arrest the progress of truth?

One victim, however, did not satisfy the persecutors; and if the first against whom their anger was let loose was but a wool-comber, the second was a gentleman of the court. It was become necessary to overawe the nobles as well as the people. The Sorbonne of Paris was unwilling to be outstripped by the Franciscans of Meaux. Berquin, "the most learned among the nobles," continuing to gather more confidence from the Scriptures, had composed certain epigrams against the "drones of the Sorbonne;" and had afterwards gone so far as to charge them with impiety.[‡]

Beda and Duchesne, who had not ventured any reply in their usual style to the witticisms of a gentleman of the court,

---

* Actes des Martyrs, p. 183.   † Ibid.
‡ Impietatis etiam accusatos, tum voce, tum scriptis.   (Bezæ Icones.)

adopted a different line of conduct when they discerned that
serious convictions were at the bottom of these attacks. Berquin had become a *Christian ;* his ruin was therefore decided
on. Beda and Duchesne having seized some of his translations, found in them sufficient to bring more than one heretic
to the stake: " He asserts," they exclaimed, " that it is wrong
to invoke the Virgin Mary in place of the Holy Spirit, and
to call her the *source of all grace!** He declares himself
against the custom of speaking of her as *our hope* and *our life*,
and says that these titles belong only to the Son of God."
There were other charges against Berquin ;—his closet was
as it were a library, whence the supposed tainted works were
diffused through the kingdom. Above all, Melancthon's
Loci Communes served to stagger the more learned. The
man of piety, entrenched amid his folios and *tracts*, had, in
his christian love, made himself translator, corrector, printer,
and bookseller. . . . . It seemed indispensable to stop the
stream at its source.

Accordingly, one day, while Berquin was quietly engaged
n his studies, the house was of a sudden surrounded by armed
men, demanding admittance. The Sorbonne and its agents,
armed with authority from the Parliament, were at his door.
Beda, the dreaded syndic, was at their head, and never did
inquisitor more perfectly perform his function. Followed by
his satellites, he made his way to Berquin's study, communicated the object of his mission, and desiring his followers to
keep an eye upon him, commenced his search. Not a volume
escaped his notice, and an exact inventory was made under
his direction. Here lay a treatise by Melancthon ; there a
pamphlet by Carlstadt; farther on a work of Luther's ;—here
'heretical' books which Berquin had translated from Latin
into French ; there—others of his own composition. With
two exceptions, all the books seized abounded with Lutheran
doctrine, and Beda quitted the house, carrying away his booty,

* Incongrue beatam Virginem invocari pro Spiritu Sancto. (Erasmi
Epp. 1279.)

and more elated than a general laden with the spoil of conquered nations.[*]

Berquin perceived that a violent storm had burst upon his head, but his courage did not falter:—he had too much contempt for his adversaries to fear them. Meanwhile, Beda lost no time. On the 31st May, 1523, the Parliament decreed that all the books seized at Berquin's house should be laid before the faculty of theology. Its decision was soon made known, and on the 25th of June, it condemned all the works, except the two already mentioned, to be burnt as heretical; and enjoined that Berquin should be required to abjure his errors. The Parliament ratified the decision. Berquin appeared at the bar of this formidable body: he knew that the next step beyond it might be to the scaffold; but, like Luther at Worms, he stood firm. It was in vain that the Parliament insisted on his retracting; he was not of those who fall away after being made partakers of the Holy Ghost. *He that is begotten of God keepeth himself, and that wicked one touched him not.*[†] Every such fall proves that conversion has either been only apparent, or else partial;[‡] now Berquin's was a real conversion. He answered the court before which he stood with decision; and the Parliament, using more severity than the Diet of Worms, directed its officers to take the accused into custody, and lead him away to prison. This took place on the 1st of August, 1523. On the 5th, the Parliament handed over the heretic to the Bishop of Paris, in order that that prelate might take cognizance of the affair, and jointly with the doctors and counsellors, pass sentence on the culprit. Berquin was forthwith transferred to the official prison.[§]

Beda, Duchesne, and their companions had their victim in their clutches; but the court bore no favour to the Sorbonne,

* Gaillard Hist. de Francois I. iv. 241. Crévier, Univ. de Paris. v. p. 171.

† Hebrews vii 4. I John v. 18.

‡ This is believed to be a faithful rendering of the original. The interpretation and the application may be open to question.—(Tr.)

§ Ductus est in carcerem, reus hæreseos periclitatus. (Erasmi Epp. 1979. Crévier, Gaillard, loc. cit.)

and Francis was more powerful than Beda. A feeling of indignation spread among the nobles: what do these monks and
priests mean, not to respect the rank of a gentleman? What
charge do they bring against him?—was the question asked
in the presence of Francis. Is it that he blames the practice
of invoking the Virgin instead of the Holy Spirit? But Erasmus and many more have censured it. Is it on such frivolous
charges they go the length of imprisoning an officer of the
king?[*] This attack of theirs is a blow struck against knowledge and true religion; an insult to nobles, knights, and
royalty itself. The king decided on again making the Sorbonne feel the weight of his authority. He issued letters summoning the parties in the cause before his council, and on the
8th of August a messenger presented himself at the official
prison, bearing a royal mandate enjoining that Berquin should
be at liberty.

It seemed at first doubtful whether the monks would yield
compliance. Francis had anticipated some difficulty, and, in
charging the messenger with the execution of his orders, had
added, " If you meet with any resistance, I authorize you to
break open the doors." There was no misunderstanding these
words. The monks and the Sorbonne submitted to the affront
put upon them ; and Berquin, released from durance, appeared
before the king's council, and was there acquitted.[†]

Thus did Francis I. humble the ecclesiastical power. Under
his reign Berquin fondly hoped that France might free herself from the Papal yoke; and he began to meditate a renewal
of hostilities. With this intent, he opened communications
with Erasmus, who at once acknowledged his right intentions.[‡]
But the philosopher, ever timid and temporizing, replied,—
" Remember to avoid irritating the drones; and pursue your

---

[*] Ob hujusmodi nœnias. (Erasm. Epp. 1279.)

[†] At judices, ubi viderunt causam esse nullius momenti, absolverunt
hominem. (Ibid.)

[‡] Ex epistola visus est mihi vir bonus. (Ibid.)

studies in peace.* Above all, do not implicate me in your affairs, for that will be of no service to either of us."†

Berquin was not discouraged. If the great genius of the age draws back, he will put his trust in God who never deserts His work. God's work *will* be effected,—either *by* humble instrumentality, or *without* it. Erasmus himself acknowledged that Berquin, like the palm tree, rose in renewed vigour from every new gust of persecution that assailed him.‡

Not such were all who had embraced the Evangelical doctrines. Martial Mazurier had been one of the most zealous of preachers. He was accused of having advocated very erroneous opinions;§ and even of having committed, while at Meaux, certain acts of violence. " This Martial Mazurier, being at Meaux,"—such are the words of a manuscript preserved in that city, and which we have already had occasion to quote,—" entering the church of the reverend Fathers, the Cordeliers, and seeing the statue of St. Francis, in high relief, outside the door of the convent, where that of St. Roch is now placed, struck it down, and broke it." Mazurier was arrested, and thrown into prison, where he at once fell back upon his own reflections and the keenest perplexity.‖ It was the Gospel rule of morals, rather than its great doctrines, that had won him over to the ranks of the Reformers; and that rule, taken alone, brought with it no strength. Terrified at the prospect of the stake awaiting him, and believing that, in France, the victory would be sure to remain with Rome, he easily persuaded himself that he should have more influence and honour by going back to the Papacy. Accordingly, he recanted his former teaching, and directed that doctrines altogether opposed to those ascribed to him should be preached in

* Sineret crabrones et suis se studiis oblectaret. (Erasmi Epp. 1279.)
† Deinde ne me involveret suæ causæ. (Ibid.)
‡ Ille, ut habebat quiddam cum palmâ commune, adversus deterrentem tollebat animos. (Ibid.) There is probably an allusion to Pliny, Hist. Naturalis, xvi. 42.
§ Historie l'Université par Crevier, v. p. 203.
‖ Gaillard, Hist. de Francois I. v. p. 234.

his parish ;* and uniting, at a later period, with most fanatical of the Romish party,—and particularly with the celebrated Ignatius Loyola,†—he became thenceforward the most zealous supporter of the Papal cause. From the days of the Emperor Julian apostates have ever been among the sternest enemies of the doctrines which they once professed.

An occasion soon offered for Mazurier to make proof of his zeal. The youthful James Pavanne had also been thrown into prison. Martial hoped to cover his own shame by involving another in the like fall. The youth, the amiable disposition, the learning, and the integrity of Pavanne, created a general interest in his favour ; and Mazurier imagined that he himself should be deemed less culpable if he could but persuade Master James to a similar course. Visiting him in his cell, he began by pretending that he had advanced further in inquiry into the truth than Pavanne had done. " You are under a mistake James," he often repeated to him : " You have not gone deep into these matters : you have made acquaintance only with the agitated surface of them."‡ Sophisms, promises, threats, were freely resorted to. The unfortunate youth, deceived, disturbed, and perplexed, yielded to these perfidious advances ; and on the morrow of Christmas day, 1524, he publicly abjured his pretended errors. But from that hour a spirit of melancholy and remorse sent by the Almighty, weighed heavy on his soul. Deep sadness consumed him, and his sighs were unceasing. " Ah !" he repeated, " for me life has nothing left but bitterness." Such are the mournful consequences of apostacy.

Nevertheless, among those Frenchmen who had received the word of God were found men of more intrepid hearts than Pavanne and Mazurier. Towards the end of 1523, Leclerc settled at Metz, in Lorraine, " and there," says Theodora Beza,

* " Comme il etait homme adroit, il esquiva la condamnation," says Creviér, v. p. 203.

† Cum Ignatio Loyolâ init amicitiam. (Launoi Navarræ gymnasii historia, p. 621.)

‡ Actes des Martyrs, p. 99.

" he acted on the example of St. Paul, who, while labouring at Corinth as a tent-maker, persuaded both the Jews and the Greeks."*   Leclerc, while pursuing his industry as a wool-comber, instructed those of his own condition; and among these last there had been several instances of real conversion. Thus did this humble artizan lay the foundations of a church which afterwards became celebrated.

But at Metz, Leclerc did not stand alone.   Among the ecclesiastics of that city was one John Châtelain, an Augustine monk of Tournay, and doctor of theology, who had been brought to the knowledge of God,† through his acquaintance with the Augustines of Antwerp.   Châtelain had gained the reverence of the people by the strictness of his morals;‡ and the doctrine of Christ, when preached by him, attired in cope and stole, appeared less strange to the inhabitants of Metz, than when it proceeded from the lips of a poor artizan, laying aside the comb with which he carded his wool, to take up and explain a French version of the Gospels.

By the active zeal of these two men the light of evangelical truth began to be diffused throughout the city.   A very devout woman named Toussaint, one of the middle class of the people, had a son called Peter, with whom, in the hours of his childish sports, she would often speak of serious things. Every one, even to the humblest, lived then in expectation of some extraordinary event.   One day the child was amusing himself in riding on a stick, in a room where his mother was conversing with some friends on the things of God, when she said, in a voice of emotion, " Antichrist will soon come with great power, and will destroy such as shall have been converted by the preaching of Elias."§   These words being fre-

---

* Acts of the Apostles, xviii. 3, 4.   Apostoli apud Corinthios exemplum secutus. (Bezæ Icones.)

† Vocatus ad cognitionem Dei. (Act. Mart. 180.)

‡ Gaillard, Hist. de Francois I. v. p. 232.

§ Cum equitabam in arundine longâ, memini sæpe audisse me a matre, venturum Antichristum cum potentiâ magnâ perditurumque eos qui essent ad Eliæ prædicationem conversi. (Tossanus Farello, 4 Sept. 1525, from a MS. of the conclave of Neufchâtel.)

quently repeated, arrested the attention of the child, and he afterwards recalled them. At the time when the doctor of heology and the wool-comber were engaged in preaching the Gospel at Metz, Peter Toussaint was grown up. His relations and friends, wondering at his precocious genius, conceived the hope of seeing him in an exalted station in the Church. An uncle on his father's side was *primicier*, or head of the chapter of Metz.* The cardinal John of Lorraine, son of Duke Réné, who kept a large establishment, expressed much regard for the *primicier* and his nephew, the latter of whom, notwithstanding his youth, had just before obtained a prebend, when his attention was drawn to the study of the Gospel. Why may not the preaching of Châtelain and Leclerc be that of Elias? It is true, Antichrist is everywhere arming against it. But what matter? "Let us," said he, "lift up our heads, looking to the Lord, who will come and will not tarry."† The light of truth was beginning to find entrance among the principal families of Metz. The knight Esch, an intimate friend of the *primicier*, or dean, and much respected, had been recently converted.‡ The friends of the Gospel were rejoicing in this event:—Pierre was accustomed to term him "our worthy master the knight;" adding with noble candour, "if we may be allowed to call any man master on earth."§

Thus Metz was about to become a focus of light when the rash zeal of Leclerc abruptly arrested its slow but sure progress, and excited a commotion which threatened ruin to the infant church. The populace of Metz had continued to observe their accustomed superstitions, and Leclerc's spirit was stirred within him at the sight of the city almost wholly given to idolatry. One of their high festivals drew nigh. About a league distant from the city stood a chapel inclosing

---

* Tossanus Farello, 21st July, 1525.

† Ibid. 4th Sept. 1525.

‡ Clarissimum illum equitem . . . cui multum familiaritæ et amicitiæ, cum primicerio Metensi, patruo meo. (Toss. Farello, 2d Aug. 1524.)

§ Ibid. 21st July, 1525. MS. of Neufchâtel.

statues of the Virgin and of the most venerated saints of the surrounding country, whither the people of Metz were in the habit of resorting in pilgrimage on a certain day in the year, to worship these images and obtain the pardon of their sins.

On the eve of this festival the pious and the courageous spirit of Leclerc was deeply agitated. Had not God said— *" Thou shalt not bow down to their gods, but thou shalt utterly overthrow them, and quite break down their images."*[*] Leclerc understood the words as addressed to himself, and without conferring with Châtelain, Esch, or any of those who he may have expected would dissuade him, quitted the city, and approached the chapel. There he collected his thoughts as he sat silently before these statues. As yet the way was open to him to retire; but to-morrow—in a few hours—the entire population of a city, which ought to be worshipping God alone, will be bowing before these blocks of wood and stone. A struggle ensued in the heart of the humble wool-carder, similar to that which was so often endured in the hearts of the early Christians. What signified the difference, that here it was the images of the saints of the neighbouring country, and not of heathen gods and goddesses—did not the worship rendered to these images belong of right to God alone? Like Polyeucte before the idols of the temple, his heart shuddered, and his courage was roused:

> Ne perdons plus le temps, le sacrifice est prêt,
> Allons y du vrai Dieu soutenir l'interet ;
> Allons fouler aux pieds ce foudre ridicule
> Dont arme un bois pourri ce peuple trop crédule
> Allons en éclairer l'aveuglement fatal,
> Allons briser ces dieux de pierre et de métal
> Abandonnons nos jours, à cette ardeur celeste—
> Faisons triompher Dieu ; qu'il dispose du reste.
>
> *Corneille, Polyeucte.*[†]

Leclerc accordingly rose from his seat, and approaching the images, removed and broke them, in his holy indignation

---

[*] Exodus xx. 4; xxiii. 24.

[†] Polyeucte, by P. Corneille. What many admire in poetry, they pass condemnation on in history.

scattering the fragments before the altar. He did not doubt that this action was by special inspiration of the spirit of the Lord, and Theodore Beza was of the same judgment.[*]—This done, Leclerc returned to Metz, re-entering it at day-break. and noticed only a few persons at the moment of his passing the gate of the city.[†]

Meanwhile all were in motion in the ancient city of Metz. The bells rang, the various religious bodies mustered, and the entire population, headed by the priests and monks, left the city, reciting prayers and chanting hymns to the saints whom they were on their way to worship. Crosses and banners went forward in orderly procession, and drums and instruments of music mingled with the hymns of the faithful. After an hours march, the procession reached the place of pilgrimage. But what was the astonishment of the priests, when advancing with censers in hand, they beheld the images they had come to worship mutilated, and their fragments strewed upon the earth. They drew back appalled,—and announced to the crowd of worshippers the sacrilege that had been committed. Instantly the hymns were hushed—the music stopped —the banners were lowered, and agitation pervaded the assembled multitude. Canons, curates, and monks, laboured still further to inflame their anger and excited them to search out the guilty person, and require that he should be put to death.[‡] A shout was raised on all sides. "Death—Death to the sacrilegious wretch." They returned in haste and disorder to the city.

Leclerc was known to all; several times he had been heard to call the images *idols;* moreover he had been observed at day-break returning from the direction of the chapel. He was apprehended, and at once confessed the fact, at the same time conjuring the people to worship God alone. But his appeal only the more inflamed the rage of the multitude, who

* Divini spiritus afflatu impulsus. (Bezæ Icones.)
† Mane apud urbis portam deprehensus.
‡ Totam civitatem concitarunt ad auctorem ejus facinoris quærendum. (Act. Mart. lat. p. 189.)

would have dragged him to instant execution.   Placed before
his judges, he courageously declared that Jesus Christ—God
manifest in the flesh—ought to be the sole object of worship;—
and was sentenced to be burnt alive!   He was conducted to
the place of execution.

Here an awful scene awaited him: his persecutors had been
devising all that could render his sufferings more dreadful
At the scaffold they were engaged heating pincers, as instru
ments of their cruelty.   Leclerc heard with calm composure
the savage yells of monks and people.   They began by cutting off his right hand; then taking up the red hot pincers,
they tore away his nose; after this, with the same instrument,
they lacerated his arms, and having thus mangled him in
many places, they ended by applying the burnings to his
breasts.*   All the while that the cruelty of his enemies was
venting itself on his body, his soul was kept in perfect peace.
He ejaculated solemnly,†—" *Their idols are silver and gold,
the work of men's hands.   They have mouths, but they speak
not: eyes have they, but they see not: they have ears, but they
hear not: noses have they, but they smell not: they have
hands, but they handle not: feet have they, but they walk not:
neither speak they through their throat.   They that make
them are like unto them; so is every one that trusteth in them.
O Israel, trust thou in the Lord: he is their help and their
shield.*"   The enemies were awed by the sight of so much
composure,—believers were confirmed in their faith,‡ and the
people, whose indignation had vented itself in the first burst
of anger, were astonished and affected.§   After undergoing
these tortures, Leclerc was burned by a slow fire in conformity
to the sentence.   Such was the death of the first martyr of the
Gospel in France.

But the priests of Metz did not rest there: in vain had they

* Naso candentibus forcipibus abrepto, iisdemque brachio utroque, ipsis
que mammis crudelissime perustis. (Bezæ Icones.) MS. of Meaux ·
Crespin, &c.

† Altissima voce recitans. (Bezæ Icones.) Psalm cxv. 4—9.

‡ Adversariis territis, piis magnopere confirmatis. (Ibid.)

§ Nemo qui non commoveretur, attonitus. (Act. Mart. lat. p. 189.)

laboured to shake the fidelity of Châtelain—" He is like the deaf adder," said they, " he refuses to hear the truth."* He was arrested by the servants of the Cardinal of Lorraine, and transferred to the castle of Nommeny.

After this he was degraded by the officers of the bishop, who stripped him of his vestments, and scraped the tips of his fingers with a piece of broken glass, saying, "' Thus do we take away the power to sacrifice, consecrate, and bless, which thou didst formerly receive by the anointing of thy hands."† Then throwing over him the habit of a layman, they handed him over to the secular power, which doomed him to be burnt alive. The fire was quickly lighted, and the servant of Christ consumed in the flames. " Nevertheless," observe the historians of the Gallican Church, who, in other respects, are loud in commendation of these acts of rigour, " Lutheranism spread through all the district of Metz."

From the moment this storm had descended on the church of Metz, distress and alarm had prevailed in the household of Touissaint. His uncle, the dean, without taking an active part in the measures resorted to against Leclerc and Châtelain, shuddered at the thought that his nephew was one among those people. His mother's fears were still more aroused: not a moment was to be lost : all who had given ear to the evangelic doctrine felt their liberty and lives to be in danger. The blood shed by the inquisitors had but increased their thirst for more. New scaffolds would ere long be erected : Pierre Touissaint, the knight Esch, and others besides, hastily quitted Metz, and sought refuge at Basle.

Thus violently did the storm of persecution rage at Meaux and at Metz. Repulsed from the northern provinces, the Gospel for a while seemed to give way; but the Reformation did but change its ground, and the south-eastern provinces became the basis and theatre of the movement.

Farel, who had retired to the foot of the Alps, was labour-

* Instar aspidis serpentis aures omni surditate affectas. (Act. Mart. lat. p. 183.)

† Utriusque manus digitos lamina vitrea erasit. (Ibid. p. 66.)

ing actively in his work. It was a small thing to him to enjoy in the bosom of his family the sweets of domestic life.
The report of the events that had taken place at Meaux and
at Paris had communicated a degree of terror to his brothers ;
but a secret influence attracted them toward those new and
wondrous truths which their brother William was in the habit
of dwelling upon. The latter, with all the earnestness of his
character, besought them to be converted to the Gospel;* and
Daniel, Walter, and Claude were at length won over to that
God whom their brother declared to them. They did not at
first relinquish the worship of their forefathers, but when persecution arose, they boldly suffered the loss of friends, property, and country, for the liberty to worship Christ.†

The brothers of Luther and Zwingle do not appear to have
been so decidedly converted to the Gospel. The Reformation
in France had from its outset a peculiarly domestic character.

Farel's exhortations were not confined to his brothers. He
made known the truth to his relatives and friends at Gap and
its vicinity. It would even appear, if we give credit to one
manuscript, that, availing himself of the friendship of certain
ecclesiastics, he began to preach the Gospel in some of the
churches;‡ but other authorities affirm that he did not at this
time occupy the pulpit. However that may be, the opinions
he professed were noised abroad, and both priests and people
insisted that he should be silenced: " What new and strange
heresy is this ?" said they ; " how can we think that all the
practices of devotion are useless ? The man is neither monk
nor priest : he has no business to preach."§

It was not long before the whole of the authorities, civil and
ecclesiastical, were combined against Farel. It was sufficiently evident he was acting with that sect which was every-

* MS. of Choupard.
† Farel, says a French MS. preserved at Geneva, was a gentleman in
station, of ample fortune, which he gave up for the sake of his religion,—
as did also three of his brothers.
‡ Il precha l'Evangile publiquement avec une grande liberté. (MS.
of Choupard.)
§ Ibid. Hist. des Evêq. de Nismes, 1738.

where spoken against. " Let us cast out from amongst us," cried they, " this firebrand of discord." Farel was summoned before the judges, roughly handled, and forcibly expelled the city."*

Yet he did not forsake his country,—the open plains and villages,—the banks of the Durance,—of the Guisanne,—of the Isere,—was there not many a soul in those localities that stood in need of the Gospel ? and if he should run any risk, were not those forests, caverns, and steep rocks, which had been the familiar haunts of his childhood, at hand to afford him their shelter ? He began therefore to traverse the country, preaching in private dwellings and secluded meadows, and retiring for shelter to the woods and overhanging torrents.† It was a training by which God was preparing him for other trials: " Crosses, persecutions, and the lyings-in-wait of Satan, of which I had intimation, were not wanting," said he ; "they were even much more than I could have borne in my own strength, but God is my father : He has ministered, and will for ever minister to me all needful strength."‡ Very many of the inhabitants of these countries received the truth from his lips ; and thus the same persecution that drove Farel from Paris and Meaux was the means of diffusing the Reformation in the countries of the Saone, the Rhone, and the Alps. In all ages, it has been found that they who have been scattered abroad, *have gone everywhere preaching the word of God.*§

Among the Frenchmen who were at this time gained over to the Gospel, was a Dauphinese gentleman, the Knight Anemond de Coct, the younger son of the auditor of Coct, the lord of Chatelard. Active, ardent, truly pious, and opposed to the generally received veneration of relics, processions and

* Il fut chassé, votre fort rudement, tant par l'eveque que par ceux de la ville. (MS. of Choupard.)

† Olim errabundus in sylvis, in nemoribus, in aquis vagatus sum. (Farel ad Capit. de Bucer· Basil 25th Oct. 1526. MS. of Neufchâtel.)

‡ Non defuere crux, persecutio et Satanæ machinamenta . . . (Farel Galeoto.)

§ Acts viii.

clergy, Anemond readily received the evangelic doctrine, and
was soon entirely devoted to it.   He could not patiently endure the formality that reigned around him, and it was his
wish to see all the ceremonies of the Church abolished.   The
religion of the heart, the inward worship of the Spirit, was
everything in his estimation : " Never," said he, " has my
mind found any rest in externals.   The sum of Christianity is
in that text,—' John truly baptized with water, but ye shall be
baptized with the Holy Ghost.'   We must become ' new
creatures.' "*

Coct, endued with the vivacity of his nation, spoke and
wrote one day in French, the next in Latin.   He read and
quoted Donatus, Thomas Aquinas, Juvenal, and the Bible !
His style was brief, and marked by abrupt transitions.   Ever
restless, he would present himself wherever a door seemed to
be open to the Gospel, or a famous teacher was to be heard.
His cordiality won the affection of all his acquaintances.
" He is a man of distinction, both for his birth and his learning," observed Zwingle, at a later period, " but yet more distinguished for his piety and obliging disposition."†   Anemond
is a sort of type of many Frenchmen of the Reformed opinions : vivacity, simplicity, a zeal which passes readily into
imprudence,—such are the qualities often recurring among
those of his countrymen who have embraced the Gospel.   But
at the very opposite extreme of the French character, we behold the grave aspect of Calvin, serving as a weighty counterpoise to the light step of Coct.   Calvin and Anemond are
as the two poles between whom the religious world of France
revolves.

No sooner had Anemond received from Farel the knowledge of Jesus Christ‡ than he set about winning souls to that
doctrine of ' spirit and life.'   His father was no more.   His

* Nunquam in externis quievit spiritus meus.   (Coetus Farello, MS.
of the Conclave of Neufchâtel.)
† Virum est genere, doctrinaque clarum, ita pietate humaniteque longe
clariorem.   (Zw. Epp. p. 319.)
‡ In a letter to Farel, he signs :—*Filius tuus humilis.*   (2 Sept. 1524.)

elder brother,—of a stern and haughty temper,—disdainfully
repulsed his advances. Laurent,—the youngest of the family,
and affectionately attached to him,—seemed but half to enter
into the understanding of his words, and Anemond, disappointed in his own family, turned his activity in another direction.

Hitherto it was among the laity only that this awakening
in Dauphiny had been known. Farel, Anemond, and their
friends, wished much to see a priest taking the lead in the
movement, which promised to make itself felt throughout the
Alps. There dwelt at Grenoble a curate,—a minorite, by
name Pierre de Sebville, famed for the eloquence of his
preaching, right-minded and simple,—" conferring not with
flesh and blood,"—and whom God, by gradual process, was
drawing to the knowledge of Himself.* It was not long before Sebville was brought to the acknowledgment that there
is no unerring Teacher save the word of the Lord; and, relinquishing such teaching as rests only on the witness of men,
he determined in his heart to preach a Gospel, at once " clear,
pure, and holy."† These three words exhibit the complete
character of the Reformation. Coct and Farel rejoiced to
hear this new preacher of Grace, raising his powerful voice
in their country ; and they concluded that their own presence
would thenceforth be less necessary.

The more the awakening spread, the more violently did opposition arise. Anemond, longing to know more of Luther,
Zwingle, and of the countries which had been the birth-place
of the Reformation,—and indignant at finding the Gospel rejected by his own countrymen, resolved to bid farewell to his
country and family. He made his will,—settling his property, then in the hands of his elder brother, the lord of Chatelard, on his brother Laurent.‡ This done, he quitted Dauphiny

---

* Pater cœlestis animum sic tuum ad se traxit. (Zwinglius Sebvillæ,
Epp. p. 320.)

† Nitide, purè, sancteque prædicare in animum inducis. (Ibid.)

‡ " My brother Anemond Coct, when setting forth from this country,
made me his heir." (MS. Letters in the Library at Neufchâtel.)

and France, and passing over, with impetuous haste, countries which were then not traversed without much difficulty, he went through Switzerland, and scarcely stopping at Basle, arrived at Wittemberg, where Luther then was. It was shortly after the second diet of Nuremberg. The French gentleman accosted the Saxon Doctor with his accustomed vivacity,—spoke with enthusiastic warmth concerning the Gospel,—and dwelt largely on the plans he had formed for the propagation of the truth. The grave Saxon smiled as he listened to the southern imagination of the speaker; and Luther,[*] who had some prejudices against the national character of the French, —was won, and carried away by Anemond. The thought that this gentleman had made the journey from France to Wittemberg, for the Gospel's sake, affected him.[†] "Certainly," remarked the Reformer to his friends, "that French knight is an excellent man, and both learned and pious:"[‡] and Zwingle formed a similar opinion of him.

Anemond having seen what had been effected by the agency of Luther and Zwingle, imagined that if they would but take in hand France and Savoy, nothing could stand against them; and accordingly, failing to persuade them to remove thither, he earnestly desired of them that, at least, they would write. He particularly besought Luther to address a letter to Charles Duke of Savoy, brother of Louisa and of Philibert, and uncle to Francis the First and Margaret. "That prince," observed he to Luther, "is much drawn to piety and true religion,[§] and he takes pleasure in conversing concerning the Reformation with certain persons at his court. He is just the one to enter into your views,—for his motto is, ' *Nihil deest timenti bus Deum ;*[‖] and that is your own maxim. Assailed alter-

---

[*] "Mire ardens in Evangelium," said Luther to Spalatin. (Epp. ii. p. 340.) "Sehr brünstig in der Herrlichkeit des Evangelii," said he to the Duke of Savoy. (Ibid. p. 401.)

[†] Evangelii gratia huc profectus e Gallia. (L. Epp. ii. p. 340.)

[‡] Hic Gallus eques . . . optimus vir est, eruditus ac pius. (Ibid.)

[§] Ein grosser Leibhaber der wahren Religion und Gottseligkeit. (Ibid. p. 401.)

[‖] "They that fear God shall want no good thing." (Hist. Gen. de la Maison de Savoie par Guichenon, ii. p. 226.)

nately by the Empire and by France, humbled, broken in spirit, and continually in danger, his heart knows its need of God and His grace: all he wants is to be impelled to action: once gained over to the Gospel, his influence would be immense in Switzerland, Savoy, and France. Pray write to him."

Luther was a thorough German, and would not have been at ease beyond the frontier of his own nation. Yet, in true catholicity of heart, his hand was immediately put out where he recognised brethren; and wherever a word might be spoken with effect, he took care to make it heard. Sometimes on the same day he would write letters to countries separated by the widest distances,—as the Netherlands, Savoy, Livonia.

"Assuredly," he answered Anemond, "a love for the Gospel is a rare and inestimable jewel in a prince's crown."* And he proceeded to write to the Duke a letter which Anemond probably carried with him as far as Switzerland.

"I beg your Highness's pardon," wrote Luther, "if I, a poor and unfriended monk, venture to address you; or rather I would ask of your Highness to ascribe this boldness of mine to the glory of the Gospel,—for I cannot see that glorious light arise and shine in any quarter, without exulting at the sight. . . . My hope is, that my Lord Jesus Christ may win over many souls by the power of your Serene Highness's example. Therefore it is I desire to instruct you in our teaching. We believe that the very beginning of salvation and the sum of Christianity consists in faith in Christ, who, by his blood alone,—and not by any works of ours,—has put away Sin, and destroyed the power of death. We believe that this faith is God's gift, formed in our hearts by the Holy Spirit, and not attained by any effort of our own;—for faith is a principle of life,* begetting man spiritually, and making him a new creature."

* Eine seltsame Gabe und hohes Kleinod unter den Fürsten. (L. Epp. ii. p. 401.)

† Der Glaube ist ein lebendig Ding . . . (Ibid. p. 509.) The Latin is wanting.

Luther passed thence to the effects of faith, and showed that it was not possible to be possessed of that faith without the superstructure of false doctrine and human merits,—built up so laboriously by the Church,—being at once swept away. " If Grace," said he, " is the purchase of Christ's blood, it follows that it is not the purchase of works of ours. Hence the whole train of works of all the cloisters in the world are, —for this purpose,—useless ; and such institutions should be abolished, as opposed to the blood of Jesus Christ, and as leading men to trust in their own good works. Ingrafted in Christ, nothing remains for us but to do good ; because being become good trees, we ought to give proof of it by bearing good fruits."

" Gracious Prince and Lord," said Luther, in conclusion : " May your Highness, having made so happy a beginning, help to spread this doctrine,—not by the sword, which would be a hindrance to the Gospel,—but by inviting to your states teachers who preach the Word. It is by the breath of His mouth that Jesus will destroy Antichrist ; so that, as Daniel describes, he may be broken without hand. Therefore, most Serene Prince, let your Highness cherish that spark that has been kindled in your heart. Let a flame go forth from the house of Savoy, as once from the house of Joseph.* May all France be as stubble before that fire. May it burn, blaze, purify,—that so that renowned kingdom may truly take the title of ' *Most Christian*,'—which it has hitherto received only in reward of blood shed in the cause of Antichrist."

Thus did Luther endeavour to diffuse the Gospel in France. We have no means of knowing the effect of this letter on the Prince ; but we do not find that he ever gave signs of a wish to detach himself from Rome. In 1523, he requested Adrian VI. to be godfather to his first-born son ; and at a later period, we find the Pope promising him a cardinal's hat for his second son. Anemond, after making an effort to be admitted to see the court and Elector of Saxony,† and, for this purpose, pro-

---

. * Das ein Feuer von dem Hause Sophoy ausgehe. (L. Epp. ii. p. 406.)
† Vult videre aulam et faciem Principis nostri. (Ibid. p. 340.)

viding himself with a letter from Luther, returned to Basle, more than ever resolved to risk his life in the cause of the Gospel. In the ardour of his purpose he would have roused the entire nation. " All that I am, or ever can be," said he,— " All I have or ever can have, it is my earnest desire to devote to the glory of God."*

At Basle Anemond found his countryman Farel. The letters of Anemond had excited in him a great desire to be personally acquainted with the Swiss and German Reformers. Moreover Farel felt the need of a sphere in which his activity might be more freely put forth. He accordingly quitted France, which already offered only the scaffold to the preachers of a pure Gospel. Taking to bye-paths, and hiding in the woods, he with difficulty escaped out of the hands of his enemies. Often had he mistaken the direction in which his route lay. " God," observes he, "designs, by my helplessness in these little matters, to teach me how helpless I am in greater things."† At length he entered Switzerland in the beginning of 1524. There he was destined to spend his life in the service of the Gospel,—and then it was that France began to pour into Switzerland those noble heralds of the Gospel who were to seat the Reformation in *Romane* Switzerland, and communicate to it a new and powerful impulse throughout and far beyond the limits of the confederated cantons.

The catholicity of the Reformation is a beautiful character in its history. The Germans pass into Switzerland—the French into Germany—and, at a somewhat later period, we see the English and the Scotch passing to the Continent, and the Continental teachers to Great Britain. The Reformations of the several countries take their rise independently of each other—but as soon as they look around them, their hands are held out to each other. To them there is one Faith, one Spirit, one Lord. It is an error to treat the history of the Refor-

* Quidquid sum, habeo, ero, habebove, ad Dei gloriam insumere mens est. (Coct. Epp. MS. of Neufchâtel.)
† Voluit Dominus per infirma hæc, docere quid possit homo in majoribus. (Farel Capitoni. Ibid.)

mation in connection with any single country;—the work was one and the same in all lands; and the Protestant Churches were from the very beginning, a "whole body fitly joined together."*

Certain persons who had fled from France and Lorraine at this time, formed in the city of Basle a French Church, whose members had escaped from the scaffold. These persons had spread the report of Lefevre, Farel, and the events that had occurred at Meaux; and when Farel entered Switzerland he was already known as one of the most fearless heralds of the truth.

He was immediately introduced to Œcolampadius, who, some time before this, had returned to Basle. Seldom does it happen that two characters more opposite are brought together. Œcolampadius charmed by his gentleness—Farel carried away his hearers by his earnestness—but from the moment they met these two men felt themselves one in heart.† It resembled the first meeting of Luther and Melancthon. Œcolampadius bade him welcome, gave him an apartment in his house, received him at his table, and introduced him to his friends; and it was not long before the learning, piety, and courage of the young Frenchman won the hearts of his new friends. Pellican, Imelia, Wolfhard, and others of the preachers of Basle, were fortified in their faith by the energy of his exhortations. Œcolampadius was just then suffering under depression of spirits:—"Alas," he wrote to Zwingle, "it is in vain I preach—I see no hope of any effect being produced. Perhaps among the *Turks* I might succeed better."‡ "Oh," added he, sighing, "I ascribe the failure to myself alone." But the more he saw of Farel the more his heart felt encouragement; and the courage he derived from the Frenchman laid the ground of an undying affection.

* Eph. iv. 16.

† Amicum semper habui a primo colloquio. (Farel ad Bulling. 27th May. 1556.)

‡ Fortasse in mediis Turcis felicius docuissem. (Zw. et Ecol. Epp. p. 200.)

" Dear Farel," said he to him, " I trust the Lord will make ours a friendship for all eternity—and if we are parted below, our joy will only be the greater when we shall be gathered in presence of Christ in the heavens!"[*]   Pious and affecting thoughts.   The coming of Farel was evidently help from above.

But whilst the Frenchman took delight in the society of Œcolampadius, he drew back with cool independence from a man at whose feet the principal nations of Christendom paid homage.   The prince of scholars—the man whose smile and words were objects of general ambition—the teacher of that age—Erasmus—was passed over by Farel.   The young Dauphinese had declined to pay his respects to the venerated philosopher of Rotterdam—having no relish for those who are never more than half-hearted for truth, and who in the clear understanding of the consequences of error, are nevertheless full of allowances for those who propagate it.   Accordingly we have in Farel that decision which has become one of the distinguishing characters of the Reformation in France, and in those cantons of Switzerland bordering on France—characters which have been by some deemed stiffness, exclusiveness, and intolerance.   A controversy had commenced between Erasmus and Lefevre, arising out of the commentaries put forth by the latter,—and in all companies parties were divided for the one and against the other.[†]   Farel had unhesitatingly ranged himself on the side of his teacher.   But that which chiefly roused his indignation was the cowardly course pursued by the philosopher toward the evangelical party;—Erasmus's doors were closed against them.   That being the case, Farel will not enter them!—to him this was felt to be no loss; convinced as he was that the very ground of a true theology—the piety of the heart—was wanting to Erasmus.   " Frobenius's *wife* knows more of theology than

* Mi Farelle, spero Dominum conservaturum amicitiam nostram immortalem; et si hic conjugi nequimus, tanto beatius alibi apud Christum erit contubernium. (Zw. et Œcol. Epp. p. 201.)

† Nullum est pene convivium . . . (Er. Epp. p. 179.)

he does," remarked Farel; and stung by the intelligence that Erasmus had written to the Pope, advising him how to set about "extinguishing the spread of Lutheranism,"[*] he publicly declared that Erasmus was endeavouring to stifle the Gospel.

This independence of young Farel disturbed the composure of the man of learning. Princes, kings, learned men, bishops, priests, and men of the world, all were ready to offer him the tribute of their admiration:—Luther himself had treated him with respect, so far as he was personally mixed up in this controversy; and this Dauphinese—a nameless refugee—ventured to brave his power. So insolent a freedom caused Erasmus more annoyance than the homage of the world at large could give him joy, and hence he lost no opportunity of venting his spite against Farel. Moreover, in assailing him he contributed to clear himself, in the judgment of the Roman Catholics, of the suspicion of heresy,—"I never met with such a liar,—such a restless seditious spirit as that man,"[†] observed he; "his heart is full of vanity, and his tongue charged with malice."[‡] But the anger of Erasmus did not stop at Farel—it was directed against all the Frenchmen who had sought refuge at Basle, and whose frankness and decision were an offence to him. They paid evidently no respect to persons; and wherever the truth was not frankly confessed, they took no notice of the man, how great soever his genius might be. Wanting, perhaps, in the graciousness of the Gospel, there was in their faithfulness that which reminds one of the prophets of old—and it is truly delightful to contemplate men who stand erect before that to which the world bows down. Erasmus, astonished by this lofty disdain, complained of it in all companies.—"What mean we," wrote he to Melancthon, "to reject pontiffs and bishops, only to submit to the insolence of more cruel ragamuffin tyrants and madmen,[§] for such it is

* Consilium quo sic extinguatur incendium Lutheranum. (Er. Epp. p. 179.)
† Quo nihil vidi mendacius, virulentius, et seditiosius. (Ibid. p. 798.)
‡ Acidæ linguæ et vanissimus. (Ibid. p. 2129.)
§ Scabiosos . . . rabiosos . . . nam nuper nobis misit Gallia. (Ibid. p. 350.)

that France has, given us."—"There are some Frenchmen," he wrote to the Pope's secretary (at the same time sending him his book on Free Will), "who are even more insane than the Germans themselves. They have ever on their lips these five words—*Gospel—Word of God—Faith—Christ—Holy Spirit*—and yet I doubt not but that it is the spirit of Satan that urges them on."[*] In place of Farellus he often wrote *Fallicus*, thus designating as a cheat and deceiver one of the most frank-hearted men of his age.

The rage and anger of Erasmus were at their height, when information arrived that Farel had termed him a *Balaam*. Farel thought that Erasmus, like that prophet, was (perhaps unconsciously) swayed by gifts to curse the people of God. The man of learning, no longer able to restrain himself, resolved to chastise the daring Dauphinese: and one day, when Farel was discussing certain topics of Christian doctrine with some friends, in the presence of Erasmus, the latter rudely interrupted him with the question,—"On what ground do you call me Balaam?"[†] Farel, who was at first disconcerted by the abruptness of the question, soon recovered himself, and made answer that it was not he who had given him that name. Being pressed to say who it was, he mentioned Du Blet of Lyons, who like himself had sought refuge at Basle.[‡] "Perhaps he may have made use of the expression," replied Erasmus, "but it is yourself who taught it him." Then ashamed to have lost his temper, he hastily changed the subject:—"Why is it," asked he, "that you assert that we are not to invoke the saints? Is it because Holy Scripture does not enjoin the practice?"—"It is," answered the Frenchman. "Well," said the man of learning, "I call on you to show from Scripture that we should invoke the Holy Ghost?" Farel gave this clear and solid answer: "If He be God, we

---

[*] Non duitem quin agantur spiritu Satanæ. (Er. Epp. p. 350.)

[†] Diremi disputationem . . . (Ibid. p. 804.)

[‡] Ut diceret negotiatorem quemdam Dupletum hoc dixisse. (Ibid. p. 2129.)

must invoke Him."[*]   "I dropt the conversation," said Erasmus, "for the night was closing in."[†]   From that time, whenever Farel's name came under his pen, the opportunity was taken to represent him as a hateful person, on every account to be shunned.   The Reformer's letters are, on the contrary, marked by moderation as regards Erasmus.   Even in those most constitutionally hasty, the Gospel is a more gracious thing than Philosophy.

The Evangelic doctrine had already many friends in Basle, in the town-council, and among the people; but the Doctors and the University opposed it to the utmost of their power. Œcolampadius and Stor, pastor at Liestal, had maintained certain theses against them.   Farel thought it well to assert in Switzerland also the great maxim of the Evangelic school of Paris and of Meaux,—*God's Word is all-sufficient.*   He requested permission of the University to maintain some theses,—"the rather," he modestly added, "to be reproved if I am in error, than to teach others."[‡]   But the University refused its permission.

Farel then appealed to the Council, and the Council issued public notice, that a Christian man, by name William Farel, having, by the inspiration of the Holy Spirit, prepared certain articles conformable to the Gospel,[§] leave was given him to maintain the same in Latin.   The University forbade all priests and students to be present at the conference, and the Council met the prohibition by one of an opposite tenor.

The following are some of the thirteen propositions that Farel put forth:—

"Christ has left us the most perfect rule of life; no one can lawfully take away, or add anything thereto."

---

* Si Deus est, inquit, invocandus est.   (Er. Epp. p. 804.)

† Omissa disputatione, nam imminebat nox.   (Ibid.)   We have only Erasmus' account of this conversation; he himself reports that Farel gave a very different account of it.

‡ Damit er gelehrt werde, oder irre.   (Fussli Beytr. iv. p. 244.)

§ Aus Eingiessung des heiligen Geistes ein christlicher Mensch und Bruder.   (Ibid.)

" To shape our lives by any other precepts than those of Christ, leads directly to impiety."

" The true ministry of priests is to attend only to the ministry of the Word; and for them there is no higher dignity."

" To take from the *certainty* of the Gospel of Christ, is to destroy it."

" He who thinks to be justified by any strength or merits of his own, and not by *faith*, puts himself in the place of God."

" Jesus Christ, who is head over all things, is our polar star, and the only guide we ought to follow."*

Thus did this native of France stand up at Basle.† A child of the mountains of Dauphiny, brought up at Paris, at the feet of Lefevre, thus boldly proclaimed in the celebrated Swiss University, and in presence of Erasmus, the great principles of the Reformation. Two leading ideas pervaded Farel's theses,—the one involved a return to the Scripture, the other a return to the Faith,—two movements distinctly condemned by the Papacy at the beginning of the eighteenth century as heretical and impious, in the celebrated constitution *Unigenitus*, and which, ever closely connected with each other, in reality overturn the whole of the Papal system. If Faith in Christ is the beginning and end of Christianity, the word of Christ, and not the voice of the Church is that to which we must adhere. Nor is this all; for if Faith unites in one the souls of believers, what signifies an external bond? Can that holy union depend for its existence on croziers, bulls, or tiaras? Faith knits together in spiritual and true oneness all those in whose hearts it has taken up its abode. Thus at one blow disappeared the triple delusion of human deservings, traditions of men, and simulated unity. And these compose the sum of Roman Catholicism.

The discussion was opened in Latin.‡ Farel and Œco-

---

* Guilelmus Farellus Christianis lectoribus, die Martis post Reminiscere. (Fussli Beytr. iv. p. 247.) Fussli does not give the Latin text.

† Schedam conclusionum a Gallo illo. (Zw. Epp. p. 333.)

‡ Schedam conclusionum latine apud nos disputatam. (Ibid.)

lampadius stated and established their articles, calling repeatedly upon those who differed from them to make answer; but none answered to, the call. The sophists, as Œcolampadius terms them, boldly denied them,—but from their skulking corners.* The people therefore began to look with contempt upon the cowardice of their priests, and learned to despise their tyranny.†

Thus did Farel take his stand among the defenders of the Reformation. So much learning and piety rejoiced the hearts of observers, and already more signal victories were looked forward to.—" He is singly more than a match for all the Sorbonne put together,"‡ said they. His openness, sincerity, and candour, charmed all.§ But in the very height of his activity he did not forget that every mission must begin at our own souls. The mild Œcolampadius made with the earnest hearted Farel an agreement, by which they mutually engaged to exercise themselves in humility and gentleness in their familiar intercourse. Thus on the very field of contention were these courageous men engaged in composing their souls to peace.—The impetuous zeal of Luther and of Farel were not unfrequently necessary virtues; for a degree of effort is required to move society and recast the Church. In our days we are very apt to forget this truth, which then was acknowledged by men of the mildest character. "Some there are," said Œcolampadius to Luther, in introducing Farel to him, "who would moderate his zeal against the opposers of the truth; but I cannot help discerning in that same zeal a wonderful virtue, and which, if but well directed, is not less needed than gentleness itself."‖ Posterity has ratified the judgment of Œcolampadius.

* Agunt tamen magnos interim thrasones, sed in angulis lucifugæ. (Zw. Epp. p. 333.)

† Incipit tamen plebs paulatim illorum ignaviam et tyrannidem verbo Dei agnoscere. (Ibid.)

‡ Ad totam Sorbonicam affligendam si non et perdendam. (Œcol. Luthero, Epp. p. 200.)

§ Farello nihil candidius est. (Ibid.)

‖ Verum ego virtutem illam admirabilem et non minus placiditate, si tempestive fuerit, necessariam. (Ibid.)

In the month of May, 1524, Farel, with some friends from Lyons, repaired to Schaffhausen, Zurich, and Constance. Zwingle and Myconius welcomed with the liveliest joy the French refugee, and Farel never forgot the kindness of that welcome. But on his return to Basle he found Erasmus and others of his enemies at work, and received an order to quit the city. His friends loudly expressed their displeasure at this stretch of authority—but in vain, and he was driven from that Swiss territory which was even then regarded as an asylum for signal misfortunes.—" Such is our hospitality !" ejaculated Œcolampadius in indignation : " We are a people like unto Sodom."*

At Basle Farel had contracted a close friendship with the knight D'Esch—the latter resolved to bear him company, and they set forth, provided by Œcolampadius with letters for Capito and Luther, to whom the doctor of Basle commended Farel as the same William who had laboured so abundantly in the work of God.† At Strasburg Farel formed an intimacy with Capito, Bucer, and Hedio—but we have no account of his having gone to Wittemberg.

When God withdraws his servants from the field of combat, it is commonly that they may be again brought forward in increased strength and more completely armed for the conflict. Farel and his companions from Meaux, from Metz, from Lyons, and from Dauphiny, driven by persecution from France, had been tempered with new firmness in Switzerland and in Germany, in the society of the earlier Reformers ; and now, like soldiers scattered by the first charge of the enemy, but instantly collecting again their force, they were about to turn round and go forward in the name of the Lord. Not only on the frontiers, but in the interior of France, the friends of the Gospel were beginning to take courage. The signal was made—the combatants were arming for the assault—the

* Adeo hospitum habemus rationem, veri Sodomitæ. (Zw. Epp. p. 434.)

† Gulielmus ille qui tam probe navavit operam. (Zw. et Œcol. Epp p. 175.)

word was given. "Jesus, his truth and grace"—a word of more power than the clang of arms in the tug of war, filled all hearts with enthusiasm, and all gave omen of a campaign pregnant with new victories and new and more wide-spreading calamities.

Montbeliard at this time stood in need of a labourer in the Gospel. Duke Ulric of Wurtemberg—young, impetuous, and cruel—having been dispossessed of his hereditary states in 1519 by the Suabian league, had retired to that province, his last remaining possession. In Switzerland he became acquainted with the Reformers. His misfortunes had a wholesome effect, and he listened to the truth.[*] Œcolampadius apprized Farel that a door was opened at Montbeliard, and the latter secretly repaired to Basle.

Farel had not regularly entered on the ministry of the word; but at this period of his life we see in him all the qualifications of a servant of the Lord. It was not lightly or rashly that he entered the service of the Church.—" If I considered my own qualifications," said he, " I would not have presumed to preach, but would have preferred to wait till the Lord should send more gifted persons."[†] But he received at this time three several calls. No sooner had he reached Basle than Œcolampadius, moved by the wants of France, besought him to give himself to the work *there*. " Consider," said he, " how little Jesus is made known in their language—will you not teach them a little in their own dialect, to enable them to understand the Scriptures."[‡] At the same time the inhabitants of Montbeliard invited him among them, and lastly, the prince of that country gave his assent to the invitation.[§] Was not this a thrice repeated call from God? . . " I did not see," said he, " how I could refuse to act upon it.[‖] It was in obe-

---

[*] Le prince qui avoit cognoissance de l'Evangile. (Farel. Summaire.)
[†] Summaire c'est à dire, briève déclaration de G. Farel, dans l'epilogue.
[‡] Ibid.
[§] Etant requis et démandé du peuple et du consentement du prince. (Ibid.)
[‖] Summaire, c'est à dire, briève déclaration de G. Farel, dans l'epilogue.

dience to God that I complied with it." Concealed in the house of Œcolampadius, little disposed to take the responsible post offered to him, and yet constrained to yield to so manifest an indication of God's will, Farel undertook the task—and Œcolampadius, calling upon the Lord, ordained him,[*] giving him at the same time some wise counsels.—" The more you find yourselves inclined to vehemence," said he, " the more must you exercise yourself to maintain a gentle bearing;—temper your lion heart with the softness of the dove."[†] The soul of Farel responded to such an appeal.

Thus Farel,—once the devoted adherent of the ancient Church,—was about to enter on the life of a servant of God, and of the Church in its renewed youth. If, in order to a valid ordination, Rome requires the imposition of the hands of a bishop deriving uninterrupted succession and descent from the Apostles, she does so—because she sets the tradition of men above the authority of the word of God. Every church in which the supremacy of the Word is not acknowledged, must needs seek authority from some other source;—and then, what more natural than to turn to the most revered servants of God, and ask *of them* what we do not know that we have in God himself? If we do not speak *in the name of Jesus Christ*, is it not at least something gained to be able to speak in the name of St. John or of St. Paul? One who has with him the voice of antiquity is indeed more than a match for the rationalist, who speaks only his own thought. But Christ's minister has a yet higher authority. He preaches,—not because he is the successor of St. Chrysostom or St. Peter,—but because the Word which he proclaims is from God. Successional authority,—venerable as it may appear,—is yet no more than a thing of man's invention, in place of God's appointment. In Farel's ordination, we see nothing of successionally derived sanction. Nay more, we do not see in it that which

---

[*] Avec l'invocation du nom de Dieu. (Ibid.)

[†] Leoninam magnanimitatem columbina modestia frangas. (Œcol. Epp. p. 198.)

becomes the congregations of the Lord,—among whom every-thing should be done "*decently and in order*," and whose God is "*not the God of confusion*." In his case there was no setting apart by the Church; but then extraordinary emer gencies justify extraordinary measures. At this eventful pe riod, God himself was interposing, and Himself ordaining, by marvellous dispensations, those whom he called to bear a part in the regeneration of society; and *that* was an ordination that abundantly compensated for the absence of the Church's seal. In Farel's ordination we see the unchanging word of God, entrusted to a man of God, to bear it to the world;—the calling of God, and of the people, and the consecration of the heart.—And perhaps no minister of Rome or of Geneva was ever more lawfully ordained for that holy ministry. Farel took his departure for Montbeliard, in company with the knight D'Esch.

Thus did Farel find himself occupying an advanced post. Behind him were Basle and Strasburg, assisting him by their advice and by the productions of their printing presses. Be-fore him lay the provinces of Franchecomté, Burgundy, Lor-raine, Lyons, and other districts of France; wherein men of God were beginning to stand up against error, in the thick darkness. He set himself immediately to preach Christ,—exhorting believers not to suffer themselves to be turned aside from the Holy Scriptures, either by threatenings or artifice. Taking the part long afterwards taken by Calvin on a grander scale, Farel, at Montbeliard, was like a general stationed on a height, surveying, with searching vigilance, the field of battle, cheering those who were actively engaged, rallying those whom the enemy's charge had forced to give way, and by his courage animating those who hung back.* Erasmus wrote directly to his Roman Catholic friends, informing them

---

* The comparison is in the words of a friend who was acquainted with Farel, during his abode at Montbeliard :—Strenuum et oculatum impera-torem, qui iis etiam animum facias qui in acie versantur. (Tossanus Farello, MS. de Neufchâtel, 2d Sept. 1524.)

that a Frenchman, escaped out of France, was making a great noise in these regions.*

The efforts of Farel were not without effect. People wrote to him: " On all sides seem to multiply men who devote their lives to the extension of Christ's kingdom."† The friends of the Gospel gave thanks to God for the daily increasing brilliancy in which the Gospel shone in France.‡ Gainsayers were confounded, and Erasmus, writing to the bishop of Rochester, observed,—"The *faction* is every day spreading, and has penetrated into Savoy, Lorraine, and France."§

For a considerable time Lyons seemed the centre of the Evangelic movement in the interior, as Basle was of that beyond the frontiers. Francis the First, called to the south, on an expedition against Charles V., arrived in those countries, attended by his mother and sister, and by his court. Margaret had with her, in her company, certain men who had embraced the Gospel. "The rest of her people she left behind," remarks a letter written at the time.|| Whilst under the eyes of Francis, 14,000 Swiss, 6,000 Frenchmen, and 1,500 noble knights, were defiling through Lyons, on their way to repel the Imperial army that had invaded Provence, and that great city resounded with the clang of arms, the tramp of cavalry, and the sound of trumpets,—the friends of the Gospel were on their way to the more peaceful triumphs. They were intent on attempting, at Lyons, what they had not been able to realize at Paris. Remote from the Sorbonne and the Parliament, a freer course might be open to God's word. Perhaps the second city of the kingdom was destined to be the first

* . . . . Tumultuatur et Burgundia nobis proxima, per Phalucum quemdam Gallum qui e Gallia profugus. (Er. Epp. p. 809.)

† Suppullulare qui omnes conatus adferant, quo possit Christi regnum quam latissime patere. (MS. de Neufchâtel, 2d Aug. 1524.)

‡ Quod in Galliis omnibus sacrosanctum Dei verbum in dies magis ac magis elucescat. (Ibid.)

§ Factio crescit in dies latius, propagata in Sabaudiam, Lothoringiam, Franciam. (Er. Epp. p. 809.)

|| De Sebville à Coct du 28th Dec. 1524. (MS. du Conclave de Neufchâtel.)

wherein the Gospel should be received. Was it not there that the excellent Peter Waldo had begun to make known the divine Word? In that earlier age he had roused the national mind. Now that God had made all things ready to emancipate His church, was there not ground to hope for more extensive and decisive results? Accordingly the Lyonese, who in general were not, it must be confessed, 'poor men,' began to handle, with more confidence, the "sword of the Spirit which is the word of God."

Among those about Margaret's person, was her almoner, Michel d'Arande. The Duchess gave direction that the Gospel should be publicly preached in Lyons, and master Michel boldly proclaimed the pure word of God to a numerous auditory,—attracted partly by the good tidings, and partly by the favour with which the preacher and his preaching were regarded by the sister of their king.*

Anthony Papillon, a man of cultivated mind, an accomplished Latinist, a friend of Erasmus, the earliest of his countrymen thoroughly instructed in the Gospel,† accompanied the Princess. At Margaret's request he had translated Luther's tract on the monks' vows, "on which account he was often called in question by that vermin of the city of Paris," remarks Sebville.‡ But Margaret had protected the scholar from the enmity of the Sorbonne, and had obtained for him the appointment of chief master of requests to the Dauphin, with a seat in the council.§ He was almost equally useful to the Gospel by the sacrifices he made for its cause as by his great prudence. Vaugris, a merchant, and Anthony Du Blet, a gentleman, and a friend of Farel, were the principal persons who took part with the Reformation at Lyons. The latter, whose activity was untiring, served as a sort of connecting link between the Christians scattered throughout those countries, and was the

* Elle a une docteur de Paris appelé maitre Michel Eleymosinarius. lequel ne prêche devant elle que purement l'Evangile. (Sebville à Coct MS. de Neufchâtel.)

† Ibid.　　　　　　　　　　　　　‡ Ibid.

‡ Ibid.

medium of their intercourse with Basle. The armed bands of Francis the First had done no more than traverse Lyons, whilst the spiritual soldiery of Jesus Christ had paused within it, and leaving the former to carry war into Provence, they commenced the 'fight' of faith' in the city of Lyons itself.

But their efforts were not confined to Lyons. Casting their eyes over the surrounding country, their operations were carried on, at one and the same time, at different points; and the Christians of Lyons supported and encouraged the confessors of Christ in the adjacent provinces, and bore His name where as yet it was not known. The new teaching reascended the banks of the Saone, and the voice of one "bringing the glad tidings" was heard in the narrow and irregular streets of Macon. Michel d'Arande, the almoner of the king's sister, himself visited that place in 1524, and, by Margaret's intercession, obtained license to preach in a town* which was afterwards deluged with blood, and became for ever memorable for its *sauteries*.

After extending their travels in the direction of the Saone, the Christians of Lyons, ever looking for an open door, reascended the acclivities of the Alps. There was, at Lyons, a Dominican named Maigret, who had been expelled from Dauphiny, where he had preached the new doctrine with singular boldness, and who earnestly requested that some one would go over and help his brethren of Grenoble and Gap. Papillon and Du Blet repaired thither.† A violent storm had just broken out there against Sebville and his preaching. The Dominicans moved heaven and earth, and, in their rage at the escape of Farel, Anemond, Maigret, and the other preachers,

---

* Arandius prêche a Mascon. (Coct à Farel, Dec. 1524, MS. de Neufchâtel.)

† Il y a eu deux grands personages à Grenoble. (Coct à Farel, Dec. 1524, MS. de Neufchâtel.) The title *Messire* is given to Du Blet, indicating a person of rank. I incline to think that that of *negotiator*, elsewhere given him, refers to his activity: yet he might be a merchant of Lyons.

sought to crush such as were within their clutches.*   **They,** therefore insisted that Sebville should be arrested.†

The friends of the Gospel at Grenoble caught the alarm. Was Sebville, also, on the eve of being lost to them?   **Margaret** interceded with her brother. Some persons of distinction at Grenoble, including the king's advocate, either secretly or avowedly favourable to the Gospel, exerted themselves in his behalf; and he was happily rescued from the fury of his enemies.‡

His life indeed was saved but his mouth was stopped. "Remain silent," said his friends, "or you will be brought to the scaffold." "Only think what it is," wrote he to De Coct "to have silence imposed upon me, under pain of death."§ Some, whose firmness had been most relied on, were over awed by these threatenings.   The king's advocate, and others, exhibited marked coldness,‖ and many returned to the Roman Catholic communion, alleging that they would still offer to God a spiritual worship in the privacy of their hearts, and give to the outward observances of Catholicism a spiritual interpretation:—a melancholy snare, and one that leads men from one act of unfaithfulness to another.   There is no false system adhesion to which may not in this way be justified. The unbeliever, taking up with fancied myths and allegories, will preach Christ from the pulpit:—and the follower of a superstition held in abhorrence among the heathen, will, by a moderate exercise of ingenuity, trace in it the symbol of a pure and elevated thought.   In religion the very first essential is truth.   There were, however, some of the Christians of Grenoble, and among them Amedee Galbert and a cousin of

---

* Conjicere potes ut post Macretum et me in Sebivillam exarserint. (Anemond à Farel, 7th Sept. 1524, MS. de Neufchâtel.)

† Les Thomistes ont voulu proceder contre moi par inquisition et caption de personne. (Lettre de Sebville. Ibid.)

‡ Si ce ne fut certains amis secrets, je estois mis entre les mains des Pharisiens. (Lettre de Sebville, MS. de Neufchâtel.)

§ Ibid.

‖ Non solum tepedi sed frigidi. (MS. de Neufchâtel.)

Anemond, who held fast to their faith.[*] These men of piety were accustomed secretly to meet together with Sebville at each other's houses, and thus "spake often one to another." Their place of meeting was chosen for the sake of its retirement; they met at night in the apartment of a brother, with closed doors, to pray to Christ,—as if they had been robbers meeting for some guilty purpose! Rumour would often follow them to their humble meeting with some groundless alarm. Their enemies winked at such secret conventicles, but they had inwardly doomed to the stake any one who should venture to open his lips in public to speak the word of God.[†]

It was at this juncture that Du Blet and Papillon arrived in Grenoble. Finding that Sebville had been silenced, they exhorted him to go to Lyons, and there preach Christ. The following Lent promised to afford him the favourable opportunity of a vast crowd of hearers. Michel d'Arande, Maigret, and Sebville agreed together to put themselves in front of the battle, and thus all was arranged for an impressive testimony to the truth in the second city of the kingdom. The rumour of the approaching Lent spread into Switzerland : " Sebville is at large, and is purposing to preach at Lyons, in the church of St. Paul," wrote Anemond to Farel.[‡] But disasters, bringing with them confusion throughout France, intervened, and prevented the spiritual contest. It is in periods of tranquillity that the Gospel achieves its blessed conquests. The battle of Pavia, which took place in the month of February, disconcerted the bold project of the Reformers.

Meanwhile, without waiting for Sebville, Maigret, amidst much opposition from the clergy and the monks,[§] had from the beginning of the winter been preaching at Lyons, Sal-

---

[*] Tuo cognato, Amedeo Galberto exceptis. (MS. de Neufchâtel.)

[†] Mais de en parler publiquement, il n'y pend que le feu. (MS. de Neufchâtel.)

[‡] Le samedi des Quatre-Temps. (Dec. 1524, ibid.)

[§] Pour vray Maigret a prêché à Lion, maulgré les prêtres et moines. (Ibid.)

vation by Christ alone.   In his sermons, he passed over the
worship of the creature,—the saints,—the Virgin,—and the
power of the priesthood.   The great mystery of Godliness,—
" God manifest in the flesh,"—was the one great doctrine exalted by him.   " The early heresies of the poor men of Lyons
were again showing themselves under a more dangerous form
than ever," it was remarked.   In spite of opposers, Maigret
continued his preaching : the faith that animated him found
utterance in emphatic words ; it is in the very nature of
Truth to embolden the heart that receives it.   Nevertheless,
it was decreed that at Lyons, as at Grenoble, Rome should get
the upper hand.   Under the very eyes of Margaret, the
preacher was arrested, dragged through the streets, and committed to prison.   Vaugris, a merchant who was just then
leaving the town on his way to Switzerland, carried with him
the news of what had happened.   One thought cheered the
melancholy these tidings diffused among the friends of the Reformation,—" Maigret is seized," said they, " but thanks be to
God, *Madame d'Alencon* is on the spot.' *

Their hopes soon left them.   The Sorbonne had formally
condemned certain propositions maintained by the faithful
preacher ;† Margaret, whose position was every day becoming more embarrassing, beheld the daring of the Reformers,
and the hatred of those in power both rising at the same moment.   Francis the First was beginning to lose patience at the
restless zeal of the preachers, and to regard them as fanatics
whom it was good policy to reduce to submission.   Margaret,
therefore, fluctuating between her desires to serve her brethren
in Christ, and the failure of her ability to preserve them, sent
them word that they were to abstain from rushing into new
difficulties, seeing that she could not again make application
to the king in their behalf.   The friends of the Gospel believed that this resolution could not be irrevocable : " God give
her grace," said they "to say and write only what is needful

* MS. de Neufchâtel.
† Histoire de François I. par Gaillard, tom. iv. p. 233.

to poor souls."[*]　But even if they should lose this help of man, Christ was with them,—and it seemed well that the soul should be stripped of other dependence, that it might lean upon God alone.

The friends of the Gospel had lost their power, and the powerful were declaring against it.　Margaret was alarmed. Soon—heavy news, received from beyond the Alps, was to plunge the whole kingdom into mourning,—absorbing attention in the one object of saving France and her king.　But if the Christians of Lyons were motionless, did not Basle contain within its walls soldiers escaped from the battle, and ready to renew it?　The exiles from France have never forgotten her: banished for three centuries by Roman fanaticism, we see their last descendants carrying to the towns and plains of their father-land, the treasure of which the Pope deprives them.　At the crisis, when the good soldiers of Christ in France dejectedly threw away their arms, we see the refugees at Basle, preparing for renewed efforts.　With the example before their eyes of the sceptre of St. Louis and of Charlemagne falling from the grasp of a Francis the First, should they not be incited· to lay hold on a " kingdom which cannot be moved ?"[†]

Farel, Anemond, Esch, Toussaint, and their friends in Switzerland, composed an Evangelical Association, having for its object the deliverance of their country from spiritual darkness.　Intelligence reached them from all sides, that there was an increasing thirst after God's word in France ;[‡] it was desirable to take advantage of it, and to water and sow the seed while yet it was seed time.　Œcolampadius, Oswald Myconius, and Zwingle, continually encouraged them to this. The Swiss teacher, Myconius, wrote thus in January[*] 1525, to De Coct : " Exiled as you are from your country by the tyranny of Antichrist, your presence amongst us is the proof

* Pierre Touissant à Farel, Basle 17 Dec. 1524.　(MS. de Neufchâtel.)
† Heb. xii. 28.
‡ Gallis verborum Dei sitientibus.　(Coctus Farello, 2 Sep. 1524.　MS. de Neufchâtel.) .

that you have courageously stood forth in the cause of Truth.
The oppressions of *Christian* Bishops will lead the people to
regard them as no better than deceivers.   Stand fast; the time
is not distant when we shall arrive in the wished for haven,
whether we be struck down by the oppressors, or they themselves be cast down,* and all will then be well with us, if we
do but continue faithful to Jesus Christ."

These cheering words were precious indeed to the French
refugees;—but just then, a blow struck by those very Christians of Switzerland, and of Germany, who sought to cheer
them, carried grief to their hearts.   In the feeling of their recent escape from the fires of persecution, they, at this time, beheld with dismay the Evangelical Christians beyond the
Rhine disturbing their repose by their deplorable differences.
The controversy, in relation to the Lord's Supper, had begun.
Deeply affected, and feeling the need of mutual love, the French
Reformers would have made any sacrifice to conciliate the
divergent parties.   It became the great object of their desire.
None more than they felt from the outset the need of Christian unity.   At a later period, Calvin afforded proof of this.
" Would to God," said Peter Toussaint, " that, by my worthless blood, I could purchase peace, concord, and union in
Christ Jesus."†   The French, gifted with quick discernment,
saw, from the very beginning, how the rising dissensions
would stand in the way of the Reformation.   " All would go
favourably beyond our hopes, if we were but agreed among
ourselves.   Many there are who would gladly come to the
light, but they are prevented by seeing such divisions among
the learned."‡

The French were the first to suggest conciliatory advances:
" Why," wrote they from Strasburg, " why not send Bucer
or some other man of learning to confer with Luther ?   The

* Non longe abest enim, quo in portum tranquillum pervenimus . . .
(Oswald Myconius à Anemond de Coct.   (MS. de Neufchâtel.)
† 21st December, 1525.   (MS. du Conclave de Neufchâtel.)
‡ Ibid.

more we delay the wider will our differences become." These
fears seemed every day more founded.*

Failing in their endeavours, these Christians turned their
eyes towards France, and the conversion of their own country
to the faith thenceforth exclusively engaged the hearts of these
generous men, whom history,—so loud in praise of men who
have sought only their own glory,—has, for three centuries,
scarcely mentioned. Cast upon a foreign soil, they threw
themselves on their knees, and, daily in their solitude, called
down blessings from God upon their fatherland.† *Prayer*
was the great instrument by which the Gospel spread through
the kingdom, and the great engine by which the conquests of
the Reformation were achieved.

But there were other men of prayer beside these. Never,
perhaps, have the ranks of the Gospel comprised combatants
more prompt to suffer in the hour of conflict. They felt the
importance of scattering the Scriptures and pious writings in
their country, which was still overclouded with the thick
darkness of superstition. A spirit of enquiry was dawning in
their nation, and it seemed necessary on all sides to unfurl the
sails to the wind. Anemond, ever prompt in action, and
Michel Bentin, another refugee, resolved to employ, in concert, their zeal and talents. Bentin decided to establish a
printing press at Balse, and the knight to turn to account the
little he knew of German, by translating into that language
the more striking tracts written by the Reformers. " Oh !"
exclaimed they, rejoicing in their project; " would to God
that France were so supplied with Gospel writings that in
cottages, and in palaces, in cloisters, and in presbyteries, and
in the inner sanctuary of all hearts, a powerful witness might
be borne for the grace of our Lord Jesus Christ."‡

* Multis jam christianis Gallis dolet, quod a Zwinglii aliorumque de
Eucharistia sententia, dissentiat Lutherus. (Tossanus Farello, 14th
July, 1525.
† Quam sollicite quotidianis precibus commendem. (Tossanus Farello,
2nd Sept. 1524, MS. de Neufchâtel.)
‡ Opto enim Galliam Evangelicis voluminibus abundare. (Coctus Fa-
rello, MS. de Neufchâtel.)

For such an undertaking funds were necessary,—and the refugees were destitute of funds. Vaugris was then at Basle. Anemond, on parting with him, gave him a letter to the brethren of Lyons, some of whom had considerable possessions in lands, and, notwithstanding they were oppressed, remained faithful to the Gospel. In his letter, he asked their assistance;* but that could not at all meet the extent of the need. The Frenchmen resolved to establish several presses at Basle, that should be worked day and night, so as to inundate all France with God's word.† At Meaux, Metz, and other places there were those rich enough to contribute to this work; and as no one could appeal to Frenchmen with more authority than Farel, it was to him that Anemond made application.‡

We do not find that the scheme of Anemond was realized; but the work was carried out by others. The presses of Basle were incessantly employed in printing French works, which were forwarded to Farel, and by him introduced into France. One of the earliest of the issues of this Religious Tract Society was Luther's *Exposition of the Lord's Prayer*. " We sell the *Pater* at four deniers de Bale to private persons," wrote Vaugris—" but to the wholesale dealer, we supply copies at the rate of 200 for two florins, which is something less."§

Anemond was accustomed to transmit from Bale to Farel any profitable books published or received in that city—at one time a tract on ordination, at another, an essay on the education of children.‖ Farel looked through them, composing, translating, and seeming, at one and the same time, all activity, and yet all meditation. Anemond urged on, and superintended the printing, and these letters, requests, and books, all these little single sheets, were among the instruments of regenera-

* Ut pecuniæ aliquid ad me mittant. (Coct. Far. MS. de Neufchâtel.)
† Ut præla multa erigere possimus. (Ibid.)
‡ An censes inveniri posse Lugduni, Meldæ, ant alibi in Galliis qui nos ad hæc juvare velint. (Ibid.)
§ Vaugris à Farel; (Bâle, 29th Aug. 1524. MS de Neufchâtel.)
‖ Mitto tibi librum de instituendis ministris Ecclesiæ cum libro de instituendis pueris. (Coctus Farello, 2d Sept. 1524, Ibid.)

tion to that age. While dissoluteness and profligacy descended from the throne to the lower orders, and darkness spread from the very steps of the altar, these writings, so inconsiderable and unnoticed, alone diffused the beams of light, and the seeds of holiness.

But it was especially God's word that the evangelic merchant of Lyons required for his fellow-countrymen. That generation of the sixteenth century, so eager for all that could satisfy the re-awakened intellect, was to receive in its vernacular tongue those early records of the first ages—redolent with the young breath of human nature,—and those holy oracles of apostolic times, bright with the fulness of the revelation of Christ. Vaugris wrote to Farel—"Pray, see if it be not possible to have the New Testament translated by some competent hand;—it would be a great blessing to France, Burgundy, and Savoy. And if you should not be already provided with the proper types, I would order some from Paris or Lyons—but if we have the types at Basle, it would be all the better."

Lefevre had previously published at Meaux, but by detached portions, the books of the New Testament in the French language. Vaugris wished some one to undertake a revision of the whole for a new edition. Lefevre undertook to do so, and, as we have already related, published the entire volume on the 12th October, 1524. Conrad, an uncle of Vaugris, who had also sought an asylum in Basle, sent for a copy. De Coct, happening to be in company with a friend on the 18th November, first saw the book, and was overjoyed. "Lose no time in going to press again," said he, "for I doubt not a vast number of copies will be called for."*

Thus was the word of God offered to France side by side with those traditions of the Church which Rome is still continually presenting to her. "How can we discern," asked the Reformers, "between what is of man in your traditions and that which is of God, save only by the Scriptures of truth?—

* MS. of the Conclave of Neufchâtel.

38*

The maxims of the Fathers, the decretals of the Church, cannot be the rule of faith: they show us what was the judgment of those earlier divines, but only from the Word can we gather the thoughts of God.   Every thing must be tested by Scripture."

In this manner, for the most part, these printed works were circulated.   Farel and his friends transmitted the sacred books to certain dealers or *colporteurs*—poor men of good character for piety, who, bearing their precious burden, went through towns and villages—from house to house—in Franchecomté, Burgundy, and the neighbouring districts, knocking at every door.   The books were sold to them at a low price, that the interest they had in the sale might make them the more industrious in disposing of them.*   Thus as early as 1524 there existed in Basle, and having France for the field of their operations, a Bible society—an association of colporteurs—and a religious tract society.   It is, then, a mistake to conceive that such efforts date only from our own age; they go back,— at least in the identity of the objects they propose,—not merely to the days of the Reformation, but still further, to the first ages of the Church.

The attention which Farel bestowed on France did not cause him to neglect the places where he resided.   Arriving at Montbeliard, towards the end of July, 1524, he had no sooner sown the seed, than, to use the language of Œcolampadius, the first-fruits of the harvest began to appear.   Farel, exulting, communicated his success to his friend.—" It is easy," replied the doctor of Basle, " to instil a few dogmas into the ears of our auditors; but God alone can change their hearts."†

De Coct, overjoyed with this intelligence, hurried to Peter Toussaint's house.   " To-morrow," said he, with his usual vivacity, " I set off to visit Farel."   Toussaint, more calm, was then writing to the evangelist of Montbeliard: " Have a care," wrote he; " the cause you have taken in hand is of

---

* Vaugris à Farel.   (MS. of Neufchâtel.)

† Animum autem immutare, divinum opus est.   (Œcol. Epp. p. 206.)

solemn importance, and should not be contaminated by the counsels of men. The great ones may promise you their favour, assistance, aye, and heaps of gold—but to put confidence in these things is to forsake Jesus Christ, and to walk in darkness."[*] Toussaint was in the act of closing his letter when De Coct entered; and the latter, taking charge of it, set off for Montbeliard.

He found all the city in commotion. Several of the nobles, in alarm, and casting a look of contempt on Farel, exclaimed, "What can this poor wretch want with us? Would that he had never come amongst us. He must not remain here, or he will bring ruin upon us as well as upon himself." These nobles, who had retired to Montbeliard in company with the duke for shelter, feared lest the stir which everywhere accompanied the spread of the Reformation should, by drawing upon them the notice of Charles V. and Ferdinand, lead to their being driven from their only remaining asylum. But the ecclesiastics were Farel's bitterest opponents. The superior of the Franciscans at Besançon hastened to Montbeliard, and concocted defensive measures with the clergy of that place. The following Sunday Farel had scarcely begun to preach when he was interrupted, and called a liar and a heretic. Immediately the whole assembly was in an uproar. The audience rose, and called for silence. The duke hastened to the spot, put both the superior and Farel under arrest, and insisted that the former should prove his charges, or else retract them. The superior chose the latter course, and an official report was published of the transaction.[†]

This attack only rendered Farel more zealous than before: thenceforward he believed it his duty fearlessly to unmask these interested priests; and, drawing the sword of the Word, he applied it unsparingly. He was now more than ever led to imitate Jesus, rather in his character as the purifier of the

* . . . A quibus si pendemus, jam a Christo defecimus. (Manuscrit de Neufchâtel.)

* Der Christliche Handel zu Mümpelgard, verlossen mit gründlichen Wahrheit.

temple, driving out thence the traffickers and money-changers,
and overthrowing their tables,—than as the one of whom prophecy declared, " *He shall not strive nor cry, neither shall his
voice be heard in the streets.*" Œcolampadius was affrighted.
These two men were the perfect types of two characters dia-
metrically opposite, and yet both worthy of our admiration—
" Your mission," wrote Œcolampadius to Farel, "is gently to
draw men to the truth, not to drag them with violence; to
preach the Gospel,—not to pronounce maledictions. Physi-
cians resort to amputation, only when external applications
have failed. Act the part of the *physician*, not of the executioner. In my judgment, it is not enough that you are gentle
towards the friends of the Truth. You must likewise *win
over the adversaries.* Or if the wolves are to be driven from
the fold, at least let the sheep hear the voice of the shepherd.
Pour oil and wine into the wounded heart—and be the herald
of *glad tidings*, not a judge or a tyrant."* The report of
these things spread both in France and Lorraine, and this
gathering together of refugees in Basle and Montbeliard began
to alarm the Sorbonne and the Cardinal. Gladly would they
have broken up so ominous an alliance; for error knows no
greater triumph than the enlisting a renegade in its ranks.
Already had Martial Mazurier and others given the popal
party in France an opportunity of rejoicing over shameful
desertions; but if they could only succeed in seducing one of
those confessors of Christ who had fled for safety to the banks
of the Rhine,—one who had suffered much for the name of
the Lord,—that were indeed a victory for the hierarchy.
Measures were concerted and directed in the first instance
against the youngest.

   The Dean, the Cardinal of Lorraine, and all the circle
which assembled at the prelate's house, deplored the sad fate
of Peter Toussaint, once the object of so many hopes. He is
at Basle, said they, living in the very house of Œcolampadius,
in close intercourse with that leader in this heresy. They

   * Quod Evangelistam, non tyrannicum legislatorem præstes. (Œcol.
Epp. p. 206.)

wrote to him movingly, as though his salvation was at stake. These letters were the more distressing to the poor young man, because they bore evident marks of sincere affection.* One of his relations, probably the Dean himself, urged him to remove to Paris, Metz, or whatever place he pleased, provided it were but at a distance from the Lutherans. This relation bearing in mind how much Toussaint was indebted to him, doubted not his immediate compliance with the injunction; when therefore he found his efforts unavailing, his affection was succeeded by violent hatred. This resistance, on the part of the young refugee exasperated against him all his family and friends. Recourse was had to his mother, who was entirely under the influence of the monks:† the priests came about her frightening her, and persuading her that her son had been guilty of crimes which could not be named without shuddering. On this the distressed parent wrote to her son an affecting letter, "full of tears," as he says, in which she described her misery in heart-rending terms. "Oh! wretched mother," said she, "Oh! unnatural son!—Cursed be the breasts that suckled thee, cursed be the knees that bare thee."‡

Poor Toussaint was overwhelmed with consternation. What was he to do? Return to France he could not. To leave Basle and proceed to Zurich or Wittemberg, beyond the reach of his kindred, would only have added to their distress. Œcolampadius suggested a middle course. "Leave my house," said he.§ With a sorrowful heart Toussaint complied, and went to lodge with a priest, both ignorant and obscure, and so‖ well fitted to quiet the fears of his relations. What a change for him! He had no intercourse with his host except at meals. At such times they were continually differing on

* Me in dies divexari legendis amicorum litteris qui me . . . ab instituto remorari nituntur. (Tossanus Farello, 2nd Sep. 1524. Manuscrit de Neufchâtel.)
† Jam capulo proxima. (MS. de Neufchâtel.)
‡ Litteras ad me dedit plenas lacrymis quibus maledicit et uberibus quæ me lactarunt, &c. (Ibid.)
§ Visum est Œcolampadio consultum . . . ut a se secederem. (Ibid.)
‖ Utor domo cujusdam sacrificuli. (Ibid.)

matters of faith, but—no sooner was his meal ended, than Toussaint hastened to shut himself in his chamber; where, undisturbed by noise and controversy, he carefully studied the word of God. " The Lord is my witness," said he, " that in this valley of tears, I have but one desire, and that is, to see Christ's kingdom extend itself, that all with one mouth may glorify God."*

One incident took place and cheered Toussaint. The enemies of the Gospel at Metz were becoming more and more powerful. At his entreaty the chevalier d'Esch, undertook a journey in July, 1525, to strengthen the Evangelical Christians of that city. He traversed the forests of Vosges, and reached the place where Leclerc had laid down his life, bringing with him several books with which Farel had supplied him.†

But the French exiles did not confine their attention to Lorraine. De Coct received letters from one of Farel's brothers, depicting, in gloomy colours, the condition of Dauphiny. He carefully avoided showing them, lest he should alarm the faint-hearted, but bore them on his heart before God in fervent prayer, for His all-powerful aid.‡ In December 1524, one Peter Verrier, a messenger from Dauphiny, entrusted with commissions for Farel and Anemond, arrived on horseback at Montbeliard. The knight, with his usual impetuosity, immediately resolved on returning into France. " If the said Peter has brought money," wrote he to Farel, " do you take it : if he has brought letters open them, take copies and send them to me. Do not however sell the horse, but keep it, since I may perhaps need it. I am minded to enter France secretly, and visit Jacobus Faber, (Lefevre) and Arandius. Write me your opinion of this plan."§

* Ut Christi regnum quam latissime pateat. (MS. de Neufchâtel.)
† Quil s'en retourne à Metz, là ou les ennemis de Dieu s'élevent journellement contre l'Evangile. (Tossanus Farello; 17th Dec. 1524. MS. de Neufchâtel.)
‡ Accepi ante horam a fratre tuo epistolam quam hic nulli manifestavi: terrentur enim infirmi. (Coctus Farello, 2nd Sept. 1524.)
† Coct à Farel, Dec. 1524. MS de Neufchâtel.

Such was the unreserved confidence which existed among these refugees. De Coct, it is true, was already indebted thirty-six crowns to Farel, whose purse was ever at the service of his friends. The knight's plan of returning to France was one of more zeal than wisdom. His habitual want of caution would have exposed him to certain death. This Farel doubtless explained to him. Leaving Basle he withdrew to a small town, having, as he said, " great hopes of acquiring the German tongue, *God willing*."*

Farel continued to preach the Gospel at Montbeliard. His spirit was grieved within him, beholding the great body of the people of that place wholly given to the worship of images. In his opinion it was no better than a return to heathen idolatry.

Nevertheless the exhortations of Œcolampadius, and the fear of compromising the truth, would, perhaps, have long restrained him, but for an unforeseen circumstance. One day, towards the end of February (it was the feast of St. Anthony,) Farel was walking near the banks of a little river that runs through the town, below the lofty rock on which stands the citadel, when, as he reached the bridge, he met a procession, reciting prayers to St. Anthony, and headed by two priests, bearing the image of that saint. He thus found himself suddenly brought into contact with these superstitions. A violent struggle took place in his soul; shall he be silent, or conceal himself? would it not be a cowardly want of faith? These dumb idols, borne on the shoulders of ignorant priests, made his blood boil. He boldly advanced, snatched from the priests' arms the shrine of the holy hermit, and threw it from the bridge into the stream. Then, turning toward the astonished crowd, he exclaimed aloud, " Poor idolaters, will ye never put away your idols?"†

The priests and people were motionless in astonishment. A holy fear for a while paralysed them; but soon recovering they exclaimed, " The image is sinking," and their motion-

* Coct à Farel, Jan. 1525. MS. de Neufchâtel.
† Revue du Dauphiné, tom. ii. p. 38. MS de Choupard.

less silence was succeeded by transports of rage. The crowd would have rushed upon the sacrilegious wretch who had hurled into the river the object of their adoration; but Farel, we know not how, escaped their fury.[*]

Many may regret that the Reformer allowed himself to be hurried into an act which tended to check the progress of the truth. We can enter into their feelings. Let no man think himself authorized to attack with violence an institution which has the public sanction. Yet is there in this zeal of the Reformer a something more noble than that cold prudence so common in the world, and which shrinks from incurring the smallest danger, or making the most trifling sacrifice for the advancement of God's kingdom. Farel well knew that by this act he was exposing himself to the death which Leclerc had suffered. But his own conscience bore testimony that he desired only to promote the glory of God, and this elevated him above all fear.

After this incident of the bridge, in which we *discern his* natural character, Farel was obliged to conceal himself, and soon afterwards to quit the city. He took refuge with Œcolampadius at Basle; but he ever retained that attachment to Montbeliard, which a servant of God never ceases to cherish for the scene of the first-fruits of his ministry.[†]

At Basle, sad tidings awaited him. Himself a *fugitive, he* now learned that Anemond de Coct was dangerously ill. Farel immediately remitted to him four gold crowns: but on the 25th of March, a letter from Oswald Myconius brought him intelligence of the knight's death. "Let *us* so live," wrote Oswald, "that we may enter into that rest which we trust the soul of Anemond has now entered upon."[‡]

[*] M. Kirchhoffer, in his Life of Farel, gives this circumstance as an uncertain tradition: but it is related by Protestant writers, and besides seems to me perfectly consistent with the character of Farel and the fears of Œcolampadius. It is our duty to admit the weaknesses of the Reformation.

[†] Ingens affectus, qui me cogit Mumpelgardum amare. (Farelii Epp.)

[‡] Quo Anemundi spiritum jam pervenisse speramus. (Myconius Farello, MS. de Neufchâtel.)

Thus prematurely died Anemond;—still young, full of activity and energy,—in himself a host,—ready to undertake every labour, and brave every danger in the hope of evangelizing France. *God's ways are not our ways.* Not long before, and near Zurich too, another noble, Ulric von Hütten, had breathed his last. Points of resemblance are not wanting between the two; but the piety and christian virtues of the native of Dauphiny entitle him to rank far above the level of the witty and intrepid enemy of the Pope and monks.

Shortly after Anemond's death, Farel, finding it impossible to remain at Basle whence he had already been expelled, joined his friends Capito and Bucer at Strasburg.

Thus at Montbeliard and at Basle, as well as at Lyons, the ranks of the Reformers were thinned. Of those who most zealously contended for the faith, some had been removed by death—others were scattered by persecution, and in exile. In vain did the combatants turn their efforts in every direction. On all sides they were repulsed. But though the forces concentrated first at Meaux, then at Lyons, and lastly at Basle, had been successively broken up, there remained here and there, in Lorraine, at Meaux, and even in Paris, good soldiers, who struggled, more or less openly, in support of God's word in France. Though the Reformation saw its ranks broken, it still had its single champions. Against these the Sorbonne and the Parliament now turned their anger. The resolution was taken to exterminate from the soil of France the devoted men who had undertaken to plant thereon the standard of Jesus Christ;—and unprecedented misfortunes seemed at this season to conspire with the enemies of the Reformation to favour the attainment of their purpose.

During the latter part of Farel's stay at Montbeliard, great events had indeed taken place on the theatre of the world. Lannoy, and Pescara, Charles's generals, having quitted France on the approach of Francis I., that Prince crossed the Alps, and blockaded Pavia. On the 24th of February 1525, Pescara attacked him. Bonnivet, la Trémouille, la Palisse and Lescure died fighting by his side. The Duke of Alençon, the first prince of the blood and husband of Margaret, fled, carrying with him the rear-guard, and died of shame and grief at Lyons. Francis himself, thrown from his horse, surrendered his sword to Charles de Lannoy, viceroy of Naples, who received it kneeling on one knee. The King of France was the Emperor's prisoner ! His captivity seemed to be the greatest of all misfortunes. "Nothing is left me but honour and life," wrote that Prince to his mother. But to none was this event more affecting than to Margaret. The glory of her country over-clouded, France without a monarch, and exposed to accumulated dangers, her beloved brother the captive of his haughty foe, her husband dishonoured and dead,—what an overflowing cup of bitterness ! But she had a Comforter : —and whilst her brother sought to comfort himself by repeating, " Tout est perdu, fors l'honneur !" (all is lost save honour !) . . She was able to say, ' Fors Jesus seul, mon frere, fils de Dieu,'—" Save Christ alone, my brother, Son of God !"*

All France, nobles, parliament, and people were overwhelmed in consternation. Ere long, as in the first three centuries of the Church, the calamity which had overtaken the state was charged upon the Christians,—and the cry of fanatics on all sides demanded their blood as the means of averting further misfortunes. The moment, therefore, was favourable to the opposers of the truth ; it was not enough to have dislodged the evangelical Christians from the three strong positions they had taken up, it was necessary to profit by the popular panic to strike while the iron was hot, and utterly to extirpate a power which was becoming so formidable to the Papacy.

At the head of this conspiracy, and loudest in these clamours, were Beda, Duchesne, and Lecouturier. These irreconcilable enemies of the Gospel flattered themselves that they might easily obtain, from public terror, the victims hitherto refused. They went immediately to work, employing fanatical he-

* Les Marguerites de la Marguerite, p. 29.

tangues, lamentations, threats, and libels, to arouse the angry
passions of the nation and its governors,—vomiting fire and
flame against their adversaries, and heaping insults upon
them.*

They stopped at nothing ;—dishonestly quoting their words,
without reference to any explanatory context, substituting expressions of their own in place of those used by the teachers
they wished to inculpate, and omitting or adding according as
was necessary to blacken the character of their opponents.†
Such is the testimony of Erasmus himself.

Nothing so much excited their anger as the doctrine of Salvation by Free Grace,—the corner-stone of Christianity and
of the Reformation. "When I contemplate," said Beda,
" these three men, Lefevre, Erasmus, and Luther, in other respects gifted with so penetrating a genius, leagued together in
a conspiracy against meritorious works, and resting all the
weight of salvation on faith alone,‡ I am no longer astonished
that thousands, led away by such teaching, begin to say,
' Why should I fast and mortify my body ?' Let us banish
from France this hateful doctrine of grace. This neglect of
good works is a fatal snare of the devil."

Thus did the syndic of the Sorbonne fight against the faith.
He would naturally find supporters in a profligate court, and
likewise in another class of people, more respectable, but not
less opposed to the Gospel ;—we mean those grave men, and
rigid moralists, who, devoted to the study of laws and judicial
forms, discern in Christianity no more than a system of laws,
and in the Church only a sort of moral police, and who, unable to make the doctrines of man's spiritual helplessness, the
new birth, and justification by faith, square with the legal
habit of their minds, are induced to regard them as fanciful
imaginations, dangerous to public morals and to national pros-

* Plus quam scurrilibus conviciis debacchantes. . . (Er. Francisco
Regi, p. 1106.)
† Pro meis verbis supponit sua, prætermittit, addit. (Ibid. p. 887.)
‡ Cum itaque cerneram tres istos . . . uno animo in opera meritoria
conspirasse. (Natalis Bedæ Apologia adversus clandestinos Lutheranos,
fol. 41.)

perity. This aversion to the doctrine of free grace, manifested itself in the 16th century under two widely different forms. In Italy and in Poland it took the form of Socinianism, so called from its originator, who was descended from a celebrated family of jurists at Sienna; while in France, it showed itself in the stern decrees and burnings of the Parliament.

Contemning the great truths of the Gospel, as promulgated by the Reformers, and thinking it necessary to do something at this season of overwhelming calamity, the Parliament presented an address to Louisa of Savoy, remonstrating strongly on the conduct of the government towards the new teaching: "Heresy," said they, "has raised its head amongst us, and the king, by his neglecting to bring the heretics to the scaffold, has drawn down upon us the wrath of heaven."

At the same time the pulpits resounded with lamentations, threatenings, and maledictions; and prompt and signal punishments were loudly demanded. Martial Mazurier took a prominent part among the preachers of Paris, and endeavouring by his violence to efface the recollection of his former connection with the partisans of the Reformation, inveighed against such as were "secretly the disciples of Luther." "Know you," cried he, "the rapid progress of this poison? Know you its strength? It acts with inconceivable rapidity; in a moment it may destroy tens of thousands of souls. Ah! well may we tremble for France."[*]

It was not difficult to excite the Queen-mother against the favourers of the Reformation. Her daughter Margaret, the chief personages of the court, she herself, Louisa of Savoy, who had ever been devoted to the Roman Pontiff, had been by certain of the fanatics charged with countenancing Lefevre, Berquin, and the other innovators. Had she not been known, insinuated her accusers, to read their tracts and translations of the Bible? The Queen-mother was not unwilling to clear herself of such dishonouring suspicions. Already she had

* Mazurius contra occultos Lutheri discipuil os declamat, ac recentis veneni celeritatem vimque denunciat. (Lannoi, regii Navarræ gymnasii historia, p. 621.

despatched her confessor to the Sorbonne to enquire of that body as to the best method of extirpating this heresy. " The detestable doctrine of Luther," said she in her message to the faculty, "every day gains new adherents." The faculty smiled on the receipt of this message. The time had been when the representations they had made were dismissed without so much as a hearing; but now their advice was humbly solicited in the matter. At length they held within their grasp that heresy which they had so long desired to stifle. They deputed Noel Beda to return an immediate answer to the Queen-Regent. "Since," said the fanatical syndic, "the sermons, discussions, and books, with which we have so often opposed heresy, have failed to arrest its progress, a proclamation ought to be put forth, prohibiting the circulation of the writings of the heretics—and if these measures should prove insufficient, force and restraint should be employed against the *persons* of the false teachers; for they who resist the light must be subdued by *punishments* and *terror*."*

But Louisa had not even waited for their answer. Scarcely had Francis fallen into the hands of Charles V., when she wrote to the Pope, consulting him as to his wishes with respect to heretics. It was important to Louisa's policy to secure to herself the favour of a pontiff who had power to raise all Italy against the conqueror of Pavia; and she did not think that favour would be too dearly bought at the cost of some French blood. The Pope, delighted at the opportunity of letting loose his vengeance in the 'most Christian kingdom,' against a heresy of which he had failed to arrest the progress either in Switzerland or Germany, gave instant directions for the establishment of the Inquisition in France, and despatched a bull to that effect to the Parliament. At the same time Duprat, whom the Pontiff had created a cardinal, at the same time bestowing upon him the archbishopric of Sens and a rich abbey, laboured to testify his gratitude for these favours, by his indefatigable opposition to the heretics. Thus the Pope, the

* Histoire de l'Université, par Crevier, v. p. 196.

39*

Regent, the doctors of the Sorbonne and the Parliament, the Chancellor and the fanatics, were now combining to ruin the Gospel and put its confessors to death.

The Parliament was first in motion. The time had arrived, when it was necessary that the first body in the state should take steps against the new doctrine: moreover, it might seem called to act, inasmuch as the public tranquillity was at stake. Accordingly, the Parliament, "under the impulse of a holy zeal against the innovations," issued an edict,* "that the Bishop of Paris, and certain other bishops, should be held responsible to M. Philippe Pott, president of requests, and Andrew Verjus, its counsellor, and to Messires William Duchesne, and Nicolas Leclerc, doctors of divinity, to institute and conduct the trial of persons tainted with the Lutheran doctrine."

"And with a purpose of making it appear that those persons were acting rather under the authority of the Church than of the Parliament, it pleased his Holiness, the Pope, to forward a brief, dated 20th May, 1525, in which he approved the commissioners that had been named."

"Accordingly, in pursuance of these measures, all who, being called before these deputies, were by the bishop or by the ecclesiastical judges, pronounced *Lutherans*, were handed over to the secular arm,—that is, to the said Parliament, who forthwith condemned them to the flames."† We quote the very words of a manuscript of that age.

Such was the dreadful court of Inquisition, appointed, during the captivity of Francis I., to take cognizance of the charge against the Evangelic Christians of France, as dangerous to the state. Its members were two laymen and two ecclesiastics; and one of these latter was Duchesne, next to Beda the most fanatical of the adverse party. Shame had prevented their

* De la religion catholique en France, par de Lezeau. MS. de la Bibliotheque de Sainte-Genevieve at Paris.

† The MS. of the Library of St. Genevieve, whence I have derived this fragment, bears the name of Lezeau, but in the catalogue that of Lefebre.

placing Beda himself in the commission, but his influence was
only the more secured by the precaution.

Thus the machinery was set up,—its various springs in
order,—and every one of its blows likely to be mortal. It
was an important point to settle against whom its first proceedings should be taken. Beda, Duchesne, and Leclerc, M.
Philip Pott, the president, and Andrew Verjus, the counsellor,
met to deliberate on this point. Was there not the Count of
Montbrun, the old friend of Louis XII., and the former ambassador at the court of Rome, Briçonnet, then Bishop of
Meaux? This committee of public safety, of 1525, thought
that by singling out its object from an elevated station, it
should strike terror through all hearts. This consideration
seems to have decided them; and the venerable bishop
received notice of trial.

Far from quailing before the persecution of 1523, Briçonnet
had persisted, in conjunction with Lefevre, in opposing the
popular superstitions. The more eminent his station in the
Church and in the State, the more fatal did the effect of his
example appear, and the more did his enemies judge it necessary to extort from him a public recantation, or to bring him
to a yet more public retribution. The court of inquisition lost
no time in collecting and preparing the evidence against him.
He was charged with harbouring the teachers of the new
heresy: it was alleged that a week after the superior of the
Cordeliers had preached in St. Martin's church at Meaux, by
direction of the Sorbonne, to restore sound doctrine,—Briçonnet had himself occupied the pulpit, and, in publicly refuting
him, had designated the preacher and his brother Cordeliers
impostors, false prophets, and hypocrites; and that, not satisfied
with that, he had, through his official, summoned the superior
to appear personally to answer to him.*

It would even seem, if we may trust to one manuscript of
the time, that the Bishop had gone much further, and that he
in person, attended by Lefevre, had in the autumn of 1524
gone over his diocese, committing to the flames, wherever he

* Hist. de l'Université, par Crevier, v. p. 904.

came, all images, the crucifix alone excepted. So daring a
conduct, which would go to prove so much decision, combined
with much timidity in the character of Briçonnet—if we give
credit to the fact—would not fix upon him the blame visited
on other *iconoclasts;* for he was at the head of that Church
whose superstitions he then sought to reform, and was therefore acting at least in the sphere of his rights and duties.*

However we may regard it, in the eyes of the enemies of
the Gospel, the charge against Briçonnet was of a very aggravated character. He had not merely impugned the
Church's authority, he had erected himself against the Sorbonne itself,—that society, all the energies of which were
directed to the perpetuation of its own greatness. Great,
therefore, was the joy in the society at the intelligence that
its adversary was to stand a trial before the Inquisition, and
John Bochart, one of the leading lawyers of the time, pleading
before the Parliament against Briçonnet, exclaimed aloud,—
" Neither the Bishop, nor any single individual can lawfully
exalt himself, or open his mouth against the faculty. Neither
is the faculty called to discuss or give its reasons at the bar
of the said Bishop, whose duty it is to offer no opposition to
the wisdom of that holy society, but to esteem it as under the
guidance of God himself."†

In conformity with this representation, the Parliament put
forth an edict on the 3d October, 1525, wherein, after author-
izing the arrest of all those who had been informed against;

---

* In the library of the pastors of Neufchâtel, is a letter of Sebville, in
which the following passage occurs: " Je te notifie que l'eveque de
Meaux en Brie pres Paris *cum Jacobo Fabro stapulensi,* depuis trois mois,
en visitant l'eveché ont brulé *actu* tous les images, reservé le crucifix, et
sont personellement ajournés à Paris a ce mois de mars venant pour re-
pondre *coram suprema curia et universitate.*" I am rather disposed to
think the fact truly stated, though Sebville was not on the spot, Mezeray,
Daniel, and Maimbourg make no mention of it. These Roman Catholic writers, who are not very circumstantial, may have had motives for
passing over the fact in silence, considering the issue of the trial; and
moreover, the report of Sebville agrees with all the known facts. However, the matter is open to question.

† Hist. de l'Université par Crevier, v. p. 204.

gave orders that the bishop should be examined by Master James Menager and Andrew Verjus, counsellors of the court, touching the matters charged against him.[*]

The order of the Parliament struck terror to the bishop's heart. Briçonnet, twice honoured with the post of ambassador at Rome,—Briçonnet, a bishop, a noble, the intimate friend of Louis XII. and Francis I.,—to undergo an interrogatory by two counsellors of the court . . . . He who had fondly dreamed that God would kindle in the hearts of the king, his mother, and his sister, a flame that would run through the kingdom, now beheld that kingdom turning against him in the endeavour to quench that fire which it had received from heaven. The king was a captive; his mother was placing herself at the head of the enemy's force; and Margaret, dismayed by the misfortunes of her country, no longer dared to avert the blow directed against her dearest friends, and falling first on the spiritual father who had so often cheered and comforted her. Not long before this, she had written to Briçonnet a letter full of pious emotions: "Oh!" she had said, "that this poor languid heart might experience some warmth of that love with which I would that it were burnt to ashes."[†] But the time had arrived when the question was one of literal burnings. Such mystical expressions were not now in season; and one who resolved to confess the faith must brave the scaffold! The poor Bishop, who had been so sanguine in the hope to see the Reformation gradually and gently winning its way in men's minds, trembled in dismay when he found, that, at the eleventh hour, it must be purchased at the sacrifice of life itself. It is possible such a thought may never before have occurred to him, and he recoiled from it in an agony of fear.

One hope, however, remained for Briçonnet; and that was, that he might be allowed to appear before the Chambers of Parliament in general assembly agreeably to the privilege

* Maimbourg Hist. du Calv. p. 14
† MS. de la Biblioth. Royale, S. F. No. 282.

belonging, by custom, to his rank. Doubtless, in that august and numerous assembly, some generous hearts would respond to his appeal, and espouse his cause. Accordingly, he humbly petitioned the court to grant him this indulgence; but his enemies had equally with himself calculated the possible issue of such a hearing. Had they not learned a lesson when Luther, in presence of the Germanic Diet, at Worms, had shaken the resolution of those who had previously seemed most decided?' Carefully closing every avenue of escape, they exerted themselves with such effect, that the Parliament on the 25th October, 1525, in an edict affirming that previously issued,* refused Briçonnet the favour he had petitioned for.

Behold the bishop of Meaux, placed like a common priest of the lowest order before Masters James Menager and Andrew Verjus. Those two jurisconsults, the obedient tools of the Sorbonne, were not likely to be swayed by those higher considerations to which the Chambers of Parliament might be accessible; they were men of facts:—was it, or was it not, a fact, that the Bishop had set himself in opposition to the society? With them, this was the only question. Accordingly Briçonnet's conviction was secured.

Whilst the sword was thus impending over the head of the Bishop, the monks, priests, and doctors, made the best use of their time;—they saw plainly that if Briçonnet could be persuaded to retract, their interest would be better served than by his martyrdom. His death would but inflame the zeal of those who were united with him in their faith, while his apostacy would plunge them in the deepest discouragement. They accordingly went to work. They visited him, and pressed him with their entreaties. Martial Mazurier especially strained every nerve to urge him to a fall, as he himself had fallen. Arguments were not wanting, which might, to Briçonnet, seem specious. Would he then take the consequence, and be rejected from his office? If he remained in the church, might he not use his influence with the king and

* Maimbourg Hist. du Calv. p. 15.

the court to an extent of good which it was not easy to estimate? What would become of his friends when his power was at an end? Was not his resistance likely to compromise the success of a Reformation which, to be salutary and lasting, ought to be carried into effect by the legitimate influence of the clergy? How many would be stumbled by his persisting in opposition to the Church; and, on the other hand how many would be won over by his concessions? His advisers pretended that they, too, were anxious for a Reformation; "All is going on by insensible steps," said they; "both at the court, in the city, and in the provinces, things are progressing:—and would he, in the mere lightness of his heart, dash the fair prospect in view! After all, he was not asked to relinquish what he had taught, but merely to comply with the established order of the Church. Could it be well, at a time when France was suffering under the pressure of so many reverses,—to stir up new confusions? "In the name of religion, country, friends—nay, even of the Reformation itself—*consent!*" said they. Such are the sophisms that are the ruin of many a noble enterprise.

Yet every one of these considerations had its influence on the Bishop's mind. The Tempter, who came to Jesus in the wilderness, presented himself to Briçonnet in fair and specious colours;—and instead of saying, with his Master, "*Get thee behind me, Satan!*" he heard, listened, and considered his suggestions. . . . Thenceforward his faithfulness was at an end.

Briçonnet had never been embarked, with all his heart, like Farel or Luther in the movement which was then remoulding the Church. There was in him a sort of mystical tendency, which enfeebles the souls in which it gains place, and takes from them the firmness and confidence which are derived from a Faith that rests simply on the word of God. The cross he was called to take up, that he might follow Christ, was too heavy for him.* Shaken in resolution,

---

* Crucis statim oblatæ terrore perculsus. (Bezæ Icones.)

alarmed, dizzy, and not knowing which way to turn, he faltered, and stumbled against the stone that had been artfully laid in his path* . . . he fell;—and, instead of throwing himself into the arms of Christ, he cast himself at the feet of Mazurier,† and, by a shameful recantation, brought a dark cloud upon the glory of a noble fidelity.‡

Thus fell Briçonnet, the friend of Lefèvre and of Margaret; and thus the earliest protector of the Gospel in France, denied that good news of Grace, in the criminal thought that his abiding faithful would compromise his influence in the Church, at the court, and in the kingdom. But what his enemies represented as the saving of his country, was, perhaps, the greatest of its misfortunes. What might not have been the consequence, if Briçonnet had possessed the courage of Luther? If one of the most eminent of the French bishops, enjoying the respect of the king and the love of the people, had ascended the scaffold, and there, like 'the poor of this world,' sealed, by a courageous confession and a christian death, the truth of the Gospel,—would not France herself have been put upon reflection? Would not the blood of the Bishop of Meaux have served, like that of Polycarp and Cyprian, as *seed of the church;* and should we not have seen those provinces, so famed for many recollections, emancipating themselves, in the sixteenth century, from the spiritual darkness in which they are still enveloped?

Briçonnet underwent the form of an interrogatory, in presence of Masters James Menager and Andrew Verjus, who declared that he had sufficiently vindicated himself from the crime charged against him. He was then put under penance, and convened a synod, at which he condemned the writings of Luther, retracted whatever he had taught at variance with the Church's teaching, restored the custom of invocation of

---

* Dementatus. (Bezæ Icones.)

† Ut Episcopus etiam desisteret suis consiliis effecit. (Launoi, regii Navarræ gymnasii hist. p. 621.)

‡ Nisi turpi palinodia gloriam hanc omnem ipse sibi invidisset. (Bezæ Icones.)

saints, persuading such as had left the rites of the Church to return to them; and as if desiring to leave no doubt as to his reconciliation with the Pope and the Sorbonne, kept a solemn fast on All-saints-eve, and issued orders for pompous processions, in which he appeared personally, evidencing still further his faith by his largesses and apparent devotion.[*]

The fall of Briçonnet is perhaps the most memorable of all those recorded of that period. There is no like example of one so deeply engaged in the work of the Reformation so abruptly turning against it; yet must we carefully consider both his character and his fall. Briçonnet stood relatively to Rome, as Lefevre stood in relation to the Reformation. Both represented a sort of *juste milieu*,—appertaining, in strictness of speech, to neither party,—as it were, one on the right and the other on the left centre. The Doctor of Etaples leans towards the Word; the Bishop inclines towards the Hierarchy;—and when these men, who touch each other, are driven to decision, we see the one range himself on the side of Christ, and the other on the side of Rome. We may add, that it is not possible to think that Briçonnet can have entirely laid aside the convictions of his faith; and at no time did the Roman doctors put confidence in him; not even after he had retracted. But he did, as did afterwards the Bishop of Cambray, whom he in some points resembled; he flattered himself he might *outwardly* submit to the Pope's authority, while he in his heart continued subject to the divine Word. Such weakness is incompatible with the principle of the Reformation. Briçonnet was one of the most distinguished of the quietist or mystic school; and it is well known that one of the leading maxims of that school has ever been to settle down in, and adapt itself to, the church in which it exists, whatever that church may be.

The mournful fall of Briçonnet was felt as a shock to the hearts of his former friends, and was the sad forerunner of those deplorable apostacies to which the friendship of the world so often led, in another age of French history. The

---

* Mezeray, ii. p. 981; Daniel, v. p. 544; Moreri, *article* Briçonnet.

man who seemed to hold the reins of the movement was abruptly precipitated from his seat, and the Reformation was, in that country, thenceforth to pursue its course without a leader or guide, in lowliness and secresy.   But the disciples of the Gospel from that time lifted up their eyes, regarding, with more fixedness of faith, their Head in heaven, whose unchanging faithfulness their souls had known.

The Sorbonne was triumphant.   A great advance toward the final ruin of the Reformation in France had been made, and it was important to follow up their success.   Lefevre stood next after Briçonnet, and Beda had, therefore, without loss of time, turned his hostility against him, publishing a tract against the celebrated doctor, full of such gross calumnies, that we have Erasmus's judgment of them, that "even cobblers and smiths could lay the finger on the falsehood of them."   What seemed above all to enrage him was that doctrine of *Justification by Faith*, which Lefevre had proclaimed in the ears of Christians.   To this Beda continually recurred as an article which, according to him, overturned the Church. " What !" he exclaimed, " Lefevre affirms that whoever ascribes to himself the power to save himself will be lost, whilst whosoever, laying aside all strength of his own, casts himself into the arms of Christ, shall be saved. . . . . Oh, what heresy ! thus to teach the uselessness of meritorious works. . . . . What hellish doctrine !—what delusion of the devil! Let us oppose it with all our power."*

Instantly that engine of persecution, which took effect in the recantation or in the death of its victims, was turned against Lefevre ; and already hopes were entertained that he would share the fate of Leclerc the wool-comber, or that of the bishop Briçonnet.   His trial was quickly gone through ; and a decree of Parliament condemned nine propositions extracted from his commentaries on the Gospels, and placed his translation of the Scriptures in the list of prohibited works.†

* Perpendens perniciosissimam demonis fallaciam. . . . Occurri quantum valui.   (Nat. Bedæ Apolog. adv. Lutheranos, fol. 42.)

† I. Lelong Biblioth. sacree, 2d part, p. 44.

These measures were felt by Lefevre to be only the prelude of others. From the first intimation of the approaching persecution he had clearly perceived, that in the absence of Francis the First he would not be able to bear up under his enemies' attacks, and that the time had arrived to act on the direction,—" *When they persecute you in one city flee ye unto another.*"[*] Lefevre quitted Meaux, where, ever since the bishop's apostacy, he had experienced nothing but bitterness of soul, and had found his efforts paralysed ; and as he looked back upon his persecutors, he shook off the dust from off his feet,—" not to call down evil upon them, but in testimony of the evils that were coming upon them : for," says he, " as that dust is shaken from off our feet, just so are they cast off from the favour and presence of the Lord."[†]

The persecutors beheld their victim at large ; but they derived comfort from the thought that, at least, France was delivered from this father of heresy.

Lefevre, a fugitive from his enemies, arrived at Strasburg under an assumed name. There he was immediately introduced to the friends of the Reformation ; and what must have been his joy, to hear publicly taught that same Gospel of which he had caught the first gleams in the Church ;—why, it was just his own faith ! It was exactly what he had intended to express ! It was as if he had been a second time born to the Christian life. Gerard Roussel, one of those Evangelical Christians, who, nevertheless, like the Doctor of Etaples, attained not to complete enfranchisement, had been likewise compelled to quit France. Both together attended the lectures of Capito and of Bucer,[‡] and met in private intercourse with those faithful teachers.[§] It was even rumoured that they had been commissioned to do so, by Margaret, the

* St. Matth. x. 14—23

† Quod excussi sunt a facie Domini sicut pulvis ille excussus est a pedibus. (Faber in Ev. Matth. p. 40.)

‡ Faber stapulensis et Gerardus Rufus, clam e Gallia profecti, Capitonem et Bucerum audierunt. (Melch. Adam. Vita Captonis p. 90.)

§ De omnibus doctrinæ præcipuis locis cum ipsis disseruerint. (Ib.)

king's sister.* But the adoring contemplation of the ways of God, rather than polemical questions, engaged Lefevre's attention. Casting a glance upon the state of Christendom, and filled with wonder at what he beheld passing on its stage, moved with feelings of gratitude, and full of hopeful anticipation, he threw himself on his knees, and prayed to the Lord "to perfect that which he saw then beginning."†

At Strasburg one especially agreeable surprise awaited him —his pupil, his 'son in the faith,' Farel,—from whom he had been parted by persecution for nearly three years,—had arrived there just before. The aged doctor of the Sorbonne found, in his young pupil, a man in the vigour of life, a christian, 'strong in the faith,'—and Farel grasped with affectionate respect the shrivelled hand which had guided his earliest steps, conscious of the liveliest joy at thus recovering his spiritual father in the society of faithful men, and in a city that had received the truth. They attended in company the pure teaching of eminent teachers,—broke bread together in the supper of the Lord, according to Christ's institution, and received touching proofs of the love of the brethren. "Do you recollect," said Farel to Lefevre, " an expression you once let fall to me, when we were both as yet in darkness, ' *William! God will renew the world; and you will live to see it!*'—See here the beginning of what you then foretold." "Yes," answered the pious old man; God is renewing the world. . . . O, my son, continue to preach boldly the holy Gospel of Jesus Christ."‡

Lefevre, from an excess of prudence doubtless, chose to remain incognito at Strasburg, and took the name of *Anthony Peregrinus*, whilst Roussel chose that of *Solnin*. But the celebrated doctor could not elude notice; and soon the whole city, even to the very children, saluted him with marks of

---

* Missi a Margaretha regis Francisci sorore. (Melch. Ad. Vit. Capitonis, p. 90.)

† Farel à tous seigneurs, peuples et pasteurs.

‡ Quod et pius senex fatebatur; meque hortabaturi pergerem in annuntiatione sacri Evangelii. (Farellus Pellicano Hotting. H. L. vi. p. 17.)

respect.[†] He did not dwell by himself, but lodged in the same house with Capito, Farel, Roussel, and Vedastus (known and loved for his retiring diffidence,) and a certain converted Jew named Simon. The houses of Capito, Œcolampadius, Zwingle, and Luther, offered a kind of open table and lodging. Such, in those days, was the attraction of 'brotherly love.' Many Frenchmen, besides, were residing in this city on the banks of the Rhine, and there composed a church in which Farel often preached the doctrine of Salvation. Such Christian communion soothed the feeling of banishment from their native land.

Whilst these brethren were thus enjoying the asylum afforded them by brotherly love, those in Paris and other parts of France were exposed to great danger. Briçonnet had recanted—Lefevre was beyond the frontier—all this was something gained, but the Sorbonne was still without those public examples of punishment which it had advised. Beda and his followers were without victims. One man there was who gave them more annoyance than either Briçonnet or Lefevre, and he was Louis Berquin. The gentleman of Artois, more fearless than his tutors, allowed no opportunity to pass of teazing the monks and theologians, and unmasking their fanaticism. Passing from the capital to the provinces, he would collect the writings of Erasmus and of Luther. These he would translate,[†] at other times himself composing controversial tracts, and defending and disseminating the new teaching with the zeal of a young convert. Louis Berquin was denounced by the bishop of Amiens, Beda seconded the accusation, and the Parliament committed him to prison. "This one," said the enemy, "shall not escape so easily as Briçonnet or Lefevre." But their bolts and bars had no effect on Berquin. In vain did the superior of the Carthusians and other persons labour to persuade him to apologise; he declared he would not retract an iota. "It seemed then,"

* Nam latere cupiunt et tamen pueris noti sunt. (Capito. Zwing. Epp. p. p. 439.)

† Erasmi Ep. p. 923.

says a chronicler, "that no way remained but to send him to the stake."*

Margaret, in consternation at what had happened to Briçonnet, dreaded to see Berquin dragged to that scaffold which the bishop had so shamefully eluded. Not daring to visit him in his prison, she endeavoured to convey a few words of consolation to him—and he may have been upon her heart—when the princess composed that touching complaint in which a prisoner thus addresses the Lord:

> O refuge free to all who feel distress !
> Their help and stay!—Judge of the fatherless !
> Exhaustless treasure of consoling grace !
> The iron doors, the moat, the massive wall
> Keep far from me,—a lone, forgotten thrall—
> Friend, kinsman, brother,—each familiar face :
> Yet mercy meets even this extremity ;
> For iron doors can never shut out *Thee !*—
> Thou, Lord! art with me here,—here in this dismal place.†

But Margaret did not rest there, she immediately wrote to her brother to solicit a pardon for her attendant. Fortunate might she deem herself if her efforts were not too late to rescue him from the hatred of his enemies.

While awaiting this victim, Beda resolved to strike terror into the adversaries of the Sorbonne and monks, by crushing the most celebrated man among them. Erasmus had declared himself against Luther:—But this mattered little ;—if the ruin of Erasmus could be accomplished then beyond all doubt the destruction of Farel, of Luther, and their associates would be sealed. The surest way of reaching our mark is to aim beyond it. Let the ecclesiastical power only set its heel on the neck of the philosopher of Rotterdam, and where was the heretical doctor who could hope to escape the vengeance of Rome? The attack had already been commenced by Lecouturier, better known by his Latin name of Sutor, who, from the solitude of a Carthusian cell, launched against Erasmus a

* Actes des Martyrs, p. 103.
† Marguerites de la Marguerite des Princesses, 1. p. 445.

publication of the most violent character, in which he called
his adversaries, theologasters, and miserable apes, and charged
them with scandalous offences, with heresy and blasphemy.
Handling subjects which he did not understand, he reminded
his readers, as Erasmus sarcastically remarks, of the old
proverb:—" Ne sutor ultra crepidam."

Beda hastened to the assistance of his confederate. He
ordered Erasmus to write no more ;* and himself taking up
the pen, which he had enjoined the greatest writer of the age
to lay down, he made a selection of all the calumnies which
the monks had invented against the philosopher, translated
them into French, and formed them into a book which he circulated at court and in the city, in the hope that all France
would join in the outcry he was raising.† This book was
the signal for a general onset ; the enemies of Erasmus started
up on every side. Nicolas D'Ecmond, an old Carmelite of
Louvain, used to exclaim, as often as he mounted the pulpit,
" There is no difference between Erasmus and Luther, unless
it be that Erasmus is the greater heretic of the two ;"‡—and
wherever the Carmelite might be,—at table or on a journey,
on the land or on the water,—he was raving against Erasmus
the heresiarch and forger.§ The faculty of Paris, excited by
these clamours, drew up a decree of censure against the illustrious writer.

Erasmus was astounded. Was this, then, the fruit of all
his politic forbearance,—was it for this that he had even engaged in hostilities against Luther ? He, with an intrepidity
which no one else had displayed, had flung himself into the
breach,—and was he now to be trampled down only that the
common enemy might be reached more safely over his prostrate body ? His indignation is raised at the thought, he turns
sharply round, and while yet warm from his attack upon
Luther, deals his retributive blows on the fanatical doctors

* Primum jubet ut desinam scribere. (Erasm. Epp. p. 921.)
† Ut totam Galliam in me concitaret. (Ib. p. 886.)
‡ Nisi quod Erasmus esset major hæreticus. (Ib. p. 915.)
§ Quoties in conviciis, in vehiculis, in navibus . . . (Ib.)

who have assailed him in the rear. Never was his correspondence more active than now. He takes a survey of his position, and his piercing eye immediately discovers in whose hands rests the balance of his fate. He hesitates not an instant;—he will at once lay his complaint and his protest at the feet of the Sorbonne,—of the Parliament,—of the King,—of the Emperor himself.—" How was this fearful flame of Lutheranism kindled?"—says he, writing to those among the divines of the Sorbonne in whose impartiality he still reposed some confidence:—" How has it been fanned into fury,—except such outrages as these which Beda has committed?* In war,—a soldier who has done his duty receives a reward from his generals,—but the only reward that you,—the generals in this war,—have to bestow upon me,—is to deliver me up to the calumnies of Beda and Lecouturier!"

" What!" he exclaims, addressing the Parliament of Paris, " when I had these Lutherans on my hands,—when, under the auspices of the Emperor, the Pope and the other princes, I was struggling against them, even at the peril of my life, must I be assailed behind my back by the foul libels of Lecouturier and Beda? Ah, if evil fortune had not deprived us of king Francis, I might have appealed to that avenger of the muses against these insults of the barbarians.† But now it rests with you to restrain their malignity."

No sooner did an opportunity present itself of conveying a letter to the king, than he wrote to him also. His penetrating glance detected in these fanatical doctors of the Sorbonne, the germs of the League, the precursors of the three Priests, who at a later period were to set up the *sixteen* against the last of the race of Valois;—his genius enabled him to warn the king of future crimes and miseries which the experience of his successors would but too fully realize.—" Religion," said he, " is their pretext,—but their true aim is despotic power, to be ex-

---

* Hoc gravissimum Lutheri incendium, unde natum, unde huc progressum, nisi ex Beddaicis intemperiis. (Erasm. Epp. p. 887.)

† Musarum vindicem adversus barbarorum incursienes.—(Ibid 2070.)

ercised even over princes.—They are moving onward with a steady step, though their path lies under ground. Should the sovereign not be inclined to submit himself in all things to their guidance, they will immediately declare that he may be deposed by the *Church*; that is to say, by a few false monks, and a few false divines conspiring together against the public peace."* Erasmus, when writing to Francis the First, could not have touched a more sensitive string.

Finally, that he might still more effectually secure himself against the malice of his enemies, Erasmus invoked the protection of Charles the Fifth himself.—" Invincible Emperor," said he, " a horrible outcry has been raised against me, by men who, under the pretence of religion, are labouring to establish their own tyrannical power, and to gratify their own sensual appetites.† I am fighting under your banner, and under the standard of Jesus Christ. It is by your wisdom and your authority that peace must be restored to the Christian world."

It was in language like this that the prince of literature addressed himself to the rulers of the age. The danger which impended over his head was averted; the secular power interposed, and the vultures were compelled to abandon the prey which in fancy they had already clutched. They then turned their eyes elsewhere in search of other victims, and they were soon found.

It was in Lorraine first that blood was appointed to flow afresh. From the earliest days of the Reformation, there had been an alliance in fanaticism between Paris and the country of the Guises. If Paris was at peace for a while, Lorraine took up the work, and then Paris began, again, to give time for Nancy and Metz to recruit their strength. The first blow, apparently, was destined to fall upon an excellent man, one of the refugees of Basle, a friend of Farel and Toussaint. The

* Nisi princeps ipsorum voluntati per omnia paruerit, dicetur fautor hæreticorum et destitui poterit per ecclesiam. (Er. Epp. p. 1108.)

† Simulato religionis prætextu, ventris tyrannidisque suæ, negotium agentes. (Ibid. p. 962.)

Chevalier d'Eseh, while residing at Metz, had not been able to screen himself from the suspicions of the priests. It was ascertained that he carried on a correspondence with Christians of the Evangelic Faith, and on that discovery he was thrown into prison at Pont-à-Mousson, a place situated five miles from Metz, on the banks of the Moselle.* The tidings filled the French refugees, and the Swiss themselves, with the deepest concern. "Alas! for that innocent heart!" exclaimed Œcolampadius: "I have full confidence in the Lord," added he, "that he will preserve this man to us, either in life as a preacher of righteousness, to make known His name; or in death to confess Him as a martyr."† But at the same time Œcolampadius censured the thoughtlessness,—the precipitancy,—and what he termed the imprudent zeal for which the French refugees were distinguished. "I wish," said he, "that my dear friends, the worthy gentlemen of France, would not be so eager to return to their own country, until they have made all due enquiries beforehand; for the devil lays his snares everywhere. Nevertheless, let them obey the Spirit of Christ, and may that Spirit never forsake them."‡

There was reason, indeed, to tremble for the fate of the chevalier. The rancour of the enemy had broken out in Lorraine with redoubled fury. Brother Bonaventure Renel, the principal of the cordeliers, and the confessor of Duke Anthony the Good, a man of an audacious temper, and of very questionable moral character, allowed that weak prince, who reigned from 1508 to 1544, a large measure of license in his pleasures; and persuaded him on the other hand, by way of atonement, as it were, to exercise a merciless severity against all innovators. "It is quite sufficient for any one," said the prince, profiting by the able instructions of Renel, "if he can repeat the *Pater* and the *Ave-Maria;* the greatest doctors are those who occasion the greatest disorders."§

* Noster captus detinetur in Bundamosa quinque millibus a Metis. (Œcol. Farello Epp. p. 201.)
† Vel vivum confessorem, vel mortuum martyrem servabit. (Ibid.)
‡ Nollem carissimos dominos meos Gallos properare in Galliam. (Ibid.)
§ Actes des Martyrs, p. 97.

Towards the end of the year 1524, information was conveyed to the Duke's court, that a pastor, named Schuch, was preaching a new kind of doctrine in the town of Saint Hippolyte, at the foot of the Vosages. " Let them return to their duty," said Anthony *the Good*, "or I will march against the town, and lay it waste with fire and sword!"*

Hereupon the faithful pastor resolved to devote himself for his flock : he repaired to Nancy, where the prince resided. Immediately on his arrival, he was lodged in a noisome prison, under the custody of brutal and cruel men :—and now at last brother Bonaventure had the heretic in his power. It was he who presided at the tribunal before which he was examined. " Heretic !" cried he, addressing the prisoner, " Judas! Devil !" Schuch, preserving the utmost tranquillity and composure, made no reply to these insults ; but holding in his hand a little Bible, all covered with notes which he had written in it, he meekly and earnestly confessed Jesus Christ and him crucified ! On a sudden, he assumed a more animated mien, —stood up boldly, raised his voice as if moved by the Spirit from on high,—and, looking his judges in the face, denounced against them the fearful judgments of God.

Brother Bonaventure and his companions, inwardly appalled, yet agitated with rage, rushed upon him at once with vehement cries, snatched away the Bible, from which he read those menacing words,—and " raging like so many mad dogs," says the chronicler, " because they could not wreak their fury on the doctrine, carried the book to their convent, and burnt it there."†

The whole court of Lorraine resounded with the obstinacy and presumption of the minister of St. Hippolyte ; and the prince, impelled by curiosity to hear the heretic, resolved to be present at his final examination,—secretly, however, and concealed from the view of the spectators. But as the interrogatory was conducted in Latin, he could not understand it ; only he was struck with the stedfast aspect of the minister,

* Actes des Martyrs, p. 95.
† Actes des Martyrs, recueillis par Crespin, en fr. p. 97.

who seemed to be neither vanquished nor abashed. Indignant at this obstinacy, Anthony the Good started from his seat, and said as he retired,—"Why dispute any longer? He denies the sacrament of the mass; let them proceed to execution against him."[*] Schuch was immediately condemned to be burnt alive. When the sentence was communicated to him, he lifted up his eyes to heaven, and mildly made answer; "I was glad when they said unto me, Let us go into the house of the Lord."[†]

On the 19th August, 1525, the whole city of Nancy was in motion. The bells gave notice of the death of a heretic. The mournful procession set out. It must pass before the convent of the Cordeliers, and there the whole fraternity were gathered in joyful expectation before the door. As soon as Schuch made his appearance, Father Bonaventure, pointing to the carved images over the convent gateway, cried out "Heretic, pay honour to God, his mother, and the saints!"— "O hypocrites!" replied Schuch, standing erect before those pieces of wood and stone, "God will destroy you, and bring your deceits to light!"

When the martyr reached the place of execution his books were first burnt in his presence, and then he was called upon to recant; but he refused, saying, "Thou, God, hast called me, and thou wilt strengthen me to the end;"[‡]—and immediately he began with a loud voice, to repeat the 51st Psalm, "Have mercy upon me, O God! according to thy loving-kindness!" Having mounted the pile, he continued to recite the psalm until the smoke and flames stifled his voice.

Thus did the persecutors in France and Lorraine behold a renewal of their triumphs,—their counsels had at length been followed. At Nancy the ashes of a heretic had been scattered to the winds: this seemed a challenge addressed to the capital of France. What! should Beda and Lecouturier be the last

* Histoire de Francois 1er par Gaillard, iv. p. 233.
† Psalm cxxii. 1.
‡ Eum auctorem vocationis suæ atque conservatorem ad extremum usque spiritum recognovit. (Acta Mart. p. 202.)

to show their zeal for the Pope?   Rather let one blazing pile
serve as the signal for another, and heresy, swept from the
soil of France, would soon be driven back beyond the Rhine.

But Beda was not to pursue his successful career, until a
contest, half serious, half ludicrous, had taken place between
him and one of those men with whom the struggle against
Popery was only a capricious effort of the intellect, not the
solemn engagement and willing duty of the heart.

Among the learned men whom Briçonnet had allured to
his diocese was a doctor of the Sorbonne, named Peter Caroli,
a man of a vain and frivolous cast of mind, and as quarrelsome
and litigious as Beda himself.   Caroli viewed the new doctrine
as the means of making an impression, and of thwarting Beda,
whose ascendancy he could not endure.—Accordingly on his
return from Meaux to Paris he caused a great sensation, by
introducing into every pulpit what was called "the new way
of preaching."   Then began a pernicious strife between the
two doctors; it was blow for blow and trick for trick.   Beda
cites Caroli before the Sorbonne, and Caroli summons him
before the episcopal court to answer for an infringement of
privilege.   The Sorbonne proceeds with the enquiry, and
Caroli gives intimation of an appeal to the Parliament.   A
provisional sentence excludes him from the pulpit, and still he
goes on preaching in all the churches of Paris.   Being
absolutely forbidden to preach in any pulpit, he takes to publicly expounding the Psalms in the college of Cambray.   The
Sorbonne prohibits him from continuing that practice, but he
asks permission to conclude the exposition of the 22d Psalm
which he has begun.   Finally, on this petition being rejected,
he posts the following placard on the college-gates :—" *Peter
Caroli, being desirous to obey the injunctions of the sacred
faculty, has ceased to teach ; he will resume his lectures,
whenever it shall please God, at the verse where he left off :
'* They have pierced my hands and my feet.' "   Thus
had Beda at length found an opponent with whom he was
fairly matched.   If Caroli had defended the truth in right
earnest, the stake would have been his reward; but he was

of too carnal a spirit to expose himself to the risk of death. How could capital punishment be inflicted on a man who laughed his judges out of countenance? Neither the episcopal court, nor the parliament, nor the council, could ever proceed to a definitive judgment in *his* cause. Two such men as Caroli would have wearied out the activity of Beda himself;— but two like him the Reformation did not produce.*

This troublesome contest concluded, Beda applied himself to matters of more serious concern. Happily for the syndic of the Sorbonne, there were men who gave persecution a better hold of them than Caroli. Briçonnet, indeed, and Erasmus, and Lefevre, and Berquin had escaped him; but since he cannot reach these distinguished personages, he will content himself with meaner victims. The poor youth, James Pavanne, ever since his abjuration at Christmas, 1524, had done nothing but weep and sigh. He was constantly seen with a gloomy brow, his eyes fixed on the ground, groaning inwardly, and muttering reproaches against himself for having denied his Lord and Saviour.†

Pavanne undoubtedly was the most retiring and the most inoffensive of men;—but what of that?—he had been at Meaux, and this, in those days, was sufficient. "Pavanne has relapsed!" was the cry: "the dog has returned to his vomit, and the swine that was washed to his wallowing in the mire." He was seized immediately, cast into prison, and after a while brought before the judges. This was all that young Pavanne desired.—He felt his mind relieved as soon as the fetters were fastened on his limbs, and recovered all his energy in the open confession of Jesus Christ!‡ The persecutors smiled when they saw that this time nothing could disappoint them of their victim,—no recantation,—no flight,—no intervention of

* Gerdesius, Historia sæculi xvi. renovati p. 52. D'Argentré, Collectio Judiciorum de novis erroribus ii. p. 21.—Gaillard, Hist. de François I. tom. iv. p. 233.

† Animi factum suum detestantis dolorem, sæpe declaraverit. (Acta Mart. p. 203.)

‡ Puram religionis Christianæ confessionem addit. (Ibid. p. 203.)

a powerful protection. The meekness of the youth, his candour, his courage, were altogether unavailing to appease the malice of his enemies. He, on the contrary, looked on them with affection,—for by loading him with chains, they had restored his peace of mind and his joy,—but that benevolent look of his only hardened their hearts the more. The proceedings against him were conducted with all despatch, and a very short time had elapsed before a pile was erected in the Place de Grève, on which Pavanne made a joyful end,—strengthening by his example all who in that great city had openly or secretly embraced the Gospel of Christ.

But this was not enough for the Sorbonne. If men of mean condition only are to be sacrificed, their number at least must make amends for their want of rank. The flames in the Place de Grève have struck terror into Paris and into the whole of France; but another pile, kindled on some other spot, will redouble that terror. It will be the subject of conversation at the court, in the colleges, in the workshop of the artisan; and tokens like these, better than all the edicts that can be issued, will prove that Louisa of Savoy, the Sorbonne, and the Parliament, are determined to sacrifice the very last heretic to the anathemas of Rome.

In the forest of Livry, three leagues distant from Paris, and not far from the site of an ancient abbey of the order of St. Augustin, lived a hermit, who, having chanced in his wanderings to fall in with some of the men of Meaux, had received the truth of the Gospel into his heart.* The poor hermit had felt himself rich indeed that day in his solitary retreat, when, along with the scanty dole of bread which public charity had afforded him, he brought home Jesus Christ and his grace. He understood from that time how much better it is to give than to receive. He went from cottage to cottage in the villages around, and as soon as he crossed the threshold, began to speak to the poor peasants of the Gospel, and the free

* Cette semence de Faber et de ses disciples, prise au grenier de Luther, germa dans le sot esprit d'un ermite qui se tenait près la ville de Paris. (Hist. Catholique de notre temps par S. Fontaine, Paris, 1562.)

pardon which it offers to every burthened soul,—a pardon infinitely more precious than any priestly absolution.[*] The good hermit of Livry was soon widely known in the neighbourhood of Paris; many came to visit him at his poor hermitage, and he discharged the office of a kind and faithful missionary to the simple-minded in all the adjacent districts.

It was not long before intelligence of what was doing by the new evangelist reached the ears of the Sorbonne, and the magistrates of Paris. The hermit was seized,—dragged from his hermitage—from his forest—from the fields he had daily traversed,—thrown into a dungeon in that great city which he had always shunned,—brought to judgment,—convicted,— and sentenced to "the exemplary punishment of being burnt by a slow fire."[†]

In order to render the example the more striking, it was determined that he should be burnt in the close of Notre Dame; before that celebrated cathedral, which typifies the majesty of the Roman Catholic Church. The whole of the clergy were convened, and a degree of pomp was displayed equal to that of the most solemn festivals.[‡] A desire was shown to attract all Paris, if possible, to the place of execution. "The great bell of the church of Notre Dame swinging heavily," says an historian, "to rouse the people all over Paris." And accordingly from every surrounding avenue, the people came flocking to the spot. The deep-toned reverberations of the bell made the workmen quit his task, the student cast aside his books, the shopkeeper forsake his traffic, the soldier start from the guard-room bench,—and already the close was filled with a dense crowd, which was continually increasing.[§] The hermit, attired in the robes appropriated to obstinate heretics, bareheaded, and with bare feet, was led out before the doors

* Lequel par les villages qu'il frequentait, sous couleur de faire ses quêtes, tenait propos heretiques. (Hist. Catholique de notre temps par S. Fontaine, Paris, 1562.)

† Histoire catholique de notre temps, par Fontaine.

‡ Avec une grande ceremonie. (Histoire des Egl. Ref. par. Theod. de Bèze, i. p. 4.)

§ Histoire des Egl. Ref. par Theod de Bèze, i. p. 4.

of the cathedral. Tranquil, firm, and collected, he replied to the exhortations of the confessors, who presented him with the crucifix, only by declaring that his hope rested solely on the mercy of God. The doctors of the Sorbonne, who stood in the front rank of the spectators, observing his constancy, and the effect it produced upon the people, cried aloud—"He is a man foredoomed to the fires of hell."[*] The clang of the great bell, which all this while was rung with a rolling stroke, while it stunned the ears of the multitude, served to heighten the solemnity of that mournful spectacle. At length the bell was silent,—and the martyr having answered the last interrogatory of his adversaries by saying that he was resolved to die in the faith of his Lord Jesus Christ, underwent his sentence of being "burnt by a slow fire." And so, in the cathedral close of Notre Dame, beneath the stately towers erected by the piety of Louis the younger, amidst the cries and tumultuous excitement of a vast population, died peaceably, a man whose name history has not deigned to transmit to us,—"the hermit of Livry."

While men were thus engaged in destroying the first confessors of Jesus Christ in France, God was raising up others gifted with ampler powers for his service. A modest student —a humble hermit—might be dragged to the stake, and Beda might almost persuade himself that the doctrine they proclaimed would perish with them. But Providence has resources which the world knows not of. The Gospel, like the fabled bird of antiquity, contains within itself a principle of life which the flames can never reach, and from the ashes in which it seemed to lie extinguished, it springs afresh, pure and vigorous as ever. Often, when the storm is at its height, when the fiery bolt of persecution appears to have laid the truth prostrate, and enduring, impenetrable darkness to have closed over it,—even at that moment there comes a gleam of light, and announces a great deliverance at hand. So, when all earthly powers were leagued together in France to effect the ruin of the Reformation, God was preparing an instru-

* Histoire des Egl. Ref. par Theod. de Bèze, i. p. 4.

41*

ment, apparently feeble, to maintain His rights at a future day, and with more than human intrepidity to defend His cause. Averting our eyes from the persecutions and cruelties which have succeeded each other so rapidly since Francis I. became the prisoner of Charles,—let us turn them on a child who shall hereafter be called forth to take his station as a leader of a mighty host in the holy warfare of Israel.

Among the inhabitants of the city and university of Paris who listened to the sound of the great bell, was a young scholar of sixteen, a native of Noyon, in Picardy, of middle stature,* and pale, and somewhat dark complexion, whose powerful and sagacious mind was indicated by the keenness and peculiar brightness of his eye, and the animated expression of his countenance. His dress, which was extremely neat, but perfectly unostentatious, corresponded to the modesty and decorum of his character.† This young man, whose name was John Cauvin or Calvin, was a student at the college of La Marche, of which Mathurin Cordier, a man celebrated for his integrity, learning, and peculiar skill in the instruction of youth, was at that time the regent. Educated in all the superstitions of Popery, the student of Noyon was blindly submissive to the Church, dutifully observant of all the practices she enjoined,‡ and fully persuaded that heretics well deserved the flames to which they were delivered. The blood which was then flowing in Paris was, in his eyes, an additional aggravation of the crime of heresy. But, although by natural disposition timid, and, to use his own words, soft and pusillanimous,§ he was endowed with that uprightness of mind, and that generosity of heart which induce men to sacrifice everything to the convictions of their conscience. Vainly, there

---

* Statura fuit mediocri, colore sub pallido et nigricante, oculis ad mortem usque limpidis, quique ingenii sagacitatem testarentur. (Bezæ Vita Calvini.)

† Cultu corporis neque culto neque sordido sed qui singularem modestiam deceret. (Ibid.)

‡ Primo quidem quum superstitionibus Papatus magis pertinaciter addictus essem. (Calv. Præf. ad Psalm.)

§ Ego qui natura timido, molli et pusillo animo me esse fateor. (Ibid.)

fore, were those appalling spectacles presented to him in his youth; vain was the example of the murderous flames kindled in the Place de Grève and in the close of Notre Dame, for the destruction of the faithful followers of the Gospel. The remembrance of such horrors could not, afterwards, deter him from entering on that "new way" which seemed to lead only to the dungeon and the scaffold. In other respects the character of the youthful Calvin afforded indications of what he was hereafter to become. The austerity of his morals was the precursor of equal austerity in his doctrine, and the scholar of sixteen already gave promise of a man who would take up in earnest all that should be imparted to him, and would rigidly exact from others what, in his own case, he felt it so much a matter of course to perform. Silent and grave while attending on the college lectures, taking no pleasure in the sports and idle frolics which others pursued during the hours of recreation;—shrinking in disgust from all participation in vice,* he sometimes censured the disorders of his fellow-pupils with severity—with a measure, even, of acrimony.† Accord‑ ingly, a canon of Noyon assures us that his companions had surnamed him the "*accusative*."‡ He stood among them as the representative of conscience and duty,—so far was he from being in reality what some calumniators endeavoured to make him. The pale aspect, the piercing eye of a student of sixteen already inspired his associates with more respect than the black gowns of their masters; and this boy from Picardy, low in stature, and timid in demeanour, who came day by day to take his seat on the benches of the college of La Marche, was, even then, by the seriousness of his conversation and sobriety of his life unconsciously discharging the office of a minister and a Reformer.

Nor was it in these particulars alone that the stripling of Noyon evinced his superiority to his compeers. His extreme

* Summam in moribus affectabat gravitatem et paucorum hominum consuetudine utebatur. (Roemundi Hist. Hæres. vii. 10.)

† Severus omnium in suis sodalibus censor. (Bezæ Vita Calv.)

‡ Annales de l'Eglise de Noyon par Levasseur, Chanoine, p. 1158.

timidity sometimes restrained him from manifesting the anti
pathy he felt to vanity and to vice; but in his studies he was
already exerting all the force of his genius, and all the inten-
sity of his will,—and any one who observed him, might have
predicted that his life would be consumed in labour. The fa-
cility of his comprehension was wonderful,—while his class-
fellows were advancing by painful steps, he was bounding
lightly over the course,—and the knowledge which others
were long in acquiring superficially, was instantaneously seized by his youthful genius, and permanently impressed on his
memory. His masters, therefore, were obliged to withdraw
him from the ranks, and introduce him singly to the higher
branches of learning.*

Among his fellow-students were the young men of the family of Mommor, a house reckoned among the first nobility
of Picardy. John Calvin was intimately connected with these
young noblemen, especially with Claude, who at a later period
was abbot of St. Eloi, and to whom he dedicated his Commentary on Seneca. It was in their company that he had
come to Paris. His father, Gerard Calvin, notary apostolic,
and procurator-fiscal of the county of Noyon, secretary of the
diocese, and proctor of the chapter,† was a man of judgment
and ability, whose talents had raised him to offices which
were sought after by the best families; and all the noblesse of
the province, but particularly the illustrious family of Mommor, entertained the highest esteem for him.‡ Gerard, who
resided at Noyon,§ had married a young woman from Cambray, named Jane Lefranq, remarkable for her beauty, and

* Exculto ipsius ingenio quod ei jam tum erat acerrimum, ita profecit
ut cæteris sodalibus in grammatices curriculo relictis ad dialecticos et alia-
rum quas vocant artium studium promoveretur. (Beza.)

† Levasseur, docteur de la Sorbonne, annales de l'Eglise Cathédrale
de Noyon, p. 1151. Drelincourt, Defense de Calvin, p. 193.

‡ Erat is Gerardus non parvi judicii et consilii homo, ideoque nobilibus
ejus regionis plerisque carus. (Beza.)

§ "On the spot where now stands a house, distinguished by the sign
of the Stag." (Desmay, Doct. de la Sorbonne. Vit. de Jean Calvin.
hemsiarque, p. 30. Levasseur, Ann. de Noyon, p. 1157.)

worthy of esteem for her humble piety, by whom he had already had a son called Charles, when on the 10th of July, 1509, she gave birth to a second son, who received the name of John, and was baptized in the church of St. Godebert [*] A third son, named Anthony, who died young, and two daughters, made up the entire family of the procurator-fiscal of Noyon.

Gerard Calvin, living in habits of familiar intercourse with the ecclesiastical dignitaries and chief men of the province, was desirous that his children should receive the same education as those of the highest rank. John, in whom he had perceived an early development of talent, was brought up with the children of the family of Mommor: he lived in the house as one of themselves, and shared in the lessons of the young Claude. The effect of early discipline and culture in such a family was to impart to his intellectual character a degree of refinement which otherwise it could scarcely have acquired.[†] He was afterwards sent to the college of Capettes, an establishment within the city of Noyon.[‡] The child had but few recreations. That severity, which was one feature in the character of the son, found a place likewise in the temperament of the father. Gerard brought him up rigidly,—from his earliest years he was obliged to bend to the inflexible rule of duty,—which after a little while became habitual to

[*] The calumnious and extravagant tales which have been circulated in regard to the person of Calvin, may be traced to a very early origin. J. Levasseur, who was afterwards dean of the chapter of Noyon, relates that when his mother brought him into the world, the birth of the child was preceded by the preternatural appearance of a swarm of large flies, —"a sure presage that he would be an evil speaker and slanderer." (Annales de la Cathedrale de Noyon, p. 115.) These absurdities and others of the same stamp, which have been invented to the prejudice of the Reformer may be safely left to refute themselves without any effort on our part. In our own day, those among the Romish doctors who are not ashamed to employ the weapons of calumny, make a selection of these coarse and ridiculous stories, not daring to repeat them all; yet they are all of equal value.

[†] Domi vestræ puer educatus, iisdem tecum studiis initiatus primam vitæ et literarum disciplinam familiæ vestræ nobilissimæ acceptam refero. (Calv. Præf. in Senecam ad Claudium.)

[‡] Desmay, Remarques, p. 31. (Drelincourt, Defense, p. 158.)

him,—and thus the influence of the father counteracted that
of the family of Mommor.   Timid by nature,—with something. as he tells us himself, of rustic bashfulness in his disposition,*—and rendered still more diffident by his father's severity, John would often escape from the splendid mansion of
his protectors, to bury himself in solitude and obscurity.†   In
hours of seclusion like this, his youthful spirit grew familiar
with lofty conceptions.   It appears that he sometimes went to
the neighbouring village of Pont l'Evêque, where his grandfather inhabited a cottage,‡ and where other relatives also,
who at a later period changed their name through hatred of
the heresiarch, then offered a kindly. welcome to the son of the
procurator-fiscal.   But it was to study, chiefly, that young
Calvin devoted his days.   While Luther, who was to act upon
the mass of the people, was brought up at first as a peasant's
son, Calvin, ordained to act chiefly as a theologian and a rea-
soner, and to become the legislator of the renovated Church,
received, even in his childhood, a more liberal education.§

A spirit of piety evinced itself betimes in the child's heart.
One of his biographers tells us that he was taught, while yet
young, to pray in the open air, under the vault of heaven,—a
practice which helped to awaken within his soul the sentiment
of an omnipresent Deity.‖   But although Calvin may, even
in his earliest years, have heard the voice of God addressed to
his heart, no one in the city of Noyon was more exact than
he in the observance of every rule established by the Church.
Gerard, therefore, remarking the bent of his mind, conceived the design of devoting his son to theology.¶   The
knowledge of his destination contributed undoubtedly to im-

* Ego qui natura subrusticus. (Præf. ad Psalm.)

† Umbram et otium semper amavi . . . latebras catare. (Præf. ap
Psalm.)

‡ " It is reported that his grandfather was a cooper." (Drelincourt,
p. 36.   Levasseur ann. de Noyon, p. 1151.)

§ Henry, das Leben Calvins, p. 29.

‖ Calvin's Leben von Fischer, Leipzig, 1794.   The author does not
quote the authority on which he relates this fact.

¶ Destinarat autem eum pater ab initio theologiæ studiis, quod in illa
etiam tenera ætate mirum in modum religiosus esset. (Beza, Vita Calv.)

press upon his mind that serious and theological cast by which it was afterwards distinguished. His intellect was formed by nature to take a decided bias from the first, and to nourish the most elevated thoughts at an early age. The report that he was a chorister boy at this time is admitted by his adversaries themselves to be destitute of foundation; but they confidently affirm that while yet a child, he was seen in religious processions carrying, instead of a cross, a sword with a cross-shaped hilt.* "A presage," they add, "of what he was one day to become." "The Lord has made my mouth like a sharp sword," says the servant of the Lord, in Isaiah. The same may be said of Calvin.

Gerard was poor: the education of his son was burthensome to him, and he wished to attach him irrevocably to the church. The Cardinal of Lorraine had been appointed coadjutor to the Bishop of Metz, when only four years old. It was then a common practice to bestow ecclesiastical titles and revenues upon children. Alphonso of Portugal was created a cardinal by Leo the Tenth, at the age of eight: Odet de Chatillon received the same dignity from Clement the Seventh at the age of eleven; and, at a later period, the celebrated Mother Angelica, of Port Royal, was made coadjutrix of that convent at the age of seven. Gerard, who died a faithful Catholic, was regarded with favour by Charles de Hangest, bishop of Noyon, and his vicars-general. Accordingly, the chaplaincy of La Gesine having become vacant by the resignation of the incumbent, the bishop, on the 15th May, 1521, bestowed that benefice on John Calvin, whose age was then nearly twelve. He was inducted by the chapter a week after. On the eve of Corpus Christi, the bishop solemnly cut the child's hair;† and by this ceremony of tonsure John was invested with the clerical character, and became capable of entering into sacred orders, and holding a benefice without residing on the spot.

Thus was it ordered that Calvin, in his childhood, should

* Levasseur, ann. de Noyon, pp. 1159, 1173.
† Vie de Calvin par Desmay, p. 31 ; Levasseur, p. 1158.

have personal experience of the abuses of the Church of Rome. There was not a tonsured head in the kingdom more sincerely pious than the chaplain of La Gesine, and the thoughtful child was himself perhaps a little astonished at the operation performed by the bishop and his vicars-general. But in the simplicity of his heart, he revered those exalted personages too highly to harbour the least suspicion regarding the lawfulness of his tonsure. He had enjoyed the distinction about two years, when Noyon was visited with a terrible pestilence. Several of the canons petitioned the chapter that they might be allowed to quit the city. Already many of the inhabitants had been struck by the " great death ;" and Gerard began to reflect with alarm that his son John, the hope of his age, might, in a moment, be snatched from his tenderness by this scourge of God. The children of the Mommor family were going to Paris to continue their studies. This was the very opportunity that the procurator-fiscal had always desired for his son. Why should he separate John from his fellow-pupils ? On the 5th August, 1523, therefore, he presented to the chapter a petition that the young chaplain might have " liberty to go whithersoever he would, during the continuance of the plague, without losing his allowances ; which was granted accordingly, until the feast of St. Remigius."* Thus it was that John Calvin, at the age of fourteen, quitted his paternal home. Calumny must be intrepid indeed, to attribute his departure to other causes, and, in sheer wantonness, provoke that disgrace which justly recoils on all who give currency to evil reports, after their falsehood has been demonstrated. It would appear, that on his arrival in Paris, Calvin was received into the house of one of his uncles, Richard Cauvin, who lived near the church of St. Germain l'Auxer-

---

* The particulars here given rest on the testimony of the priest, and vicar-general Desmay, (Jean Calvin, heresiarque, p. 32,) and the canon Levasseur, (Ann. de Noyon, p. 1160,) who found them, as they assure us, in the registers of the chapter of Noyon. These Romish authors, therefore, refute the inventions or mistakes of Richelieu and other writers.— See the preface.

rois. " And so, while flying from the plague," says the canon
of Noyon, " he encountered a more fatal pestilence."

A new world opened itself to the young man in this metropolis of literature. He determined to profit by his fortune,
applied himself to study, and made great progress in latinity.
He became intimately acquainted with the writings of Cicero,
and learned from that great master to employ the language
of the Romans with an ease, a purity, an idiomatic grace
which excited the admiration of his enemies themselves. But
he also discovered in that language a store of wealth which
he was afterwards to transfer into his own.

Hitherto the Latin had been the sole language of literature.
It was, and even to our own days it has continued, the language of the Romish Church. The modern tongues of.
Europe were created,—at least they were emancipated,—by
the Reformation. The exclusive agency of the priests was
now at an end; the people were called upon to learn and to
know for themselves. In this single fact was involved the
abrogation of the language of the priests,—the inauguration
of the language of the people. It is not to the Sorbonne alone,
—it is not to a few monks, a few divines, a few men of letters,
that the new doctrine is to be addressed; it is to the noble, to
the burgher, to the artisan,—all men now are to be preached
to: nay, more,—all men now are to become preachers; wool-
combers and knights no less than curates and doctors. A new
language, therefore, is wanted, or, at any rate, the ordinary
language of the people must undergo a mighty transformation,—must experience a happy deliverance from its shackles:
drawn from the common uses of life, it must be indebted to a
renovated Christianity for its patent of nobility. The Gospel,
so long laid to sleep, is now awake again : it appeals to the
nation at large; it kindles the most generous affections of the
soul; it opens the treasures of heaven to a generation whose
thoughts were all confined within the petty circle of the world
below; it agitates the masses ; it speaks to them of God, of
man, of good and evil, of the Pope, of the Bible, of a crown

in heaven,—it may be, also, of a scaffold upon earth. The popular idiom, which hitherto had been employed only by the chronicler and the minstrel, was summoned, by the Reformation, to act a new part, and consequently to receive a new development. Society finds a new world rising up around it; and for this new world there must needs be new languages. The Reformation freed the French language from the swaddling bands in which it had hitherto been confined, and reared it to a speedy and vigorous maturity. Since then, that language has had full possession of all the exalted privileges that belong to a dialect conversant with the operations of mind and the great concerns of heaven,—privileges which, under the tutelage of Rome, it had never enjoyed. True it is that the people form their own language; they, and they alone, invent those happy words,—those figurative and energetic phrases, which give colouring and animation to human speech. But there are latent powers in language which they know not how to elicit, and which men of cultivated intellect can alone call into action. When the time arrived for Calvin to engage in discussion and controversy, he was forced, by the exigency of the case to enrich his native tongue with modes of expression hitherto unknown to it,—indicating the dependence, the connection, the minute diversity of ideas, the transition from one to another, and the various steps in the process of logical deductions.

The elements of all this were already working in the brain of the young student of the college of La Marche. This child, who was to exert so powerful a mastery over the human heart, was destined to exhibit equal power in bending and moulding to his will the idiom which was to serve as his instrument. The French of Calvin eventually became the language of Protestant France, and when we speak of Protestant France, we speak of the most cultivated portion of the French nation; since out of that portion arose those families of scholars and dignified magistrates, who contributed so much to the refinement of the national character —out of that portion arose

also the society of Port Royal,* one of the great agents by
which the prose and even the poetry of France have been
modelled,—a society which aimed at introducing into the
catholicism of the Gallican Church both the *doctrine* and the
language of the Reformation, and failing in one of these objects, succeeded in the other; for who can deny that Roman
Catholic France had to learn from her antagonists among the
Jansenists and Reformers how to handle those weapons of
style, without which it would have been impossible for her to
maintain her ground against them?†

In the mean time, while the future Reformer of religion
and of language, was ripening in the college of La Marche, all
was in commotion around that young and thoughtful scholar,
without his being at all affected by the mighty movement
which agitated society. The flames that consumed the hermit
and Pavanne, shed dismay over Paris. But the persecutors
were not satisfied; a system of terror was set on foot throughout the whole of France. The friends of the Reformation no
longer dared to correspond with each other, lest their letters
should be intercepted, and so betray to the vengeance of the
tribunals, not only those who had written them, but those also
to whom they were addressed.‡ One man, however, was
bold enough to undertake the office of conveying intelligence
of what was passing in Paris and in France, to the refugees
at Basle,—by means of an unsigned letter sewed up in his
doublet. He escaped the scattered parties of arquebusiers,—
the marechaussée of the different districts,—the strict exami-
nations of the provosts and their lieutenants,—and arrived at
Basle with the doublet on his back and its hidden deposit untouched. The tidings of which he was the bearer, struck

* M. A. Arnauld, the grandfather of Mother Angelica and of all the
Arnaulds of Port Royal, was a Protestant,—see "Port Royal, par M.
Sainte-Beuve."

† Etudes Liter. sur Calvin, par M. A. Sayers, Genève, 1839, art. iv.
This work has been followed by similar enquiries regarding Farel, Viret,
and Beza.

‡ "Not a person dares to write to me.'—(Toussaint to Farel, 4th
Sept. 1525. MS. of Neufchâtel.'

terror into the hearts of Toussaint and his friends.—" It is
piteous to hear of the cruelties they are committing yonder !"*
—exclaims Toussaint.   A little before this, two Franciscan
friars had arrived at Basle closely pursued by the officers of
justice.   One of these friars, named Iohn Prevost, had preached
at Meaux, and had afterwards been thrown into prison in
Paris.†—The accounts they brought from the capital, as well
as from Lyons, through which city they had passed on their
way, excited the deepest compassion in the minds of the refugees: " May our Lord visit them with his grace !" said Toussaint, writing to Farel ;—" believe me when I tell you that at
times I am in great anxiety and tribulation."

These excellent men did not lose heart, however.   In vain
were all the Parliaments on the watch ; in vain did the spies
of the Sorbonne and the monks creep into churches and colleges, and even into private families, to catch up any word of
Evangelic doctrine that might be dropped there; in vain did
the king's *gens d'armes* patrol the highways to intercept everything that seemed to bear the impress of the Reformation ;—
these Frenchmen, thus hunted and trodden on by Rome and
her myrmidons, had faith in better days to come ; and even
now, the termination of what they called the Babylonish captivity was greeted by them afar.   " At length," said they,
" the seventieth year will arrive—the year of deliverance, and
liberty of spirit and conscience will be ours."‡   But the seventy
years were to be extended to nearly three centuries, and unheard-of calamities were to be endured before these hopes
should be realized.   It was not in man, however, that the
refugees put their trust.   " They who have begun the dance,"
said Toussaint, " will not stop short in the middle of it."   But
they believed that the Lord " knew those whom he had chosen,
and would accomplish the deliverance of His people by the
hand of His power."§

* Toussaint to Farel, 4th Sept. 1525.
† Ibid, 21st July, 1525.
‡ Sane venit annus septuagesimus, et tempus appetit ut tandem vin-
dicemur in libertatem spiritus et conscientiæ.   (Ibid.)
§ Sed novit Dominus quos elegerit.   (Toussaint to Farel, 21 July, 1525.)

The Chevalier d'Esch had actually tasted the mercy of
deliverance. Being dismissed from the prison of Pont-à-Mousson, he had hastened to Strasburg; but his stay there was
short. For "the honour of God," wrote Toussaint to Farel,
"immediately prevail on our worthy master,* the Chevalier,
to return as quickly as possible, for our other brethren have
need of such a leader." In fact, the French refugees had now
fresh cause of alarm. They were apprehensive that the dispute respecting the Lord's Supper, which had afflicted them
so grievously in Germany, would find its way across the
Rhine, and prove the source of new troubles in France.
Francis Lambert, the monk of Avignon, after visiting Zurich
and Wittemberg, had arrived at Metz, where he was regarded
with a measure of distrust, for it was feared that he might introduce the sentiments of Luther, and by fruitless, and, as
Toussaint calls them, "monstrous" controversies, impede the
progress of the Reformation.† Esch, therefore, returned to
Lorraine, to be again exposed to great dangers, "in common
with all in that region who were seeking the glory of Christ."‡

But Toussaint was not the man who would invite others to
join the battle, while he himself kept aloof from it. Deprived
of the comfort of daily intercourse with Œcolampadius,
reduced to the society of an ill-nurtured priest, he had sought
more communion with Christ, and had gained an accession
of courage. If he could not return to Metz, might he not at
least go to Paris? True,—the smoke that ascended from- the
piles on which Pavanne and the hermit of Livry had been
sacrificed was scarcely yet cleared away, and its dark shadow
might seem to repel from the capital all whose faith bore any
resemblance to their's. But if, as he had heard, the terror
that prevailed in the colleges of Paris and amidst her streets
was such, that none dared even to name the Gospel or the

* Si nos magistrum in terris habere deceat," he adds. (Tossanus
Farello, MS. of Neufchâtel.)
† Vereor ne aliquid monstri alat. (Ibid 27 Sept. 1525.)
‡ Audio etiam equitem periclitari, simul et omnes qui
favent. (Ibid. 27 Dec. 1525.)

42*

Reformation,—was not this a reason why he should repair thither? Toussaint quitted Basle, and took up his abode within those perilous walls, heretofore the seat of revelry and licentious pleasure, now the stronghold of fanaticism. His desire was to pursue his studies in Christian literature, and at the same time to form a connection with the brethren who were in the colleges, particularly with those who were in the college of Cardinal Lemoine, where Lefevre and Farel had taught.* But he was not long left at liberty to prosecute his design. The tyranny of the parliamentary commissaries and the doctors of the Sorbonne now reigned supreme over the capital, and whosoever was obnoxious to these was sure to be accused of heresy.† A duke and an abbot, whose names are not upon record, denounced Toussaint as a heretic; and, one day, the king's sergeants arrested the young Lorrainer, and threw him into prison. Separated from all his friends, and treated as a criminal. Toussaint felt his helplessness more as a sinner than a captive. "O Lord!" cried he, "withdraw not thy Spirit from me, for without that Holy Spirit I am altogether carnal, and a sink of iniquity." While his body was held in chains, his heart turned for solace to the remembrance of those who were still at large to struggle for the Gospel. There was Œcolampadius, his father, "whose work," says he, "we are in the Lord."‡ There was Lefevre, whom (obviously on account of his age,) he deemed "unmeet to bear the burthen of the Gospel;"§ there was Roussel, "by whom he trusted that the Lord would do great things;"‖ and Vaugris, who had manifested all the zeal "of the most affectionate brother," in his efforts to rescue him from the power of his

* Fratres qui in collegio Cardinalis Monachi sunt te salutant. (Tossanus Farello, MS. of Neufchatel.)
† Regnante hic tyrannide commissariorum et theologorum. (Ibid.)
‡ Patrem nostrum cujus nos opus sumus in Domino. (Ibid.) This letter is without a date, but it appears to have been written shortly after the liberation of Toussaint, and it shows the thoughts which occupied him at that period.
§ Faber est impar oneri evangelico ferendo. (Ibid.)
‖ Per Rufum magna operabitur Dominus. (Ibid.)

enemies.* There was Farel also, to whom he wrote—"I
entreat your prayers on my behalf, that I may not faint in this
conflict."† How effectual must he have found the repetition
of those beloved names in awakening thoughts which mitigated
the bitterness of his captivity—for he showed no signs of
fainting. Death, it is true, seemed to be impending over his
head, in a city where the blood of multitudes of his brethren
was afterwards to be poured out like water;‡ and, on the
other hand, offers of the most lavish kind were made by the
friends of his mother, and of his uncle the dean of Metz, as
well as by the Cardinal of Lorraine, to induce him to recant.§
But his reply to such offers was—"I despise them all. I
know that God is now putting me to the trial. I would
rather endure hunger—I would rather be a very abject in the
house of the Lord, than dwell with great riches in the palaces
of the ungodly."‖ At the same time he made a clear and
open confession of his faith: "I glory," he said, "in being called
a heretic by those whose lives and doctrine I see to be directly opposite to those of Christ."¶ And the young man subscribed himself, "Peter Toussaint, unworthy of his name of *Christian*."

Thus, in the absence of the monarch, new attacks were
levelled against the Reformation. Berquin, Toussaint, and
many others were in bonds; Schuch, Pavanne, and the hermit
of Livry had been put to death; Farel, Lefevre, Roussel, and
many other defenders of sound doctrine were in exile; and the
tongues of the most eloquent were chained. The light of the
Gospel waxed dim; the storm roared around, bending, and
shaking as if it would uproot that tree which the hand of God
had so recently planted on the French soil.

To those humbler victims who had already fallen, others

* Fidelissimi fratris officio functum. (Tossanus Farello, MS. of
Neufchâtel.)
† Commendo me vestris precibus, ne succumbam in hac militia. (Ibid.)
‡ Me periclitari de vita. (Ibid.)
§ Offerebantur hic mihi conditiones amplissimæ. (Ibid.)
‖ Malo esurire et abjectus esse in domo Domini. (Ibid.)
¶ Hæc, hæc gloria mea quod habeor hæreticus ab his quorum vitam et
doctrinam video pugnare cum Christo. (Ibid.)

of more note were now to succeed. The enemy, failing in their efforts when directed against persons of distinction, had submitted to work from beneath upwards; hoping gradually to bring to bear on the more eminent in station the sentence of condemnation and death. It was a sort of countermarch which answered the purpose they had in view. Scarcely had the wind scattered the ashes with which persecution strewed the Place de Grève and the close of Notre Dame, when further blows were struck. The excellent Messire Anthony Du Blet, the "negociateur" of Lyons, sunk under the persecutions of the enemies of the truth; as did also another disciple, Francis Moulin. No detailed account of their deaths has come down to us.* Not stopping there, the persecutors proceeded to take a higher aim. One there was whose eminent rank placed her beyond their reach—but who might yet be stricken in the persons of those dear to her.—This was the Duchess of Alençon. Michel d'Arande, her chaplain,—for the sake of whom Margaret had dismissed her other preachers, and who was accustomed in her presence to publish a pure Gospel,—was singled out for attack, and threatened with imprisonment and death.† About the same time Anthony Papillon, for whom the princess had obtained the office of Chief Master of Requests to the Dauphin, died suddenly, and a report, generally prevalent even among the enemies, ascribed his death to poison.‡

The persecution was spreading through the kingdom, and drawing nearer to the person of Margaret. The isolated champions of truth were, one after another, stretched upon the field. A few more such victories, and the soil of France would be purged from heresy. Underhand contrivances and secret practices took the place of clamour and the stake. The war

* Periit Franciscus Molinus ac Dubletus. (Erasm. Epp. p. 1109.) Erasmus, in his letter addressed to Francis I., in July, 1526, names all those who, during the captivity of that prince, fell victims to the Romish fanatics.

† Periclitatus est Michael Arantius. (Ibid.)

‡ "Periit Papilio non sine gravi suspicione veneni," says Erasmus. (Ibid.)

was conducted in open day; but it was decided that it should also be carried on darkly and in secrecy. If, in dealing with the common people, fanaticism employs the tribunal and the scaffold, it has in reserve poison and the dagger for those of more note. The doctors of a celebrated school are but too well known for having patronized the use of such means; and kings themselves have fallen victims to the steel of the assassins. But if France has had in every age its *Seides*, it has also had its Vincents de Paul and its Fenelons. Strokes falling in darkness and silence were well fitted to spread terror on all sides; and to this perfidious policy and these fanatical persecutions, in the interior of the kingdom, were now added the fatal reverses experienced beyond the frontier. A dark cloud was spread over the whole nation. Not a family, especially among the higher classes, but was either mourning for a father, a husband, or a son, who had fallen on the plains of Italy,[*] or trembling for the liberty or life of one of its members. The signal misfortunes which had burst upon the nation diffused everywhere a leaven of hatred against the heretics. The people, the parliament, the Church, and even the throne, were joined hand in hand.

Was there not enough to bow the heart of Margaret in the defeat at Pavia, the death of her husband, and the captivity of her brother? Was she doomed to witness the final extinction of that soft light of the Gospel in which her heart had found such joy? News arrived from Spain which added to the general distress. Mortification and sickness had reduced the haughty Francis to the brink of the grave. If the king should continue a captive, or die, and the regency of his mother be protracted for some years, there was apparently an end of all prospect of a Reformation. "But when all seems lost," observed, at a later period, the young scholar of Noyon, "God interposes to deliver and guard His church in His own wondrous way."[†] The Church of France, which was as if tra-

[*] Gaillard Histoire de Francois 1er tom. 2, p. 255.

[†] Nam habet Deus modum, quo electos suos mirabiliter custodiat, ubi omnia perdita videntur. (Calvinus in Ep. ad Rom. xi. 2.)

vailing in birth, was to have a brief interval of ease before its
pains returned upon it; and God made use of a weak woman,
—one who never openly declared for the Gospel,—in order to
give to the Church this season of rest.   Margaret herself, at
this time, thought more of saving the king and the kingdom,
than of delivering the comparatively unknown Christians, who
were yet resting many hopes upon her interference.*   But
under the dazzling surface of human affairs, God often hides
the mysterious ways in which He rules His people.   A generous project was suggested to the mind of the Duchess of
Alençon; it was, to cross the sea, or traverse the Pyrenees,
and rescue Francis I. from the power of Charles V.   Such
was the object to which her thoughts were henceforth
directed.

Margaret announced her intention, and France hailed it
with grateful acclamation.   Her genius, her great reputation,
and the attachment existing between herself and her brother,
helped much to counterbalance, in the eyes of Louisa and of
Duprat, her partiality for the new doctrines.   All eyes were
turned upon her, as the only person capable of extricating the
nation from its perilous position.   Let Margaret in person
make an appeal to the powerful emperor and his ministers,
and employ the admirable genius with which she was gifted,
in the effort to give liberty to her brother and her king.

Yet very various feelings existed among the nobility and
the people in the prospect of the Duchess trusting herself in
the centre of the enemies' councils, and among the stern
soldiery of the Catholic king.   All admired, but without sharing in her confidence and devotedness: her friends had fears
for her, which, in the result, were but too near being realized:
but the evangelical party were full of hope.   The king's captivity had been to them the occasion of hitherto unprecedented
severities—his restoration to liberty they expected would put
a period to those rigours.   Let the king once find himself
beyond the Spanish frontier,—and the gates of those prison

* . . . . Beneficio illustrissimæ Ducus Alanconiæ.   (Toussaint à
Farel.)

houses and castles, wherein the servants of God's word were immured, would instantly be set open. Margaret was more and more confirmed in a project to which she felt herself drawn by so many and various motives.

> My heart is fixed; and not the heavens above
> From its firm purpose can my spirit move;
> Nor hell, with all its powers, my course withstand,
> For Jesus holds its keys within his hand.*

Her woman's heart was strengthened with that faith which overcomes the world, and her resolution was irrevocably settled. Preparation was accordingly made for her journey.

The archbishop of Embrun, afterwards cardinal of Tournon, and the president of Selves, had already repaired to Madrid to treat for the ransom of the king. They were placed under the direction of Margaret, as was also the bishop of Tarbes, afterwards cardinal of Grammont; full powers being given to the Princess. At the same time Montmorency, afterwards so hostile to the Reformation, was despatched in haste to Spain to solicit a safe-conduct for the king's sister.† The Emperor at first hesitated, alleging that it was for his ministers to arrange terms.—"One hour's conference between your majesty, the king my master, and Madame d'Alençon," remarked Selves, "would forward matters more than a month's discussion between the diplomatists."‡ Margaret, impatient to attain her object, set out unprovided with a safe-conduct, accompanied by a splendid retinue.§ She took leave of the court and passed through Lyons, taking the direction of the Mediterranean; but on her road she was joined by Montmorency, who was the bearer of letters from Charles, guaranteeing her liberty for a period of three months. She reached

* Marguerites de la Marguerite des princesses, tom. i. p. 125.
† Memoires de Du Bellay, p. 124.
‡ Histoire de France, par Garnier, tom. xxiv
§ Pour taster au vif la volunté de l'ésleu empereur . . . madame Marguerite, duchesse d'Alencon, tres-notablement accompaignée de plusieurs ambassadeurs . . . (Les gestes de Francoise de Valois, par E. Dolet, 1540.)

Aigues-Mortes,* and at that port the sister of Francis the First embarked on board a vessel prepared for her. Led by Providence into Spain rather for the deliverance of nameless and oppressed Christians, than for the liberation of the powerful monarch of France, Margaret committed herself to that sea whose waves had borne her brother when taken prisoner after the fatal battle of Pavia.

* Jam in itinere erat Margarita, Francisci soror . . e fossis Marianis solvens, Barcinonem primum, deinde Cæsar Augustum appulerat. (Belcarius, Rerum Gallicarum Comment. p. 566.)

END OF VOL. III.

CPSIA information can be obtained
at www.ICGtesting.com
Printed in the USA
BVHW082351110819
555624BV00022B/3363/P

9 781318 672417